15.95

THE FACTS ON FILE
Visual Dictionary

Jean-Claude Corbeil & Martin Manser

THE FACTS ON FILE
Visual Dictionary

**Facts On File
Publications**

Oxford • New York

British Library Cataloguing in Publication Data

Corbeil, Jean-Claude
  The visual dictionary.
   1. English language — Dictionaries.
   I. Title. II. Manser, Martin H.
423   PE1625
ISBN 0-948894-06-7

Printed in Canada

EDITORIAL STAFF

Jacques Fortin
publisher

Jean-Claude Corbeil
editor-in-chief

Martin H. Manser
managing editor

Ariane Archambault
assistant editor

ASSOCIATE RESEARCH EDITORS
Édith Girard
René Saint-Pierre
Christiane Vachon
Marielle Hébert
Ann Céro

GRAPHICS STAFF
Sylvie Lévesque
Francine Giroux
Emmanuelle Rousseau
Emmanuel Blanc

COPY EDITORS
Jean-Pierre Fournier
Philip Stratford
Michel Veyron
Diane Martin
Ann Céro
Guy Connolly
Joseph Reilly
Mandy Briars
Sharon Buckland
Rosalind Desmond

*The editors are grateful for the assistance provided by
the following manufacturers, organizations, and individuals:*

Anderson Strathclyde plc — Art & Archery — BBC Television — British Airways — British
National Space Centre — Burgess Office Equipment — I.A.Z. International (U.K.) Ltd — London
Planetarium — Moseley Group (PSV) Ltd.

Roy M. Adams — Chris Axtell — Jean Baker — David Bayly — Paul F. Binder — Dr. K.R. Bond —
C.J. Briars — Angela D. Bowman — Dan Childs — Christopher L. Clarke — Roger Cook — R.A.
Dennis — Heather A. Dewar — C.P. Dowding — H.S. Dukes — Paul J. East — Raymond Ewers —
J.P. Gill — Sandy J. Goodworth — J. Hanson — Arthur J. Harland M. Inst. P.S. — G.C. Lamb —
Doreen A. Lister — N.R. Manser — Yusandra Manser — John Marcus — Gary A. Martin M.L.A. —
Karyn J. Mazillius — M.J. Miller — Andrew R. Nobbs — Brian Norten — Karen M. Payne E.N.G. —
J.S. Pate — Clare Paxton — L.C. Pierce — Wendy Sharpe — Rodney P. Shepherd — John Slater
— J.K. Snell — S.T. Stephens — Christopher Sugg — Paul F.J. Thompson — R.T. Upton —
Maurice Waite — M.R. Walden.

Air Canada — Archambault Musique — Aréo-feu Ltée — ASEA Inc. — Atelier Lise Dubois —
Atomic Energy of Canada Ltd — Automobiles Renault Canada Ltée — Banque de terminologie
du Québec — Bell Canada — Bombardier Inc. — Botanical Garden of Montreal — Camco Inc. —
Canada Mortgage and Housing Corporation — Canadian Broadcasting Corporation — Canadian
Coleman Supply Inc. — Canadian General Electric Company Ltd — Canadian Government
Terminology Bank — Canadian National — Canadian Pacific — François Caron Inc. — CKAC
Radio — CNCP Telecommunications — Control Data Canada Ltd — Department of National
Defence — Dow Planetarium — Eaton — Fédération québécoise de badminton — Fédération
québécoise de canot-camping — Fédération québécoise de handball olympique — Fédération
québécoise de la montagne — Fédération de ski nautique — Fédération québécoise de soccer
football — Fédération québécoise des sports aériens Inc. — Fédération québécoise de tennis —
Fédération de tennis de table du Québec — Ford du Canada Ltée — General Motors of Canada
Ltd — G.T.E. Sylvania Canada Ltée — Gulf Canada Ltd — Hewitt Equipment Ltd — Hippodrome
Blue Bonnets Inc. — Honeywell Ltd — Hudson's Bay Company — Hydro-Québec — IBM Canada
Ltd — Imperial Oil Ltd — Institut de recherche d'Hydro-Québec (IREQ) — Institut Teccart Inc. —
Institut de tourisme et d'hôtellerie du Québec — International Civil Aviation Organization —
Johnson & Johnson Inc. — La Maison Casavant — Office de la langue française du Québec —
J. Pascal Inc. — Petro-Canada Inc. — Quebec Cartier Mining Company — RCA Inc. — Shell
Canada Products Company Ltd — Smith-Corona Division of SMC (Canada) Ltd — Société
d'énergie de la Baie James — Société de transport de la Communauté Urbaine de Montréal —
Teleglobe Canada — Translation Bureau: Department of the Secretary of State of Canada — Via
Rail Canada Inc. — Volvo Canada Inc. — Wild Leitz Canada Ltd — Xerox Canada Inc. — Yamaha
Canada Music Ltd.

TABLE OF CONTENTS

PREFACE 15

INTRODUCTION 17

THE FACTS ON FILE
VISUAL DICTIONARY
USAGE GUIDE 23

ASTRONOMY 25
   Earth co-ordinate system 27
   Celestial co-ordinate system 27
   Seasons of the year 27
   Planets of the solar system 28
   Symbols of the planets 28
   Sun 29
     Structure of the Sun, solar eclipse
   Moon 30
     Lunar features, lunar eclipse, phases of the Moon
   Galaxy, Hubble's classification 31
   Comet 31
   Constellations of the northern hemisphere 32
   Constellations of the southern hemisphere 33
   Astronomical observatory 34
   Planetarium 35
   Planetarium projector 35

GEOGRAPHY 37
   Structure of the Earth 39
   Profile of the Earth's atmosphere 39
   Space achievements 39
   Section of the Earth's crust 40
   Configuration of the continents 41
   Ocean floor 42
   Wave 43
   Common coastal features 43
   Clouds and meteorological symbols 44
   Volcano 45
   Earthquake 45
   Mountain 46
   Cave 46
   Desert 47
   Glacier 48

Water forms 49
   Classification of snow crystals, kinds of precipi-
   tation
Hydrologic cycle 50
Climates of the world 51
International weather symbols 52
   Fronts, cloud amount, wind
Meteorology 54
   Weather map, station model, meteorological
   ground
Meteorological measuring instruments 56
   Direct-reading rain gauge, sunshine recorder
Meteorological satellite 57

VEGETABLE KINGDOM 59
   Structure of a plant 61
     Root, stem, leaf, leaf margin, types of leaves,
     simple leaves, compound leaves
   Structure of a tree 63
     Tree, cross section of a trunk, stump
   Structure of a flower 64
     Types of inflorescences
   Mushrooms 65
     Structure of a mushroom, edible mushrooms,
     poisonous mushroom, deadly mushroom
   Fleshy fruits : berry fruits 66
     Section of a berry : grape, major types of berries
   Compound fleshy fruits 66
     Section of a strawberry, section of a wild black-
     berry or raspberry
   Stone fleshy fruits 67
     Section of a stone fruit : peach, major types of
     stone fruits
   Pome fleshy fruits 68
     Section of a pome fruit : apple, principal types of
     pome fruits
   Fleshy fruits : citrus fruits 69
     Section of a citrus fruit : orange, major types of
     citrus fruits
   Dry fruits : nuts 70
     Section of a hazelnut, section of a walnut, major
     types of nuts
   Various dry fruits 71
     Section of a follicle : star anise, section of a
     legume : pea, section of a silique : mustard, section
     of a capsule : poppy, section of a grain of wheat

Table of Contents

Tropical fruits 72
  Major types of tropical fruits
Vegetables 73
  Fruit vegetables, inflorescent vegetables, leaf vege-
  tables, section of a bulb, bulb vegetables, tuber
  vegetables, root vegetables, stalk vegetables, seed
  vegetables
ANIMAL KINGDOM 79
Deer family 81
  Deer antlers, kinds of deer
Types of jaws 82
  Carnivore's jaw : leopard, rodent's jaw : beaver,
  herbivore's jaw : horse
Horse 83
  Morphology, skeleton, hoof, plantar surface of
  the hoof, horseshoe
Cat 86
  Head, foreleg, retracted claw, extended claw
Bird 87
  Morphology, wing, contour feather, principal types
  of bills, principal types of feet, egg
Fish 90
  Morphology, gills, anatomy
Butterfly 92
  Caterpillar, chrysalis, butterfly
Univalve shell 93
Bivalve shell 93
  Left valve, dorsal view
Edible molluscs 94
  Oyster, principal edible molluscs
Edible crustaceans 95
  Lobster, principal edible crustaceans
Edible gastropods 96
  Snail, principal edible gastropods
Amphibian 97
  Frog, life cycle of the frog, skeleton of the hind-
  limb
Honeybee 98
  Worker, queen, drone, hind legs of the worker,
  hive, honeycomb section
Bat 100
Reptile 101
  Venomous snake's head, turtle
HUMAN BEING 103
Cell 105
  Plant cell, animal cell
Human body 106
  Front view, back view
Genital organs, male 108
  Sagittal section, spermatozoon
Genital organs, female 109
  Sagittal section, anterior view
Breast, sagittal section 109
Muscles 110
  Front view, back view
Skeleton 112
  Front view, back view
Osteology of skull 114
  Lateral view, front view, superior view, inferior
  view
Teeth 115
  Cross section of a molar, human denture

Blood circulation 116
  Schema of circulation, heart, principal veins and
  arteries
Respiratory system, lungs 118
Digestive system 119
Urinary system 120
Nervous system 121
  Peripheral nervous system, central nervous
  system, cross section of lumbar vertebra
Sense organs : sight 123
  Eye, eyeball
Sense organs : hearing 124
  External ear, internal and middle ear
Sense organs : smell 125
  External nose, nasal fossae, sense of smell and
  taste
Sense organs : taste 126
  Mouth, dorsum of tongue
Sense organs : touch 127
  Skin, sensory impulse
Neuron 127
Skin 128
Nail 129
Hair 129
Family relationships 130
FOOD 133
Herbs 135
Pasta 136
Bread 138
Veal 139
  British cut, Parisian cut
Beef 140
  British cut, Parisian cut
Pork 142
  British cut, Parisian cut
Lamb 143
  British cut, Parisian cut
British cheeses 144
Continental cheeses 145
Desserts 146
FARMING 149
Buildings 151
Agricultural machinery 152
ARCHITECTURE 157
Traditional houses 159
Architecture styles 160
  Doric order, ionic order, corinthian order, column
  base
Greek temple 161
  Basic plan of the Greek temple
Arches 162
  Semicircular arch, types of arches
Roman house 163
Gothic cathedral 164
  Cathedral, plan, façade, vault
Vauban fortification 166
Castle 167
Urban scene 168
Theatre 169
  Hall, wings, cross section of a stage

Table of Contents

Lift 171
Escalator 172
House styles 173
HOUSE 175
Exterior of a house 177
Plan 178
Site plan, ground floor, first floor
Rooms of the house 179
Ground floor, first floor, basement
Structure of the house 180
Roof structure, types of roofs, frame, foundations
Building materials 183
Wood flooring 186
*Wood flooring on wooden structure, wood flooring
on cement screed, wood flooring arrangements*
Stairs 187
Door 188
Exterior door, types of doors, plan symbols
Window 189
Composite window, types of windows
Heating 190
*Fireplace, wood burning stove, fire irons, log car-
rier, fire-dog, forced warm-air system, chimney,
single pipe heating system, heating unit, convector,
column radiator, skirting convector, boiler, split
system heating pump, electric heating unit, oil
burner*
Air conditioning 196
Room air conditioner, ceiling fan, dehumidifier
HOUSE FURNITURE 197
Table 199
Gate-leg table, types of tables
Chairs and couches 200
Parts, principal types
Seats 202
Side chair 203
Parts, stretchers, types of chairs
Bed 204
Parts, linen
Storage furniture 205
Window accessories 207
*Curtain, pole, rod, track, roller blind, roll-up blind,
shutters, Venetian blind*
Lights 210
Glassware 212
Dinnerware 213
Silverware 214
*Knife, major types of knives, fork, major types of
forks, spoon, major types of spoons*
Kitchen utensils 217
*Kitchen knife, types of kitchen knives, utensils
for straining and draining, utensils for grinding
and grating, set of utensils, utensils for opening,
utensils for measuring, baking utensils, miscel-
laneous utensils*
Cooking utensils 222
Coffee makers 224
Domestic appliances 225
*Blender, mixer, hand mixer, hand blender, beaters,
food processor, ice-cream freezer, juice extractor,
citrus juicer, microwave oven, electric grill, toaster,*

*griddle, electric cooker, fridge-freezer, washing
machine, tumble dryer, dishwasher, steam iron,
tin-opener, kettle, canister vacuum cleaner, clean-
ing tools*
GARDENING 235
Garden 237
Tools and equipment 238
Chainsaw 243
TOOLS AND EQUIPMENT 245
Carpentry tools 247
*Claw hammer, mallet, plane, screwdriver, spanners,
chisel, spirit level, bradawl, pliers, vice, G-clamp,
brace, hand drill, router, pedestal drill, electric drill,
bench saw, hacksaw, handsaw, circular saw*
Carpentry : fasteners 254
Nail, screw, bolt, nut, washer
Carpentry 255
Board, peeled veneer, plywood, chipboard
Lock 256
Mortise lock, cylinder lock, tubular lock
Plumbing 257
*Plumbing system, toilet, bathroom, sink, tap,
branching, electric water-heater tank, connectors,
union, fittings, plumbing tools, septic tank, sump
pump*
Painting upkeep 268
*Ladders and stepladders, spray paint gun, brush,
scraper, paint roller*
Soldering and welding 271
*Soldering iron, soldering gun, blowlamp, oxy-
acetylene welding, arc welding, welding torch,
cutting torch, butt welding, pressure regulator,
protective clothing*
Electricity 274
*Light bulb, mercury-vapour lamp, fluorescent tube,
three-pin plug, fuse, electrician's tools*
CLOTHING 279
Men's clothing 281
*Trench coat, raincoat, sheepskin jacket, duffle
coat, parka, inverness cape, three-quarter coat,
waistcoat, double-breasted jacket, single-breasted
coat, trousers, braces, belt, shirt, collar, necktie,
cravat, bow tie, V-neck cardigan, pullovers,
sock, underwear, headgear*
Glove 289
Women's clothing 290
*Coats, dresses, skirts, pockets, blouses, sleeves,
waistcoats and pullovers, types of collars, necklines and necks, trousers, nightwear, hose, underwear, headgear*
Children's clothing 305
*Christening set, all-in-one vest, hooded towelling
robe, babygro, nylon frilly tights, plastic pants,
nappy, vest, bib, crossover back straps dungarees,
high-back dungarees, jumpsuit, sleeping bag, sleepsuit, one-piece sleepsuit, pyjamas, leotard, pinafore, snowsuit*
Shoes 308
*Parts of a shoe, principal types of shoes, acces-
sories for shoes*
Costumes 311
Bullfighter, ballerina

9

Table of Contents

PERSONAL ADORNMENT 313
  Jewellery 315
    Diversity of jewellery, bracelets, charms, rings,
    necklaces, cuts for gemstones, brilliant cut facets
  Eyeglasses 318
    Front, temple, nose pad, principal types of eye-
    glasses
  Hair styles 320
    Kinds of hair, components of hair styles, wigs
    and hairpieces
  Make-up 322
    Make-up kit, make-up products, make-up acces-
    sories

PERSONAL ARTICLES 325
  Razors 327
  Scissors 328
  Combs 328
  Hairbrushes 328
  Toothbrush 329
  Electric toothbrush 329
  Hair dryer 330
  Lighted mirror 330
  Salon-style hair dryer 330
  Curling iron 331
  Curling brush 331
  Hairsetter 331
  Manicure set 332
  Manicuring instruments 333
  Hairstyling implements 333
  Smoking accessories 334
  Umbrella 336
  Luggage 337
  Handbags 338
  Leather goods 340

COMMUNICATIONS 343
  Writing styles of the world 345
  Braille alphabet 346
  Deaf-mute alphabet 347
  Punctuation marks 347
  Diacritic symbols 347
  International phonetic alphabet 348
  Typical letter 349
  Proofreading 350
  Writing instruments 352
  Photography 353
    Single-lens reflex camera, still cameras, acces-
    sories, Polaroid Land camera, films, flash unit,
    exposure meter, spotmeter, studio lighting, pho-
    tographic accessories, studio accessories, dark-
    room, enlarger, slide projector, projection screen
  Sound reproducing system 363
    System elements, amplifier-tuner, turntable,
    record, tape deck
  Video tape recorder 367
  Cinematography 368
    Sound camera, sound projector, video camera,
    dynamic microphone
  Telegraph 370
    Diagram of a circuit, receiver, transmitter, Morse
    code

  Telex : teleprinter 371
  Telephone set 372
    Receiver, transmitter, types of telephones, tele-
    phone answering machine
  Television 374
    Studio and control rooms, studio floor, produc-
    tion control room, television set, picture tube
  Telecommunication satellites 378
    Hermes satellite, examples of satellites, trajectory
    of a satellite, telecommunications network

TRANSPORT 381

Road Transport 383
  Car 383
    Body, types of body, headlight, rear of estate car,
    windscreen wiper, dashboard, instrument panel,
    door, steering, seats
  Service station 387
    Petrol pump
  Semi-trailer 388
    Tractor unit
  Engines 390
    Diesel engine, turbo-charged engine, petrol
    engine
  Battery 392
  Radiator 392
  Spark plug 392
  Exhaust system 392
  Tyres 393
  Brakes 393
  Long-distance coach 394
  Motorcycle 395
  Bicycle 397
  Cross section of a street 399
  Cross section of a road 399
  Fixed bridges 400
  Movable bridges 403

Rail Transport 404
  Diesel-electric locomotive 404
  Bogie wagon 405
  Freight wagons 406
  Types of passenger coaches 407
    Saloon open coach, sleeping car, dining car
  Railway track 408
  Level crossing 409
  Railway station 410
  Train yard 411
  Container 411
  Station concourse 412
  Station platform 413
  Underground station 414
  Underground railway 415
    Underground train, passenger car interior, bogie
    and track

Maritime Transport 416
  Four-masted bark 416
    Masting and standing, sail plan
  Types of sails 418
  Types of rigs 418
  Passenger liner 419

Table of Contents

Inter-island ferry 420
Container ship 420
Hovercraft 421
Hydrofoil, jetfoil 422
Submersible 423
Submarine 424
Frigate 425
Canal lock 426
Harbour 427
Navigational aids 428
   Echo sounder, sextant, liquid compass
Maritime signals 430
   Buoys, lighthouse, lantern of lighthouse, cardinal
   system of marking, lateral system of marking
Anchor 433
   Ship's anchor, types of anchors

Air Transport 434
Long-range aircraft 434
Wing structure 435
Wing shape 435
Tail shape 435
Turbo-jet engine 436
Flight deck 437
Airport 438
   Ground airport equipment
Passenger terminal 440
Helicopter 441

Space Travel 442
Rocket 442
Space shuttle 443
   Space shuttle at take-off, space shuttle in orbit
Spacesuit 444

OFFICE SUPPLIES AND EQUIPMENT 445
Stationery 447
Office furniture 451
Typewriter 452
Microcomputer 454
   Functions in a system, configuration of a system,
   keyboard, peripheral equipment, dot matrix
   printer, acoustic coupler, joystick
Computer room 458

MUSIC 459
Musical notation 461
Stringed instruments 463
   Violin family, violin, bow, harp
Keyboard instruments 465
   Upright piano, upright piano action
Organ 467
   Production of sound, console, mechanism of the
   organ, organ pipes
Wind instruments 469
   Woodwind family, saxophone, reeds, brass family,
   trumpet
Percussion instruments 471
Traditional musical instruments 473
Instrumental groups 476
Musical accessories 478
Symphony orchestra 479
Electric guitar 480

Classical guitar 481
CREATIVE LEISURE ACTIVITIES 483
Sewing 485
   Sewing machine: tension dial, presser foot,
   needle, sewing accessories, fasteners, zip, fabric
   structure, underlying fabrics, pattern
Knitting 490
   Knitting machine: tension block, needle bed,
   carriage, latch needle
Bobbin lace 492
Embroidery 493
   Frame, groups of stitches
Weaving 494
   Horizontal floor loom, upright floor loom, acces-
   sories, diagram of weaving principle, basic
   weaves
Fine bookbinding 498
   Bound book
Engraving and etching tools 501
Relief printing 502
   Equipment, intaglio press
Lithography 503
   Equipment, litho press
Printing 504
   Diagram of letterpress printing, diagram of gravure
   printing, diagram of lithographic printing
Pottery 505
   Kick wheel, tools, firing
Stained glass 507

SPORTS AND LEISURE 509

Team Games 511
Soccer 511
   Field, ball
Rugby 512
   Field, ball
Rugby union 512
   Scrum, team playing positions, line out, line out
   plan
Cricket 514
   Field, pitch, wicket, cricket player, bat, ball
Hockey 516
   Field, stick, ball, player, goalkeeper
Ice hockey 517
   Rink
American football 518
   Scrimmage, protective equipment, playing field
Baseball 520
   Field, catcher, player, bat, glove
Netball 522
   Court, goalpost, netball player, netball
Basketball 523
   Court, basket
Tennis 524
   Court, tennis player, tennis racquet
Badminton 526
   Court, shuttlecock
Squash 527
   International singles court, squash racquet
Table tennis 528
   Table

Table of Contents

Volleyball 529
Court, ball
Bowls 530
Green, mat position on green, bowl, jack, delivery

Water Sports 531
Water polo 531
Playing area
Swimming 532
Swimming competition, starting position, types of strokes
Diving 534
Diving installations, starting positions, groups of dives
Skin diving 536
Sailboard 537
Dinghy 538
Points of sailing, fixtures
Water skiing 540
Rowing 541
Types of boat, types of oar

Aerial Sports 542
Gliding 542
Glider, cockpit
Hang gliding 543
Hang glider
Parachuting 544
Parachute, free fall

Winter Sports 545
Skiing 545
Skier, ski boot, safety binding, ski resort
Skating 548
Figure skate, hockey skate, speed skate, roller skate
Bobsleigh 549
Toboggan 549

Pub Sports 550
Darts, dartboard, playing area

Equestrian Sports 551
Riding 551
Dress and equipment, obstacles, competition ring, bridle, saddle
Horse racing 554
Horse and jockey, racing programme, race course

Athletics 556
Track and field athletics 556
Arena, field events
Gymnastics 559
Weightlifting 561

Combat Sports 562
Fencing 562
Piste, fencer, parts of the weapon, fencing weapons, positions
Judo 564
Mat, judo suit, holds
Boxing 565
Ring

Leisure Sports 566

Fishing 566
Fly rod, spinning rod, fly reel, open-face spinning reel, fishhook, float, lures, accessories
Snooker and Billiards 568
Snooker and billiards equipment, tables
Archery 570
Bow, arrow, archer
Golf 571
Course, hole, types of golf clubs, golf accessories
Mountaineering 574
Equipment, mountaineer
Tenpin bowling 576

Indoor Games 577
Chess 577
Men, chessboard, chess notation
Backgammon 578
Card games 578
Dice 579
Dominoes 579
Mah-jong 579
Roulette table 580
French roulette wheel, betting layout

Camping 581
Caravan 581
Tents 582
Family tents, ridge tent, types of tents
Sleeping bags 584
Bed-mattress and accessories 584
Butane accessories 585
Cooking set 585
Penknife 585
Tools 586
Knots 587

MEASURING DEVICES 589
Measure of time 591
Mechanical watch, tuning fork watch, hourglass, sundial, weight-driven clock mechanism, grandfather clock
Measure of weight 594
Steelyard, beam balance, spring balance, Roberval's balance, analytical balance, self-indicating scales, bathroom scales, electronic scales
Measure of temperature 597
Bimetallic thermometer, clinical thermometer, room thermostat
Measure of pressure 598
Aneroid barometer, sphygmomanometer
Measure of length and width 599
Tape measure, pedometer, micrometer
Theodolite 600
Watt-hour meter 601
Horizontal seismograph 602
Vertical seismograph 602

OPTICAL INSTRUMENTS 603
Binocular microscope 605
Electron microscope 606
Prism binoculars 607
Telescopic sight 607

Table of Contents

Reflector telescope 608
Refractor telescope 609
Lens 610
   Converging lens, diverging lens
Magnetic compass 610
Radar 611

HEALTH 613
First aid kit 615
Syringes 615
Walking aids 616
   Crutches, sticks
Wheelchair 617

ENERGY 619
Coal mine 621
   *Open-pit mine, strip mine, mining, underground
   mine, pithead, pneumatic hammer, jackleg drill*
Oil 626
   *Drilling rig, beam pump, gas lift, Christmas tree,
   offshore drilling and rigs, production platform,
   pipeline, tanker, oil transport, oil storage, refinery,
   refinery products, oil sands mining plant*
Electricity 637
   *Hydroelectric complex, cross section of an em-
   bankment dam, cross section of a concrete dam,
   major types of dams, steps in production of electricity, cross section of a hydroelectric power
   station, generator, cross section of a hydraulic
   turbine, suspension tower, overhead connection,
   tidal power plant, power station: coal fired power
   station, nuclear power station, turbo-generator*
Nuclear energy 650
   *Magnox reactor, advance gas-cooled reactor, pres-
   surized water reactor, fast reactor, control room,
   production of electricity by nuclear energy, nuclear
   fuel cycle*
Solar energy 654
   *Solar furnace, tower-type solar power station,
   solar house, solar cell, solar collector*
Windmill 657
   Tower mill, post mill
Wind turbine 658
   *Horizontal-axis wind turbine, vertical-axis wind
   turbine, wind turbine electricity production*

HEAVY MACHINERY AND PLANT 659
Dragline 661
Fire appliance 662
   Turntable ladder, water-tender
Bulldozer 664
Wheel loader 665
Grader 666
Hydraulic shovel 667
Tractor-scraper 668

Dumper truck 668
Freight handling 669
   Crane, forklift trucks, handling appliances

WEAPONS 673
Stone Age arms 675
African warrior 675
Roman legionary 675
Armour 676
Bows and crossbow 677
Swords 678
Bayonets 679
   Major types of bayonets, parts of a hilted bayonet
Ship's cannon 680
   *Muzzle loading, barrel, projectiles, accessories
   for firing*
Arquebus 682
   Flintlock, loading
Hand grenade 682
Mortar 683
Submachine gun 683
Modern howitzer 684
Automatic rifle 685
Bazooka 686
Recoilless rifle 686
Heavy machine gun 687
Light machine gun 687
Hunting weapons 688
   Rifle, shotgun, cartridge
Pistol 689
Revolver 689
Tank 690
Combat aircraft 691
Missiles 692
   *Structure of a missile, command system, major
   types of modern missiles*

SYMBOLS 693
Heraldry 695
   *Flag and shield, examples of symbols, flag
   shapes*
Signs of the zodiac 698
Information symbols 699
   *Graphic elements for symbols, international road
   signs, common symbols, crosses*
Scientific symbols 708

GENERAL INDEX 711

THEMATIC INDEXES 745

SPECIALIZED INDEXES 781

SELECTIVE BIBLIOGRAPHY 795

CONTENTS 797

13

PREFACE

There are many dictionaries available whose titles readily spring to mind and whose merits are beyond question.

Why then a new dictionary?

It has become increasingly evident that there is a notable absence of dictionaries which provide a reliable terminology for the many objects, devices, machines and tools of modern life.

It is also evident that few, if any, dictionaries are available to those whose learning disabilities, or approach to the English language from a less than regimented manner, prevent them from accessing words by alphabetical sequence alone.

Given this situation it was logical that a dictionary should be originated to answer those needs. The original edition of the VISUAL DICTIONARY was the brainchild of Éditions Québec/Amérique of Canada, whose terminologists, linguists, researchers and illustrators, under the supervision of prominent terminologist Jean-Claude Corbeil, spent fully four years devising and compiling an impressive work of reference. This British English edition of the VISUAL DICTIONARY is based on that original work to which many new, revised and improved drawings have been made to ensure its accuracy and applicability to the British reader or student of English.

Its clarity of presentation, carefully selected content, crisp illustrations, and yet simplicity of use make it a unique tool for anyone concerned with using the right term in all circumstances. It is a work intended to promote clear, efficient communication, encourage learning and to develop and enrich everyone's vocabulary.

Alan GOODWORTH
Facts On File Publications
Oxford, England

INTRODUCTION

PURPOSE OF THE DICTIONARY

Initially, we set ourselves two goals:
a) List all the terms and notions which designate or portray the many elements of everyday life in an industrial, post-industrial or developing society, and which one needs to know to buy an object, discuss a repair, read a book or a newspaper, etc.
b) Visualize them through graphic representation; i.e., assign to an illustration the role played by the written definition in a conventional dictionary.

The latter implies a constraint: The selected notions must lend themselves to graphic representation. Hence, the list must omit abstract words, adjectives, verbs and adverbs, even though they are part of the specialized vocabulary. Terminologists have not yet adequately solved this problem.

Following a series of tests and consultations, technical graphics were deemed the best form of visual presentation because they stress the essential features of a notion and leave out the accessories, like the fashion details of clothing. The resulting illustration gains in conceptual clarity what it loses in detail and provides a better definition.

To achieve our goals, we assembled two production teams, one of terminologists and another of graphic artists, who worked together under one scientific supervisor.

THE INTENDED USER

The VISUAL DICTIONARY is meant for the active member of the modern industrial society who needs to be acquainted with a wide range of technical terms from many assorted areas, but not to be specialist in any.

The profile of the typical user guided our selection of items in every category. We included what may be of use to everybody and deliberately left out what is in the exclusive realm of the specialist.

Varying levels of specialization will be noted from one category to another, however, depending on one's degree of familiarity with a subject or the very constraints of specialization. Thus, the vocabulary of clothing or electricity is more familiar to us than that of nuclear energy. Or again, to describe the human anatomy, one is confined to medical terminology but to describe the structure of a fruit, one may use both the scientific and popular terms. Familiarity with a subject also varies from one user to another or with the degree of penetration of a speciality. The best example no doubt is the propagation of the vocabulary of data processing brought on by the widespread use of the personal computer.

Be that as it may, the aim was to reflect as best as possible the specialized vocabulary currently used in every field.

CHARACTERISTICS OF THE DICTIONARY

What distinguishes THE FACTS ON FILE VISUAL DICTIONARY from other lexicons?

Conventional works

Dictionaries come in four basic types:
a) Language dictionaries

Language dictionaries are divided into two parts.

The first is the nomenclature, i.e., the list of words that are the object of a lexicographical commentary. It forms the macrostructure of the dictionary. For practical purposes, words are listed in alphabetical order. The nomenclature generally includes words of the common modern

Introduction

language, archaic words — often incorporated in a text — whose knowledge is useful to understand the language's history, and some technical terms that are fairly widespread.

The second is a lexicographical commentary whose microstructure varies according to lexicographical tradition. It generally deals with the word's grammatical category, its pronunciation, in the international phonetic alphabet, its etymology, its various meanings, often in chronological order, and, finally, its uses according to a rather impressionistic typology that includes the *colloquial*, the *popular* and the *vulgar*.

b) Encyclopedic dictionaries

These add on to the former type of dictionary commentaries on the nature, the function or the history of things, allowing the layman or the specialist to better understand the import of a word. They devote much more space to technical terms and closely follow the development of science and technology. Illustrations are assigned an important role. These works are more or less bulky, depending on the extent of the nomenclature, the importance of the commentaries and the space allotted to proper nouns.

c) Encyclopedias

Contrary to the preceding, encyclopedias do not include a full word list. They are essentially concerned with the scientific, technical, geographical, historical and economic aspects of their subjects. The structure of the nomenclature is arbitrary since every classification, be it alphabetical, notional, chronological or otherwise, is legitimate. The number of such works is potentially unlimited as are the activities of civilization, although a distinction must be drawn between universal and specialized encyclopedias.

d) Specialized lexicons or vocabularies

These works are generally meant to enhance communications or to answer particular needs arising from the evolution of science or technology. They vary from one another in every respect : the method of compilation, the relationship of the authors to the subject, the size of the nomenclature, the number of languages dealt with at once and the manner of establishing equivalents, either through translation or comparison between unilingual terminologies. There is intense activity in this field nowadays. Works abound in every area and in every language combination deemed useful.

THE FACTS ON FILE VISUAL DICTIONARY is not an encyclopedia. For one, it does not describe but names items. Secondly, it avoids the enumeration of items within a category. Rather than list the different types of trees, for instance, it selects a typical representative of the tree family and lists each of its parts.

It is even less a language dictionary. It contains mostly nouns — without written definitions — few adjectives, and some complex terms.

Neither is it a compendium of specialized vocabularies —, as it favours words useful to the average person over terms known only to specialists, who may find it too elementary.

The VISUAL DICTIONARY is the first basic dictionary of terminological orientation, comprising within a single volume, with high regard for accuracy and easy access, thousands of more or less technical terms for which knowledge becomes a necessity in this modern world where science, technology and their by-products permeate and influence daily life.

METHODOLOGY

The preparation of this dictionary followed the methodology of systematic and comparative terminological research developed in Quebec in the early Seventies, now widespread in the whole of Canada, Europe, South America, North Africa and Sub-Saharan Africa.

We worked in the two languages, English and French, that are the most widely used throughout the world. The research available in both languages ensures a comprehensive stock of notions and terms, thanks to the interrelationship of approaches and specialities proper to each language and their different perception and expression of the same realities. Eventually, we propose to apply the same methods to other languages, particularly Arab and Spanish.

The methodology of systematic terminological research involves many stages that follow one another in logical order. This progression applies to each language under study, their comparison intervening only at the end of the process with the compilation of terminological files. Thus, the pitfalls of literal translation are avoided.

A brief description of each stage follows:

Field delimitation

First, the content and size of the project must be carefully determined according to its goals and its prospective users.

In the case of the VISUAL DICTIONARY, we selected the major themes we felt should be dealt with, then divided each one into categories and sub-categories, keeping sight of our initial goal to steer clear of encyclopedism and ultraspecialization. The result was a detailed interim table of contents, providing the structure of the dictionary, to be used as a guide and refined in subsequent stages. The actual table of contents emerged from this process.

A dummy was then submitted to the contributing editors, lexicographers and terminologists, for their opinion on the content and the graphic style of the illustrations. Enriched from their comments, the project moved onto the production stage.

The collection of documentary sources

The production plan first called for researching and collecting the material likely to yield the required information on each subject. The research covered both French and English texts.

Here, without prejudice, is the list of documentary sources in order of the confidence placed in them for reflecting correct usage:
— English-French language dictionaries.
— Specialized dictionaries or vocabularies, whether unilingual, bilingual (French-English) or multilingual, whose quality and reliability should be carefully appraised.
— Encyclopedias or encyclopedic dictionaries, language dictionaries.
— Catalogues, commercial texts, advertisements in specialized magazines and large dailies.
— Technical documents from the International Standard Organization (ISO), the American Standard Association (ASA) and the Association française de normalisation (AFNOR); directions for use of commercial products; comparative product analyses; technical information supplied by manufacturers; official government publications, etc.
— French or English articles or works by specialists with an adequate level of competence in their field. In translation, these prove highly instructive as to word usage, although caution should be exercised.

On the whole, some four to five thousand references. The selective bibliography contained in the dictionary lists only the general reference works, not the specialized sources.

Sifting through the documentation

For every subject, the terminologist must sift through the documentation, searching for specific notions and the words used by various authors to express them. From this process emerges the notional structure of the subject, its standard or differing designations. In the latter case, the terminologist pursues his research, recording each term with supporting references, until he has formed a well-documented opinion on each of the competing terms.

Since the dictionary is visual, terminologists at this stage searched for appropriate ways of graphically depicting each coherent group of notions in one or several illustrations depending on the subject. The graphic artists drew from these elements to design each page of the dictionary.

Introduction

The make-up of documentary files

The elements of each terminological file were assembled from the mass of documentation.

Once identified and defined through illustration, each notion was assigned the term most frequently used by the best authors and the most reliable sources to express it. If the terminological file suggested competing terms, one was selected upon discussion and agreement between the terminologist and the scientific director.

Specialists were called upon to discuss highly technical files subject to a greater risk of error.

Graphic visualization

The terminological file, along with a proposal for graphic representation, was then turned over to the graphics team for the design and production of the final illustrated page.

Each terminologist revised the plates pertaining to his files to ensure the accuracy of illustrations, terms and spelling.

General revision of plates

The terminological research was carried out subject by subject following a plan, but not necessarily in order.

The final version of the original edition of the dictionary underwent two complete verifications. Three revisers in each language were first asked to proofread the entire work, with emphasis on the spelling, without disregarding the terminology. With the help of their commentaries, the written form was standardized throughout the dictionary. Each instance of every word or notion was checked to ensure the greatest possible degree of coherence.

All the documentation and terminological files on which the dictionary is based remain in archives.

PARTICULAR PROBLEMS

British English

The whole of the text of the original edition of the dictionary was then submitted to a further stage of revision. The text was divided into different subject areas and sections were sent to specialists to check the terminology and illustrations for their accuracy in British usage.

Once checked, all the items were then discussed by the Managing Editor and the Publisher, and changes were agreed and then implemented in this edition.

Terminological variation

Our research revealed a number of cases of terminological variation, i.e., designation of a notion by different terms.

Here is a partial list of such cases:

— A particular term may have been used by only one author or occurred only once throughout the documentation; we then chose the most frequent competing term;

— Technical terms are often in compound form, hyphenated or not, incorporating a preposition or preceded by a noun. This characteristic gives rise to at least two types of terminological variants:

a) The compound technical term may be shortened by the deletion of one or many of its elements, especially when the context is significant. Within limits, the shorter term becomes the usual designation of the notion. For instance, *objective lens* becomes *objective, fine adjustment knob* becomes *fine adjustment, revolving nose piece, nose piece*. We retained the compound form, leaving it to the user to shorten it according to the context.

b) One of the elements of the compound may itself have equivalent forms, generally synonyms in the common language. For instance, *magnetic needle* is equivalent to *magnetized needle, eye lens* to *ocular lens.* We then retained the most frequent form.
— Finally, the variation may stem from a difference of opinion, with no bearing on terminology, making it unnecessary to give up the best known term. For instance, the *first condenser lens* and *second condenser lens* of the electronic microscope are called *upper condenser lens* and *lower condenser lens* by some authors. The difference is not sufficient to cause a problem. In these cases, the most frequent or best known form was preferred.

Terminological sense

This calls for a brief commentary on the terminological sense as compared to the lexicographical sense.

The long history of language dictionaries, the fact that they are familiar reference works, known and used by everyone from schooldays, means that a certain tradition has been set that is known and accepted by all. We know how variants designating the same notion are classified and treated ; therefore, we know how to interpret the dictionary and how to use the information it gives or does not give us.

Terminological dictionaries are either recent or intended for a specialized few. There is no real tradition guiding the preparation of such dictionaries. If the specialist knows how to interpret a dictionary pertaining to his own area of expertise because he is familiar with its terminology, the same cannot be said of the layman who may be confused by variants. Finally, language dictionaries have to some extent disciplined their users to a standard vocabulary. But since they relate to recent specialities, the terms listed in specialized vocabularies are far from set.

This aspect of the vocabulary sciences must be taken into account in the evaluation of the VISUAL DICTIONARY.

Spelling variations

The spelling of English words varies considerably. It sometimes differs according to the variety of English : for instance, *center* is American while *centre* is British. Often, the problem lies in determining whether a word should be written as a single word or in two words, with or without a hyphen : for example, *wave length* and *wavelength, grand-mother* and *grandmother*. In most cases the spelling favoured by the *Collins English Dictionary* and the *Longman Dictionary of the English Language* has been adopted.

Jean-Claude CORBEIL
Martin H. MANSER

THE FACTS ON FILE VISUAL DICTIONARY
FOR A *NEW* DICTIONARY A *NEW* USAGE GUIDE

THE FACTS ON FILE VISUAL DICTIONARY is divided into three parts:
- — TABLE OF CONTENTS
- — ILLUSTRATIONS depicting the ENTRIES
- — ALPHABETICAL INDEXES
  - — GENERAL
  - — THEMATIC
  - — SPECIALIZED

There are two ways of finding what you are looking for. You may refer either to the illustration or the word.

Starting from the **illustration**	Starting from the **word**
You want to know what an object is called	You want to know what a word stands for
Look in the **table of contents** for the **theme** which best corresponds to your query	Look for the word in the **general** index or in the **thematic** or **specialized** indexes, depending on the area of research
You will find **references** to **illustrations**	You will find **references** to the **illustrations** in which the word appears
Alongside the illustration, you will find the corresponding **word**	You will see from the **illustration** what the word stands for

ASTRONOMY

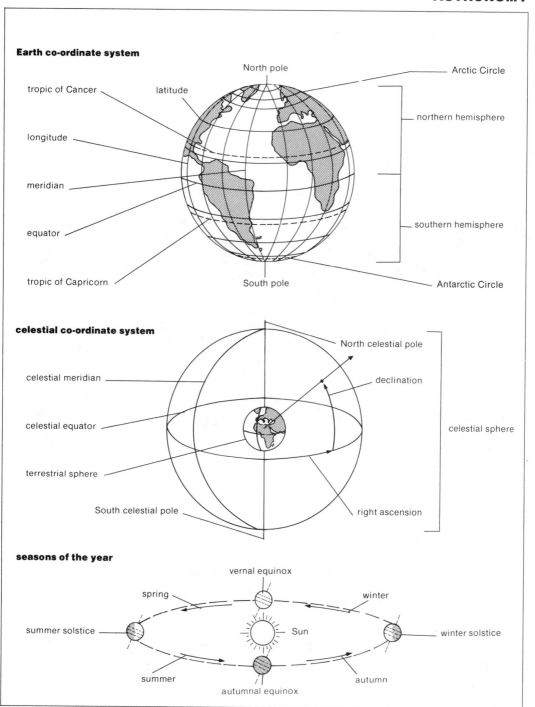

Earth co-ordinate system

- North pole
- Arctic Circle
- tropic of Cancer
- latitude
- northern hemisphere
- longitude
- meridian
- southern hemisphere
- equator
- tropic of Capricorn
- South pole
- Antarctic Circle

celestial co-ordinate system

- celestial meridian
- North celestial pole
- declination
- celestial equator
- celestial sphere
- terrestrial sphere
- South celestial pole
- right ascension

seasons of the year

- vernal equinox
- spring
- winter
- summer solstice
- Sun
- winter solstice
- summer
- autumn
- autumnal equinox

planets of the solar system

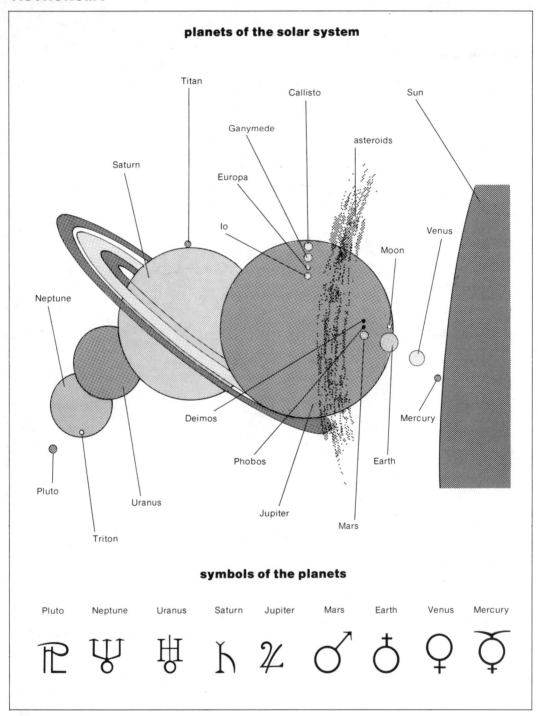

Titan

Callisto

Sun

Ganymede

asteroids

Saturn

Europa

Venus

Io

Moon

Neptune

Deimos

Mercury

Pluto

Phobos

Earth

Uranus

Jupiter

Triton

Mars

symbols of the planets

Pluto	Neptune	Uranus	Saturn	Jupiter	Mars	Earth	Venus	Mercury

Sun

structure of the Sun

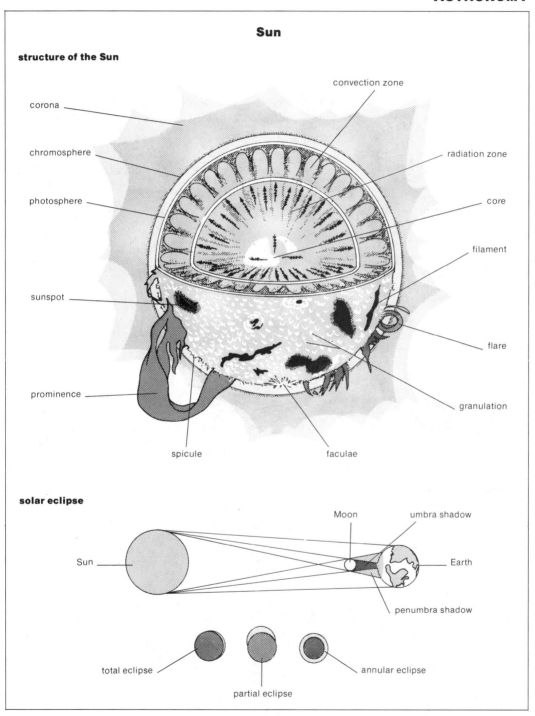

corona

convection zone

chromosphere

radiation zone

photosphere

core

filament

sunspot

flare

prominence

granulation

spicule

faculae

solar eclipse

Moon

umbra shadow

Sun

Earth

penumbra shadow

total eclipse

annular eclipse

partial eclipse

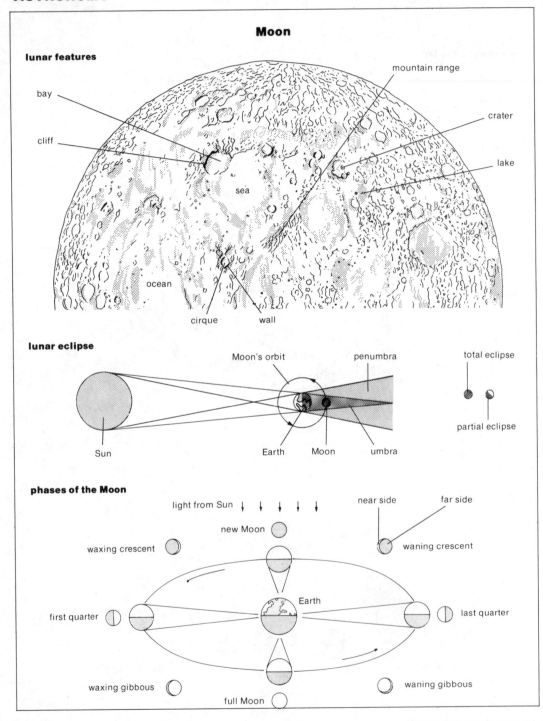

Moon

lunar features

mountain range

bay

cliff

crater

lake

sea

ocean

cirque   wall

lunar eclipse

Moon's orbit   penumbra   total eclipse

partial eclipse

Sun   Earth   Moon   umbra

phases of the Moon

light from Sun   near side   far side

new Moon

waxing crescent   waning crescent

first quarter   Earth   last quarter

waxing gibbous   waning gibbous

full Moon

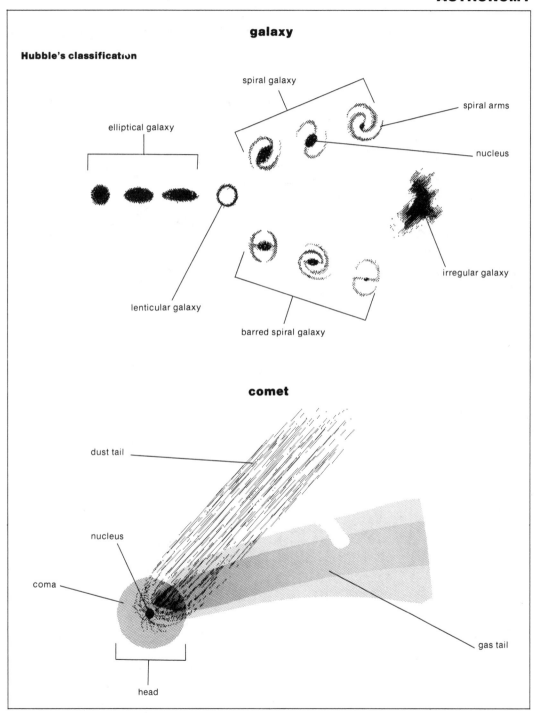

galaxy

Hubble's classification

elliptical galaxy

spiral galaxy

spiral arms

nucleus

lenticular galaxy

barred spiral galaxy

irregular galaxy

comet

dust tail

nucleus

coma

gas tail

head

constellations of the northern hemisphere

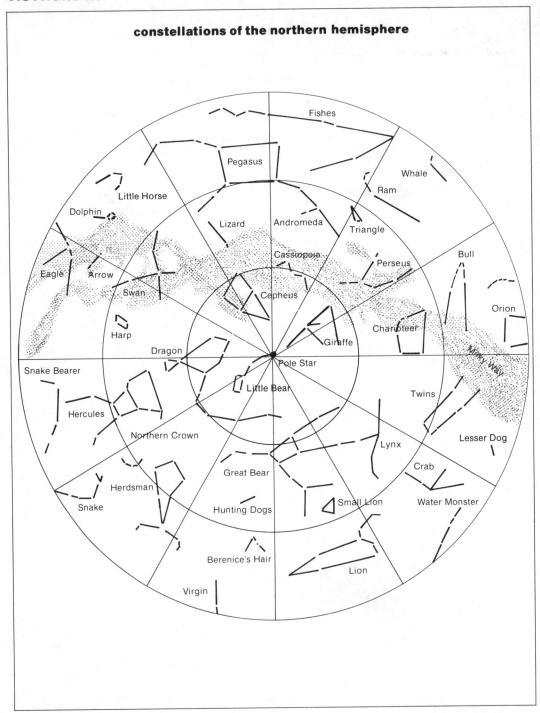

constellations of the southern hemisphere

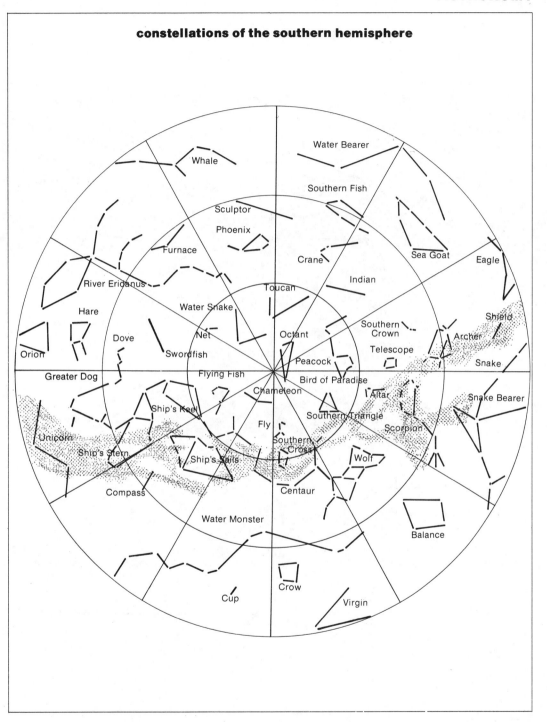

astronomical observatory

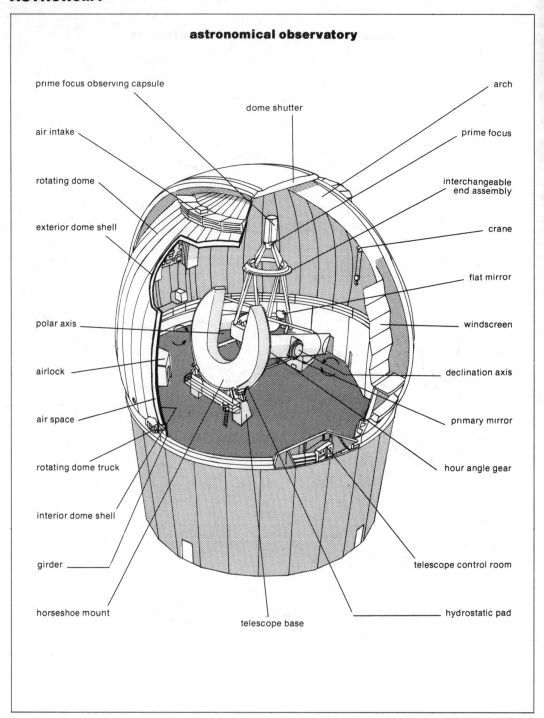

prime focus observing capsule

arch

dome shutter

air intake

prime focus

rotating dome

interchangeable end assembly

exterior dome shell

crane

flat mirror

polar axis

windscreen

airlock

declination axis

air space

primary mirror

rotating dome truck

hour angle gear

interior dome shell

girder

telescope control room

horseshoe mount

hydrostatic pad

telescope base

planetarium

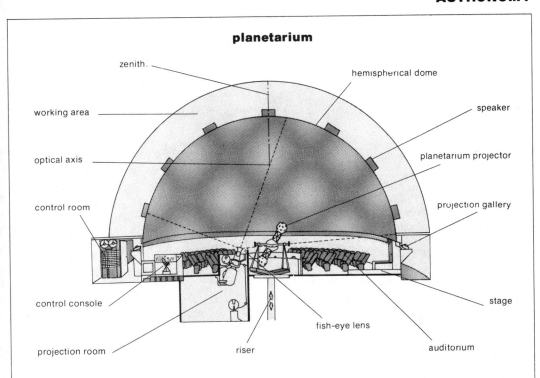

zenith

hemispherical dome

working area

speaker

optical axis

planetarium projector

control room

projection gallery

control console

stage

projection room

riser

fish-eye lens

auditorium

planetarium projector

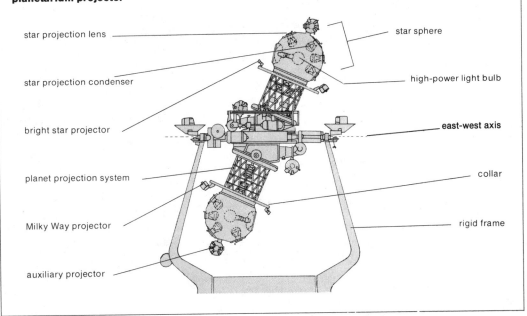

star projection lens

star sphere

star projection condenser

high-power light bulb

bright star projector

east-west axis

planet projection system

collar

Milky Way projector

rigid frame

auxiliary projector

GEOGRAPHY

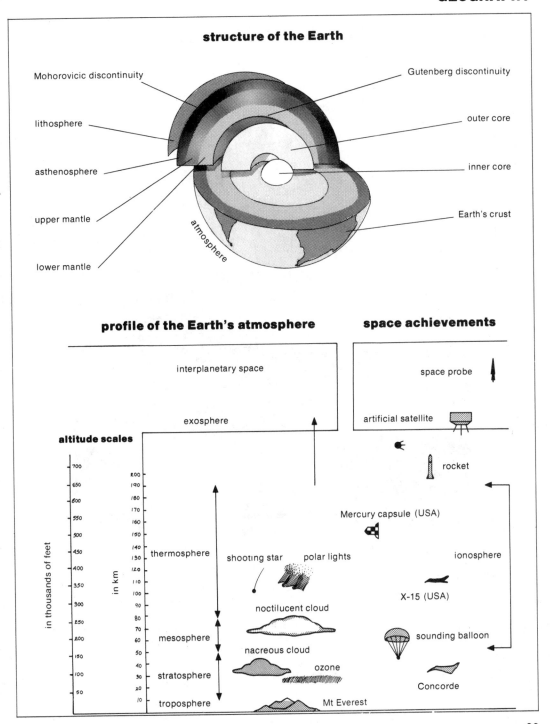

structure of the Earth

Mohorovicic discontinuity

lithosphere

asthenosphere

upper mantle

lower mantle

Gutenberg discontinuity

outer core

inner core

Earth's crust

atmosphere

profile of the Earth's atmosphere

interplanetary space

exosphere

altitude scales

in thousands of feet

in km

thermosphere

shooting star   polar lights

noctilucent cloud

mesosphere

nacreous cloud

stratosphere

ozone

troposphere

Mt Everest

space achievements

space probe

artificial satellite

rocket

Mercury capsule (USA)

ionosphere

X-15 (USA)

sounding balloon

Concorde

section of the Earth's crust

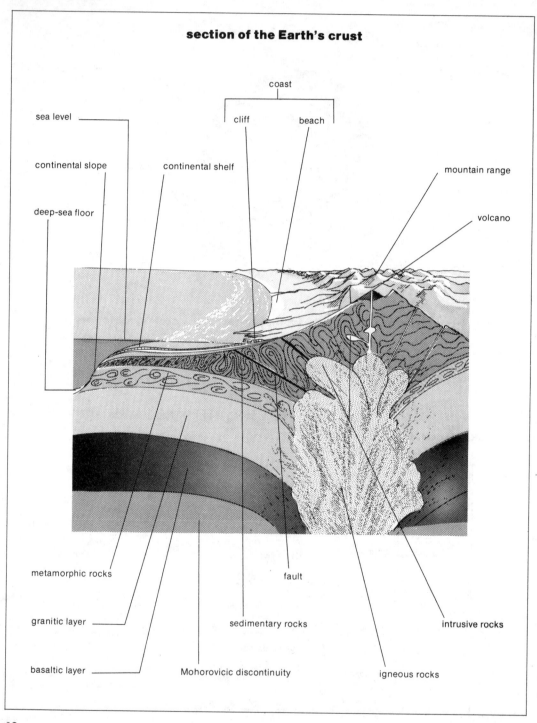

coast

sea level

cliff   beach

continental slope   continental shelf

mountain range

deep-sea floor

volcano

metamorphic rocks   fault

granitic layer   sedimentary rocks   intrusive rocks

basaltic layer   Mohorovicic discontinuity   igneous rocks

configuration of the continents

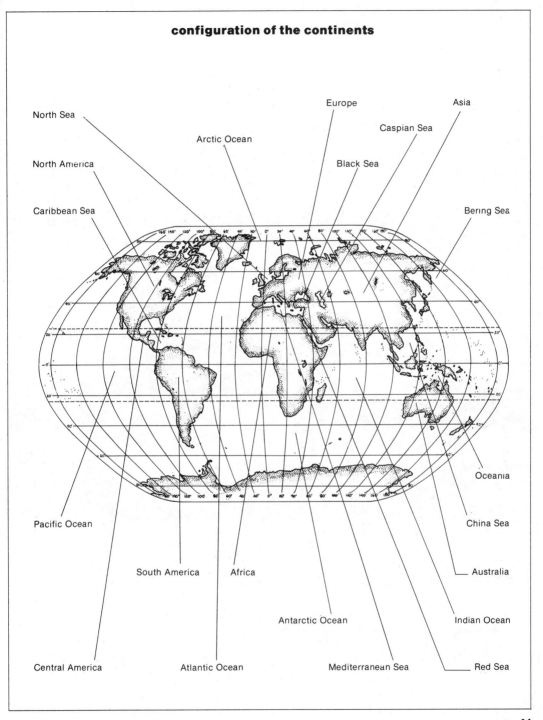

North Sea

North America

Caribbean Sea

Arctic Ocean

Europe

Caspian Sea

Asia

Black Sea

Bering Sea

Pacific Ocean

Oceania

China Sea

South America

Africa

Australia

Central America

Atlantic Ocean

Antarctic Ocean

Mediterranean Sea

Indian Ocean

Red Sea

continental plate on ocean floor

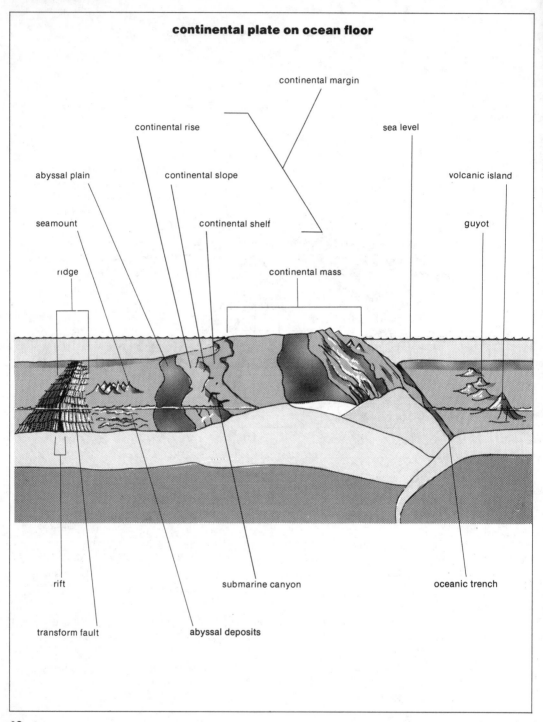

continental margin

continental rise

sea level

abyssal plain

continental slope

volcanic island

continental shelf

guyot

seamount

ridge

continental mass

rift

submarine canyon

oceanic trench

transform fault

abyssal deposits

wave

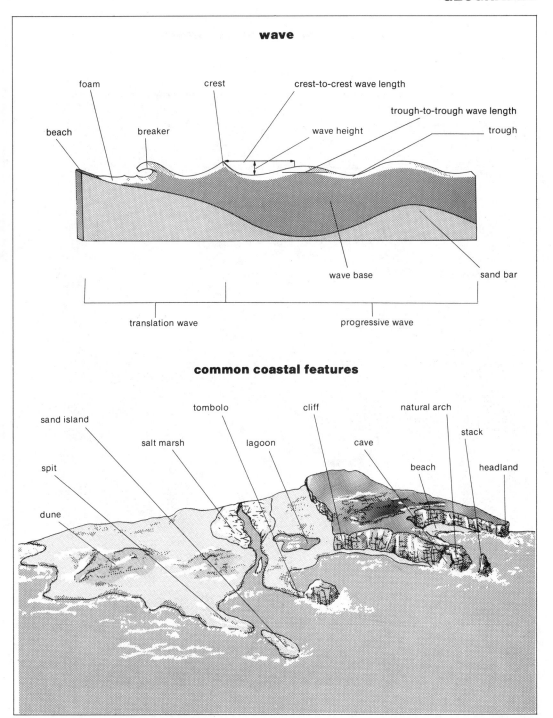

foam

crest

crest-to-crest wave length

trough-to-trough wave length

beach

breaker

wave height

trough

wave base

sand bar

translation wave

progressive wave

common coastal features

tombolo

cliff

natural arch

sand island

stack

salt marsh

lagoon

cave

beach

headland

spit

dune

clouds and meteorological symbols

high clouds

clouds of vertical development

cirrus

cirrocumulus

cirrostratus

middle clouds

altostratus

cumulonimbus

altocumulus

stratocumulus

low clouds

nimbostratus

cumulus

stratus

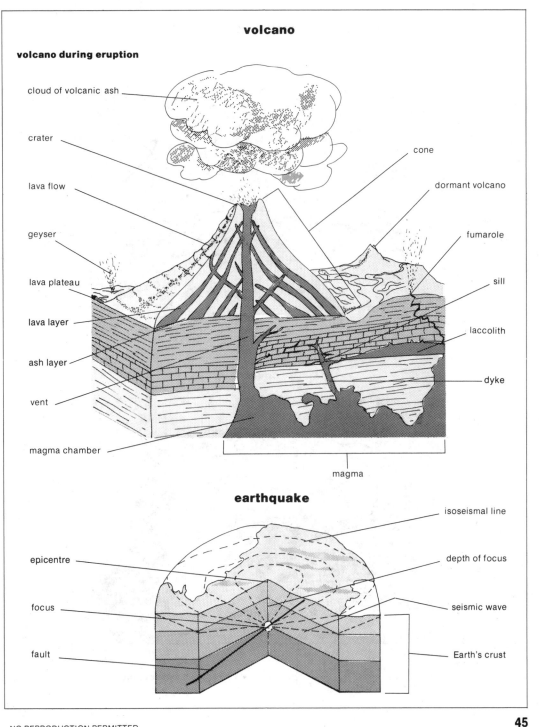

volcano

volcano during eruption

cloud of volcanic ash

crater

cone

lava flow

dormant volcano

geyser

fumarole

lava plateau

sill

lava layer

laccolith

ash layer

dyke

vent

magma chamber

magma

earthquake

isoseismal line

epicentre

depth of focus

focus

seismic wave

fault

Earth's crust

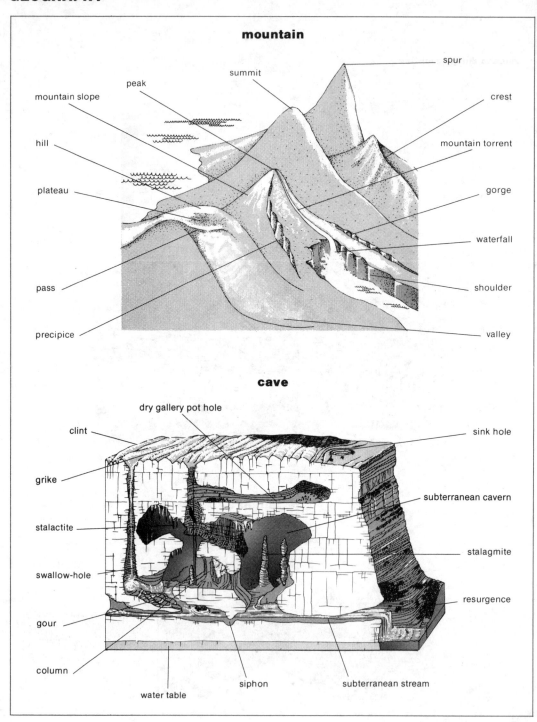

mountain

spur

summit

peak

crest

mountain slope

mountain torrent

hill

gorge

plateau

waterfall

pass

shoulder

precipice

valley

cave

dry gallery pot hole

sink hole

clint

grike

subterranean cavern

stalactite

stalagmite

swallow-hole

resurgence

gour

column

siphon

subterranean stream

water table

desert

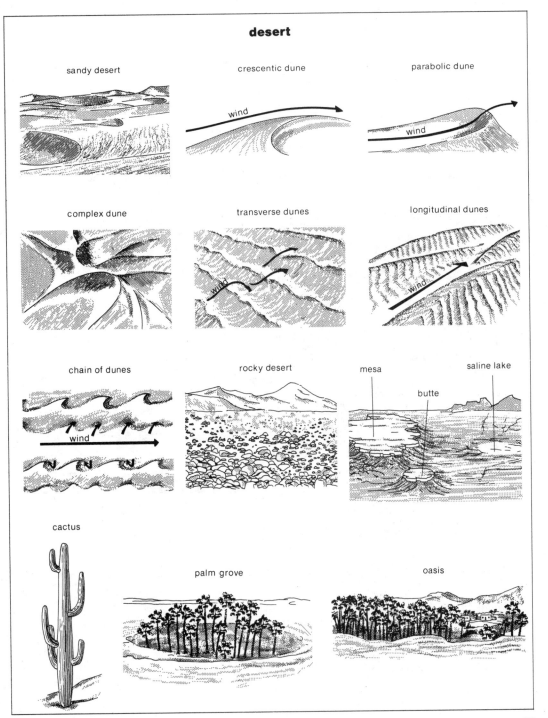

sandy desert

crescentic dune

wind

parabolic dune

wind

complex dune

transverse dunes

wind

longitudinal dunes

wind

chain of dunes

wind

rocky desert

mesa

butte

saline lake

cactus

palm grove

oasis

glacier

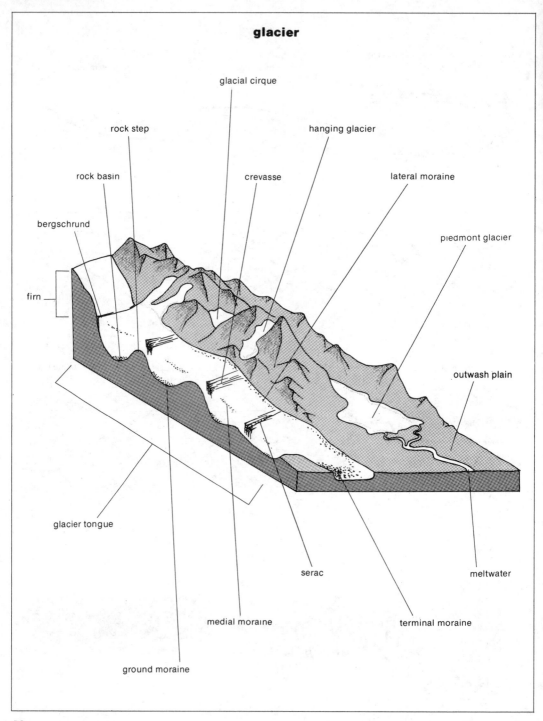

glacial cirque

rock step

hanging glacier

rock basin

crevasse

lateral moraine

bergschrund

piedmont glacier

firn

outwash plain

glacier tongue

serac

meltwater

medial moraine

terminal moraine

ground moraine

water forms

classification of snow crystals

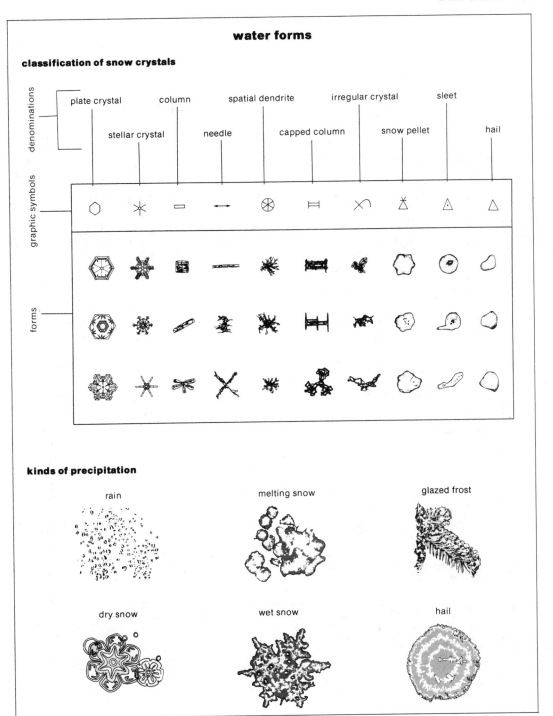

denominations

plate crystal

stellar crystal

column

needle

spatial dendrite

capped column

irregular crystal

snow pellet

sleet

hail

graphic symbols

forms

kinds of precipitation

rain

melting snow

glazed frost

dry snow

wet snow

hail

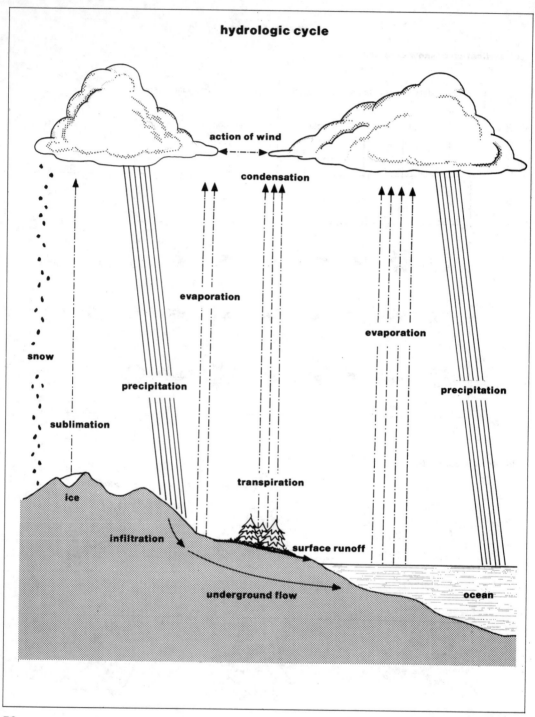

hydrologic cycle

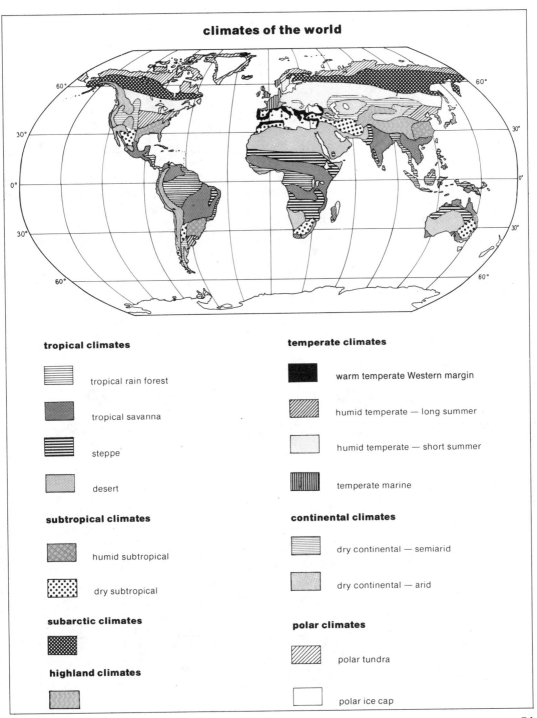

climates of the world

tropical climates

- tropical rain forest
- tropical savanna
- steppe
- desert

subtropical climates

- humid subtropical
- dry subtropical

subarctic climates

highland climates

temperate climates

- warm temperate Western margin
- humid temperate — long summer
- humid temperate — short summer
- temperate marine

continental climates

- dry continental — semiarid
- dry continental — arid

polar climates

- polar tundra
- polar ice cap

international weather symbols

● intermittent rain

● ● continuous rain

◗ intermittent drizzle

❜❜ continuous drizzle

✶ intermittent snow

✶ ✶ continuous snow

rain shower

snow shower

thunderstorm

heavy thunderstorm

 freezing rain

tropical storm

hurricane

= mist

≡ fog

sleet

 hail shower

 sandstorm or dust storm

 squall

smoke

✛ drifting snow

✚ blowing snow

international weather symbols

fronts

surface warm front   upper warm front   surface cold front   upper cold front

occluded front   quasi-stationary front

cloud amount

clear sky   scattered sky   slightly covered sky   cloudy sky

very cloudy sky   overcast sky   obscured sky

wind

station circle

calm

wind arrow

shaft	half barb	barb	pennant
1-2 knots	5 knots	10 knots	50 knots

wind scale

wind speed in knots

meteorology

weather map

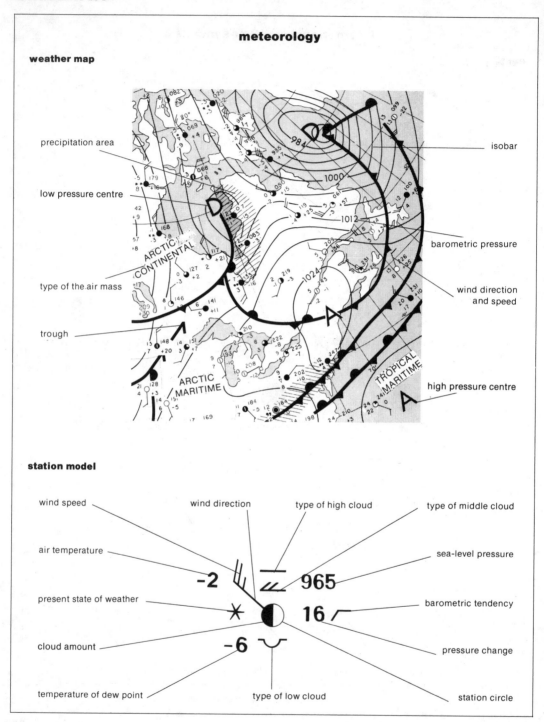

precipitation area

low pressure centre

type of the air mass

trough

ARCTIC CONTINENTAL

ARCTIC MARITIME

TROPICAL MARITIME

isobar

barometric pressure

wind direction and speed

high pressure centre

station model

wind speed

air temperature

present state of weather

cloud amount

temperature of dew point

wind direction

type of high cloud

type of middle cloud

sea-level pressure

barometric tendency

pressure change

type of low cloud

station circle

-2   965

16

-6

meteorology

meteorological ground

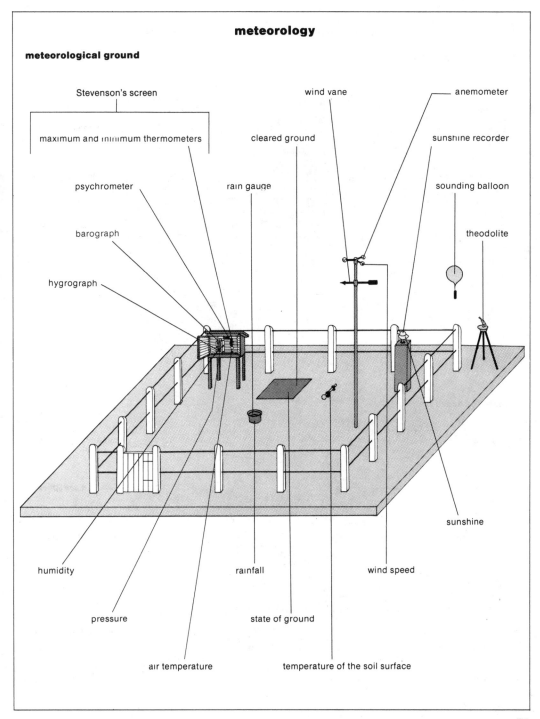

Stevenson's screen

wind vane

anemometer

maximum and minimum thermometers

cleared ground

sunshine recorder

psychrometer

rain gauge

sounding balloon

barograph

theodolite

hygrograph

sunshine

humidity

rainfall

wind speed

pressure

state of ground

air temperature

temperature of the soil surface

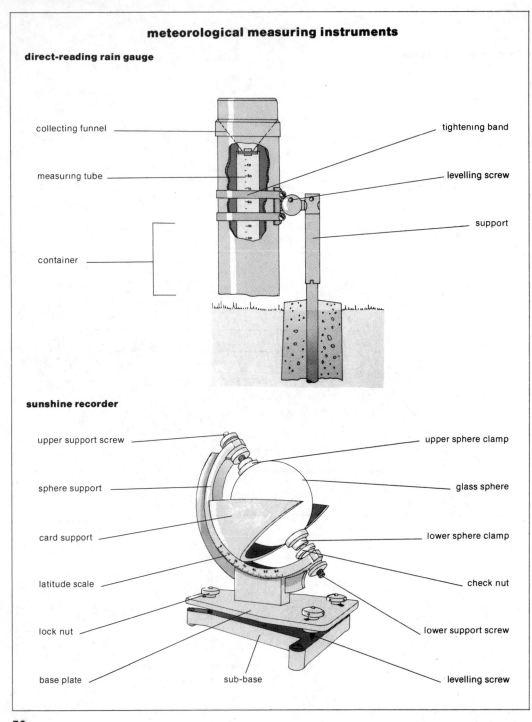

meteorological measuring instruments

direct-reading rain gauge

collecting funnel

measuring tube

container

tightening band

levelling screw

support

sunshine recorder

upper support screw

sphere support

card support

latitude scale

lock nut

base plate

sub-base

upper sphere clamp

glass sphere

lower sphere clamp

check nut

lower support screw

levelling screw

NIMBUS III meteorological satellite

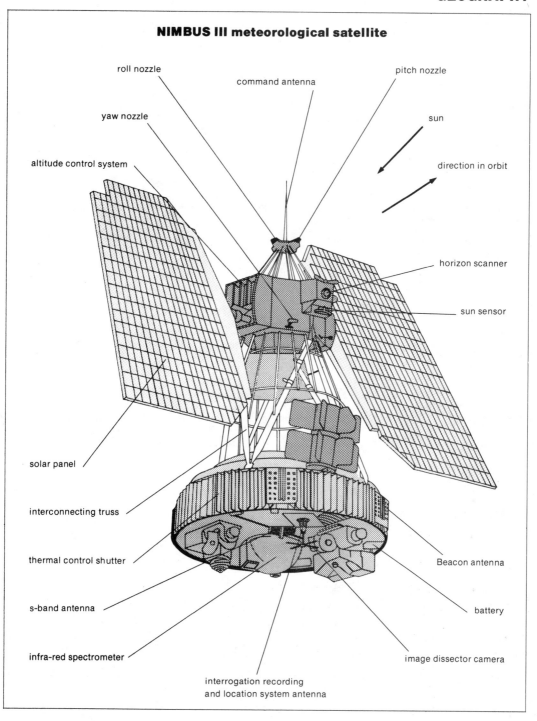

roll nozzle

command antenna

pitch nozzle

yaw nozzle

sun

altitude control system

direction in orbit

horizon scanner

sun sensor

solar panel

interconnecting truss

thermal control shutter

Beacon antenna

s-band antenna

battery

infra-red spectrometer

image dissector camera

interrogation recording
and location system antenna

VEGETABLE KINGDOM

structure of a plant

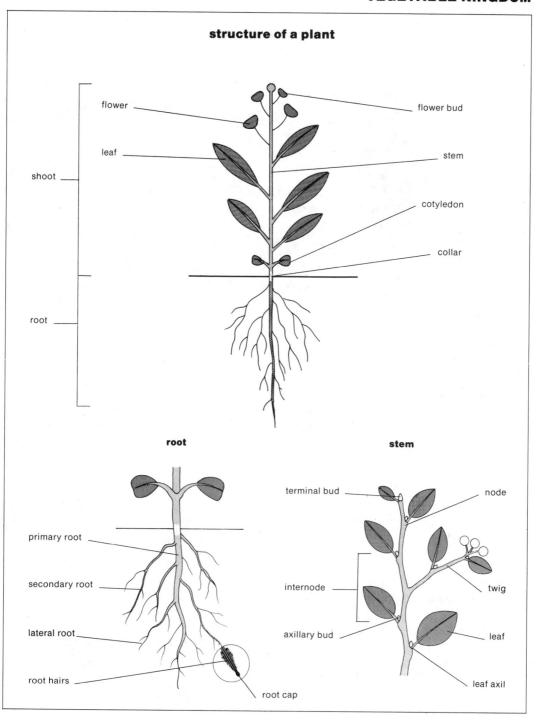

flower

flower bud

leaf

stem

shoot

cotyledon

collar

root

root

stem

terminal bud

node

primary root

secondary root

internode

twig

lateral root

axillary bud

leaf

root hairs

leaf axil

root cap

VEGETABLE KINGDOM

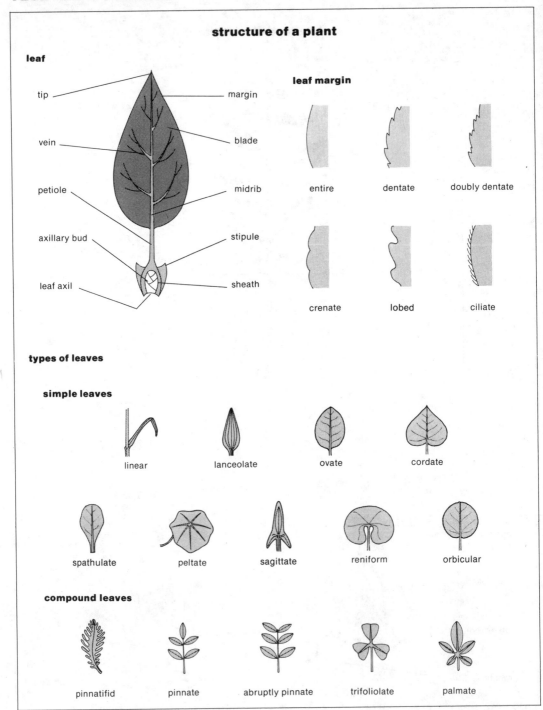

structure of a plant

leaf

tip
margin
vein
blade
petiole
midrib
axillary bud
stipule
leaf axil
sheath

leaf margin

entire
dentate
doubly dentate
crenate
lobed
ciliate

types of leaves

simple leaves

linear
lanceolate
ovate
cordate
spathulate
peltate
sagittate
reniform
orbicular

compound leaves

pinnatifid
pinnate
abruptly pinnate
trifoliolate
palmate

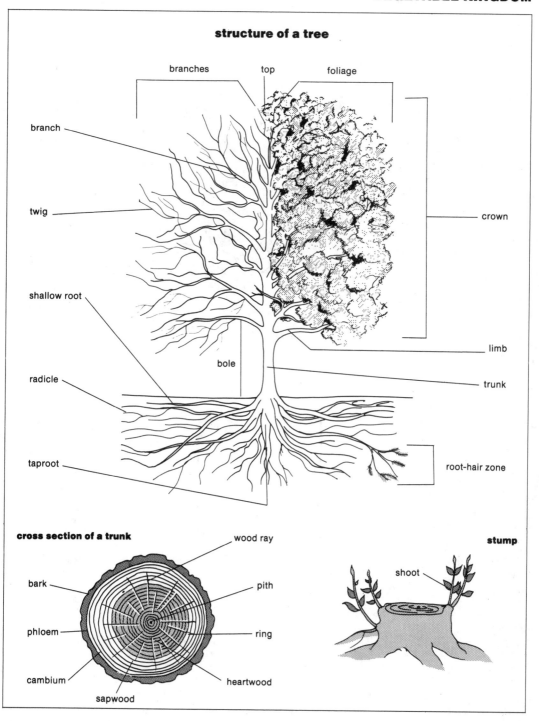

structure of a tree

branches   top   foliage

branch

twig

shallow root

radicle

taproot

bole

crown

limb

trunk

root-hair zone

cross section of a trunk

wood ray

bark

phloem

cambium

sapwood

pith

ring

heartwood

stump

shoot

VEGETABLE KINGDOM

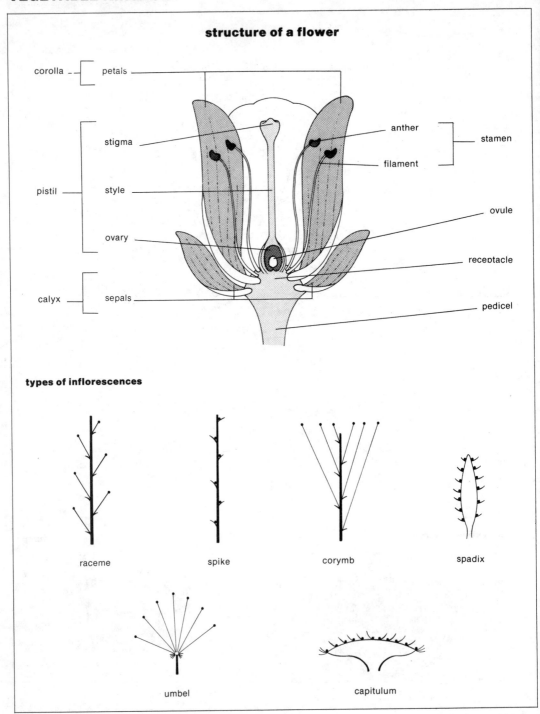

structure of a flower

corolla -- [petals

pistil

stigma

anther

filament

stamen

style

ovule

ovary

receptacle

calyx [sepals

pedicel

types of inflorescences

raceme

spike

corymb

spadix

umbel

capitulum

mushrooms

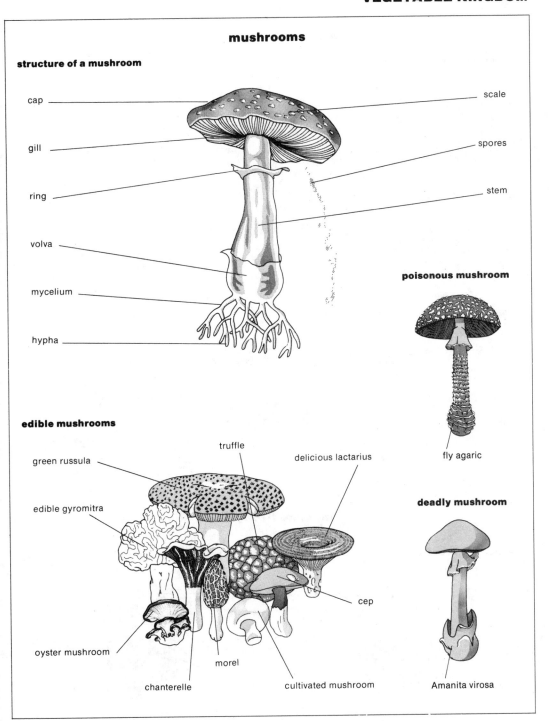

structure of a mushroom

cap

gill

ring

volva

mycelium

hypha

scale

spores

stem

poisonous mushroom

fly agaric

edible mushrooms

green russula

edible gyromitra

truffle

delicious lactarius

cep

oyster mushroom

chanterelle

morel

cultivated mushroom

deadly mushroom

Amanita virosa

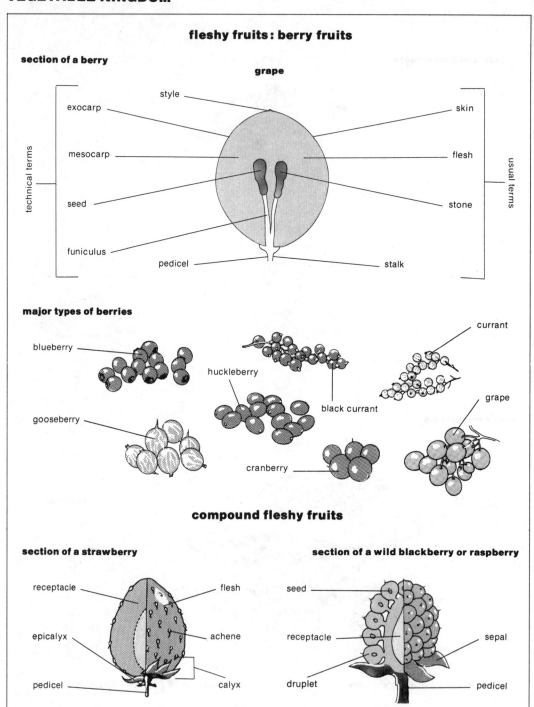

fleshy fruits: berry fruits

section of a berry

grape

technical terms

style
exocarp
mesocarp
seed
funiculus
pedicel

skin
flesh
stone
stalk

usual terms

major types of berries

blueberry

huckleberry

gooseberry

currant

black currant

grape

cranberry

compound fleshy fruits

section of a strawberry

receptacle
epicalyx
pedicel

flesh
achene
calyx

section of a wild blackberry or raspberry

seed
receptacle
druplet

sepal
pedicel

stone fleshy fruits

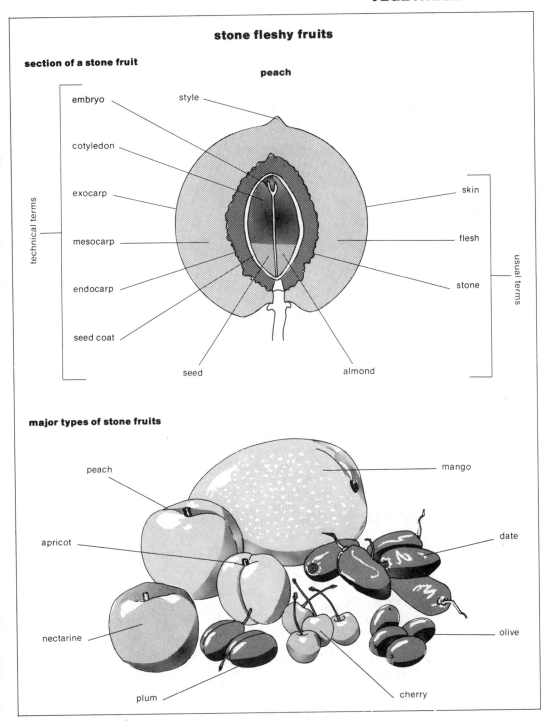

section of a stone fruit

peach

technical terms

- embryo
- cotyledon
- exocarp
- mesocarp
- endocarp
- seed coat
- seed
- style
- almond

usual terms

- skin
- flesh
- stone

major types of stone fruits

- peach
- apricot
- nectarine
- plum
- mango
- date
- olive
- cherry

VEGETABLE KINGDOM

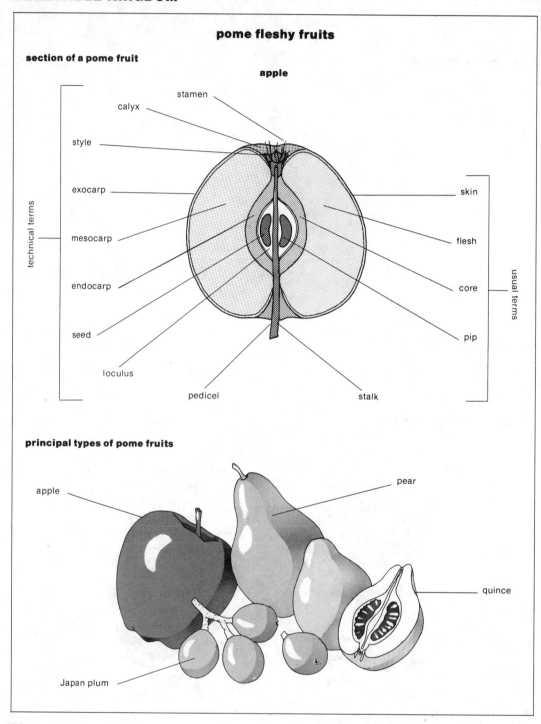

pome fleshy fruits

section of a pome fruit

apple

technical terms

- stamen
- calyx
- style
- exocarp
- mesocarp
- endocarp
- seed
- loculus
- pedicel
- stalk

usual terms

- skin
- flesh
- core
- pip

principal types of pome fruits

- apple
- pear
- quince
- Japan plum

fleshy fruits: citrus fruits

section of a citrus fruit

orange

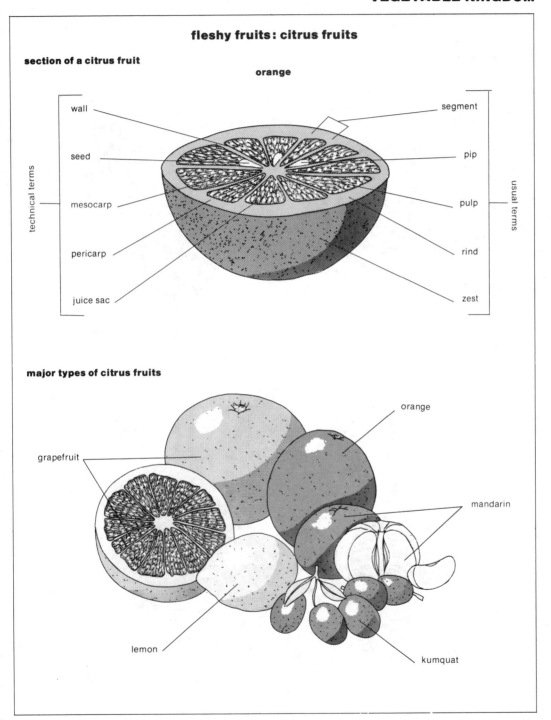

technical terms

wall
seed
mesocarp
pericarp
juice sac

usual terms

segment
pip
pulp
rind
zest

major types of citrus fruits

orange

grapefruit

mandarin

lemon

kumquat

VEGETABLE KINGDOM

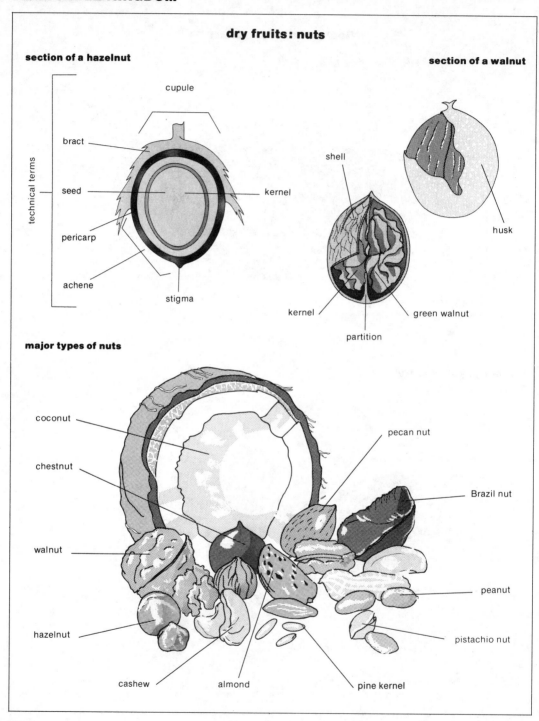

dry fruits: nuts

section of a hazelnut

cupule

bract

technical terms

seed

kernel

pericarp

achene

stigma

section of a walnut

shell

husk

kernel

green walnut

partition

major types of nuts

coconut

chestnut

walnut

hazelnut

cashew

almond

pine kernel

pecan nut

Brazil nut

peanut

pistachio nut

various dry fruits

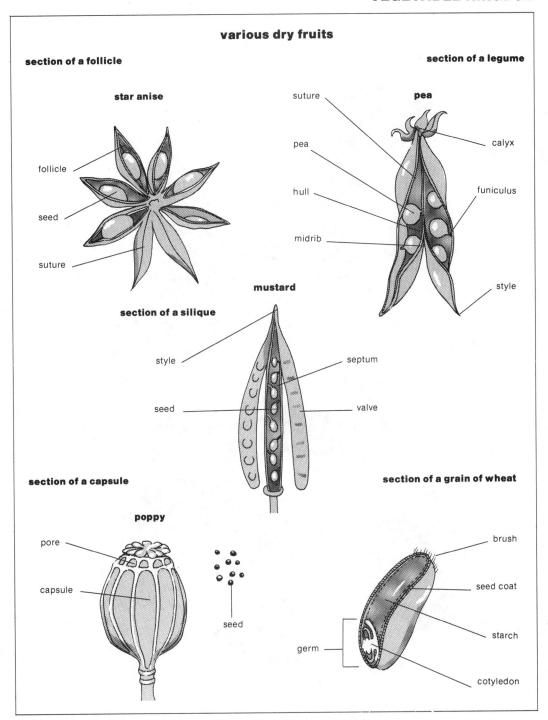

section of a follicle

star anise

follicle

seed

suture

section of a legume

pea

suture

pea

hull

midrib

calyx

funiculus

style

section of a silique

mustard

style

seed

septum

valve

section of a capsule

poppy

pore

capsule

seed

section of a grain of wheat

brush

seed coat

starch

germ

cotyledon

tropical fruits

major types of tropical fruits

pineapple

banana

papaya

pomegranate

Indian fig

cherimoya

guava

Japanese persimmon

avocado

litchi

kiwi

vegetables

fruit vegetables

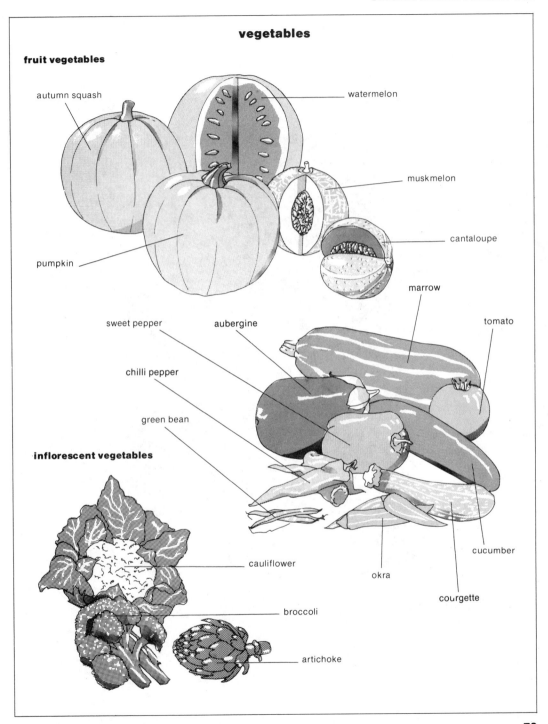

- autumn squash
- watermelon
- muskmelon
- cantaloupe
- pumpkin
- marrow
- sweet pepper
- aubergine
- tomato
- chilli pepper
- green bean
- cucumber
- cauliflower
- okra
- courgette
- broccoli
- artichoke

inflorescent vegetables

VEGETABLE KINGDOM

vegetables

leaf vegetables

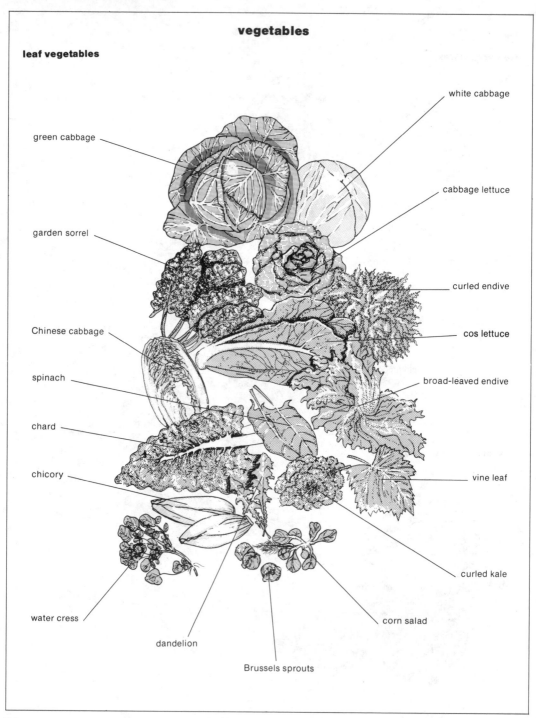

green cabbage

white cabbage

cabbage lettuce

garden sorrel

curled endive

Chinese cabbage

cos lettuce

spinach

broad-leaved endive

chard

chicory

vine leaf

water cress

curled kale

dandelion

corn salad

Brussels sprouts

vegetables

section of a bulb

bulb vegetables

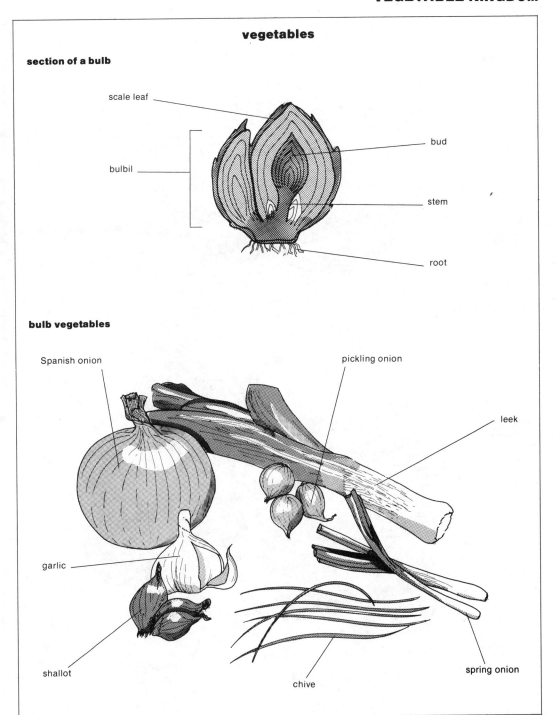

scale leaf

bud

bulbil

stem

root

Spanish onion

pickling onion

leek

garlic

shallot

chive

spring onion

VEGETABLE KINGDOM

vegetables

tuber vegetables

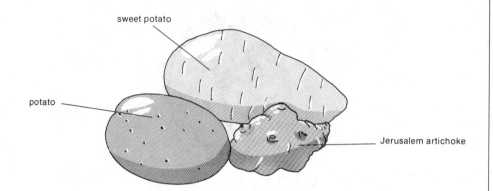

sweet potato

potato

Jerusalem artichoke

root vegetables

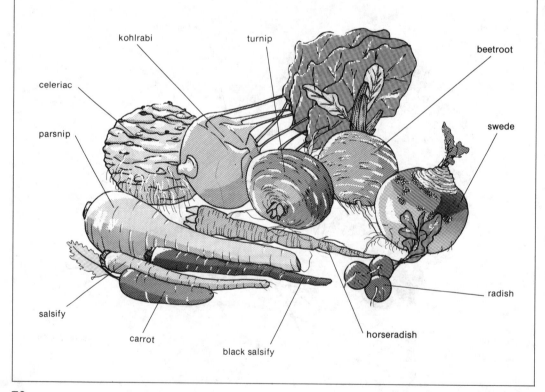

kohlrabi

turnip

beetroot

celeriac

swede

parsnip

salsify

carrot

black salsify

horseradish

radish

vegetables

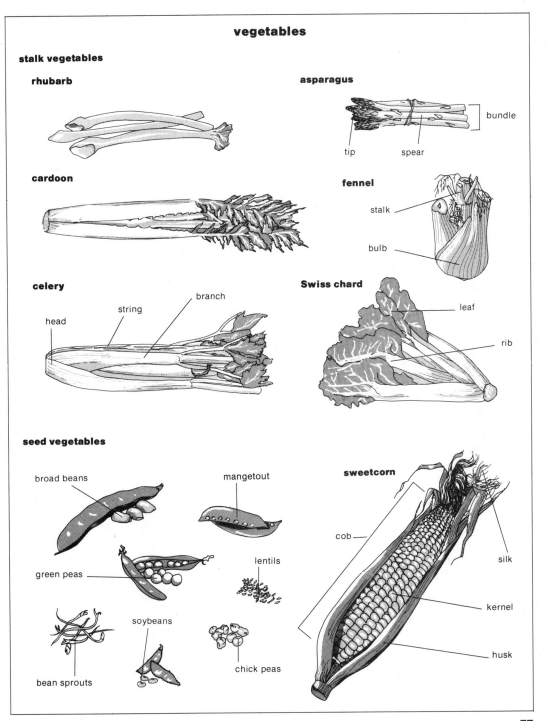

stalk vegetables

rhubarb

asparagus

bundle

tip   spear

cardoon

fennel

stalk

bulb

celery

branch

string

head

Swiss chard

leaf

rib

seed vegetables

broad beans

mangetout

sweetcorn

green peas

lentils

cob

silk

bean sprouts

soybeans

chick peas

kernel

husk

ANIMAL KINGDOM

deer family

deer antlers

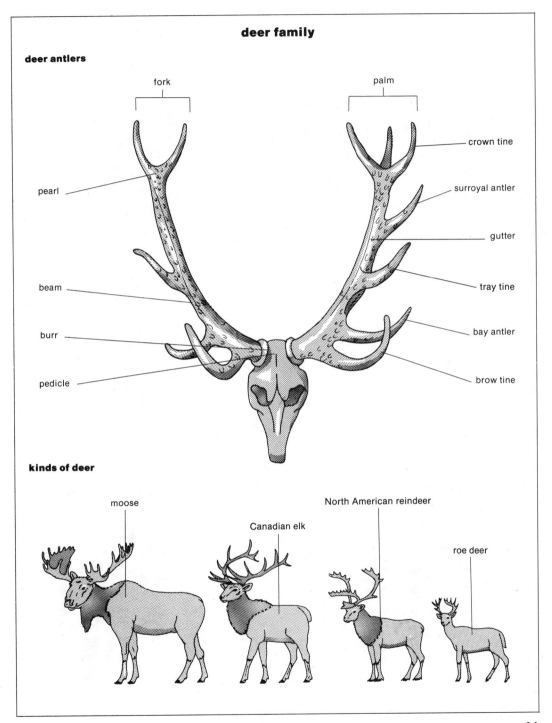

fork

palm

crown tine

surroyal antler

pearl

gutter

beam

tray tine

burr

bay antler

pedicle

brow tine

kinds of deer

moose

Canadian elk

North American reindeer

roe deer

ANIMAL KINGDOM

types of jaws

carnivore's jaw

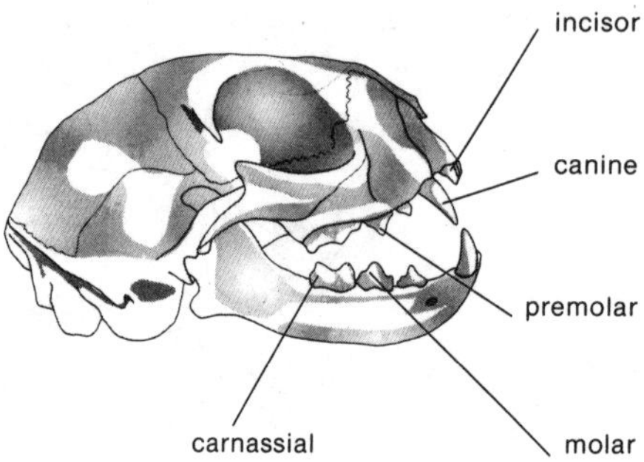

incisor

canine

premolar

carnassial

molar

leopard

rodent's jaw

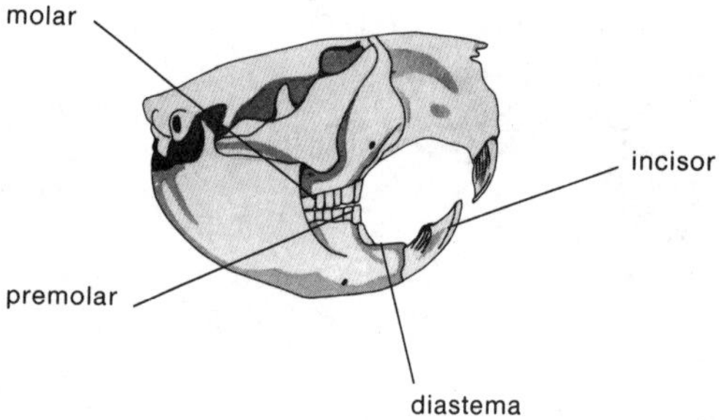

molar

premolar

incisor

diastema

beaver

herbivore's jaw

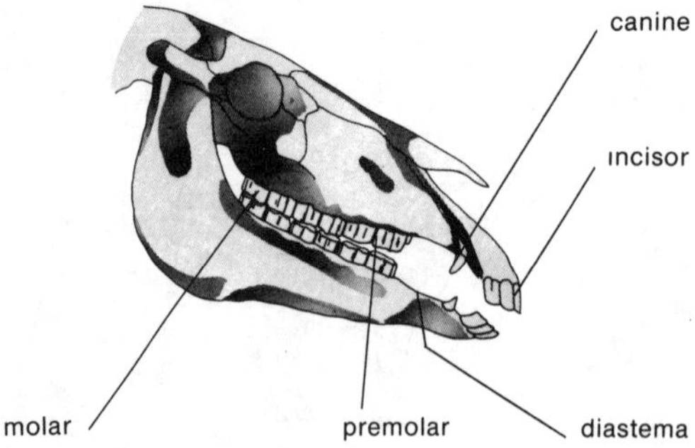

canine

incisor

molar

premolar

diastema

horse

horse

morphology

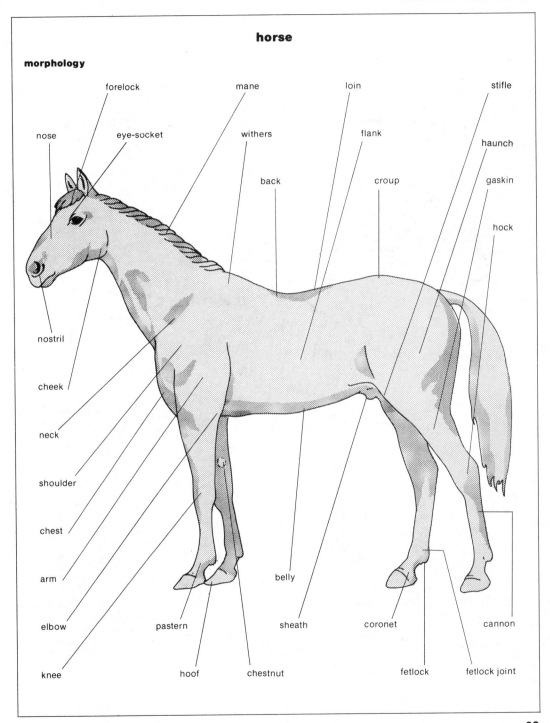

forelock

mane

loin

stifle

nose

eye-socket

withers

flank

haunch

back

croup

gaskin

hock

nostril

cheek

neck

shoulder

chest

arm

belly

elbow

pastern

sheath

coronet

cannon

knee

hoof

chestnut

fetlock

fetlock joint

horse

skeleton

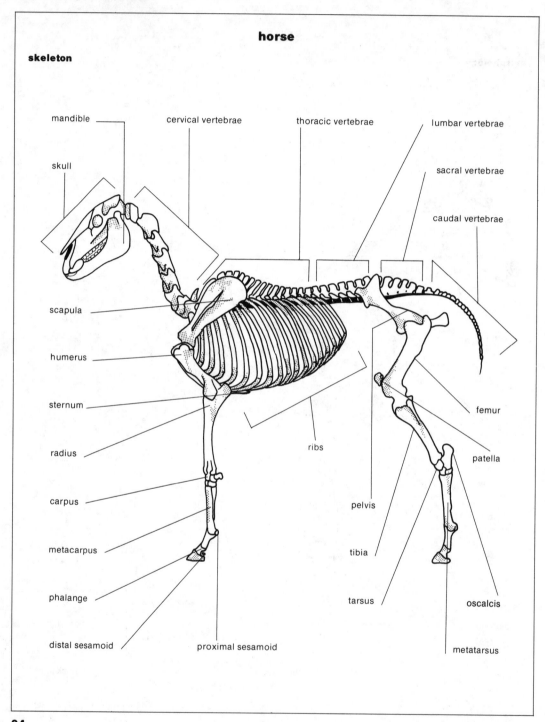

mandible

cervical vertebrae

thoracic vertebrae

lumbar vertebrae

skull

sacral vertebrae

caudal vertebrae

scapula

humerus

sternum

femur

radius

patella

carpus

pelvis

metacarpus

tibia

phalange

tarsus

oscalcis

distal sesamoid

proximal sesamoid

metatarsus

ribs

horse

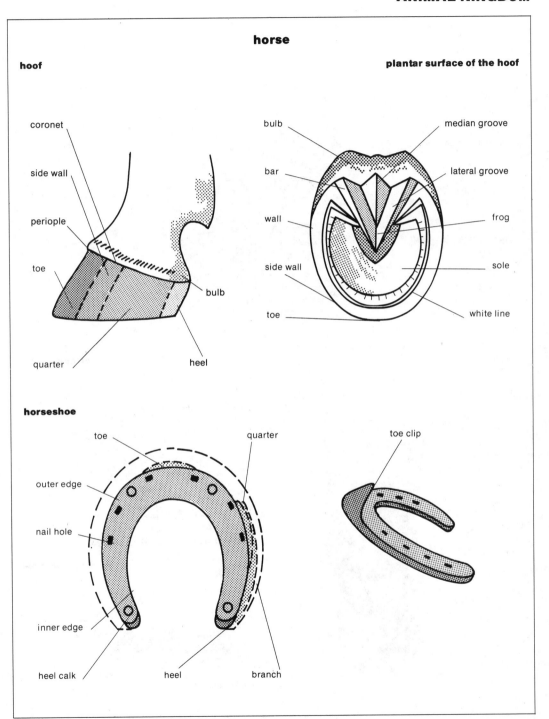

hoof

coronet

side wall

periople

toe

bulb

quarter

heel

plantar surface of the hoof

bulb

bar

wall

side wall

toe

median groove

lateral groove

frog

sole

white line

horseshoe

toe

outer edge

nail hole

inner edge

heel calk

heel

quarter

branch

toe clip

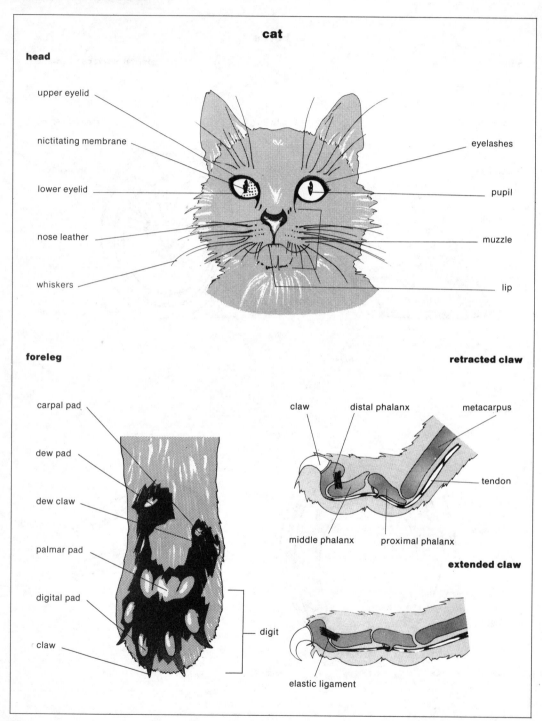

cat

head

upper eyelid

nictitating membrane

lower eyelid

nose leather

whiskers

eyelashes

pupil

muzzle

lip

foreleg

carpal pad

dew pad

dew claw

palmar pad

digital pad

claw

digit

retracted claw

claw

distal phalanx

metacarpus

tendon

middle phalanx

proximal phalanx

extended claw

elastic ligament

bird

morphology

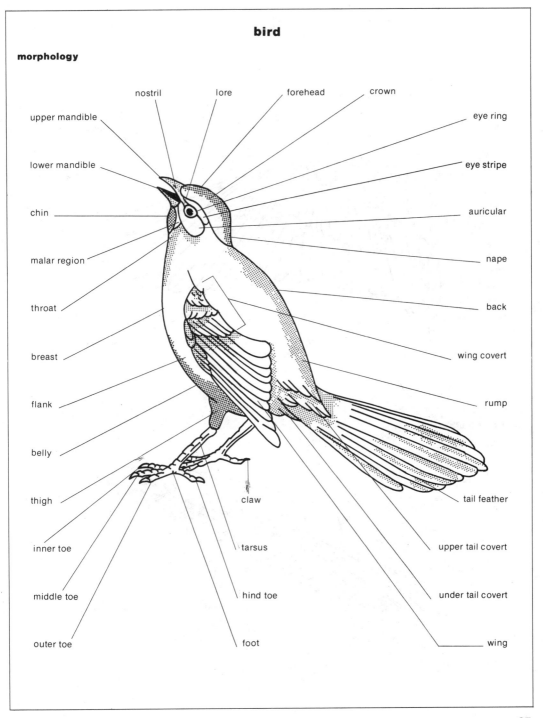

nostril

lore

forehead

crown

upper mandible

eye ring

lower mandible

eye stripe

chin

auricular

malar region

nape

throat

back

breast

wing covert

flank

rump

belly

thigh

claw

tail feather

inner toe

tarsus

upper tail covert

middle toe

hind toe

under tail covert

outer toe

foot

wing

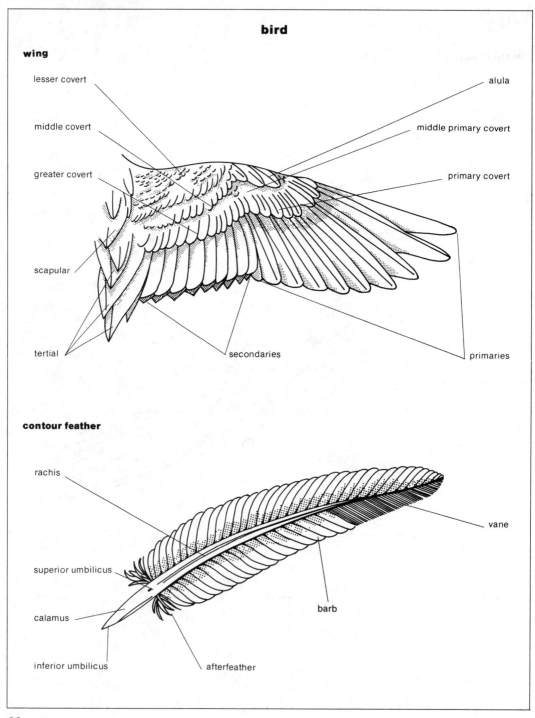

bird

wing

lesser covert

alula

middle covert

middle primary covert

greater covert

primary covert

scapular

tertial

secondaries

primaries

contour feather

rachis

vane

superior umbilicus

calamus

barb

inferior umbilicus

afterfeather

bird

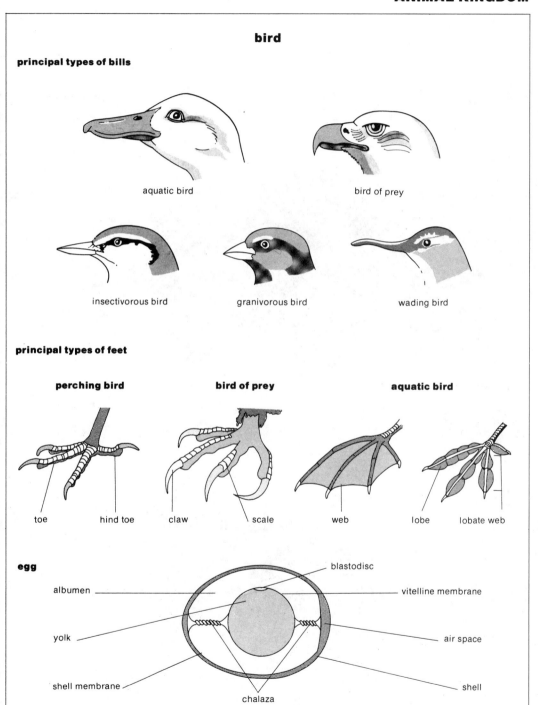

principal types of bills

aquatic bird

bird of prey

insectivorous bird

granivorous bird

wading bird

principal types of feet

perching bird

bird of prey

aquatic bird

toe

hind toe

claw

scale

web

lobe

lobate web

egg

albumen

blastodisc

vitelline membrane

yolk

air space

shell membrane

chalaza

shell

fish

morphology

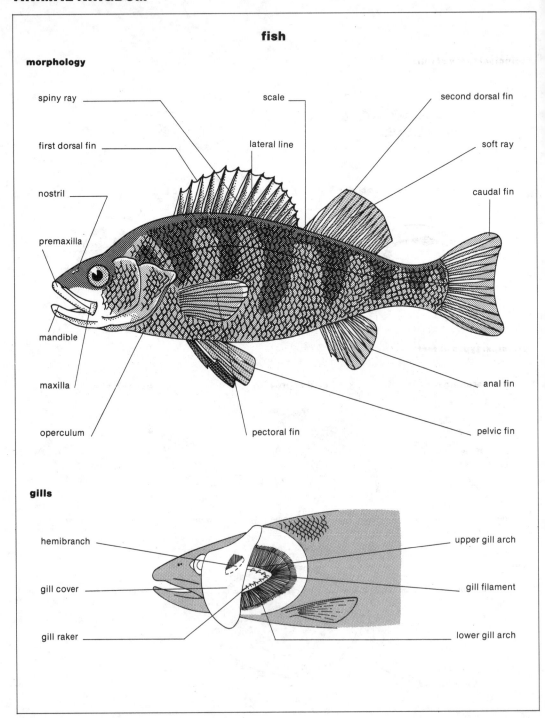

spiny ray

first dorsal fin

nostril

premaxilla

mandible

maxilla

operculum

scale

lateral line

pectoral fin

second dorsal fin

soft ray

caudal fin

anal fin

pelvic fin

gills

hemibranch

gill cover

gill raker

upper gill arch

gill filament

lower gill arch

fish

anatomy

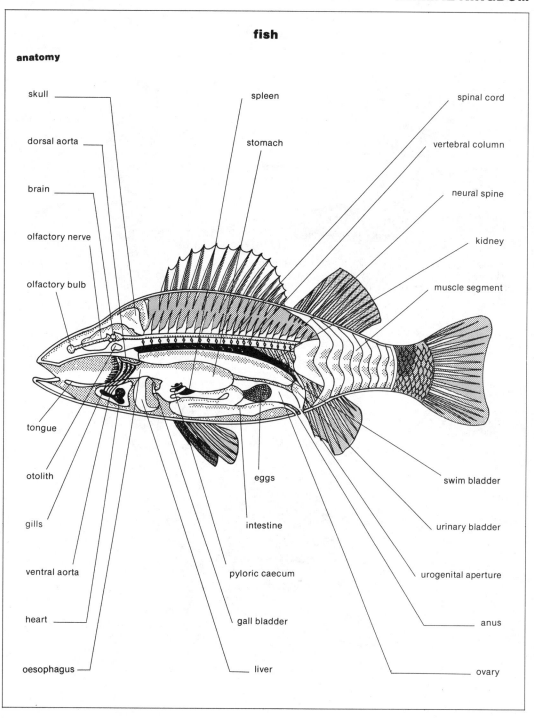

skull

dorsal aorta

brain

olfactory nerve

olfactory bulb

tongue

otolith

gills

ventral aorta

heart

oesophagus

spleen

stomach

eggs

intestine

pyloric caecum

gall bladder

liver

spinal cord

vertebral column

neural spine

kidney

muscle segment

swim bladder

urinary bladder

urogenital aperture

anus

ovary

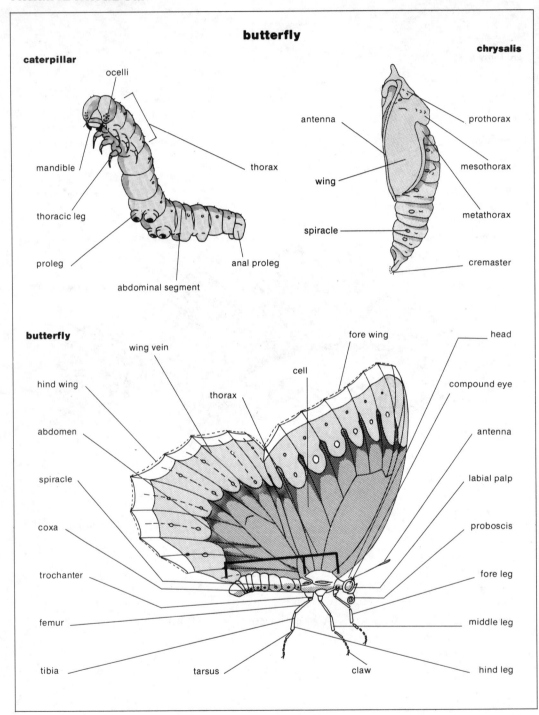

butterfly

caterpillar

ocelli

thorax

mandible

thoracic leg

proleg

abdominal segment

anal proleg

chrysalis

antenna

wing

spiracle

prothorax

mesothorax

metathorax

cremaster

butterfly

wing vein

hind wing

abdomen

spiracle

coxa

trochanter

femur

tibia

thorax

cell

tarsus

fore wing

claw

head

compound eye

antenna

labial palp

proboscis

fore leg

middle leg

hind leg

univalve shell

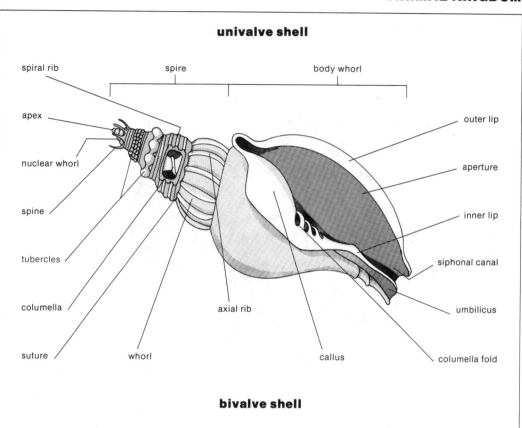

spiral rib

spire

body whorl

apex

nuclear whorl

spine

tubercles

columella

suture

whorl

axial rib

callus

outer lip

aperture

inner lip

siphonal canal

umbilicus

columella fold

bivalve shell

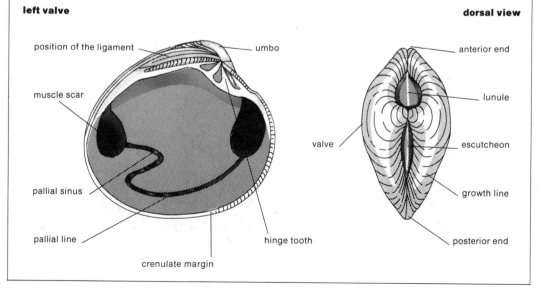

left valve

dorsal view

position of the ligament

umbo

muscle scar

pallial sinus

pallial line

hinge tooth

crenulate margin

valve

anterior end

lunule

escutcheon

growth line

posterior end

edible molluscs

oyster

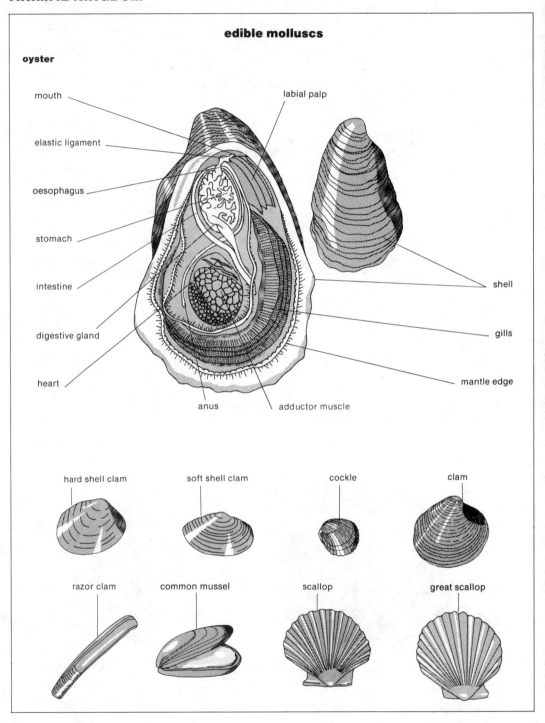

mouth

labial palp

elastic ligament

oesophagus

stomach

intestine

shell

digestive gland

gills

heart

mantle edge

anus

adductor muscle

hard shell clam

soft shell clam

cockle

clam

razor clam

common mussel

scallop

great scallop

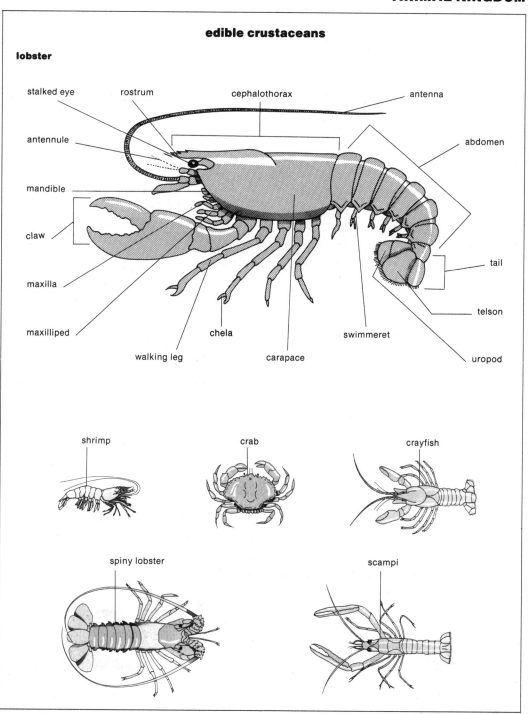

edible crustaceans

lobster

stalked eye

rostrum

cephalothorax

antenna

antennule

abdomen

mandible

claw

maxilla

tail

telson

maxilliped

chela

uropod

walking leg

carapace

swimmeret

shrimp

crab

crayfish

spiny lobster

scampi

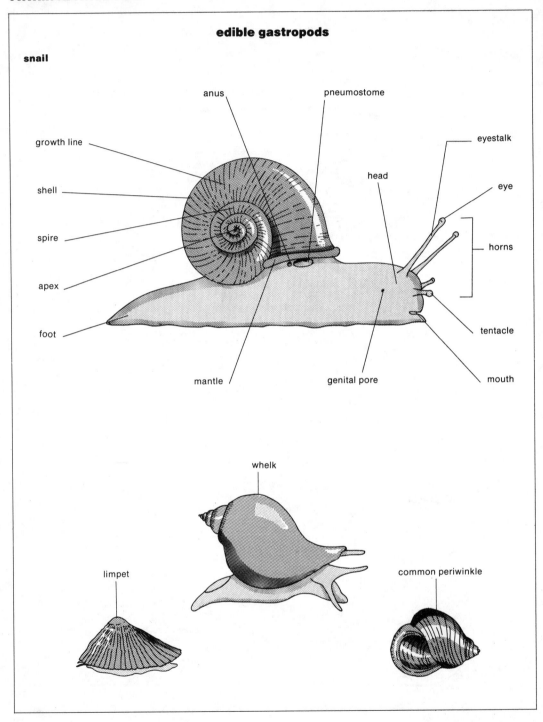

edible gastropods

snail

anus

pneumostome

growth line

eyestalk

head

eye

shell

spire

horns

apex

foot

tentacle

mantle

genital pore

mouth

whelk

limpet

common periwinkle

amphibian

frog

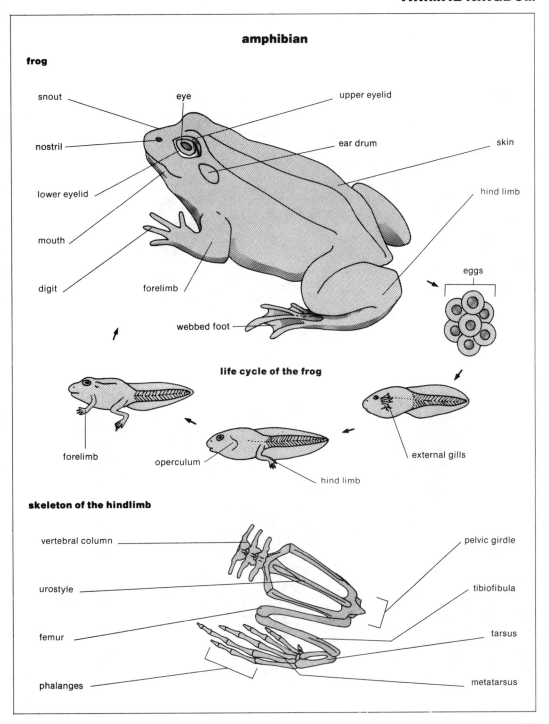

snout

eye

upper eyelid

nostril

ear drum

skin

lower eyelid

hind limb

mouth

eggs

digit

forelimb

webbed foot

life cycle of the frog

forelimb

operculum

hind limb

external gills

skeleton of the hindlimb

vertebral column

pelvic girdle

urostyle

tibiofibula

femur

tarsus

phalanges

metatarsus

honeybee

worker

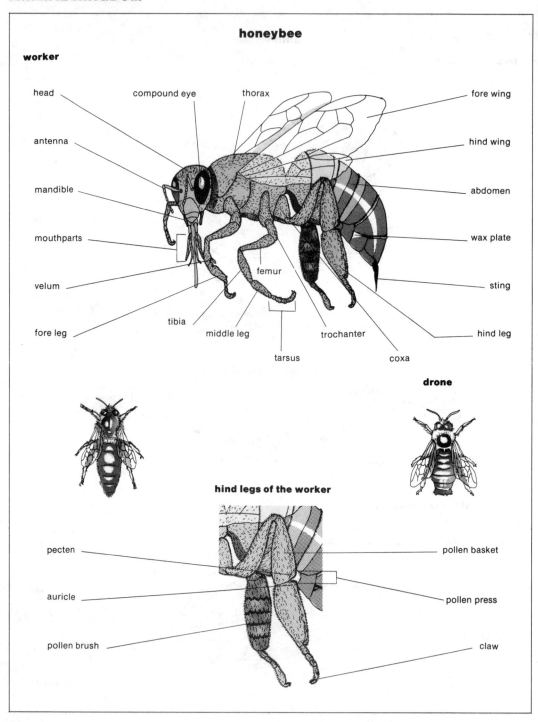

head

compound eye

thorax

fore wing

antenna

hind wing

mandible

abdomen

mouthparts

wax plate

velum

sting

fore leg

tibia

middle leg

trochanter

hind leg

femur

tarsus

coxa

drone

hind legs of the worker

pecten

pollen basket

auricle

pollen press

pollen brush

claw

honeybee

hive

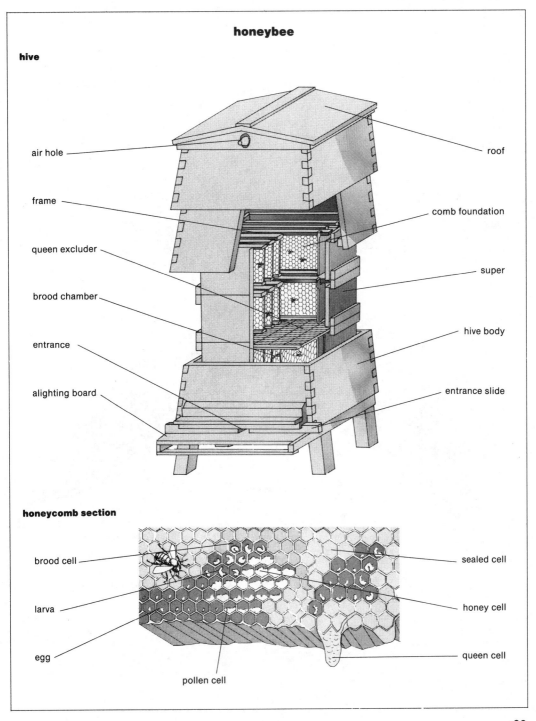

air hole — roof

frame — comb foundation

queen excluder — super

brood chamber — hive body

entrance —

alighting board — entrance slide

honeycomb section

brood cell — sealed cell

larva — honey cell

egg — queen cell

pollen cell

bat

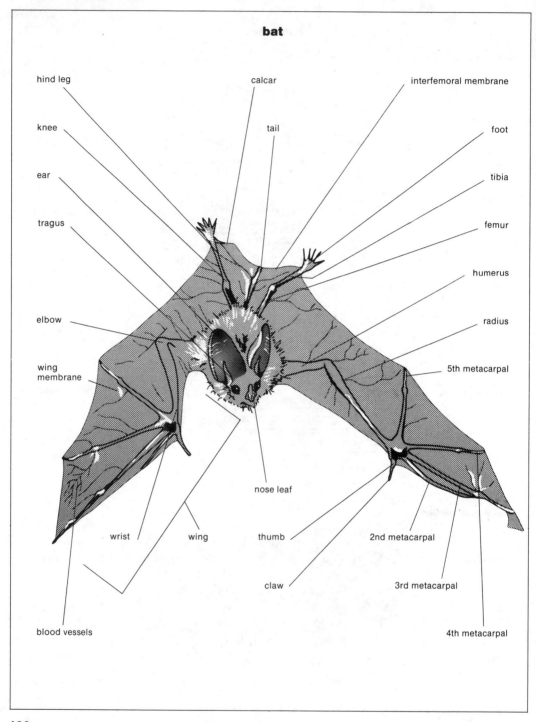

hind leg

calcar

interfemoral membrane

knee

tail

foot

ear

tibia

tragus

femur

humerus

elbow

radius

wing membrane

5th metacarpal

nose leaf

wrist

wing

thumb

2nd metacarpal

claw

3rd metacarpal

blood vessels

4th metacarpal

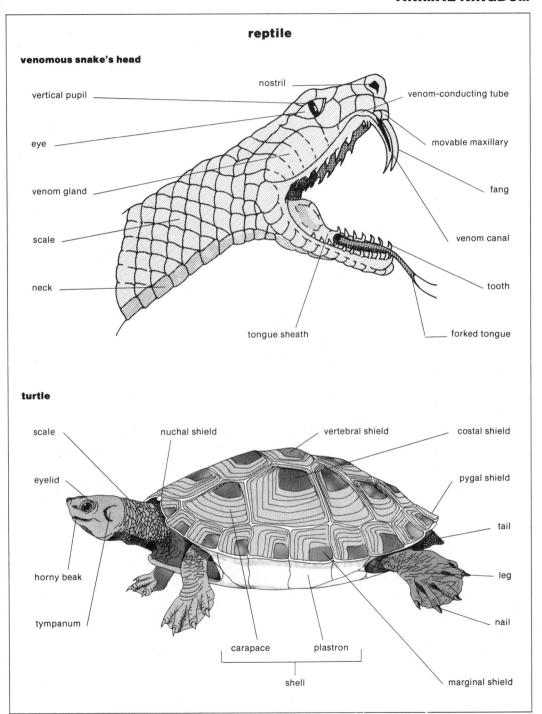

reptile

venomous snake's head

- vertical pupil
- nostril
- venom-conducting tube
- eye
- movable maxillary
- venom gland
- fang
- scale
- venom canal
- neck
- tooth
- tongue sheath
- forked tongue

turtle

- scale
- nuchal shield
- vertebral shield
- costal shield
- eyelid
- pygal shield
- horny beak
- tail
- tympanum
- leg
- nail
- carapace
- plastron
- shell
- marginal shield

HUMAN BEING

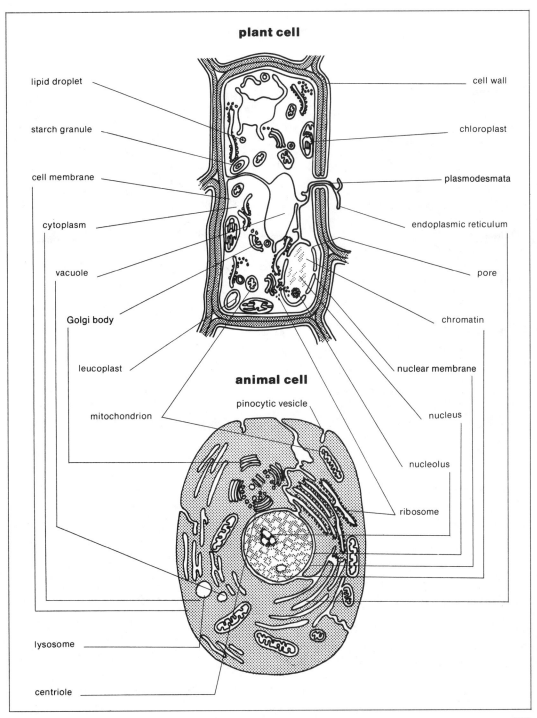

plant cell

lipid droplet

starch granule

cell membrane

cytoplasm

vacuole

Golgi body

leucoplast

mitochondrion

cell wall

chloroplast

plasmodesmata

endoplasmic reticulum

pore

chromatin

nuclear membrane

animal cell

pinocytic vesicle

nucleus

nucleolus

ribosome

lysosome

centriole

HUMAN BEING

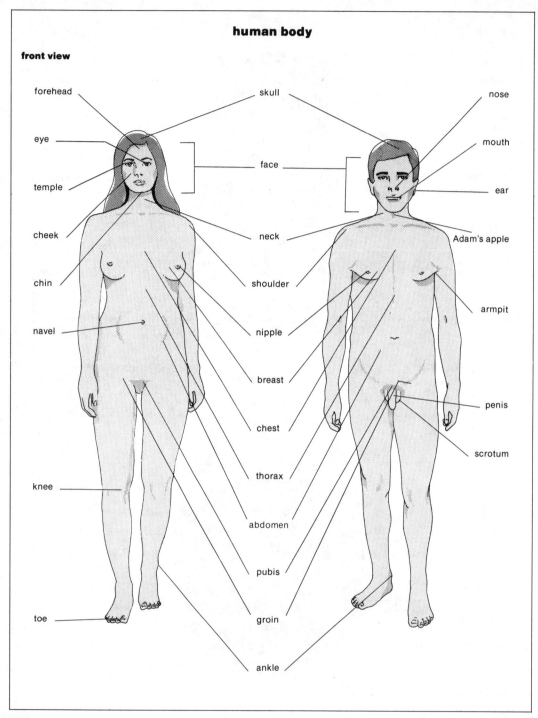

human body

front view

forehead

eye

temple

cheek

chin

navel

knee

toe

skull

face

neck

shoulder

nipple

breast

chest

thorax

abdomen

pubis

groin

ankle

nose

mouth

ear

Adam's apple

armpit

penis

scrotum

human body

back view

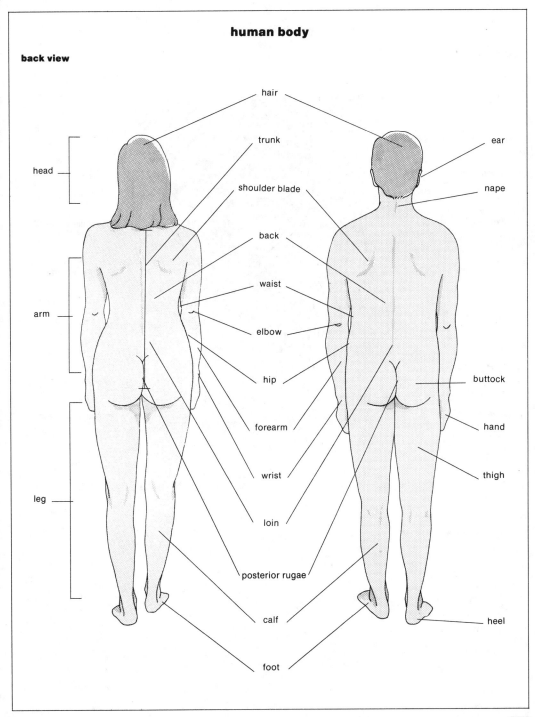

hair

trunk

shoulder blade

back

waist

elbow

hip

forearm

wrist

loin

posterior rugae

calf

foot

head

arm

leg

ear

nape

buttock

hand

thigh

heel

genital organs
male

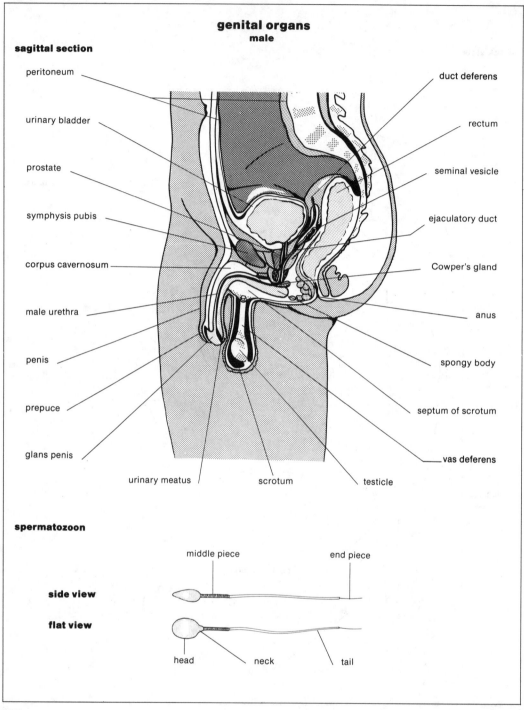

sagittal section

peritoneum

urinary bladder

prostate

symphysis pubis

corpus cavernosum

male urethra

penis

prepuce

glans penis

urinary meatus

scrotum

testicle

duct deferens

rectum

seminal vesicle

ejaculatory duct

Cowper's gland

anus

spongy body

septum of scrotum

vas deferens

spermatozoon

middle piece

end piece

side view

flat view

head

neck

tail

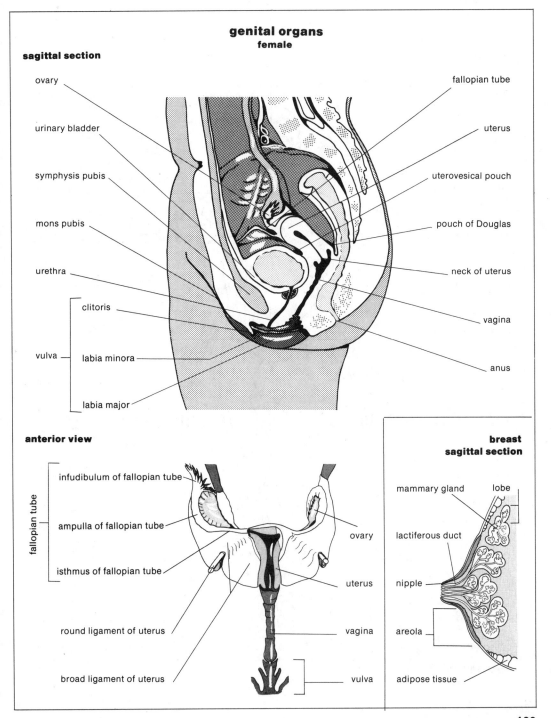

genital organs
female

sagittal section

ovary

urinary bladder

symphysis pubis

mons pubis

urethra

clitoris

vulva

labia minora

labia major

fallopian tube

uterus

uterovesical pouch

pouch of Douglas

neck of uterus

vagina

anus

anterior view

fallopian tube

infudibulum of fallopian tube

ampulla of fallopian tube

isthmus of fallopian tube

round ligament of uterus

broad ligament of uterus

ovary

uterus

vagina

vulva

breast
sagittal section

mammary gland

lobe

lactiferous duct

nipple

areola

adipose tissue

HUMAN BEING

muscles

front view

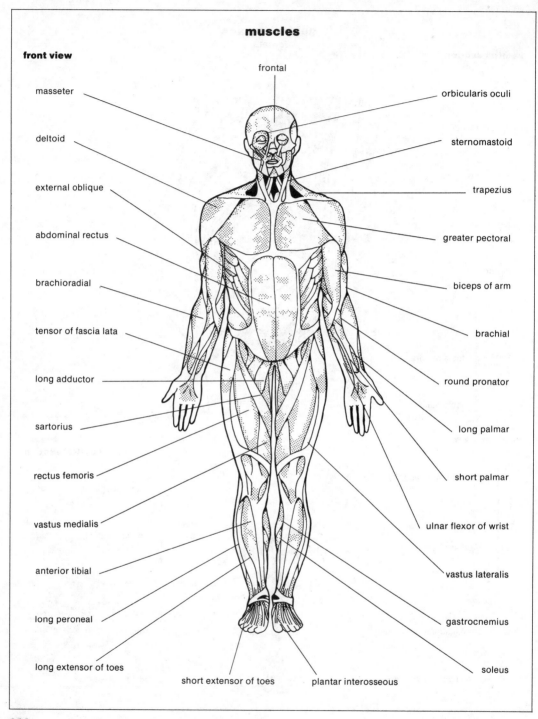

frontal

masseter

orbicularis oculi

deltoid

sternomastoid

external oblique

trapezius

abdominal rectus

greater pectoral

brachioradial

biceps of arm

tensor of fascia lata

brachial

long adductor

round pronator

sartorius

long palmar

rectus femoris

short palmar

vastus medialis

ulnar flexor of wrist

anterior tibial

vastus lateralis

long peroneal

gastrocnemius

long extensor of toes

soleus

short extensor of toes

plantar interosseous

110

muscles

back view

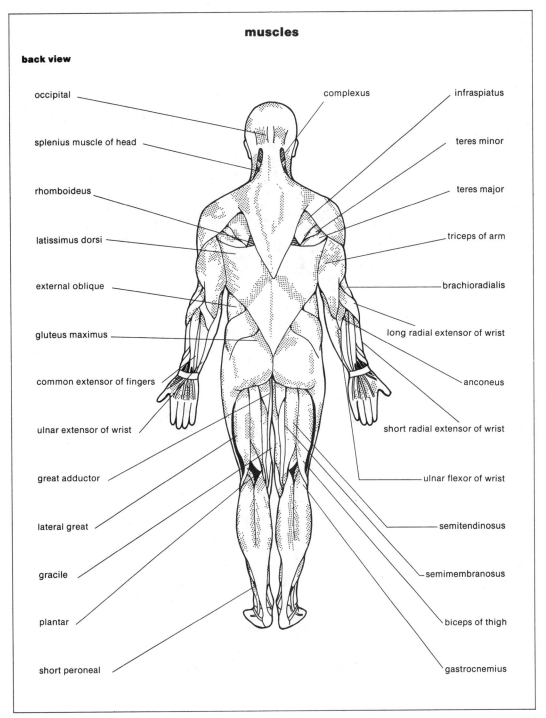

occipital

complexus

infraspiatus

splenius muscle of head

teres minor

rhomboideus

teres major

latissimus dorsi

triceps of arm

external oblique

brachioradialis

gluteus maximus

long radial extensor of wrist

common extensor of fingers

anconeus

ulnar extensor of wrist

short radial extensor of wrist

great adductor

ulnar flexor of wrist

lateral great

semitendinosus

gracile

semimembranosus

plantar

biceps of thigh

short peroneal

gastrocnemius

HUMAN BEING

skeleton

front view

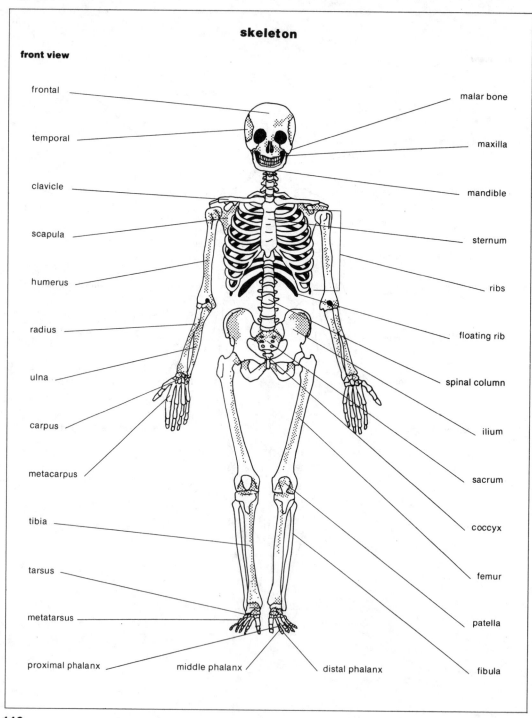

frontal

temporal

clavicle

scapula

humerus

radius

ulna

carpus

metacarpus

tibia

tarsus

metatarsus

proximal phalanx

middle phalanx

distal phalanx

malar bone

maxilla

mandible

sternum

ribs

floating rib

spinal column

ilium

sacrum

coccyx

femur

patella

fibula

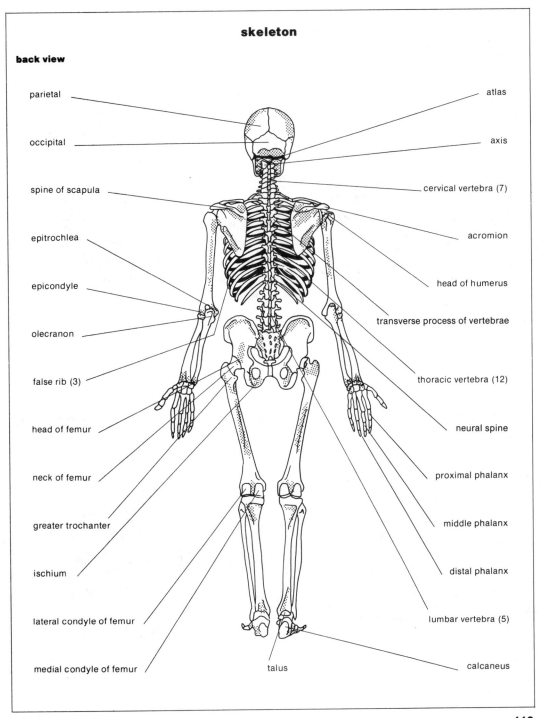

skeleton

back view

parietal

occipital

spine of scapula

epitrochlea

epicondyle

olecranon

false rib (3)

head of femur

neck of femur

greater trochanter

ischium

lateral condyle of femur

medial condyle of femur

atlas

axis

cervical vertebra (7)

acromion

head of humerus

transverse process of vertebrae

thoracic vertebra (12)

neural spine

proximal phalanx

middle phalanx

distal phalanx

lumbar vertebra (5)

talus

calcaneus

osteology of skull

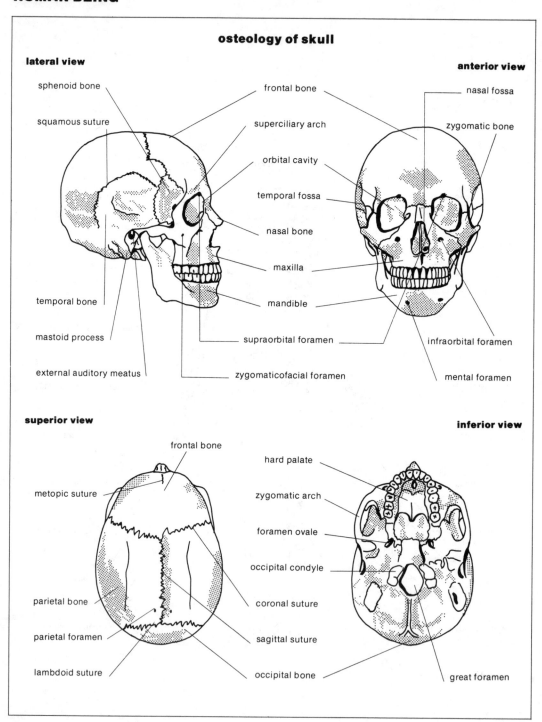

lateral view

sphenoid bone

squamous suture

frontal bone

superciliary arch

orbital cavity

temporal fossa

nasal bone

maxilla

mandible

temporal bone

mastoid process

external auditory meatus

supraorbital foramen

zygomaticofacial foramen

anterior view

nasal fossa

zygomatic bone

infraorbital foramen

mental foramen

superior view

frontal bone

metopic suture

parietal bone

parietal foramen

lambdoid suture

hard palate

zygomatic arch

foramen ovale

occipital condyle

coronal suture

sagittal suture

occipital bone

inferior view

great foramen

teeth

cross section of a molar

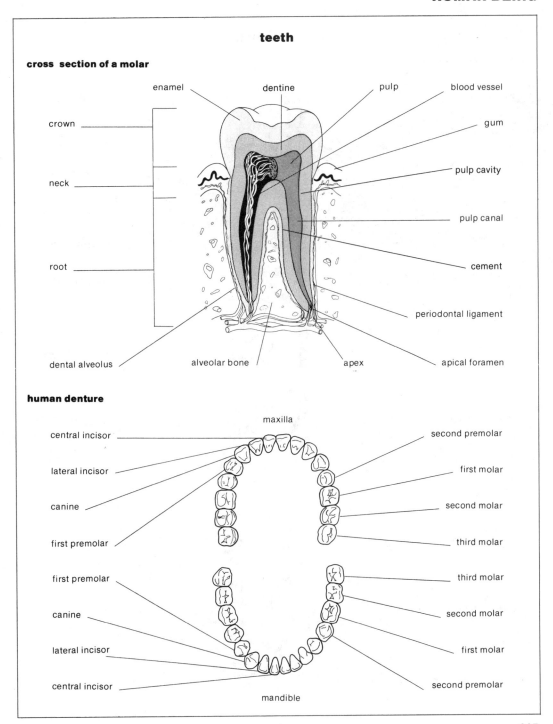

enamel

dentine

pulp

blood vessel

crown

gum

neck

pulp cavity

pulp canal

root

cement

periodontal ligament

dental alveolus

alveolar bone

apex

apical foramen

human denture

maxilla

central incisor

second premolar

lateral incisor

first molar

canine

second molar

first premolar

third molar

first premolar

third molar

canine

second molar

lateral incisor

first molar

central incisor

second premolar

mandible

blood circulation

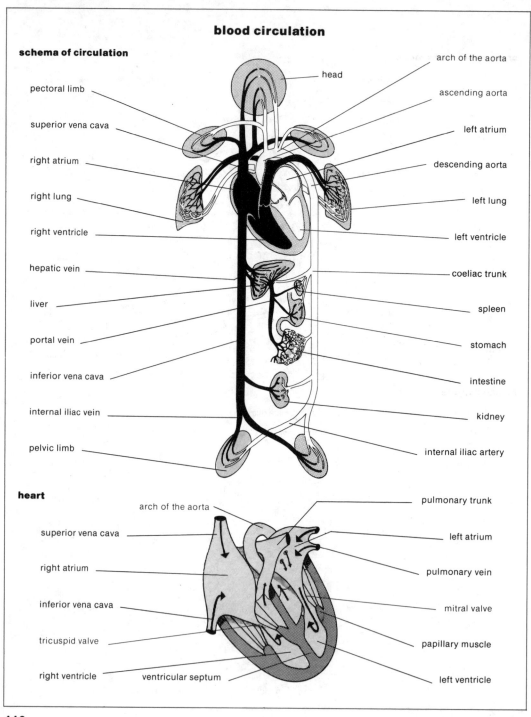

schema of circulation

pectoral limb

superior vena cava

right atrium

right lung

right ventricle

hepatic vein

liver

portal vein

inferior vena cava

internal iliac vein

pelvic limb

head

arch of the aorta

ascending aorta

left atrium

descending aorta

left lung

left ventricle

coeliac trunk

spleen

stomach

intestine

kidney

internal iliac artery

heart

arch of the aorta

superior vena cava

right atrium

inferior vena cava

tricuspid valve

right ventricle   ventricular septum

pulmonary trunk

left atrium

pulmonary vein

mitral valve

papillary muscle

left ventricle

blood circulation

principal veins and arteries

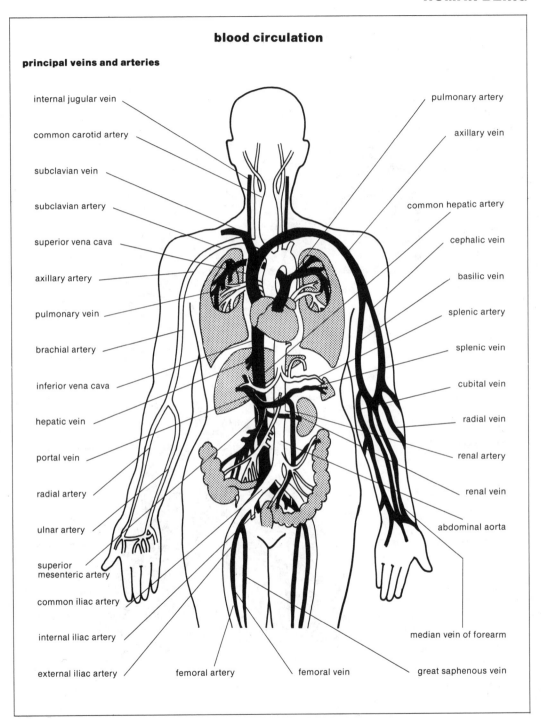

internal jugular vein

common carotid artery

subclavian vein

subclavian artery

superior vena cava

axillary artery

pulmonary vein

brachial artery

inferior vena cava

hepatic vein

portal vein

radial artery

ulnar artery

superior
mesenteric artery

common iliac artery

internal iliac artery

external iliac artery

femoral artery

femoral vein

pulmonary artery

axillary vein

common hepatic artery

cephalic vein

basilic vein

splenic artery

splenic vein

cubital vein

radial vein

renal artery

renal vein

abdominal aorta

median vein of forearm

great saphenous vein

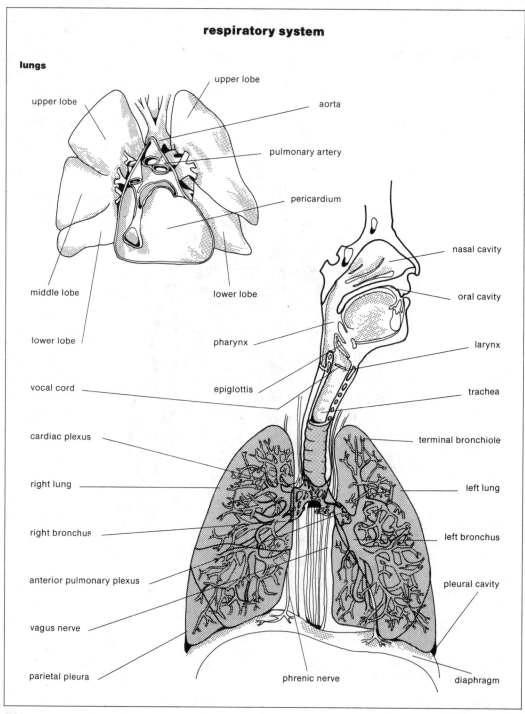

respiratory system

lungs

- upper lobe
- upper lobe
- aorta
- pulmonary artery
- pericardium
- nasal cavity
- oral cavity
- middle lobe
- lower lobe
- larynx
- lower lobe
- pharynx
- vocal cord
- epiglottis
- trachea
- cardiac plexus
- terminal bronchiole
- right lung
- left lung
- right bronchus
- left bronchus
- anterior pulmonary plexus
- pleural cavity
- vagus nerve
- parietal pleura
- phrenic nerve
- diaphragm

digestive system

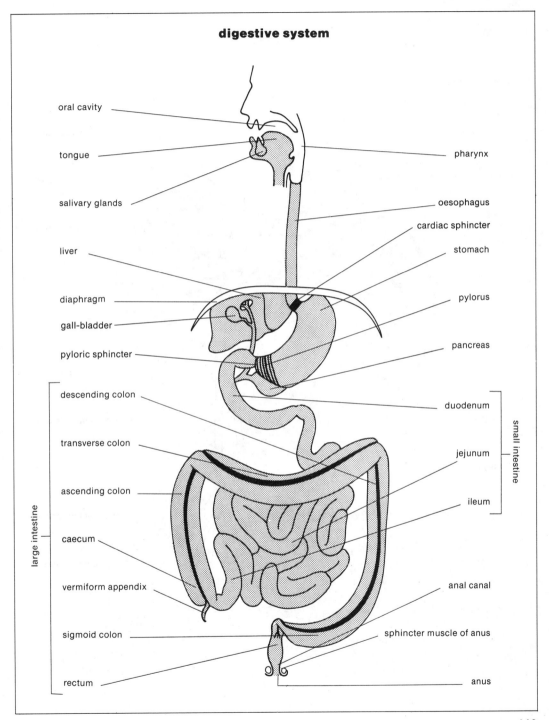

oral cavity

tongue

salivary glands

liver

diaphragm

gall-bladder

pyloric sphincter

descending colon

transverse colon

ascending colon

caecum

vermiform appendix

sigmoid colon

rectum

large intestine

pharynx

oesophagus

cardiac sphincter

stomach

pylorus

pancreas

duodenum

jejunum

ileum

small intestine

anal canal

sphincter muscle of anus

anus

urinary system

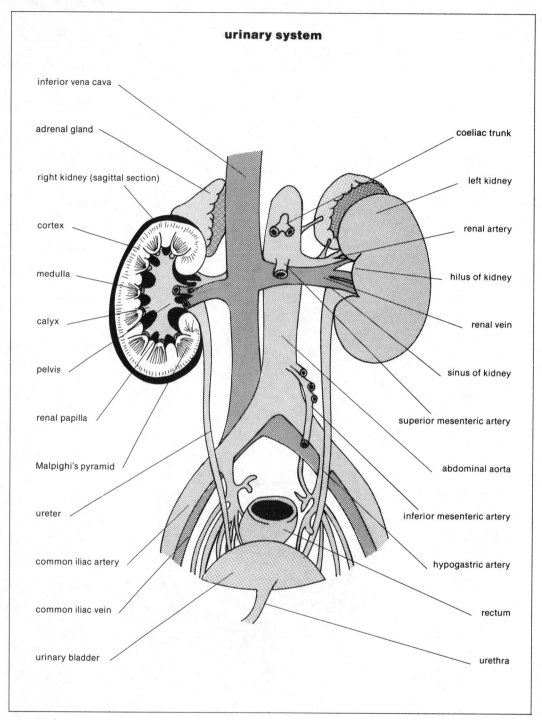

inferior vena cava

adrenal gland

right kidney (sagittal section)

cortex

medulla

calyx

pelvis

renal papilla

Malpighi's pyramid

ureter

common iliac artery

common iliac vein

urinary bladder

coeliac trunk

left kidney

renal artery

hilus of kidney

renal vein

sinus of kidney

superior mesenteric artery

abdominal aorta

inferior mesenteric artery

hypogastric artery

rectum

urethra

nervous system

peripheral nervous system

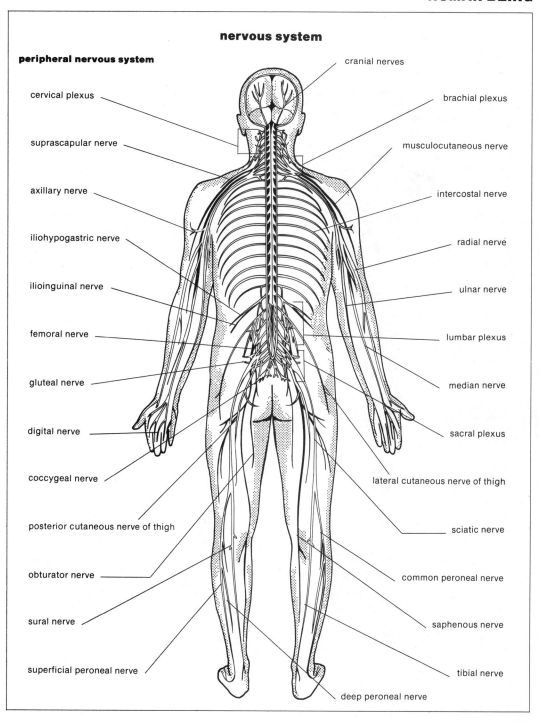

cranial nerves

cervical plexus

brachial plexus

suprascapular nerve

musculocutaneous nerve

axillary nerve

intercostal nerve

iliohypogastric nerve

radial nerve

ilioinguinal nerve

ulnar nerve

femoral nerve

lumbar plexus

gluteal nerve

median nerve

digital nerve

sacral plexus

coccygeal nerve

lateral cutaneous nerve of thigh

posterior cutaneous nerve of thigh

obturator nerve

sciatic nerve

sural nerve

common peroneal nerve

superficial peroneal nerve

saphenous nerve

tibial nerve

deep peroneal nerve

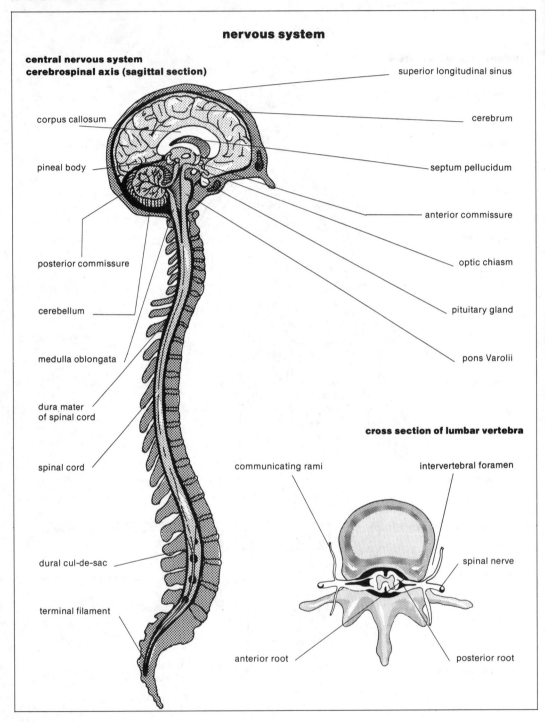

nervous system

central nervous system
cerebrospinal axis (sagittal section)

superior longitudinal sinus

corpus callosum

cerebrum

pineal body

septum pellucidum

anterior commissure

posterior commissure

optic chiasm

cerebellum

pituitary gland

medulla oblongata

pons Varolii

dura mater
of spinal cord

cross section of lumbar vertebra

spinal cord

communicating rami

intervertebral foramen

spinal nerve

dural cul-de-sac

terminal filament

anterior root

posterior root

sense organs : sight

eye

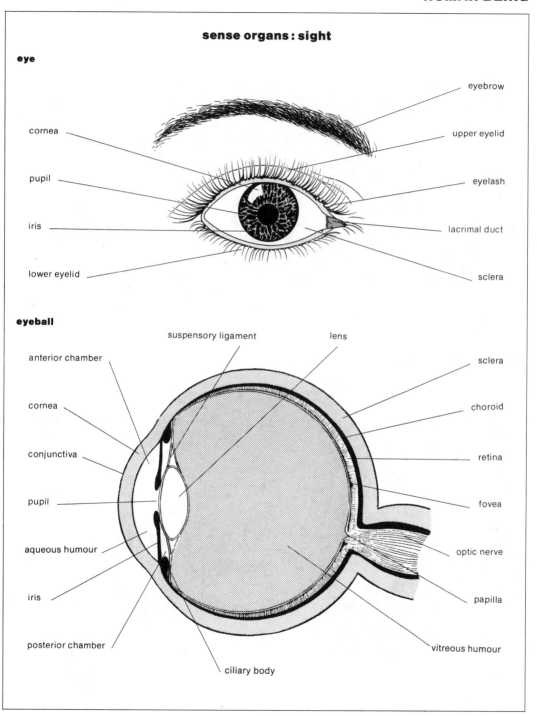

cornea

pupil

iris

lower eyelid

eyebrow

upper eyelid

eyelash

lacrimal duct

sclera

eyeball

suspensory ligament

lens

anterior chamber

cornea

conjunctiva

pupil

aqueous humour

iris

posterior chamber

ciliary body

sclera

choroid

retina

fovea

optic nerve

papilla

vitreous humour

sense organs : hearing

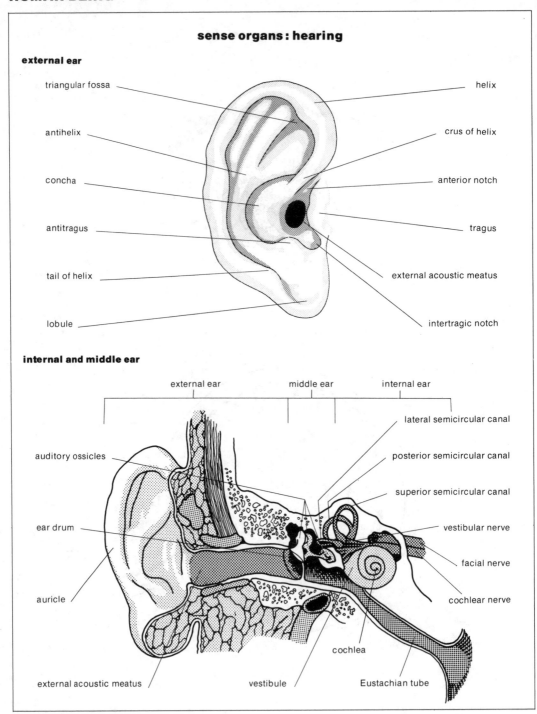

external ear

triangular fossa

helix

antihelix

crus of helix

concha

anterior notch

antitragus

tragus

tail of helix

external acoustic meatus

lobule

intertragic notch

internal and middle ear

external ear

middle ear

internal ear

auditory ossicles

lateral semicircular canal

posterior semicircular canal

superior semicircular canal

ear drum

vestibular nerve

facial nerve

cochlear nerve

auricle

cochlea

external acoustic meatus

vestibule

Eustachian tube

sense organs : smell

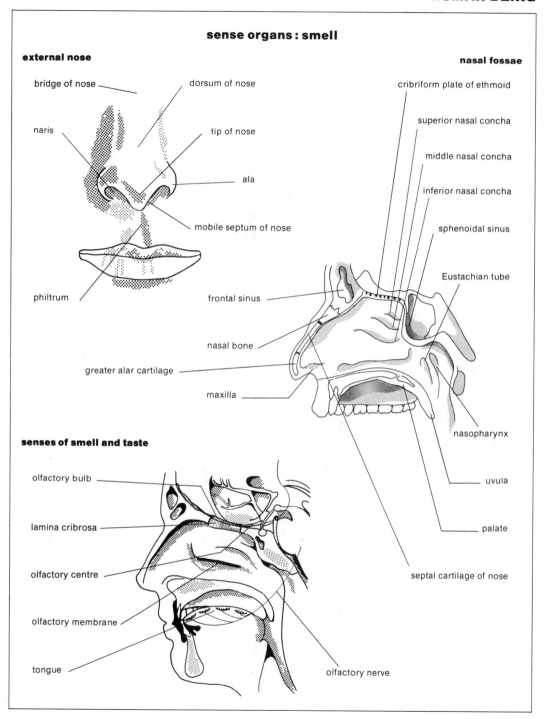

external nose

bridge of nose

dorsum of nose

naris

tip of nose

ala

mobile septum of nose

philtrum

nasal fossae

cribriform plate of ethmoid

superior nasal concha

middle nasal concha

inferior nasal concha

sphenoidal sinus

Eustachian tube

frontal sinus

nasal bone

greater alar cartilage

maxilla

nasopharynx

uvula

palate

senses of smell and taste

olfactory bulb

lamina cribrosa

olfactory centre

olfactory membrane

tongue

septal cartilage of nose

olfactory nerve

sense organs : taste

mouth

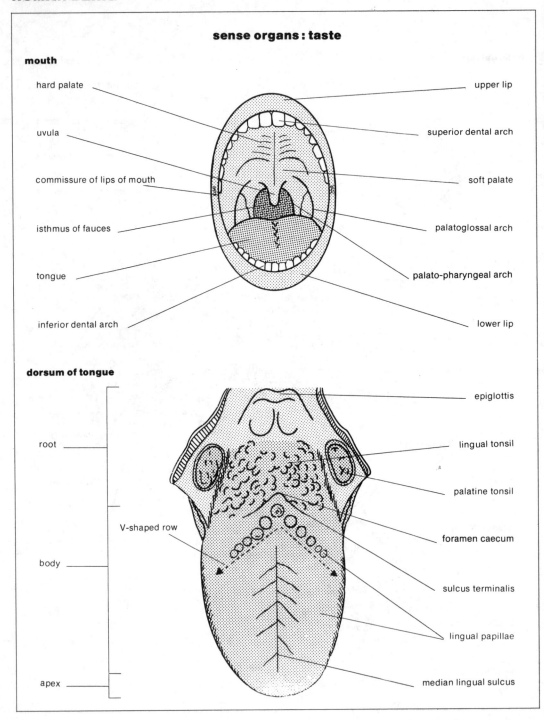

hard palate

uvula

commissure of lips of mouth

isthmus of fauces

tongue

inferior dental arch

upper lip

superior dental arch

soft palate

palatoglossal arch

palato-pharyngeal arch

lower lip

dorsum of tongue

root

V-shaped row

body

apex

epiglottis

lingual tonsil

palatine tonsil

foramen caecum

sulcus terminalis

lingual papillae

median lingual sulcus

sense organs : touch

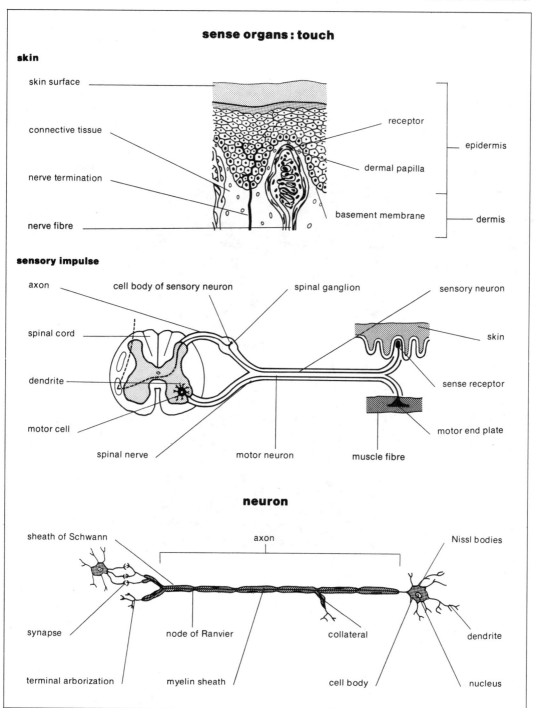

skin

- skin surface
- connective tissue
- nerve termination
- nerve fibre
- receptor
- dermal papilla
- basement membrane
- epidermis
- dermis

sensory impulse

- axon
- cell body of sensory neuron
- spinal ganglion
- sensory neuron
- spinal cord
- skin
- dendrite
- sense receptor
- motor cell
- motor end plate
- spinal nerve
- motor neuron
- muscle fibre

neuron

- sheath of Schwann
- axon
- Nissl bodies
- synapse
- node of Ranvier
- collateral
- dendrite
- terminal arborization
- myelin sheath
- cell body
- nucleus

skin

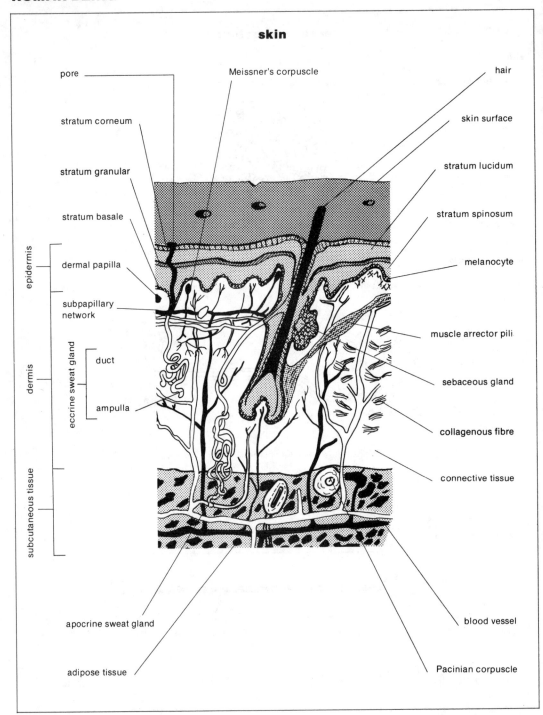

pore

Meissner's corpuscle

hair

stratum corneum

skin surface

stratum granular

stratum lucidum

stratum basale

stratum spinosum

dermal papilla

melanocyte

subpapillary network

muscle arrector pili

epidermis

eccrine sweat gland

duct

sebaceous gland

dermis

ampulla

collagenous fibre

subcutaneous tissue

connective tissue

apocrine sweat gland

blood vessel

adipose tissue

Pacinian corpuscle

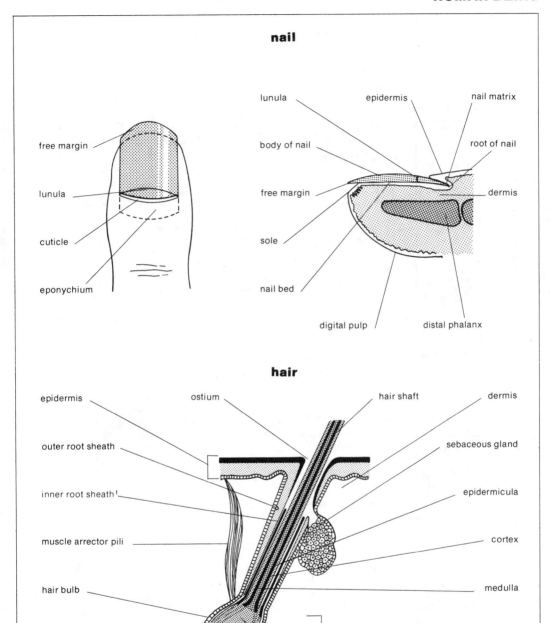

nail

free margin

lunula

cuticle

eponychium

lunula

body of nail

free margin

sole

nail bed

epidermis

nail matrix

root of nail

dermis

digital pulp

distal phalanx

hair

epidermis

outer root sheath

inner root sheath¹

muscle arrector pili

hair bulb

papilla

blood vessel

nerve

ostium

hair shaft

hair follicle

dermis

sebaceous gland

epidermicula

cortex

medulla

root of hair

indifferent cells

HUMAN BEING

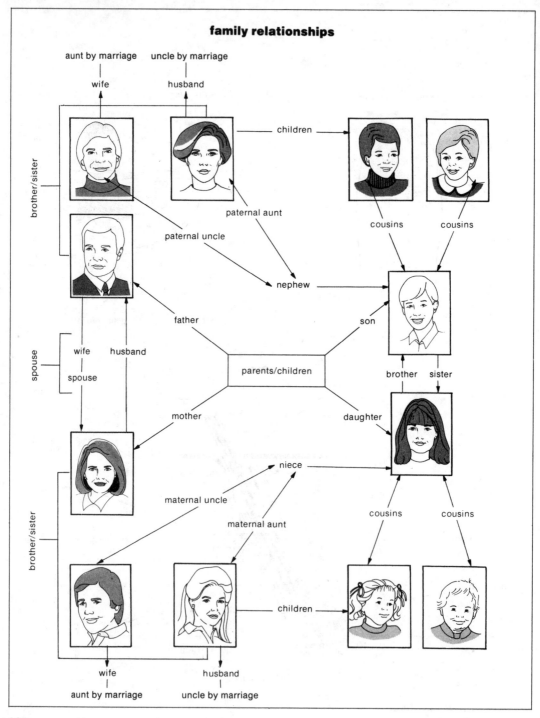

family relationships

family relationships

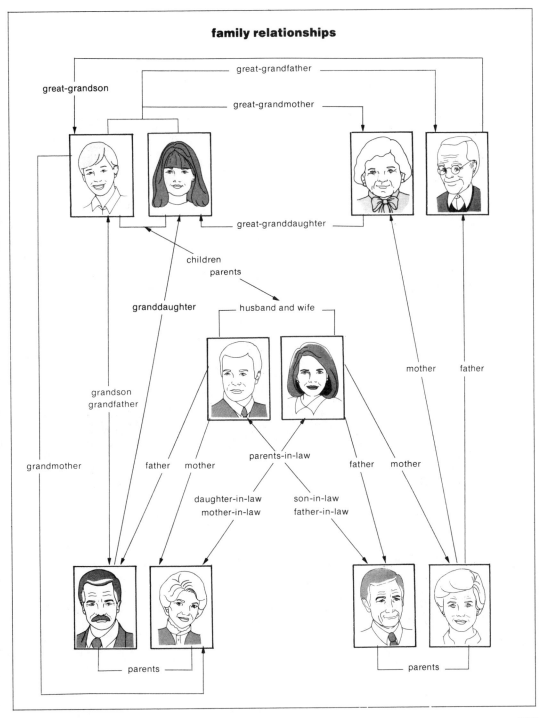

great-grandfather

great-grandson

great-grandmother

great-granddaughter

children

parents

granddaughter

husband and wife

grandson
grandfather

mother   father

grandmother

father   mother

parents-in-law

father   mother

daughter-in-law
mother-in-law

son-in-law
father-in-law

parents

parents

FOOD

herbs

basil

tarragon

chervil

parsley

marjoram

oregano

sage

rosemary

savory

thyme

sweet bay

dill

mint

lovage

hyssop

borage

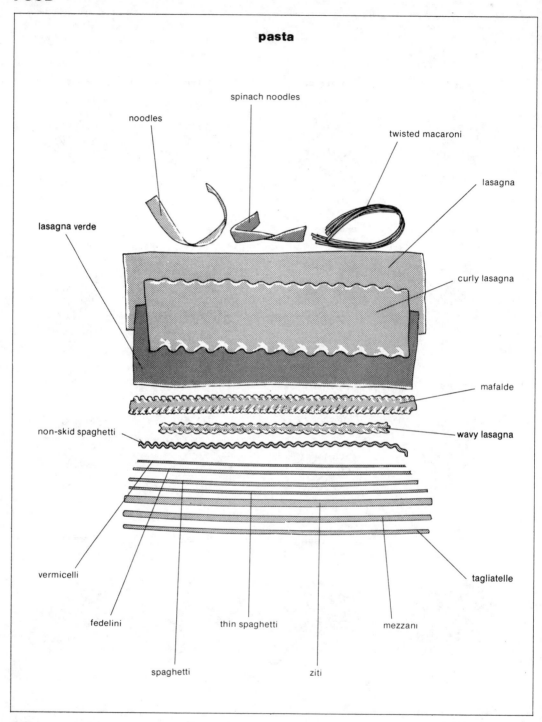

pasta

spinach noodles

noodles

twisted macaroni

lasagna

lasagna verde

curly lasagna

mafalde

non-skid spaghetti

wavy lasagna

vermicelli

tagliatelle

fedelini

thin spaghetti

mezzanı

spaghetti

ziti

pasta

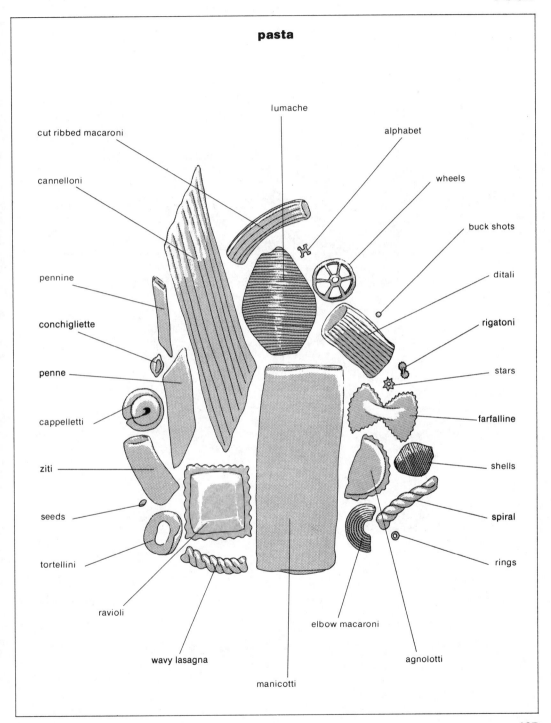

cut ribbed macaroni

cannelloni

lumache

alphabet

wheels

buck shots

ditali

rigatoni

pennine

conchigliette

penne

cappelletti

stars

farfalline

ziti

seeds

shells

spiral

tortellini

rings

ravioli

elbow macaroni

wavy lasagna

agnolotti

manicotti

137

bread

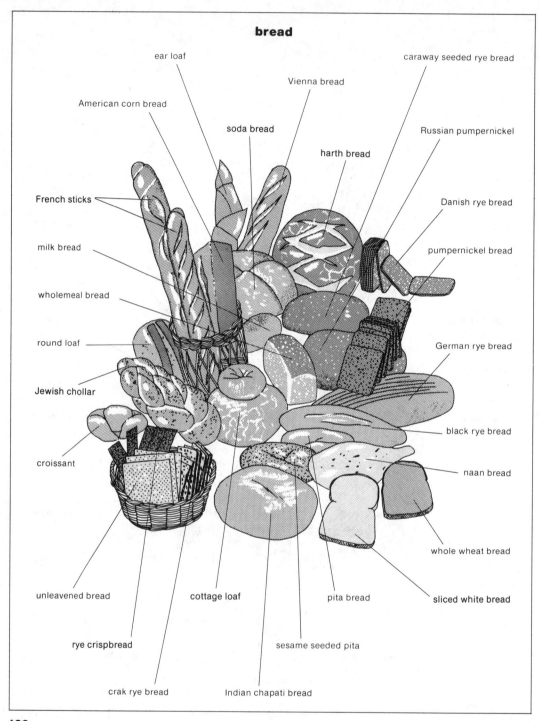

ear loaf

caraway seeded rye bread

Vienna bread

American corn bread

Russian pumpernickel

soda bread

harth bread

Danish rye bread

French sticks

pumpernickel bread

milk bread

wholemeal bread

German rye bread

round loaf

Jewish chollar

black rye bread

croissant

naan bread

whole wheat bread

unleavened bread

cottage loaf

pita bread

sliced white bread

rye crispbread

sesame seeded pita

crak rye bread

Indian chapati bread

veal

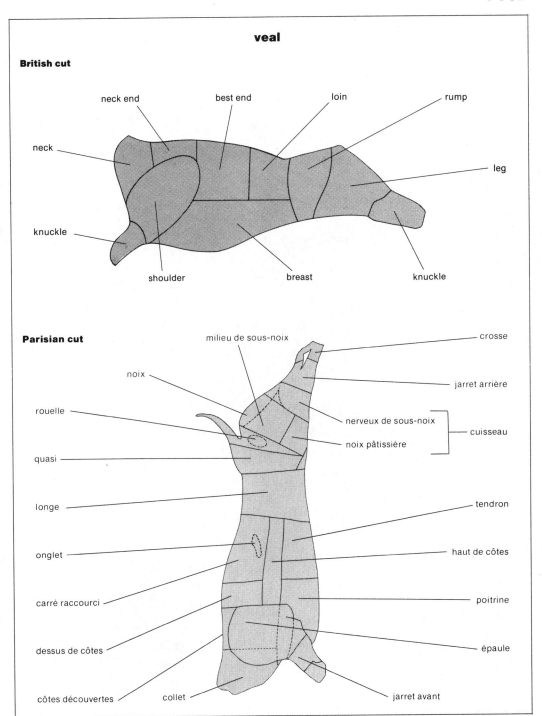

British cut

neck end

best end

loin

rump

neck

leg

knuckle

shoulder

breast

knuckle

Parisian cut

milieu de sous-noix

crosse

noix

jarret arrière

rouelle

nerveux de sous-noix

cuisseau

noix pâtissière

quasi

longe

tendron

onglet

haut de côtes

carré raccourci

poitrine

dessus de côtes

épaule

côtes découvertes

collet

jarret avant

beef

British cut

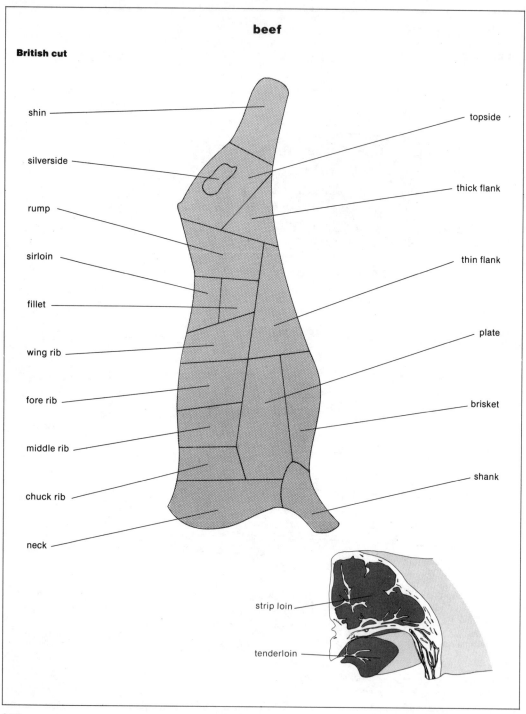

shin

silverside

rump

sirloin

fillet

wing rib

fore rib

middle rib

chuck rib

neck

topside

thick flank

thin flank

plate

brisket

shank

strip loin

tenderloin

beef

Parisian cut

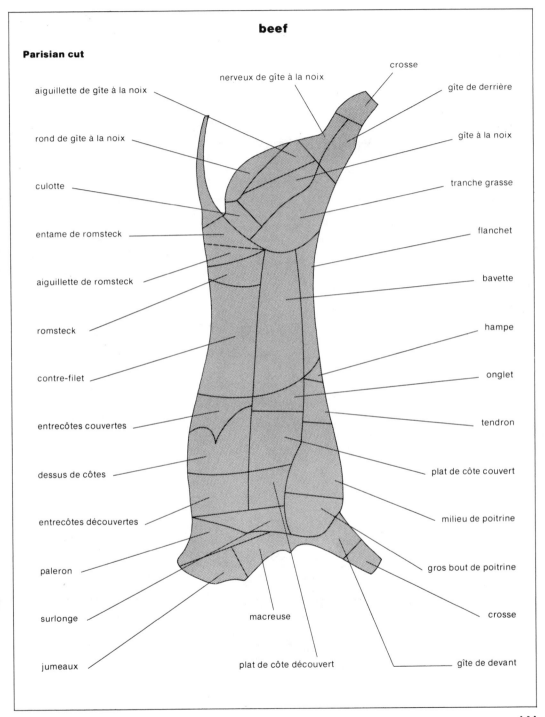

nerveux de gîte à la noix

crosse

aiguillette de gîte à la noix

gîte de derrière

rond de gîte à la noix

gîte à la noix

culotte

tranche grasse

entame de romsteck

flanchet

aiguillette de romsteck

bavette

romsteck

hampe

contre-filet

onglet

entrecôtes couvertes

tendron

dessus de côtes

plat de côte couvert

entrecôtes découvertes

milieu de poitrine

paleron

gros bout de poitrine

surlonge

crosse

jumeaux

macreuse

plat de côte découvert

gîte de devant

FOOD

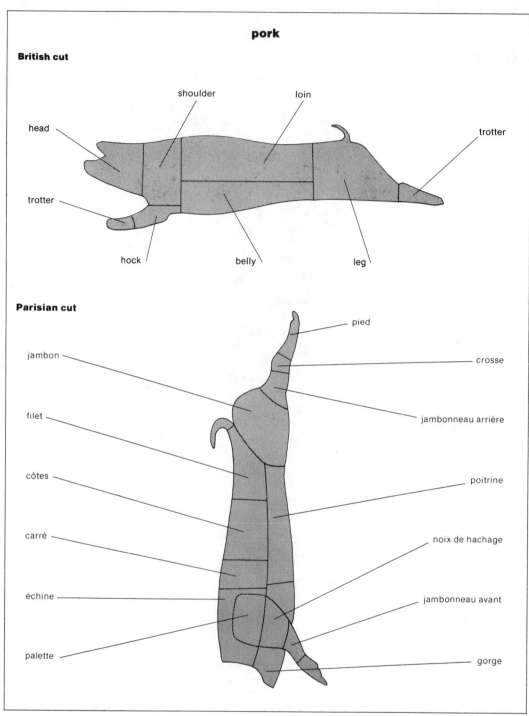

pork

British cut

- head
- shoulder
- loin
- trotter
- trotter
- hock
- belly
- leg

Parisian cut

- pied
- jambon
- crosse
- filet
- jambonneau arrière
- côtes
- poitrine
- carré
- noix de hachage
- échine
- jambonneau avant
- palette
- gorge

lamb

British cut

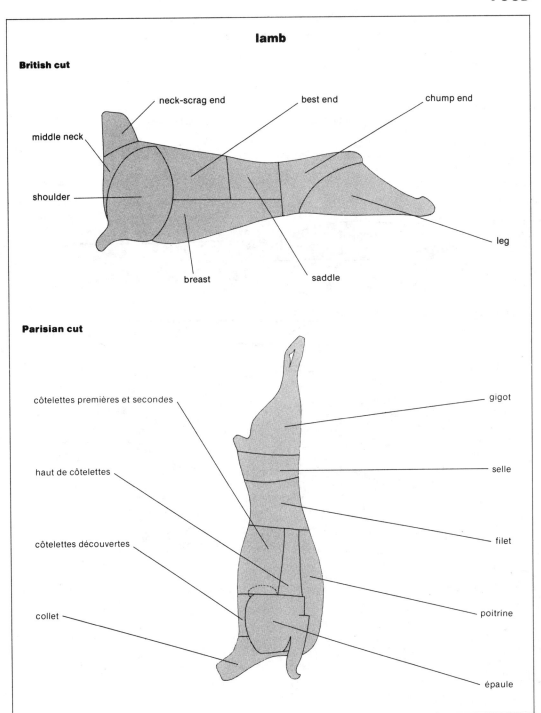

neck-scrag end

best end

chump end

middle neck

shoulder

leg

breast

saddle

Parisian cut

côtelettes premières et secondes

gigot

haut de côtelettes

selle

côtelettes découvertes

filet

collet

poitrine

épaule

British cheeses

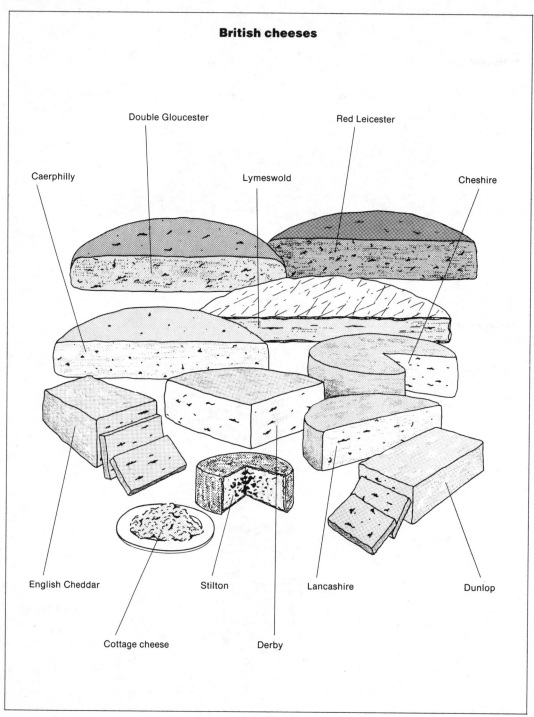

Double Gloucester

Red Leicester

Caerphilly

Lymeswold

Cheshire

English Cheddar

Stilton

Lancashire

Dunlop

Cottage cheese

Derby

Continental cheeses

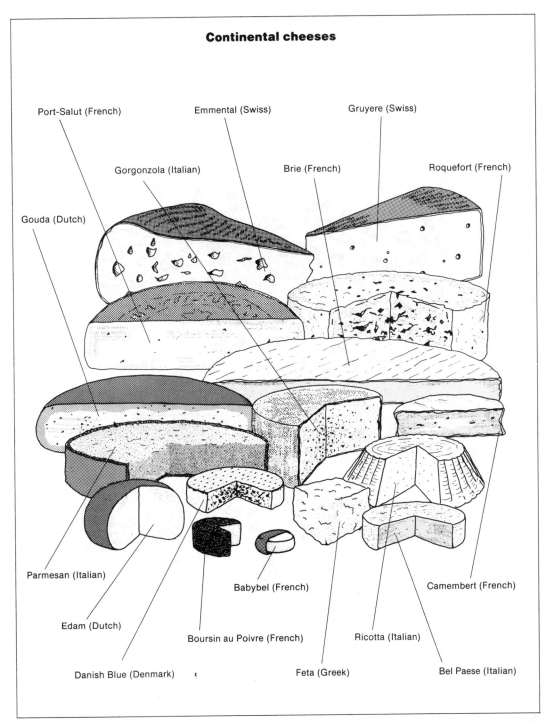

Port-Salut (French)

Emmental (Swiss)

Gruyere (Swiss)

Gorgonzola (Italian)

Brie (French)

Roquefort (French)

Gouda (Dutch)

Parmesan (Italian)

Babybel (French)

Camembert (French)

Edam (Dutch)

Boursin au Poivre (French)

Ricotta (Italian)

Danish Blue (Denmark)

Feta (Greek)

Bel Paese (Italian)

desserts

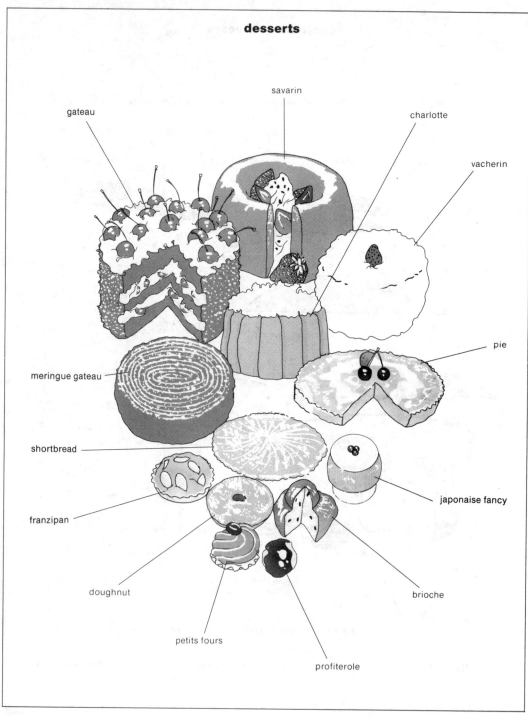

savarin

gateau

charlotte

vacherin

pie

meringue gateau

shortbread

japonaise fancy

franzipan

doughnut

petits fours

profiterole

brioche

desserts

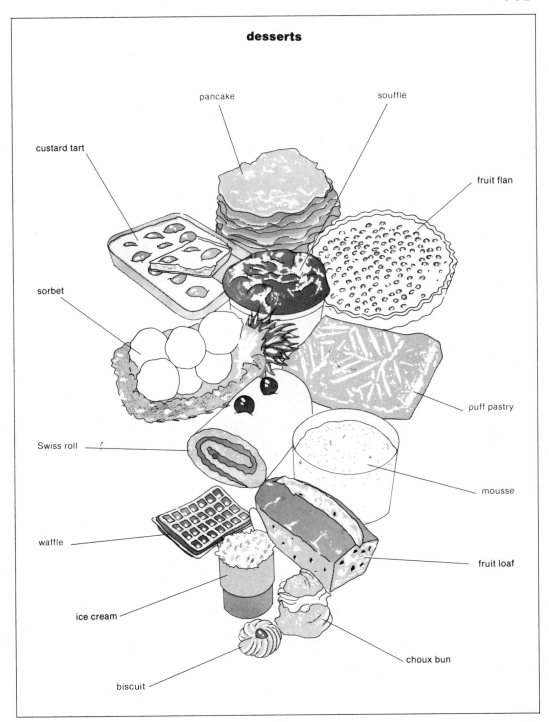

pancake

soufflé

custard tart

fruit flan

sorbet

puff pastry

Swiss roll

mousse

waffle

fruit loaf

ice cream

choux bun

biscuit

FARMING

buildings

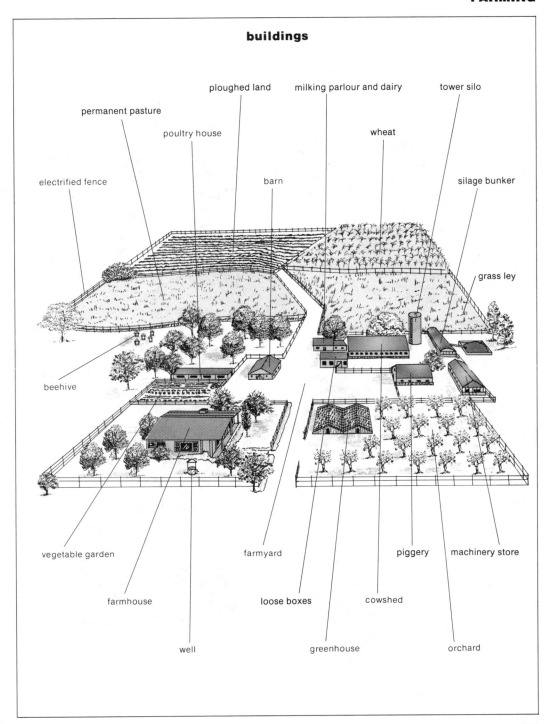

permanent pasture

ploughed land

milking parlour and dairy

tower silo

poultry house

wheat

electrified fence

barn

silage bunker

grass ley

beehive

vegetable garden

farmyard

piggery

machinery store

farmhouse

loose boxes

cowshed

well

greenhouse

orchard

agricultural machinery

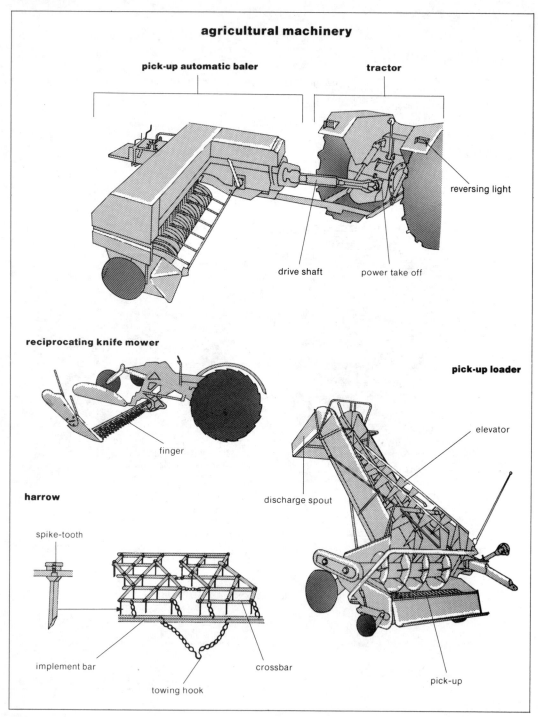

pick-up automatic baler

tractor

reversing light

drive shaft

power take off

reciprocating knife mower

pick-up loader

elevator

finger

discharge spout

harrow

spike-tooth

implement bar

towing hook

crossbar

pick-up

agricultural machinery

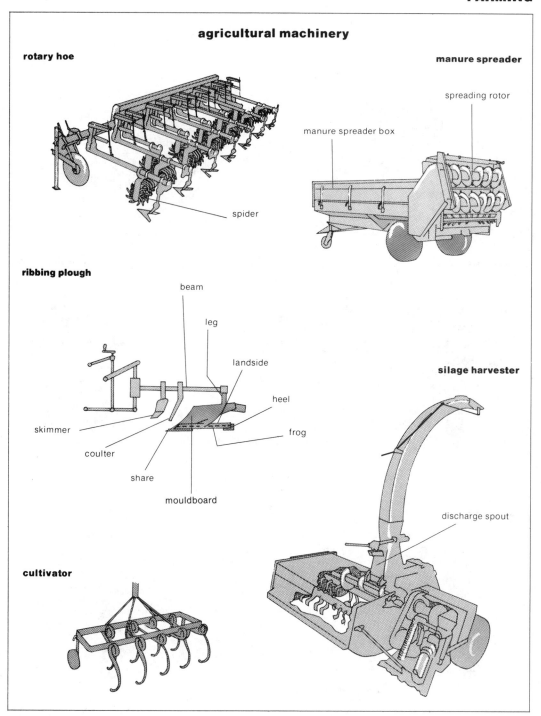

rotary hoe

spider

manure spreader

spreading rotor

manure spreader box

ribbing plough

beam

leg

landside

heel

skimmer

frog

coulter

share

mouldboard

silage harvester

discharge spout

cultivator

agricultural machinery

field heap spreader

seed drill

hopper

toothed rotor

hay turner

reel

subsoil plough

fertilizer distributor

tooth

potato planter

cup conveyor

tandem disc harrow

hopper

covering disc

machinery

combine harvester

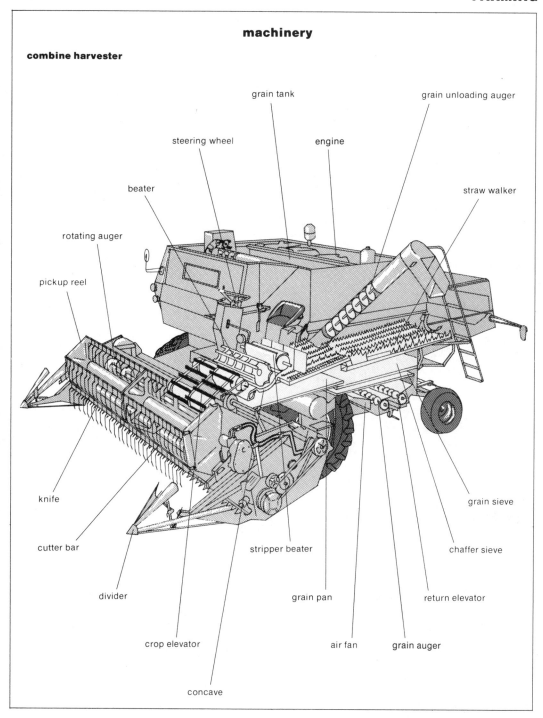

grain tank

grain unloading auger

steering wheel

engine

beater

straw walker

rotating auger

pickup reel

knife

cutter bar

grain sieve

stripper beater

chaffer sieve

divider

grain pan

return elevator

crop elevator

air fan

grain auger

concave

ARCHITECTURE

traditional houses

hut

hut

wigwam

igloo

yurt

tepee

isba

architectural styles

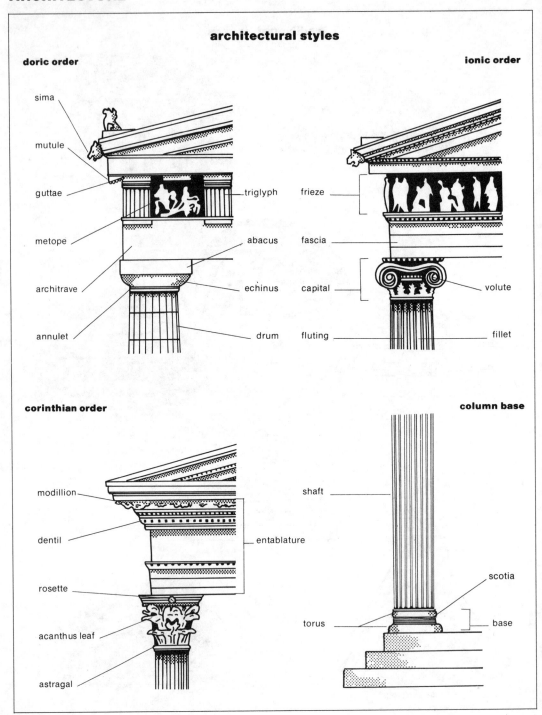

doric order

- sima
- mutule
- guttae
- metope
- architrave
- annulet
- triglyph
- abacus
- echinus
- drum

ionic order

- frieze
- fascia
- capital
- fluting
- volute
- fillet

corinthian order

- modillion
- dentil
- rosette
- acanthus leaf
- astragal
- entablature

column base

- shaft
- scotia
- torus
- base

Greek temple

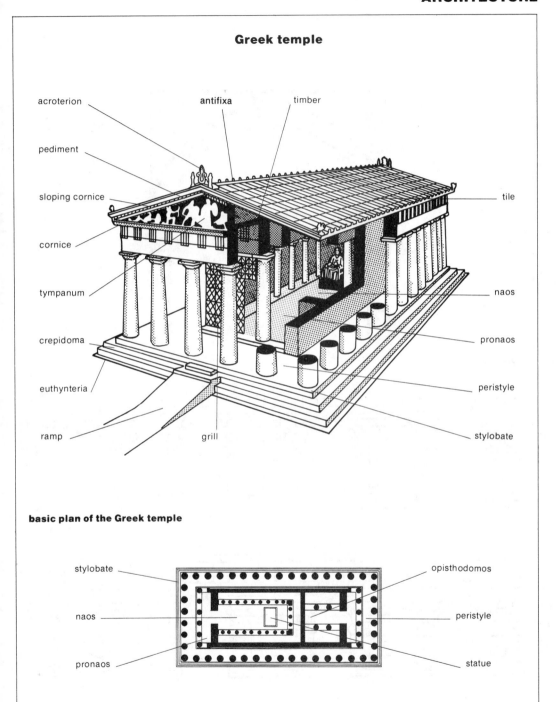

acroterion

antifixa

timber

pediment

sloping cornice

tile

cornice

tympanum

naos

crepidoma

pronaos

euthynteria

peristyle

ramp

grill

stylobate

basic plan of the Greek temple

stylobate

opisthodomos

naos

peristyle

pronaos

statue

ARCHITECTURE

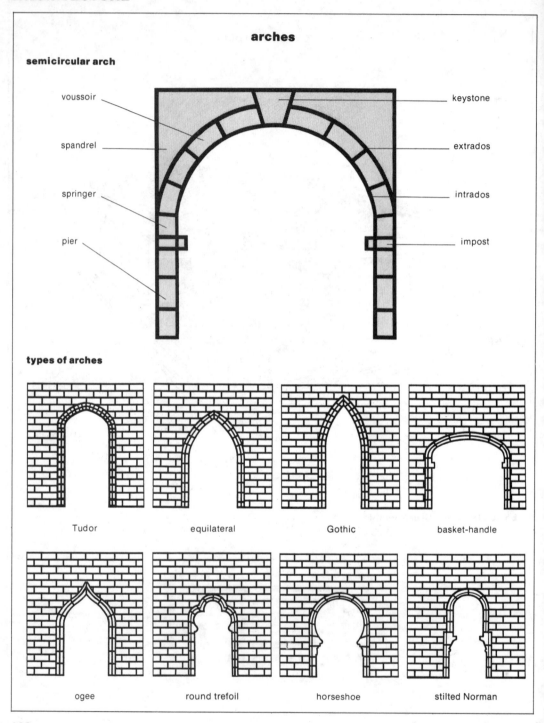

arches

semicircular arch

voussoir

keystone

spandrel

extrados

springer

intrados

pier

impost

types of arches

Tudor

equilateral

Gothic

basket-handle

ogee

round trefoil

horseshoe

stilted Norman

Roman house

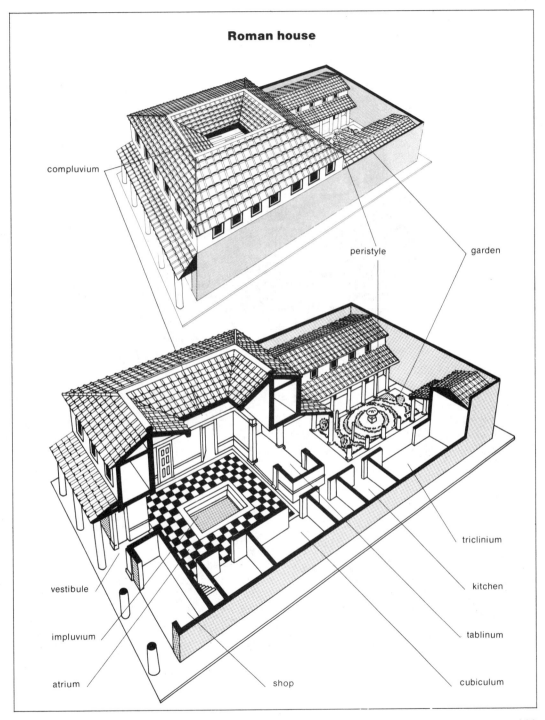

compluvium

peristyle

garden

triclinium

kitchen

vestibule

tablinum

impluvium

atrium

shop

cubiculum

ARCHITECTURE

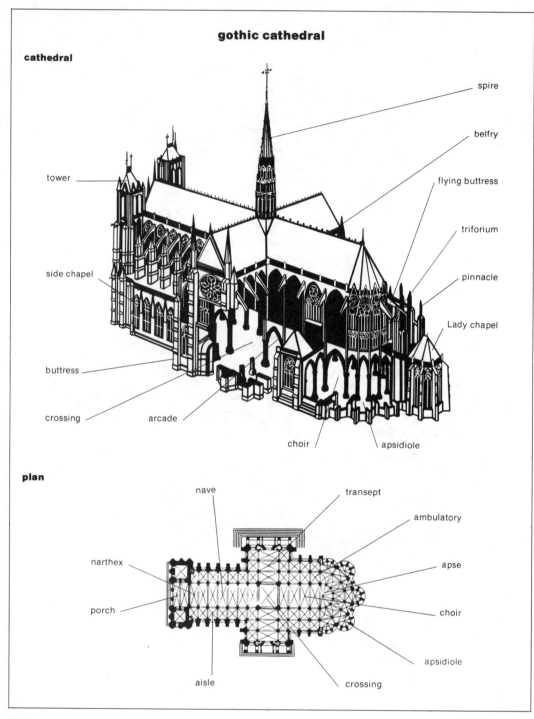

gothic cathedral

cathedral

spire

belfry

tower

flying buttress

triforium

side chapel

pinnacle

Lady chapel

buttress

crossing

arcade

choir

apsidiole

plan

nave

transept

ambulatory

narthex

apse

porch

choir

apsidiole

aisle

crossing

gothic cathedral

façade

gallery

rose window

gable

archivolt

tympanum

order

splay

piers

portal

bell tower

louvre-board

triforium

trefoil

lintel

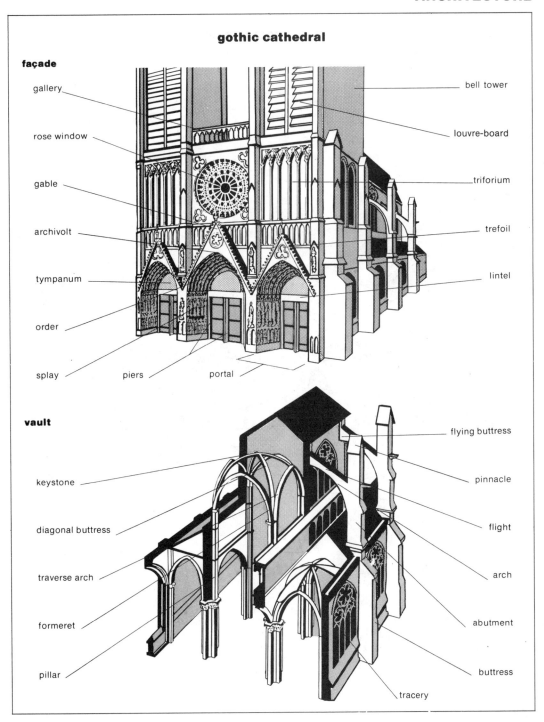

vault

keystone

diagonal buttress

traverse arch

formeret

pillar

flying buttress

pinnacle

flight

arch

abutment

buttress

tracery

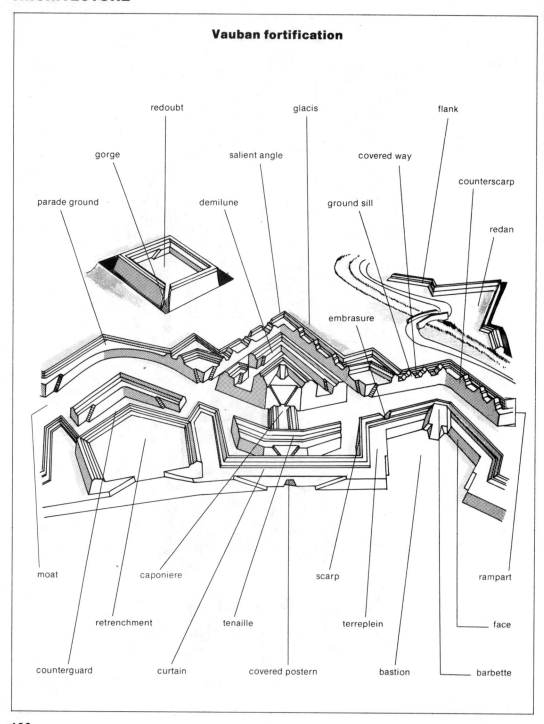

Vauban fortification

redoubt

glacis

flank

gorge

salient angle

covered way

counterscarp

parade ground

demilune

ground sill

redan

embrasure

moat

caponiere

scarp

rampart

retrenchment

tenaille

terreplein

face

counterguard

curtain

covered postern

bastion

barbette

castle

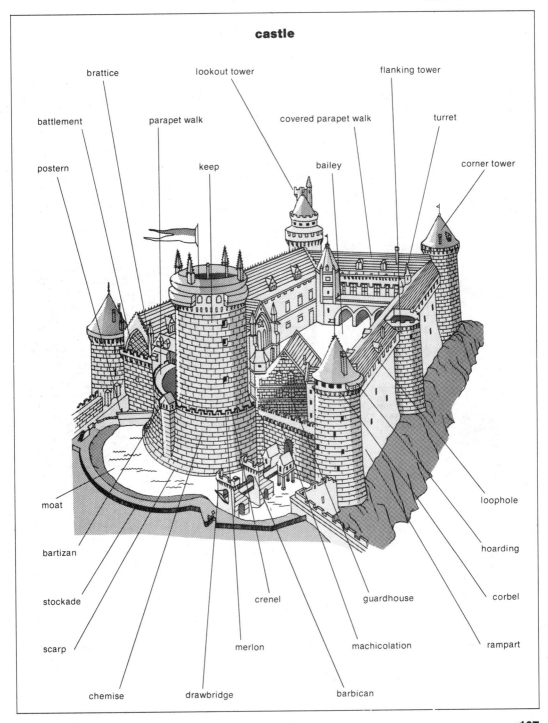

brattice

lookout tower

flanking tower

battlement

parapet walk

covered parapet walk

turret

postern

keep

bailey

corner tower

loophole

moat

hoarding

bartizan

stockade

crenel

guardhouse

corbel

scarp

merlon

machicolation

rampart

chemise

drawbridge

barbican

ARCHITECTURE

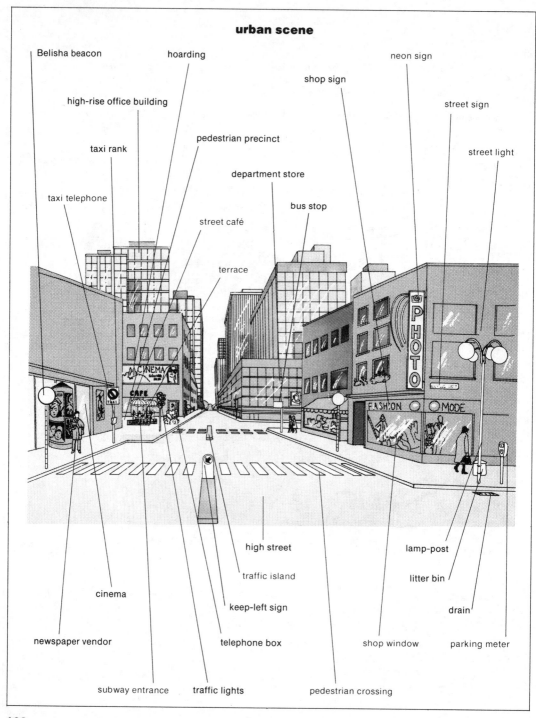

urban scene

Belisha beacon

hoarding

neon sign

high-rise office building

shop sign

street sign

taxi rank

pedestrian precinct

street light

taxi telephone

department store

street café

bus stop

terrace

PHOTO

FASHION MODE

CINEMA

CAFE

TAXI

high street

lamp-post

traffic island

litter bin

cinema

keep-left sign

drain

newspaper vendor

telephone box

shop window

parking meter

subway entrance

traffic lights

pedestrian crossing

theatre

hall

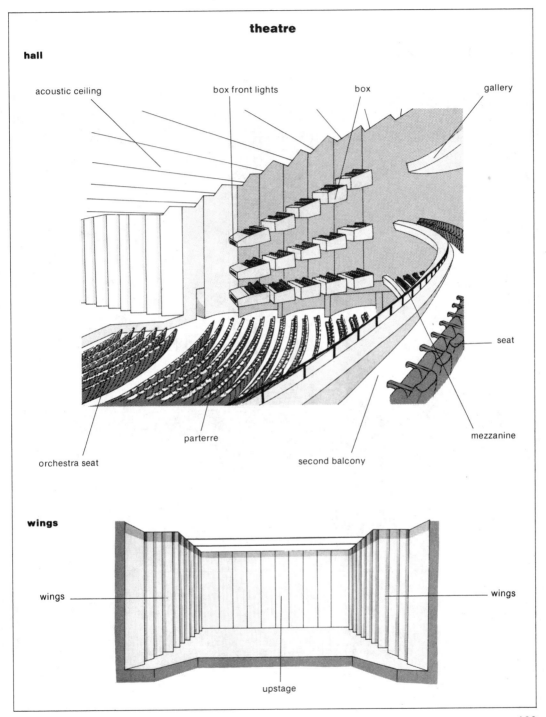

acoustic ceiling

box front lights

box

gallery

seat

parterre

mezzanine

orchestra seat

second balcony

wings

wings

wings

upstage

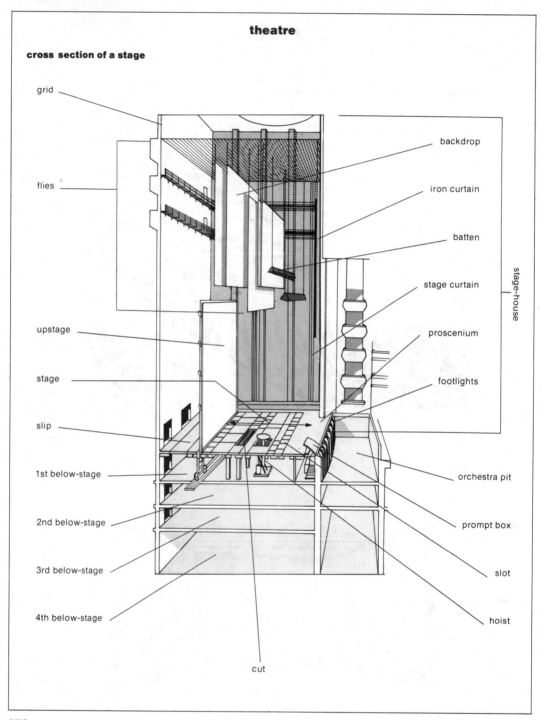

theatre

cross section of a stage

grid

flies

upstage

stage

slip

1st below-stage

2nd below-stage

3rd below-stage

4th below-stage

backdrop

iron curtain

batten

stage curtain

proscenium

footlights

orchestra pit

prompt box

slot

hoist

stage-house

cut

lift

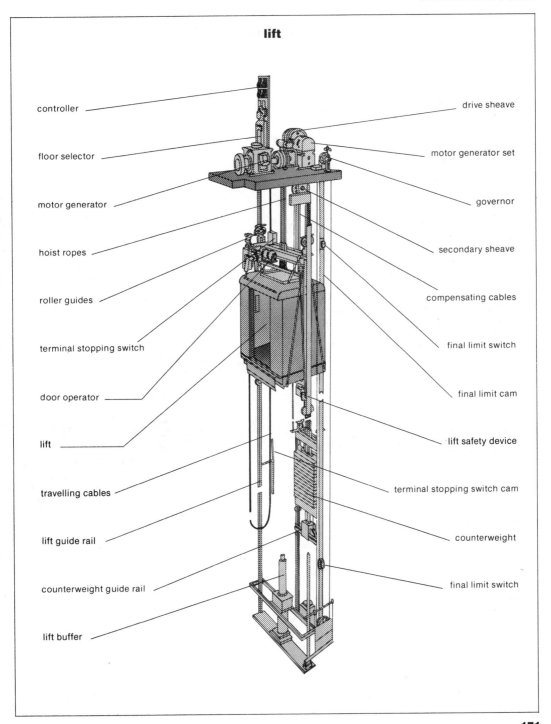

controller

floor selector

motor generator

hoist ropes

roller guides

terminal stopping switch

door operator

lift

travelling cables

lift guide rail

counterweight guide rail

lift buffer

drive sheave

motor generator set

governor

secondary sheave

compensating cables

final limit switch

final limit cam

lift safety device

terminal stopping switch cam

counterweight

final limit switch

ARCHITECTURE

escalator

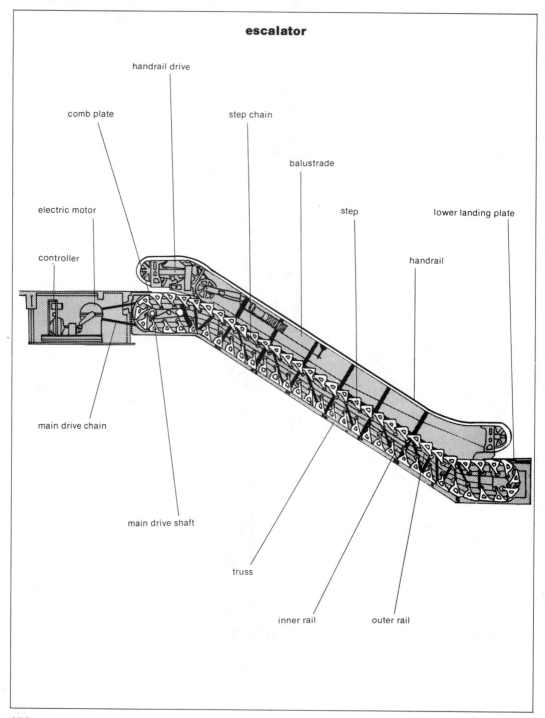

handrail drive

comb plate

step chain

balustrade

electric motor

step

lower landing plate

controller

handrail

main drive chain

main drive shaft

truss

inner rail

outer rail

house styles

bungalow

chalet bungalow

terraced

semi-detached

maisonette

detached

town house

high-rise block

cottage

low-rise apartments

HOUSE

exterior of a house

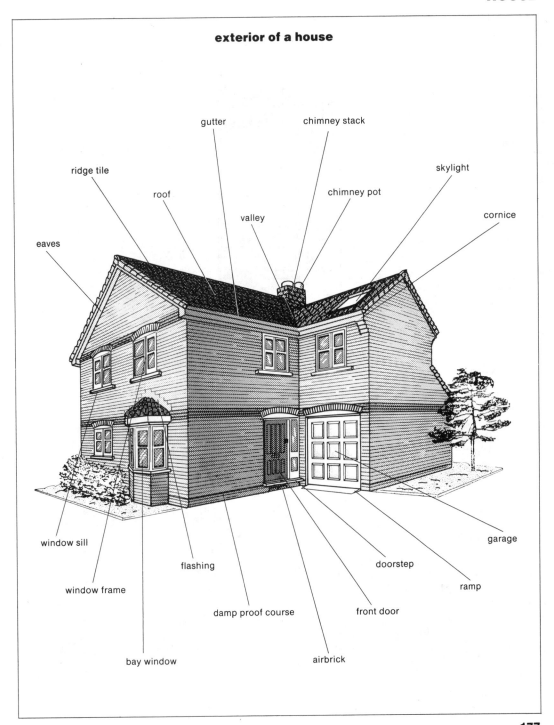

gutter

chimney stack

ridge tile

skylight

roof

chimney pot

valley

cornice

eaves

window sill

flashing

doorstep

garage

window frame

ramp

damp proof course

front door

bay window

airbrick

HOUSE

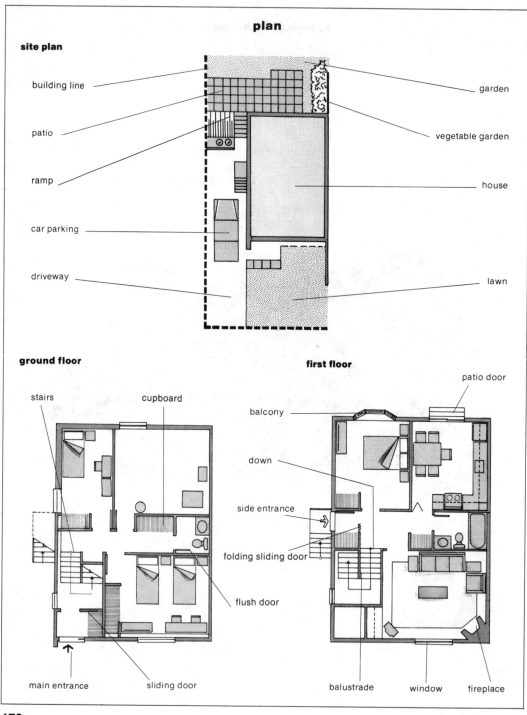

plan

site plan

building line

patio

ramp

car parking

driveway

garden

vegetable garden

house

lawn

ground floor

stairs

cupboard

main entrance

sliding door

flush door

first floor

patio door

balcony

down

side entrance

folding sliding door

balustrade

window

fireplace

178

rooms of the house

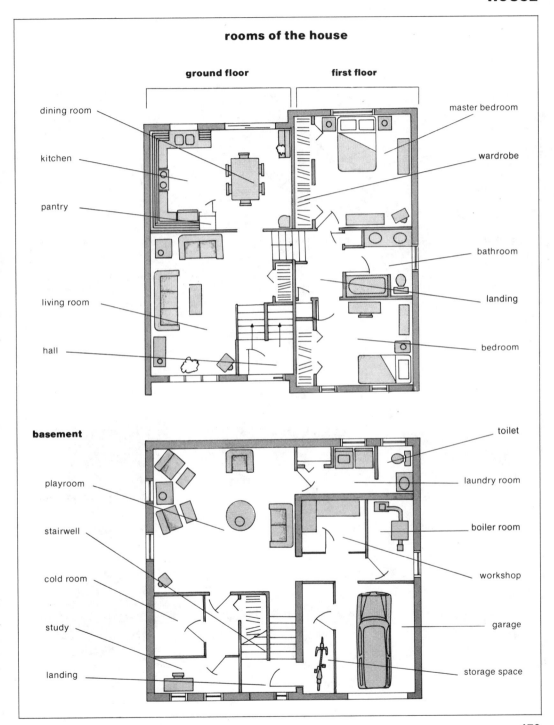

ground floor

first floor

dining room

kitchen

pantry

living room

hall

master bedroom

wardrobe

bathroom

landing

bedroom

basement

playroom

stairwell

cold room

study

landing

toilet

laundry room

boiler room

workshop

garage

storage space

HOUSE

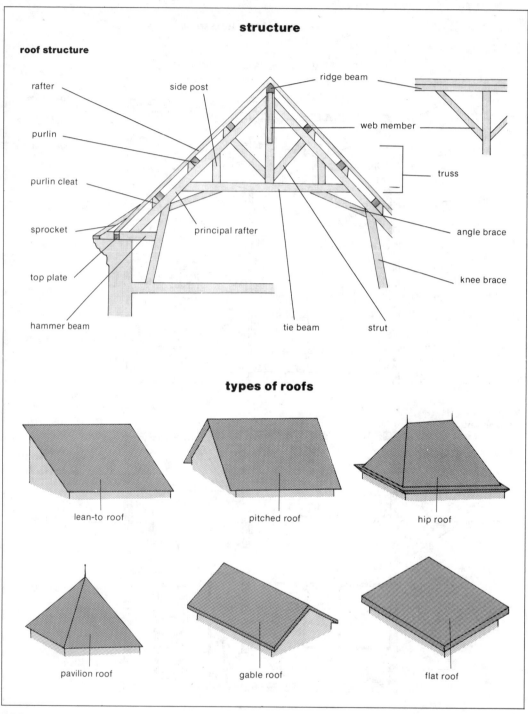

structure

roof structure

rafter

side post

ridge beam

web member

purlin

truss

purlin cleat

sprocket

principal rafter

angle brace

top plate

knee brace

hammer beam

tie beam

strut

types of roofs

lean-to roof

pitched roof

hip roof

pavilion roof

gable roof

flat roof

types of roofs

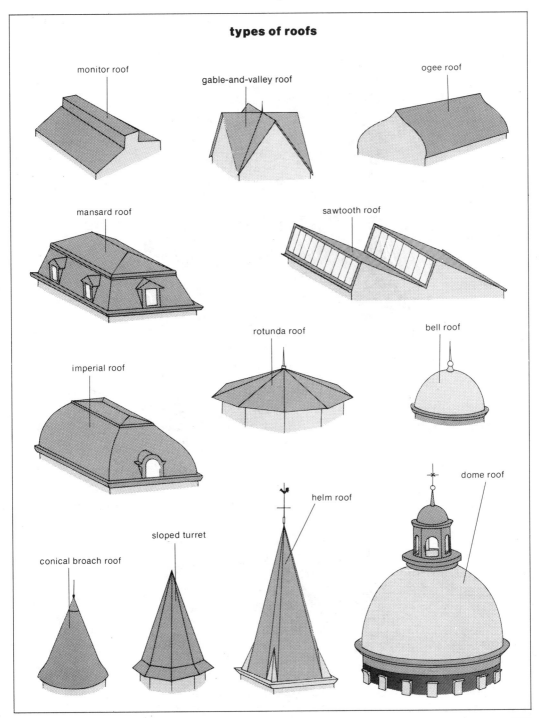

monitor roof

gable-and-valley roof

ogee roof

mansard roof

sawtooth roof

rotunda roof

bell roof

imperial roof

dome roof

helm roof

sloped turret

conical broach roof

HOUSE

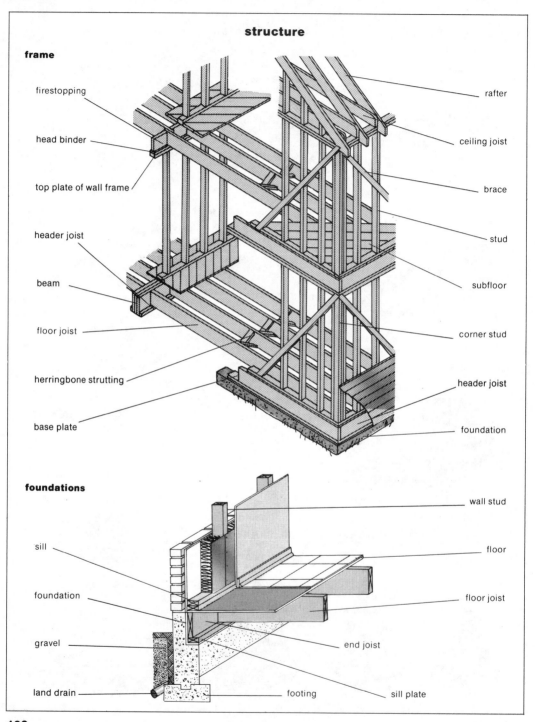

structure

frame

firestopping

head binder

top plate of wall frame

header joist

beam

floor joist

herringbone strutting

base plate

rafter

ceiling joist

brace

stud

subfloor

corner stud

header joist

foundation

foundations

wall stud

sill

floor

foundation

floor joist

gravel

end joist

land drain

footing

sill plate

building materials

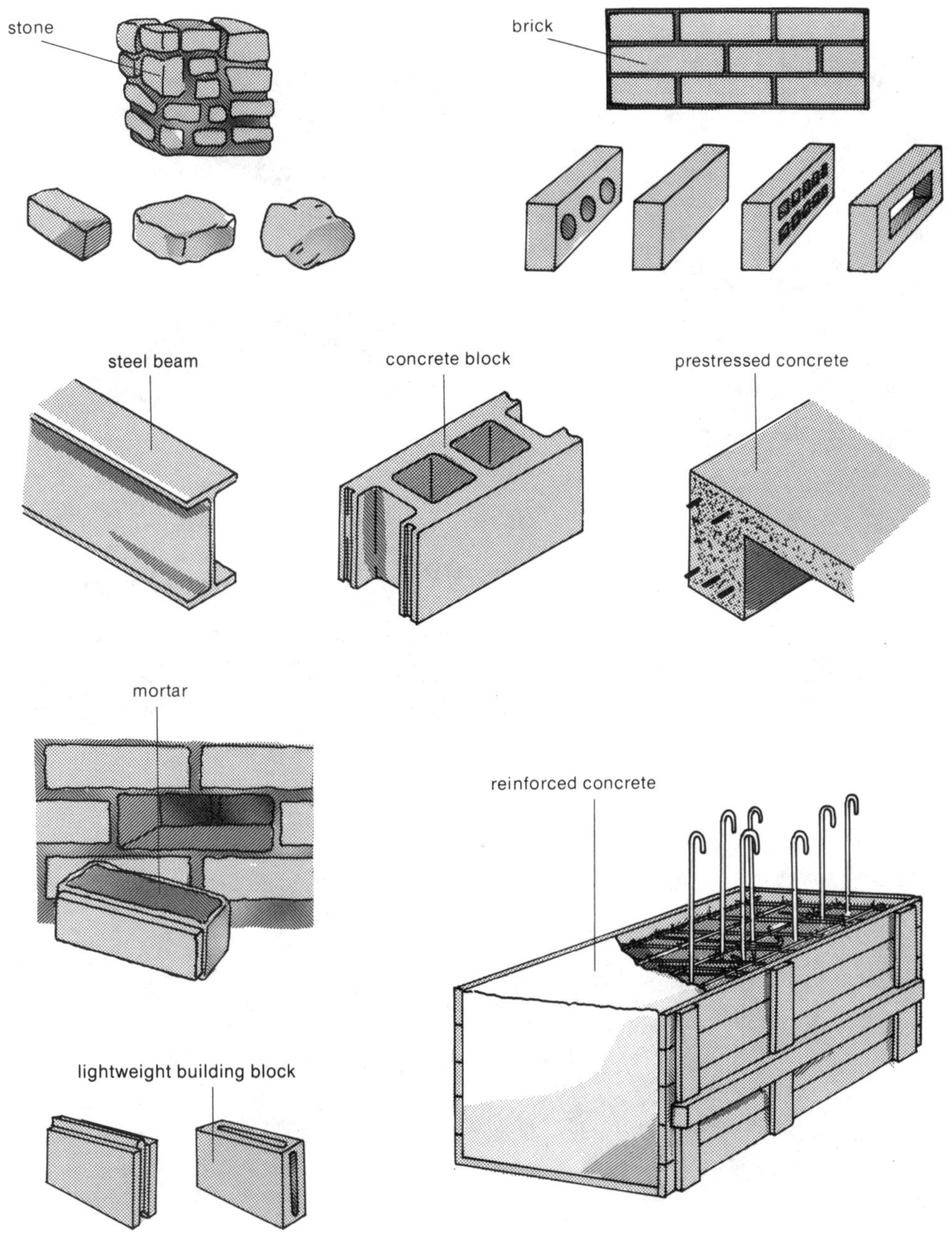

stone

brick

steel beam

concrete block

prestressed concrete

mortar

reinforced concrete

lightweight building block

building materials

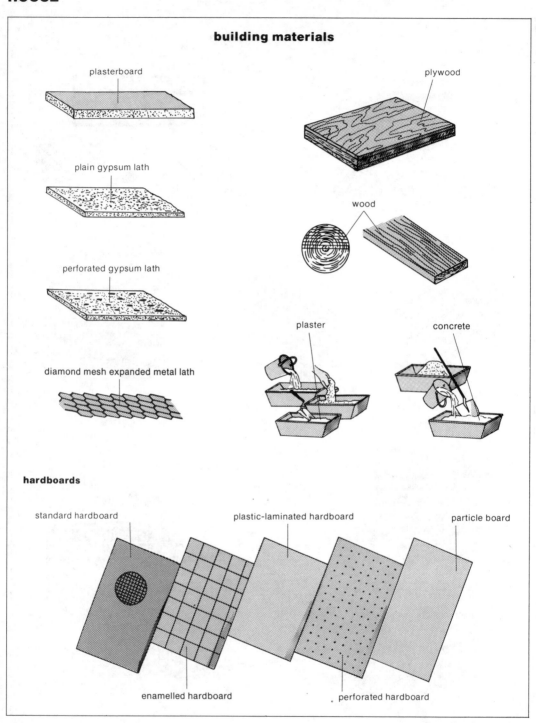

plasterboard

plywood

plain gypsum lath

wood

perforated gypsum lath

plaster

concrete

diamond mesh expanded metal lath

hardboards

standard hardboard

plastic-laminated hardboard

particle board

enamelled hardboard

perforated hardboard

building materials

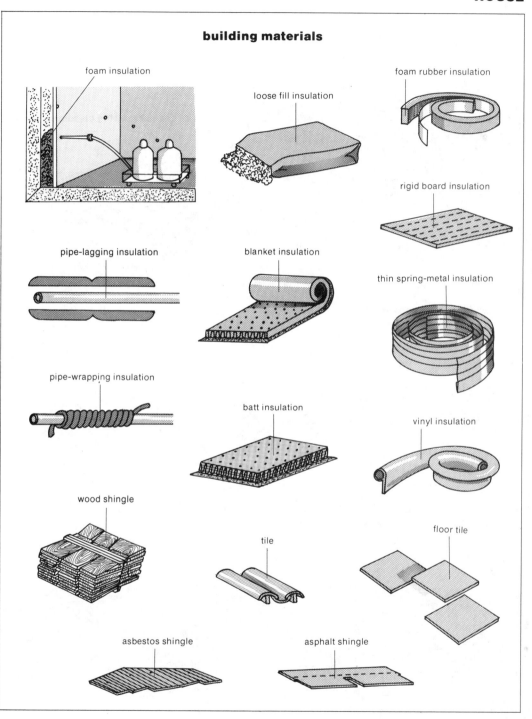

foam insulation

loose fill insulation

foam rubber insulation

rigid board insulation

pipe-lagging insulation

blanket insulation

thin spring-metal insulation

pipe-wrapping insulation

batt insulation

vinyl insulation

wood shingle

tile

floor tile

asbestos shingle

asphalt shingle

wood flooring

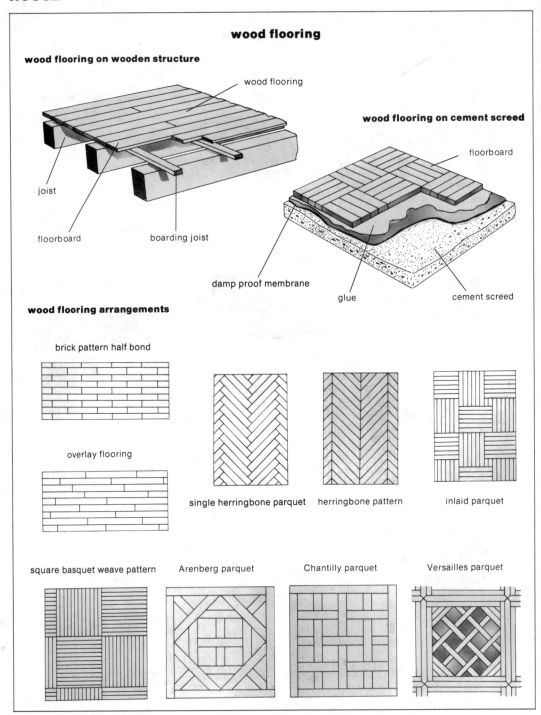

wood flooring on wooden structure

wood flooring

joist

floorboard

boarding joist

wood flooring on cement screed

floorboard

damp proof membrane

glue

cement screed

wood flooring arrangements

brick pattern half bond

overlay flooring

single herringbone parquet

herringbone pattern

inlaid parquet

square basquet weave pattern

Arenberg parquet

Chantilly parquet

Versailles parquet

stairs

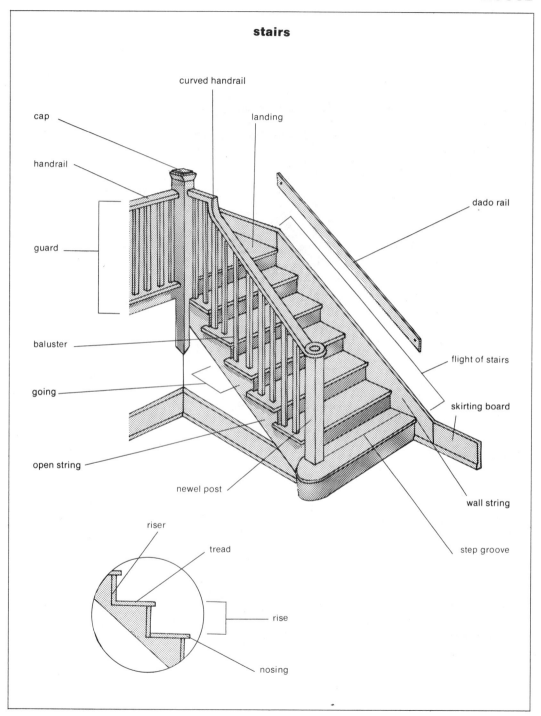

cap

curved handrail

landing

handrail

dado rail

guard

baluster

going

open string

flight of stairs

skirting board

newel post

wall string

step groove

riser

tread

rise

nosing

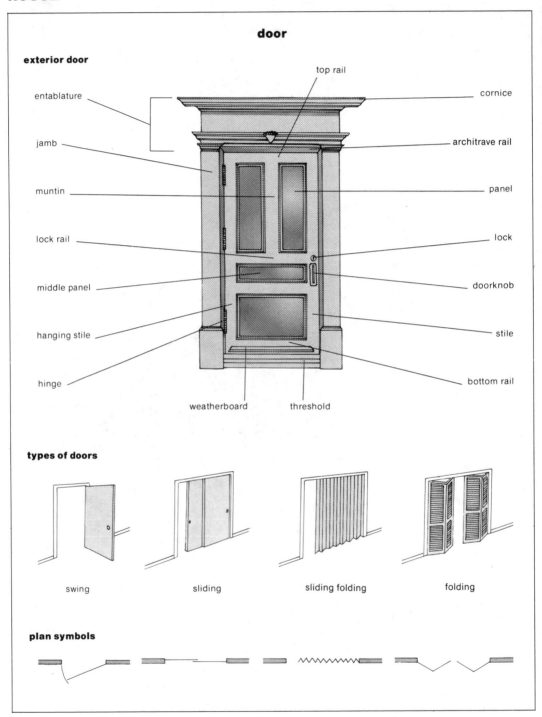

door

exterior door

top rail

entablature

cornice

jamb

architrave rail

muntin

panel

lock rail

lock

middle panel

doorknob

hanging stile

stile

hinge

bottom rail

weatherboard

threshold

types of doors

swing

sliding

sliding folding

folding

plan symbols

window

composite window

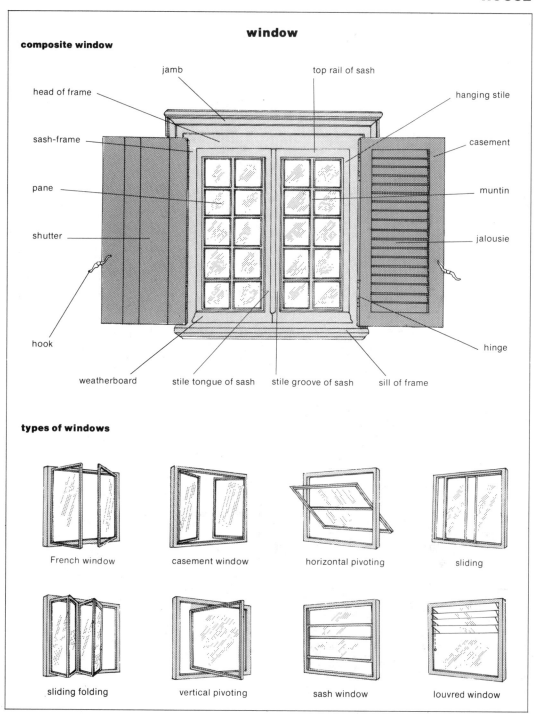

jamb

top rail of sash

head of frame

hanging stile

sash-frame

casement

pane

muntin

shutter

jalousie

hook

hinge

weatherboard   stile tongue of sash   stile groove of sash   sill of frame

types of windows

French window   casement window   horizontal pivoting   sliding

sliding folding   vertical pivoting   sash window   louvred window

heating

fireplace

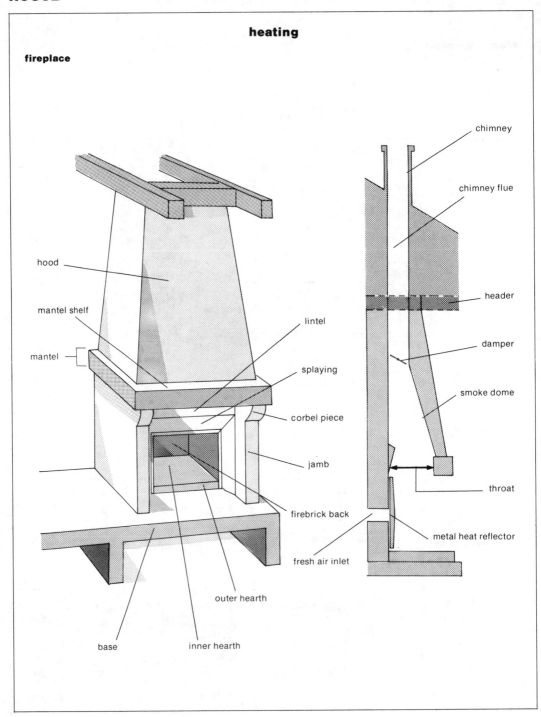

chimney

chimney flue

hood

mantel shelf

mantel

lintel

splaying

corbel piece

jamb

header

damper

smoke dome

firebrick back

throat

fresh air inlet

metal heat reflector

outer hearth

base

inner hearth

heating

wood burning stove

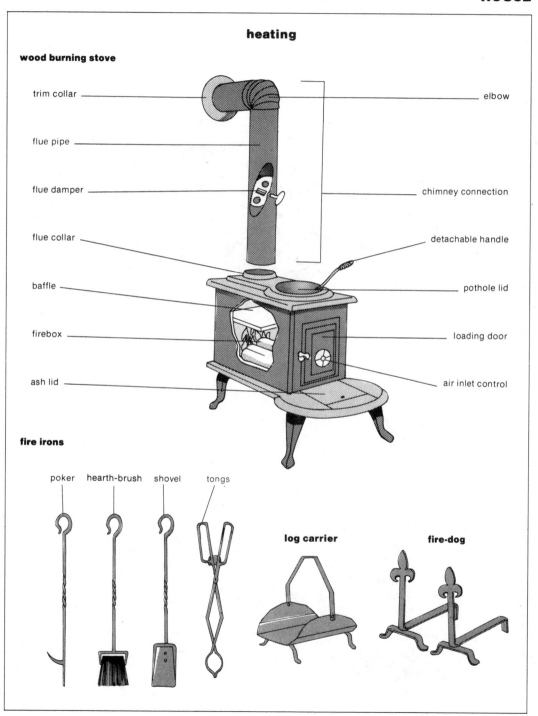

trim collar

elbow

flue pipe

flue damper

chimney connection

flue collar

detachable handle

baffle

pothole lid

firebox

loading door

ash lid

air inlet control

fire irons

poker hearth-brush shovel tongs

log carrier

fire-dog

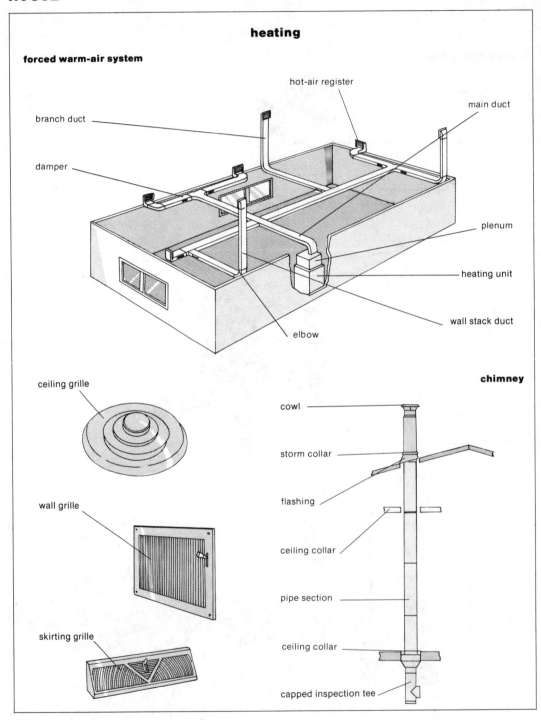

heating

forced warm-air system

hot-air register

branch duct

main duct

damper

plenum

heating unit

wall stack duct

elbow

ceiling grille

chimney

cowl

storm collar

flashing

wall grille

ceiling collar

pipe section

ceiling collar

skirting grille

capped inspection tee

heating

single pipe heating system

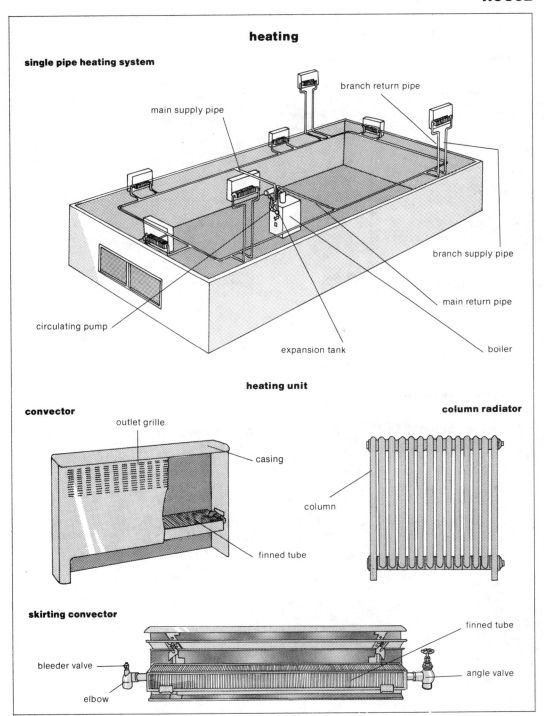

branch return pipe

main supply pipe

branch supply pipe

main return pipe

circulating pump

expansion tank

boiler

heating unit

convector

column radiator

outlet grille

casing

column

finned tube

skirting convector

finned tube

bleeder valve

angle valve

elbow

heating

boiler

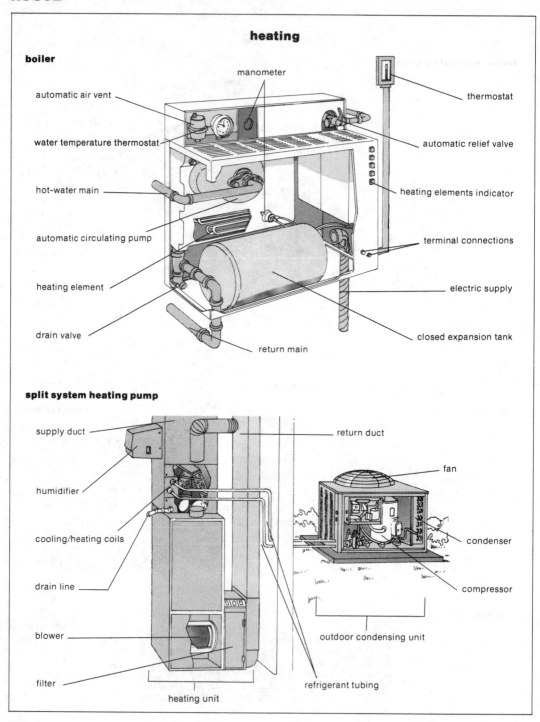

manometer

automatic air vent

thermostat

water temperature thermostat

automatic relief valve

hot-water main

heating elements indicator

automatic circulating pump

terminal connections

heating element

electric supply

drain valve

closed expansion tank

return main

split system heating pump

supply duct

return duct

fan

humidifier

cooling/heating coils

condenser

drain line

compressor

blower

outdoor condensing unit

filter

refrigerant tubing

heating unit

heating

electric heating unit

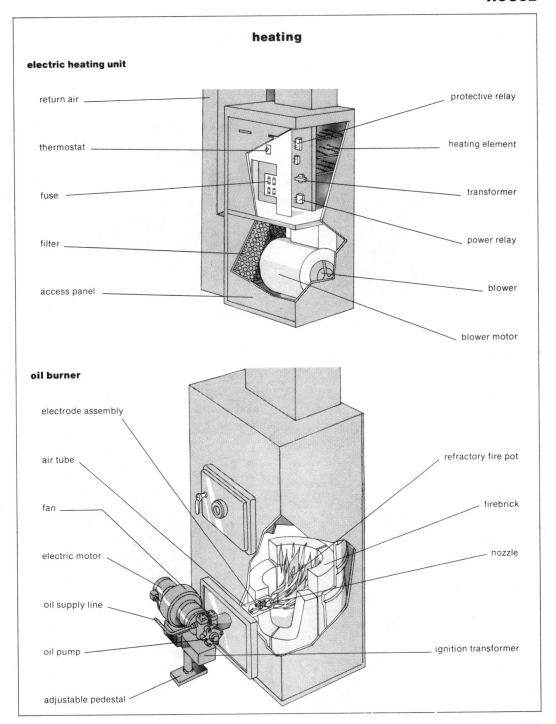

return air

thermostat

fuse

filter

access panel

protective relay

heating element

transformer

power relay

blower

blower motor

oil burner

electrode assembly

air tube

fan

electric motor

oil supply line

oil pump

adjustable pedestal

refractory fire pot

firebrick

nozzle

ignition transformer

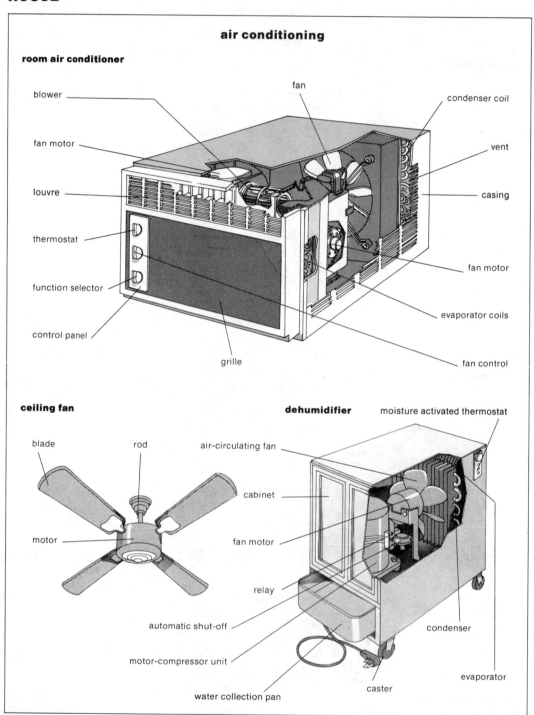

air conditioning

room air conditioner

- fan
- blower
- condenser coil
- fan motor
- vent
- louvre
- casing
- thermostat
- fan motor
- function selector
- evaporator coils
- control panel
- grille
- fan control

ceiling fan

- blade
- rod
- motor

dehumidifier

- moisture activated thermostat
- air-circulating fan
- cabinet
- fan motor
- relay
- condenser
- automatic shut-off
- motor-compressor unit
- evaporator
- water collection pan
- caster

HOUSE FURNITURE

table

gate-leg table

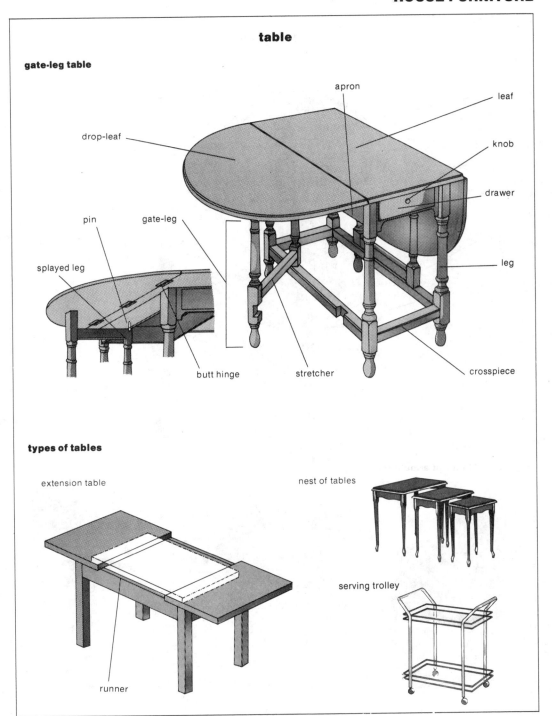

apron

leaf

knob

drawer

drop-leaf

leg

pin

gate-leg

splayed leg

butt hinge

stretcher

crosspiece

types of tables

extension table

nest of tables

serving trolley

runner

HOUSE FURNITURE

armchair

parts

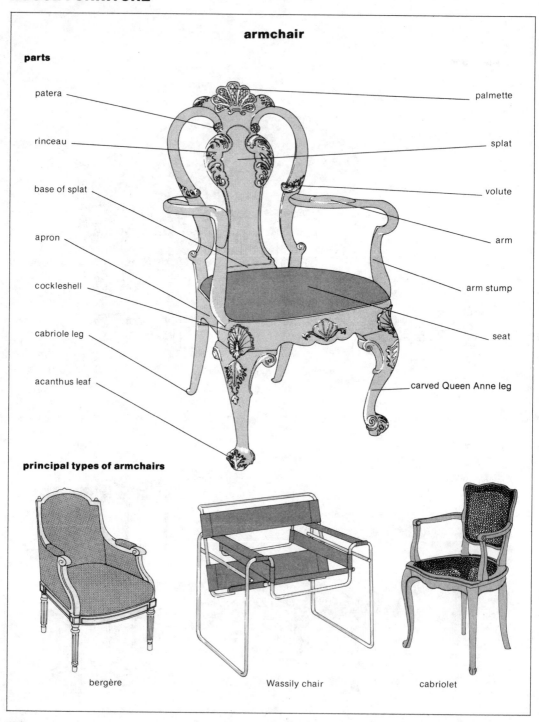

patera

rinceau

base of splat

apron

cockleshell

cabriole leg

acanthus leaf

palmette

splat

volute

arm

arm stump

seat

carved Queen Anne leg

principal types of armchairs

bergère

Wassily chair

cabriolet

chairs and couches

principal types

récamier

three-seater settee

two-seater settee

director's chair

club chair

chesterfield

rocking chair

méridienne

seats

banquette

pouffe

bean bag chair

bench

step chair

stool

footstool

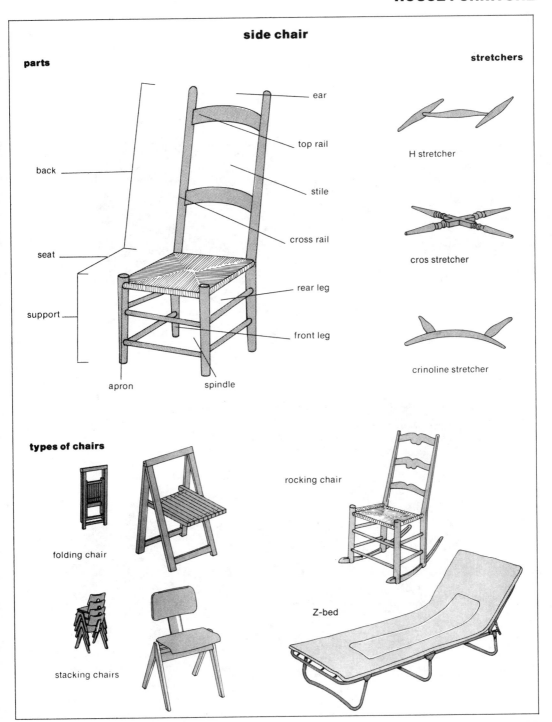

side chair

parts

stretchers

ear

top rail

back

stile

cross rail

seat

rear leg

support

front leg

apron

spindle

H stretcher

cros stretcher

crinoline stretcher

types of chairs

folding chair

rocking chair

stacking chairs

Z-bed

HOUSE FURNITURE

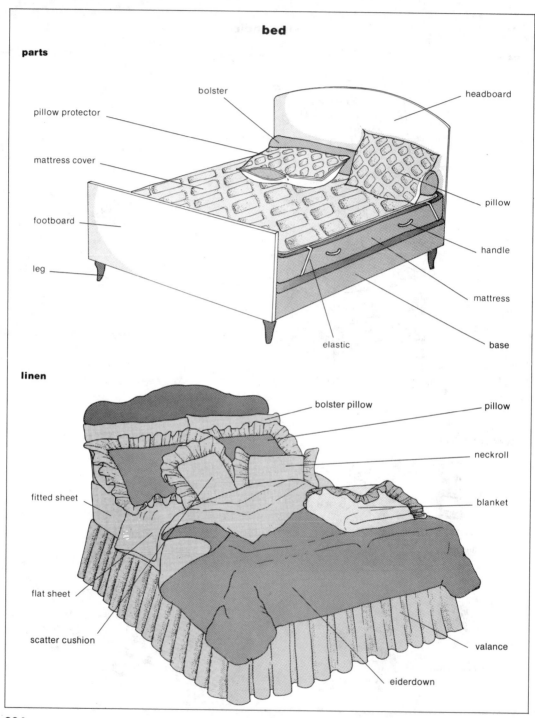

bed

parts

bolster

pillow protector

mattress cover

footboard

leg

headboard

pillow

handle

mattress

base

elastic

linen

bolster pillow

pillow

neckroll

blanket

fitted sheet

flat sheet

scatter cushion

valance

eiderdown

204

storage furniture

armoire

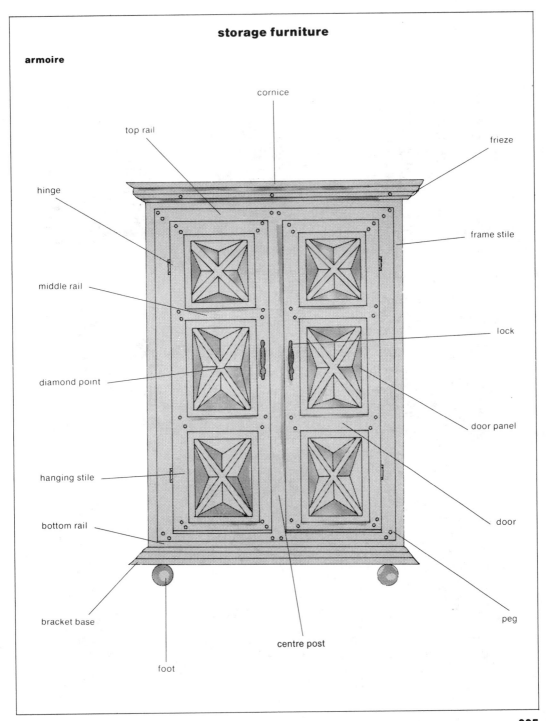

cornice

top rail

frieze

hinge

frame stile

middle rail

lock

diamond point

door panel

hanging stile

bottom rail

door

bracket base

peg

centre post

foot

HOUSE FURNITURE

storage furniture

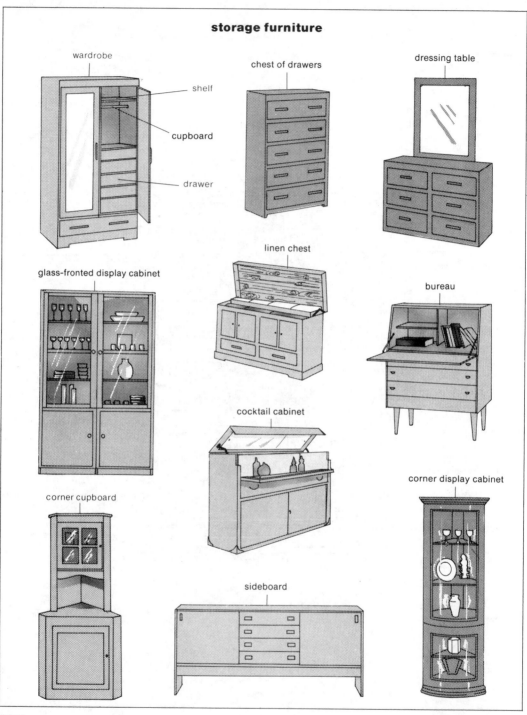

wardrobe

shelf

cupboard

drawer

chest of drawers

dressing table

linen chest

glass-fronted display cabinet

bureau

cocktail cabinet

corner display cabinet

corner cupboard

sideboard

window accessories

curtain

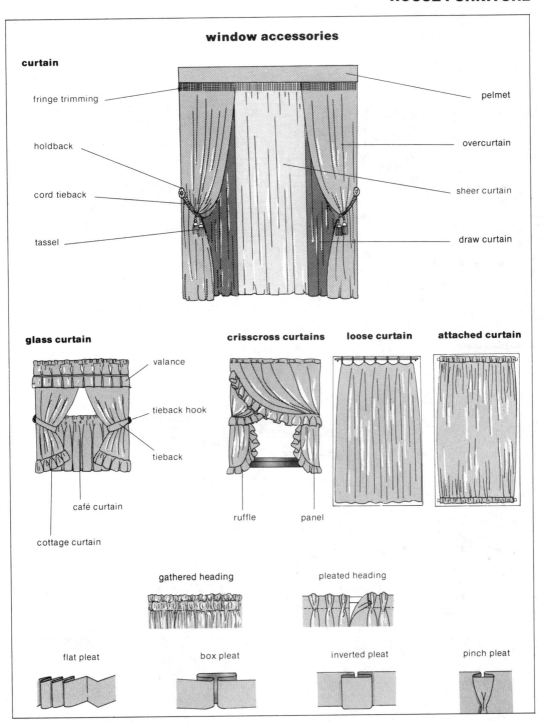

fringe trimming

pelmet

holdback

overcurtain

cord tieback

sheer curtain

tassel

draw curtain

glass curtain

valance

tieback hook

tieback

café curtain

cottage curtain

crisscross curtains

ruffle

panel

loose curtain

attached curtain

gathered heading

pleated heading

flat pleat

box pleat

inverted pleat

pinch pleat

HOUSE FURNITURE

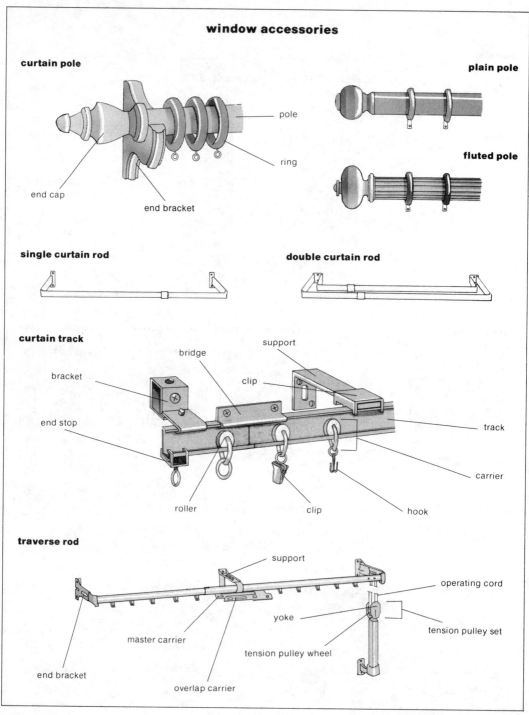

window accessories

curtain pole

plain pole

pole

ring

end cap

end bracket

fluted pole

single curtain rod

double curtain rod

curtain track

bridge

support

bracket

clip

end stop

track

carrier

roller

clip

hook

traverse rod

support

operating cord

yoke

tension pulley set

master carrier

tension pulley wheel

end bracket

overlap carrier

208

window accessories

roller blind

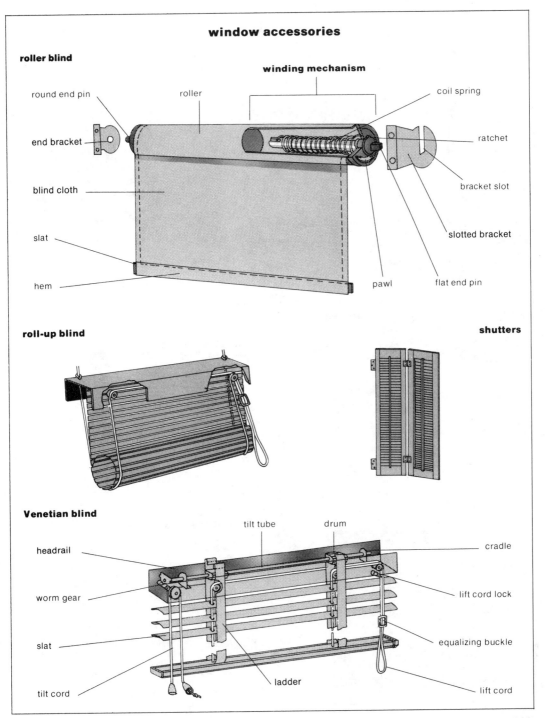

winding mechanism

round end pin

roller

coil spring

end bracket

ratchet

blind cloth

bracket slot

slat

slotted bracket

hem

pawl

flat end pin

roll-up blind

shutters

Venetian blind

tilt tube

drum

cradle

headrail

worm gear

lift cord lock

slat

equalizing buckle

tilt cord

ladder

lift cord

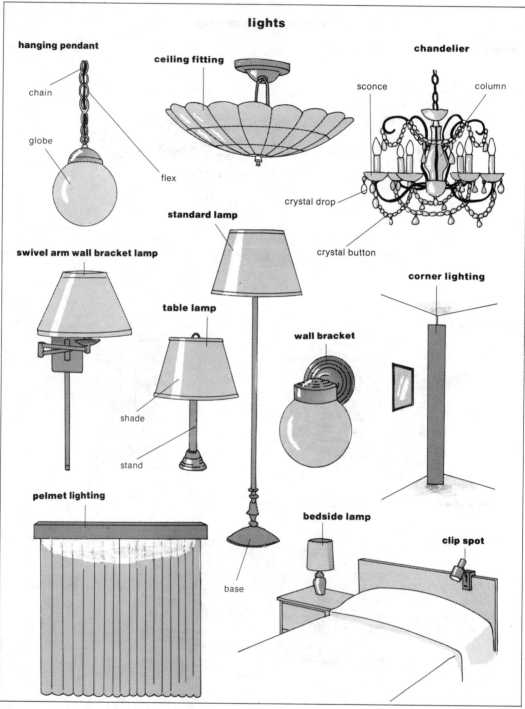

lights

hanging pendant

chain

globe

flex

ceiling fitting

chandelier

sconce

column

crystal drop

crystal button

standard lamp

swivel arm wall bracket lamp

table lamp

wall bracket

corner lighting

shade

stand

pelmet lighting

bedside lamp

base

clip spot

lights

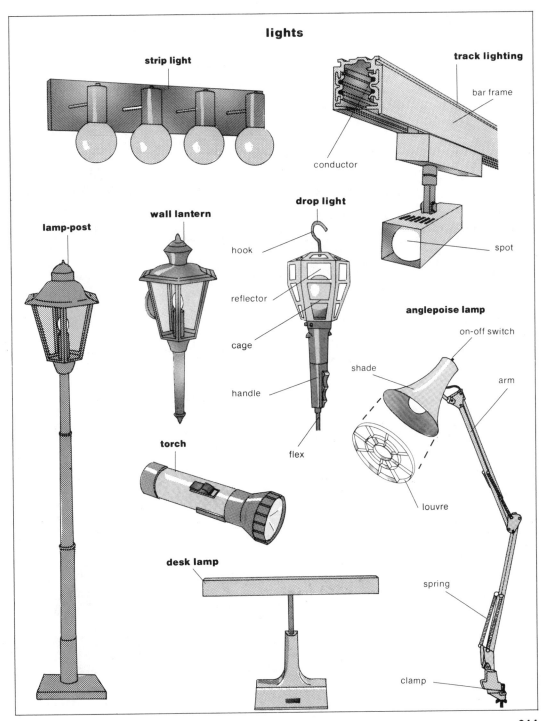

strip light

track lighting

bar frame

conductor

lamp-post

wall lantern

drop light

hook

reflector

cage

handle

flex

spot

anglepoise lamp

on-off switch

shade

arm

louvre

torch

desk lamp

spring

clamp

glassware

champagne flute	champagne glass	bordeaux	burgundy
white wine	Alsace glass	water goblet	cocktail
port	brandy	liqueur	
tumbler	tall tumbler	beer mug	decanter

dinnerware

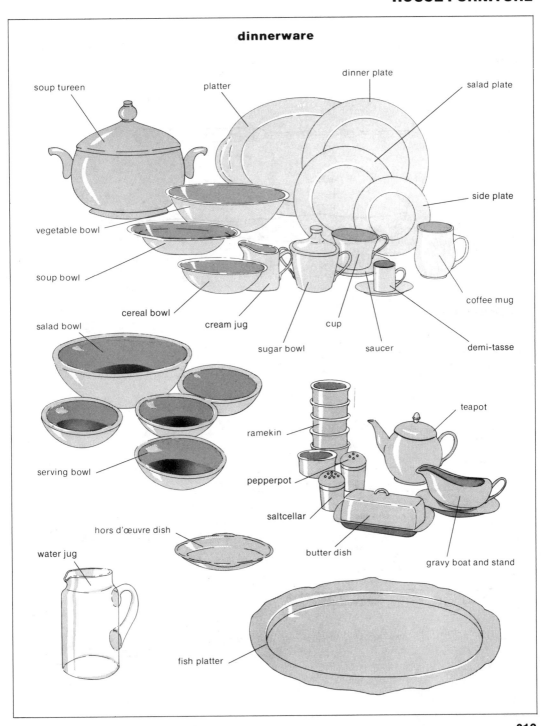

soup tureen

platter

dinner plate

salad plate

side plate

vegetable bowl

soup bowl

coffee mug

cereal bowl

cream jug

cup

salad bowl

sugar bowl

saucer

demi-tasse

ramekin

teapot

serving bowl

pepperpot

saltcellar

hors d'œuvre dish

water jug

butter dish

gravy boat and stand

fish platter

silverware

knife

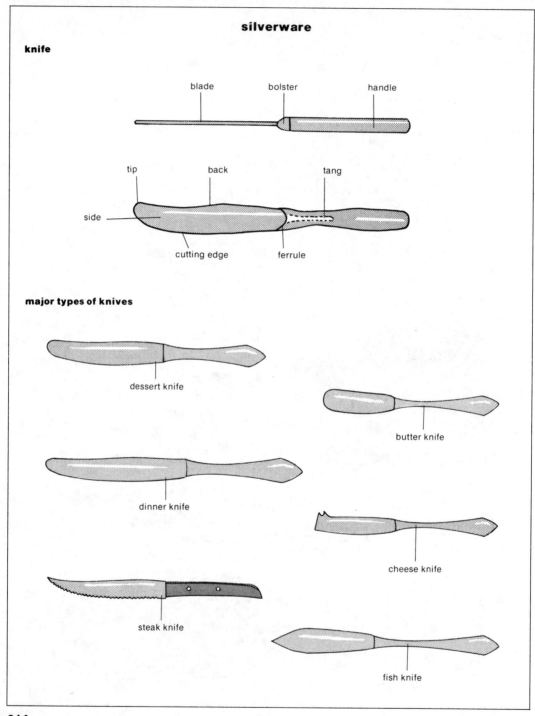

blade   bolster   handle

tip   back   tang

side

cutting edge   ferrule

major types of knives

dessert knife

butter knife

dinner knife

cheese knife

steak knife

fish knife

silverware

fork

major types of forks

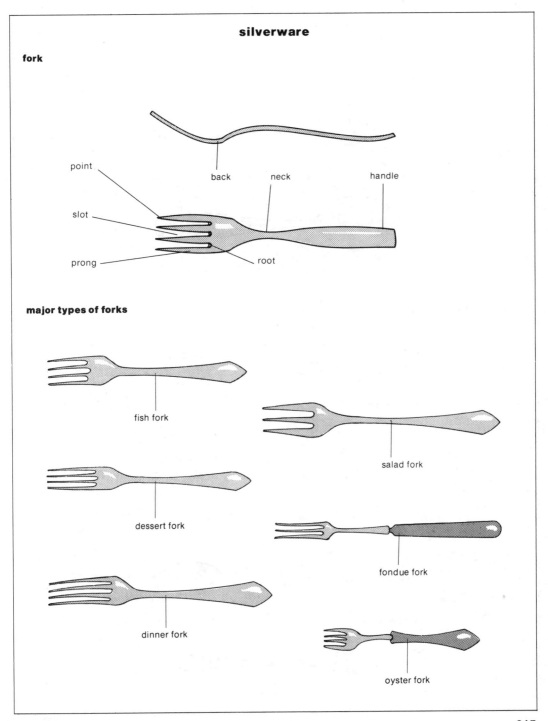

fish fork

salad fork

dessert fork

fondue fork

dinner fork

oyster fork

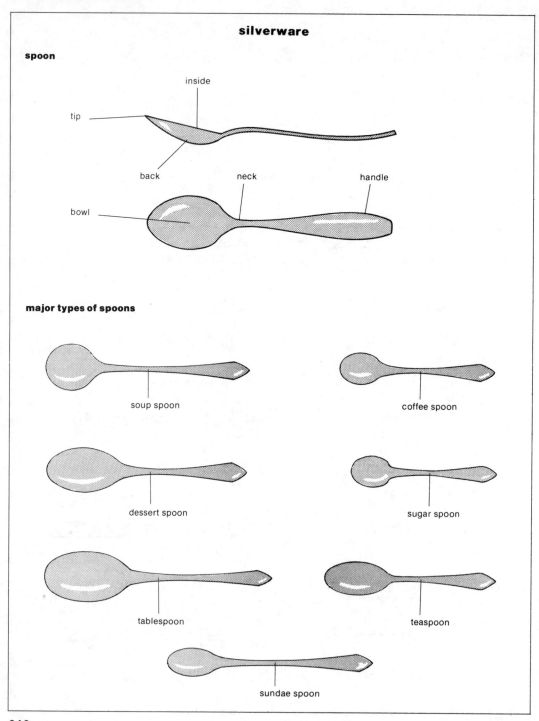

silverware

spoon

inside

tip

back   neck   handle

bowl

major types of spoons

soup spoon

coffee spoon

dessert spoon

sugar spoon

tablespoon

teaspoon

sundae spoon

kitchen utensils

kitchen knife

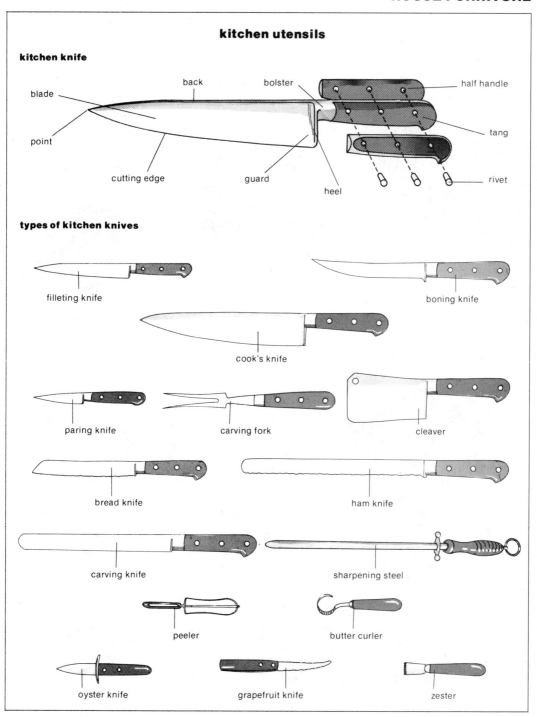

back · bolster · half handle · blade · tang · point · cutting edge · guard · heel · rivet

types of kitchen knives

filleting knife

boning knife

cook's knife

paring knife

carving fork

cleaver

bread knife

ham knife

carving knife

sharpening steel

peeler

butter curler

oyster knife

grapefruit knife

zester

kitchen utensils

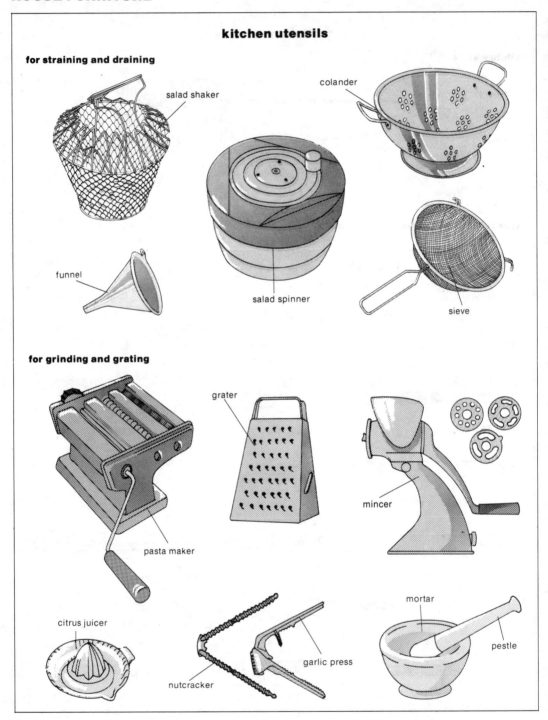

for straining and draining

salad shaker

colander

funnel

salad spinner

sieve

for grinding and grating

grater

mincer

pasta maker

citrus juicer

nutcracker

garlic press

mortar

pestle

kitchen utensils

set of utensils

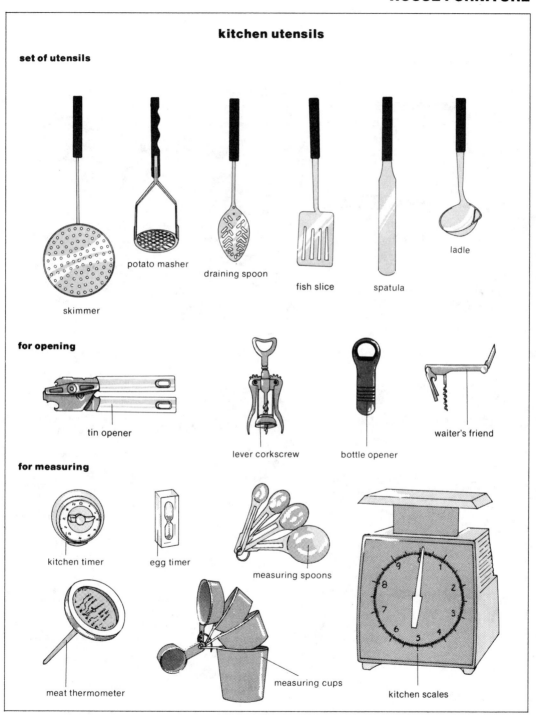

skimmer

potato masher

draining spoon

fish slice

spatula

ladle

for opening

tin opener

lever corkscrew

bottle opener

waiter's friend

for measuring

kitchen timer

egg timer

measuring spoons

meat thermometer

measuring cups

kitchen scales

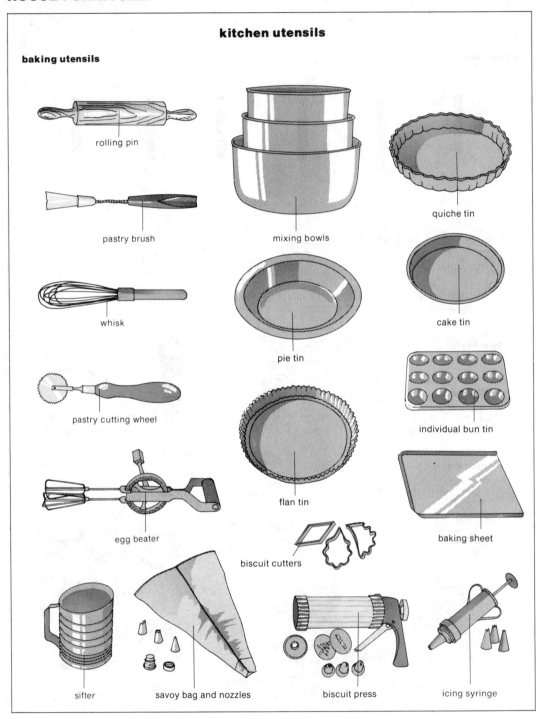

kitchen utensils

baking utensils

rolling pin

pastry brush

whisk

pastry cutting wheel

egg beater

sifter

savoy bag and nozzles

mixing bowls

pie tin

flan tin

biscuit cutters

biscuit press

quiche tin

cake tin

individual bun tin

baking sheet

icing syringe

kitchen utensils

miscellaneous utensils

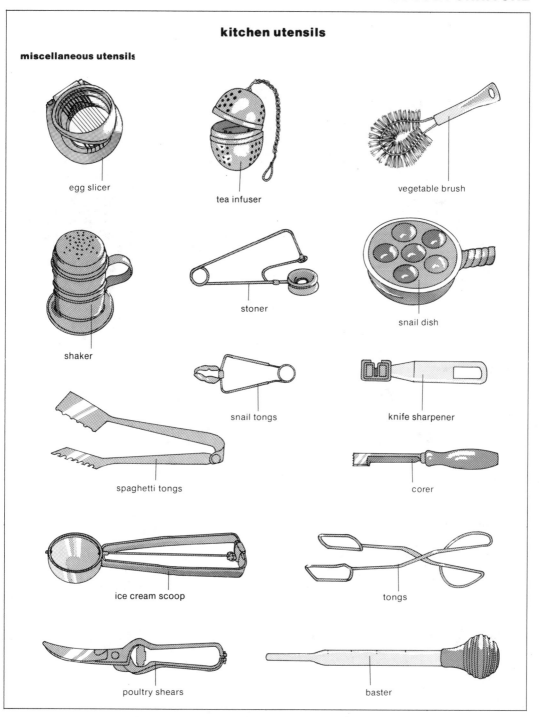

egg slicer

tea infuser

vegetable brush

shaker

stoner

snail dish

snail tongs

knife sharpener

spaghetti tongs

corer

ice cream scoop

tongs

poultry shears

baster

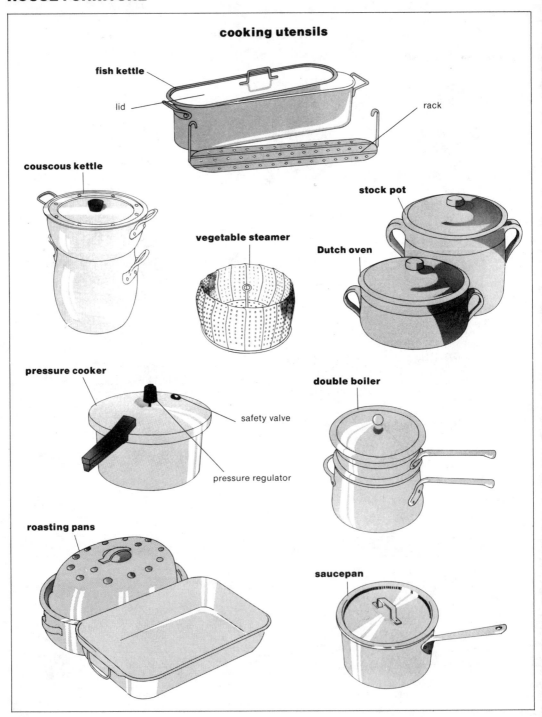

cooking utensils

fish kettle

lid

rack

couscous kettle

stock pot

vegetable steamer

Dutch oven

pressure cooker

double boiler

safety valve

pressure regulator

roasting pans

saucepan

cooking utensils

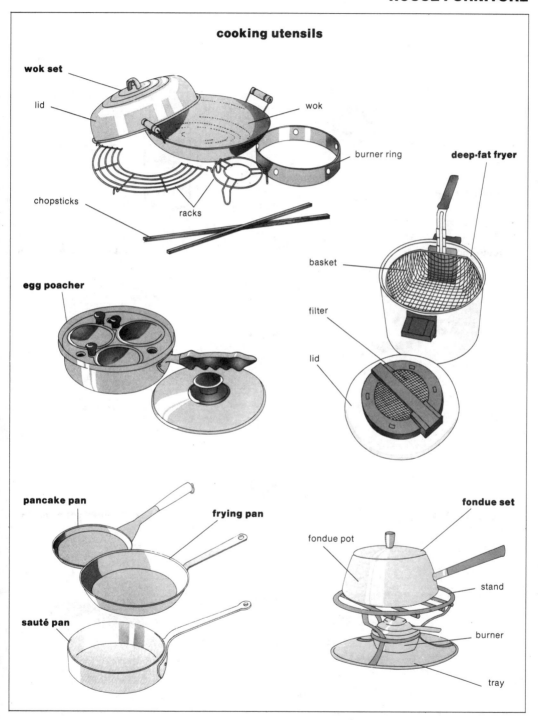

wok set

lid

wok

burner ring

deep-fat fryer

chopsticks

racks

basket

filter

egg poacher

lid

pancake pan

frying pan

fondue set

fondue pot

stand

sauté pan

burner

tray

HOUSE FURNITURE

coffee makers

coffee mill

lid

blade

motor unit

percolator

filter basket

spout

stem

vacuum coffee maker

upper bowl

lower bowl

plunger

espresso coffee maker

filter coffee maker

lid

filter

carafe

reservoir

warming plate

Neapolitan coffee maker

domestic appliances

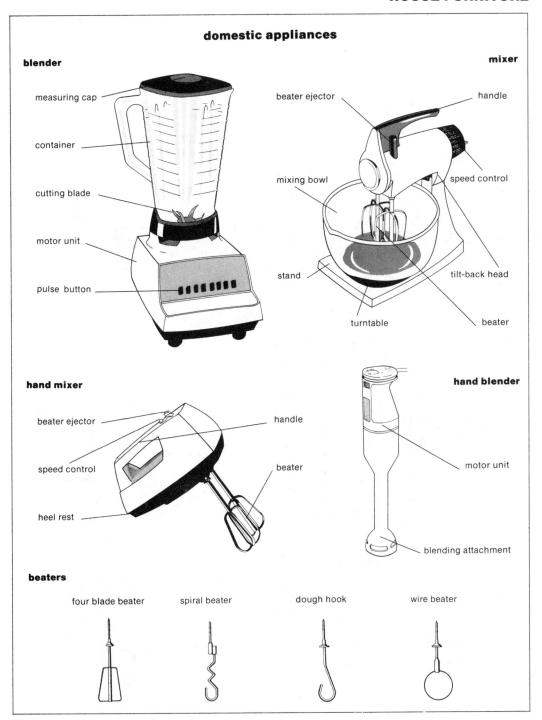

blender

measuring cap

container

cutting blade

motor unit

pulse button

mixer

beater ejector

handle

mixing bowl

speed control

stand

tilt-back head

turntable

beater

hand mixer

beater ejector

handle

speed control

beater

heel rest

hand blender

motor unit

blending attachment

beaters

four blade beater   spiral beater   dough hook   wire beater

HOUSE FURNITURE

domestic appliances

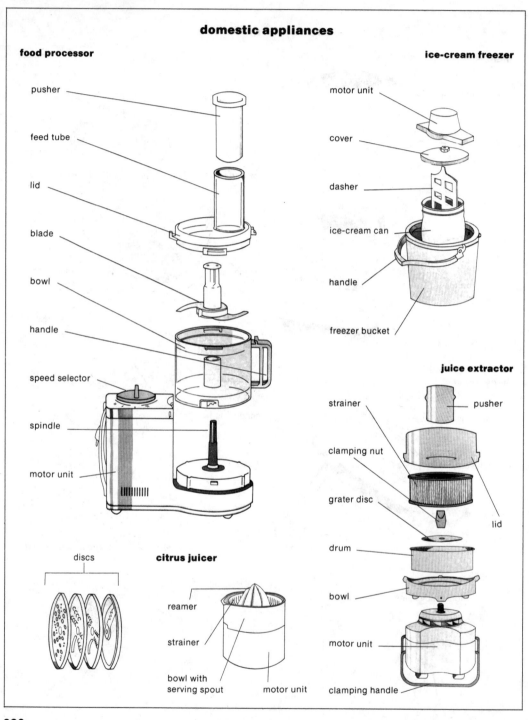

food processor

- pusher
- feed tube
- lid
- blade
- bowl
- handle
- speed selector
- spindle
- motor unit

ice-cream freezer

- motor unit
- cover
- dasher
- ice-cream can
- handle
- freezer bucket

juice extractor

- strainer
- pusher
- clamping nut
- grater disc
- lid
- drum
- bowl
- motor unit
- clamping handle

discs

citrus juicer

- reamer
- strainer
- bowl with serving spout
- motor unit

226

domestic appliances

microwave oven

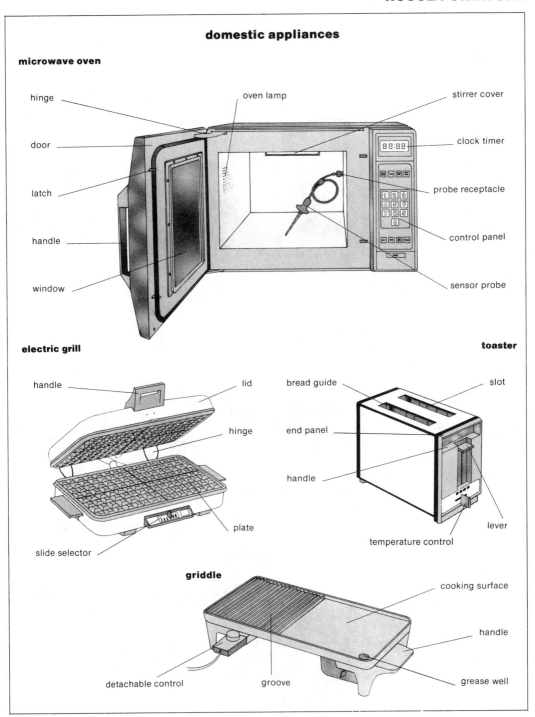

hinge

oven lamp

stirrer cover

door

clock timer

latch

probe receptacle

handle

control panel

window

sensor probe

electric grill

toaster

handle

lid

bread guide

slot

hinge

end panel

handle

plate

handle

slide selector

temperature control

lever

griddle

cooking surface

handle

detachable control

groove

grease well

227

domestic appliances

electric cooker

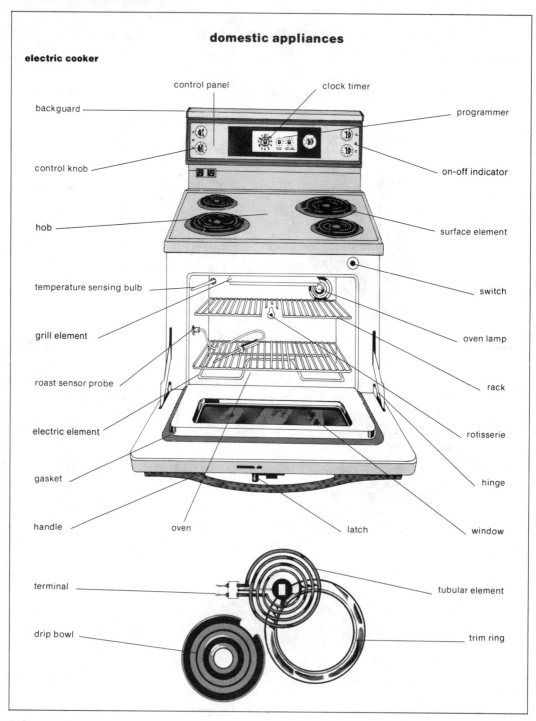

control panel

clock timer

backguard

programmer

control knob

on-off indicator

hob

surface element

temperature sensing bulb

switch

grill element

oven lamp

roast sensor probe

rack

electric element

rotisserie

gasket

hinge

handle

oven

latch

window

terminal

tubular element

drip bowl

trim ring

domestic appliances

fridge-freezer

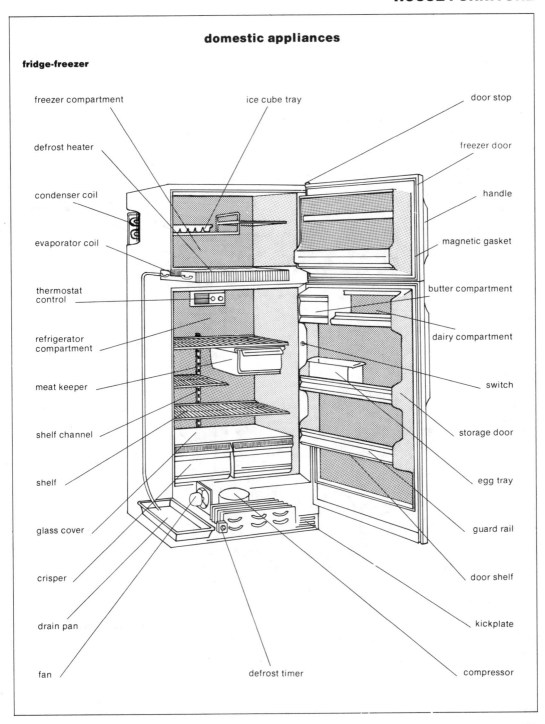

freezer compartment

ice cube tray

door stop

defrost heater

freezer door

condenser coil

handle

evaporator coil

magnetic gasket

thermostat control

butter compartment

refrigerator compartment

dairy compartment

meat keeper

switch

shelf channel

storage door

shelf

egg tray

glass cover

guard rail

crisper

door shelf

drain pan

kickplate

fan

defrost timer

compressor

domestic appliances

washing machine

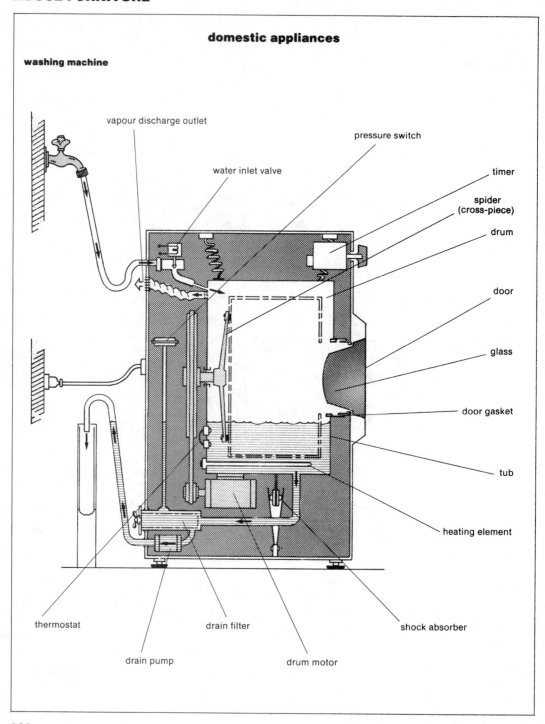

vapour discharge outlet

pressure switch

water inlet valve

timer

spider
(cross-piece)

drum

door

glass

door gasket

tub

heating element

thermostat

drain filter

shock absorber

drain pump

drum motor

domestic appliances

tumble dryer

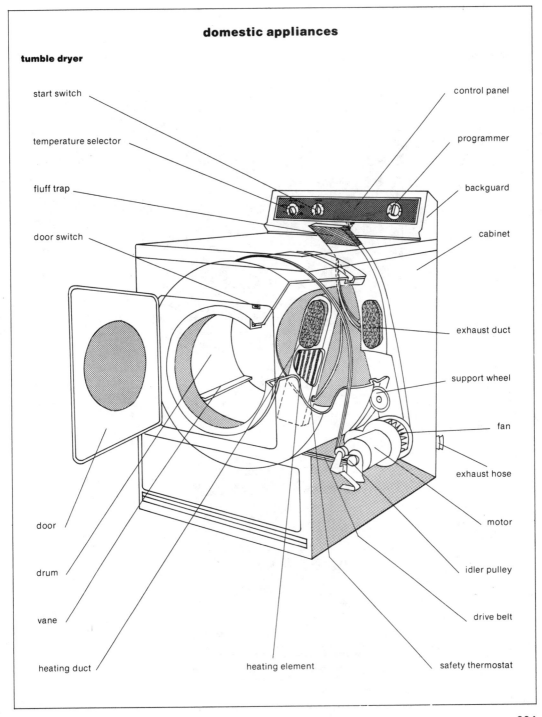

start switch

control panel

temperature selector

programmer

fluff trap

backguard

door switch

cabinet

exhaust duct

support wheel

fan

exhaust hose

door

motor

drum

idler pulley

vane

drive belt

heating duct

heating element

safety thermostat

HOUSE FURNITURE

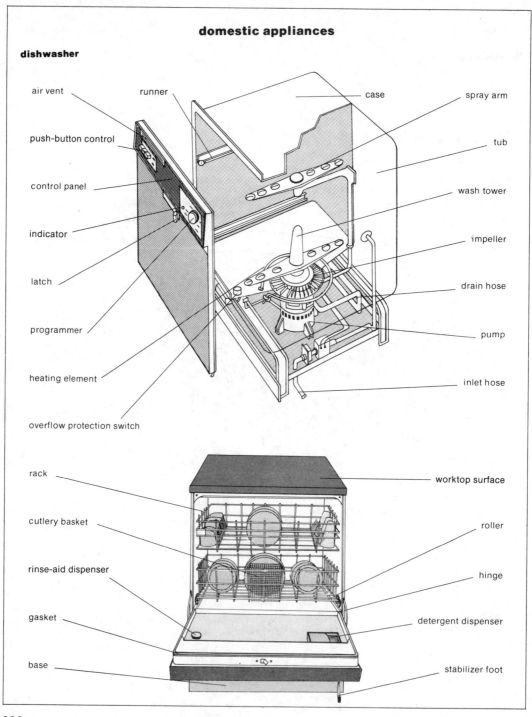

domestic appliances

dishwasher

air vent

runner

case

spray arm

push-button control

tub

control panel

wash tower

indicator

impeller

latch

drain hose

programmer

pump

heating element

inlet hose

overflow protection switch

rack

worktop surface

cutlery basket

roller

rinse-aid dispenser

hinge

gasket

detergent dispenser

base

stabilizer foot

domestic appliances

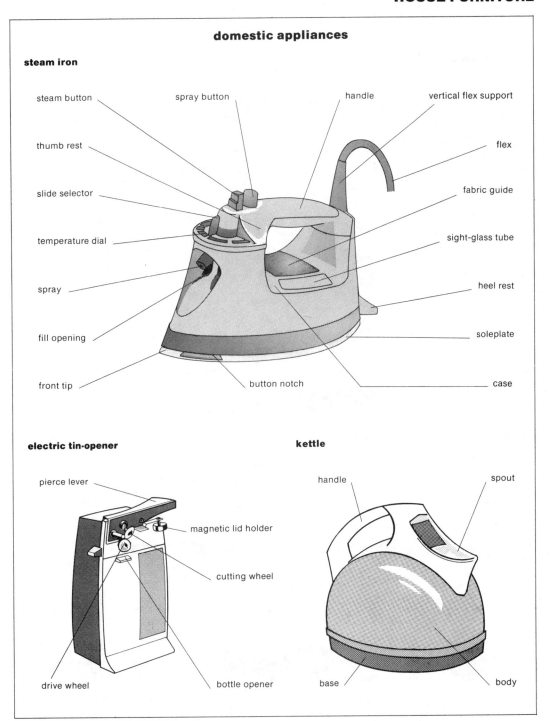

steam iron

steam button

spray button

handle

vertical flex support

thumb rest

flex

slide selector

fabric guide

temperature dial

sight-glass tube

spray

heel rest

fill opening

soleplate

front tip

button notch

case

electric tin-opener

kettle

pierce lever

handle

spout

magnetic lid holder

cutting wheel

drive wheel

bottle opener

base

body

HOUSE FURNITURE

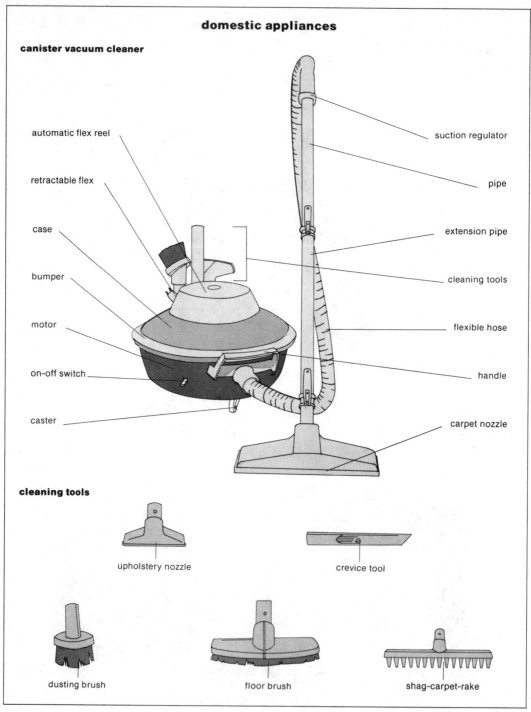

domestic appliances

canister vacuum cleaner

automatic flex reel

retractable flex

case

bumper

motor

on-off switch

caster

suction regulator

pipe

extension pipe

cleaning tools

flexible hose

handle

carpet nozzle

cleaning tools

upholstery nozzle

crevice tool

dusting brush

floor brush

shag-carpet-rake

GARDENING

garden

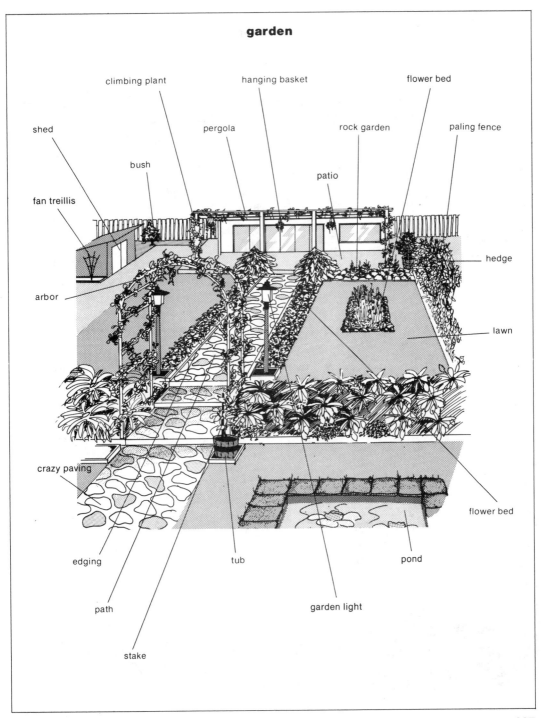

climbing plant

hanging basket

flower bed

shed

pergola

rock garden

paling fence

bush

patio

fan treillis

hedge

arbor

lawn

crazy paving

flower bed

edging

tub

pond

path

garden light

stake

GARDENING

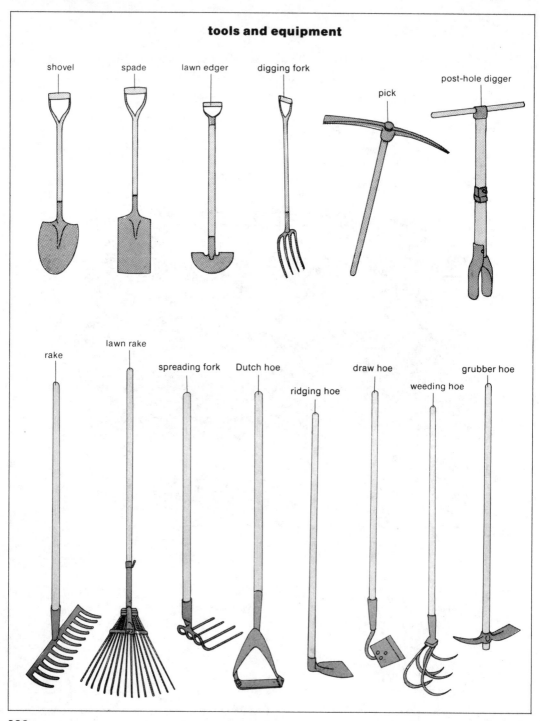

tools and equipment

shovel · spade · lawn edger · digging fork · pick · post-hole digger

rake · lawn rake · spreading fork · Dutch hoe · ridging hoe · draw hoe · weeding hoe · grubber hoe

tools and equipment

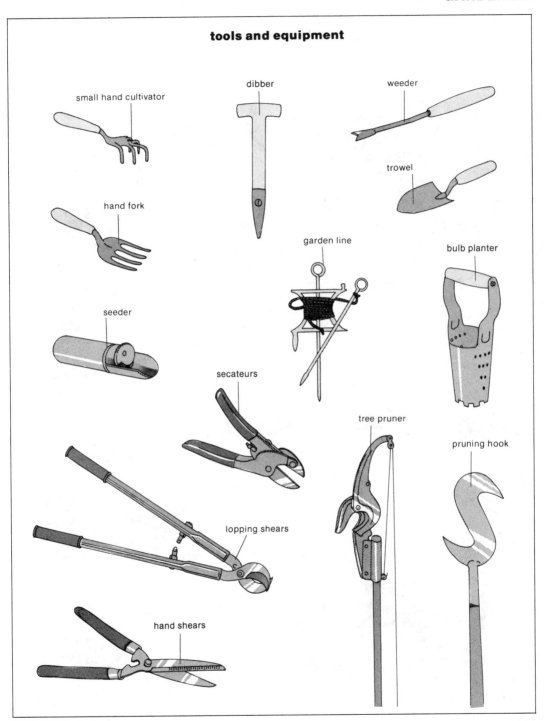

small hand cultivator

dibber

weeder

hand fork

trowel

garden line

seeder

bulb planter

secateurs

tree pruner

pruning hook

lopping shears

hand shears

tools and equipment

watering can

mist sprayer

tank sprayer

rose

revolving sprinkler

pistol spray

oscillating sprinkler

garden hose

hose reel

sprinkler hose

hose nozzle

tools and equipment

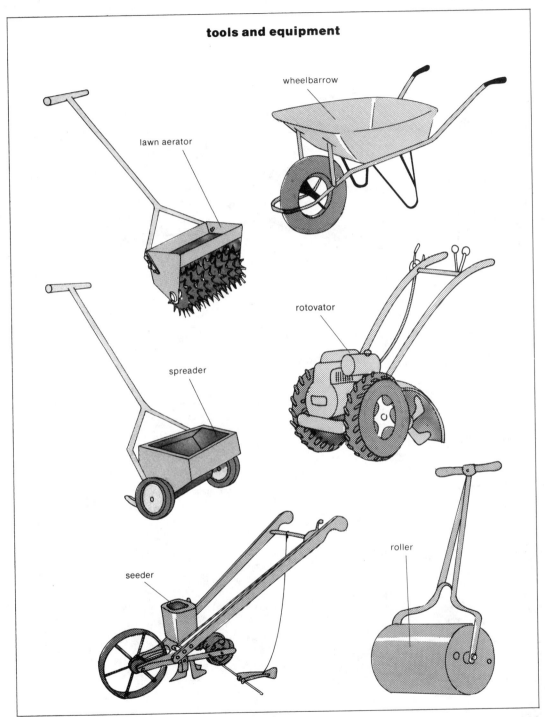

lawn aerator

wheelbarrow

rotovator

spreader

seeder

roller

GARDENING

tools and equipment

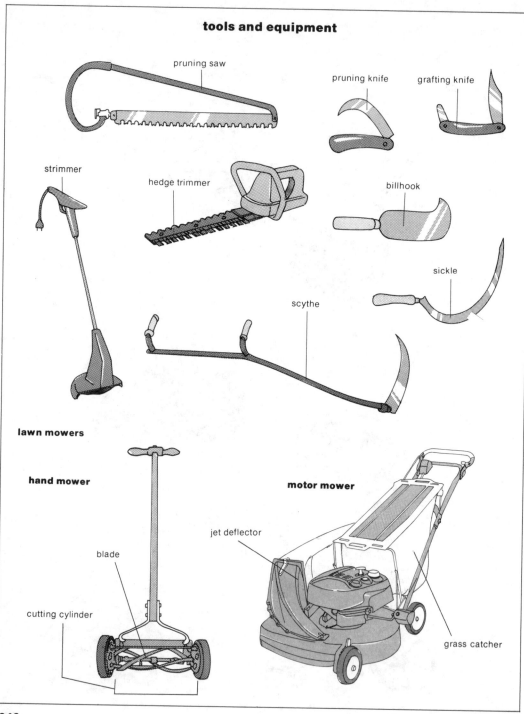

pruning saw

pruning knife

grafting knife

strimmer

hedge trimmer

billhook

sickle

scythe

lawn mowers

hand mower

motor mower

jet deflector

blade

cutting cylinder

grass catcher

chainsaw

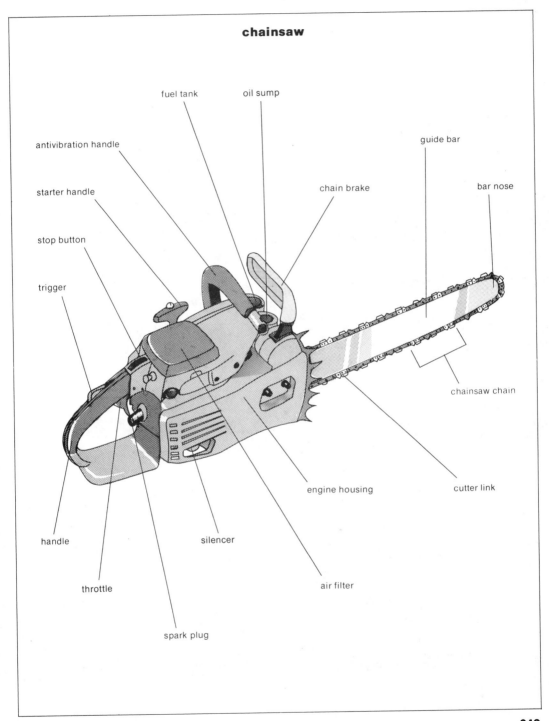

fuel tank

oil sump

guide bar

antivibration handle

chain brake

bar nose

starter handle

stop button

trigger

chainsaw chain

handle

silencer

cutter link

throttle

engine housing

air filter

spark plug

TOOLS AND EQUIPMENT

carpentry: tools

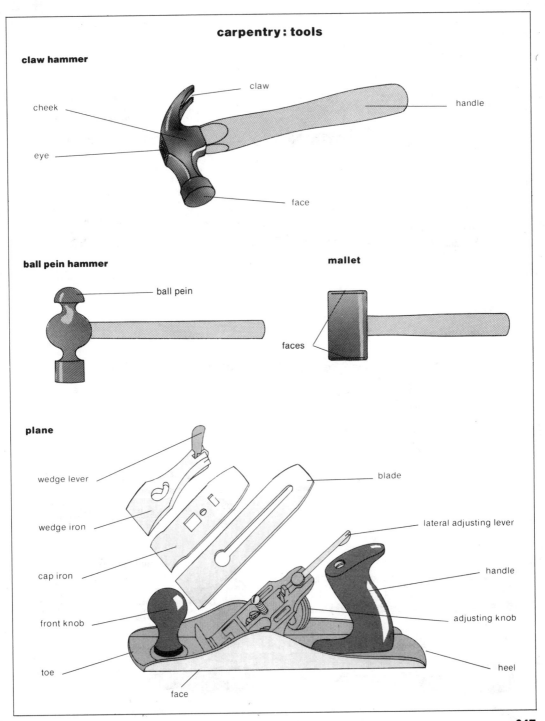

claw hammer

claw

cheek

handle

eye

face

ball pein hammer

ball pein

mallet

faces

plane

wedge lever

blade

wedge iron

lateral adjusting lever

cap iron

handle

front knob

adjusting knob

toe

heel

face

247

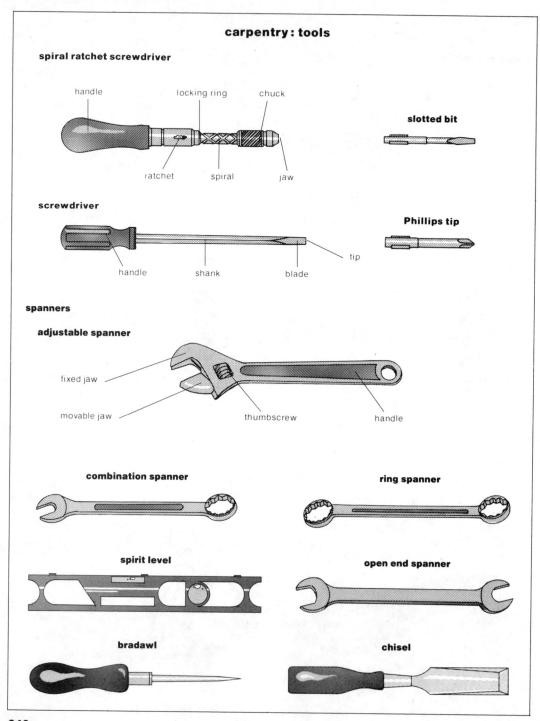

carpentry : tools

spiral ratchet screwdriver

handle   locking ring   chuck

slotted bit

ratchet   spiral   jaw

screwdriver

Phillips tip

handle   shank   blade   tip

spanners

adjustable spanner

fixed jaw

movable jaw   thumbscrew   handle

combination spanner   **ring spanner**

spirit level   **open end spanner**

bradawl   **chisel**

carpentry : tools

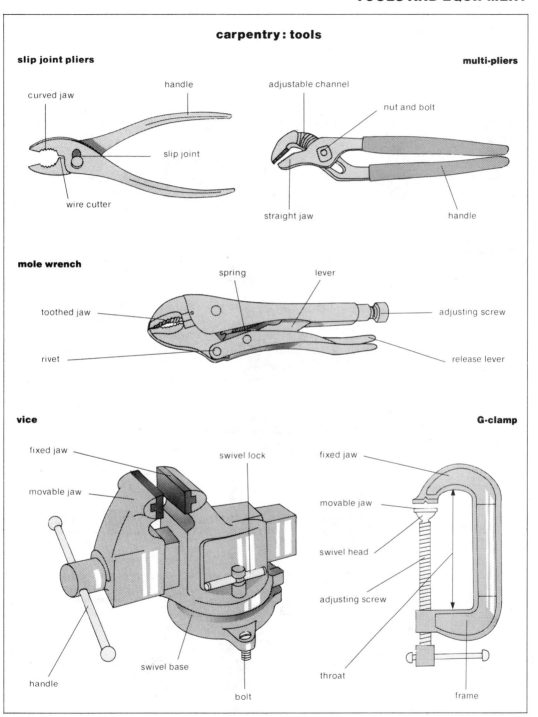

slip joint pliers

multi-pliers

curved jaw

handle

adjustable channel

nut and bolt

slip joint

wire cutter

straight jaw

handle

mole wrench

spring

lever

toothed jaw

adjusting screw

rivet

release lever

vice

G-clamp

fixed jaw

swivel lock

fixed jaw

movable jaw

movable jaw

swivel head

adjusting screw

swivel base

throat

handle

bolt

frame

carpentry: tools

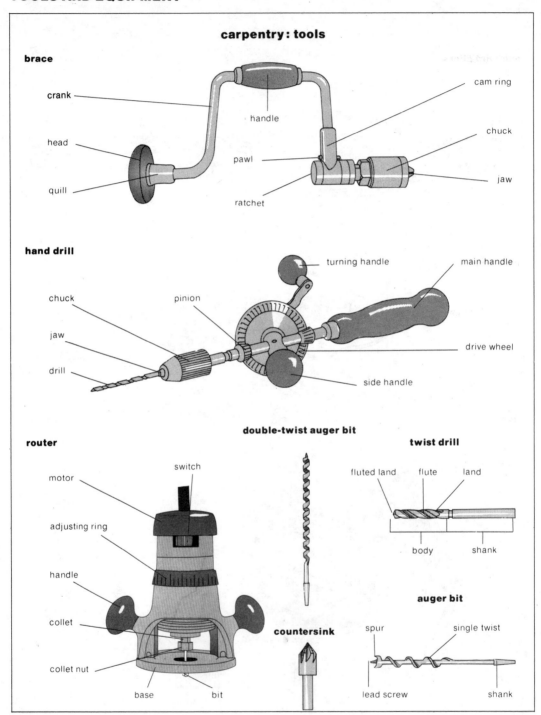

brace

crank

handle

cam ring

head

pawl

chuck

quill

jaw

ratchet

hand drill

turning handle

main handle

chuck

pinion

jaw

drive wheel

drill

side handle

router

double-twist auger bit

twist drill

motor

switch

fluted land

flute

land

adjusting ring

handle

body

shank

collet

auger bit

collet nut

countersink

spur

single twist

base

bit

lead screw

shank

carpentry : tools

pedestal drill

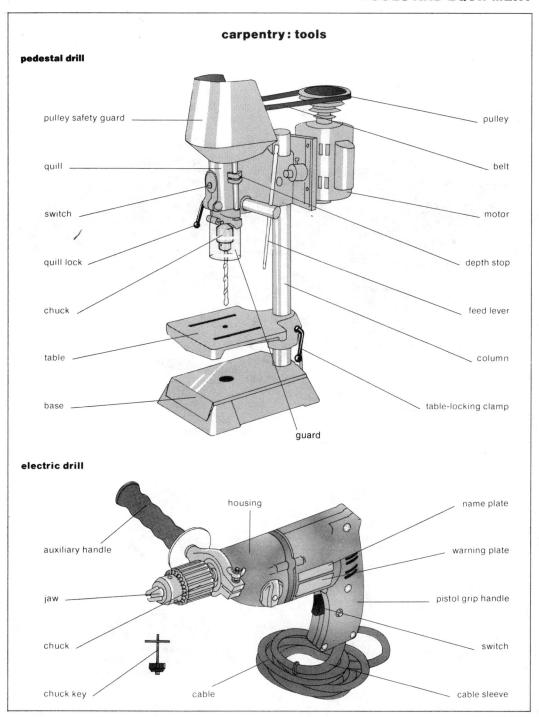

pulley safety guard

quill

switch

quill lock

chuck

table

base

pulley

belt

motor

depth stop

feed lever

column

table-locking clamp

guard

electric drill

housing

auxiliary handle

jaw

chuck

chuck key

cable

name plate

warning plate

pistol grip handle

switch

cable sleeve

TOOLS AND EQUIPMENT

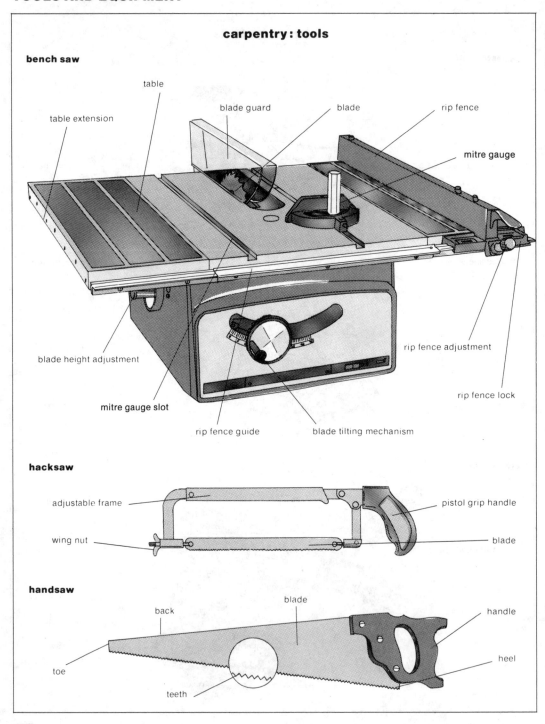

carpentry: tools

bench saw

table extension

table

blade guard

blade

rip fence

mitre gauge

blade height adjustment

mitre gauge slot

rip fence guide

blade tilting mechanism

rip fence adjustment

rip fence lock

hacksaw

adjustable frame

pistol grip handle

wing nut

blade

handsaw

back

blade

handle

toe

heel

teeth

carpentry: tools

circular saw

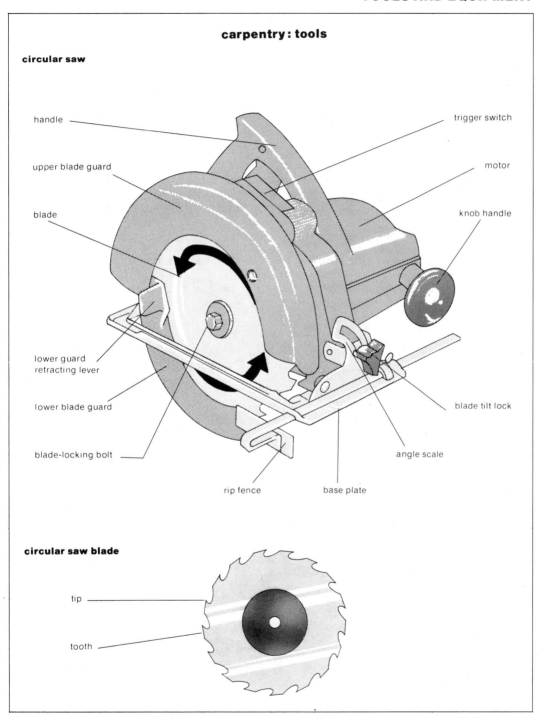

handle

trigger switch

upper blade guard

motor

blade

knob handle

lower guard
retracting lever

lower blade guard

blade tilt lock

blade-locking bolt

angle scale

rip fence

base plate

circular saw blade

tip

tooth

carpentry: fasteners

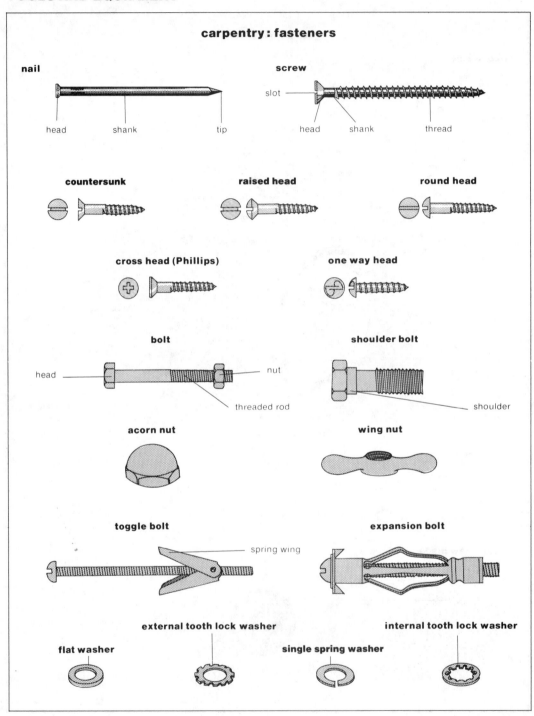

nail

head   shank   tip

screw

slot   head   shank   thread

countersunk

raised head

round head

cross head (Phillips)

one way head

bolt

head   nut   threaded rod

shoulder bolt

shoulder

acorn nut

wing nut

toggle bolt

spring wing

expansion bolt

flat washer

external tooth lock washer

single spring washer

internal tooth lock washer

carpentry

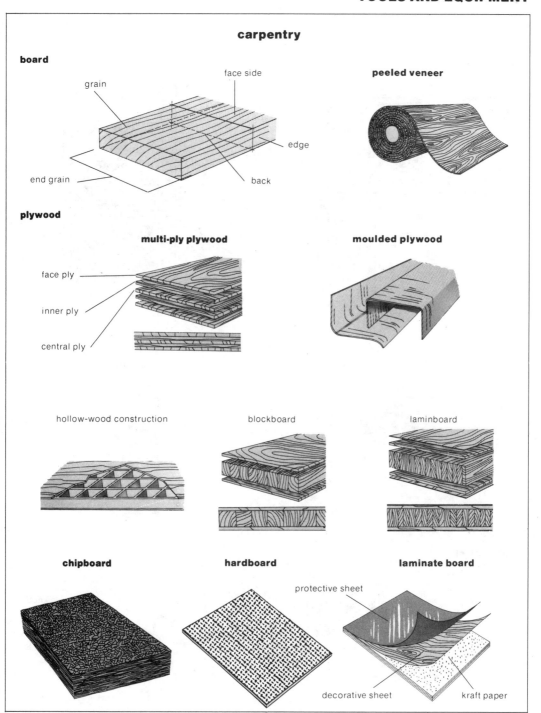

board

grain

face side

edge

end grain

back

peeled veneer

plywood

multi-ply plywood

face ply

inner ply

central ply

moulded plywood

hollow-wood construction

blockboard

laminboard

chipboard

hardboard

laminate board

protective sheet

decorative sheet

kraft paper

lock

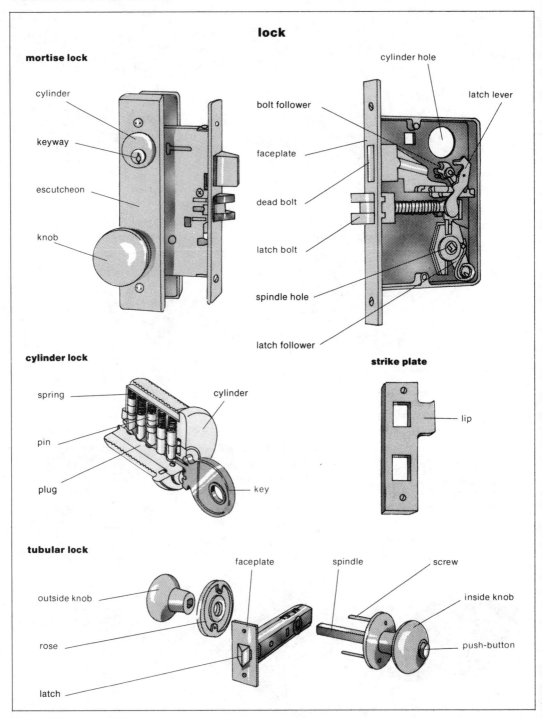

mortise lock

cylinder

keyway

escutcheon

knob

cylinder hole

latch lever

bolt follower

faceplate

dead bolt

latch bolt

spindle hole

latch follower

cylinder lock

spring

pin

plug

cylinder

key

strike plate

lip

tubular lock

outside knob

rose

latch

faceplate

spindle

screw

inside knob

push-button

plumbing

plumbing system

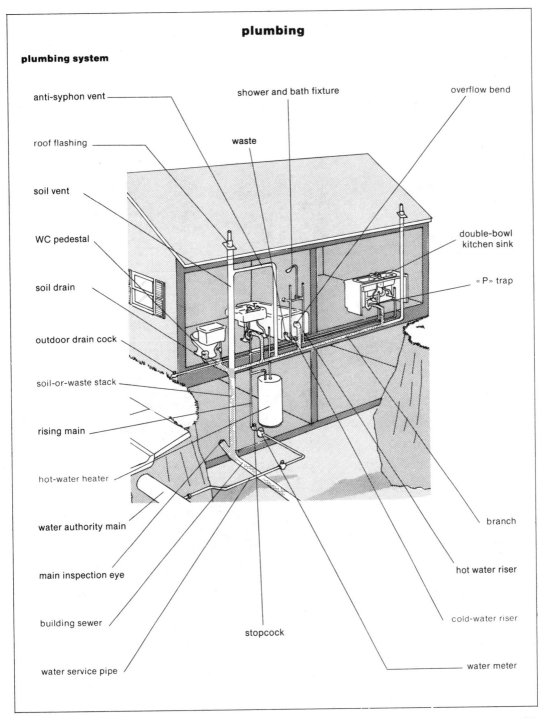

anti-syphon vent

roof flashing

soil vent

WC pedestal

soil drain

outdoor drain cock

soil-or-waste stack

rising main

hot-water heater

water authority main

main inspection eye

building sewer

water service pipe

shower and bath fixture

waste

stopcock

overflow bend

double-bowl kitchen sink

« P » trap

branch

hot water riser

cold-water riser

water meter

plumbing

toilet

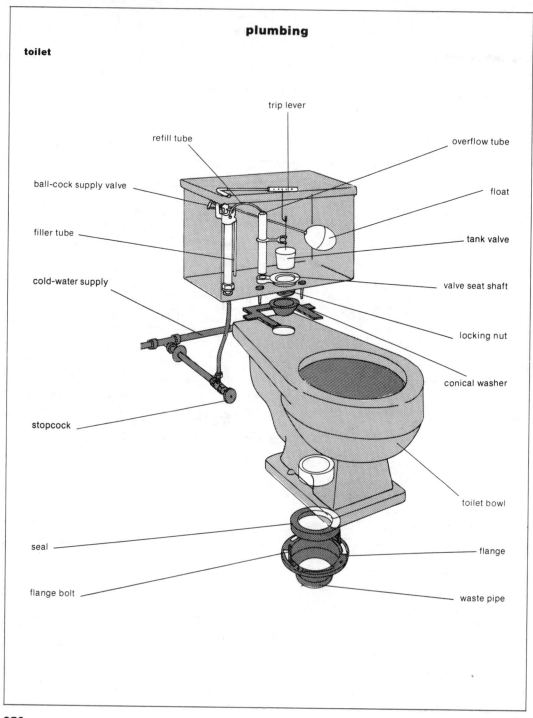

trip lever

refill tube

overflow tube

ball-cock supply valve

float

filler tube

tank valve

cold-water supply

valve seat shaft

locking nut

conical washer

stopcock

toilet bowl

seal

flange

flange bolt

waste pipe

plumbing

bathroom

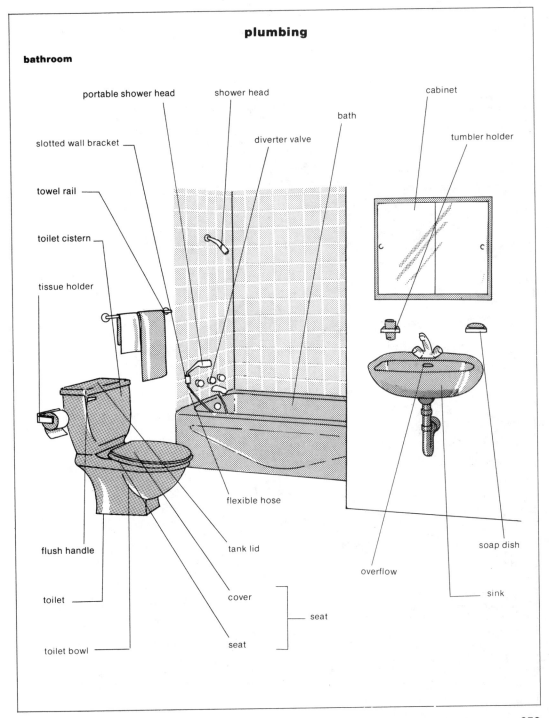

portable shower head

shower head

cabinet

slotted wall bracket

bath

diverter valve

tumbler holder

towel rail

toilet cistern

tissue holder

flexible hose

tank lid

flush handle

overflow

soap dish

toilet

cover

seat

sink

toilet bowl

seat

plumbing

sink

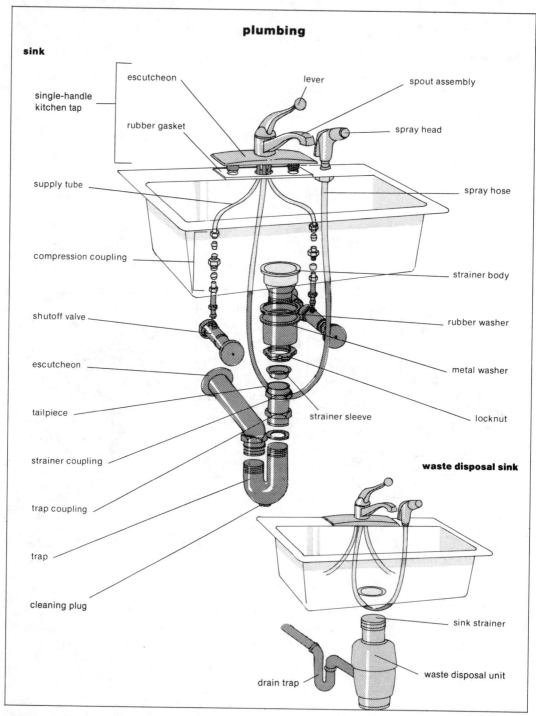

escutcheon

lever

spout assembly

single-handle kitchen tap

rubber gasket

spray head

supply tube

spray hose

compression coupling

strainer body

shutoff valve

rubber washer

escutcheon

metal washer

tailpiece

strainer sleeve

locknut

strainer coupling

waste disposal sink

trap coupling

trap

cleaning plug

sink strainer

waste disposal unit

drain trap

plumbing

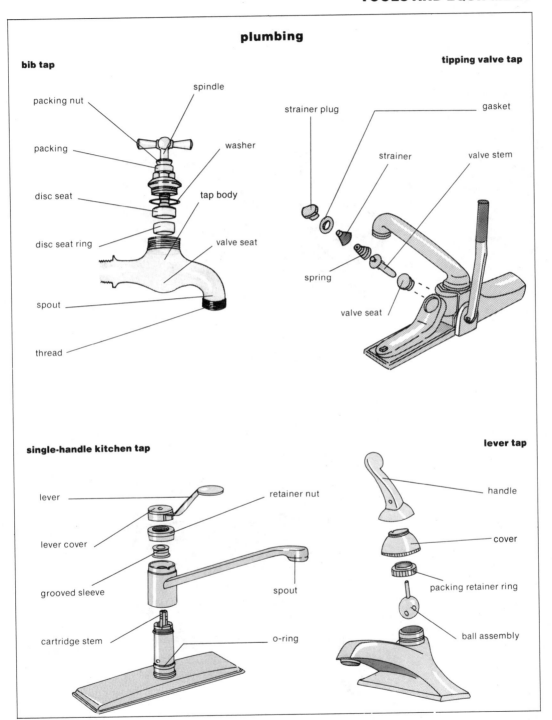

bib tap

packing nut

spindle

packing

washer

disc seat

tap body

disc seat ring

valve seat

spout

thread

tipping valve tap

strainer plug

gasket

strainer

valve stem

spring

valve seat

single-handle kitchen tap

lever

retainer nut

lever cover

grooved sleeve

spout

cartridge stem

o-ring

lever tap

handle

cover

packing retainer ring

ball assembly

plumbing

examples of branching

domestic sink

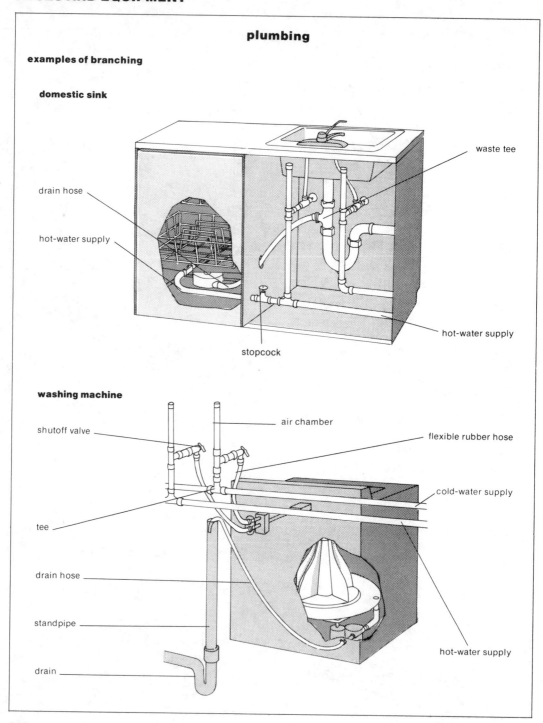

waste tee

drain hose

hot-water supply

hot-water supply

stopcock

washing machine

shutoff valve

air chamber

flexible rubber hose

cold-water supply

tee

drain hose

standpipe

drain

hot-water supply

plumbing

electric water-heater tank

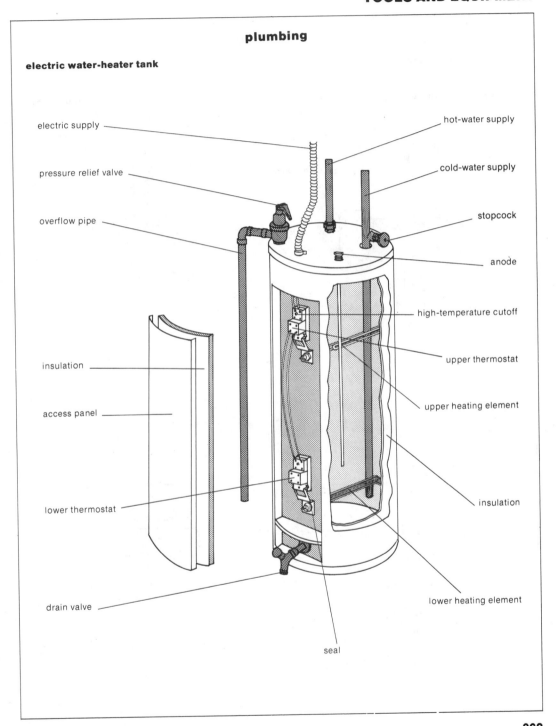

electric supply

pressure relief valve

overflow pipe

insulation

access panel

lower thermostat

drain valve

hot-water supply

cold-water supply

stopcock

anode

high-temperature cutoff

upper thermostat

upper heating element

insulation

lower heating element

seal

TOOLS AND EQUIPMENT

plumbing

mechanical connectors

compression fitting

flare joint

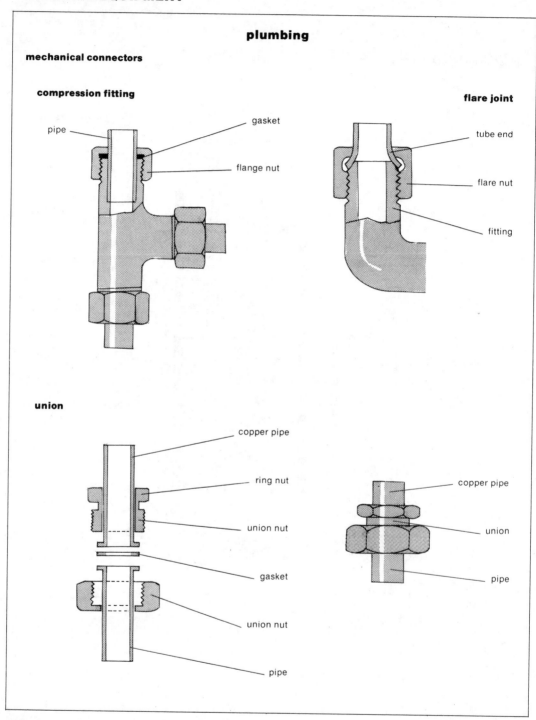

pipe

gasket

flange nut

tube end

flare nut

fitting

union

copper pipe

ring nut

union nut

gasket

union nut

pipe

copper pipe

union

pipe

plumbing

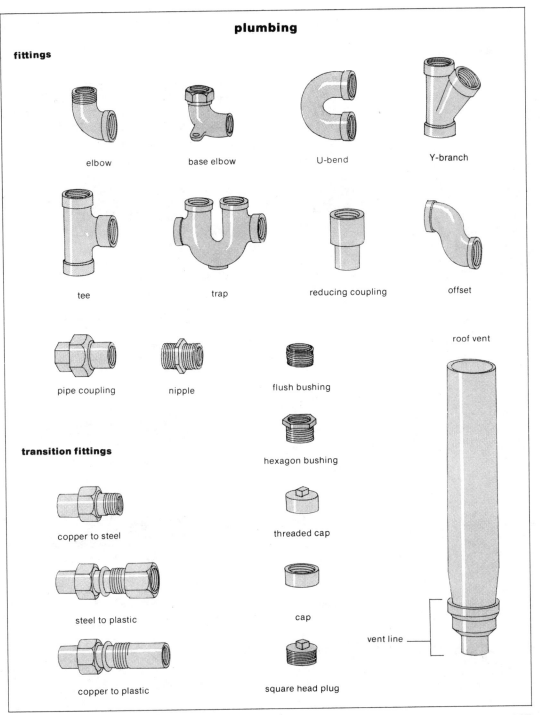

fittings

elbow

base elbow

U-bend

Y-branch

tee

trap

reducing coupling

offset

pipe coupling

nipple

flush bushing

hexagon bushing

transition fittings

copper to steel

threaded cap

steel to plastic

cap

copper to plastic

square head plug

roof vent

vent line

TOOLS AND EQUIPMENT

plumbing

plumbing tools

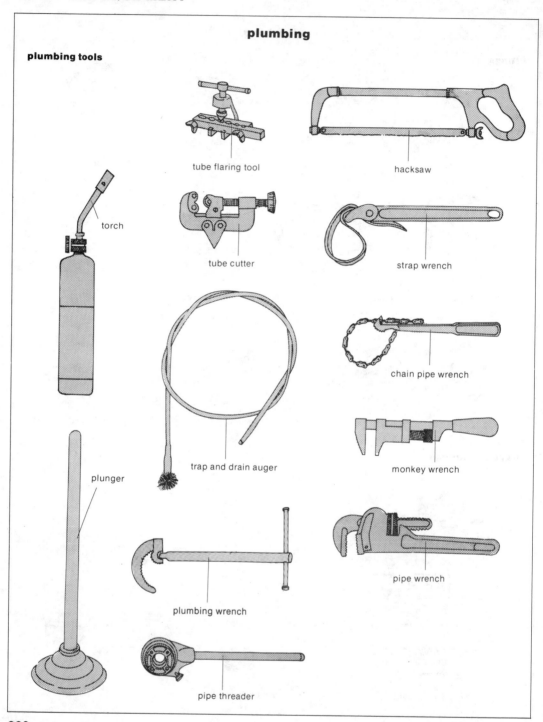

tube flaring tool

hacksaw

torch

tube cutter

strap wrench

chain pipe wrench

trap and drain auger

monkey wrench

plunger

pipe wrench

plumbing wrench

pipe threader

plumbing

septic tank

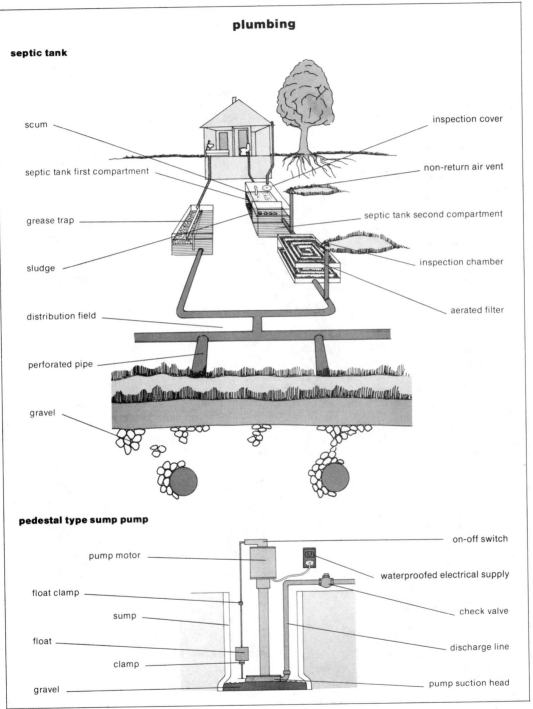

scum

septic tank first compartment

grease trap

sludge

distribution field

perforated pipe

gravel

inspection cover

non-return air vent

septic tank second compartment

inspection chamber

aerated filter

pedestal type sump pump

pump motor

float clamp

sump

float

clamp

gravel

on-off switch

waterproofed electrical supply

check valve

discharge line

pump suction head

painting upkeep

ladders and stepladders

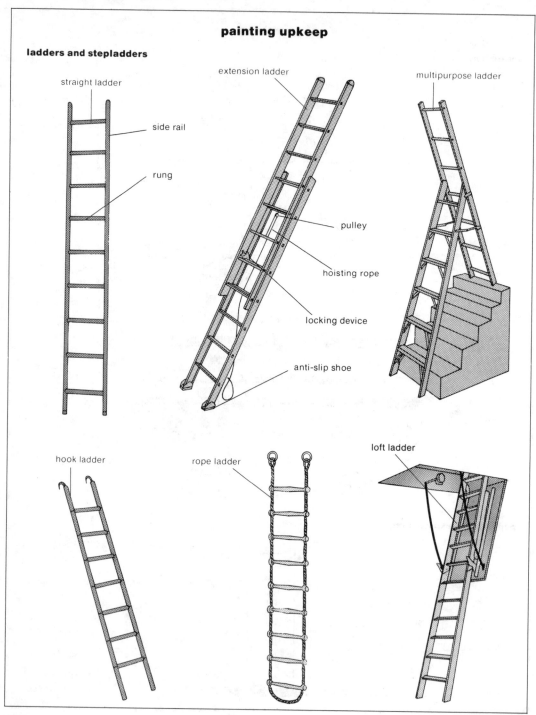

straight ladder

side rail

rung

extension ladder

pulley

hoisting rope

locking device

anti-slip shoe

multipurpose ladder

hook ladder

rope ladder

loft ladder

painting upkeep

ladders and stepladders

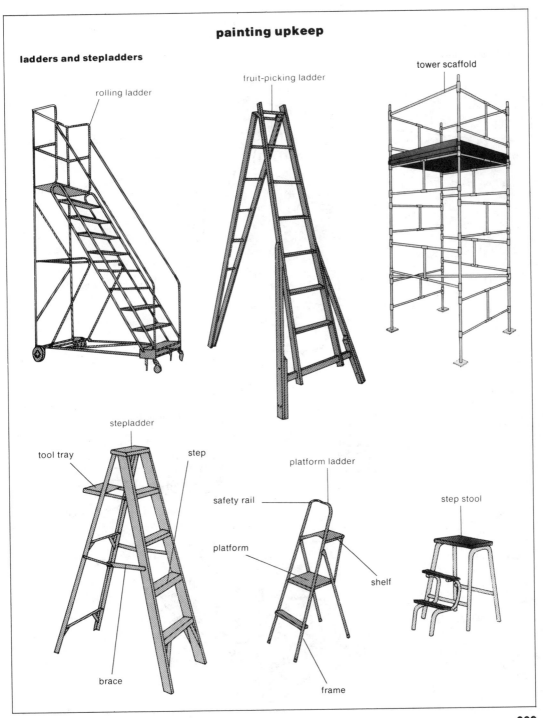

rolling ladder

fruit-picking ladder

tower scaffold

stepladder

tool tray

step

platform ladder

safety rail

platform

shelf

step stool

brace

frame

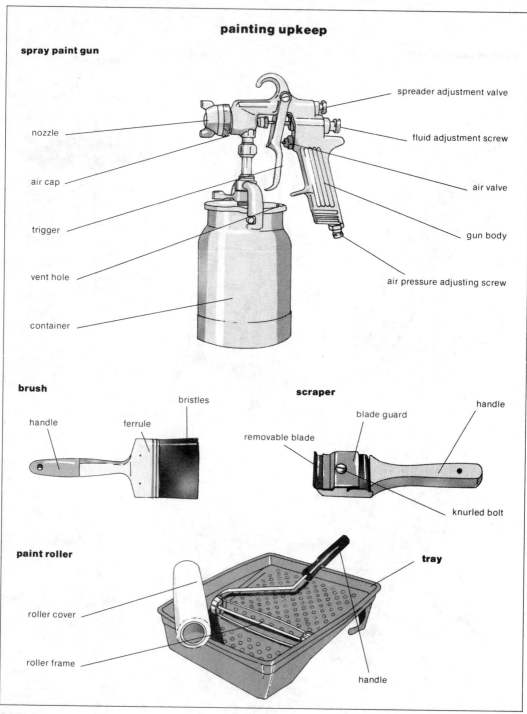

painting upkeep

spray paint gun

spreader adjustment valve

nozzle

fluid adjustment screw

air cap

air valve

trigger

gun body

vent hole

air pressure adjusting screw

container

brush

bristles

handle

ferrule

scraper

handle

blade guard

removable blade

knurled bolt

paint roller

roller cover

roller frame

tray

handle

soldering and welding

soldering iron

soldering gun

tip

blowlamp

pencil point tip

adjustable valve

flame spreader tip

oxyacetylene welding

bottle cart

pressure regulator

cap

disposable gas cylinder

hose

welding torch

oxygen cylinder

acetylene cylinder

arc welding

electrode holder

earth clamp

electrode

electric arc

weld bead

arc welding machine

metal bench top

electrode lead

work lead

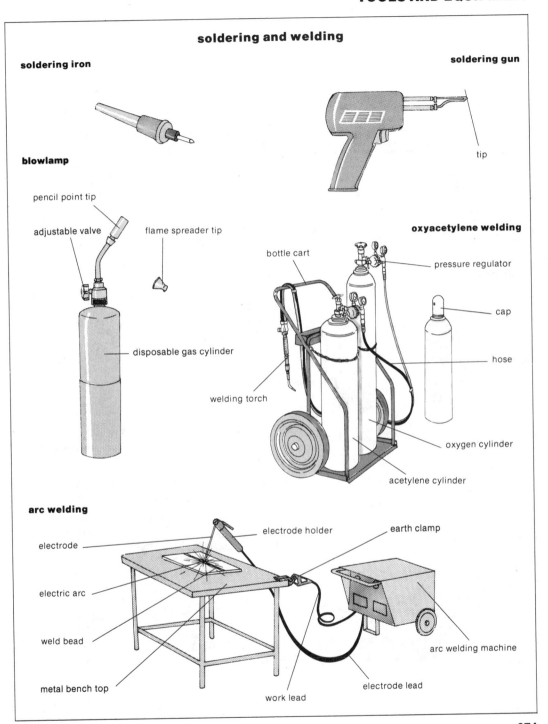

TOOLS AND EQUIPMENT

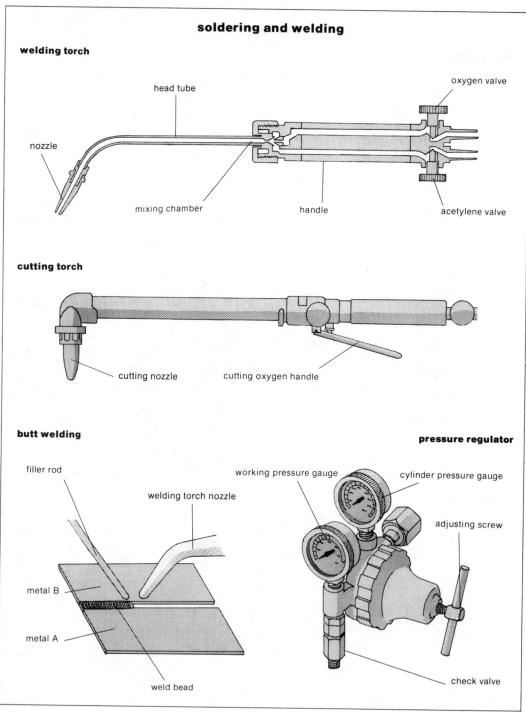

soldering and welding

welding torch

head tube

oxygen valve

nozzle

mixing chamber

handle

acetylene valve

cutting torch

cutting nozzle

cutting oxygen handle

butt welding

pressure regulator

filler rod

working pressure gauge

cylinder pressure gauge

welding torch nozzle

adjusting screw

metal B

metal A

weld bead

check valve

soldering and welding

protective clothing

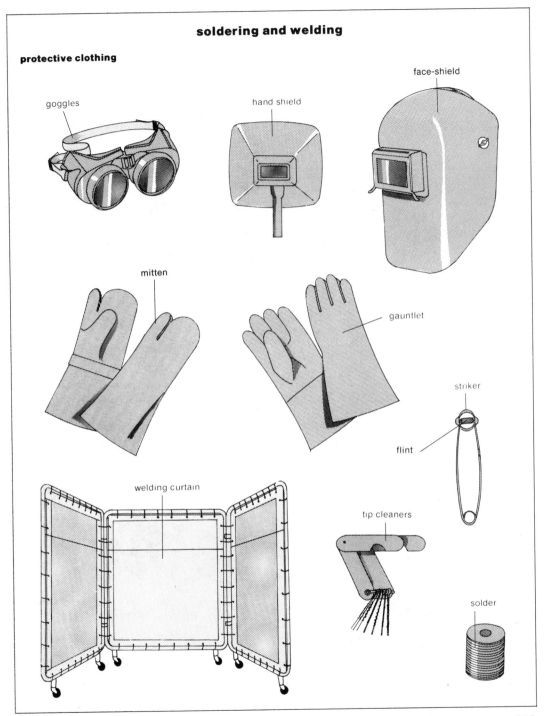

goggles

hand shield

face-shield

mitten

gauntlet

striker

flint

welding curtain

tip cleaners

solder

electricity

light bulb

mercury-vapour lamp

inert gas

bulb

bulb

arc tube mount structure

filament

stem

reflector

support

heat deflecting disc

arc tube

lead-in wire

nitrogen

button

exhaust tube

screw base

main electrode

starting electrode

screw base

starting resistor

fluorescent tube

phosphor coating

electrode

pin

bulb

lead-in wire

exhaust tube

cap

mercury

gas

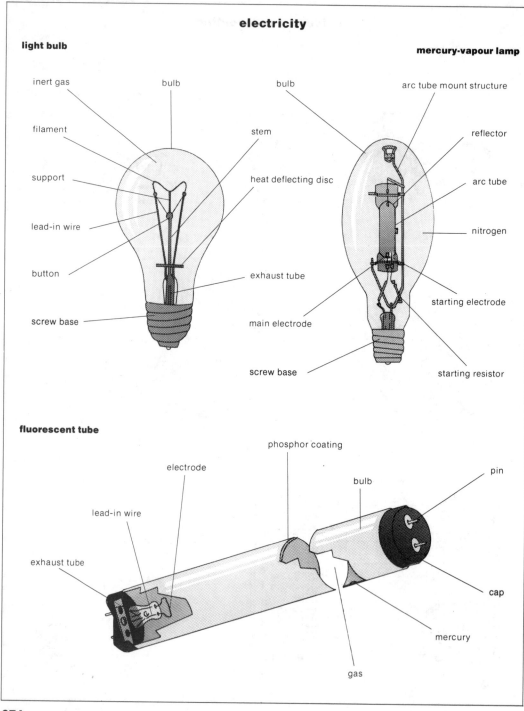

electricity

three-pin plug

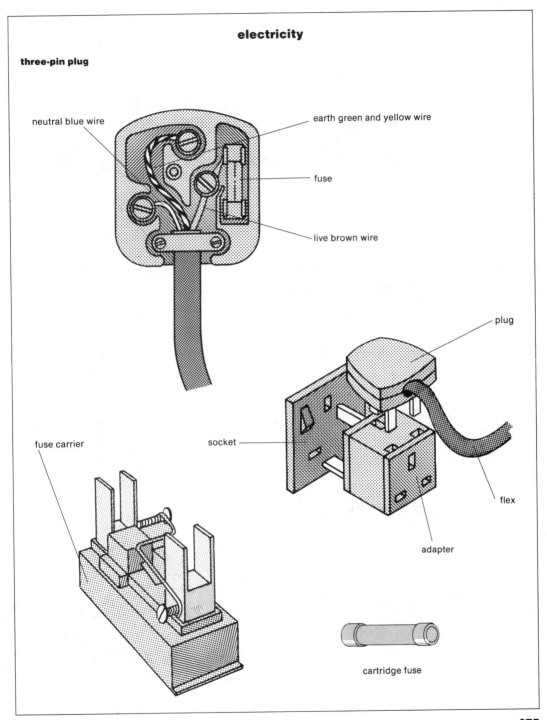

neutral blue wire

earth green and yellow wire

fuse

live brown wire

plug

fuse carrier

socket

flex

adapter

cartridge fuse

electricity

electrician's tools

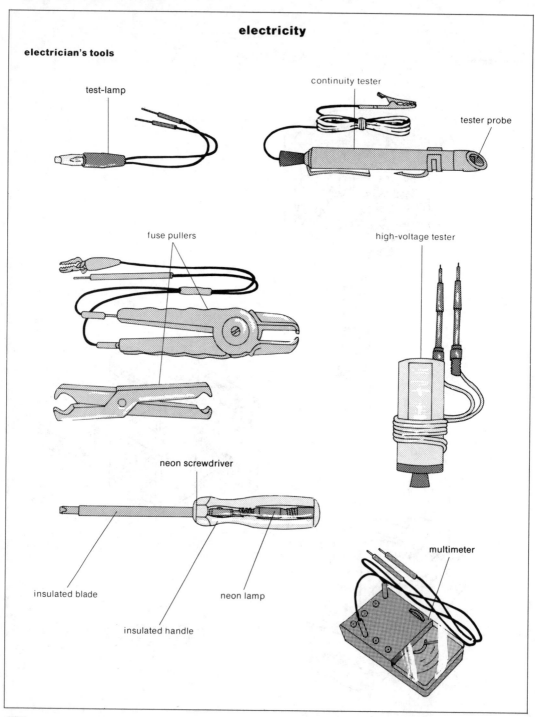

test-lamp

continuity tester

tester probe

fuse pullers

high-voltage tester

neon screwdriver

insulated blade

neon lamp

insulated handle

multimeter

electricity

electrician's tools

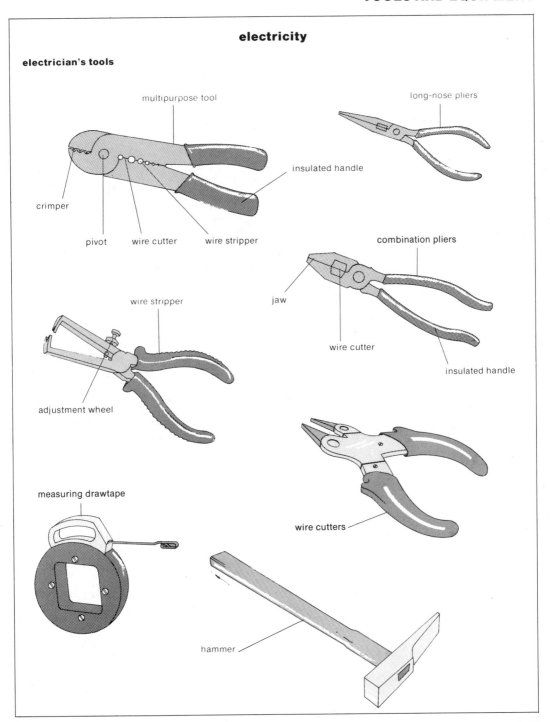

multipurpose tool

long-nose pliers

insulated handle

crimper

pivot   wire cutter   wire stripper

combination pliers

wire stripper

jaw

wire cutter

insulated handle

adjustment wheel

measuring drawtape

wire cutters

hammer

CLOTHING

men's clothing

trench coat   **raincoat**

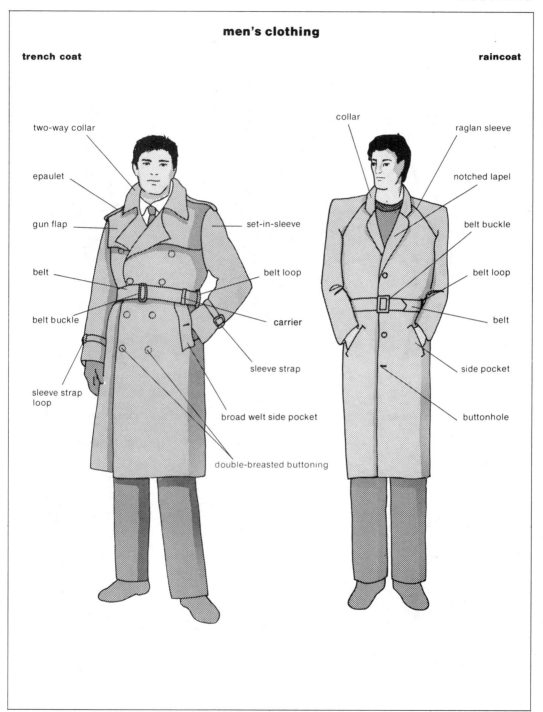

two-way collar

epaulet

gun flap

belt

belt buckle

sleeve strap loop

collar

raglan sleeve

notched lapel

belt buckle

belt loop

belt

side pocket

buttonhole

set-in-sleeve

belt loop

carrier

sleeve strap

broad welt side pocket

double-breasted buttoning

CLOTHING

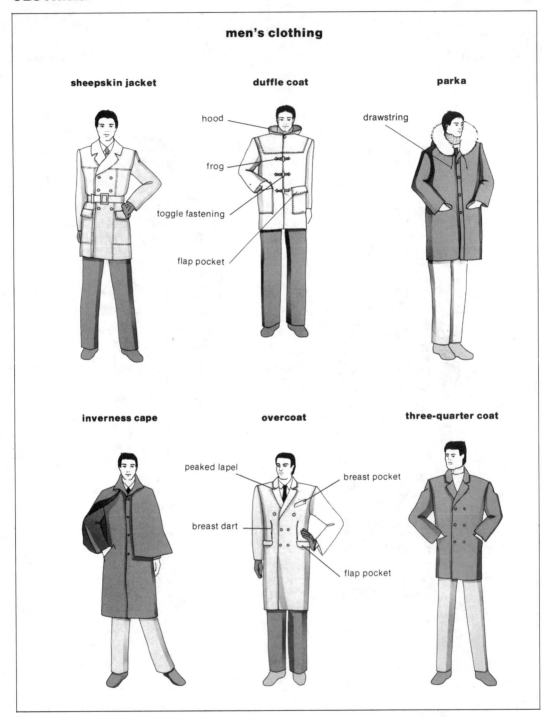

men's clothing

sheepskin jacket

duffle coat

hood

frog

toggle fastening

flap pocket

parka

drawstring

inverness cape

overcoat

peaked lapel

breast pocket

breast dart

flap pocket

three-quarter coat

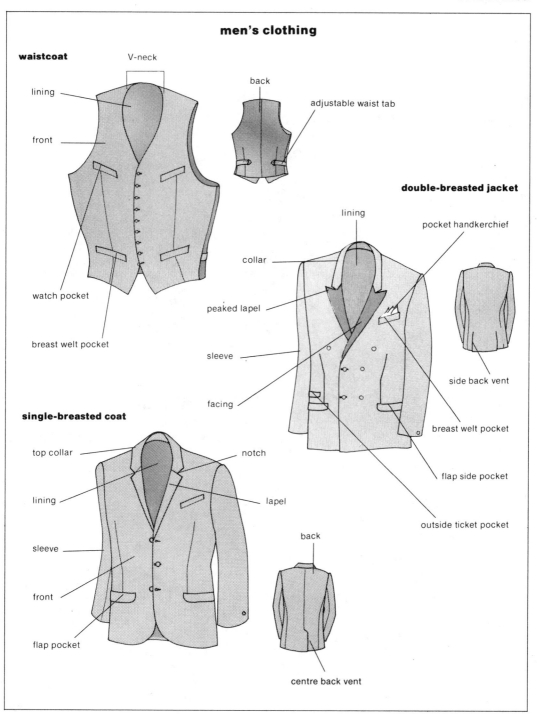

men's clothing

waistcoat

V-neck

lining

front

back

adjustable waist tab

watch pocket

breast welt pocket

double-breasted jacket

lining

pocket handkerchief

collar

peaked lapel

sleeve

facing

side back vent

breast welt pocket

flap side pocket

outside ticket pocket

single-breasted coat

top collar

notch

lining

lapel

sleeve

front

back

flap pocket

centre back vent

CLOTHING

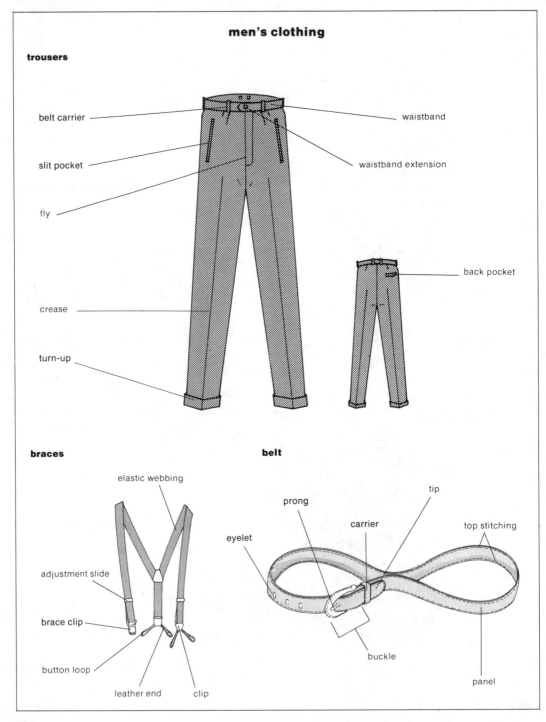

men's clothing

trousers

belt carrier

slit pocket

fly

waistband

waistband extension

crease

turn-up

back pocket

braces

elastic webbing

adjustment slide

brace clip

button loop

leather end

clip

belt

prong

tip

eyelet

carrier

top stitching

buckle

panel

men's clothing

shirt

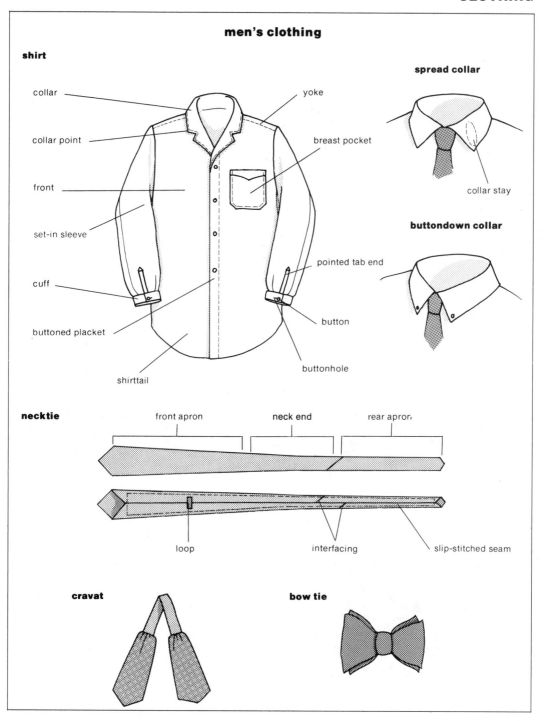

collar

collar point

front

set-in sleeve

cuff

buttoned placket

shirttail

yoke

breast pocket

pointed tab end

button

buttonhole

spread collar

collar stay

buttondown collar

necktie

front apron

neck end

rear apron

loop

interfacing

slip-stitched seam

cravat

bow tie

CLOTHING

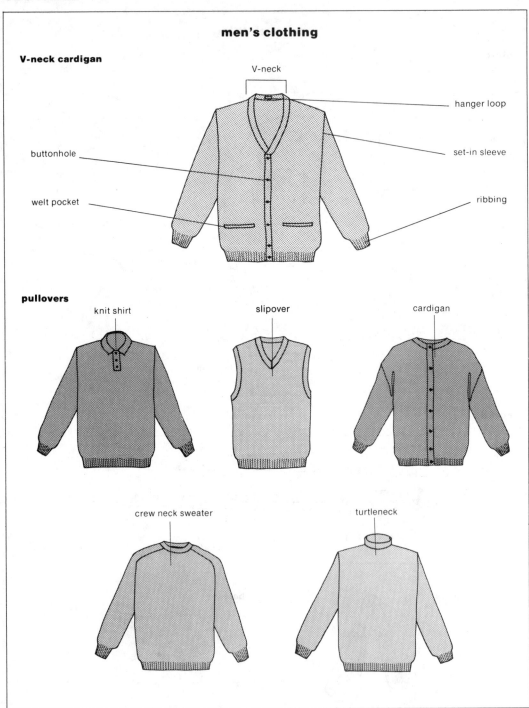

men's clothing

V-neck cardigan

V-neck

hanger loop

set-in sleeve

buttonhole

welt pocket

ribbing

pullovers

knit shirt

slipover

cardigan

crew neck sweater

turtleneck

men's clothing

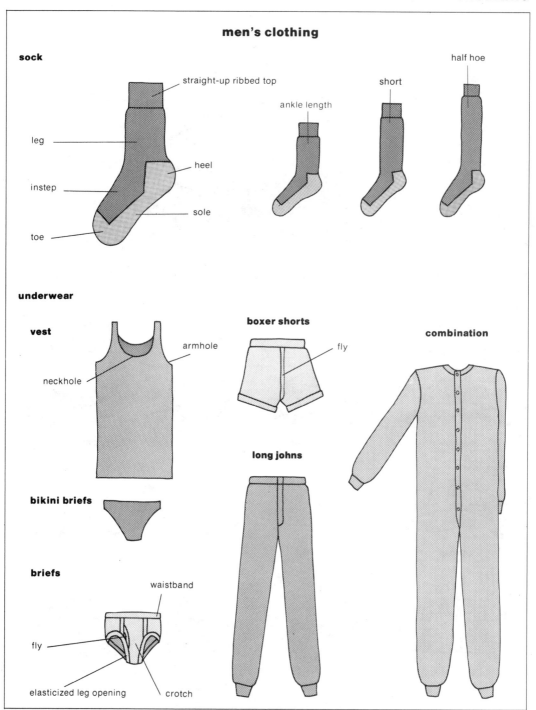

sock

straight-up ribbed top

ankle length

short

half hoe

leg

heel

instep

sole

toe

underwear

vest

armhole

neckhole

boxer shorts

fly

combination

long johns

bikini briefs

briefs

waistband

fly

elasticized leg opening

crotch

CLOTHING

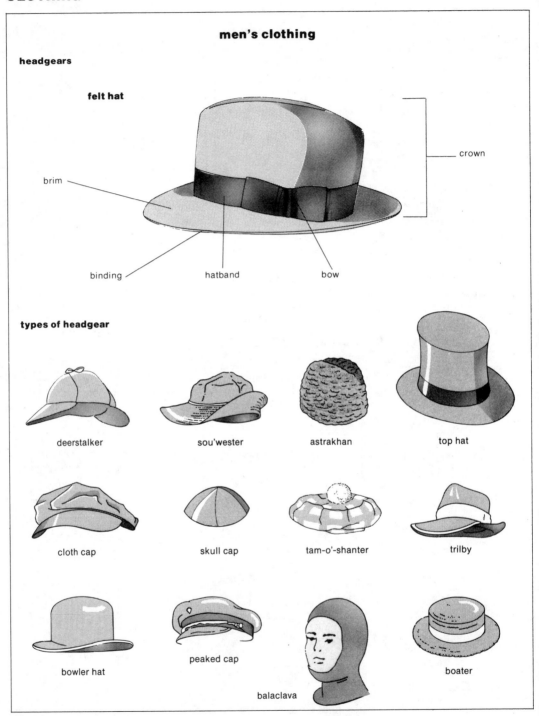

men's clothing

headgears

felt hat

crown

brim

binding

hatband

bow

types of headgear

deerstalker

sou'wester

astrakhan

top hat

cloth cap

skull cap

tam-o'-shanter

trilby

bowler hat

peaked cap

balaclava

boater

glove

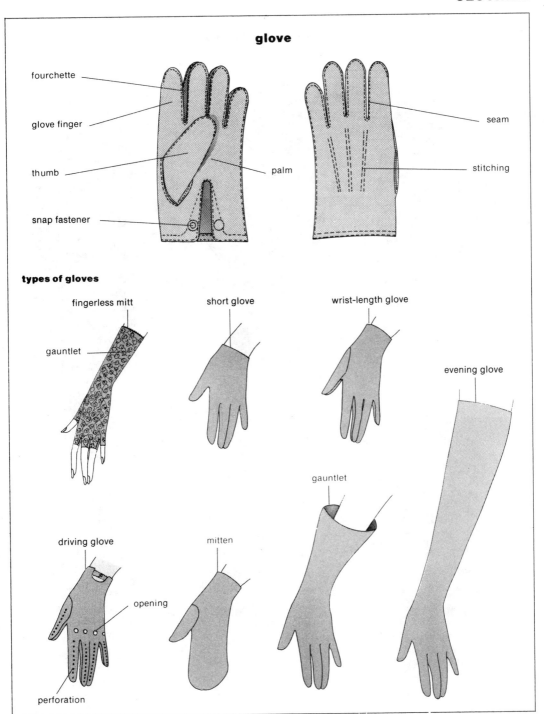

fourchette

glove finger

thumb

palm

snap fastener

seam

stitching

types of gloves

fingerless mitt

gauntlet

short glove

wrist-length glove

evening glove

gauntlet

driving glove

mitten

opening

perforation

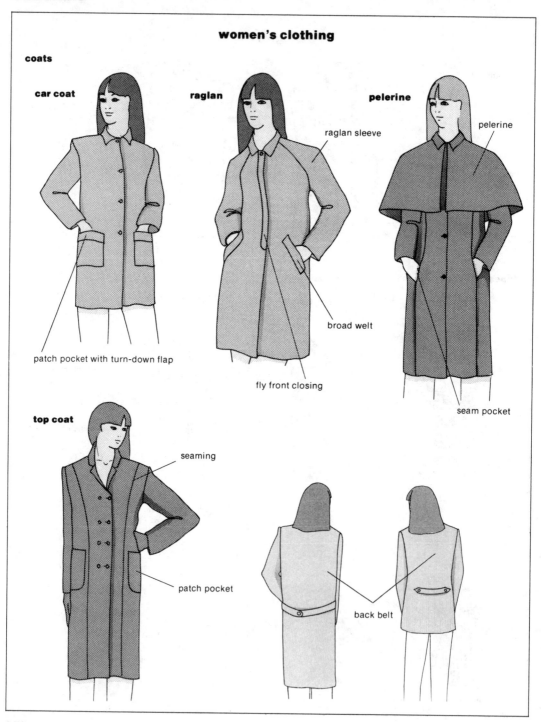

women's clothing

coats

car coat

raglan

pelerine

raglan sleeve

pelerine

patch pocket with turn-down flap

broad welt

seam pocket

fly front closing

top coat

seaming

patch pocket

back belt

women's clothing

coats

cape

buttoned placket

arm slit

tailored collar

pea jacket

notched lapel

hand warmer pocket

mock pocket

poncho

double breasted buttoning

windcheater

blouson

ribbing

waistband

women's clothing

dresses

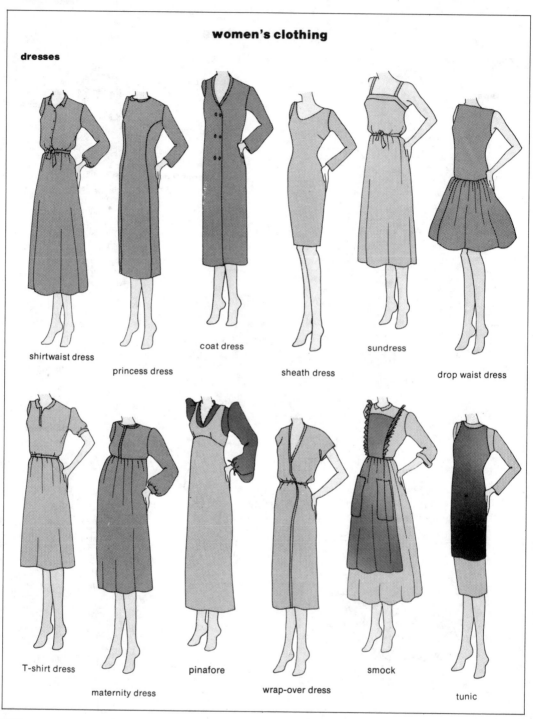

shirtwaist dress

princess dress

coat dress

sheath dress

sundress

drop waist dress

T-shirt dress

maternity dress

pinafore

wrap-over dress

smock

tunic

women's clothing

skirts

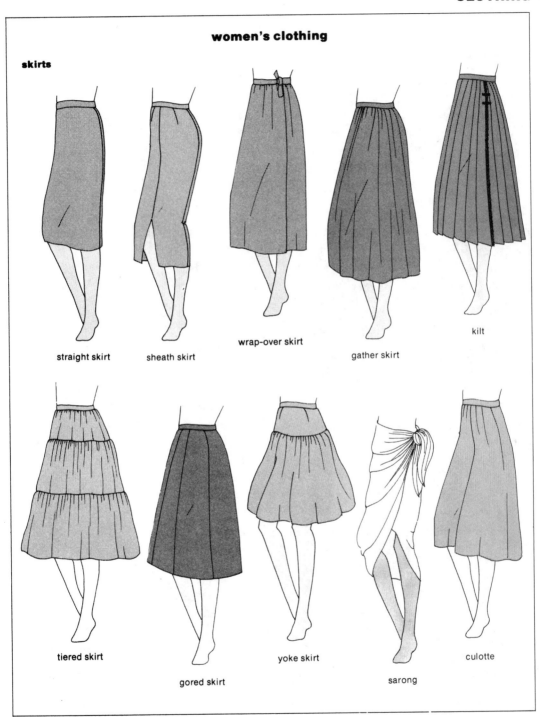

straight skirt

sheath skirt

wrap-over skirt

gather skirt

kilt

tiered skirt

gored skirt

yoke skirt

sarong

culotte

CLOTHING

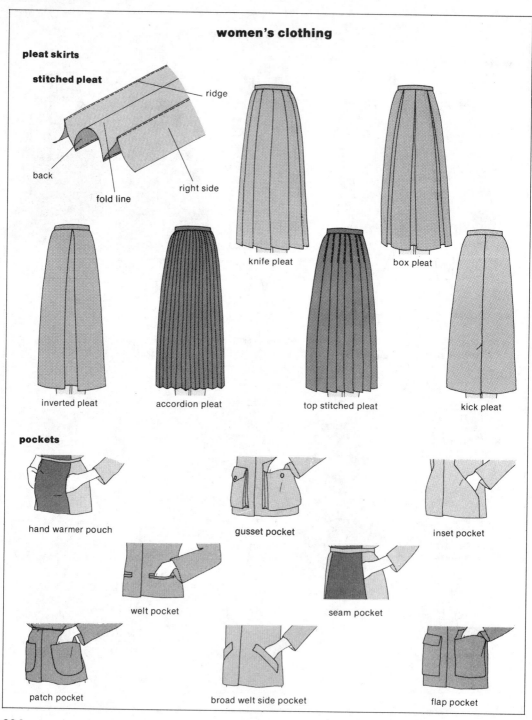

women's clothing

pleat skirts

stitched pleat

ridge

back

fold line

right side

knife pleat

box pleat

inverted pleat

accordion pleat

top stitched pleat

kick pleat

pockets

hand warmer pouch

gusset pocket

inset pocket

welt pocket

seam pocket

patch pocket

broad welt side pocket

flap pocket

women's clothing

blouses

classic

smock

sailor tunic

button-through smock

yoke

gather

T-shirt

buttoned placket

breast pocket

wrap-over top

tunic

overshirt

shirt collar

bottom of collar

shirt-tail

shirt sleeve

body shirt

crotch piece

CLOTHING

women's clothing

sleeves

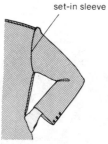

set-in sleeve

tailored sleeve

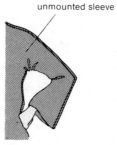

unmounted sleeve

kimono sleeve

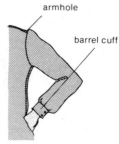

armhole

barrel cuff

shirtwaist sleeve

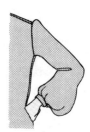

bishop sleeve

three-quarter sleeve

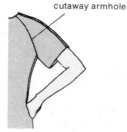

cutaway armhole

raglan sleeve

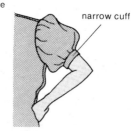

narrow cuff

puff sleeve

cap sleeve

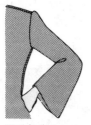

pagoda sleeve

batwing sleeve

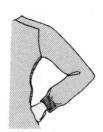

epaulet sleeve

leg-of-mutton sleeve

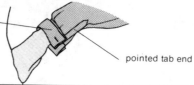

double cuff

pointed tab end

women's clothing

waistcoats and pullovers

cardigan

turtleneck

pullover

long cardigan

twin-set

slipover

crew sweater

gusset pocket

safari jacket

blazer

waistcoat

welt pocket

bolero

box jacket

CLOTHING

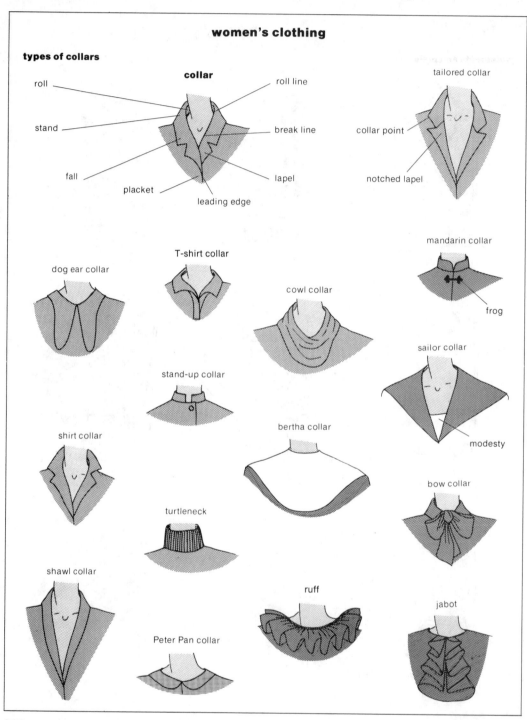

women's clothing

types of collars

collar

roll

roll line

stand

break line

fall

lapel

placket

leading edge

tailored collar

collar point

notched lapel

dog ear collar

T-shirt collar

cowl collar

mandarin collar

frog

stand-up collar

sailor collar

modesty

shirt collar

bertha collar

bow collar

turtleneck

shawl collar

ruff

jabot

Peter Pan collar

women's clothing

necklines and necks

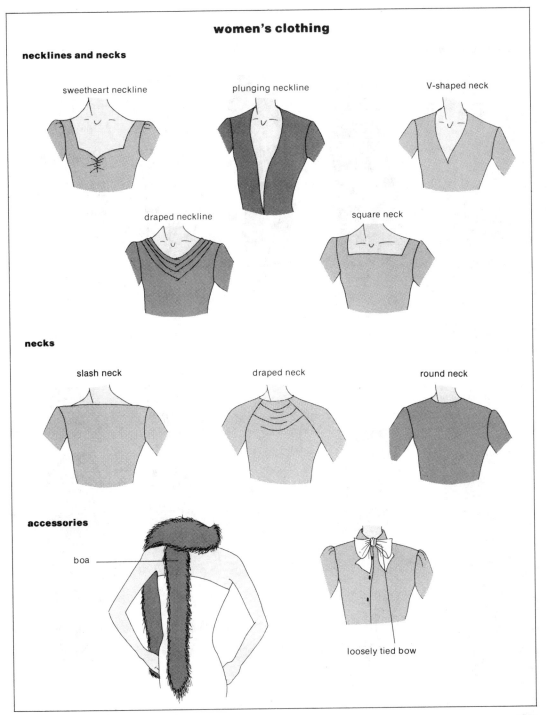

sweetheart neckline

plunging neckline

V-shaped neck

draped neckline

square neck

necks

slash neck

draped neck

round neck

accessories

boa

loosely tied bow

CLOTHING

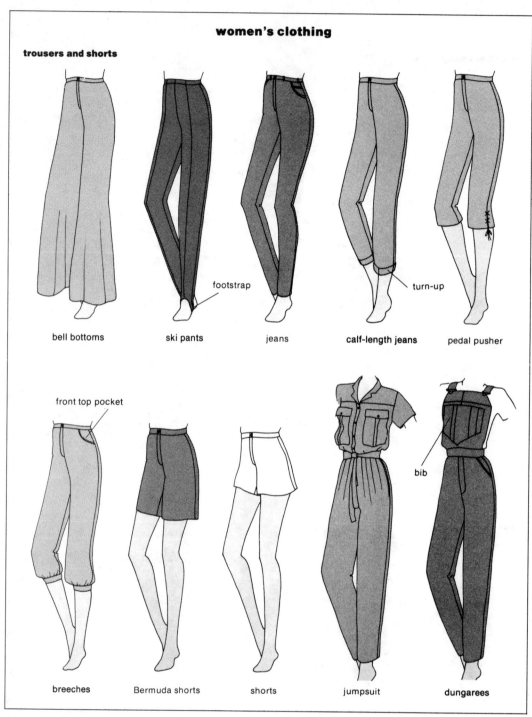

women's clothing

trousers and shorts

bell bottoms

ski pants

footstrap

jeans

calf-length jeans

turn-up

pedal pusher

front top pocket

breeches

Bermuda shorts

shorts

jumpsuit

bib

dungarees

women's clothing

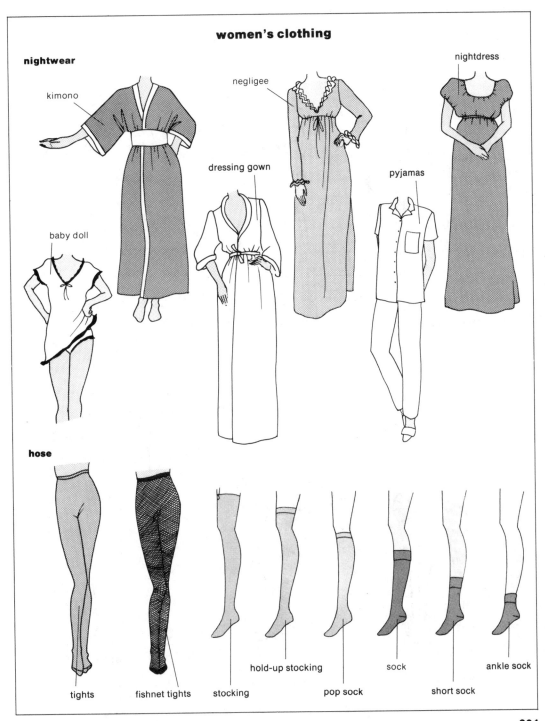

nightwear

kimono

negligee

nightdress

dressing gown

pyjamas

baby doll

hose

tights

fishnet tights

stocking

hold-up stocking

pop sock

short sock

sock

ankle sock

women's clothing

underwear

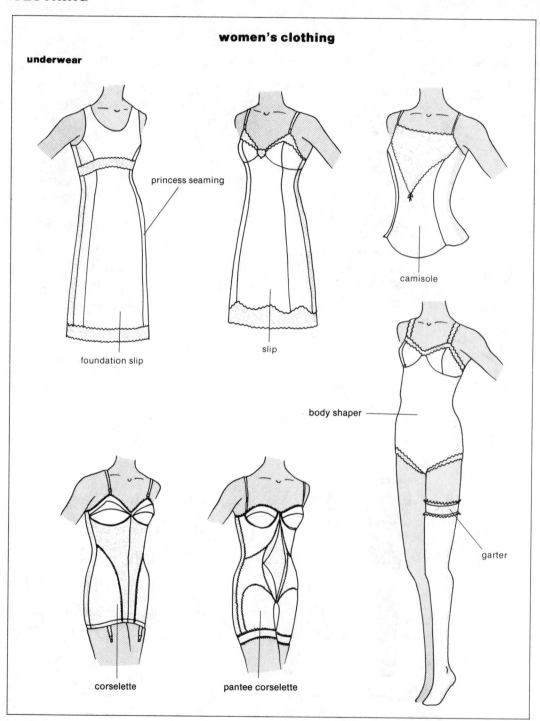

princess seaming

camisole

foundation slip

slip

body shaper

garter

corselette

pantee corselette

women's clothing

underwear

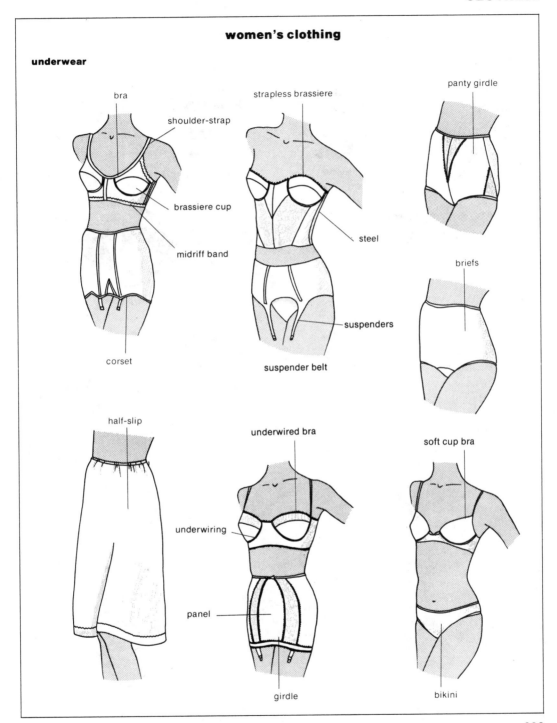

bra

shoulder-strap

strapless brassiere

panty girdle

brassiere cup

steel

midriff band

briefs

suspenders

corset

suspender belt

half-slip

underwired bra

soft cup bra

underwiring

panel

girdle

bikini

CLOTHING

women's clothing

headgear

fur hood

balaclava

stocking cap

scarf turban

pompom

head band

tam-o'-shanter

sou'wester

string

crown

brim

showerproof hat

toque

hat veil

pillbox hat

mob-cap

turban

boater

cartwheel hat

trilby

cap

beret

cloche

304

children's clothing

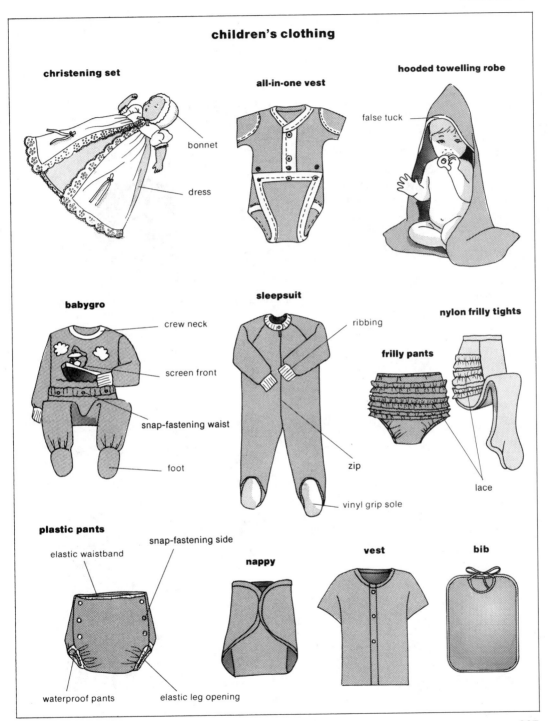

christening set

bonnet

dress

all-in-one vest

hooded towelling robe

false tuck

babygro

crew neck

screen front

snap-fastening waist

foot

sleepsuit

ribbing

zip

vinyl grip sole

nylon frilly tights

frilly pants

lace

plastic pants

elastic waistband

snap-fastening side

nappy

vest

bib

waterproof pants

elastic leg opening

CLOTHING

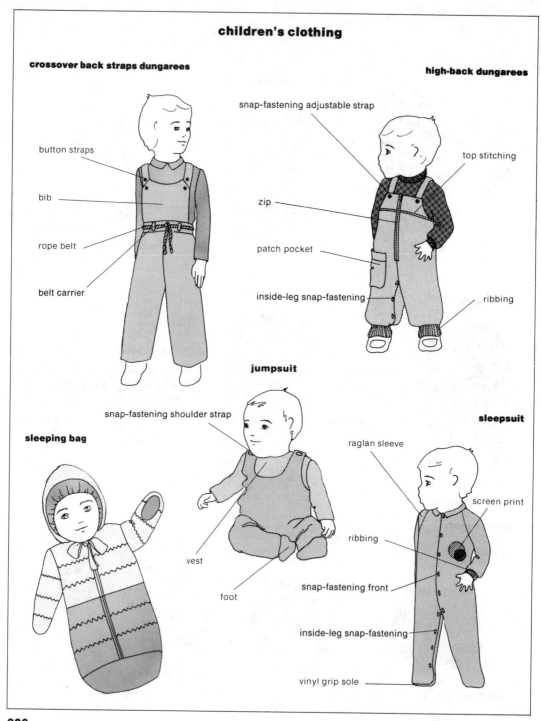

children's clothing

crossover back straps dungarees

high-back dungarees

snap-fastening adjustable strap

button straps

top stitching

bib

zip

rope belt

patch pocket

belt carrier

inside-leg snap-fastening

ribbing

jumpsuit

snap-fastening shoulder strap

sleepsuit

sleeping bag

raglan sleeve

screen print

ribbing

vest

snap-fastening front

foot

inside-leg snap-fastening

vinyl grip sole

children's clothing

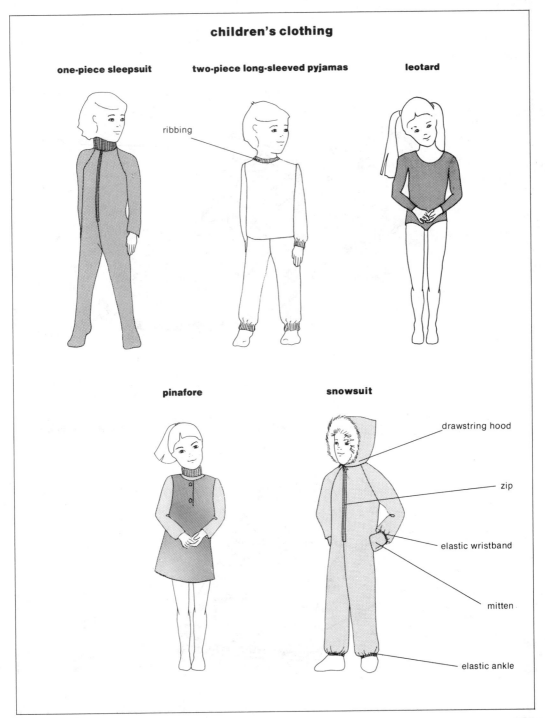

one-piece sleepsuit

two-piece long-sleeved pyjamas

leotard

ribbing

pinafore

snowsuit

drawstring hood

zip

elastic wristband

mitten

elastic ankle

CLOTHING

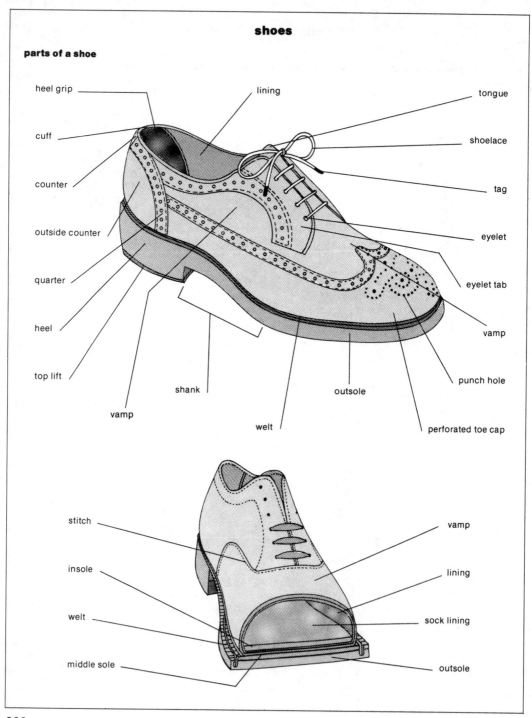

shoes

parts of a shoe

heel grip

lining

tongue

cuff

shoelace

counter

tag

outside counter

eyelet

quarter

eyelet tab

heel

vamp

top lift

punch hole

vamp

shank

outsole

perforated toe cap

welt

stitch

vamp

insole

lining

welt

sock lining

middle sole

outsole

shoes

principal types of shoes

mule

training shoe

T-strap shoe

moccasin

clog

sandal

sneaker

flip-flop

tennis shoe

pump

toe-strap

espadrille

ankle-strap sandal

court

one-bar shoe

CLOTHING

shoes

principal types of shoes

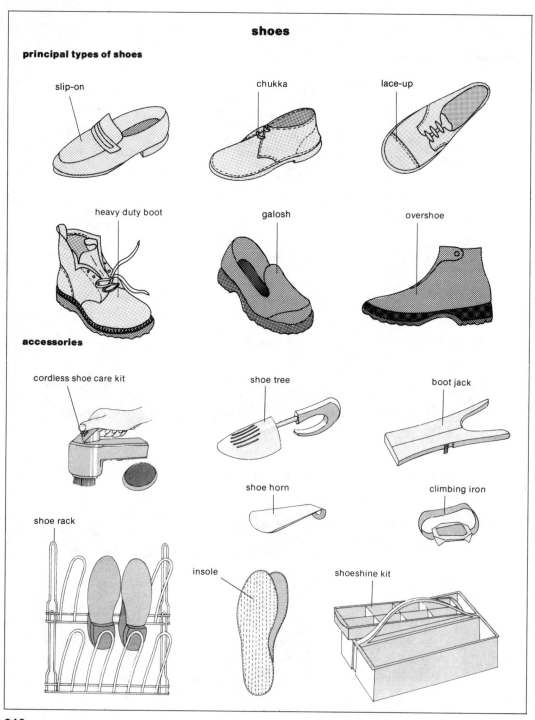

slip-on

chukka

lace-up

heavy duty boot

galosh

overshoe

accessories

cordless shoe care kit

shoe tree

boot jack

shoe horn

climbing iron

shoe rack

insole

shoeshine kit

costumes

bullfighter

shirt — montera

tie — pigtail

chaleco — epaulet

sash — torero

cairel — cape

breeches

tassel

pink stocking

slippers

ballerina

ballet shoes

tights — tutu

ribbon

drawstring — toe

sole

ballet shoes

PERSONAL ADORNMENT

jewellery

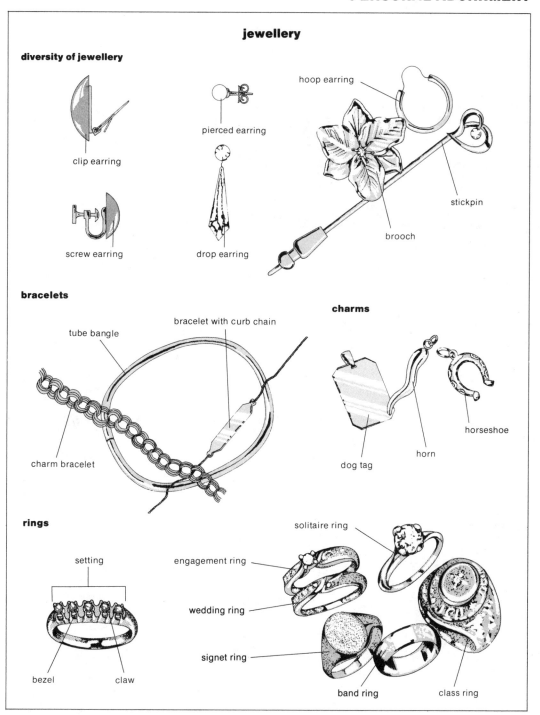

diversity of jewellery

clip earring

screw earring

pierced earring

drop earring

hoop earring

stickpin

brooch

bracelets

tube bangle

bracelet with curb chain

charm bracelet

charms

dog tag

horn

horseshoe

rings

setting

bezel

claw

engagement ring

wedding ring

signet ring

solitaire ring

band ring

class ring

jewellery

necklaces

velvet band choker

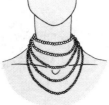

tiered necklace

choker

pendant

locket pendant

matinee length necklace
(22 in.)

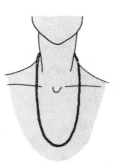

opera length necklace (30 in.)

rope (45 in.)

miscellaneous

collar bar

tie tack

tie slide

jewellery

cuts for gemstones

| brilliant full cut | eight cut | rose cut | step cut | scissors cut |

| emerald cut | table cut | cabochon cut | oval cut | baguette cut |

| French cut | pear-shaped cut | navette cut | briolette cut |

brilliant cut facets

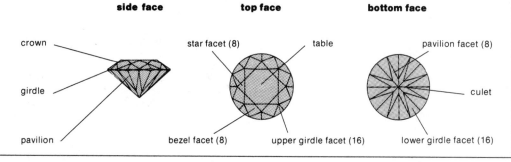

side face **top face** **bottom face**

crown
girdle
pavilion

star facet (8)
table
bezel facet (8)
upper girdle facet (16)

pavilion facet (8)
culet
lower girdle facet (16)

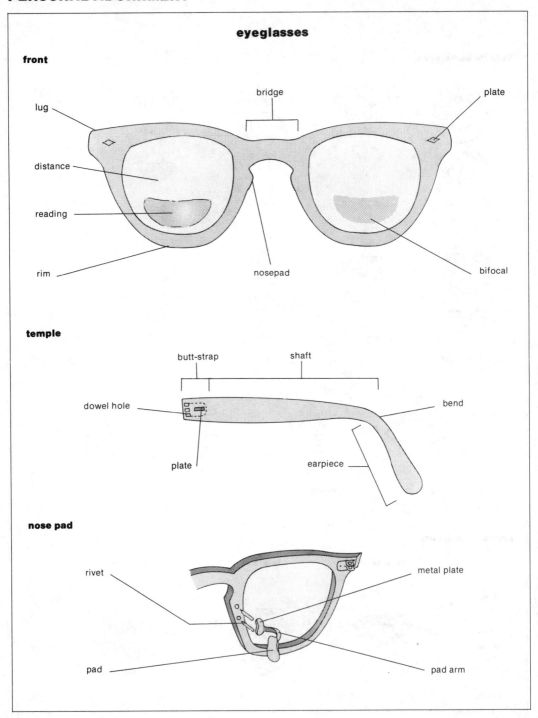

eyeglasses

front

lug

distance

reading

rim

bridge

nosepad

plate

bifocal

temple

butt-strap

shaft

dowel hole

plate

bend

earpiece

nose pad

rivet

pad

metal plate

pad arm

eyeglasses

principal types of eyeglasses

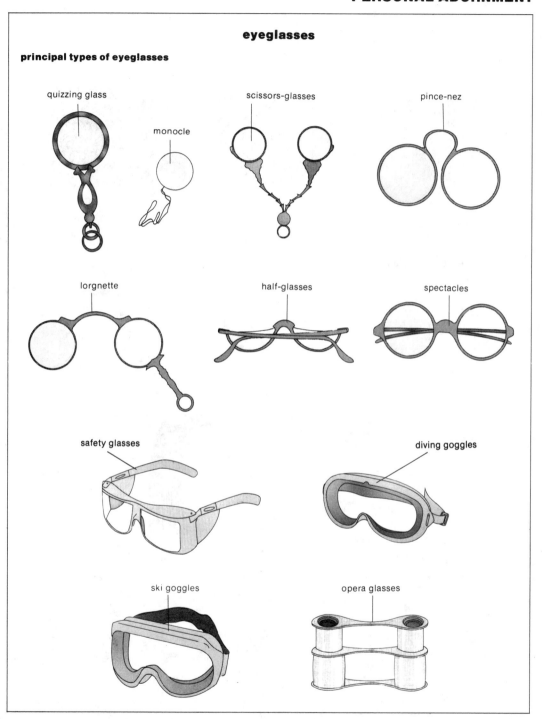

quizzing glass

monocle

scissors-glasses

pince-nez

lorgnette

half-glasses

spectacles

safety glasses

diving goggles

ski goggles

opera glasses

PERSONAL ADORNMENT

hair styles

kinds of hair

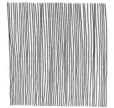

straight hair

wavy hair

curly hair

components of hair styles

bun

bouffant

page boy

ringlets

braids

plaits

pony tail

fingerwaves

hair styles

components of hair styles

shag

poodle cut

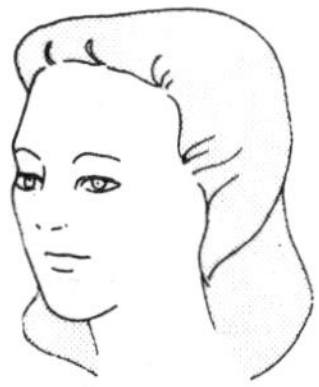

women's pompadour

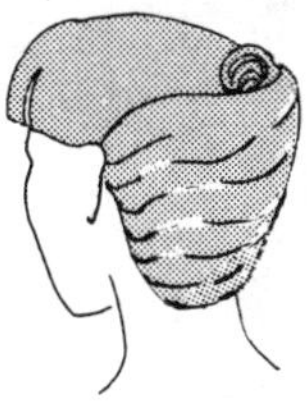

French pleat

fringe

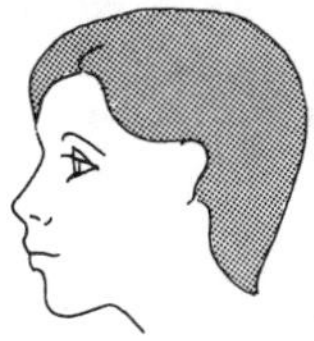

bob

crew cut

Beatle cut

men's pompadour

Afro

wigs and hairpieces

capless wig

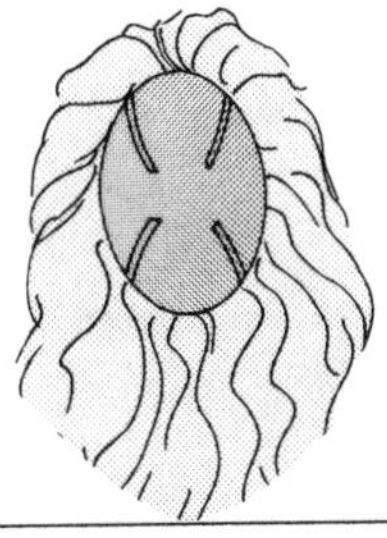

hairpieces

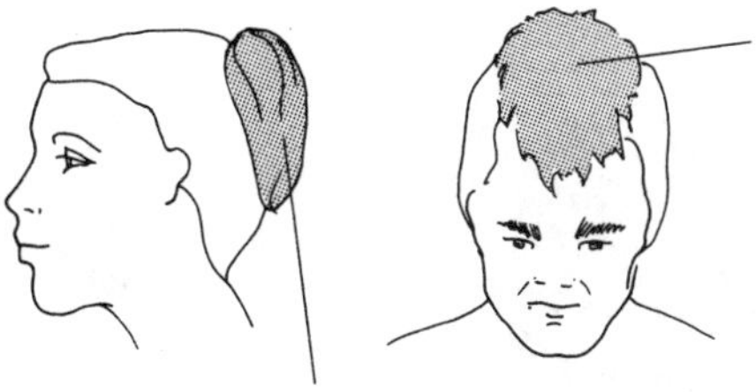

toupee

bun

make-up

make-up kit

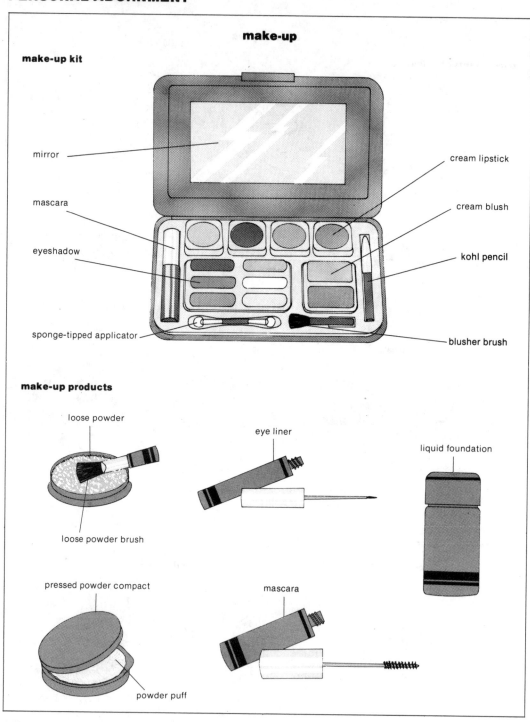

mirror

mascara

eyeshadow

sponge-tipped applicator

cream lipstick

cream blush

kohl pencil

blusher brush

make-up products

loose powder

loose powder brush

pressed powder compact

powder puff

eye liner

mascara

liquid foundation

make-up

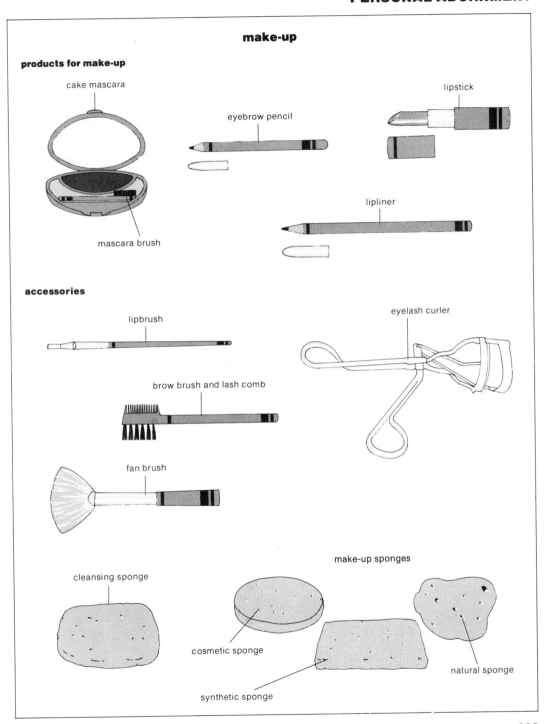

products for make-up

cake mascara

eyebrow pencil

lipstick

mascara brush

lipliner

accessories

lipbrush

eyelash curler

brow brush and lash comb

fan brush

make-up sponges

cleansing sponge

cosmetic sponge

natural sponge

synthetic sponge

PERSONAL ARTICLES

razors

electric razor

floating head

trimmer

screen

push-button release

housing

case

closeness setting

charging light

on-off switch

cleaning brush

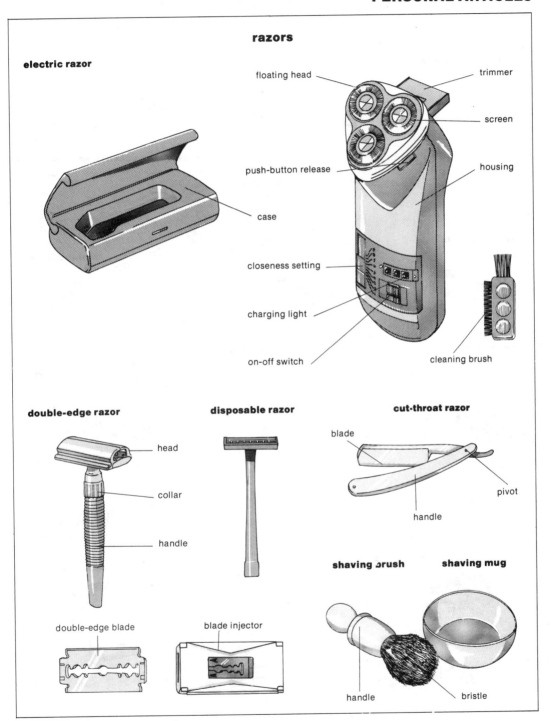

double-edge razor

head

collar

handle

double-edge blade

disposable razor

blade injector

cut-throat razor

blade

pivot

handle

shaving brush   **shaving mug**

handle

bristle

PERSONAL ARTICLES

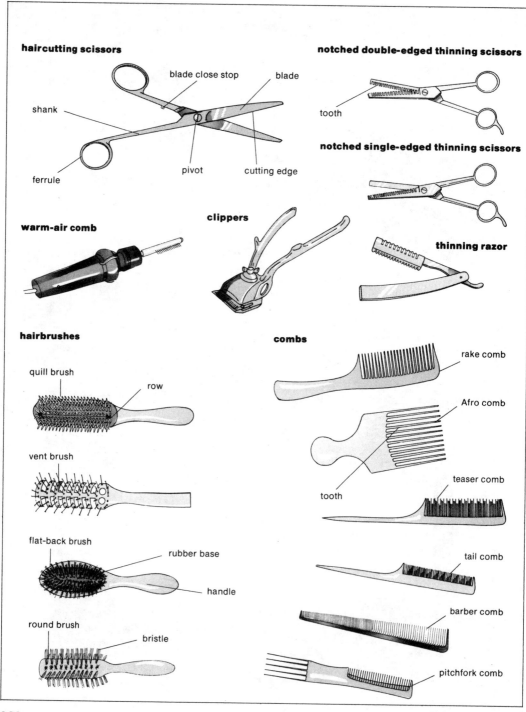

haircutting scissors

blade close stop

blade

shank

pivot

ferrule

cutting edge

notched double-edged thinning scissors

tooth

notched single-edged thinning scissors

warm-air comb

clippers

thinning razor

hairbrushes

quill brush

row

vent brush

flat-back brush

rubber base

handle

round brush

bristle

combs

rake comb

Afro comb

tooth

teaser comb

tail comb

barber comb

pitchfork comb

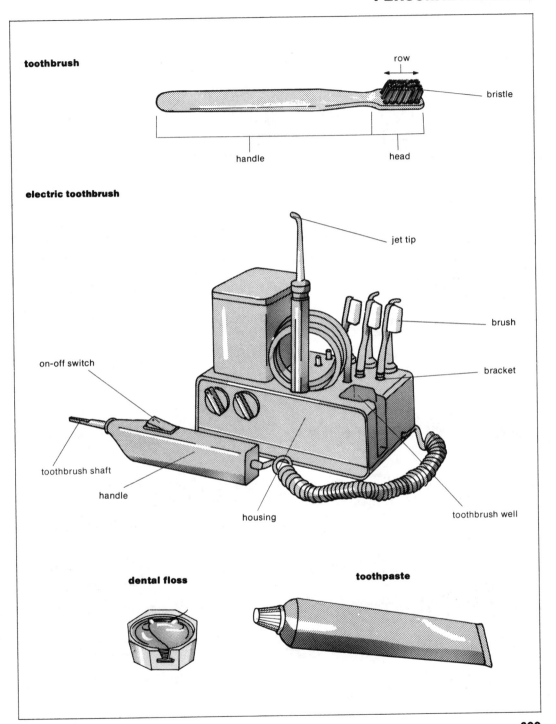

toothbrush

row

bristle

handle

head

electric toothbrush

jet tip

brush

on-off switch

bracket

toothbrush shaft

handle

housing

toothbrush well

dental floss

toothpaste

PERSONAL ARTICLES

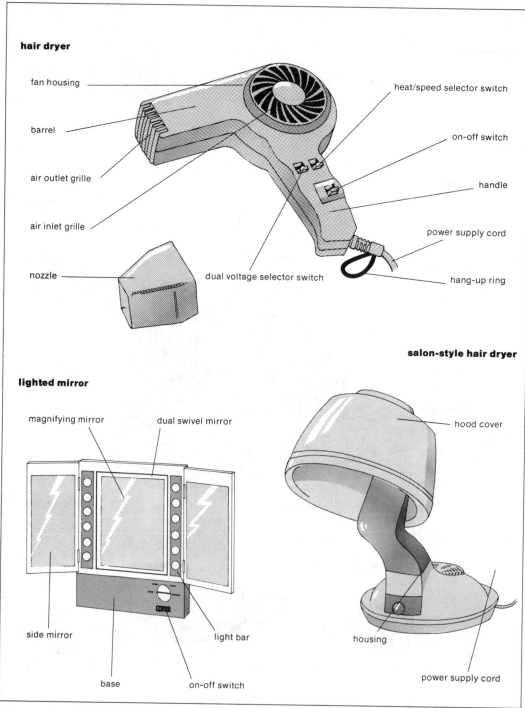

hair dryer

fan housing

barrel

air outlet grille

air inlet grille

nozzle

dual voltage selector switch

heat/speed selector switch

on-off switch

handle

power supply cord

hang-up ring

salon-style hair dryer

lighted mirror

magnifying mirror

dual swivel mirror

hood cover

side mirror

light bar

base

on-off switch

housing

power supply cord

330

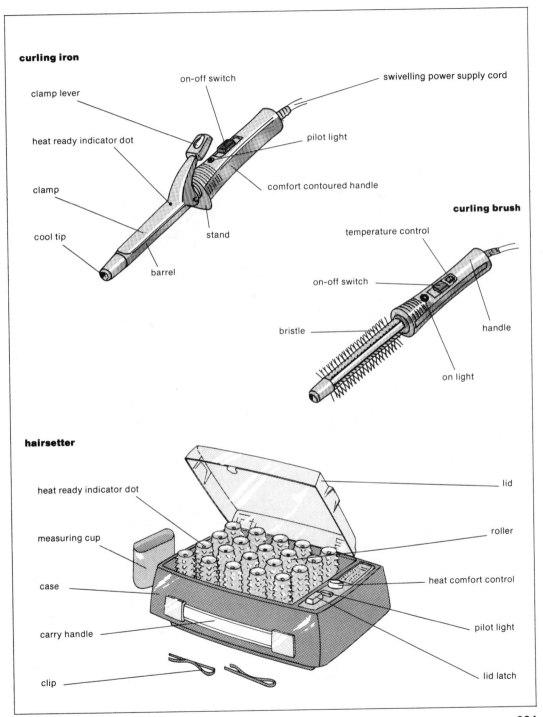

curling iron

on-off switch

swivelling power supply cord

clamp lever

heat ready indicator dot

pilot light

clamp

comfort contoured handle

curling brush

cool tip

stand

temperature control

barrel

on-off switch

bristle

handle

on light

hairsetter

heat ready indicator dot

lid

measuring cup

roller

case

heat comfort control

carry handle

pilot light

clip

lid latch

manicure set

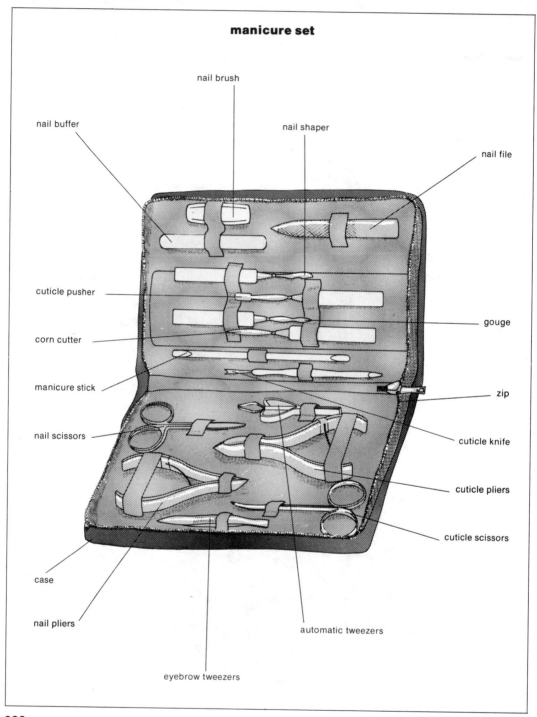

nail brush

nail buffer

nail shaper

nail file

cuticle pusher

gouge

corn cutter

manicure stick

zip

nail scissors

cuticle knife

cuticle pliers

cuticle scissors

case

nail pliers

automatic tweezers

eyebrow tweezers

manicuring instruments

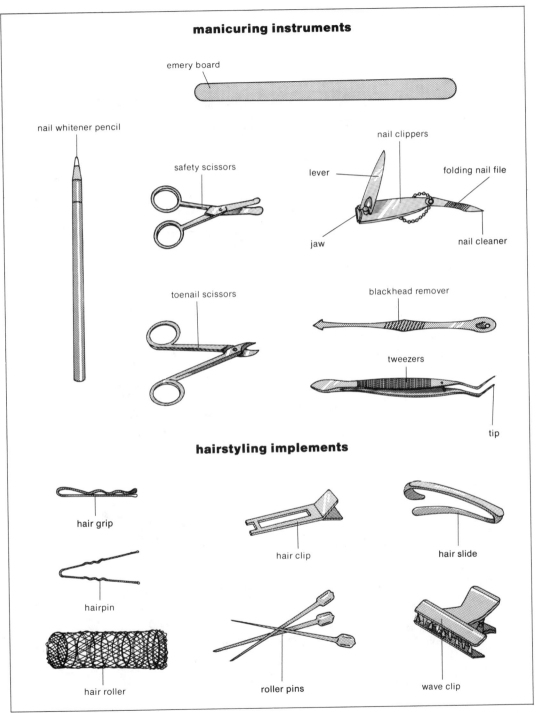

emery board

nail whitener pencil

safety scissors

nail clippers

lever

folding nail file

jaw

nail cleaner

toenail scissors

blackhead remover

tweezers

tip

hairstyling implements

hair grip

hair clip

hair slide

hairpin

hair roller

roller pins

wave clip

PERSONAL ARTICLES

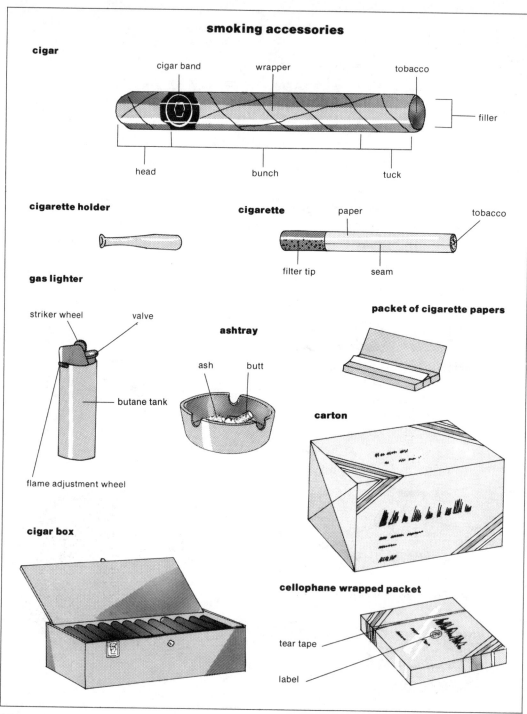

smoking accessories

cigar

cigar band

wrapper

tobacco

filler

head

bunch

tuck

cigarette holder

cigarette

paper

tobacco

filter tip

seam

gas lighter

striker wheel

valve

packet of cigarette papers

ashtray

ash

butt

butane tank

carton

flame adjustment wheel

cigar box

cellophane wrapped packet

tear tape

label

334

smoking accessories

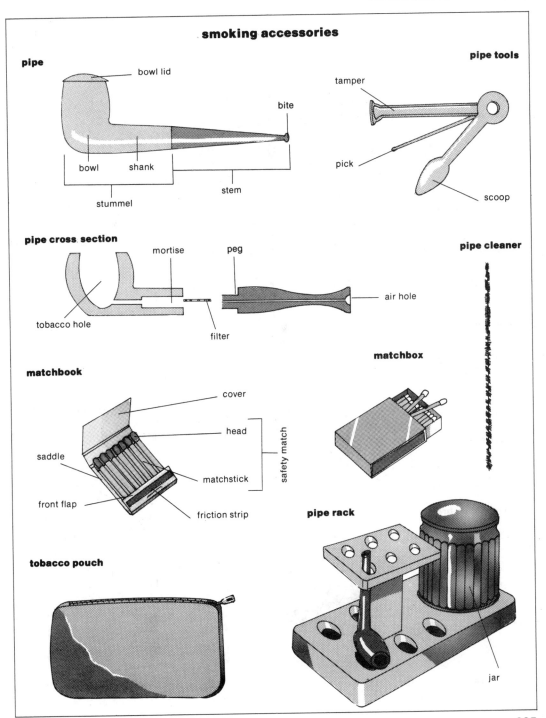

pipe

bowl lid

bite

bowl

shank

stem

stummel

pipe tools

tamper

pick

scoop

pipe cross section

mortise

peg

air hole

tobacco hole

filter

pipe cleaner

matchbook

cover

head

saddle

matchstick

safety match

front flap

friction strip

matchbox

pipe rack

tobacco pouch

jar

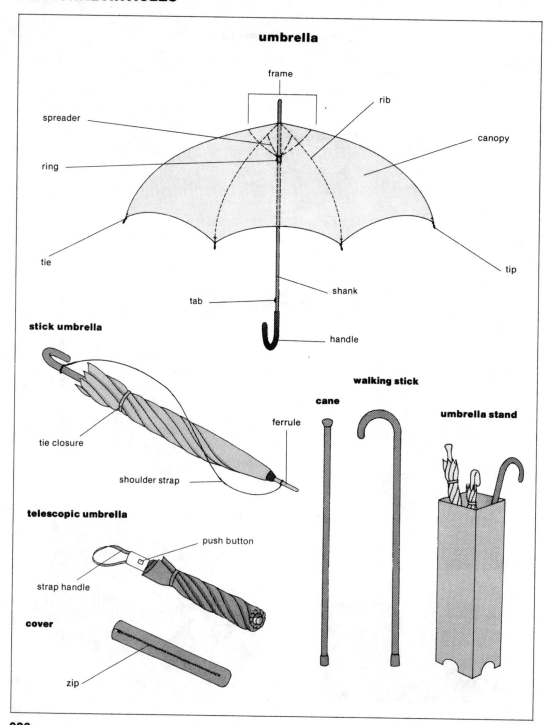

umbrella

frame

rib

spreader

canopy

ring

tie

tip

shank

tab

handle

stick umbrella

tie closure

ferrule

walking stick

cane

umbrella stand

shoulder strap

telescopic umbrella

push button

strap handle

cover

zip

336

luggage

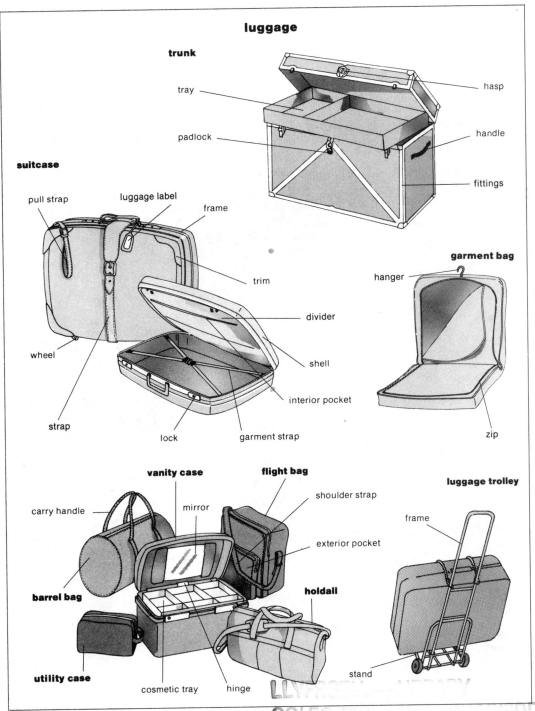

trunk

tray

hasp

padlock

handle

fittings

suitcase

pull strap

luggage label

frame

trim

divider

shell

wheel

interior pocket

strap

lock

garment strap

garment bag

hanger

zip

vanity case

flight bag

luggage trolley

carry handle

mirror

shoulder strap

frame

exterior pocket

barrel bag

holdall

utility case

cosmetic tray

hinge

stand

handbags

barrel bag

zip

clutch bag

press-stud

flapover bag

box bag

gusset

tote bag

lining

beach bag

carrier bag

shopping bag

handbags

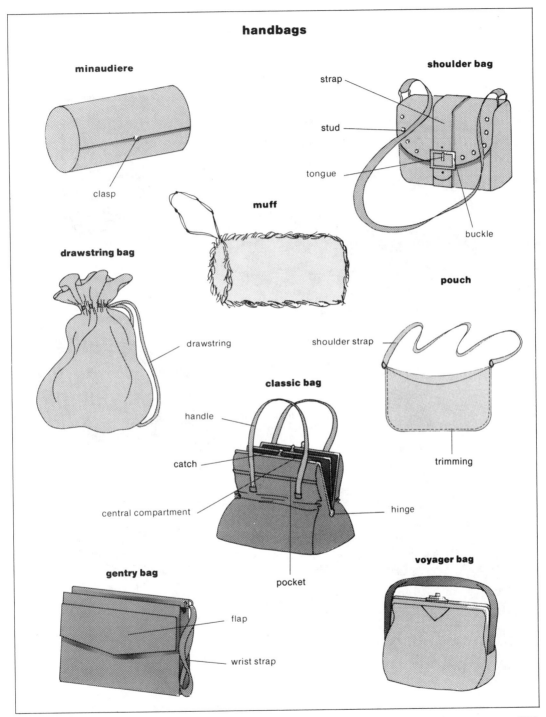

minaudiere

clasp

shoulder bag

strap

stud

tongue

buckle

muff

drawstring bag

drawstring

pouch

shoulder strap

classic bag

handle

catch

central compartment

hinge

trimming

gentry bag

flap

wrist strap

pocket

voyager bag

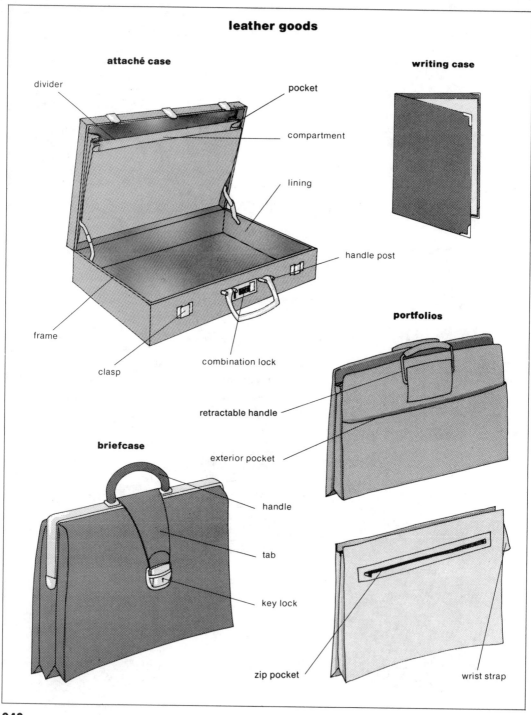

leather goods

attaché case

divider

pocket

compartment

lining

handle post

frame

combination lock

clasp

writing case

portfolios

retractable handle

exterior pocket

briefcase

handle

tab

key lock

zip pocket

wrist strap

leather goods

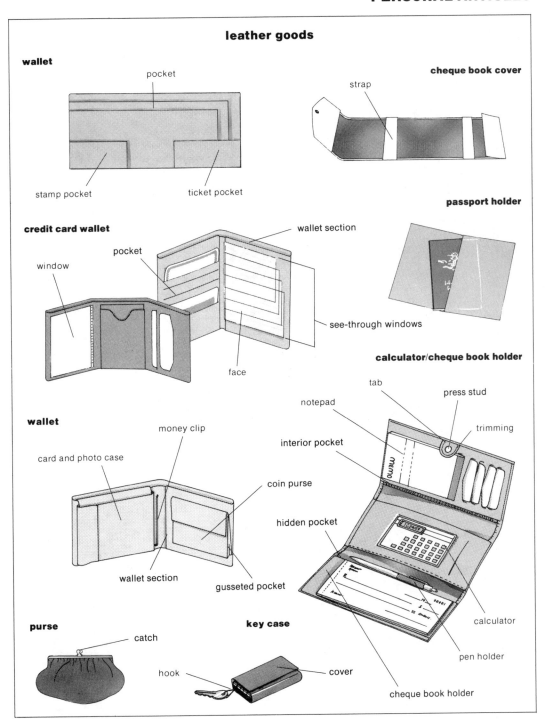

wallet

pocket

stamp pocket

ticket pocket

cheque book cover

strap

passport holder

credit card wallet

wallet section

pocket

window

see-through windows

face

calculator/cheque book holder

tab

press stud

notepad

trimming

interior pocket

wallet

money clip

card and photo case

coin purse

hidden pocket

wallet section

gusseted pocket

calculator

pen holder

cheque book holder

purse

catch

key case

hook

cover

COMMUNICATIONS

writing styles of the world

Merry Christmas
Happy New Year

Olde English

Joyeux Noël
Bonne année

French

クリスマス
おめでとう

初光り

Japanese

God
Jul
Godt
Nytt Ar

Norwegian

Vrolijk Kerstfeest
en een
Gelukkig Nieuwjaar

Dutch

Feliz
Navidad
Próspero
Año Nuevo

Spanish

C Рождеством
С новым годом

Russian

חג שמח
שנה טובה

Hebrew

عید شما مبارک
کریسمس مبارک

Iranian

BUON
NATALE
FELICE
ANNO NUOVO

Italian

Glædelig Jul
og
Godt Nytaar

Danish

Hyvaa Joulua Ja
Onnellista
Uutta Vuotta

Finnish

ΚΑΛΑ ΧΡΙΣΤΟΥΓΕΝΝΑ
ΚΑΙ ΕΥΤΥΧΙΣΜΕΝΟΣ Ο
ΚΑΙΝΟΥΡΓΙΟΣ ΧΡΟΝΟΣ

Greek

CHÚC MỪNG GIÁNG SINH
CONG CHÚC TÂN XUÂN

Vietnamese

God Jul
och
Gott Nytt
År

Swedish

عام سعيد
وكل عام وانتم بخير

Arabic

नव वर्ष की शुभकामनाऐं

Hindi

Շնորհավոր Սուրբ
Ծնունդ և Նոր տարի

Armenian

SĂRBĂTORI FERICITE
ŞI
LA MULŢI ANI

Romanian

ХРИСТОС
РОДИВСЯ
ШАСЛИВОГО
НОВОГО РОКУ

Ukrainian

FELIZ NATAL.
PROSPERO ANO NOVO

Portuguese

Fröhliche Weihnachten
und alles Gute
zum Neuen Jahr

German

සුබ නත්තලක් වේවා
සුබ අලුත් අවුරුද්දක් වේවා

Sinhalese

Wesołych Świąt
i
Szczęśliwego
Nowego Roku

Polish

聖誕快樂
新年愉快

Chinese

Nadolig Llawen
Blwyddyn Newydd
Dda

Welsh

KELLEMES KARÁCSONYI
ÜNNEPEKE
BOLDOG ÚJÉVET

Hungarian

ᖃᓄᐃᑦᑐᖅ ᖃᓄᐃᑦᑐᖅ
ᖃᓄᐃᑦᑐᖅ ᒥᑦᑐᖅ ᐅᑉᐊᒃ

Inuktitut

COMMUNICATIONS

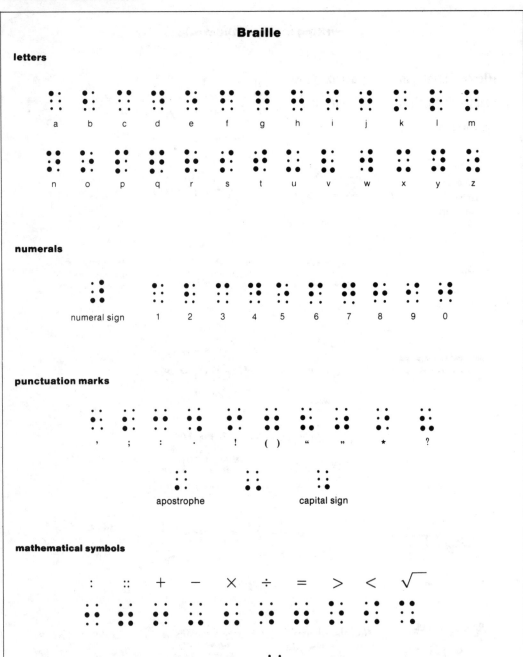

Braille

letters

a b c d e f g h i j k l m

n o p q r s t u v w x y z

numerals

numeral sign 1 2 3 4 5 6 7 8 9 0

punctuation marks

, ; : . ! ( ) " " ★ ?

apostrophe   capital sign

mathematical symbols

: :: + − × ÷ = > < √

maths symbol sign

deaf-mute alphabet

letters

a b c d e f g h i

j k l m n o p q r

s t u v w x y z

numbers

1 2 3 4 5 6 7 8 9 10

punctuation marks

. **full stop**

? **question mark**

! **exclamation mark**

, **comma**

; **semicolon**

: **colon**

... **ellipsis**

( ) **parentheses**

[ ] **brackets**

* **asterisk**

— **dash**

/ **slash**

" " **quotation marks**

' ' **single quotation marks**

diacritic symbols

é **acute accent**

à **grave accent**

â **circumflex accent**

ç **cedilla**

s' **apostrophe**

ä **umlaut**

- **hyphen**

international phonetic alphabet

signs	English	signs	English
vowels		**fricative consonants**	
[æ]	bad	[f]	life
[a:]	father	[v]	live
[i:]	see	[θ]	thin
[ı]	it	[ð]	then
[ɛ]	get	[h]	hot
[ɒ]	hot	[s]	pass
[ɔ:]	saw	[z]	zoo
[ʊ]	push	[ʒ]	rouge
[u:]	zoo	[ʃ]	she
[ʌ]	up	**liquid consonants**	
[ɜ:]	bird	[l]	real
[ə]	driver	[r]	rue
glides		[m]	him
[j]	you	[n]	in
[w]	we	[ŋ]	rang
diphthongs		**stop consonants**	
[aı]	try	[p]	mop
[aʊ]	now	[b]	bat
[eı]	may	[d]	do
[ɛə]	dare	[t]	too
[ıə]	here	[k]	lake
[əʊ]	no	[g]	bag
[ɔı]	boy	**affricate consonants**	
[ʊə]	cure	[ʧ]	chin
		[dʒ]	joke

typical letter

British model

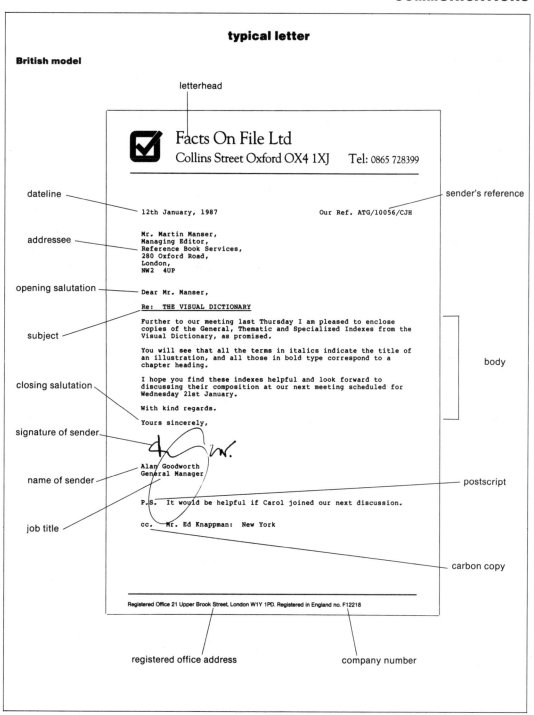

letterhead

Facts On File Ltd
Collins Street Oxford OX4 1XJ   Tel: 0865 728399

dateline

12th January, 1987   Our Ref. ATG/10056/CJH

sender's reference

addressee

Mr. Martin Manser,
Managing Editor,
Reference Book Services,
280 Oxford Road,
London,
NW2 4UP

opening salutation — Dear Mr. Manser,

subject — Re: THE VISUAL DICTIONARY

Further to our meeting last Thursday I am pleased to enclose
copies of the General, Thematic and Specialized Indexes from the
Visual Dictionary, as promised.

You will see that all the terms in italics indicate the title of
an illustration, and all those in bold type correspond to a
chapter heading.

body

I hope you find these indexes helpful and look forward to
discussing their composition at our next meeting scheduled for
Wednesday 21st January.

With kind regards.

closing salutation — Yours sincerely,

signature of sender

name of sender — Alan Goodworth
General Manager

postscript

P.S. It would be helpful if Carol joined our next discussion.

job title

cc. Mr. Ed Knappman: New York

carbon copy

Registered Office 21 Upper Brook Street, London W1Y 1PD. Registered in England no. F12218

registered office address   company number

COMMUNICATIONS

proofreading

corrections of errors

align vertically	‖	take back to previous line	*move up*⌉
align horizontal	=	let it stand	(stet)
begin a new paragraph	⌐_	move to left	⎮←⌐⌐
centre	[ ]	move to right	⌐→⎮
correct a letter	*a/*	something omitted	(see copy)
correct a word	heel /	reduce space	↑
insert space	Y	delete	ℯ
run on	heel. The doctor	transpose two words	⌐order⌐ the
insert here	*h*	transpose lines	⊃
close up	⌣	transpose two letters	�
take over to next line	⌐break		

corrections of punctuation marks

full stop	⊙
comma	⌃
apostrophe	⌄
colon	⊙
semicolon	;/
hyphen	⊢–⊣
quotation marks	⌄ / ⌄
parentheses	(/)

corrections of diacritic symbols

superscript	⌄ e^2
subscript	⌃ H_2O

corrections of type

set in lowercase	≠ *lc*	set in italic	—
set in capitals	≡	set in roman	4/
set in small capitals	=	set in boldface	⌇⌇⌇

proofreading

indication of types

italic	bible	*bible*
bold	bible	**bible**
small capitals	bible	BIBLE
capitals	bible	BIBLE
italic capitals	bible	*BIBLE*
bold capitals	bible	**BIBLE**
ital. bold	bible	***bible***
capitals for initials small capitals for the rest	HENRY MILLER	HENRY MILLER

1.1 – The phoneme. It is important to keep in mind that the sounds of human language are more that just sounds. The p of pin is exploded with a puff of air following it, whereas the p of capture is not; those sound are quite different as mere sounds. But english we say they are the same, and they are, because they function as the same unit in the sound system of English.

The functioning units like English /p/ are called phonemes by structural linguists and usually be enclosed in slant bars in the text.

Robert Lado

from Linguistics across cultures

COMMUNICATIONS

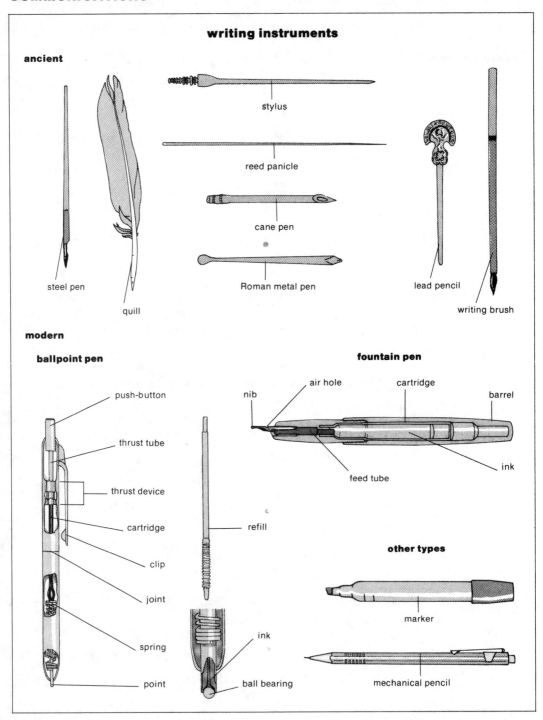

writing instruments

ancient

stylus

reed panicle

cane pen

Roman metal pen

steel pen

quill

lead pencil

writing brush

modern

ballpoint pen

push-button

thrust tube

thrust device

cartridge

clip

joint

spring

point

refill

ink

ball bearing

fountain pen

nib

air hole

cartridge

barrel

feed tube

ink

other types

marker

mechanical pencil

photography

single-lens reflex camera

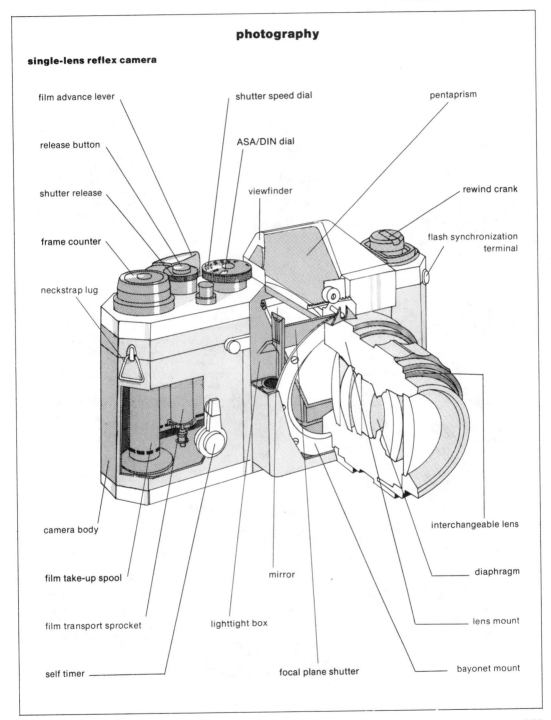

film advance lever

release button

shutter release

frame counter

neckstrap lug

shutter speed dial

ASA/DIN dial

viewfinder

pentaprism

rewind crank

flash synchronization terminal

camera body

film take-up spool

film transport sprocket

self timer

mirror

lighttight box

focal plane shutter

interchangeable lens

diaphragm

lens mount

bayonet mount

353

photography

still cameras

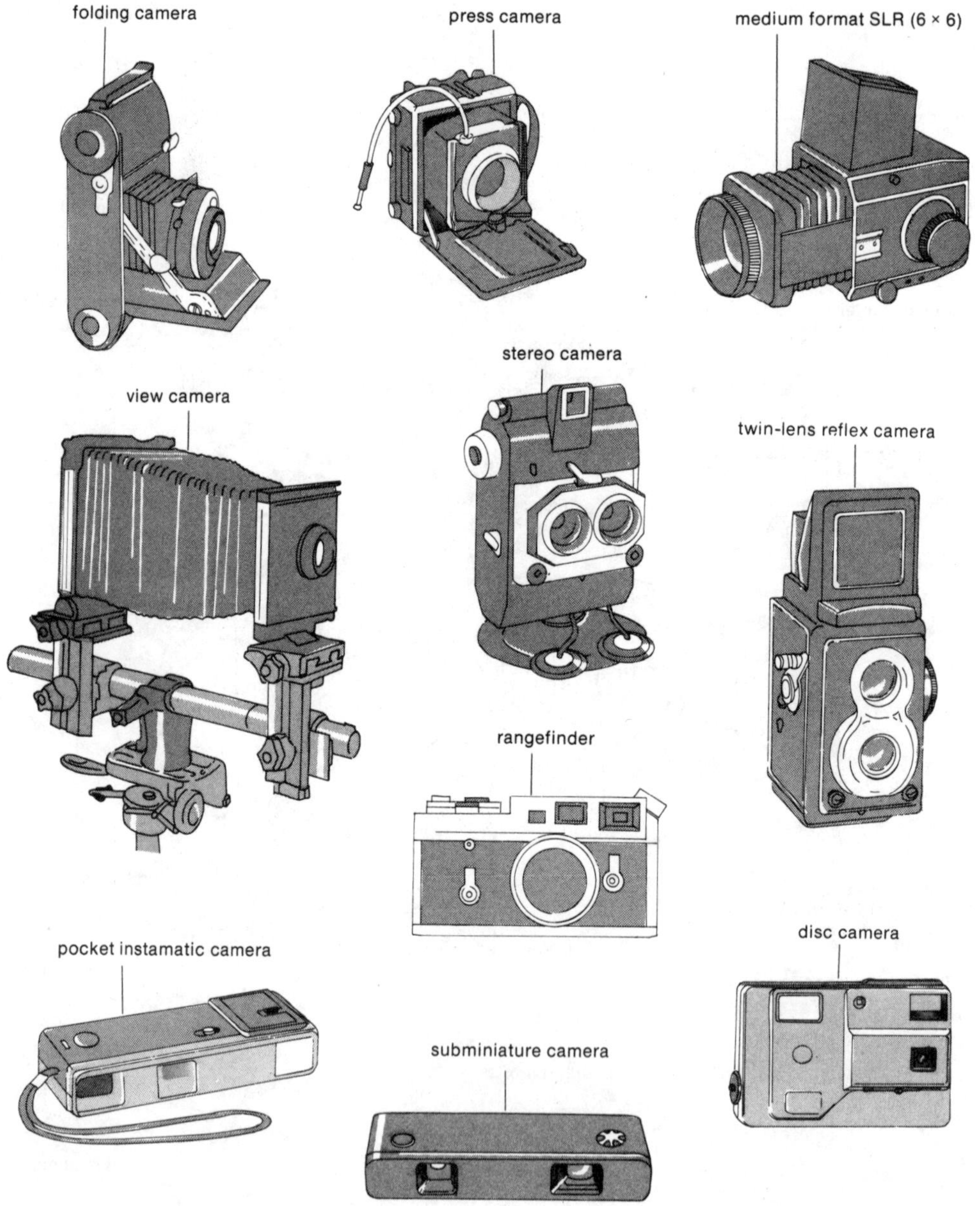

folding camera

press camera

medium format SLR (6 × 6)

view camera

stereo camera

twin-lens reflex camera

rangefinder

pocket instamatic camera

disc camera

subminiature camera

photography

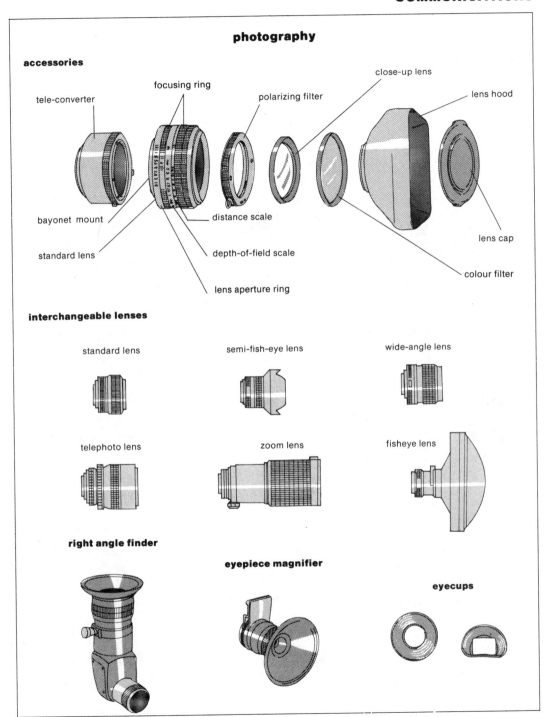

accessories

tele-converter

focusing ring

polarizing filter

close-up lens

lens hood

bayonet mount

distance scale

standard lens

depth-of-field scale

lens aperture ring

lens cap

colour filter

interchangeable lenses

standard lens

semi-fish-eye lens

wide-angle lens

telephoto lens

zoom lens

fisheye lens

right angle finder

eyepiece magnifier

eyecups

photography

Polaroid Land camera

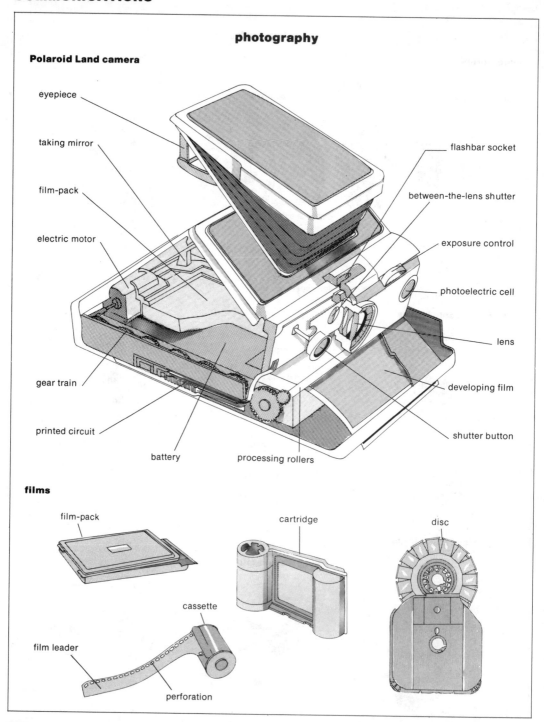

eyepiece

taking mirror

film-pack

electric motor

flashbar socket

between-the-lens shutter

exposure control

photoelectric cell

lens

gear train

developing film

printed circuit

shutter button

battery

processing rollers

films

film-pack

cartridge

disc

cassette

film leader

perforation

photography

flash unit

electronic flash

flash outlet

lens

flash sensor

calculator

fastening screw

hot shoe

flash bracket

wide angle adapter

synchro cord

flash lamp

magnesium wire

glass bulb

lead-in wire

base of lamp

battery

flashcube

exposure meter

incident-light measuring diffuser

exposure-time scale

indicator needle

light-reading scale

aperture scale

cine scale

transfer scale

exposure value

calculator dial

ASA/DIN exposure index

spotmeter

exposure value scale

objective lens

eyepiece

switch

grip

photography

studio lighting

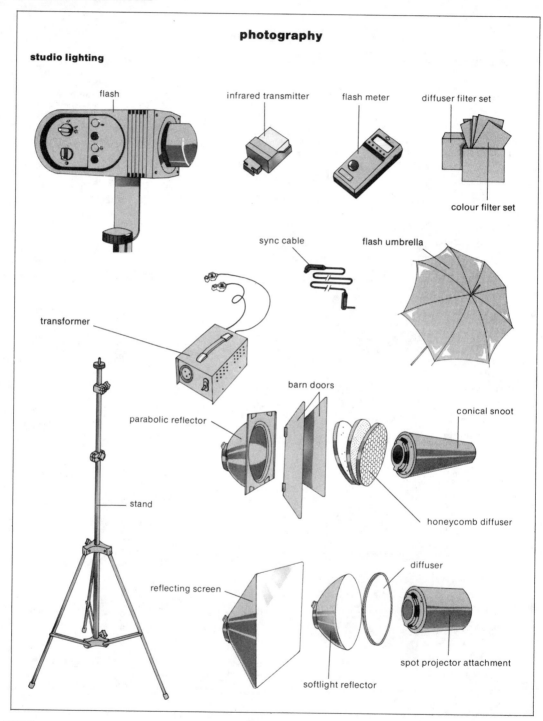

flash

infrared transmitter

flash meter

diffuser filter set

colour filter set

sync cable

flash umbrella

transformer

barn doors

conical snoot

parabolic reflector

stand

honeycomb diffuser

diffuser

reflecting screen

spot projector attachment

softlight reflector

photography

photographic accessories

air shutter release

cable release

tripod

- side-tilt lock
- camera screw
- camera platform
- pan handle
- telescoping leg
- panoramic and tilting head
- column lock
- column crank
- column
- collet

lower pan-head mounting screw

studio accessories

- boom arm
- stand
- reflector
- background

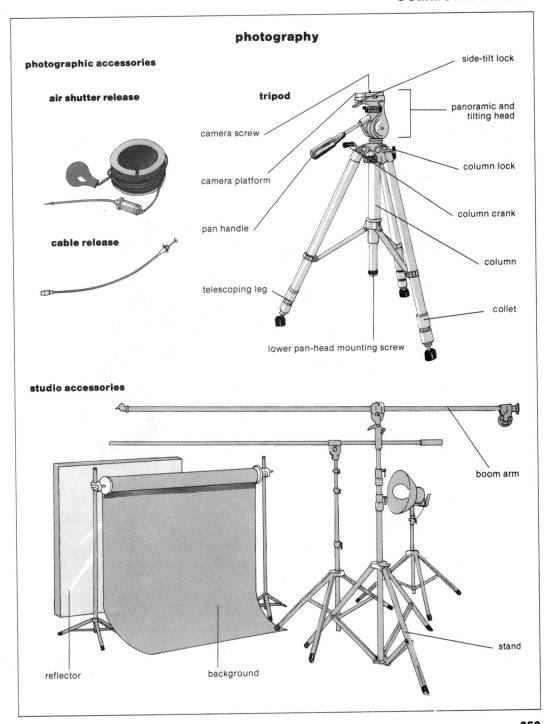

photography

darkroom

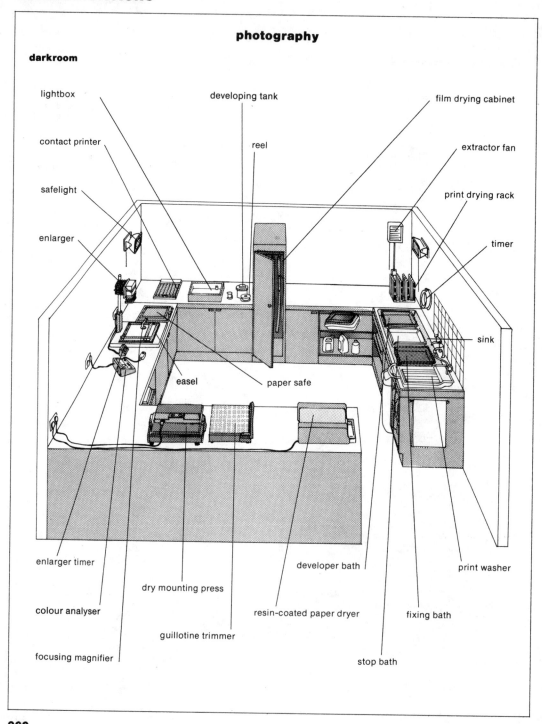

lightbox

developing tank

film drying cabinet

contact printer

reel

extractor fan

safelight

print drying rack

enlarger

timer

sink

easel

paper safe

enlarger timer

developer bath

print washer

colour analyser

dry mounting press

fixing bath

resin-coated paper dryer

guillotine trimmer

focusing magnifier

stop bath

photography

enlarger

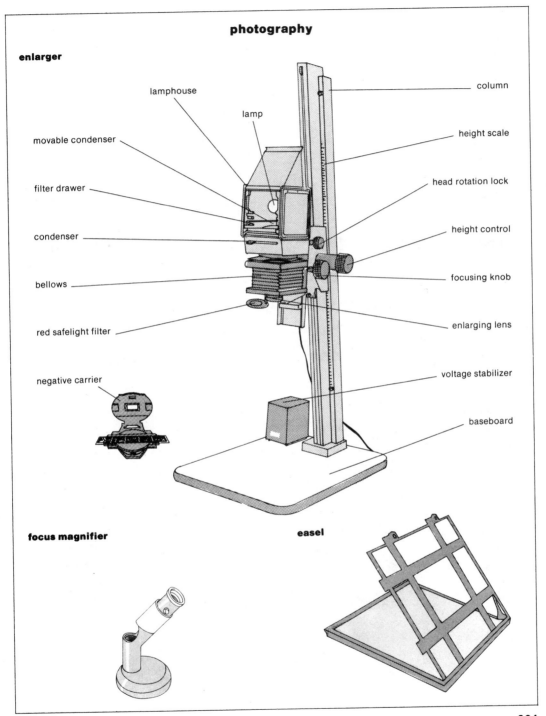

lamphouse

lamp

column

movable condenser

height scale

filter drawer

head rotation lock

condenser

height control

bellows

focusing knob

red safelight filter

enlarging lens

negative carrier

voltage stabilizer

baseboard

focus magnifier

easel

COMMUNICATIONS

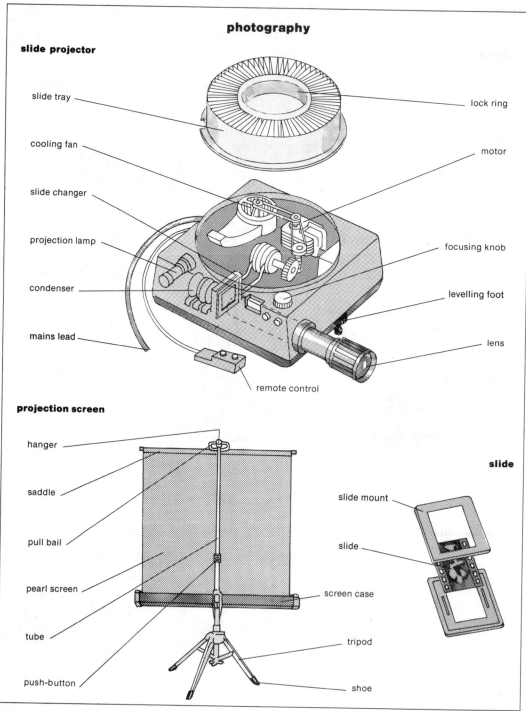

photography

slide projector

- slide tray
- cooling fan
- slide changer
- projection lamp
- condenser
- mains lead
- lock ring
- motor
- focusing knob
- levelling foot
- lens
- remote control

projection screen

- hanger
- saddle
- pull bail
- pearl screen
- tube
- push-button
- screen case
- tripod
- shoe

slide

- slide mount
- slide

362

sound reproducing system

system elements

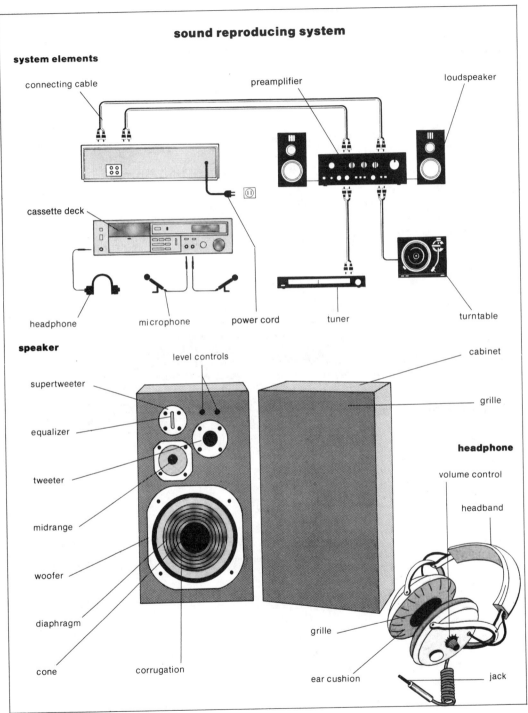

connecting cable

preamplifier

loudspeaker

cassette deck

headphone

microphone

power cord

tuner

turntable

speaker

level controls

cabinet

supertweeter

grille

equalizer

tweeter

headphone

volume control

headband

midrange

woofer

diaphragm

grille

cone

corrugation

ear cushion

jack

COMMUNICATIONS

sound reproducing system

amplifier-tuner

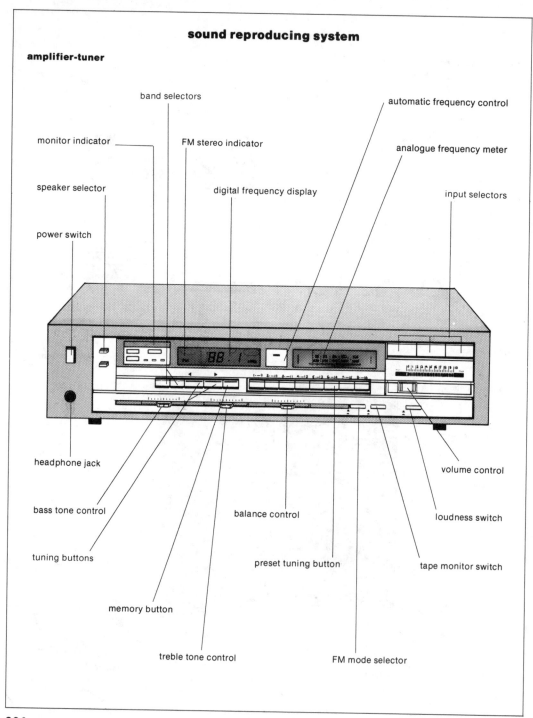

band selectors

automatic frequency control

monitor indicator

FM stereo indicator

analogue frequency meter

speaker selector

digital frequency display

input selectors

power switch

headphone jack

volume control

bass tone control

balance control

loudness switch

tuning buttons

preset tuning button

tape monitor switch

memory button

treble tone control

FM mode selector

sound reproducing system

turntable

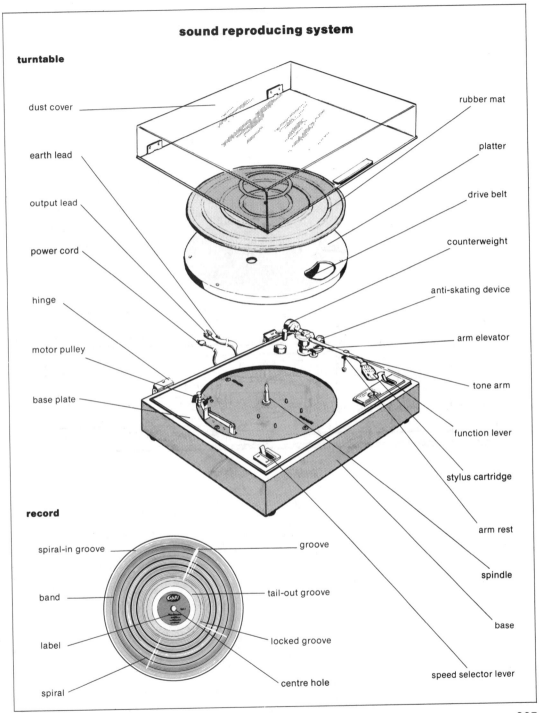

dust cover

earth lead

output lead

power cord

hinge

motor pulley

base plate

rubber mat

platter

drive belt

counterweight

anti-skating device

arm elevator

tone arm

function lever

stylus cartridge

arm rest

spindle

base

speed selector lever

record

spiral-in groove

band

label

spiral

groove

tail-out groove

locked groove

centre hole

sound reproducing system

tape deck

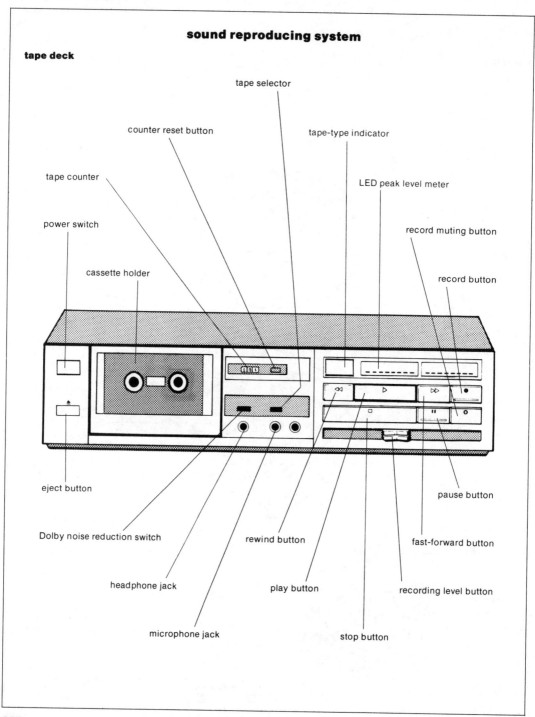

tape selector

counter reset button

tape-type indicator

tape counter

LED peak level meter

power switch

record muting button

cassette holder

record button

eject button

pause button

Dolby noise reduction switch

rewind button

fast-forward button

headphone jack

play button

recording level button

microphone jack

stop button

video tape recorder

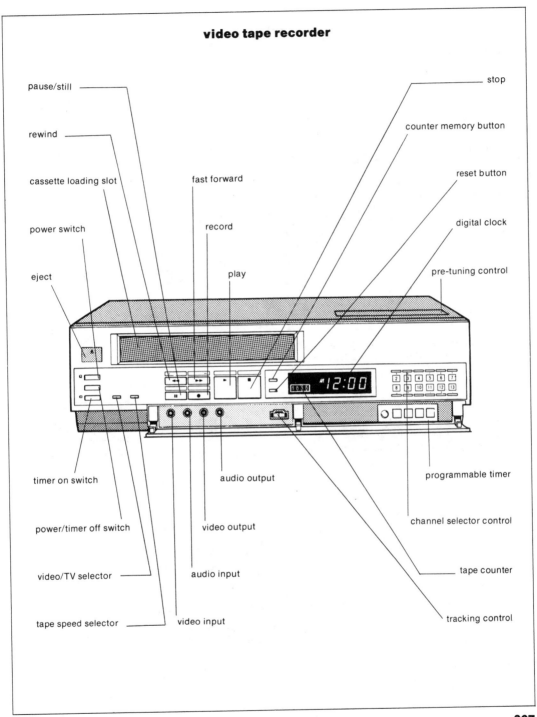

pause/still

stop

rewind

counter memory button

cassette loading slot

fast forward

reset button

power switch

record

digital clock

eject

play

pre-tuning control

timer on switch

audio output

programmable timer

power/timer off switch

video output

channel selector control

video/TV selector

audio input

tape counter

tape speed selector

video input

tracking control

cinematography

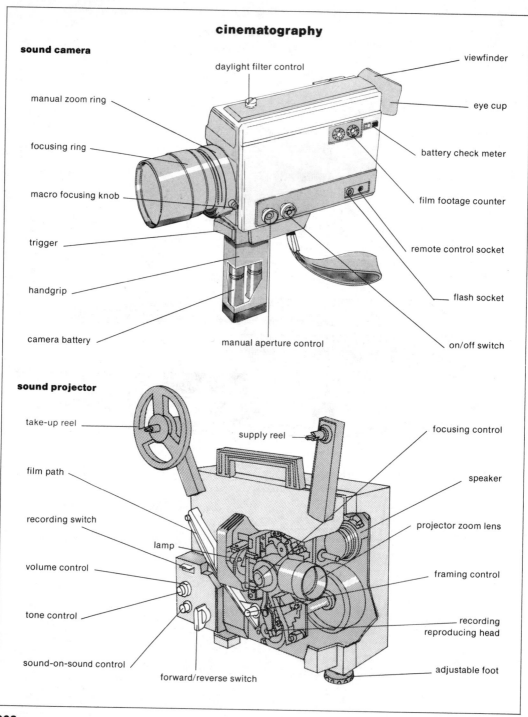

sound camera

- daylight filter control
- viewfinder
- eye cup
- manual zoom ring
- focusing ring
- battery check meter
- macro focusing knob
- film footage counter
- trigger
- remote control socket
- handgrip
- flash socket
- camera battery
- manual aperture control
- on/off switch

sound projector

- take-up reel
- supply reel
- focusing control
- film path
- speaker
- recording switch
- lamp
- projector zoom lens
- volume control
- framing control
- tone control
- recording reproducing head
- sound-on-sound control
- forward/reverse switch
- adjustable foot

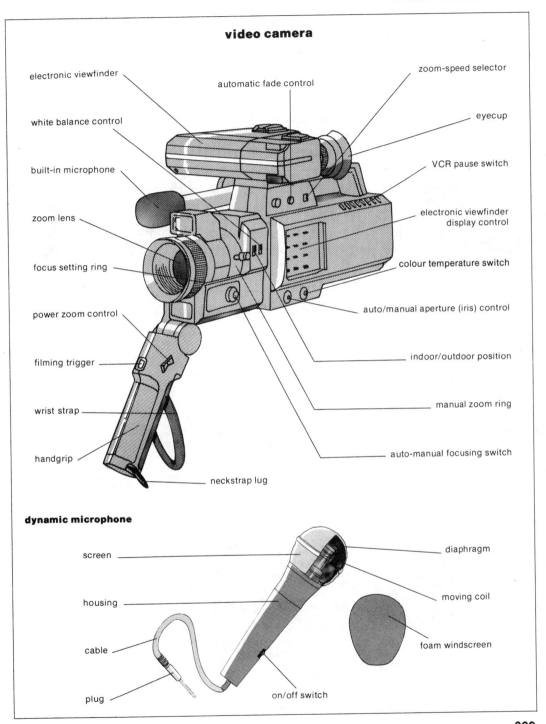

video camera

electronic viewfinder

automatic fade control

zoom-speed selector

white balance control

eyecup

built-in microphone

VCR pause switch

zoom lens

electronic viewfinder display control

focus setting ring

colour temperature switch

power zoom control

auto/manual aperture (iris) control

filming trigger

indoor/outdoor position

wrist strap

manual zoom ring

handgrip

auto-manual focusing switch

neckstrap lug

dynamic microphone

screen

diaphragm

housing

moving coil

cable

foam windscreen

plug

on/off switch

369

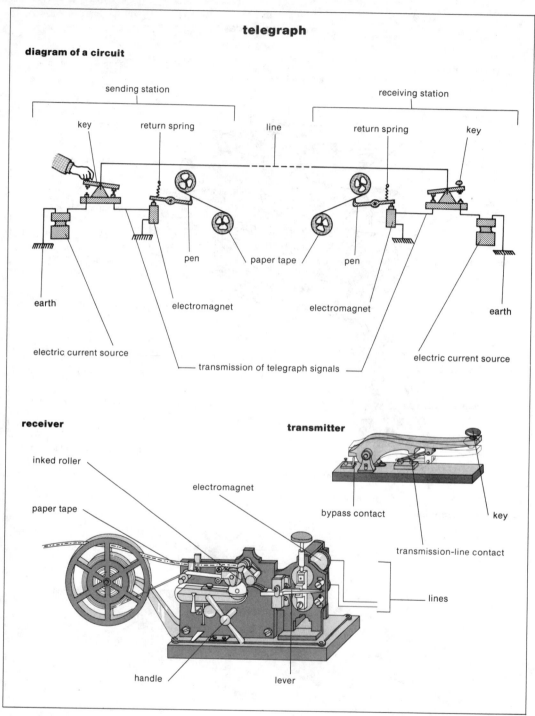

telegraph

diagram of a circuit

sending station

receiving station

key

return spring

line

return spring

key

pen

paper tape

pen

earth

electromagnet

electromagnet

earth

electric current source

transmission of telegraph signals

electric current source

receiver

transmitter

inked roller

electromagnet

paper tape

bypass contact

key

transmission-line contact

lines

handle

lever

telegraph

Morse code

alphabet

A	• ▬
B	▬ • • •
C	▬ • ▬ •
D	▬ • •
E	•
F	• • ▬ •
G	▬ ▬ •
H	• • • •
I	• •
J	• ▬ ▬ ▬
K	▬ • ▬
L	• ▬ • •
M	▬ ▬
N	▬ •
O	▬ ▬ ▬
P	• ▬ ▬ •
Q	▬ ▬ • ▬
R	• ▬ •
S	• • •
T	▬
U	• • ▬

V	• • • ▬
W	• ▬ ▬
X	▬ • • ▬
Y	▬ • ▬ ▬
Z	▬ ▬ • •

numerals

1	• ▬ ▬ ▬ ▬
2	• • ▬ ▬ ▬
3	• • • ▬ ▬
4	• • • • ▬
5	• • • • •
6	▬ • • • •
7	▬ ▬ • • •
8	▬ ▬ ▬ • •
9	▬ ▬ ▬ ▬ •
0	▬ ▬ ▬ ▬ ▬

punctuation

full stop (.)	• ▬ • ▬ • ▬
comma (,)	▬ ▬ • • ▬ ▬
question mark (?)	• • ▬ ▬ • •
colon (:)	▬ ▬ ▬ • • •
semicolon (;)	▬ • ▬ • ▬ •
hyphen (-)	▬ • • • • ▬
slash (/)	▬ • • ▬ •
quotation marks (")	• ▬ • • ▬ •
dash	▬
dot	•

telex: teleprinter

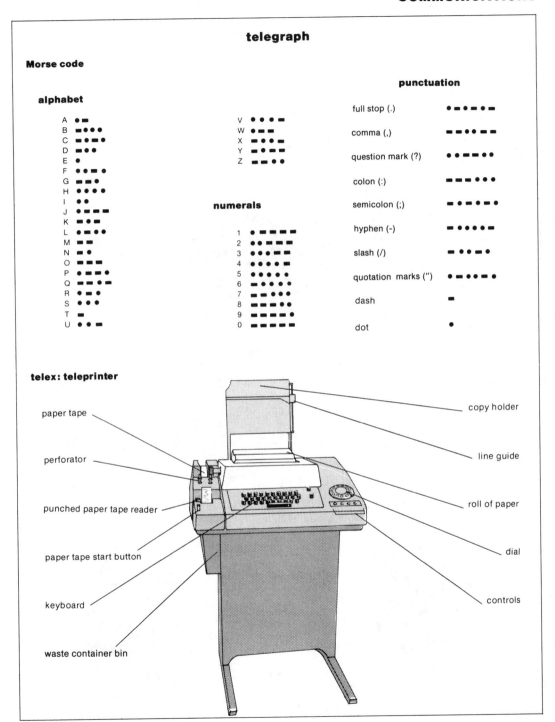

paper tape

perforator

punched paper tape reader

paper tape start button

keyboard

waste container bin

copy holder

line guide

roll of paper

dial

controls

telephone set

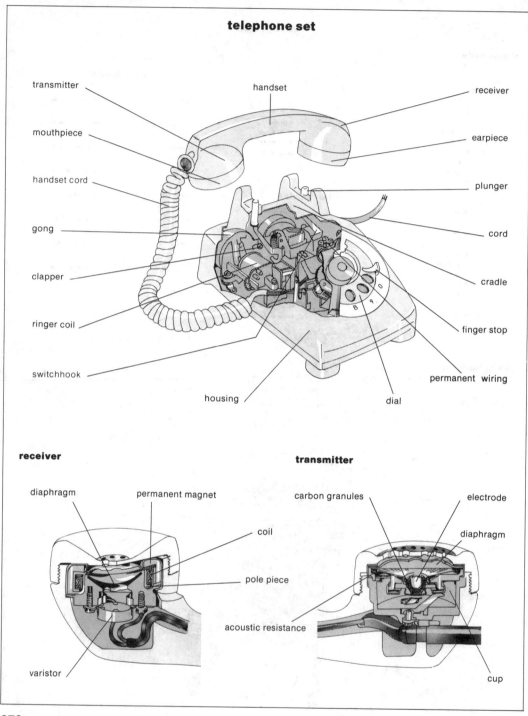

transmitter

handset

receiver

mouthpiece

earpiece

handset cord

plunger

gong

cord

clapper

cradle

ringer coil

finger stop

switchhook

permanent wiring

housing

dial

receiver

diaphragm

permanent magnet

coil

pole piece

acoustic resistance

varistor

transmitter

carbon granules

electrode

diaphragm

cup

types of telephones

facility telephone system

coinbox telephone

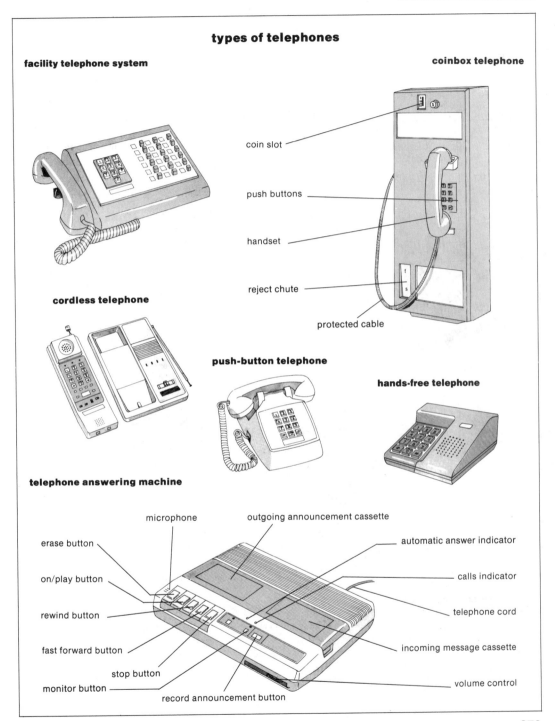

coin slot

push buttons

handset

reject chute

protected cable

cordless telephone

push-button telephone

hands-free telephone

telephone answering machine

microphone

outgoing announcement cassette

erase button

automatic answer indicator

on/play button

calls indicator

rewind button

telephone cord

fast forward button

incoming message cassette

stop button

monitor button

volume control

record announcement button

television

studio and control rooms

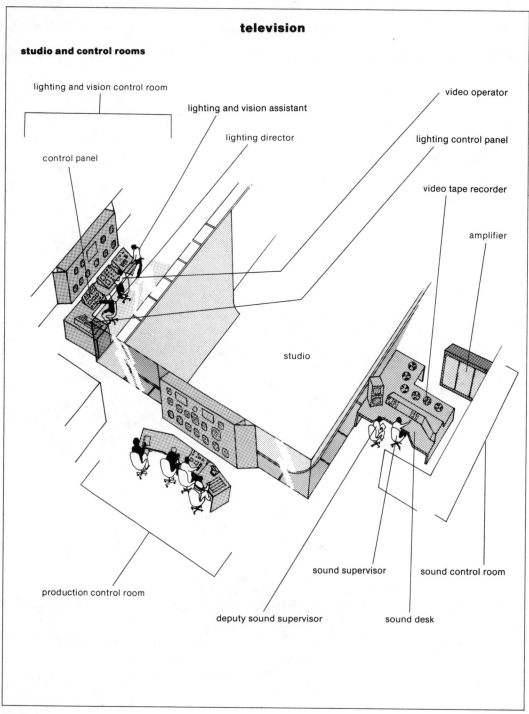

lighting and vision control room

lighting and vision assistant

lighting director

control panel

video operator

lighting control panel

video tape recorder

amplifier

studio

sound supervisor

sound control room

production control room

deputy sound supervisor

sound desk

television

studio floor

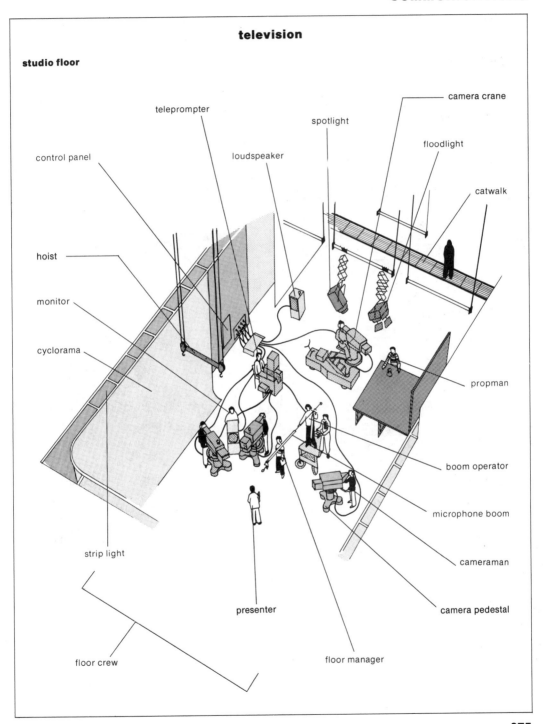

camera crane

teleprompter

spotlight

floodlight

control panel

loudspeaker

catwalk

hoist

monitor

cyclorama

propman

boom operator

microphone boom

strip light

cameraman

camera pedestal

presenter

floor crew

floor manager

television

production control room

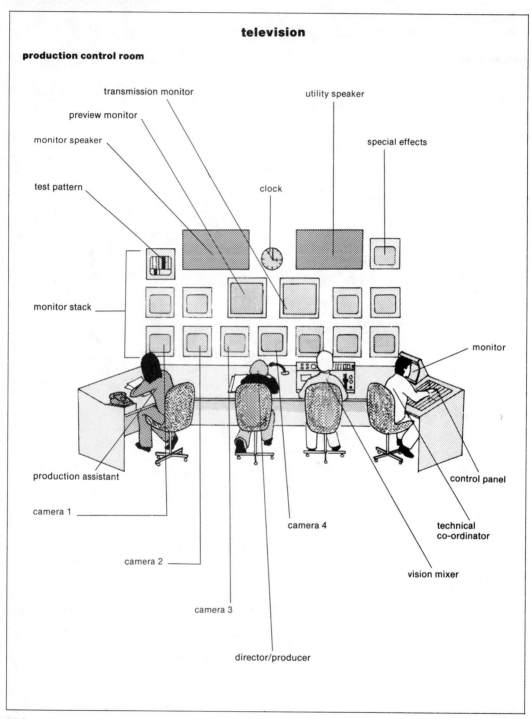

transmission monitor

utility speaker

preview monitor

special effects

monitor speaker

test pattern

clock

monitor stack

monitor

production assistant

control panel

camera 1

technical
co-ordinator

camera 4

camera 2

vision mixer

camera 3

director/producer

television

television set

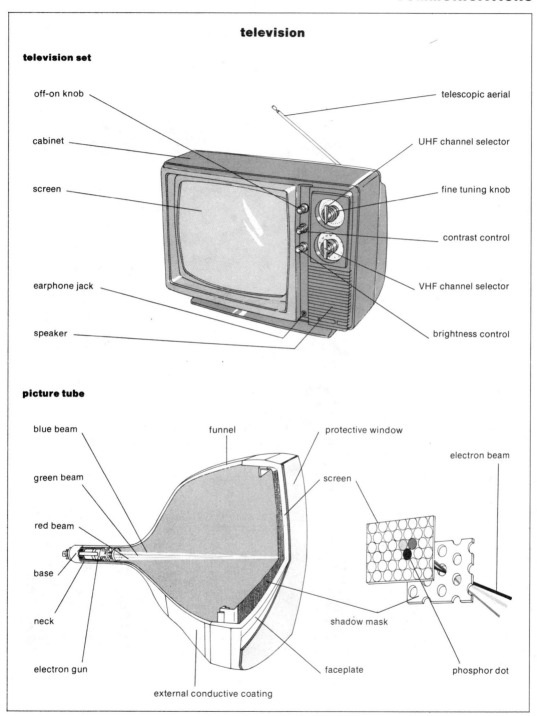

off-on knob

cabinet

screen

earphone jack

speaker

telescopic aerial

UHF channel selector

fine tuning knob

contrast control

VHF channel selector

brightness control

picture tube

blue beam

green beam

red beam

base

neck

electron gun

funnel

protective window

screen

electron beam

shadow mask

faceplate

phosphor dot

external conductive coating

COMMUNICATIONS

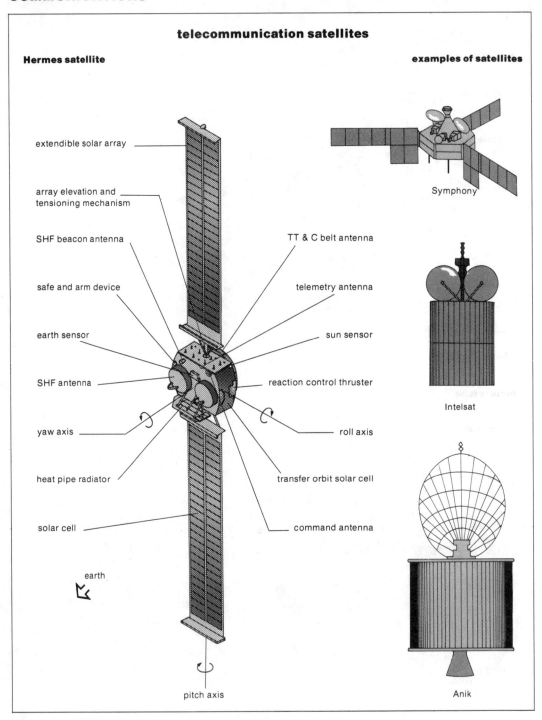

telecommunication satellites

Hermes satellite

examples of satellites

extendible solar array

array elevation and tensioning mechanism

SHF beacon antenna

safe and arm device

earth sensor

SHF antenna

yaw axis

heat pipe radiator

solar cell

TT & C belt antenna

telemetry antenna

sun sensor

reaction control thruster

roll axis

transfer orbit solar cell

command antenna

earth

pitch axis

Symphony

Intelsat

Anik

telecommunication satellites

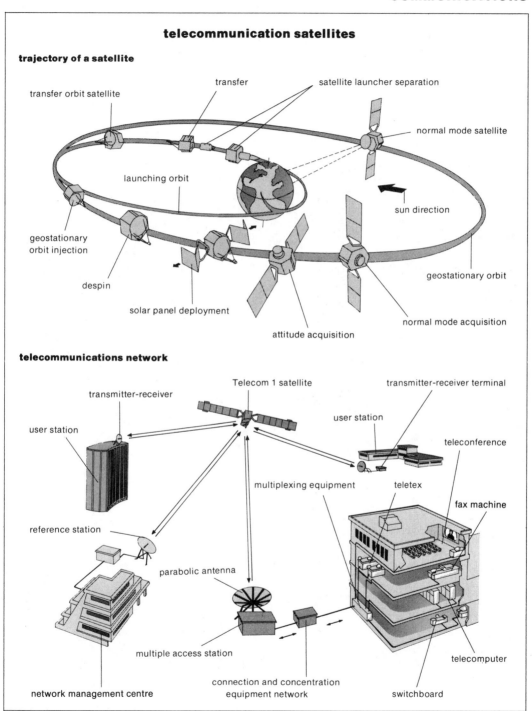

trajectory of a satellite

transfer orbit satellite

transfer

satellite launcher separation

normal mode satellite

launching orbit

sun direction

geostationary orbit injection

despin

geostationary orbit

solar panel deployment

normal mode acquisition

attitude acquisition

telecommunications network

transmitter-receiver

Telecom 1 satellite

transmitter-receiver terminal

user station

user station

teleconference

multiplexing equipment

teletex

fax machine

reference station

parabolic antenna

telecomputer

multiple access station

network management centre

connection and concentration equipment network

switchboard

TRANSPORT

car

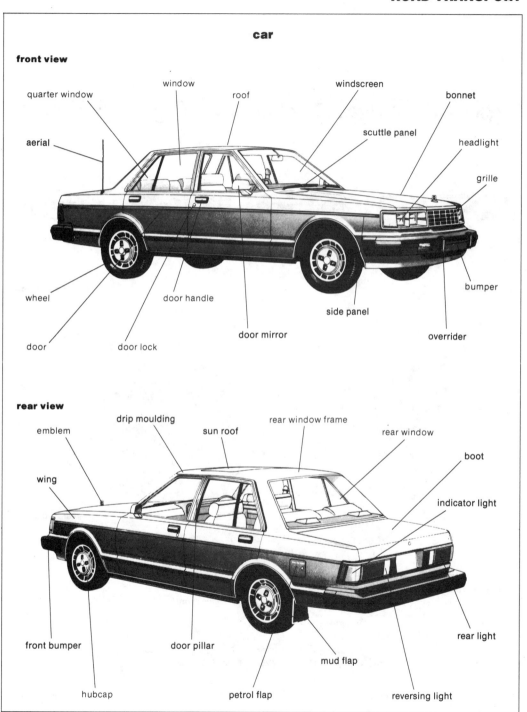

front view

quarter window

window

roof

windscreen

bonnet

scuttle panel

headlight

aerial

grille

wheel

door handle

side panel

bumper

door

door lock

door mirror

overrider

rear view

drip moulding

rear window frame

emblem

sun roof

rear window

boot

wing

indicator light

front bumper

door pillar

mud flap

rear light

hubcap

petrol flap

reversing light

ROAD TRANSPORT

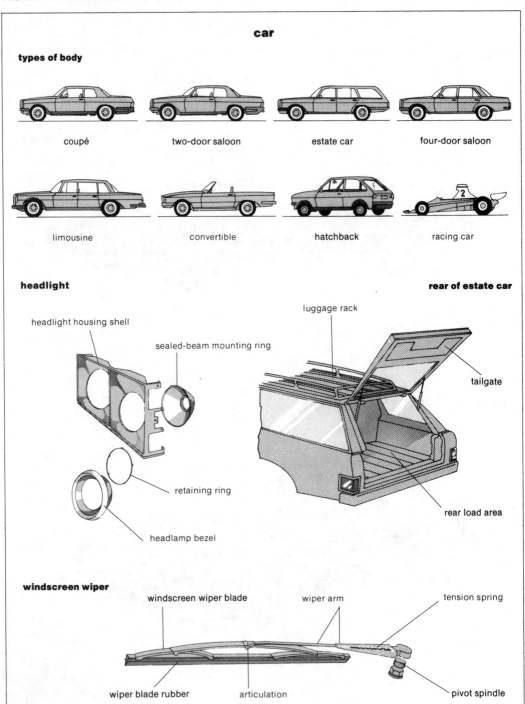

car

types of body

coupé

two-door saloon

estate car

four-door saloon

limousine

convertible

hatchback

racing car

headlight

headlight housing shell

sealed-beam mounting ring

retaining ring

headlamp bezel

rear of estate car

luggage rack

tailgate

rear load area

windscreen wiper

windscreen wiper blade

wiper arm

tension spring

wiper blade rubber

articulation

pivot spindle

car

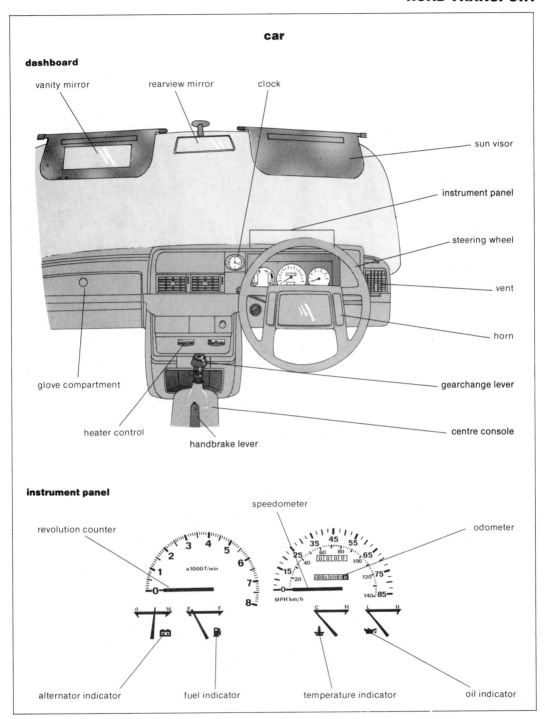

dashboard

vanity mirror

rearview mirror

clock

sun visor

instrument panel

steering wheel

vent

horn

glove compartment

gearchange lever

heater control

centre console

handbrake lever

instrument panel

speedometer

revolution counter

odometer

a 1000 T/min

MPH km/h

alternator indicator

fuel indicator

temperature indicator

oil indicator

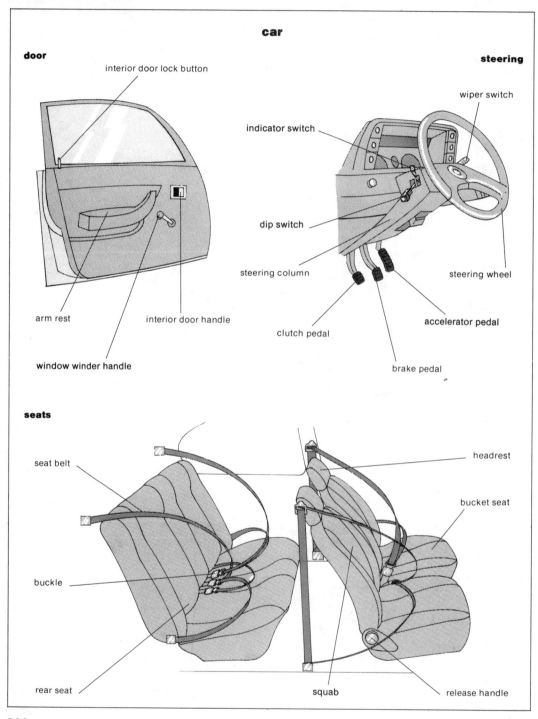

car

door

interior door lock button

arm rest

interior door handle

window winder handle

steering

wiper switch

indicator switch

dip switch

steering column

clutch pedal

brake pedal

steering wheel

accelerator pedal

seats

seat belt

buckle

rear seat

headrest

bucket seat

squab

release handle

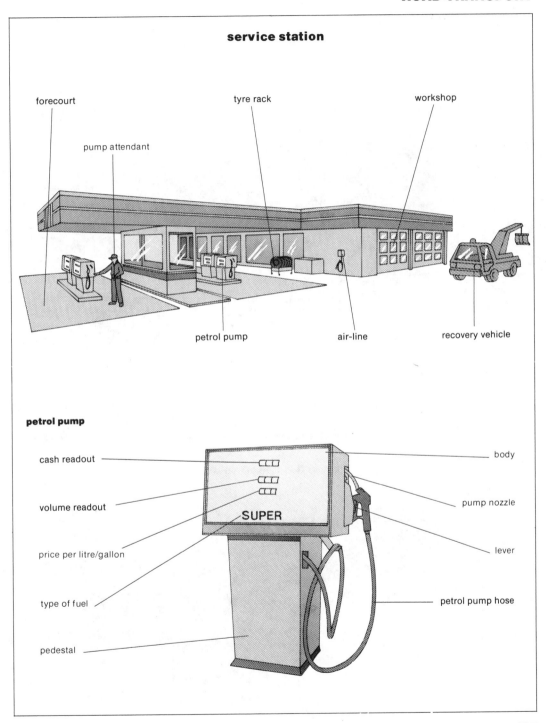

service station

forecourt

pump attendant

tyre rack

workshop

petrol pump

air-line

recovery vehicle

petrol pump

cash readout

body

volume readout

pump nozzle

price per litre/gallon

SUPER

type of fuel

lever

petrol pump hose

pedestal

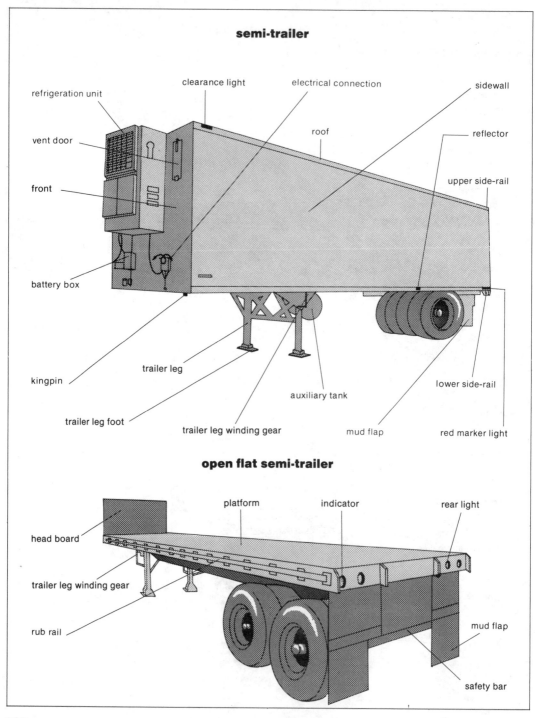

semi-trailer

refrigeration unit

clearance light

electrical connection

sidewall

vent door

roof

reflector

front

upper side-rail

battery box

kingpin

trailer leg

auxiliary tank

lower side-rail

trailer leg foot

trailer leg winding gear

mud flap

red marker light

open flat semi-trailer

platform

indicator

rear light

head board

trailer leg winding gear

rub rail

mud flap

safety bar

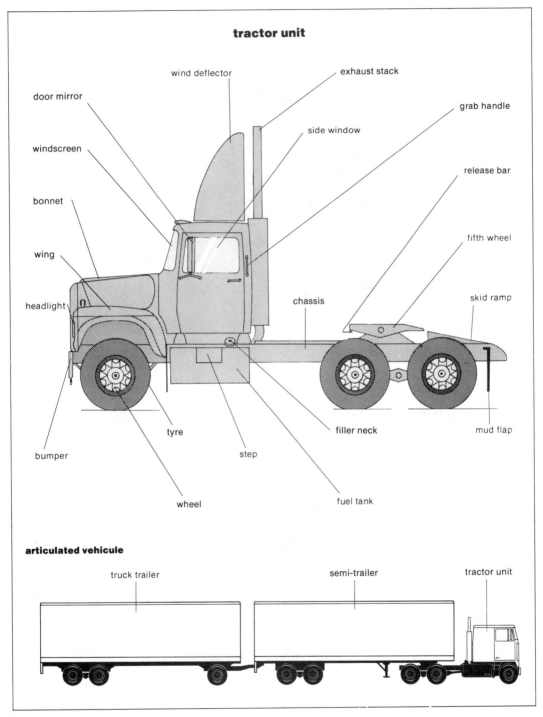

tractor unit

wind deflector

exhaust stack

door mirror

grab handle

windscreen

side window

release bar

bonnet

fifth wheel

wing

skid ramp

headlight

chassis

filler neck

mud flap

bumper

tyre

step

wheel

fuel tank

articulated vehicle

truck trailer

semi-trailer

tractor unit

engines

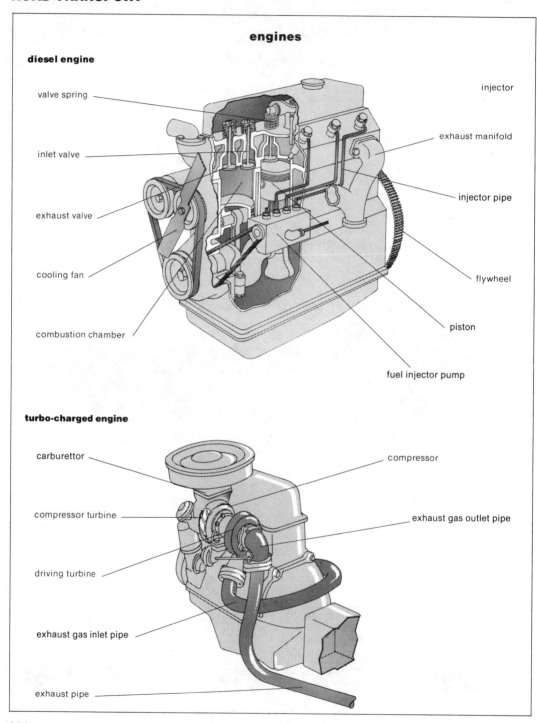

diesel engine

valve spring

inlet valve

exhaust valve

cooling fan

combustion chamber

injector

exhaust manifold

injector pipe

flywheel

piston

fuel injector pump

turbo-charged engine

carburettor

compressor turbine

driving turbine

exhaust gas inlet pipe

exhaust pipe

compressor

exhaust gas outlet pipe

engine

petrol engine

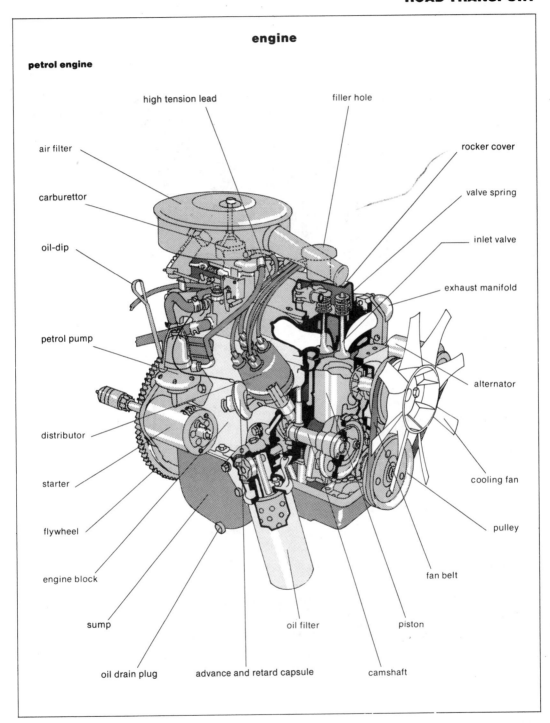

high tension lead

filler hole

air filter

rocker cover

carburettor

valve spring

oil-dip

inlet valve

exhaust manifold

petrol pump

alternator

distributor

starter

cooling fan

flywheel

pulley

engine block

fan belt

sump

oil filter

piston

oil drain plug

advance and retard capsule

camshaft

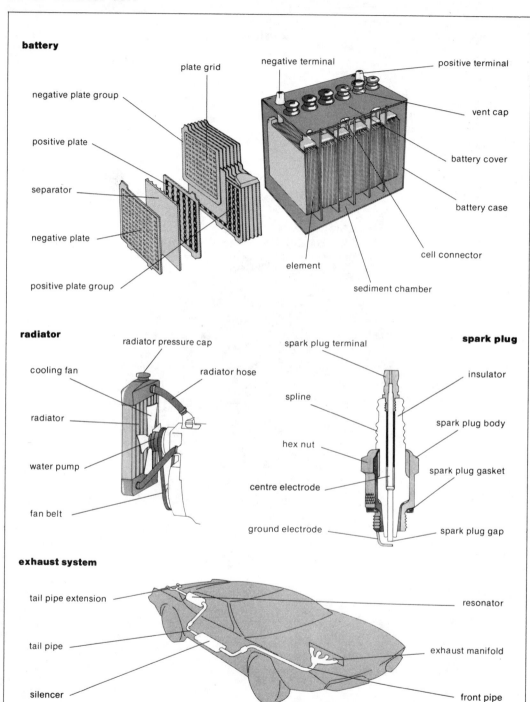

battery

plate grid

negative terminal

positive terminal

negative plate group

vent cap

positive plate

battery cover

separator

battery case

negative plate

battery case

positive plate group

cell connector

element

sediment chamber

radiator

radiator pressure cap

spark plug terminal

spark plug

cooling fan

radiator hose

insulator

radiator

spline

spark plug body

water pump

hex nut

spark plug gasket

centre electrode

fan belt

ground electrode

spark plug gap

exhaust system

tail pipe extension

resonator

tail pipe

exhaust manifold

silencer

front pipe

392

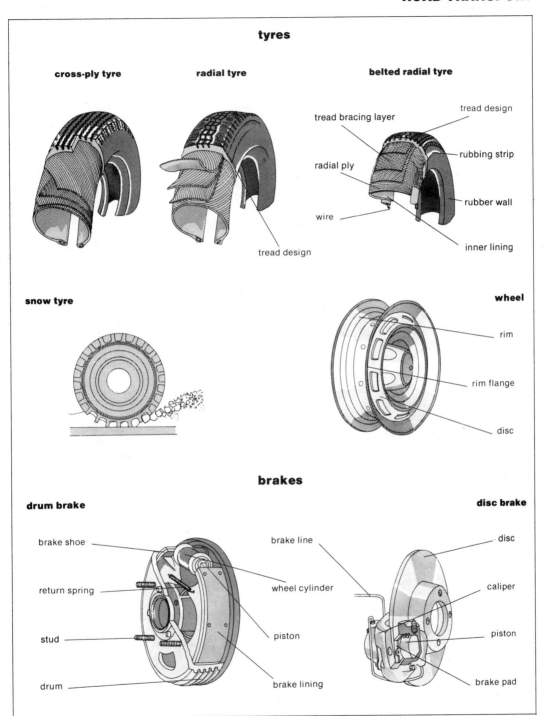

tyres

cross-ply tyre

radial tyre

belted radial tyre

tread bracing layer

tread design

radial ply

rubbing strip

wire

rubber wall

inner lining

tread design

snow tyre

wheel

rim

rim flange

disc

brakes

drum brake

disc brake

brake shoe

brake line

disc

return spring

wheel cylinder

caliper

stud

piston

piston

drum

brake lining

brake pad

long-distance coach

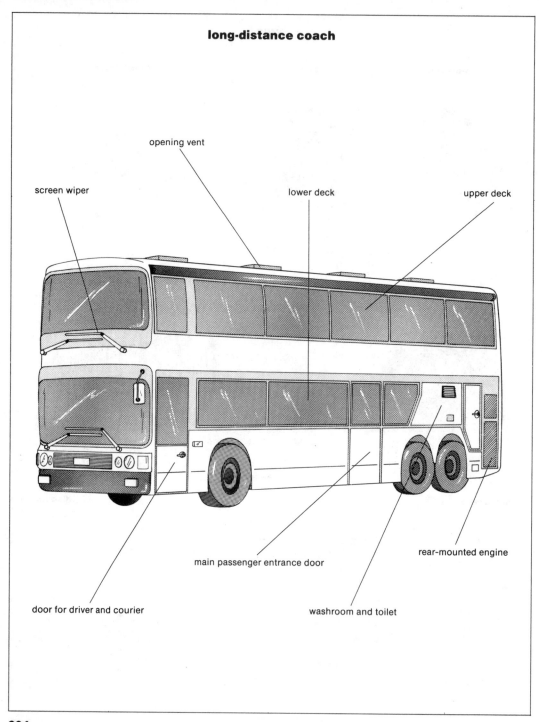

opening vent

screen wiper

lower deck

upper deck

main passenger entrance door

rear-mounted engine

door for driver and courier

washroom and toilet

motorcycle

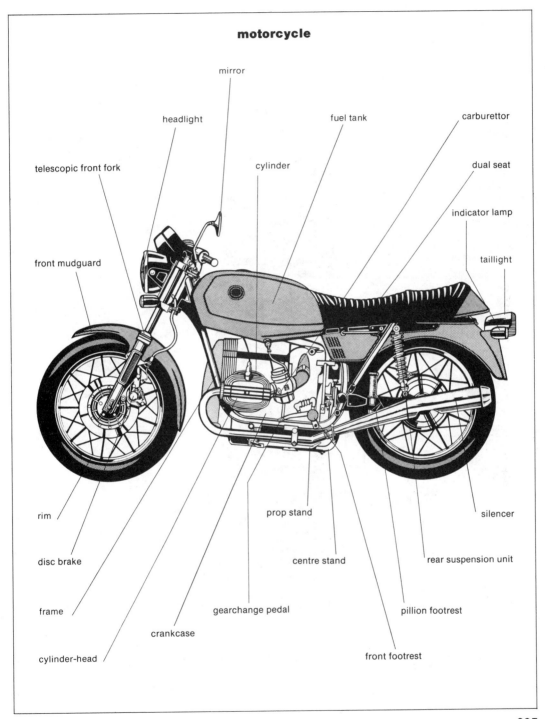

mirror

headlight

fuel tank

carburettor

telescopic front fork

cylinder

dual seat

front mudguard

indicator lamp

taillight

rim

prop stand

silencer

disc brake

centre stand

rear suspension unit

frame

gearchange pedal

pillion footrest

crankcase

cylinder-head

front footrest

motorcycle

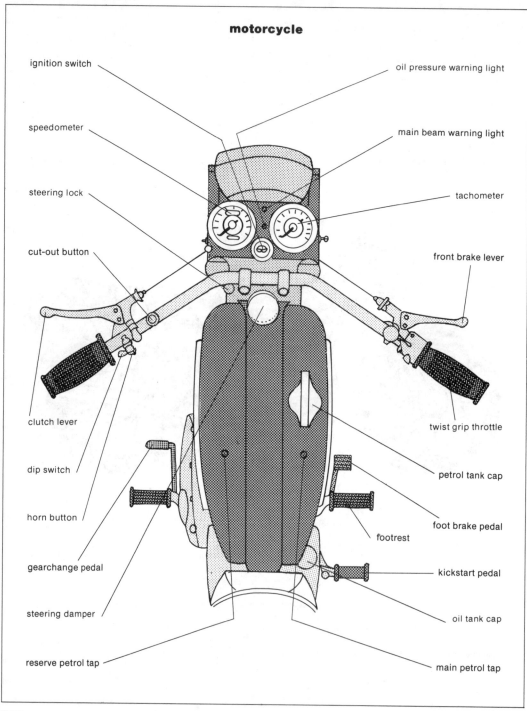

ignition switch

oil pressure warning light

speedometer

main beam warning light

steering lock

tachometer

cut-out button

front brake lever

clutch lever

twist grip throttle

dip switch

petrol tank cap

horn button

foot brake pedal

footrest

gearchange pedal

kickstart pedal

steering damper

oil tank cap

reserve petrol tap

main petrol tap

bicycle

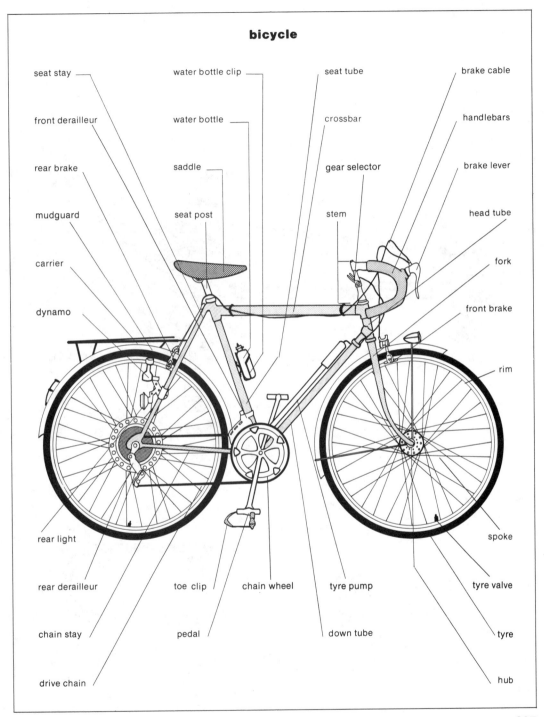

seat stay

water bottle clip

seat tube

brake cable

front derailleur

water bottle

crossbar

handlebars

rear brake

saddle

gear selector

brake lever

mudguard

seat post

stem

head tube

carrier

fork

dynamo

front brake

rim

rear light

spoke

rear derailleur

toe clip

chain wheel

tyre pump

tyre valve

chain stay

pedal

down tube

tyre

drive chain

hub

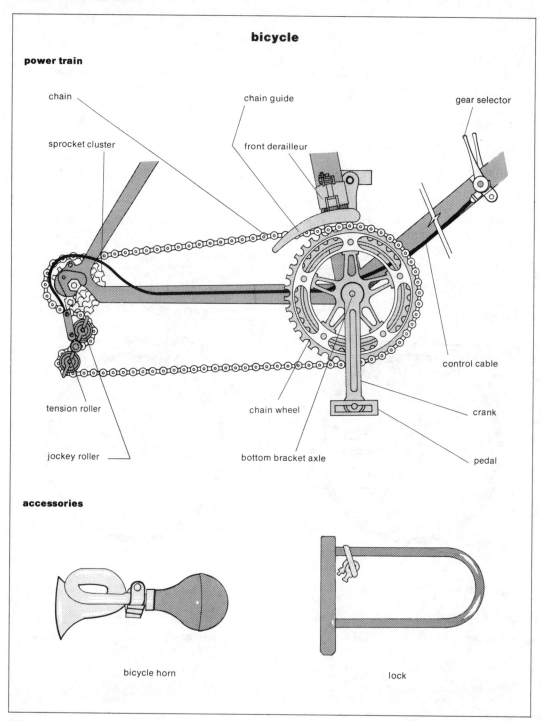

bicycle

power train

chain

sprocket cluster

chain guide

gear selector

front derailleur

control cable

tension roller

chain wheel

crank

jockey roller

bottom bracket axle

pedal

accessories

bicycle horn

lock

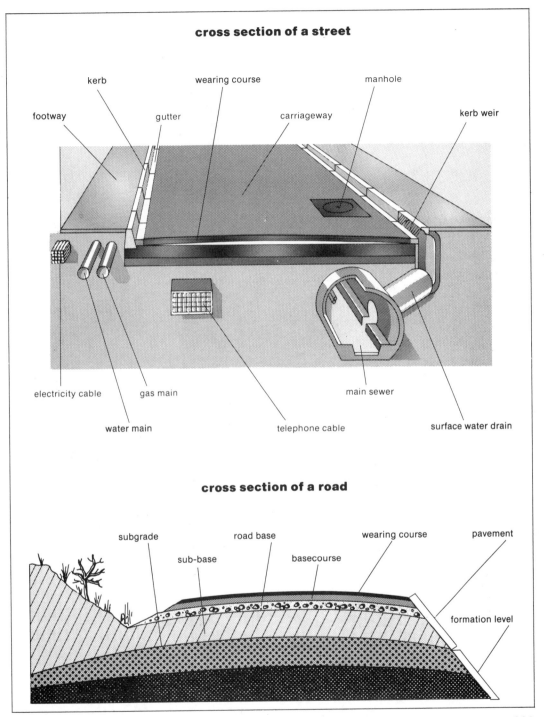

cross section of a street

kerb
wearing course
manhole
footway
gutter
carriageway
kerb weir
electricity cable
gas main
main sewer
water main
telephone cable
surface water drain

cross section of a road

subgrade
road base
wearing course
pavement
sub-base
basecourse
formation level

fixed bridges

beam bridge

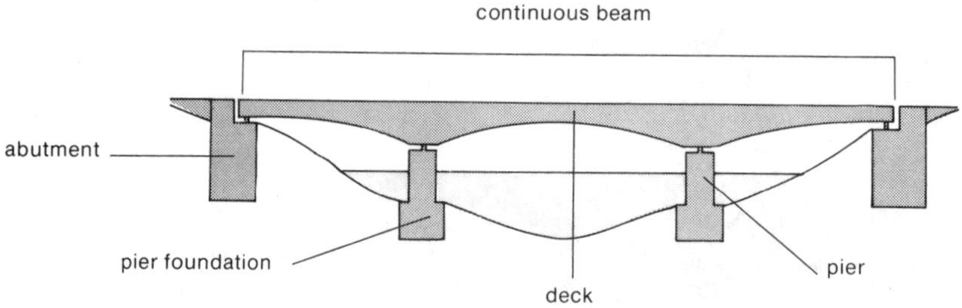

continuous beam

abutment

pier foundation

deck

pier

types of beam bridges

multiple-span beam bridge

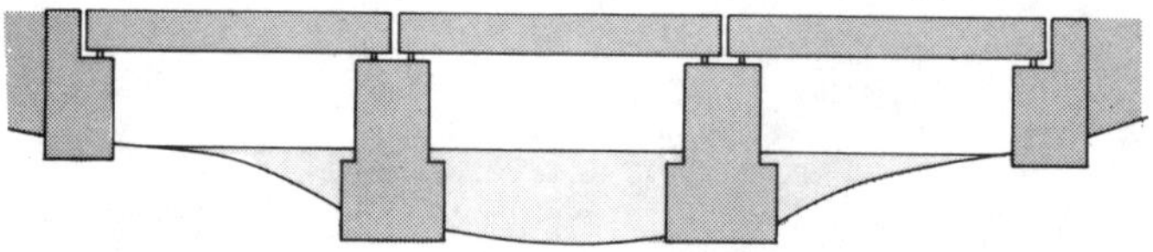

simple-span beam bridge

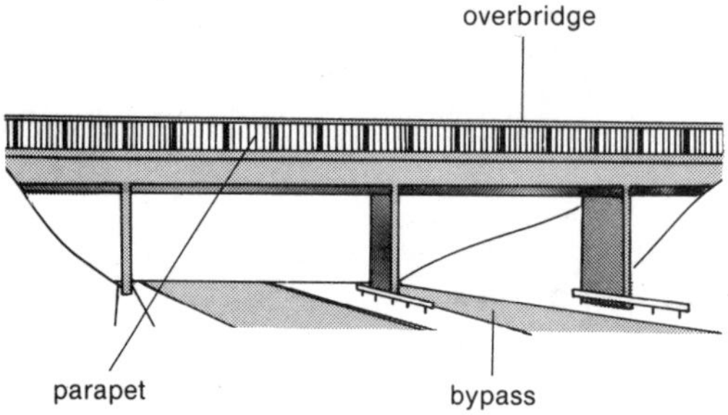

overbridge

viaduct

parapet

bypass

cantilever bridge

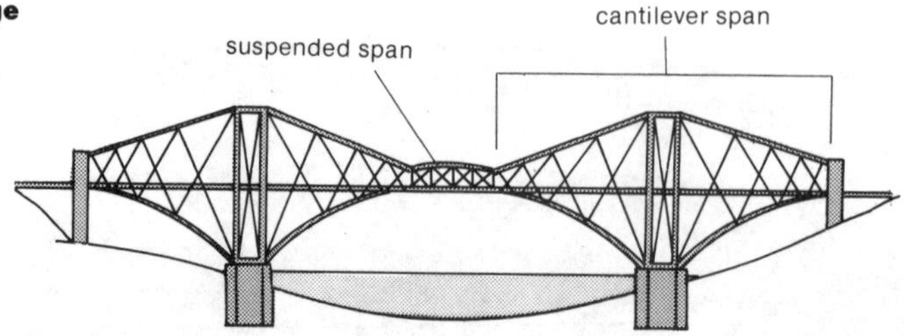

suspended span

cantilever span

fixed bridges

arch bridge

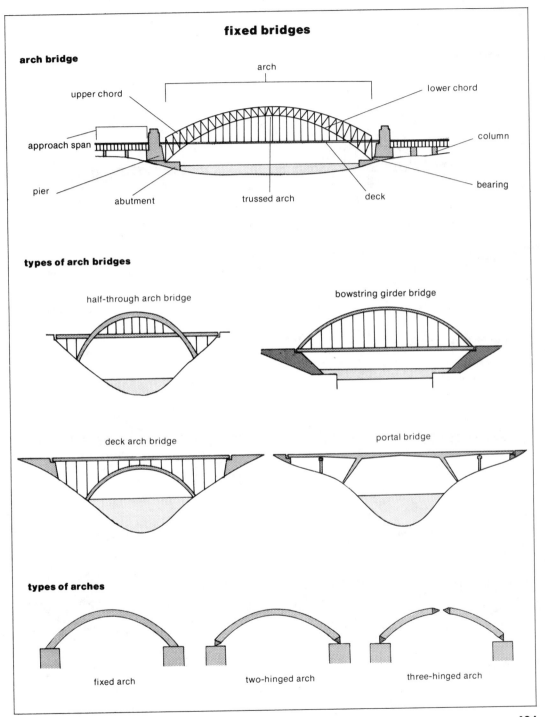

types of arch bridges

half-through arch bridge

bowstring girder bridge

deck arch bridge

portal bridge

types of arches

fixed arch

two-hinged arch

three-hinged arch

fixed bridges

suspension bridge

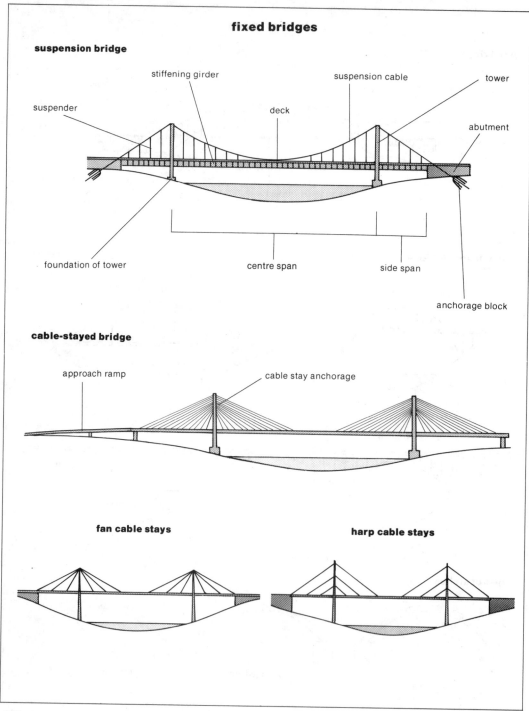

suspender

stiffening girder

deck

suspension cable

tower

abutment

foundation of tower

centre span

side span

anchorage block

cable-stayed bridge

approach ramp

cable stay anchorage

fan cable stays

harp cable stays

movable bridges

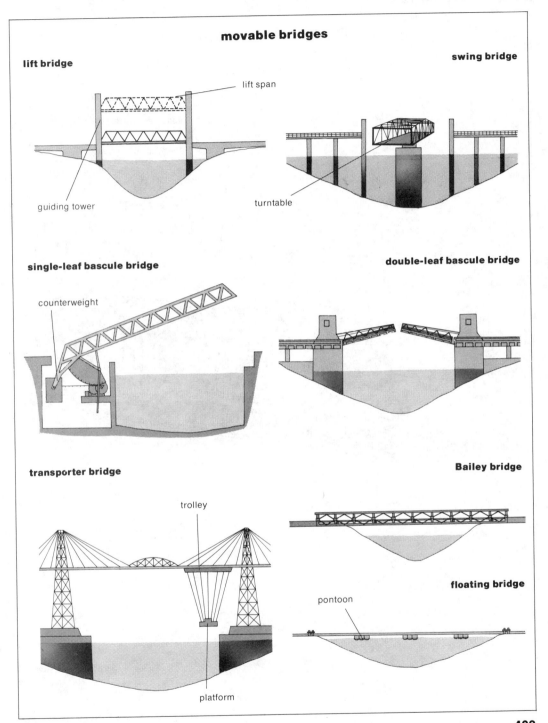

lift bridge

lift span

guiding tower

swing bridge

turntable

single-leaf bascule bridge

counterweight

double-leaf bascule bridge

transporter bridge

trolley

platform

Bailey bridge

floating bridge

pontoon

diesel-electric locomotive

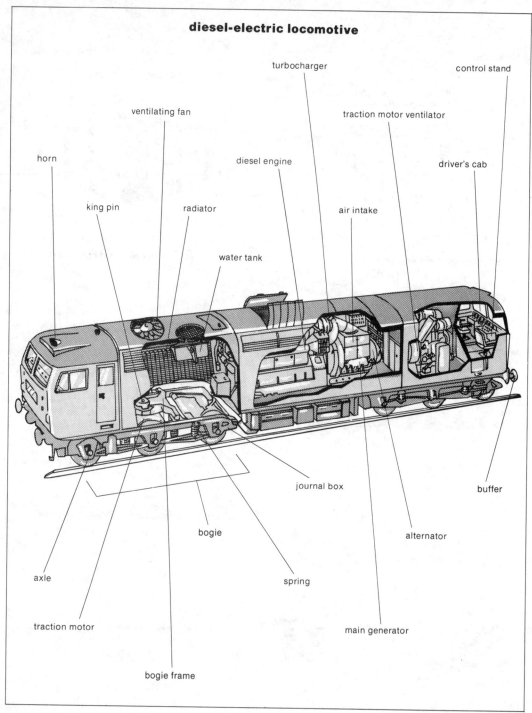

turbocharger

control stand

ventilating fan

traction motor ventilator

horn

driver's cab

diesel engine

king pin

radiator

air intake

water tank

journal box

buffer

bogie

alternator

axle

spring

traction motor

main generator

bogie frame

bogie wagon

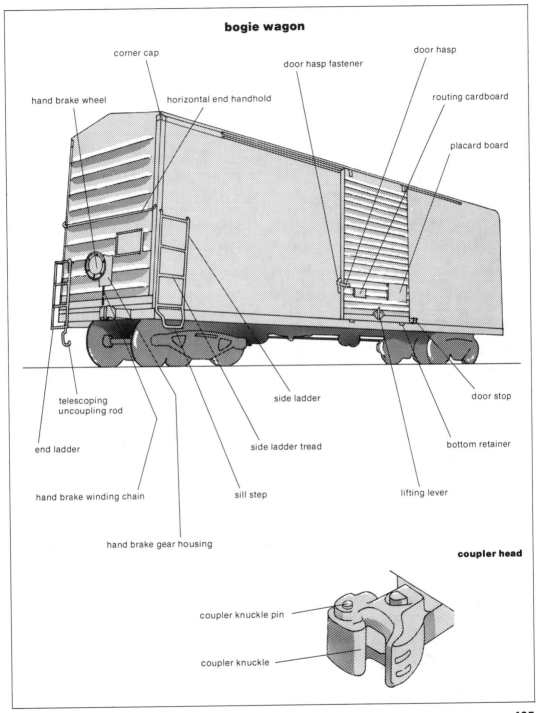

corner cap

hand brake wheel

door hasp fastener

door hasp

routing cardboard

horizontal end handhold

placard board

telescoping uncoupling rod

side ladder

door stop

end ladder

side ladder tread

bottom retainer

hand brake winding chain

sill step

lifting lever

hand brake gear housing

coupler head

coupler knuckle pin

coupler knuckle

types of freight wagons

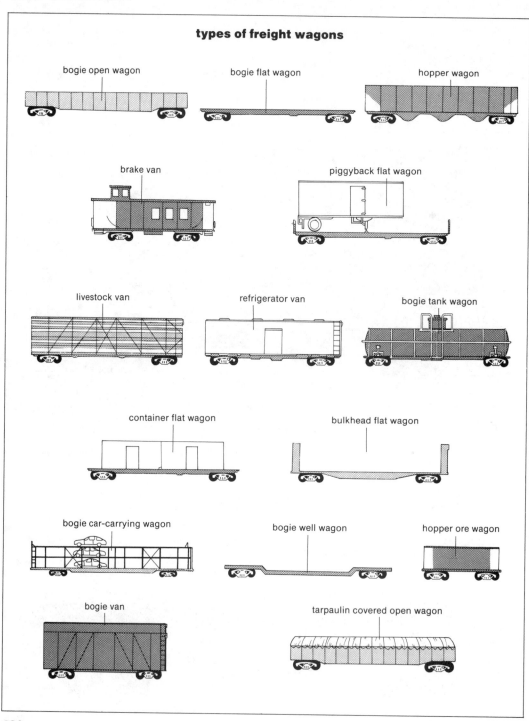

bogie open wagon

bogie flat wagon

hopper wagon

brake van

piggyback flat wagon

livestock van

refrigerator van

bogie tank wagon

container flat wagon

bulkhead flat wagon

bogie car-carrying wagon

bogie well wagon

hopper ore wagon

bogie van

tarpaulin covered open wagon

types of passenger coaches

saloon open coach

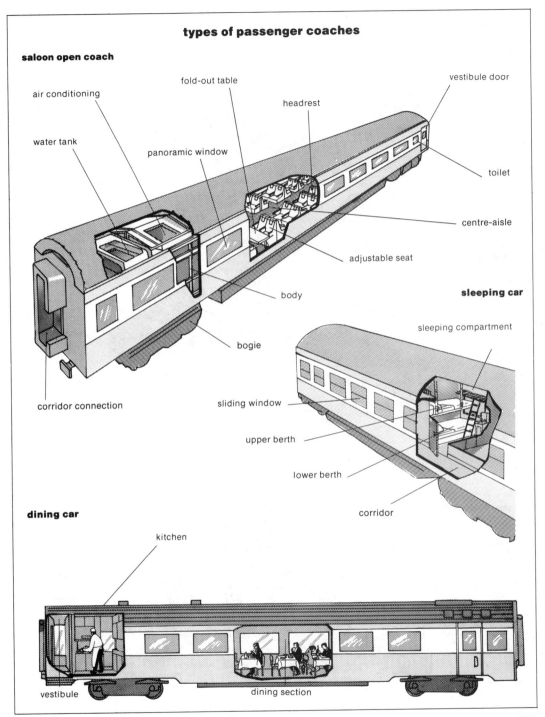

air conditioning

fold-out table

headrest

vestibule door

water tank

panoramic window

toilet

centre-aisle

adjustable seat

body

sleeping car

bogie

sleeping compartment

corridor connection

sliding window

upper berth

lower berth

corridor

dining car

kitchen

vestibule

dining section

407

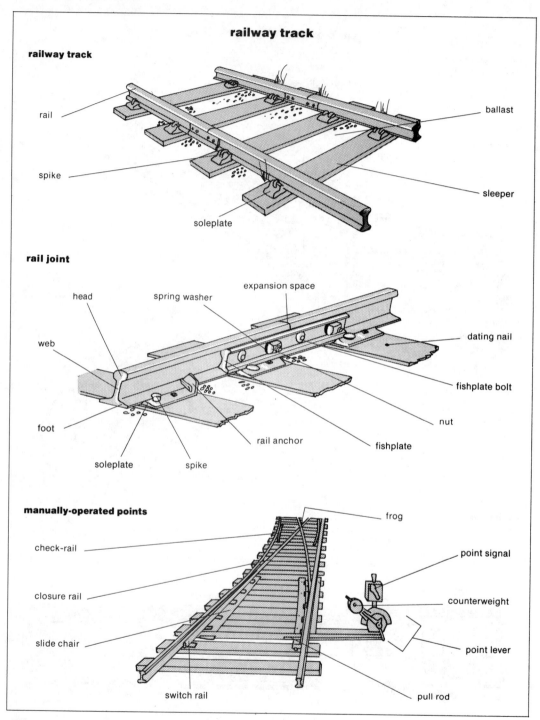

railway track

railway track

- rail
- ballast
- spike
- sleeper
- soleplate

rail joint

- head
- spring washer
- expansion space
- web
- dating nail
- foot
- fishplate bolt
- soleplate
- spike
- rail anchor
- nut
- fishplate

manually-operated points

- frog
- check-rail
- point signal
- closure rail
- counterweight
- slide chair
- point lever
- switch rail
- pull rod

railway track

remote-controlled points

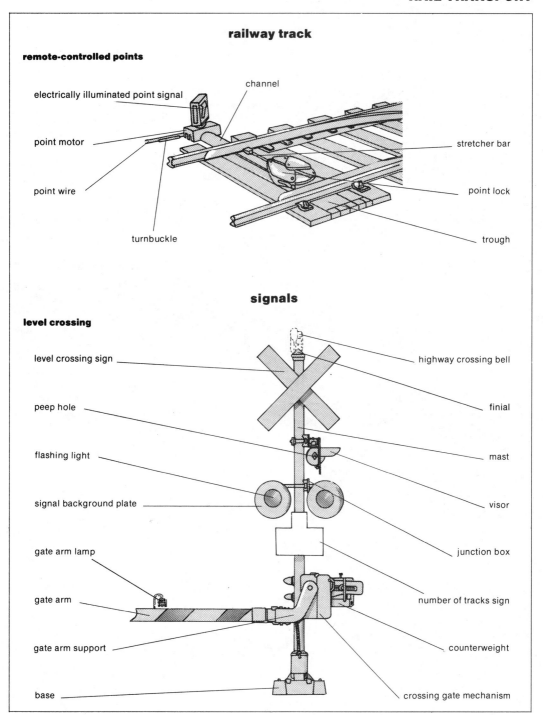

electrically illuminated point signal

channel

point motor

stretcher bar

point wire

point lock

turnbuckle

trough

signals

level crossing

level crossing sign

highway crossing bell

peep hole

finial

flashing light

mast

signal background plate

visor

gate arm lamp

junction box

gate arm

number of tracks sign

gate arm support

counterweight

base

crossing gate mechanism

railway station

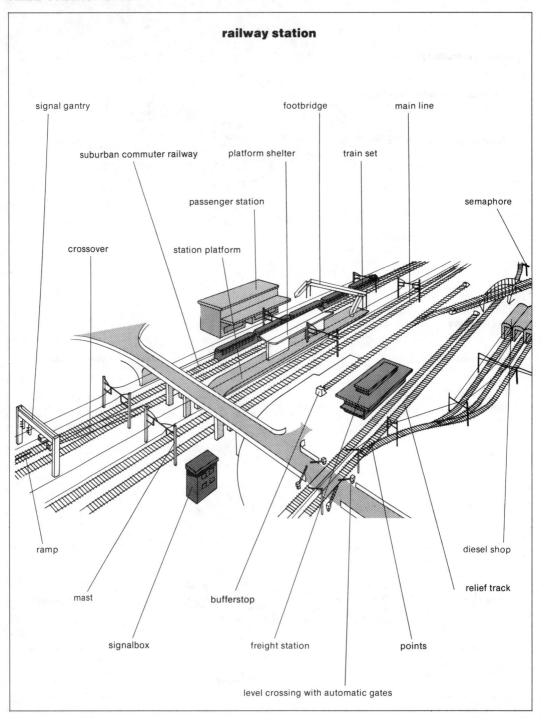

signal gantry

footbridge

main line

suburban commuter railway

platform shelter

train set

passenger station

semaphore

crossover

station platform

ramp

diesel shop

relief track

mast

bufferstop

signalbox

freight station

points

level crossing with automatic gates

container

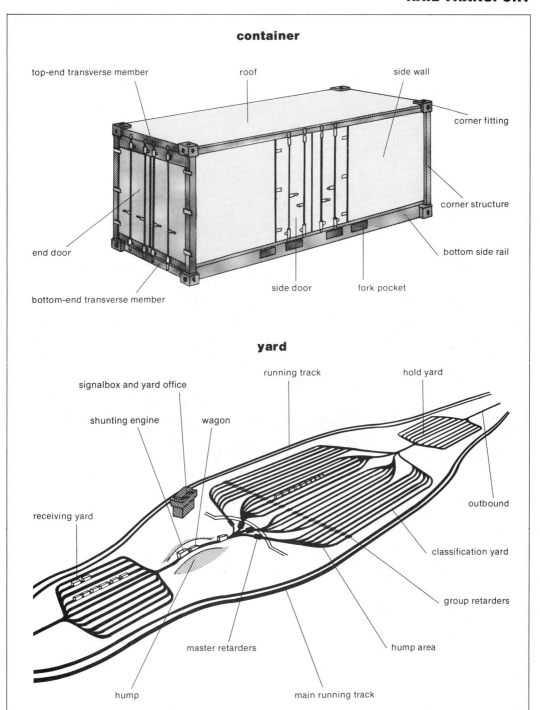

top-end transverse member

roof

side wall

corner fitting

corner structure

end door

bottom side rail

bottom-end transverse member

side door

fork pocket

yard

running track

hold yard

signalbox and yard office

shunting engine

wagon

receiving yard

outbound

classification yard

group retarders

master retarders

hump area

hump

main running track

RAIL TRANSPORT

station concourse

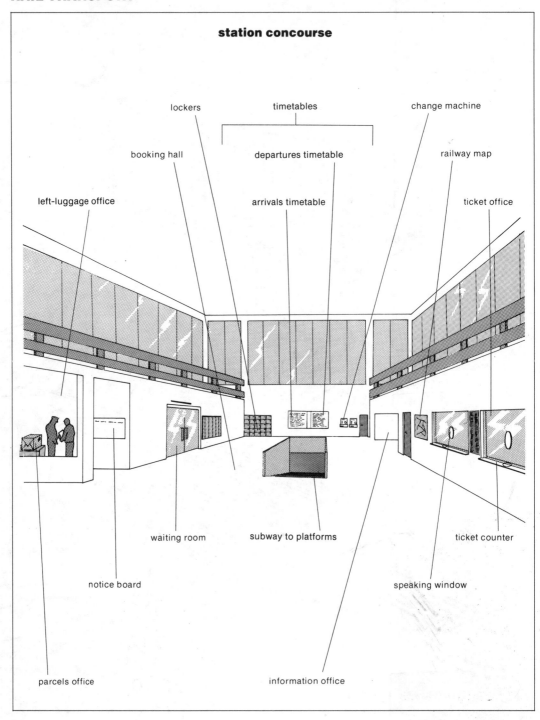

lockers

timetables

change machine

booking hall

departures timetable

railway map

left-luggage office

arrivals timetable

ticket office

waiting room

subway to platforms

ticket counter

notice board

speaking window

parcels office

information office

station platform

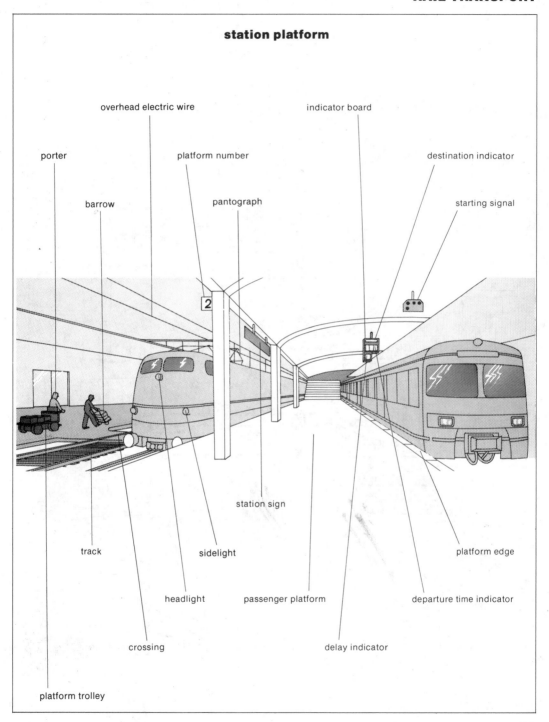

overhead electric wire

indicator board

porter

platform number

destination indicator

barrow

pantograph

starting signal

2

station sign

track

sidelight

platform edge

headlight

passenger platform

departure time indicator

crossing

delay indicator

platform trolley

RAIL TRANSPORT

underground station

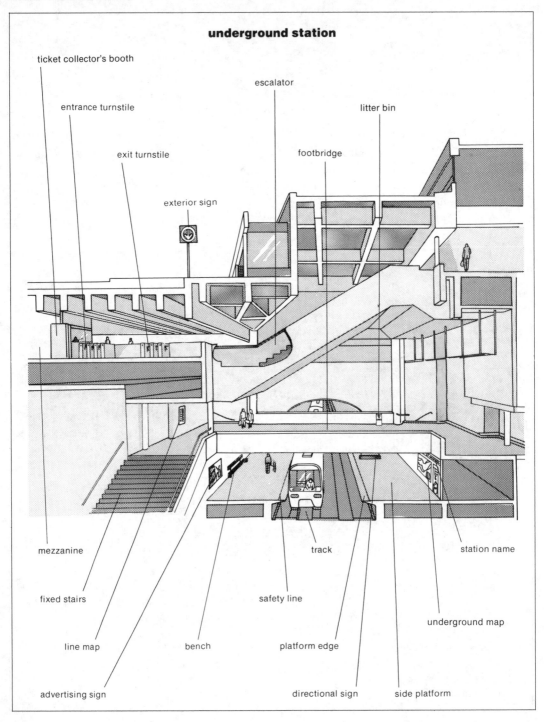

ticket collector's booth

entrance turnstile

escalator

litter bin

exit turnstile

footbridge

exterior sign

mezzanine

track

station name

fixed stairs

safety line

underground map

line map

bench

platform edge

advertising sign

directional sign

side platform

underground railway

underground train

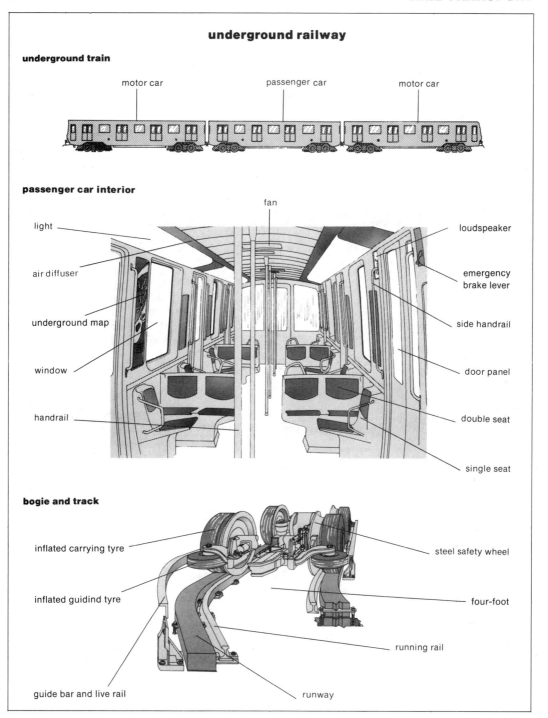

motor car   passenger car   motor car

passenger car interior

fan

light

air diffuser

underground map

window

handrail

loudspeaker

emergency
brake lever

side handrail

door panel

double seat

single seat

bogie and track

inflated carrying tyre

inflated guidind tyre

guide bar and live rail

steel safety wheel

four-foot

running rail

runway

four-masted bark

masting and standing rigging

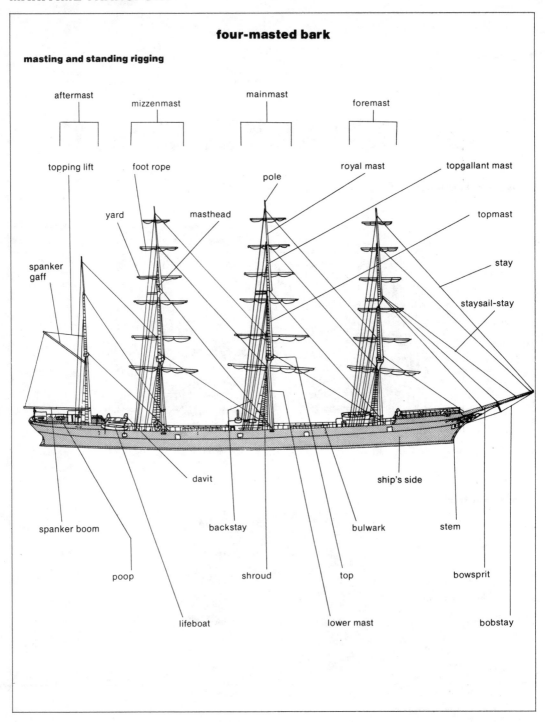

aftermast

mizzenmast

mainmast

foremast

topping lift

foot rope

pole

royal mast

topgallant mast

yard

masthead

topmast

spanker gaff

stay

staysail-stay

davit

ship's side

spanker boom

backstay

bulwark

stem

poop

shroud

top

bowsprit

lifeboat

lower mast

bobstay

four-masted bark

sail plan

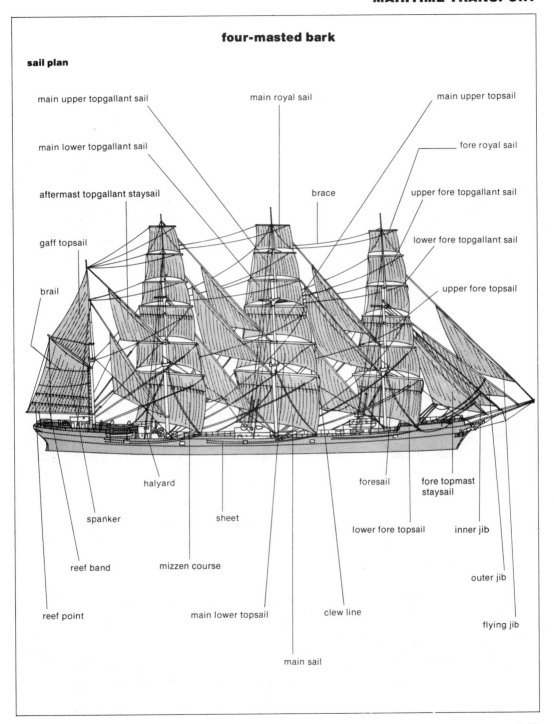

main upper topgallant sail

main royal sail

main upper topsail

main lower topgallant sail

fore royal sail

aftermast topgallant staysail

brace

upper fore topgallant sail

gaff topsail

lower fore topgallant sail

brail

upper fore topsail

halyard

foresail

fore topmast staysail

spanker

sheet

lower fore topsail

inner jib

reef band

mizzen course

outer jib

reef point

main lower topsail

clew line

flying jib

main sail

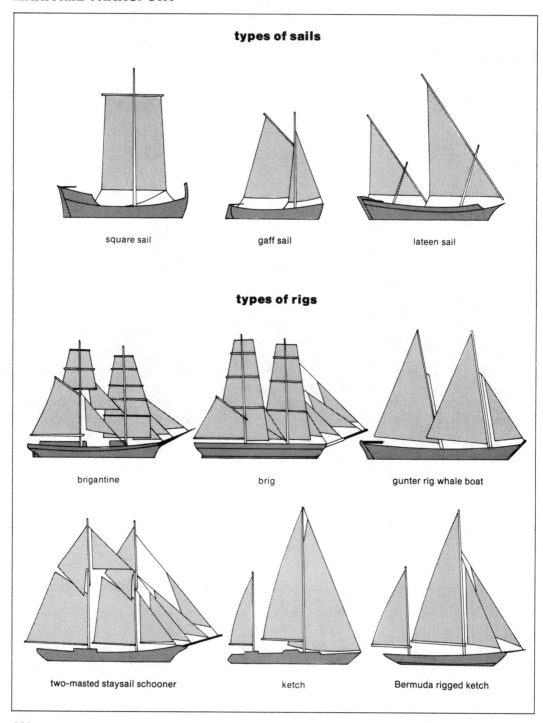

types of sails

square sail

gaff sail

lateen sail

types of rigs

brigantine

brig

gunter rig whale boat

two-masted staysail schooner

ketch

Bermuda rigged ketch

passenger liner

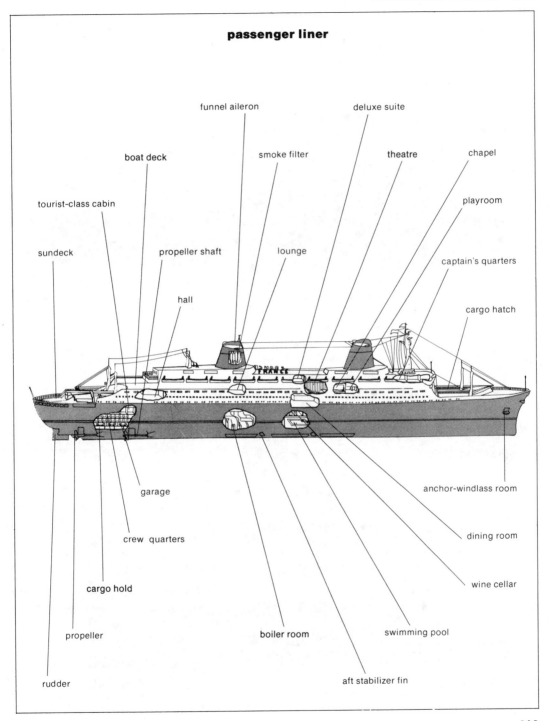

funnel aileron

deluxe suite

boat deck

smoke filter

theatre

chapel

tourist-class cabin

playroom

sundeck

propeller shaft

lounge

captain's quarters

hall

cargo hatch

garage

anchor-windlass room

crew quarters

dining room

cargo hold

wine cellar

propeller

boiler room

swimming pool

rudder

aft stabilizer fin

MARITIME TRANSPORT

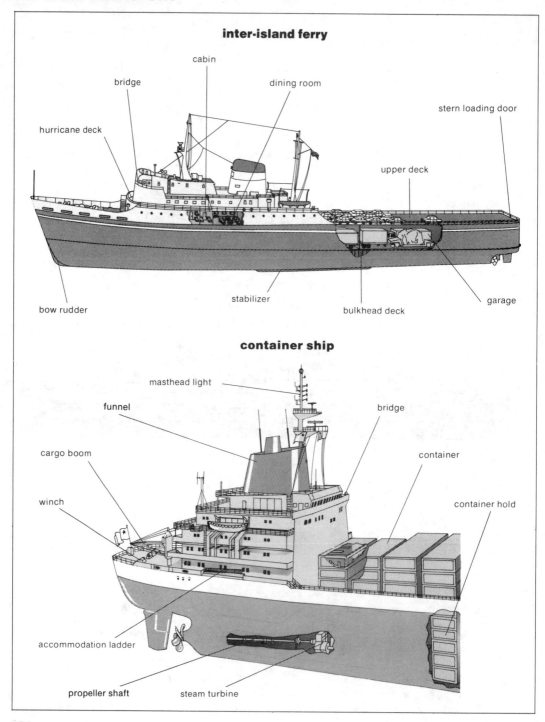

inter-island ferry

cabin

bridge

dining room

stern loading door

hurricane deck

upper deck

bow rudder

stabilizer

bulkhead deck

garage

container ship

masthead light

funnel

bridge

cargo boom

container

winch

container hold

accommodation ladder

propeller shaft

steam turbine

hovercraft

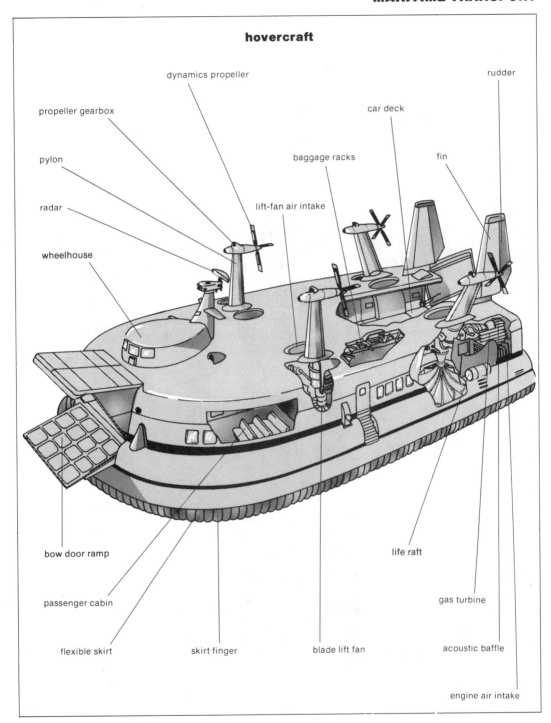

dynamics propeller

rudder

propeller gearbox

car deck

pylon

baggage racks

fin

radar

lift-fan air intake

wheelhouse

bow door ramp

life raft

passenger cabin

gas turbine

flexible skirt

skirt finger

blade lift fan

acoustic baffle

engine air intake

hydrofoil boat

hydrofoil

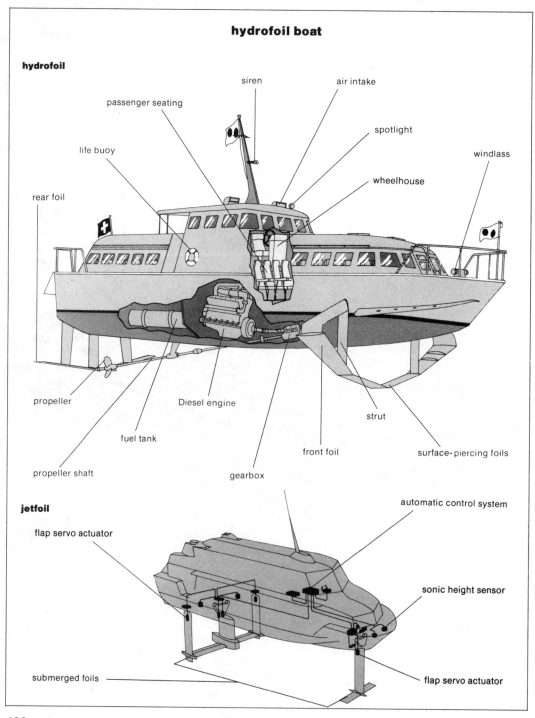

siren

air intake

passenger seating

spotlight

life buoy

windlass

wheelhouse

rear foil

propeller

Diesel engine

strut

fuel tank

front foil

surface-piercing foils

propeller shaft

gearbox

jetfoil

automatic control system

flap servo actuator

sonic height sensor

submerged foils

flap servo actuator

422

submersible

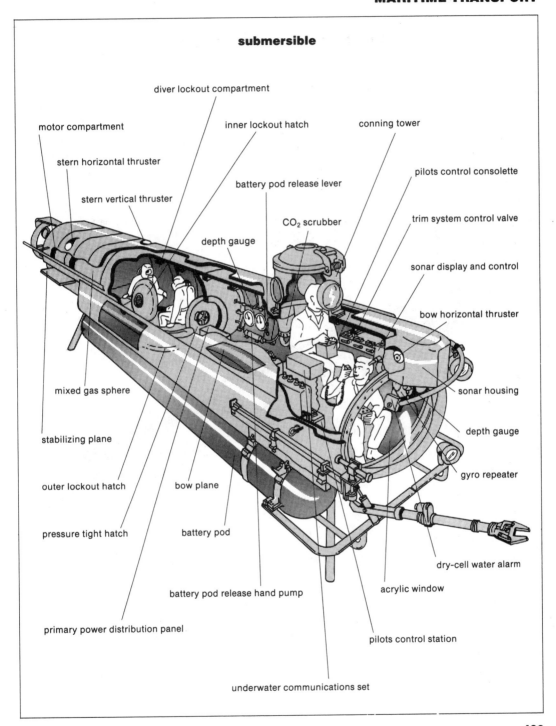

diver lockout compartment

motor compartment

inner lockout hatch

conning tower

stern horizontal thruster

pilots control consolette

battery pod release lever

stern vertical thruster

trim system control valve

CO_2 scrubber

depth gauge

sonar display and control

bow horizontal thruster

mixed gas sphere

sonar housing

stabilizing plane

depth gauge

outer lockout hatch

bow plane

gyro repeater

pressure tight hatch

battery pod

dry-cell water alarm

battery pod release hand pump

acrylic window

primary power distribution panel

pilots control station

underwater communications set

ballistic missile nuclear submarine

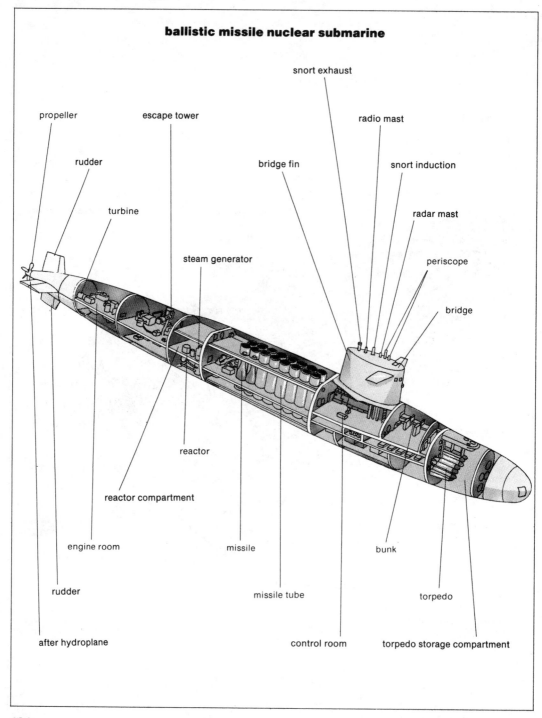

snort exhaust

propeller

escape tower

radio mast

rudder

snort induction

bridge fin

turbine

radar mast

steam generator

periscope

bridge

reactor

reactor compartment

engine room

missile

bunk

rudder

missile tube

torpedo

after hydroplane

control room

torpedo storage compartment

frigate

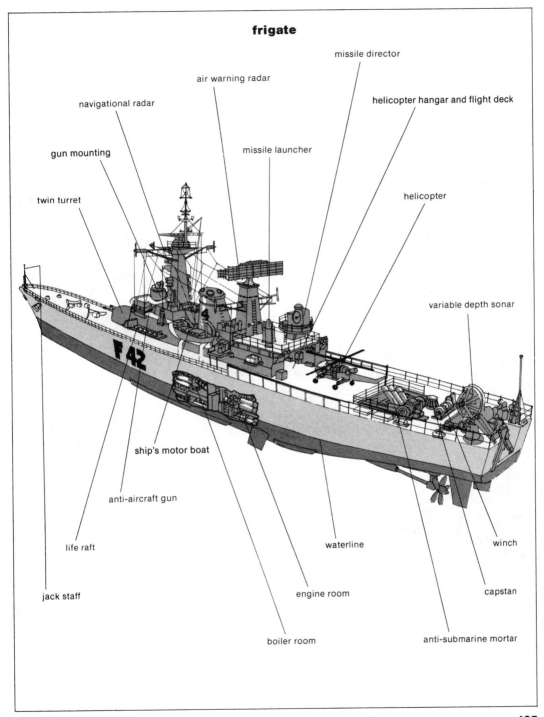

missile director

air warning radar

helicopter hangar and flight deck

navigational radar

missile launcher

gun mounting

helicopter

twin turret

variable depth sonar

ship's motor boat

anti-aircraft gun

life raft

winch

waterline

jack staff

capstan

engine room

boiler room

anti-submarine mortar

canal lock

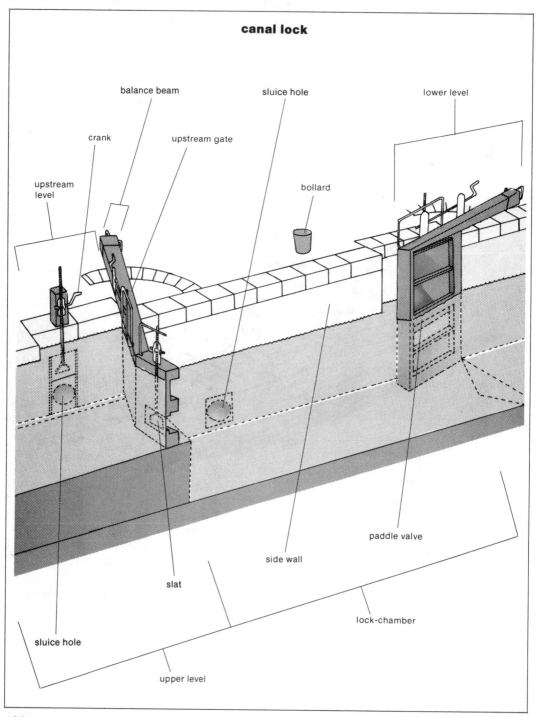

balance beam

sluice hole

lower level

crank

upstream gate

bollard

upstream level

paddle valve

side wall

slat

lock-chamber

sluice hole

upper level

harbour

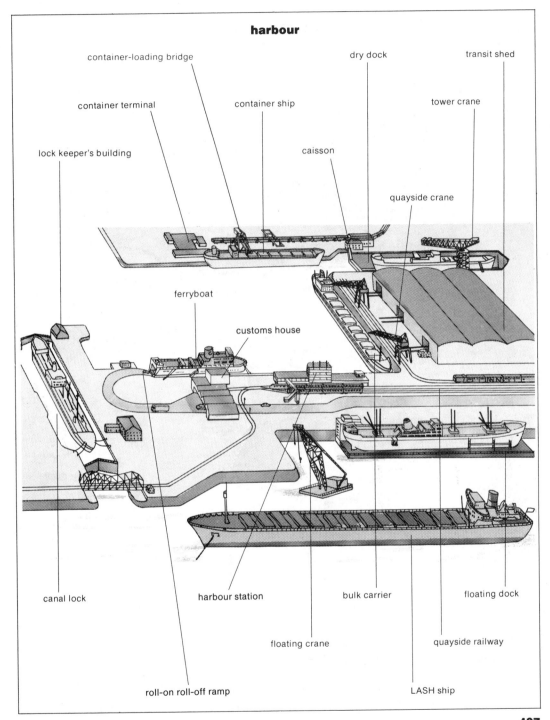

container-loading bridge

dry dock

transit shed

container terminal

container ship

tower crane

lock keeper's building

caisson

quayside crane

ferryboat

customs house

canal lock

harbour station

bulk carrier

floating dock

floating crane

quayside railway

roll-on roll-off ramp

LASH ship

MARITIME TRANSPORT

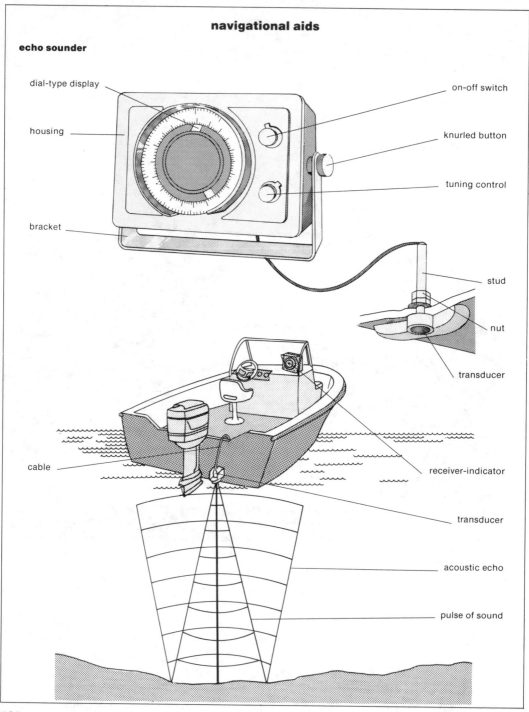

navigational aids

echo sounder

dial-type display

housing

bracket

on-off switch

knurled button

tuning control

stud

nut

transducer

cable

receiver-indicator

transducer

acoustic echo

pulse of sound

navigational aids

sextant

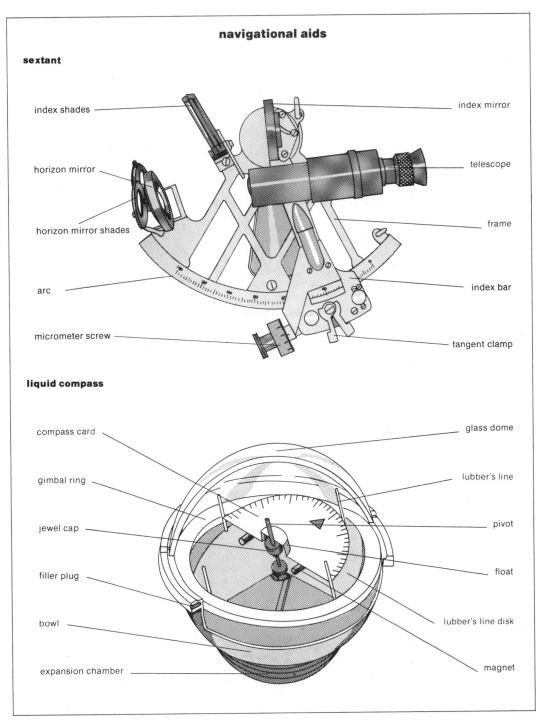

index shades — index mirror

horizon mirror — telescope

horizon mirror shades — frame

arc — index bar

micrometer screw — tangent clamp

liquid compass

compass card — glass dome

gimbal ring — lubber's line

jewel cap — pivot

filler plug — float

bowl — lubber's line disk

expansion chamber — magnet

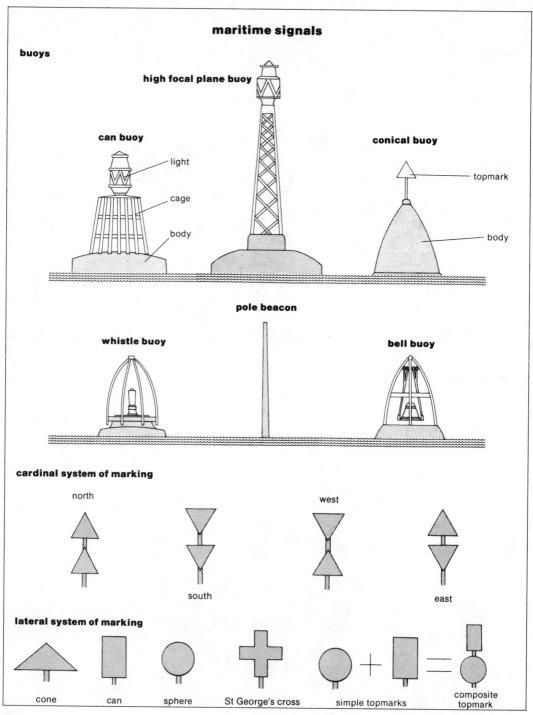

maritime signals

buoys

high focal plane buoy

can buoy

light

cage

body

conical buoy

topmark

body

pole beacon

whistle buoy

bell buoy

cardinal system of marking

north

west

south

east

lateral system of marking

cone

can

sphere

St George's cross

simple topmarks

composite topmark

maritime signals

lighthouse

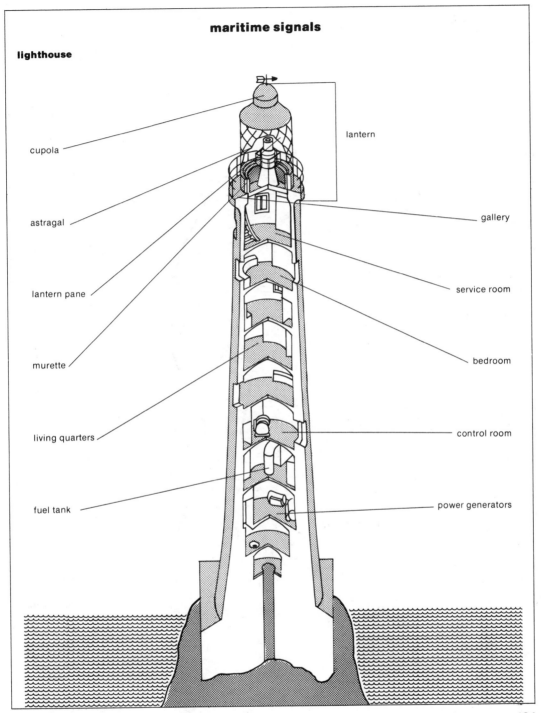

cupola

astragal

lantern pane

murette

living quarters

fuel tank

lantern

gallery

service room

bedroom

control room

power generators

maritime signals

lantern of lighthouse

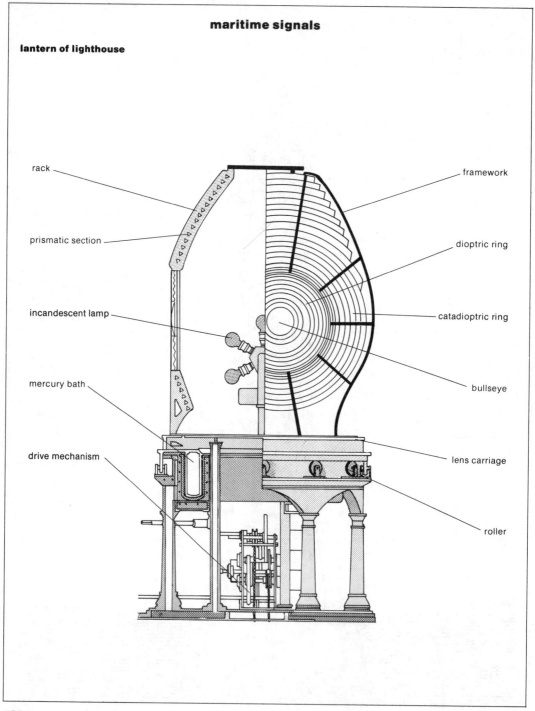

rack

prismatic section

incandescent lamp

mercury bath

drive mechanism

framework

dioptric ring

catadioptric ring

bullseye

lens carriage

roller

anchor

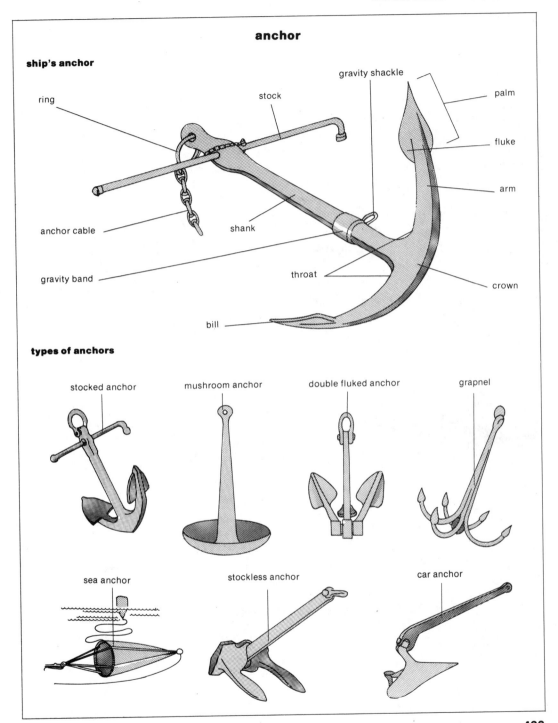

ship's anchor

ring

stock

gravity shackle

palm

fluke

arm

anchor cable

shank

throat

crown

gravity band

bill

types of anchors

stocked anchor

mushroom anchor

double fluked anchor

grapnel

sea anchor

stockless anchor

car anchor

433

long-range aircraft

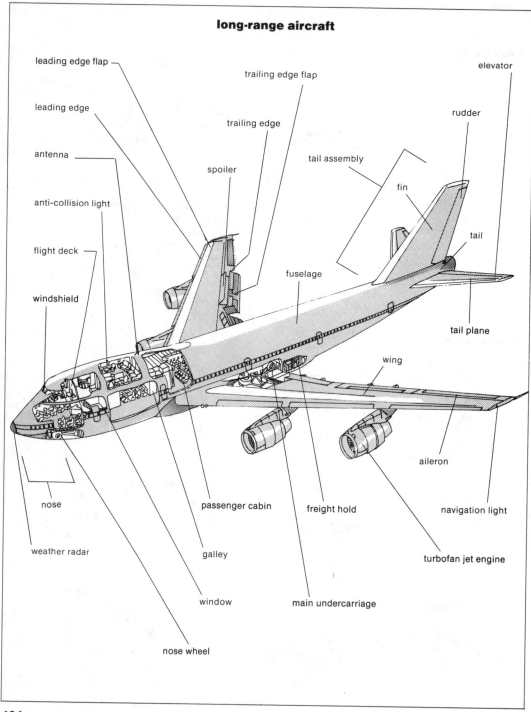

leading edge flap

trailing edge flap

elevator

leading edge

trailing edge

rudder

antenna

spoiler

tail assembly

anti-collision light

fin

flight deck

tail

windshield

fuselage

tail plane

wing

nose

aileron

weather radar

passenger cabin

freight hold

navigation light

galley

turbofan jet engine

window

main undercarriage

nose wheel

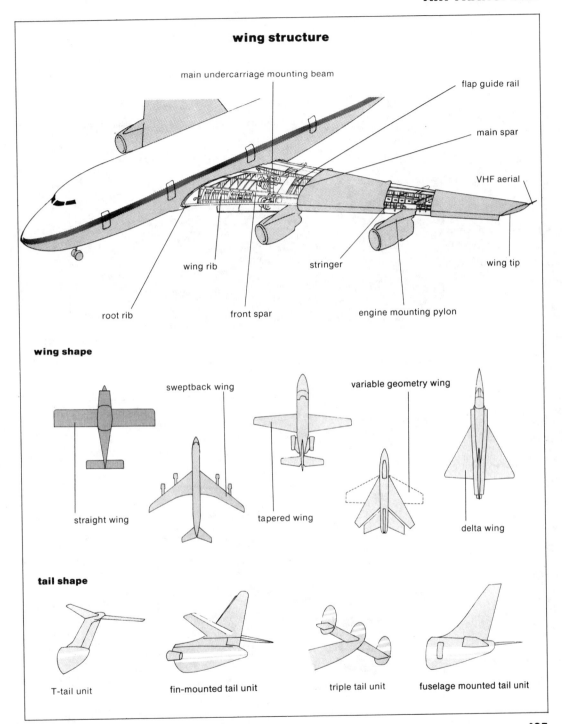

wing structure

main undercarriage mounting beam

flap guide rail

main spar

VHF aerial

wing rib

stringer

wing tip

root rib

front spar

engine mounting pylon

wing shape

sweptback wing

variable geometry wing

straight wing

tapered wing

delta wing

tail shape

T-tail unit

fin-mounted tail unit

triple tail unit

fuselage mounted tail unit

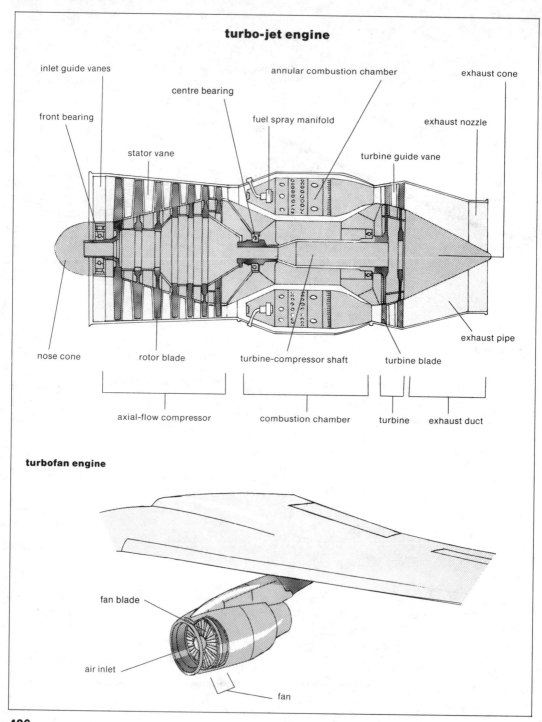

turbo-jet engine

inlet guide vanes

annular combustion chamber

exhaust cone

centre bearing

front bearing

fuel spray manifold

exhaust nozzle

stator vane

turbine guide vane

nose cone

rotor blade

turbine-compressor shaft

turbine blade

exhaust pipe

axial-flow compressor

combustion chamber

turbine

exhaust duct

turbofan engine

fan blade

air inlet

fan

flight deck

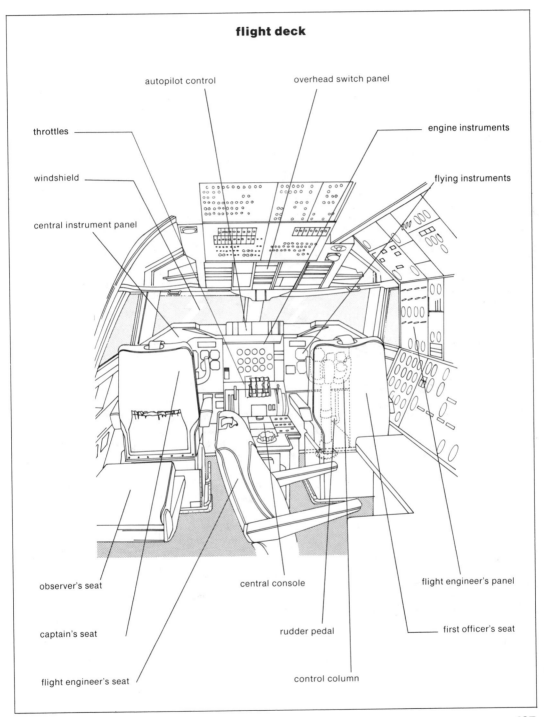

autopilot control

overhead switch panel

throttles

engine instruments

windshield

flying instruments

central instrument panel

observer's seat

central console

flight engineer's panel

captain's seat

rudder pedal

first officer's seat

flight engineer's seat

control column

airport

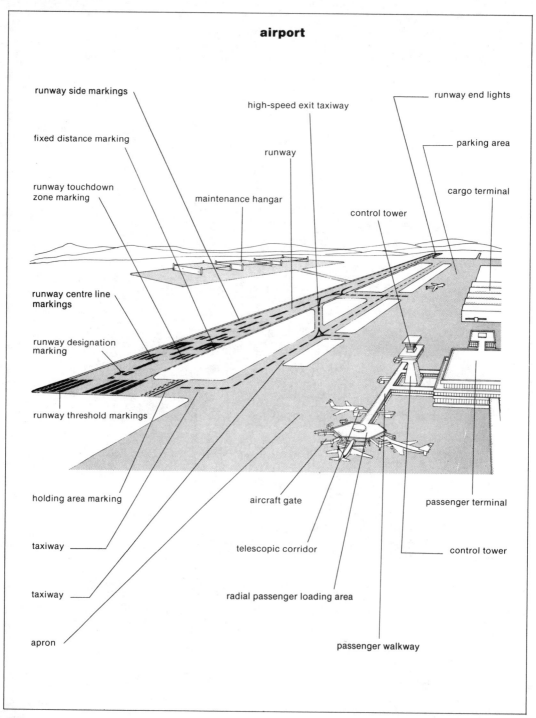

runway side markings

high-speed exit taxiway

runway end lights

fixed distance marking

runway

parking area

runway touchdown zone marking

maintenance hangar

cargo terminal

control tower

runway centre line markings

runway designation marking

runway threshold markings

holding area marking

aircraft gate

passenger terminal

taxiway

telescopic corridor

control tower

taxiway

radial passenger loading area

apron

passenger walkway

airport

ground airport equipment

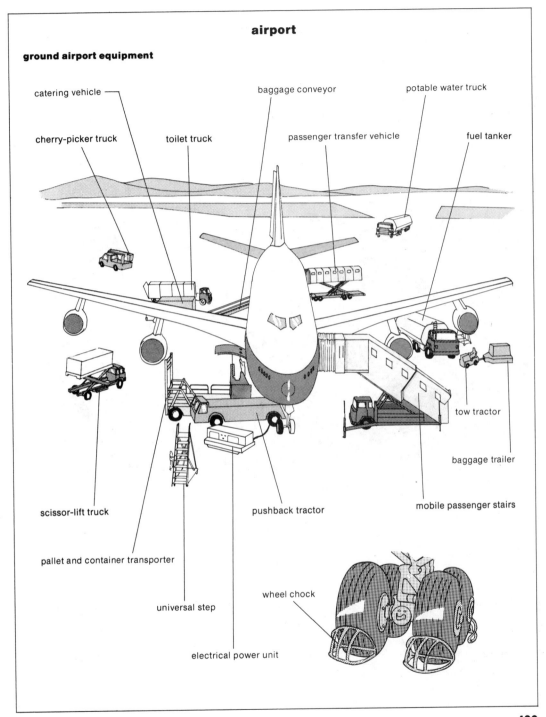

catering vehicle

cherry-picker truck

toilet truck

baggage conveyor

passenger transfer vehicle

potable water truck

fuel tanker

tow tractor

baggage trailer

mobile passenger stairs

scissor-lift truck

pushback tractor

pallet and container transporter

universal step

wheel chock

electrical power unit

AIR TRANSPORT

passenger terminal

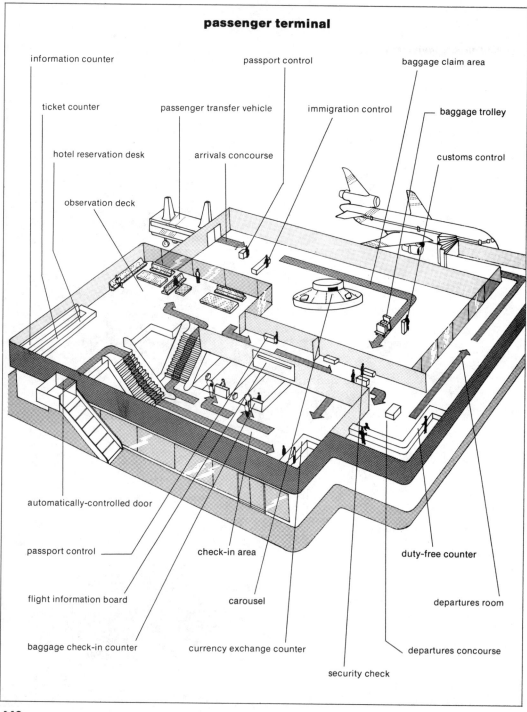

information counter

ticket counter

hotel reservation desk

observation deck

passport control

passenger transfer vehicle

arrivals concourse

immigration control

baggage claim area

baggage trolley

customs control

automatically-controlled door

passport control

flight information board

baggage check-in counter

check-in area

carousel

currency exchange counter

security check

duty-free counter

departures room

departures concourse

helicopter

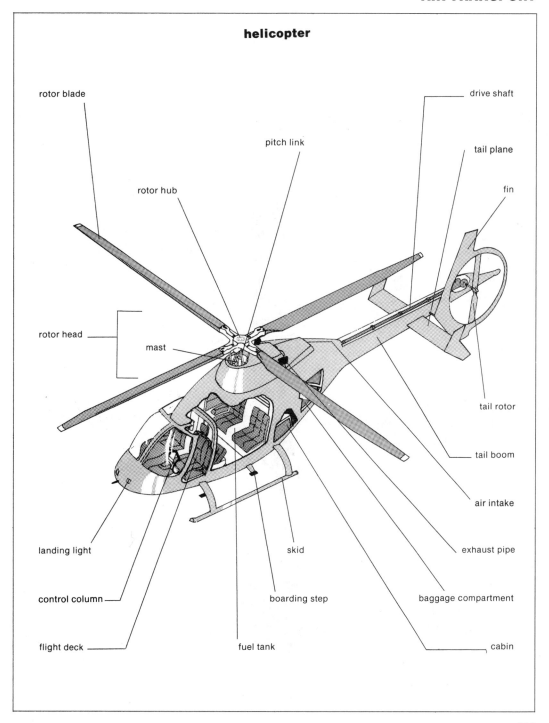

rotor blade

drive shaft

pitch link

tail plane

rotor hub

fin

rotor head

mast

tail rotor

tail boom

air intake

landing light

exhaust pipe

skid

control column

boarding step

baggage compartment

flight deck

fuel tank

cabin

rocket

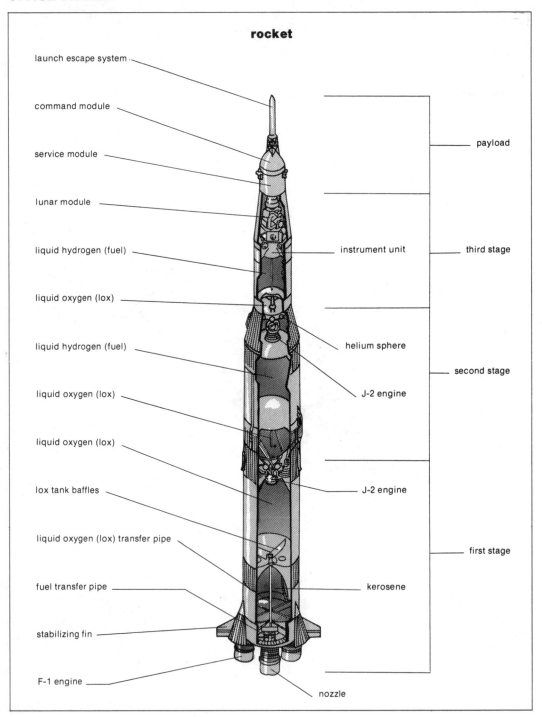

launch escape system

command module

service module

lunar module

liquid hydrogen (fuel)

liquid oxygen (lox)

liquid hydrogen (fuel)

liquid oxygen (lox)

liquid oxygen (lox)

lox tank baffles

liquid oxygen (lox) transfer pipe

fuel transfer pipe

stabilizing fin

F-1 engine

instrument unit

helium sphere

J-2 engine

J-2 engine

kerosene

nozzle

payload

third stage

second stage

first stage

space shuttle

space shuttle at take-off

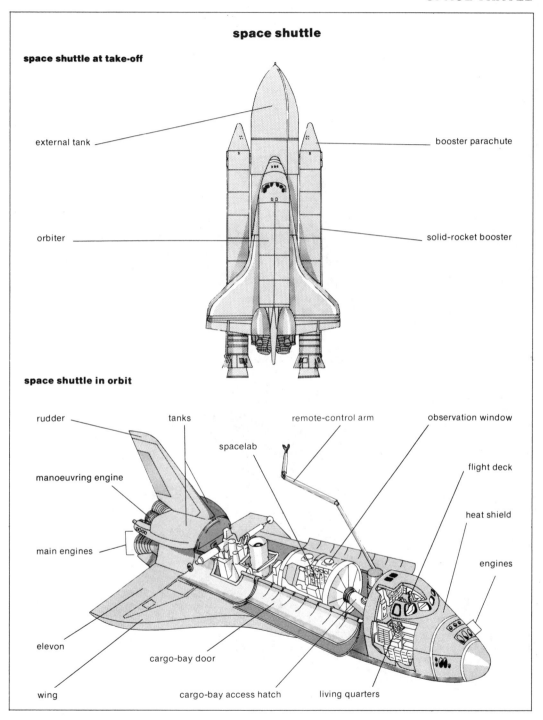

external tank

booster parachute

orbiter

solid-rocket booster

space shuttle in orbit

rudder

tanks

remote-control arm

observation window

spacelab

flight deck

manoeuvring engine

heat shield

main engines

engines

elevon

cargo-bay door

wing

cargo-bay access hatch

living quarters

spacesuit

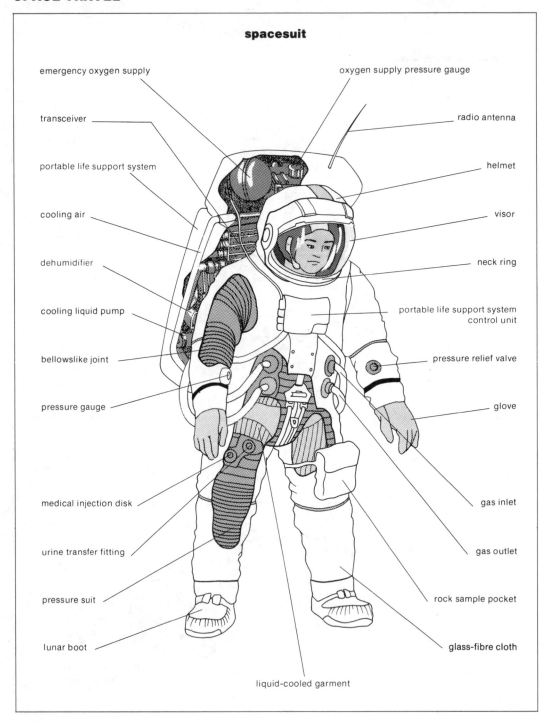

emergency oxygen supply

oxygen supply pressure gauge

transceiver

radio antenna

portable life support system

helmet

cooling air

visor

dehumidifier

neck ring

cooling liquid pump

portable life support system control unit

bellowslike joint

pressure relief valve

pressure gauge

glove

medical injection disk

gas inlet

urine transfer fitting

gas outlet

pressure suit

rock sample pocket

lunar boot

glass-fibre cloth

liquid-cooled garment

OFFICE SUPPLIES AND EQUIPMENT

stationery

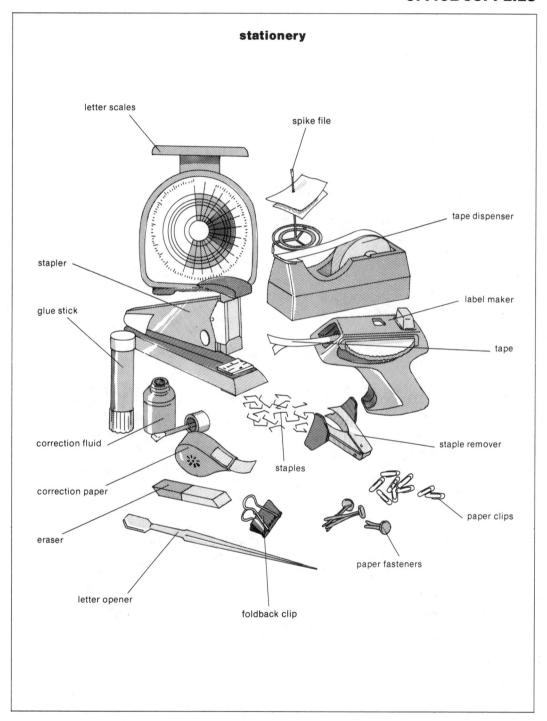

letter scales

spike file

tape dispenser

stapler

glue stick

label maker

tape

correction fluid

correction paper

staples

staple remover

eraser

paper clips

letter opener

paper fasteners

foldback clip

stationery

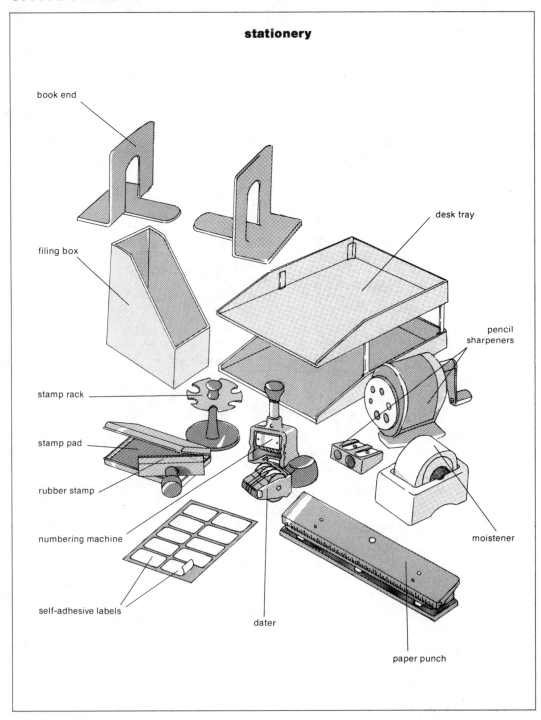

book end

desk tray

filing box

pencil sharpeners

stamp rack

stamp pad

rubber stamp

numbering machine

moistener

self-adhesive labels

dater

paper punch

stationery

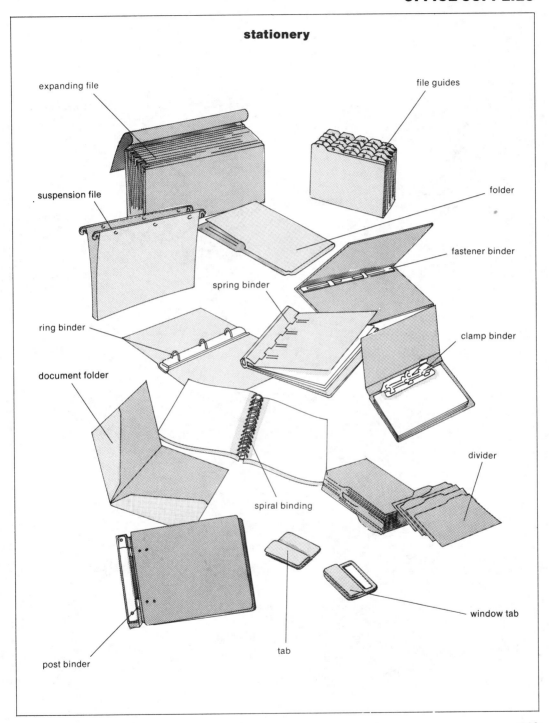

expanding file

file guides

suspension file

folder

fastener binder

spring binder

ring binder

clamp binder

document folder

divider

spiral binding

window tab

post binder

tab

449

stationery

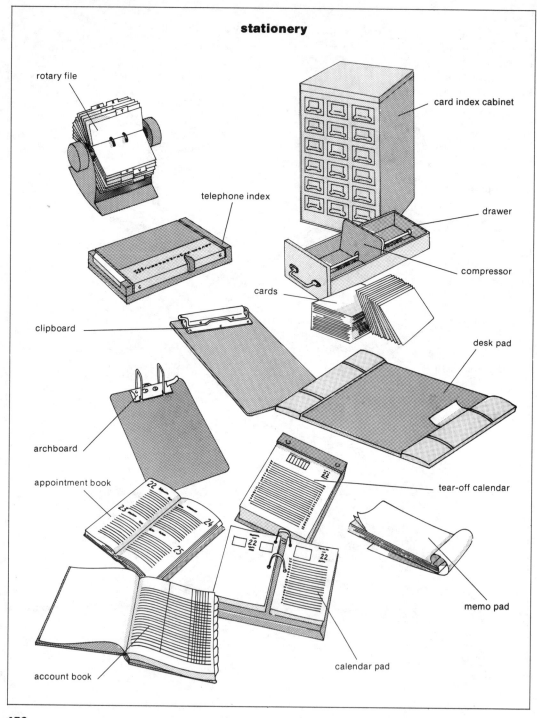

rotary file

card index cabinet

telephone index

drawer

compressor

cards

clipboard

desk pad

archboard

appointment book

tear-off calendar

memo pad

calendar pad

account book

office furniture

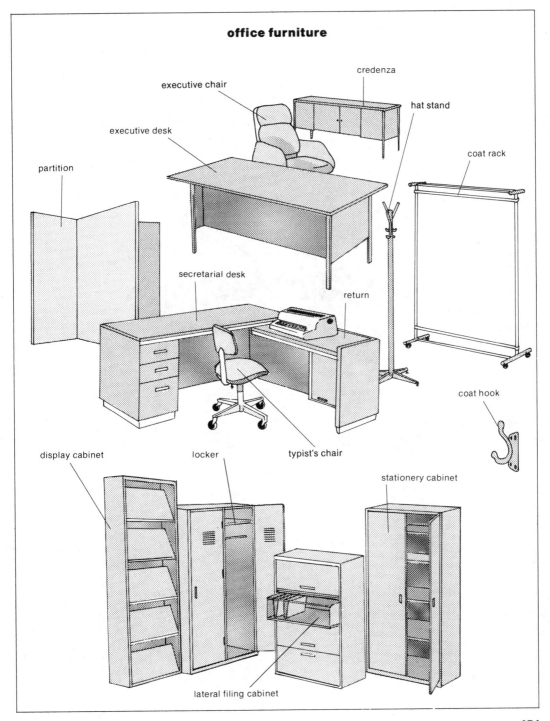

credenza

executive chair

hat stand

executive desk

coat rack

partition

secretarial desk

return

coat hook

display cabinet

locker

typist's chair

stationery cabinet

lateral filing cabinet

typewriter

golfball element

golfball element

golfball release lever

typestyle

card holder

ribbon

separator wire

correcting tape

impression control

roller

supply spool

take-up spool

guide post

ribbon guide

ribbon end indicator

tape load lever

character

ribbon cartridge

ribbon load lever

take-up knob

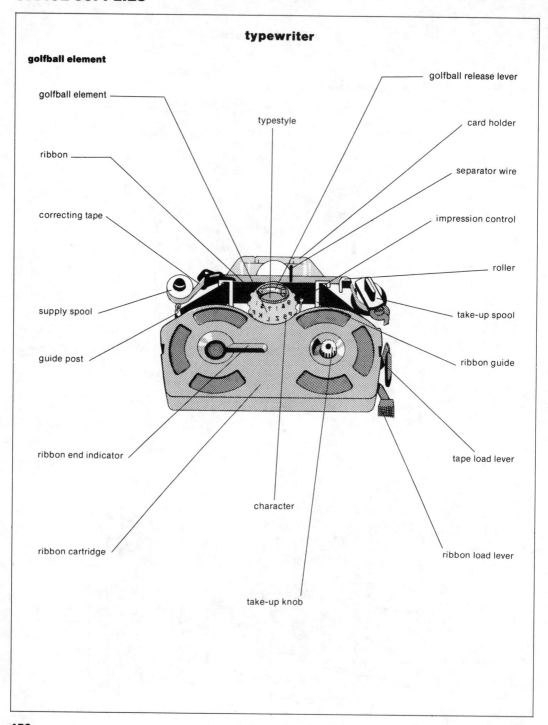

typewriter

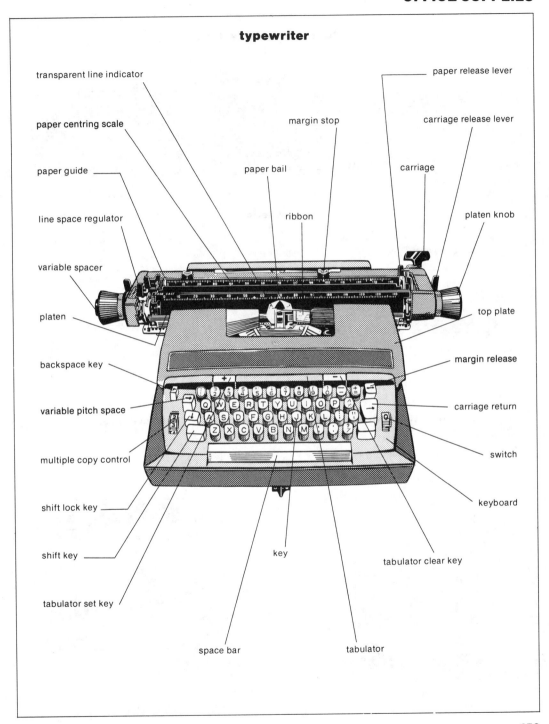

transparent line indicator

paper centring scale

paper guide

line space regulator

variable spacer

platen

backspace key

variable pitch space

multiple copy control

shift lock key

shift key

tabulator set key

space bar

margin stop

paper bail

ribbon

key

tabulator

paper release lever

carriage release lever

carriage

platen knob

top plate

margin release

carriage return

switch

keyboard

tabulator clear key

MICROCOMPUTER

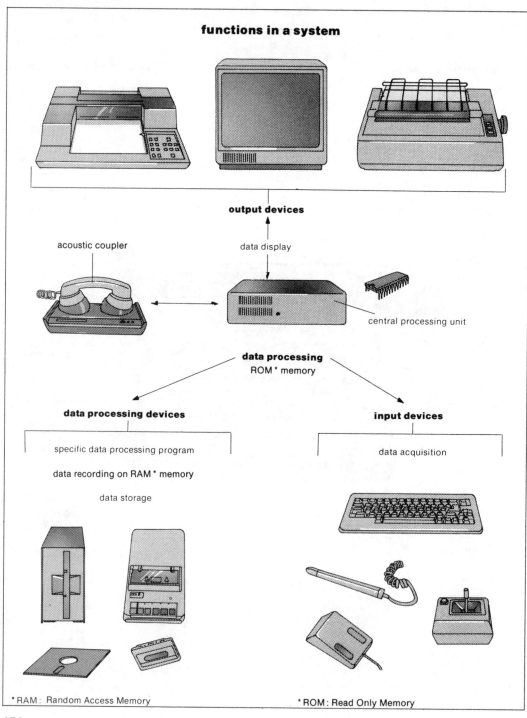

functions in a system

output devices

acoustic coupler

data display

central processing unit

data processing
ROM * memory

data processing devices

specific data processing program

data recording on RAM * memory

data storage

input devices

data acquisition

* RAM : Random Access Memory

* ROM : Read Only Memory

454

configuration of a system

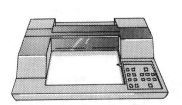

plotter

visual display unit

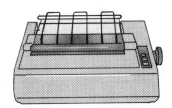

printer

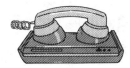

acoustic coupler

central processing unit

microprocessor

disk

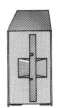

disk drive

keyboard

mouse

joystick

cassette

cassette recorder

light pen

MICRO-COMPUTER

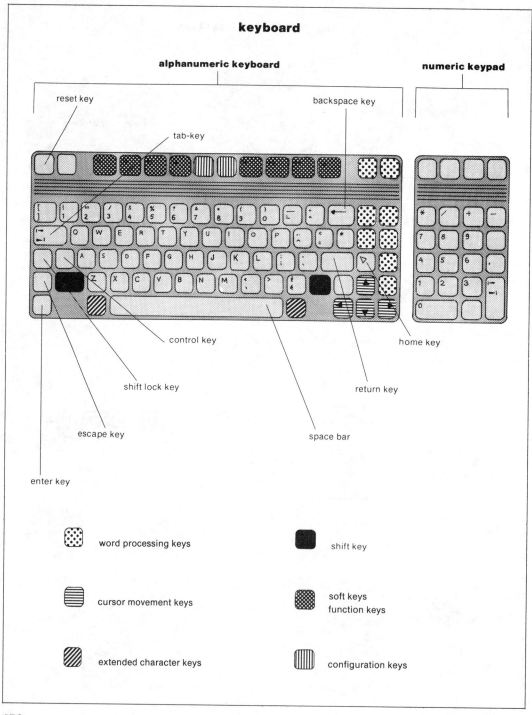

keyboard

alphanumeric keyboard

numeric keypad

reset key

backspace key

tab-key

control key

home key

shift lock key

return key

escape key

space bar

enter key

	word processing keys		shift key
	cursor movement keys		soft keys function keys
	extended character keys		configuration keys

peripheral equipment

dot matrix printer

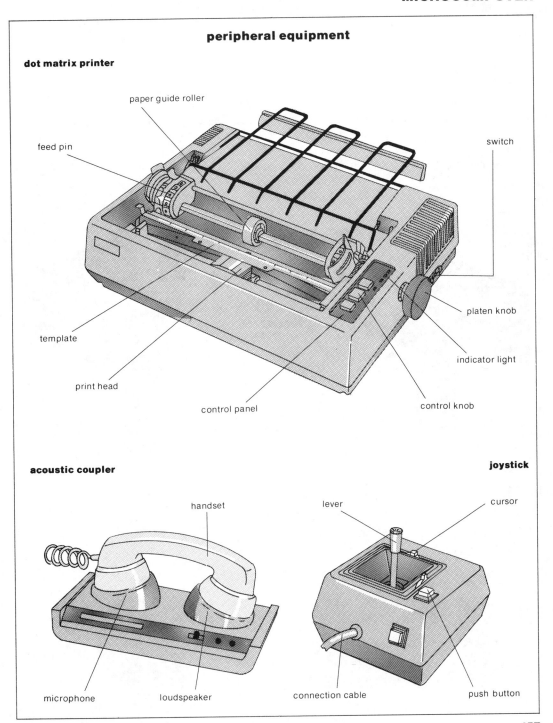

paper guide roller

feed pin

switch

template

platen knob

print head

indicator light

control panel

control knob

acoustic coupler

joystick

handset

lever

cursor

microphone

loudspeaker

connection cable

push button

COMPUTER

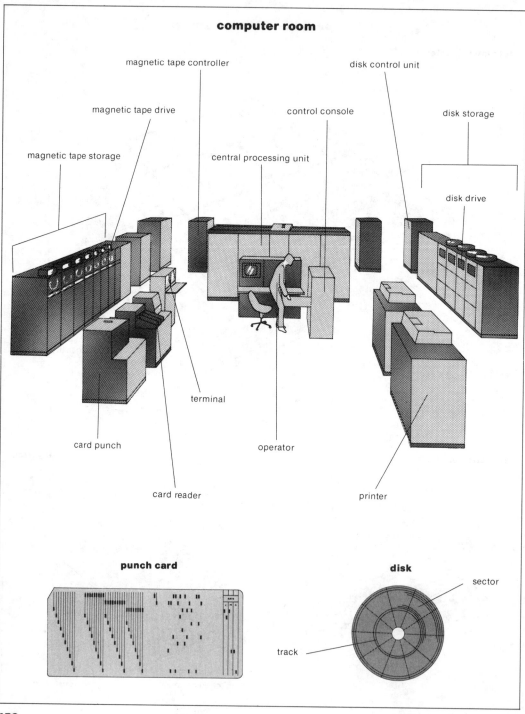

computer room

magnetic tape controller

disk control unit

magnetic tape drive

control console

disk storage

magnetic tape storage

central processing unit

disk drive

terminal

card punch

operator

card reader

printer

punch card

disk

sector

track

MUSIC

musical notation

staff

line · space · ledger line

clefs

g clef · f clef · c clef

scale

c · d · e · f · g · a · b · c

note symbols

breve · semi-breve · minim · crotchet · quaver · semi-quaver · demi-semi-quaver · hemi-demi-semi-quaver

rest symbols

breve rest · semi-breve rest · minim rest · crotchet rest · quaver rest · semi-quaver rest · demi-semi-quaver rest · hemi-demi-semi-quaver rest

musical notation

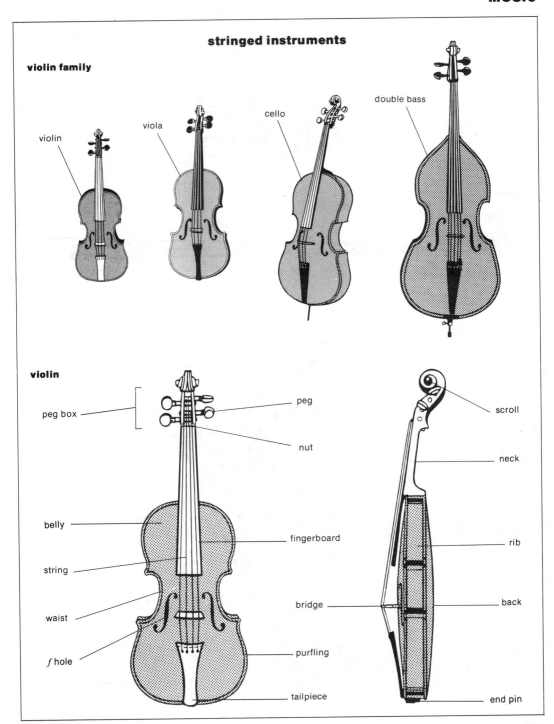

stringed instruments

violin family

violin

viola

cello

double bass

violin

peg box

peg

nut

scroll

neck

belly

fingerboard

string

waist

f hole

bridge

rib

back

purfling

tailpiece

end pin

stringed instruments

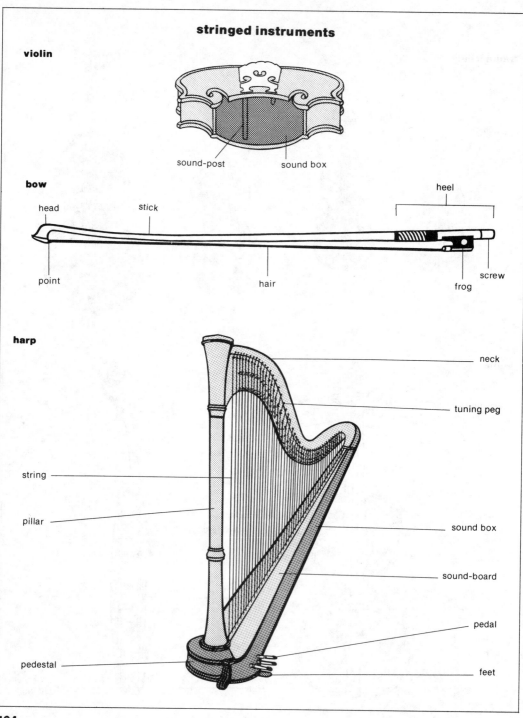

violin

sound-post   sound box

bow

heel

head   stick

point   hair   frog   screw

harp

neck

tuning peg

string

pillar

sound box

sound-board

pedal

pedestal   feet

keyboard instruments

upright piano

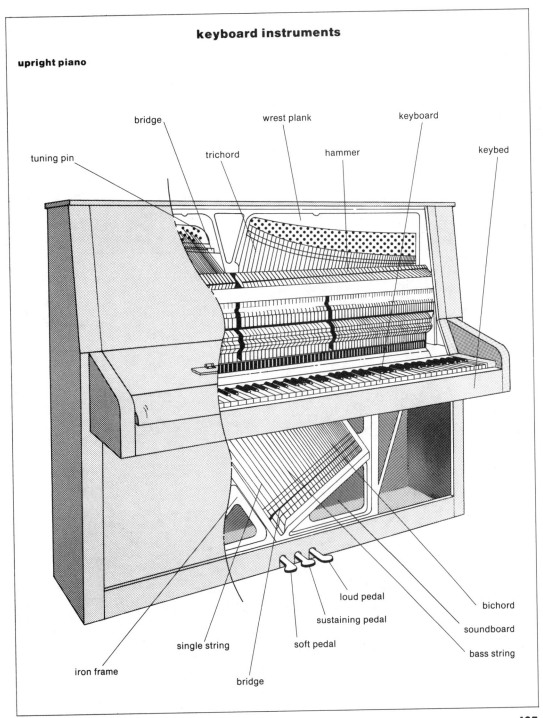

bridge

wrest plank

keyboard

tuning pin

trichord

hammer

keybed

loud pedal

sustaining pedal

soft pedal

bichord

soundboard

bass string

iron frame

single string

bridge

keyboard instruments

upright piano action

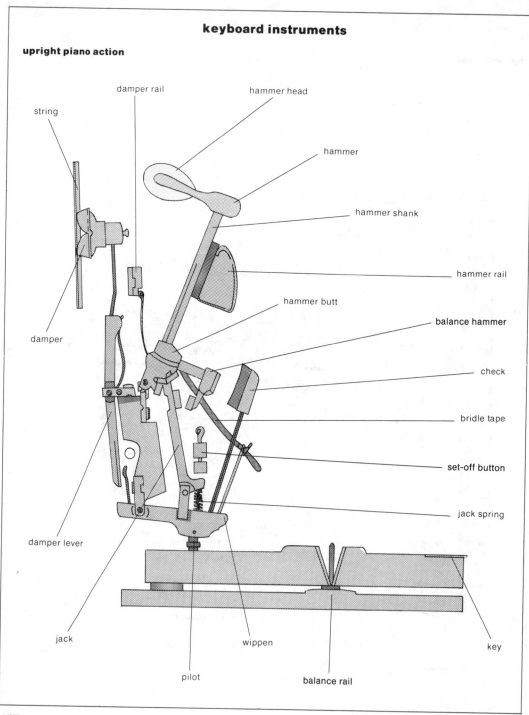

organ

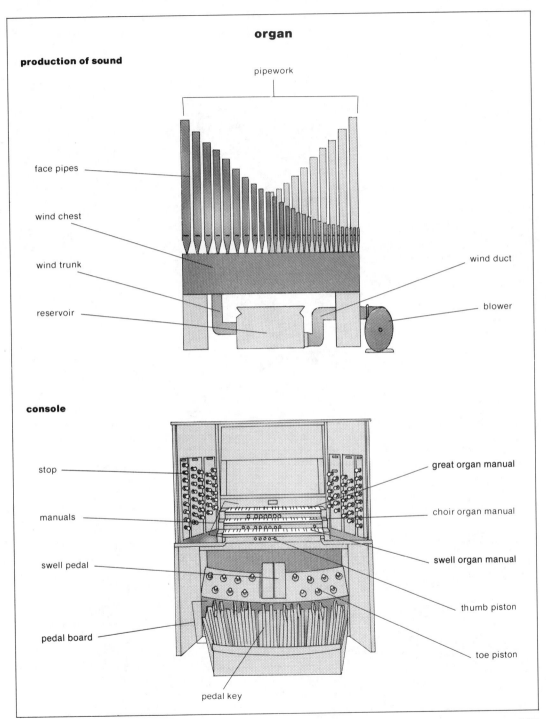

production of sound

pipework

face pipes

wind chest

wind trunk

reservoir

wind duct

blower

console

stop

manuals

swell pedal

pedal board

pedal key

great organ manual

choir organ manual

swell organ manual

thumb piston

toe piston

organ

mechanism of the organ

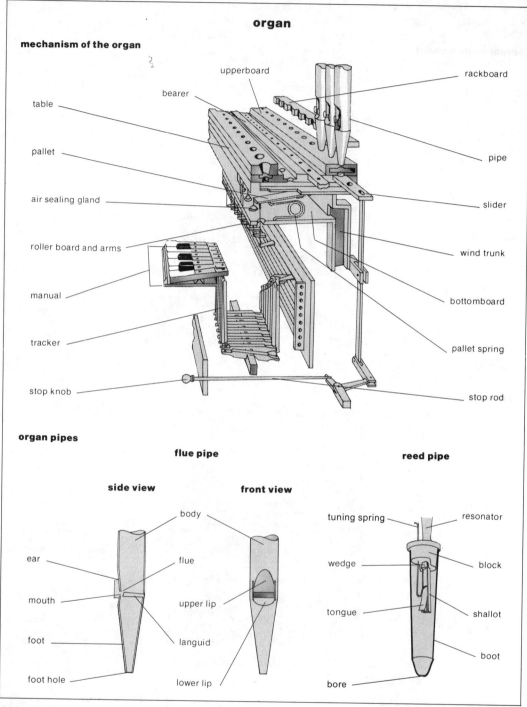

upperboard

bearer

rackboard

table

pallet

pipe

air sealing gland

slider

roller board and arms

wind trunk

manual

bottomboard

tracker

pallet spring

stop knob

stop rod

organ pipes

flue pipe

reed pipe

side view

front view

body

tuning spring

resonator

ear

flue

wedge

block

mouth

upper lip

tongue

shallot

foot

languid

boot

foot hole

lower lip

bore

468

wind instruments

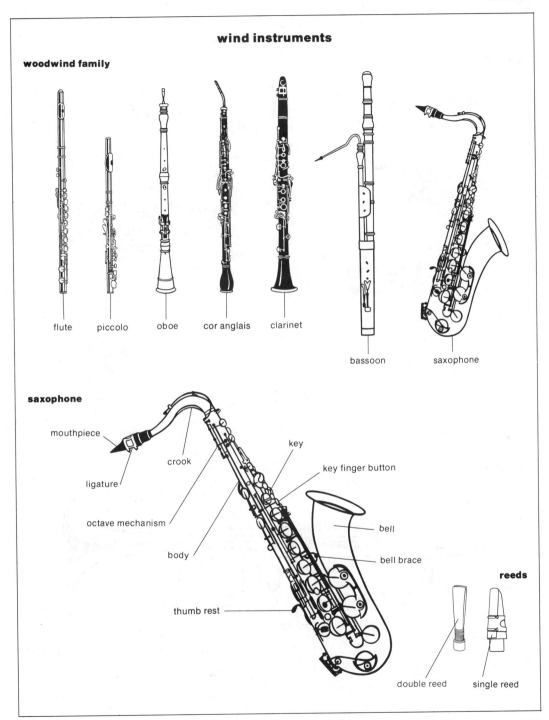

woodwind family

flute piccolo oboe cor anglais clarinet

bassoon saxophone

saxophone

mouthpiece

crook

key

key finger button

ligature

octave mechanism

bell

body

bell brace

reeds

thumb rest

double reed single reed

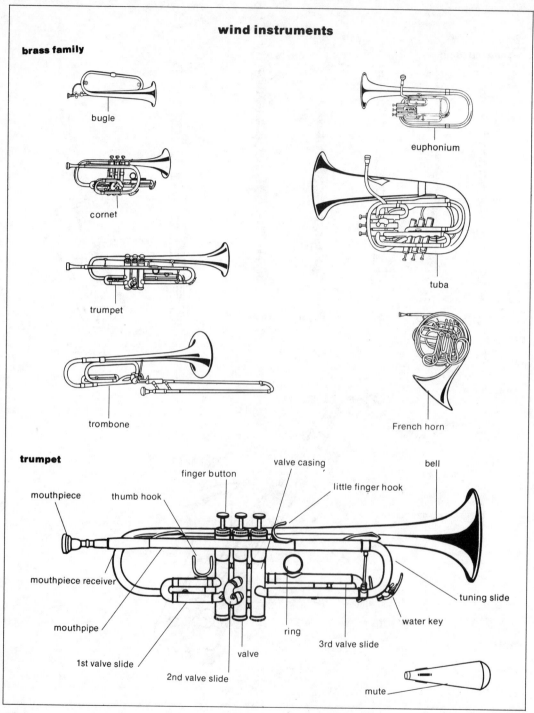

wind instruments

brass family

bugle

euphonium

cornet

tuba

trumpet

trombone

French horn

trumpet

mouthpiece

thumb hook

finger button

valve casing

little finger hook

bell

mouthpiece receiver

mouthpipe

1st valve slide

2nd valve slide

valve

ring

3rd valve slide

water key

tuning slide

mute

percussion instruments

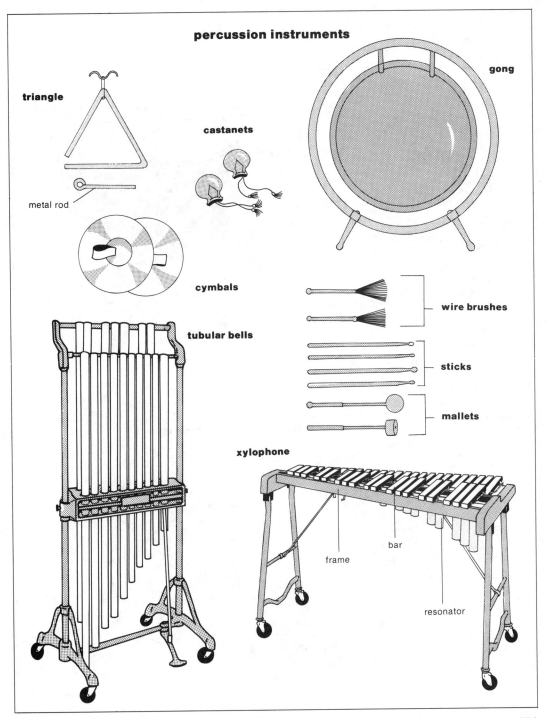

gong

triangle

castanets

metal rod

cymbals

tubular bells

wire brushes

sticks

mallets

xylophone

frame

bar

resonator

percussion instruments

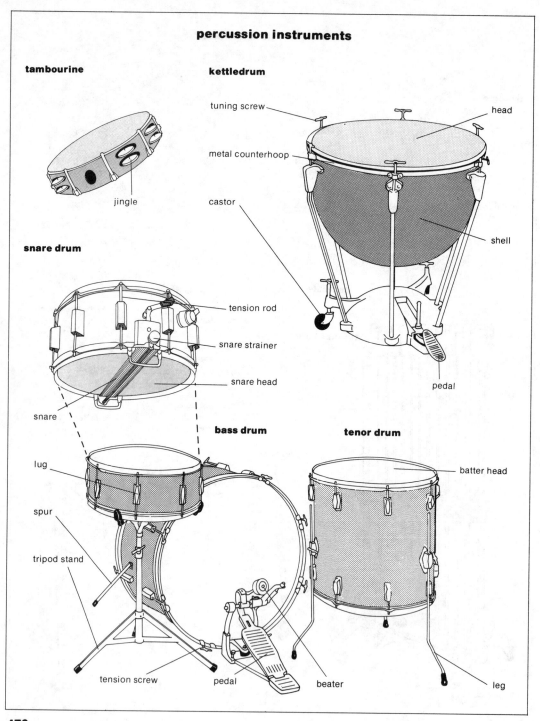

tambourine

jingle

kettledrum

tuning screw

head

metal counterhoop

castor

shell

snare drum

tension rod

snare strainer

snare head

snare

pedal

bass drum

tenor drum

lug

batter head

spur

tripod stand

tension screw

pedal

beater

leg

traditional musical instruments

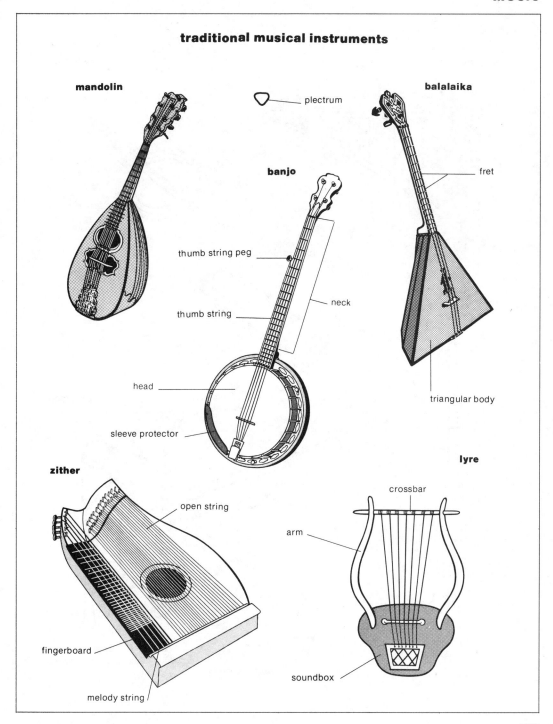

mandolin

plectrum

balalaika

banjo

fret

thumb string peg

thumb string

neck

triangular body

head

sleeve protector

lyre

zither

crossbar

open string

arm

fingerboard

soundbox

melody string

traditional musical instruments

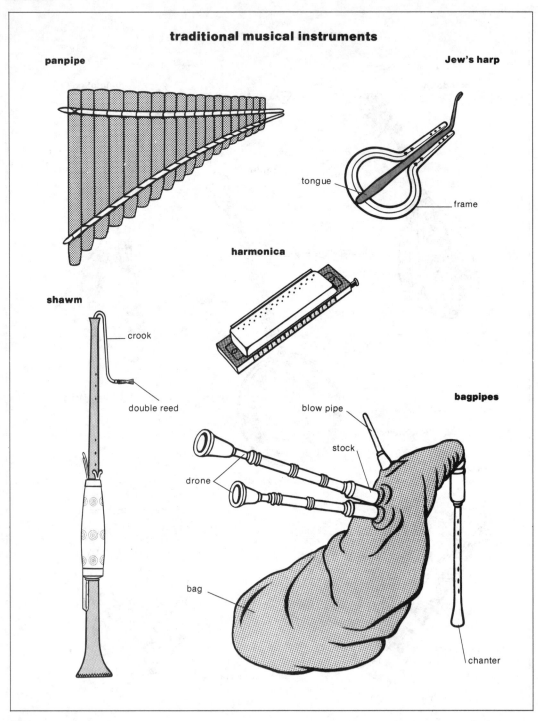

panpipe

Jew's harp

tongue

frame

harmonica

shawm

crook

double reed

bagpipes

blow pipe

stock

drone

bag

chanter

traditional musical instruments

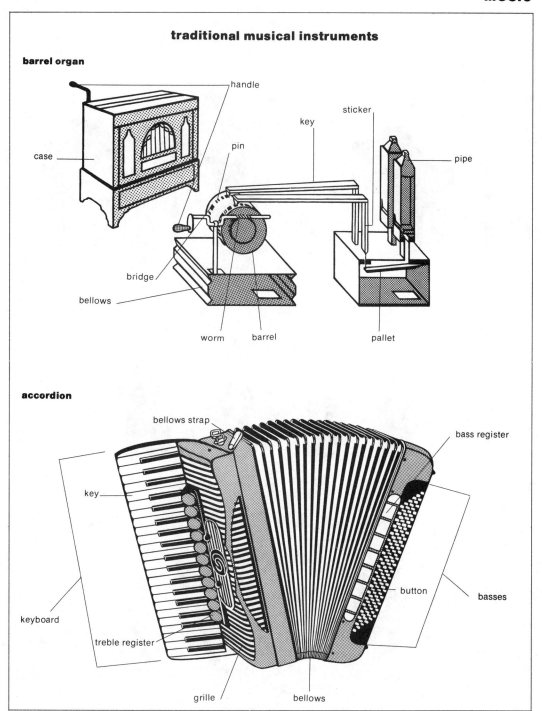

barrel organ

handle

key

sticker

pin

case

pipe

bridge

bellows

worm

barrel

pallet

accordion

bellows strap

bass register

key

keyboard

treble register

grille

bellows

button

basses

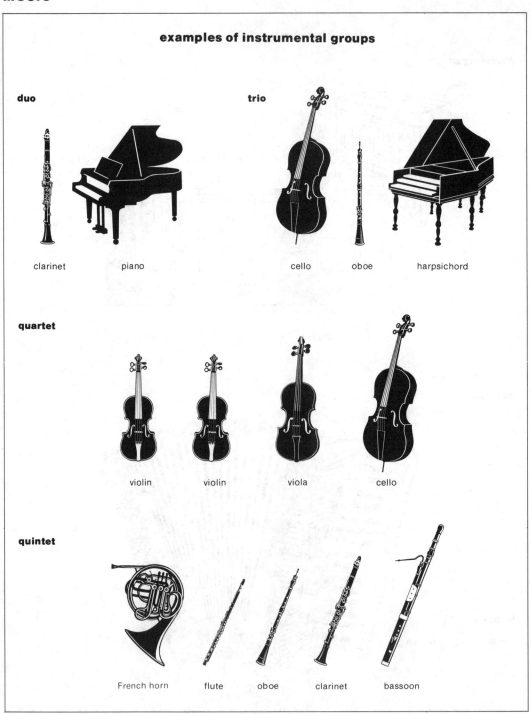

examples of instrumental groups

duo

clarinet   piano

trio

cello   oboe   harpsichord

quartet

violin   violin   viola   cello

quintet

French horn   flute   oboe   clarinet   bassoon

examples of instrumental groups

sextet

clarinet   clarinet   French horn   French horn   bassoon   bassoon

jazz band

drum kit

bass drum   tenor drum   snare drum   cymbals   piano

double bass   clarinet   saxophone   trombone   trumpet   cornet

MUSIC

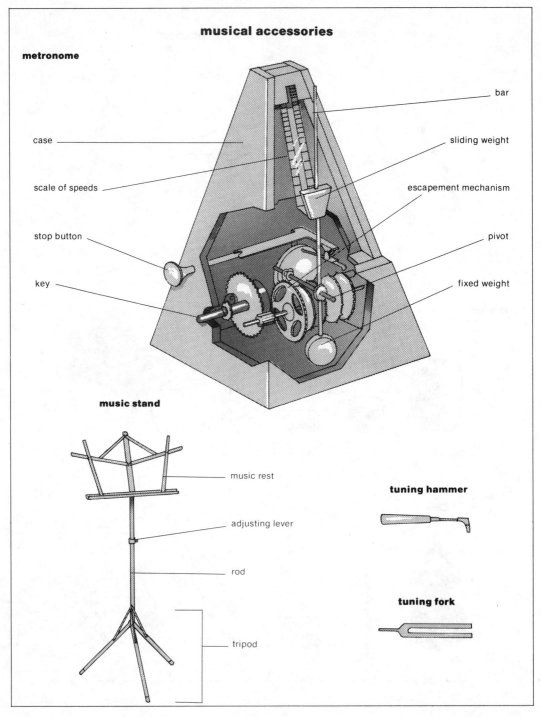

musical accessories

metronome

bar

case

sliding weight

scale of speeds

escapement mechanism

stop button

pivot

key

fixed weight

music stand

music rest

tuning hammer

adjusting lever

rod

tuning fork

tripod

symphony orchestra

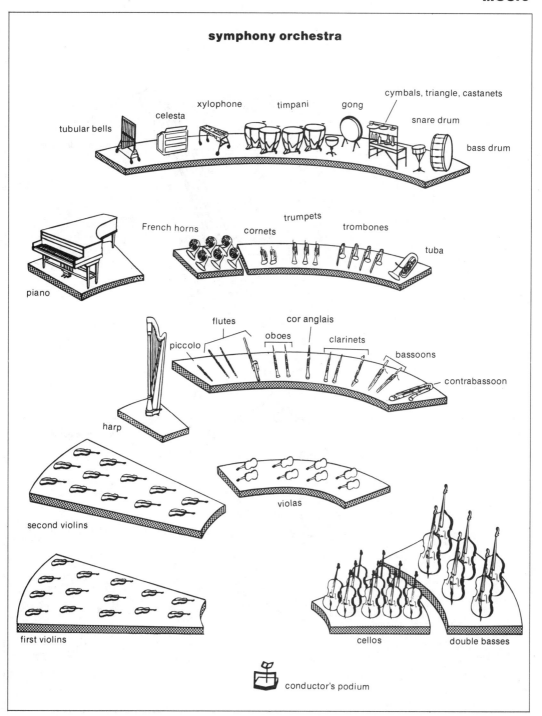

tubular bells

celesta

xylophone

timpani

gong

cymbals, triangle, castanets

snare drum

bass drum

French horns

cornets

trumpets

trombones

tuba

piano

flutes

cor anglais

piccolo

oboes

clarinets

bassoons

contrabassoon

harp

second violins

violas

first violins

cellos

double basses

conductor's podium

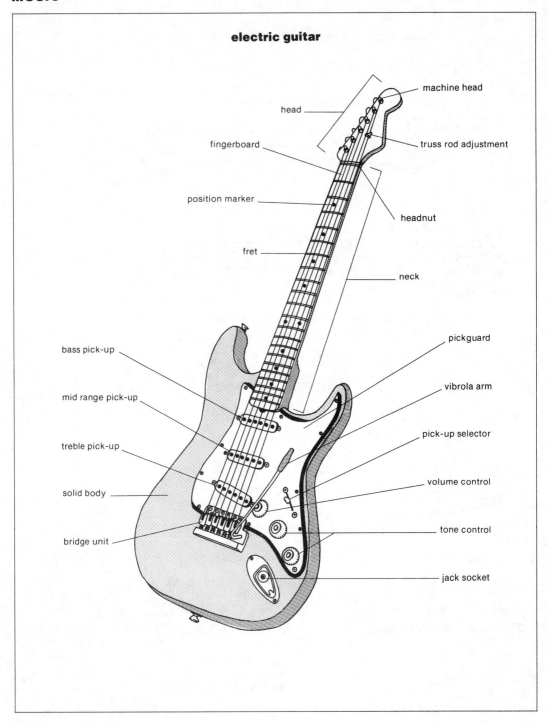

electric guitar

head

machine head

fingerboard

truss rod adjustment

position marker

headnut

fret

neck

bass pick-up

pickguard

mid range pick-up

vibrola arm

treble pick-up

pick-up selector

solid body

volume control

bridge unit

tone control

jack socket

classical guitar

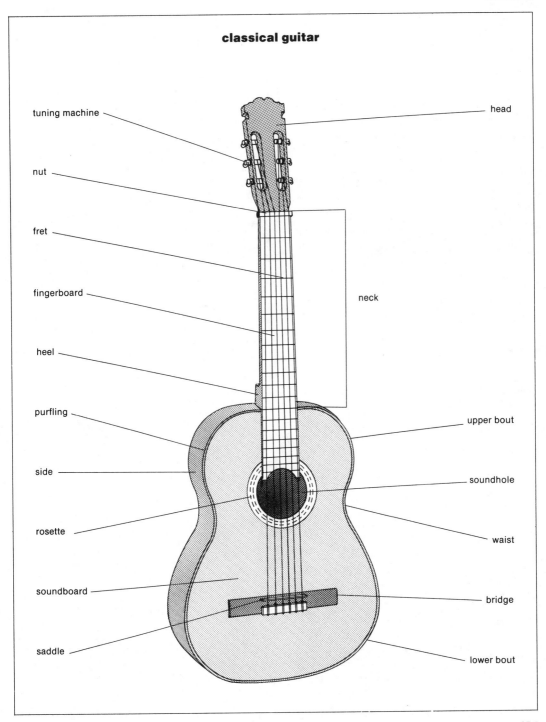

tuning machine

head

nut

fret

fingerboard

neck

heel

purfling

upper bout

side

soundhole

rosette

waist

soundboard

bridge

saddle

lower bout

CREATIVE LEISURE ACTIVITIES

sewing

sewing machine

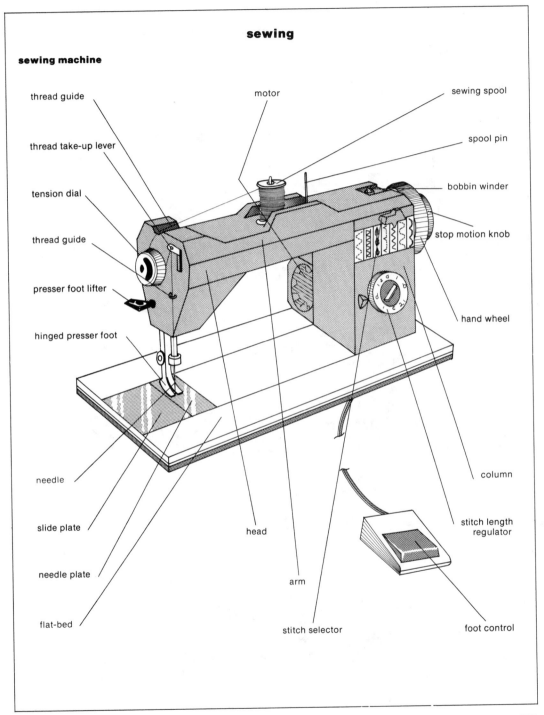

thread guide

motor

sewing spool

thread take-up lever

spool pin

tension dial

bobbin winder

thread guide

stop motion knob

presser foot lifter

hand wheel

hinged presser foot

needle

column

slide plate

stitch length
regulator

head

needle plate

flat-bed

arm

stitch selector

foot control

sewing

sewing machine

tension dial

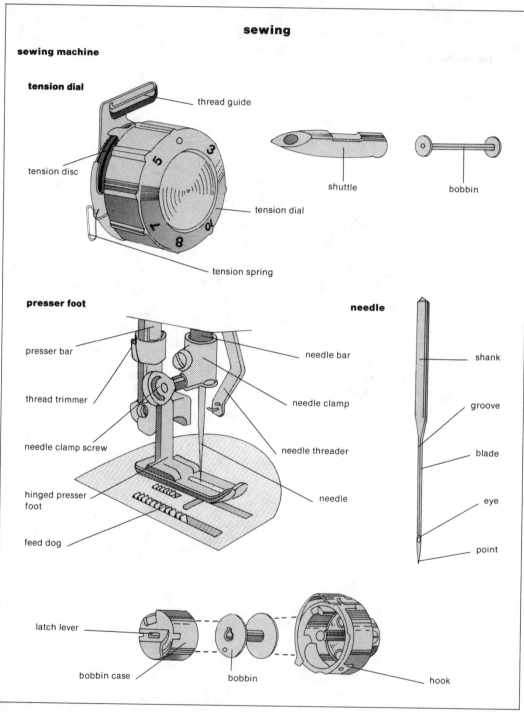

thread guide

tension disc

3

5

tension dial

7

10

8

tension spring

shuttle

bobbin

presser foot

needle

presser bar

needle bar

thread trimmer

needle clamp

needle clamp screw

needle threader

hinged presser foot

needle

feed dog

shank

groove

blade

eye

point

latch lever

bobbin case

bobbin

hook

sewing

accessories

pin cushion

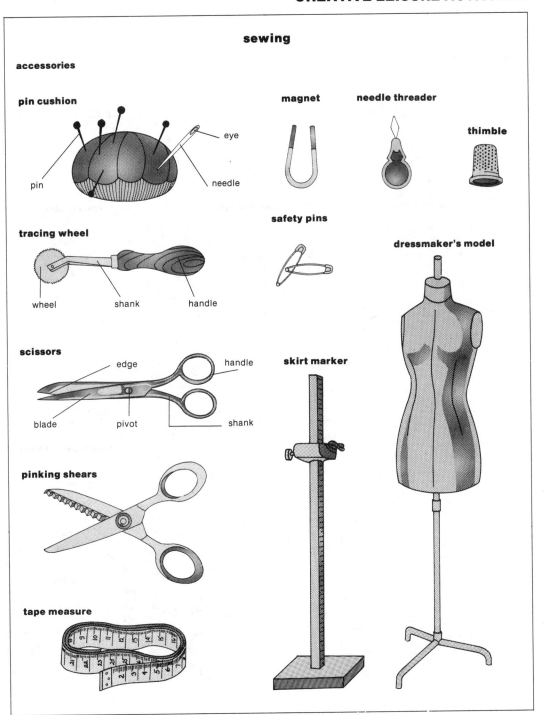

eye

pin

needle

magnet

needle threader

thimble

safety pins

tracing wheel

wheel shank handle

dressmaker's model

scissors

edge handle

blade pivot shank

skirt marker

pinking shears

tape measure

CREATIVE LEISURE ACTIVITIES

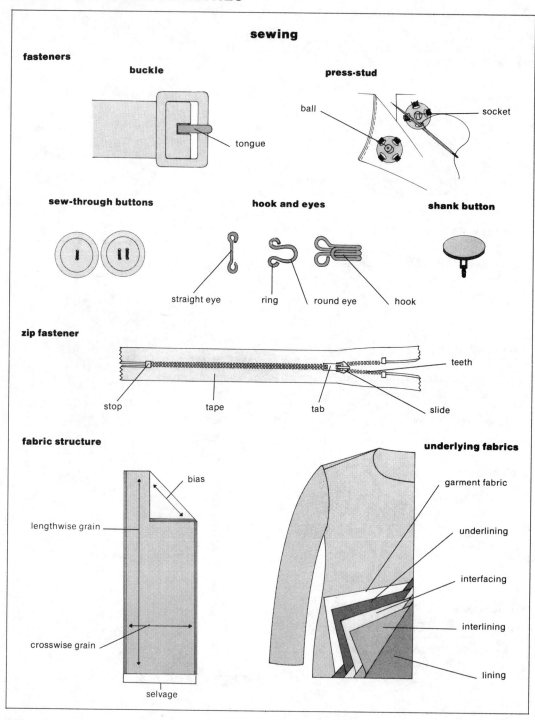

sewing

fasteners

buckle

tongue

press-stud

ball

socket

sew-through buttons

hook and eyes

straight eye

ring

round eye

hook

shank button

zip fastener

teeth

stop

tape

tab

slide

fabric structure

bias

lengthwise grain

crosswise grain

selvage

underlying fabrics

garment fabric

underlining

interfacing

interlining

lining

sewing

pattern

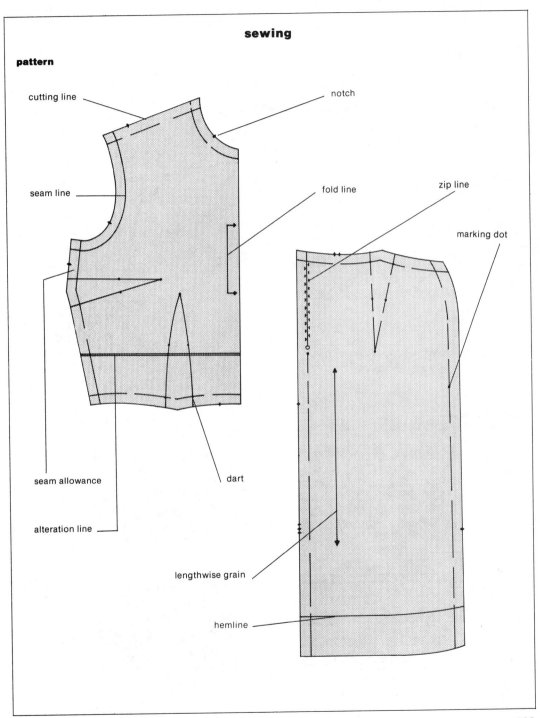

cutting line

notch

seam line

fold line

zip line

marking dot

seam allowance

dart

alteration line

lengthwise grain

hemline

CREATIVE LEISURE ACTIVITIES

knitting

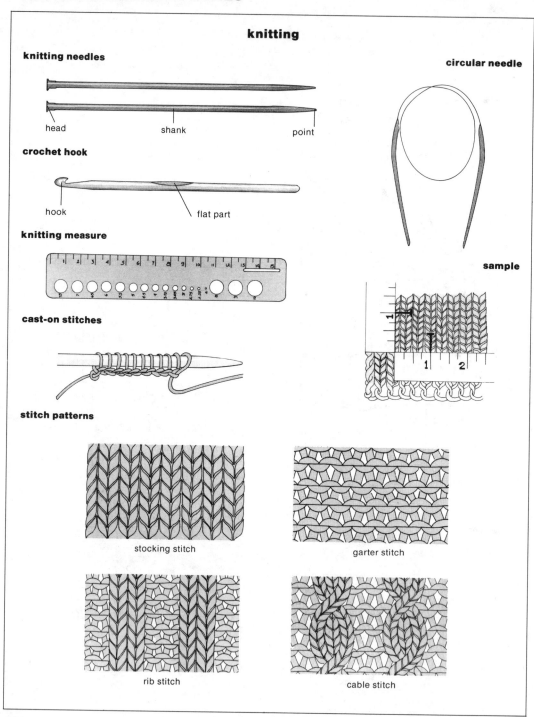

knitting needles

head shank point

crochet hook

hook flat part

knitting measure

cast-on stitches

stitch patterns

stocking stitch

garter stitch

rib stitch

cable stitch

circular needle

sample

knitting machine

tension block

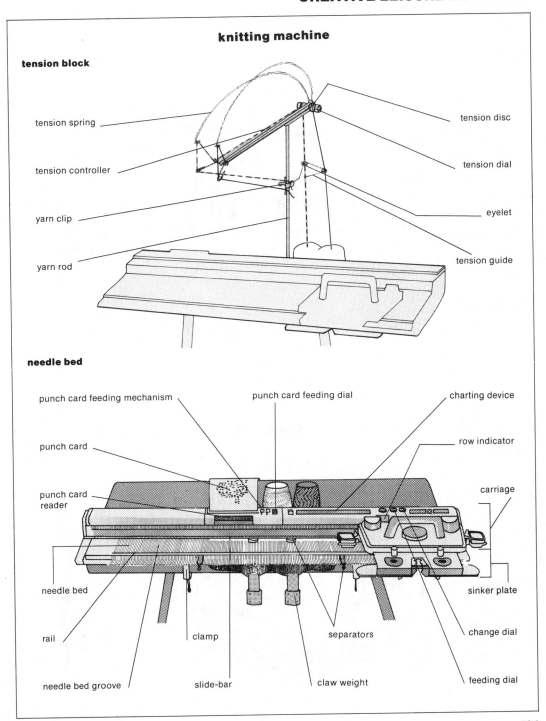

tension spring

tension controller

yarn clip

yarn rod

tension disc

tension dial

eyelet

tension guide

needle bed

punch card feeding mechanism

punch card feeding dial

charting device

punch card

row indicator

punch card reader

carriage

needle bed

rail

clamp

separators

sinker plate

change dial

needle bed groove

slide-bar

claw weight

feeding dial

491

CREATIVE LEISURE ACTIVITIES

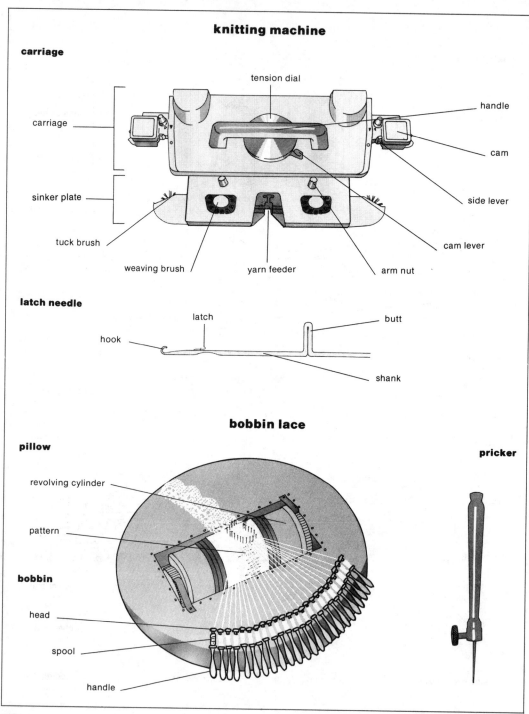

knitting machine

carriage

tension dial

handle

carriage

cam

side lever

sinker plate

cam lever

tuck brush

weaving brush

yarn feeder

arm nut

latch needle

latch

butt

hook

shank

bobbin lace

pillow

pricker

revolving cylinder

pattern

bobbin

head

spool

handle

492

embroidery

frame

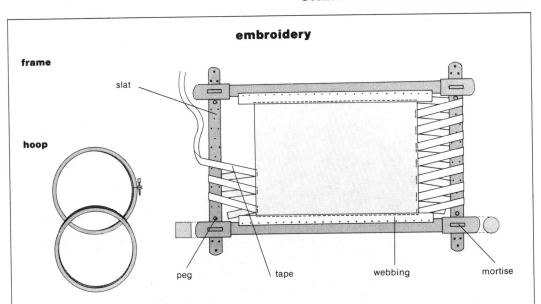

slat

hoop

peg   tape   webbing   mortise

groups of stitches

knot stitches group

French knot stitch   bullion stitch

flat stitches group

couched stitches

long and short stitch   fishbone stitch   Romanian couching stitch   Oriental couching stitch

cross stitches group

loop stitches group

chevron stitch   herringbone stitch   chain stitch   feather stitch

493

weaving

horizontal floor loom

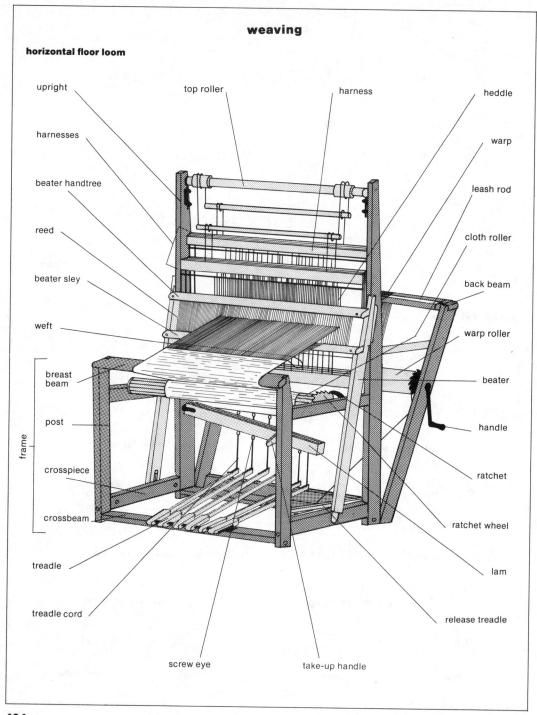

upright

top roller

harness

heddle

harnesses

warp

beater handtree

leash rod

reed

cloth roller

beater sley

back beam

weft

warp roller

breast beam

beater

post

handle

frame

crosspiece

ratchet

crossbeam

ratchet wheel

treadle

lam

treadle cord

release treadle

screw eye

take-up handle

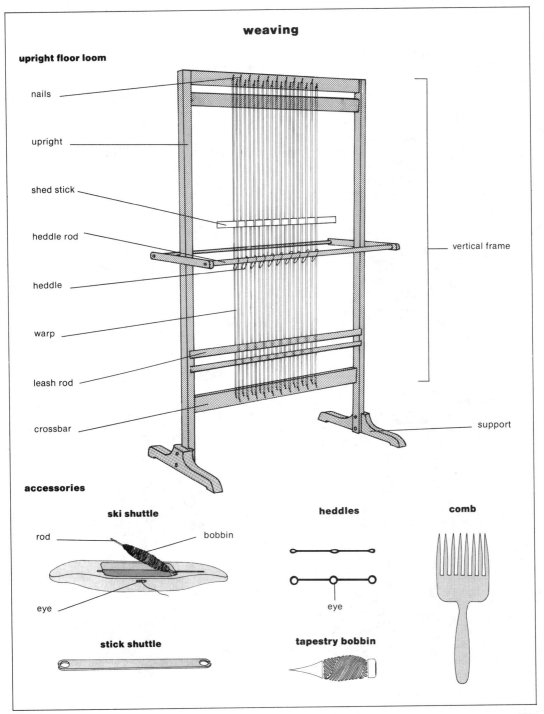

weaving

upright floor loom

nails

upright

shed stick

heddle rod

heddle

warp

leash rod

crossbar

vertical frame

support

accessories

ski shuttle

rod

bobbin

eye

heddles

eye

comb

stick shuttle

tapestry bobbin

CREATIVE LEISURE ACTIVITIES

weaving

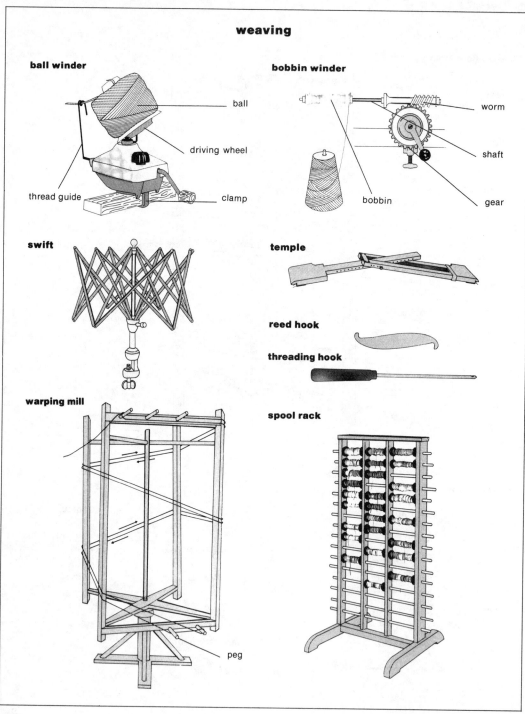

ball winder

ball

driving wheel

thread guide

clamp

bobbin winder

worm

shaft

gear

bobbin

swift

temple

reed hook

threading hook

warping mill

peg

spool rack

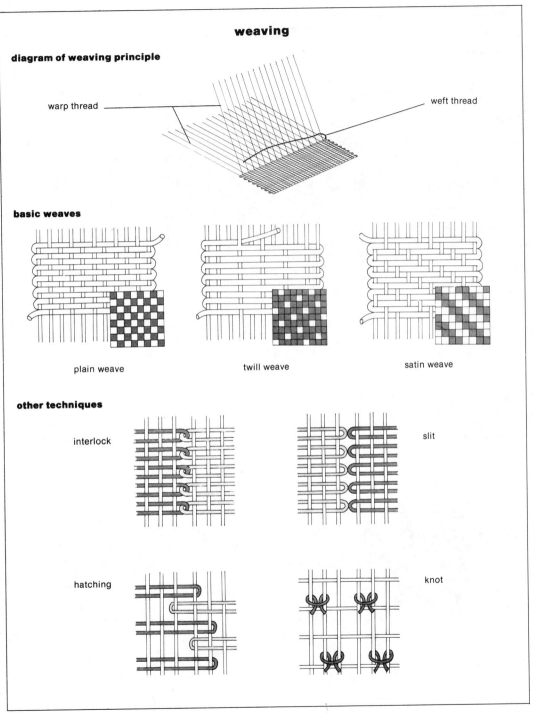

weaving

diagram of weaving principle

warp thread

weft thread

basic weaves

plain weave

twill weave

satin weave

other techniques

interlock

slit

hatching

knot

CREATIVE LEISURE ACTIVITIES

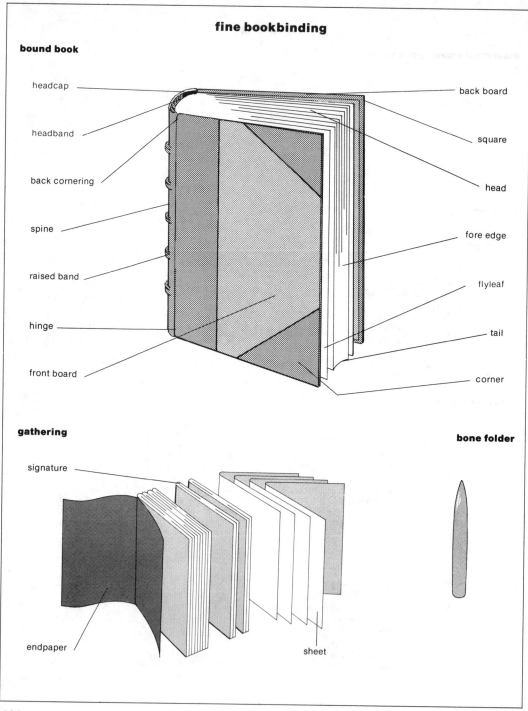

fine bookbinding

bound book

headcap

headband

back cornering

spine

raised band

hinge

front board

back board

square

head

fore edge

flyleaf

tail

corner

gathering

signature

endpaper

sheet

bone folder

fine bookbinding

trimming

board cutter

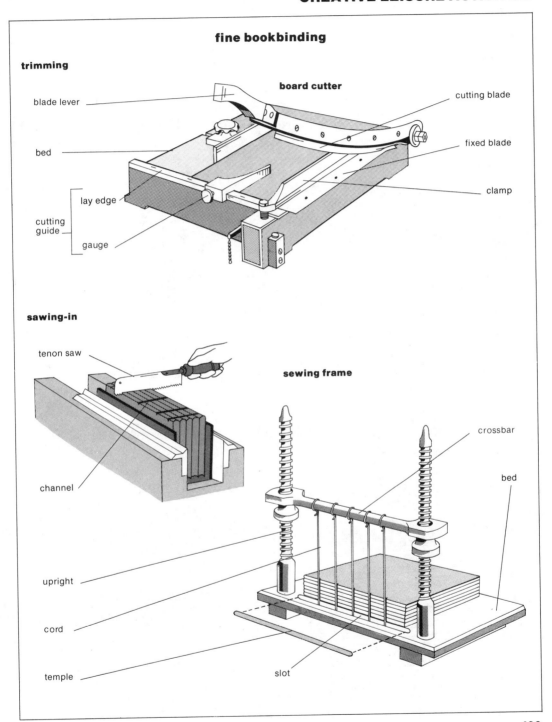

blade lever

cutting blade

bed

fixed blade

clamp

lay edge

cutting guide

gauge

sawing-in

tenon saw

sewing frame

crossbar

bed

channel

upright

cord

temple

slot

CREATIVE LEISURE ACTIVITIES

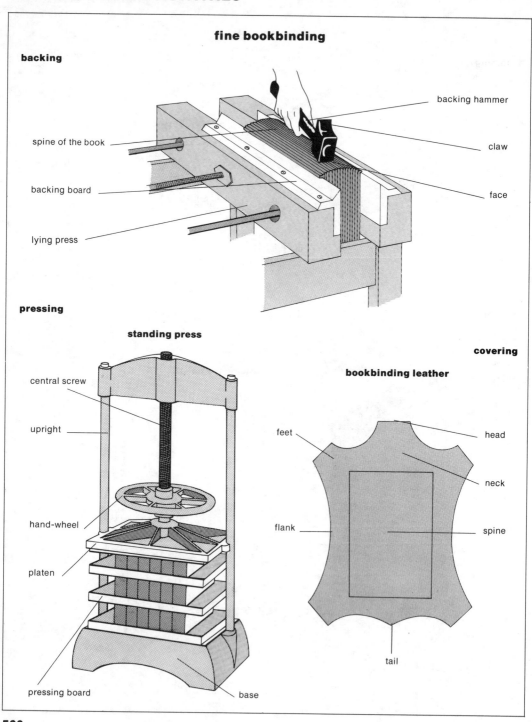

fine bookbinding

backing

- spine of the book
- backing board
- lying press
- backing hammer
- claw
- face

pressing

standing press

- central screw
- upright
- hand-wheel
- platen
- pressing board
- base

covering

bookbinding leather

- feet
- flank
- head
- neck
- spine
- tail

engraving and etching tools

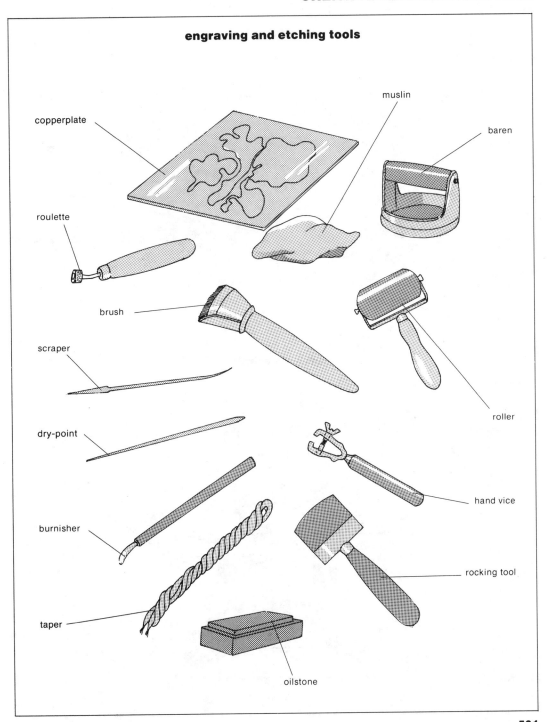

muslin

copperplate

baren

roulette

brush

scraper

dry-point

burnisher

taper

oilstone

roller

hand vice

rocking tool

CREATIVE LEISURE ACTIVITIES

relief printing

equipment

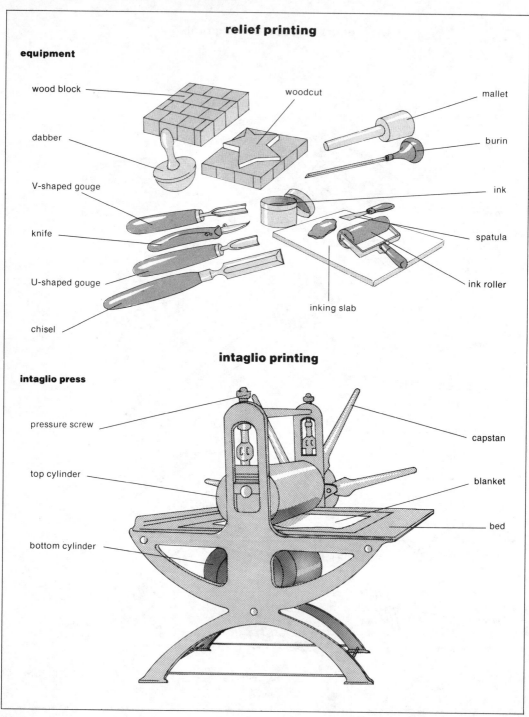

wood block

woodcut

mallet

dabber

burin

V-shaped gouge

ink

knife

spatula

U-shaped gouge

ink roller

chisel

inking slab

intaglio printing

intaglio press

pressure screw

capstan

top cylinder

blanket

bed

bottom cylinder

lithography

equipment

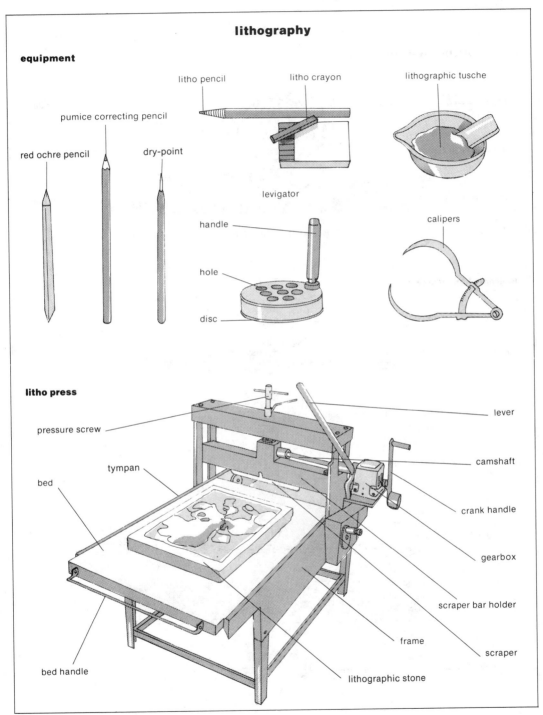

litho pencil

litho crayon

lithographic tusche

pumice correcting pencil

red ochre pencil

dry-point

levigator

handle

hole

disc

calipers

litho press

lever

pressure screw

camshaft

tympan

bed

crank handle

gearbox

scraper bar holder

frame

scraper

bed handle

lithographic stone

printing

diagram of letterpress printing

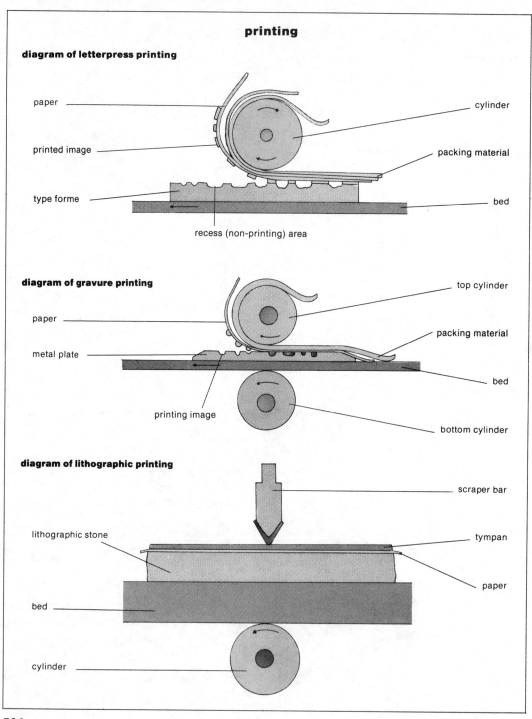

paper
cylinder

printed image
packing material

type forme
bed

recess (non-printing) area

diagram of gravure printing

top cylinder

paper
packing material

metal plate
bed

printing image

bottom cylinder

diagram of lithographic printing

scraper bar

lithographic stone
tympan

paper

bed

cylinder

pottery

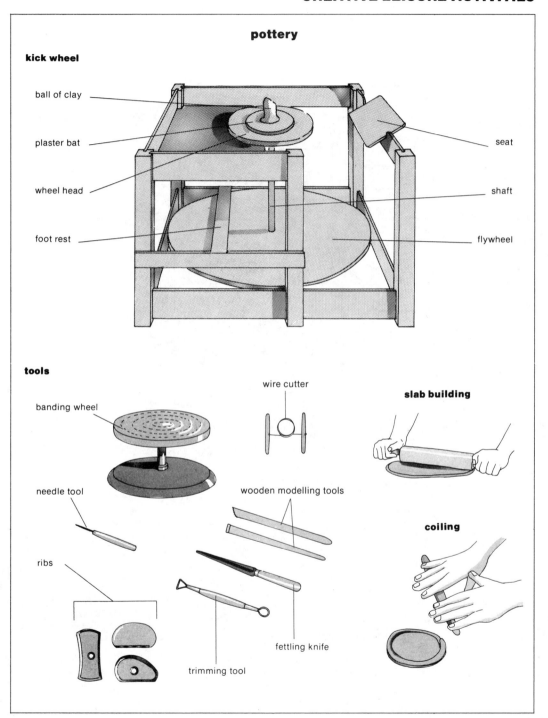

kick wheel

ball of clay

plaster bat

wheel head

foot rest

seat

shaft

flywheel

tools

wire cutter

banding wheel

slab building

needle tool

wooden modelling tools

ribs

coiling

fettling knife

trimming tool

CREATIVE LEISURE ACTIVITIES

pottery

electric kiln

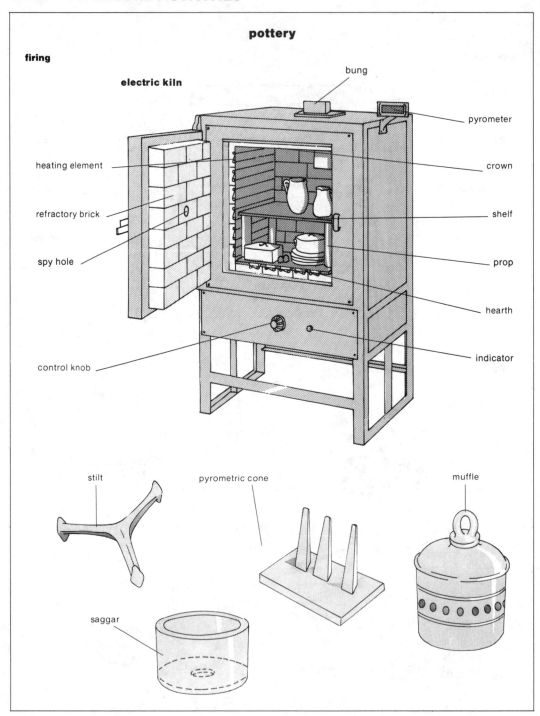

bung

pyrometer

heating element

crown

refractory brick

shelf

spy hole

prop

hearth

indicator

control knob

stilt

pyrometric cone

muffle

saggar

stained glass

sketch

layout

cartoon

layout paper

pattern

carbon

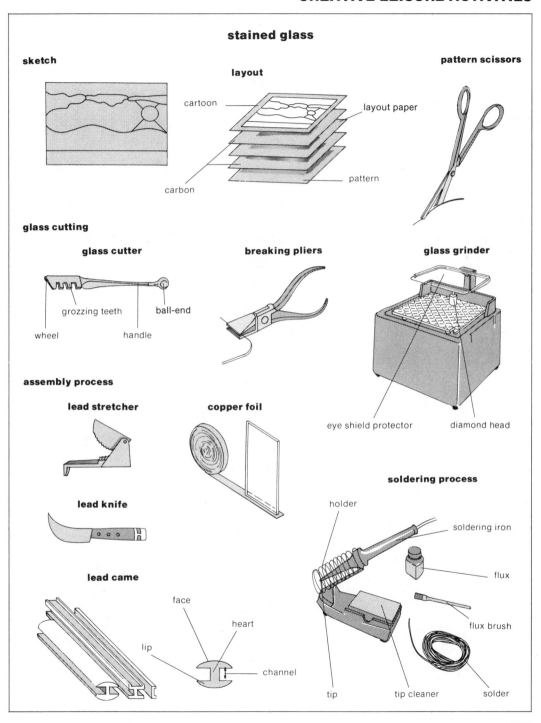

pattern scissors

glass cutting

glass cutter

grozzing teeth

ball-end

wheel

handle

breaking pliers

glass grinder

eye shield protector

diamond head

assembly process

lead stretcher

copper foil

lead knife

lead came

face

heart

lip

channel

soldering process

holder

soldering iron

flux

flux brush

tip

tip cleaner

solder

SPORTS & LEISURE

soccer

playing field (showing modern line-up)

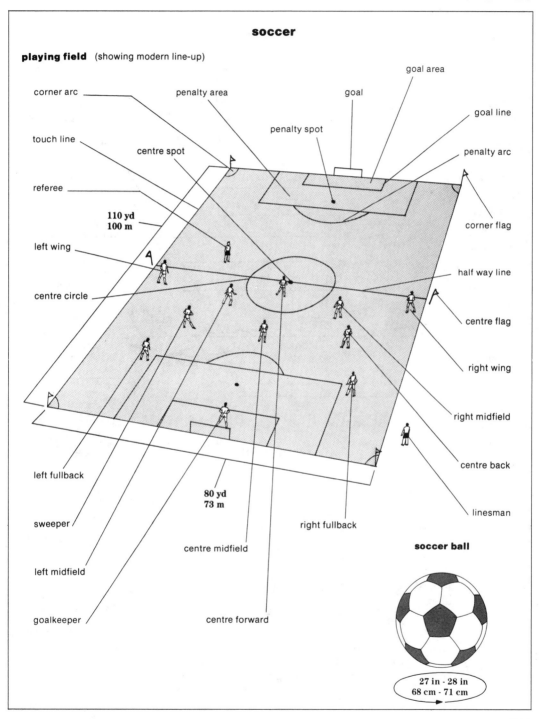

corner arc

penalty area

goal

goal area

goal line

touch line

penalty spot

centre spot

penalty arc

referee

**110 yd
100 m**

corner flag

left wing

half way line

centre circle

centre flag

right wing

right midfield

left fullback

centre back

sweeper

linesman

**80 yd
73 m**

right fullback

left midfield

centre midfield

soccer ball

goalkeeper

centre forward

27 in - 28 in
68 cm - 71 cm

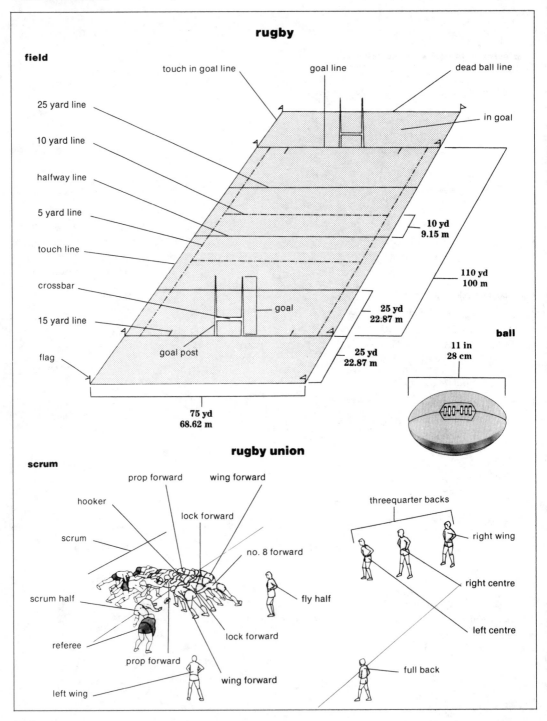

rugby

field

touch in goal line

goal line

dead ball line

25 yard line

10 yard line

halfway line

5 yard line

touch line

crossbar

15 yard line

flag

in goal

goal

goal post

**10 yd
9.15 m**

**110 yd
100 m**

**25 yd
22.87 m**

**25 yd
22.87 m**

**75 yd
68.62 m**

ball

**11 in
28 cm**

rugby union

scrum

prop forward

wing forward

hooker

lock forward

scrum

no. 8 forward

scrum half

referee

prop forward

wing forward

left wing

fly half

threequarter backs

right wing

right centre

left centre

full back

lock forward

rugby union

team playing positions

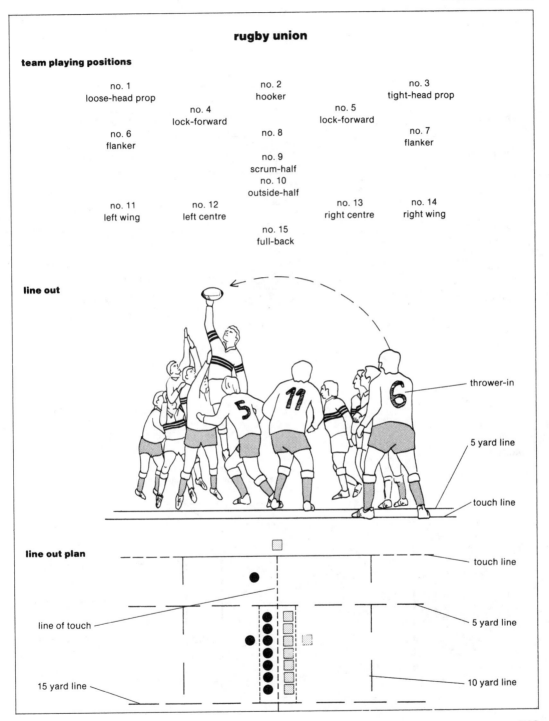

| no. 1 | | no. 2 | | no. 3 |
| loose-head prop | | hooker | | tight-head prop |

| | no. 4 | | no. 5 | |
| | lock-forward | | lock-forward | |

| no. 6 | | no. 8 | | no. 7 |
| flanker | | | | flanker |

no. 9
scrum-half
no. 10
outside-half

| no. 11 | no. 12 | | no. 13 | no. 14 |
| left wing | left centre | | right centre | right wing |

no. 15
full-back

line out

thrower-in

5 yard line

touch line

line out plan

touch line

line of touch

5 yard line

15 yard line

10 yard line

cricket

field

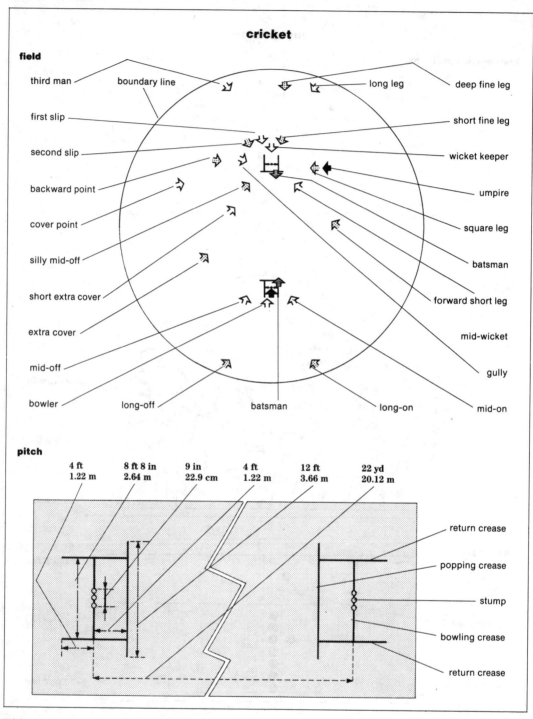

third man

boundary line

long leg

deep fine leg

first slip

short fine leg

second slip

wicket keeper

backward point

umpire

cover point

square leg

silly mid-off

batsman

short extra cover

forward short leg

extra cover

mid-wicket

mid-off

gully

bowler   long-off   batsman   long-on   mid-on

pitch

4 ft
1.22 m

8 ft 8 in
2.64 m

9 in
22.9 cm

4 ft
1.22 m

12 ft
3.66 m

22 yd
20.12 m

return crease

popping crease

stump

bowling crease

return crease

cricket

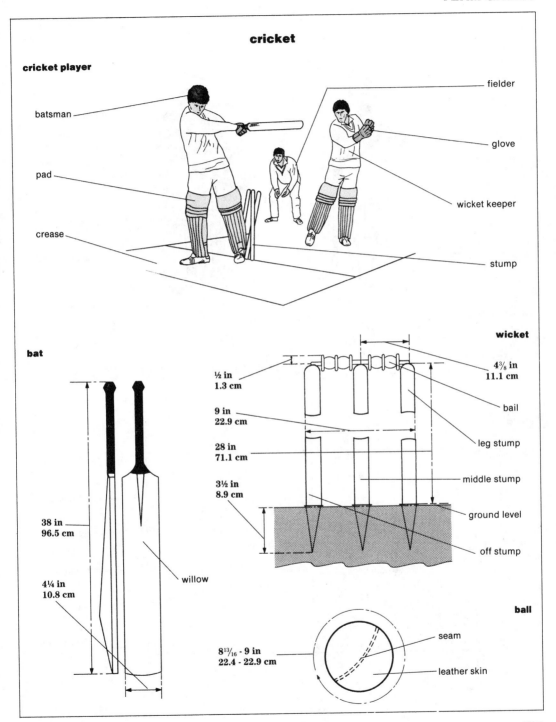

cricket player

batsman

pad

crease

fielder

glove

wicket keeper

stump

bat

wicket

½ in
1.3 cm

9 in
22.9 cm

28 in
71.1 cm

3½ in
8.9 cm

4⅜ in
11.1 cm

bail

leg stump

middle stump

ground level

off stump

38 in
96.5 cm

4¼ in
10.8 cm

willow

ball

8¹³⁄₁₆ - 9 in
22.4 - 22.9 cm

seam

leather skin

hockey

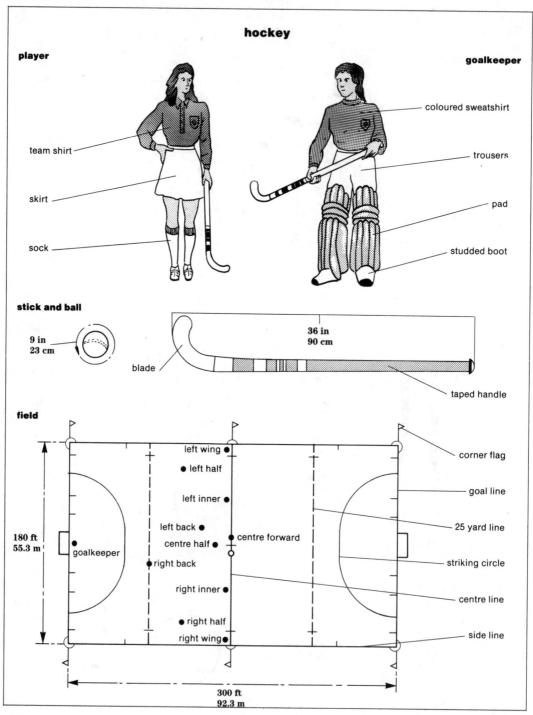

player

goalkeeper

team shirt

skirt

sock

coloured sweatshirt

trousers

pad

studded boot

stick and ball

9 in
23 cm

36 in
90 cm

blade

taped handle

field

left wing

left half

left inner

left back

centre half

right back

right inner

right half

right wing

centre forward

goalkeeper

180 ft
55.3 m

300 ft
92.3 m

corner flag

goal line

25 yard line

striking circle

centre line

side line

516

ice hockey

rink

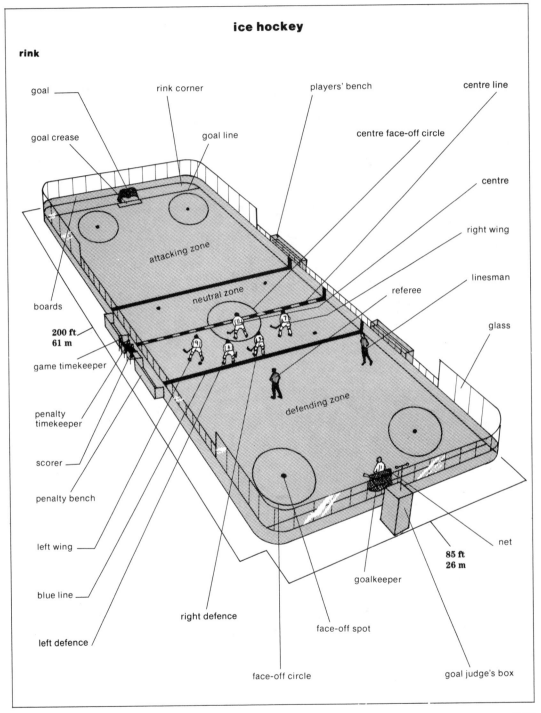

goal

goal crease

rink corner

goal line

players' bench

centre line

centre face-off circle

centre

right wing

linesman

referee

glass

boards

attacking zone

neutral zone

200 ft.
61 m

game timekeeper

penalty
timekeeper

scorer

penalty bench

left wing

blue line

defending zone

net

85 ft
26 m

goalkeeper

right defence

face-off spot

left defence

face-off circle

goal judge's box

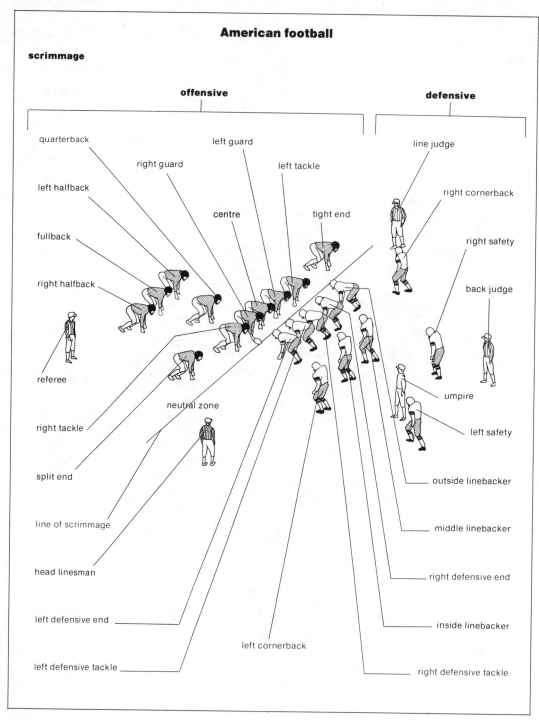

American football

scrimmage

offensive

defensive

quarterback

left guard

right guard

left tackle

line judge

right cornerback

left halfback

centre

tight end

right safety

fullback

back judge

right halfback

referee

umpire

neutral zone

left safety

right tackle

split end

outside linebacker

line of scrimmage

middle linebacker

head linesman

right defensive end

left defensive end

inside linebacker

left cornerback

left defensive tackle

right defensive tackle

American football

protective equipment

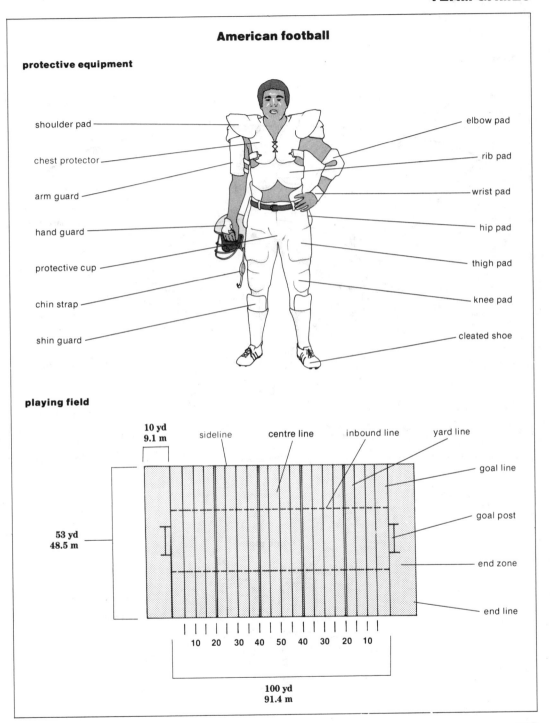

shoulder pad

chest protector

arm guard

hand guard

protective cup

chin strap

shin guard

elbow pad

rib pad

wrist pad

hip pad

thigh pad

knee pad

cleated shoe

playing field

10 yd
9.1 m

sideline   centre line   inbound line   yard line

goal line

goal post

53 yd
48.5 m

end zone

end line

10 20 30 40 50 40 30 20 10

100 yd
91.4 m

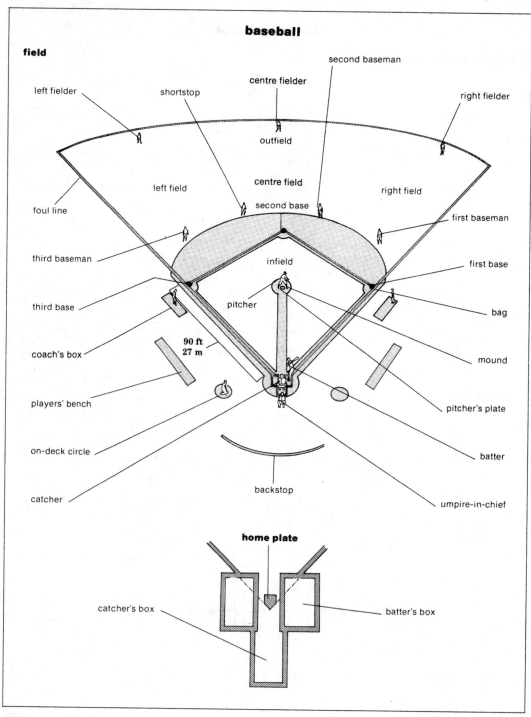

baseball

field

left fielder

shortstop

centre fielder

second baseman

right fielder

outfield

left field

centre field

right field

foul line

second base

first baseman

third baseman

infield

first base

third base

pitcher

bag

coach's box

90 ft
27 m

mound

players' bench

pitcher's plate

on-deck circle

batter

catcher

backstop

umpire-in-chief

home plate

catcher's box

batter's box

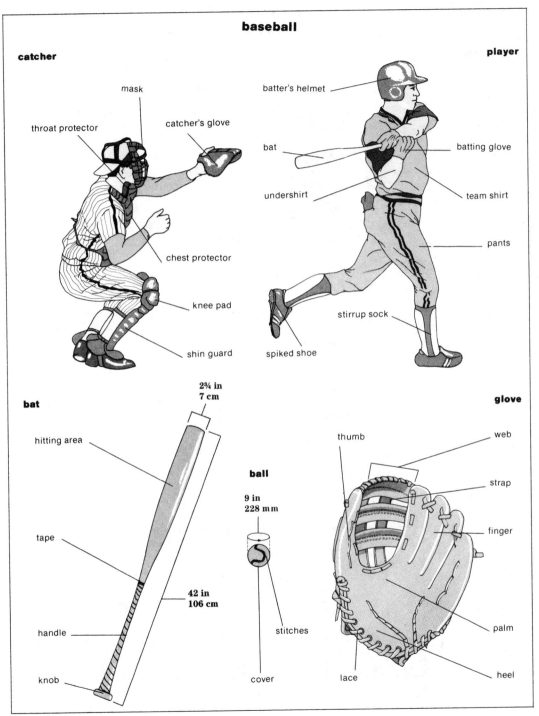

baseball

catcher

- mask
- throat protector
- catcher's glove
- chest protector
- knee pad
- shin guard

player

- batter's helmet
- bat
- batting glove
- undershirt
- team shirt
- pants
- stirrup sock
- spiked shoe

bat

2¾ in
7 cm

- hitting area
- tape
- handle
- knob

42 in
106 cm

ball

9 in
228 mm

- stitches
- cover

glove

- thumb
- web
- strap
- finger
- palm
- heel
- lace

netball

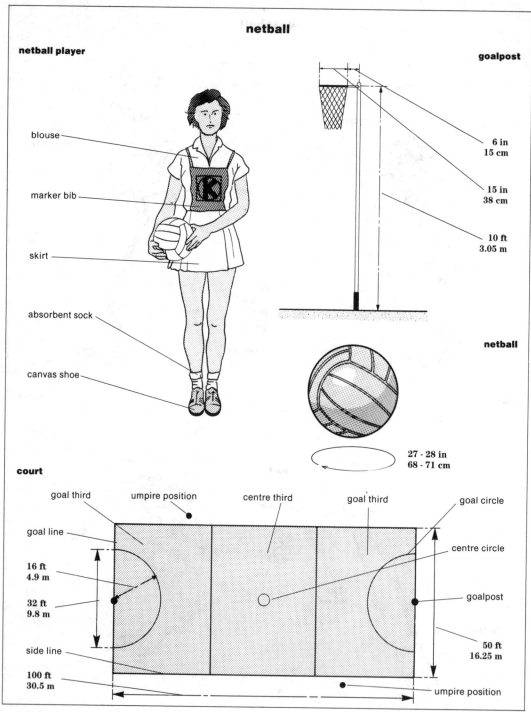

netball player

blouse

marker bib

skirt

absorbent sock

canvas shoe

goalpost

6 in
15 cm

15 in
38 cm

10 ft
3.05 m

netball

27 - 28 in
68 - 71 cm

court

goal third

umpire position

centre third

goal third

goal circle

goal line

centre circle

16 ft
4.9 m

32 ft
9.8 m

goalpost

side line

50 ft
16.25 m

100 ft
30.5 m

umpire position

basketball

court

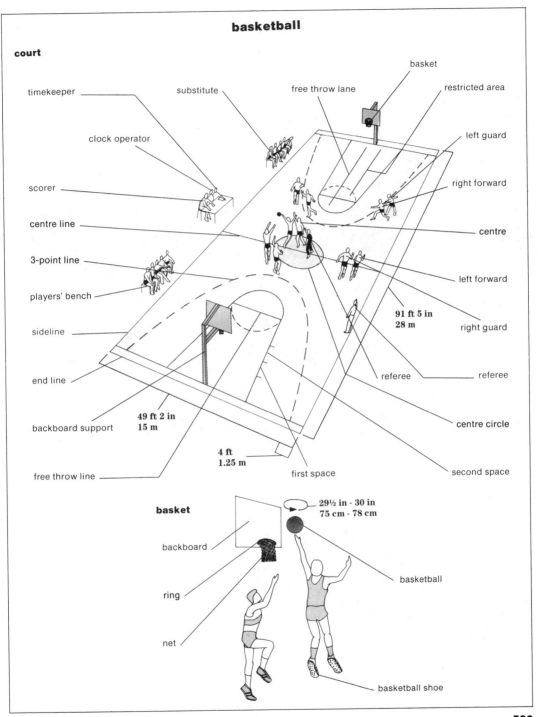

timekeeper

clock operator

scorer

centre line

3-point line

players' bench

sideline

end line

backboard support

free throw line

substitute

basket

free throw lane

restricted area

left guard

right forward

centre

left forward

91 ft 5 in
28 m

right guard

referee — referee

centre circle

49 ft 2 in
15 m

4 ft
1.25 m

first space

second space

basket

backboard

ring

net

29½ in - 30 in
75 cm - 78 cm

basketball

basketball shoe

523

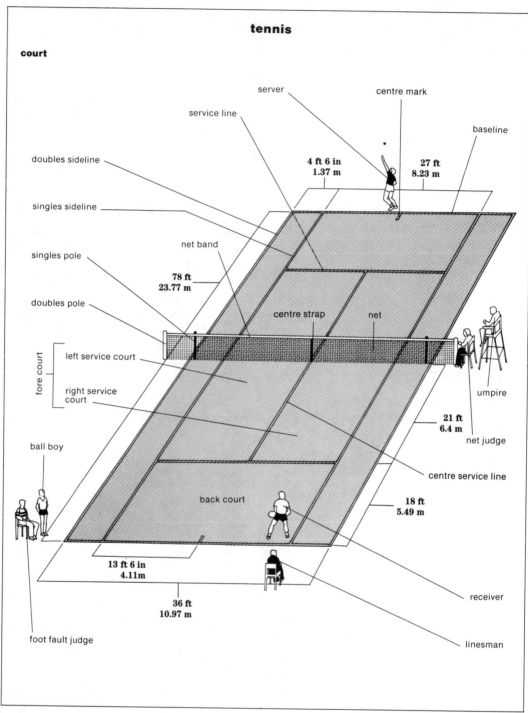

tennis

court

server

centre mark

service line

baseline

doubles sideline

4 ft 6 in
1.37 m

27 ft
8.23 m

singles sideline

singles pole

net band

78 ft
23.77 m

doubles pole

centre strap

net

fore court

left service court

right service
court

umpire

net judge

ball boy

21 ft
6.4 m

centre service line

back court

18 ft
5.49 m

13 ft 6 in
4.11m

receiver

36 ft
10.97 m

foot fault judge

linesman

tennis

tennis players

headband

shirt

wristband

shorts

blouse

skirt

tennis shoe

sock

tennis racquet

shoulder

throat

top

bevel

flat side of the grip

frame

stringing

handle

head

shaft

tennis ball

63.5 mm - 66.7 mm
2½ in - 2⅝ in

press

badminton

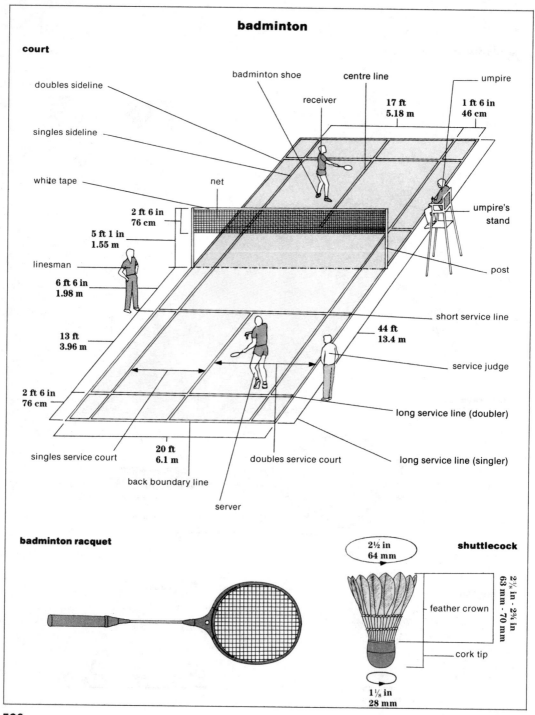

court

doubles sideline

badminton shoe

centre line

umpire

receiver

**17 ft
5.18 m**

**1 ft 6 in
46 cm**

singles sideline

white tape

net

umpire's
stand

**2 ft 6 in
76 cm**

**5 ft 1 in
1.55 m**

linesman

post

**6 ft 6 in
1.98 m**

short service line

**13 ft
3.96 m**

**44 ft
13.4 m**

service judge

**2 ft 6 in
76 cm**

long service line (doubler)

singles service court

**20 ft
6.1 m**

doubles service court

long service line (singler)

back boundary line

server

badminton racquet

**2½ in
64 mm**

shuttlecock

feather crown

**2⅜ in - 2¾ in
63 mm - 70 mm**

cork tip

**1⅛ in
28 mm**

squash

international singles court

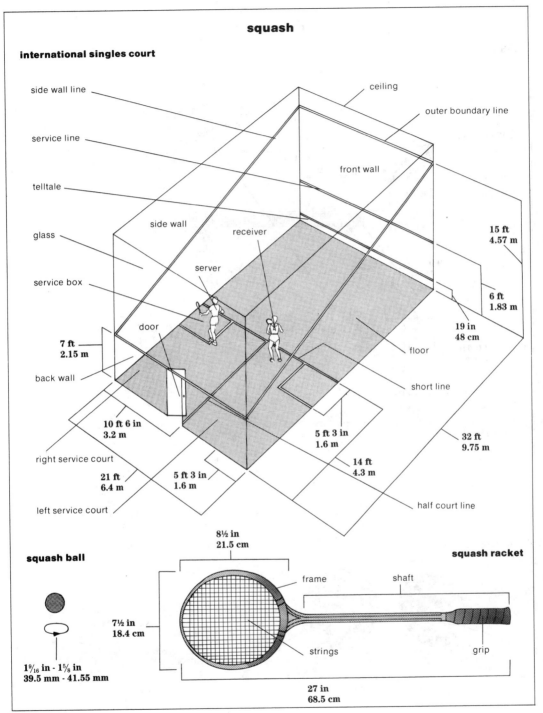

side wall line

service line

telltale

glass

service box

door

7 ft
2.15 m

back wall

ceiling

outer boundary line

front wall

side wall

receiver

server

15 ft
4.57 m

6 ft
1.83 m

19 in
48 cm

floor

short line

10 ft 6 in
3.2 m

right service court

21 ft
6.4 m

left service court

5 ft 3 in
1.6 m

5 ft 3 in
1.6 m

14 ft
4.3 m

32 ft
9.75 m

half court line

squash ball

1⁹/₁₆ in - 1⁵/₈ in
39.5 mm - 41.55 mm

8½ in
21.5 cm

7½ in
18.4 cm

frame

strings

shaft

grip

27 in
68.5 cm

squash racket

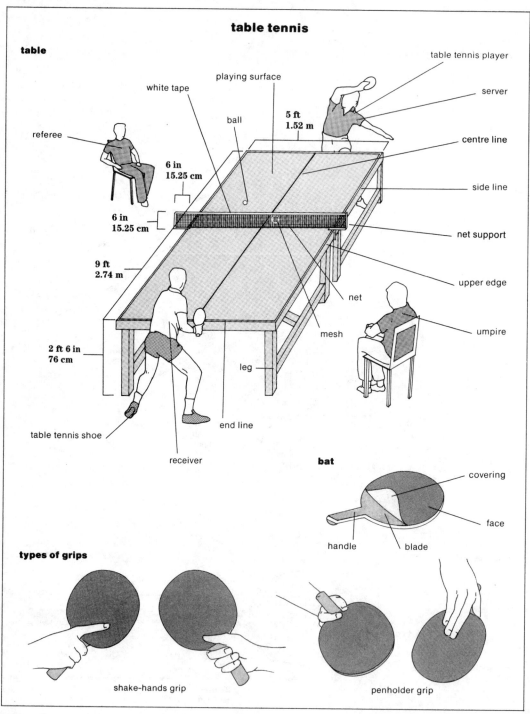

table tennis

table

referee

white tape

playing surface

ball

6 in
15.25 cm

6 in
15.25 cm

9 ft
2.74 m

2 ft 6 in
76 cm

table tennis shoe

receiver

end line

leg

mesh

net

5 ft
1.52 m

table tennis player

server

centre line

side line

net support

upper edge

umpire

bat

covering

face

handle

blade

types of grips

shake-hands grip

penholder grip

volleyball

court

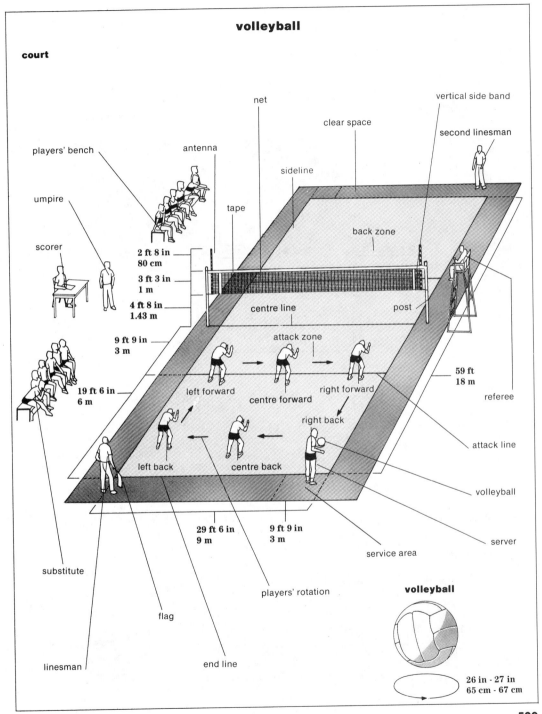

net

vertical side band

clear space

second linesman

players' bench

antenna

sideline

umpire

tape

back zone

scorer

2 ft 8 in
80 cm

3 ft 3 in
1 m

4 ft 8 in
1.43 m

centre line

post

9 ft 9 in
3 m

attack zone

19 ft 6 in
6 m

left forward

centre forward

right forward

59 ft
18 m

referee

right back

attack line

left back

centre back

volleyball

substitute

29 ft 6 in
9 m

9 ft 9 in
3 m

service area

server

players' rotation

flag

volleyball

linesman

end line

26 in - 27 in
65 cm - 67 cm

bowls

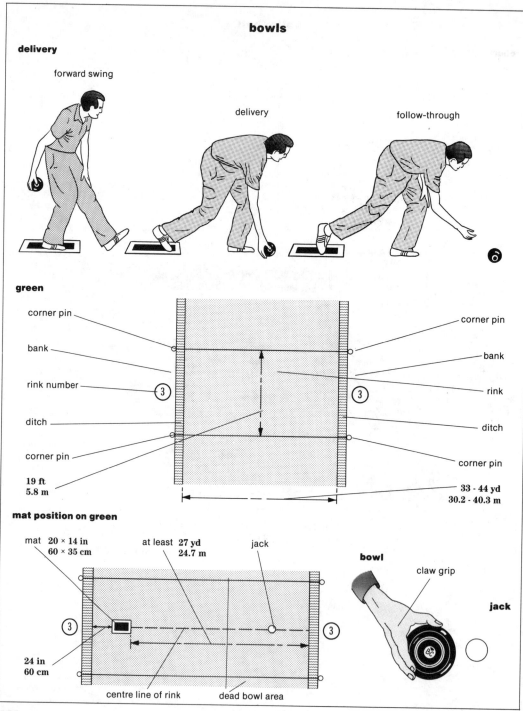

delivery

forward swing

delivery

follow-through

green

corner pin

bank

rink number ③

ditch

corner pin

**19 ft
5.8 m**

corner pin

bank

rink

③

ditch

corner pin

**33 - 44 yd
30.2 - 40.3 m**

mat position on green

mat 20 × 14 in
60 × 35 cm

at least 27 yd
24.7 m

jack

③

**24 in
60 cm**

③

centre line of rink

dead bowl area

bowl

claw grip

jack

water polo

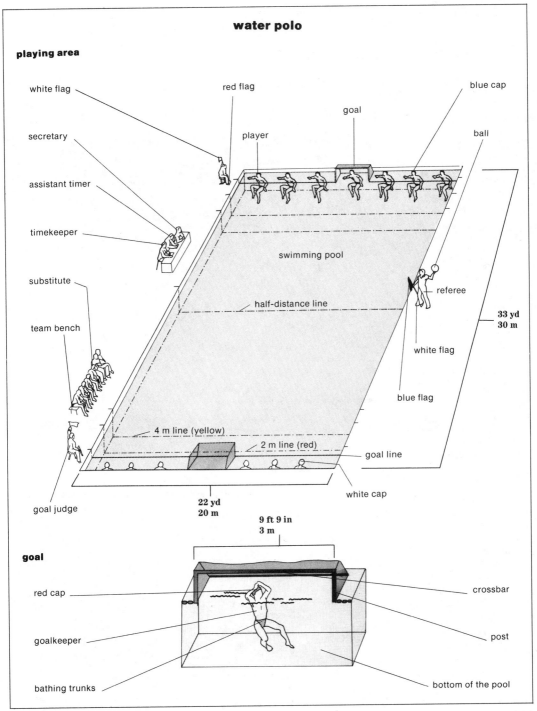

playing area

white flag

red flag

blue cap

secretary

goal

player

ball

assistant timer

timekeeper

swimming pool

substitute

referee

half-distance line

team bench

white flag

33 yd
30 m

blue flag

4 m line (yellow)

2 m line (red)

goal line

goal judge

white cap

22 yd
20 m

9 ft 9 in
3 m

goal

red cap

crossbar

goalkeeper

post

bathing trunks

bottom of the pool

531

swimming

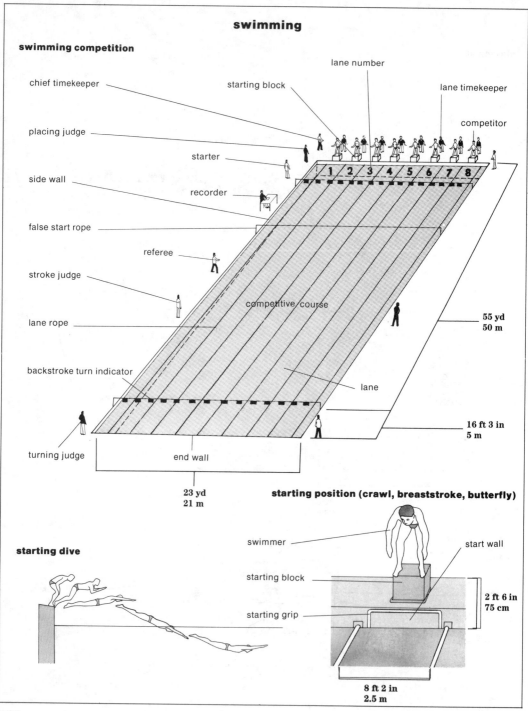

swimming competition

chief timekeeper

placing judge

side wall

false start rope

referee

stroke judge

lane rope

backstroke turn indicator

turning judge

starting block

lane number

lane timekeeper

competitor

starter

recorder

competitive course

lane

end wall

55 yd
50 m

16 ft 3 in
5 m

23 yd
21 m

1 2 3 4 5 6 7 8

starting dive

starting position (crawl, breaststroke, butterfly)

swimmer

starting block

starting grip

start wall

2 ft 6 in
75 cm

8 ft 2 in
2.5 m

types of strokes

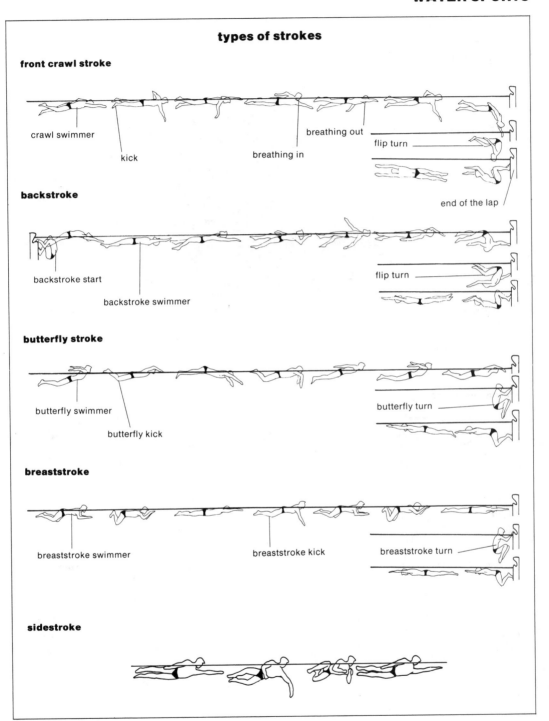

front crawl stroke

crawl swimmer

kick

breathing in

breathing out

flip turn

end of the lap

backstroke

backstroke start

backstroke swimmer

flip turn

butterfly stroke

butterfly swimmer

butterfly kick

butterfly turn

breaststroke

breaststroke swimmer

breaststroke kick

breaststroke turn

sidestroke

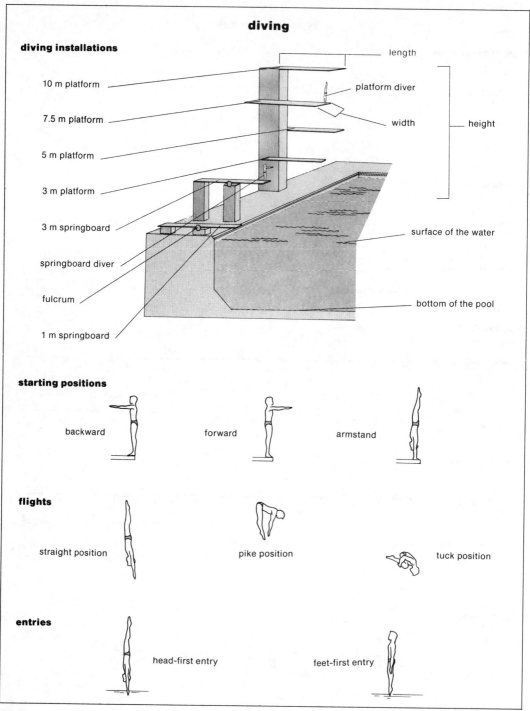

diving

diving installations

length

10 m platform

platform diver

7.5 m platform

width

height

5 m platform

3 m platform

surface of the water

3 m springboard

springboard diver

fulcrum

bottom of the pool

1 m springboard

starting positions

backward

forward

armstand

flights

straight position

pike position

tuck position

entries

head-first entry

feet-first entry

534

groups of dives

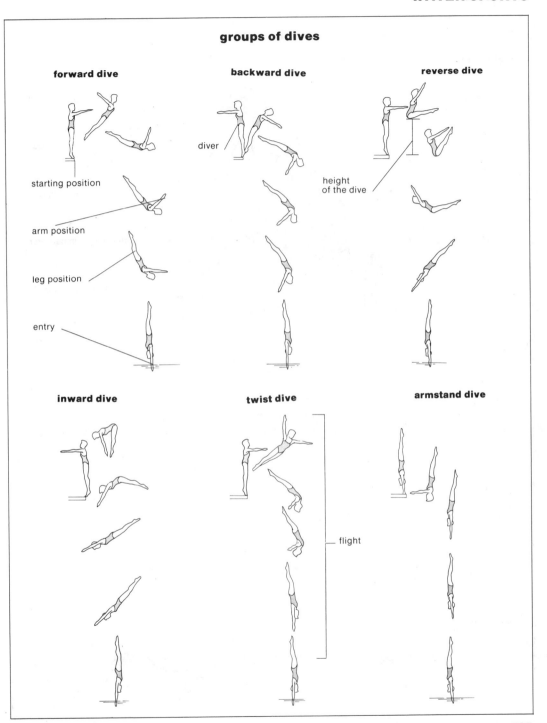

forward dive

starting position

arm position

leg position

entry

backward dive

diver

reverse dive

height
of the dive

inward dive

twist dive

flight

armstand dive

skin diving

scuba diver

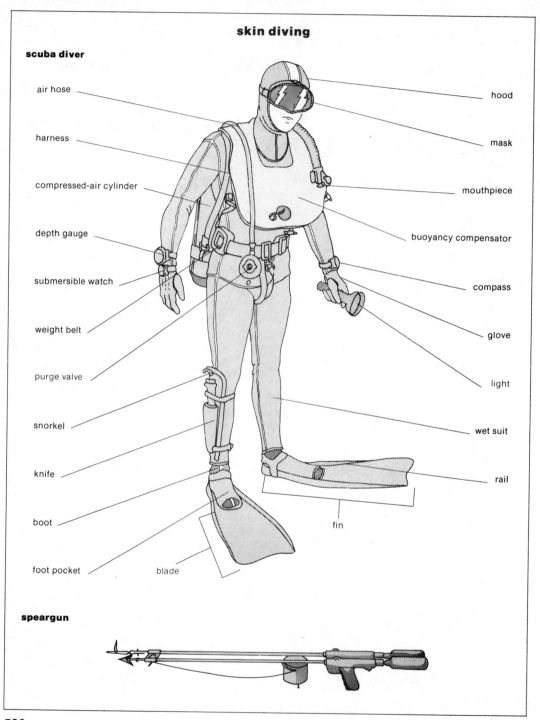

air hose

harness

compressed-air cylinder

depth gauge

submersible watch

weight belt

purge valve

snorkel

knife

boot

foot pocket

blade

hood

mask

mouthpiece

buoyancy compensator

compass

glove

light

wet suit

rail

fin

speargun

sailboard

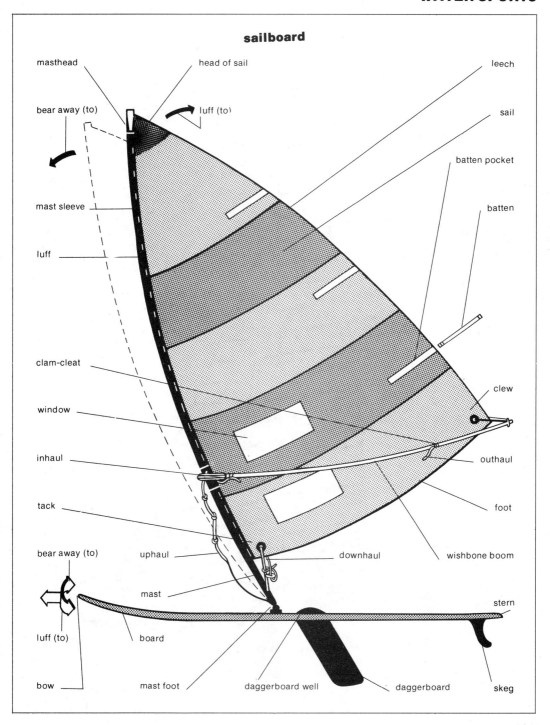

masthead

head of sail

leech

bear away (to)

luff (to)

sail

batten pocket

mast sleeve

batten

luff

clam-cleat

clew

window

inhaul

outhaul

tack

foot

bear away (to)

uphaul

downhaul

wishbone boom

mast

stern

luff (to)

board

bow

mast foot

daggerboard well

daggerboard

skeg

dinghy

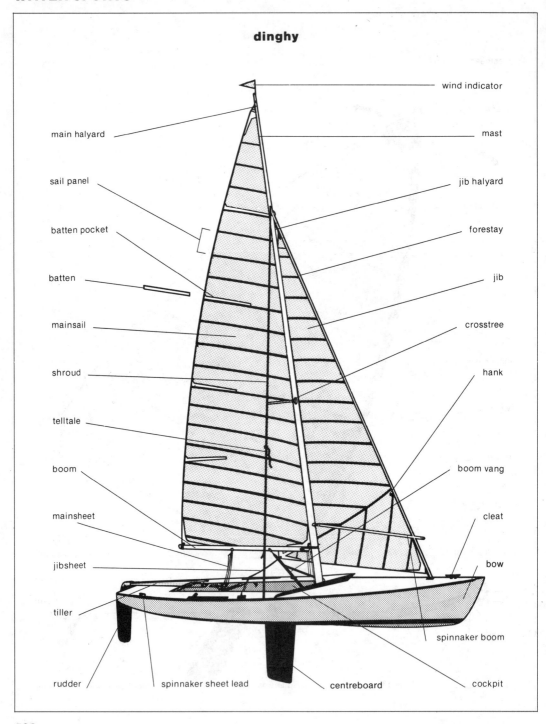

wind indicator

main halyard

mast

sail panel

jib halyard

batten pocket

forestay

batten

jib

mainsail

crosstree

shroud

hank

telltale

boom

boom vang

mainsheet

cleat

jibsheet

bow

tiller

spinnaker boom

rudder

spinnaker sheet lead

centreboard

cockpit

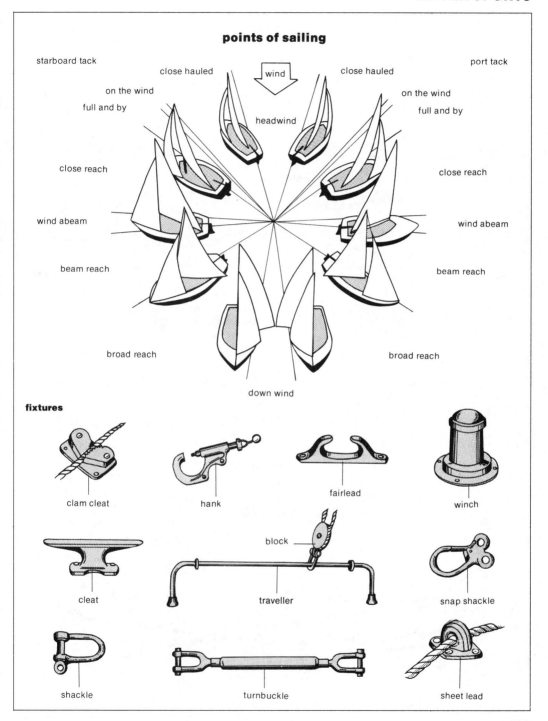

points of sailing

starboard tack

close hauled

wind

close hauled

port tack

on the wind

on the wind

full and by

headwind

full and by

close reach

close reach

wind abeam

wind abeam

beam reach

beam reach

broad reach

broad reach

down wind

fixtures

clam cleat

hank

fairlead

winch

block

cleat

traveller

snap shackle

shackle

turnbuckle

sheet lead

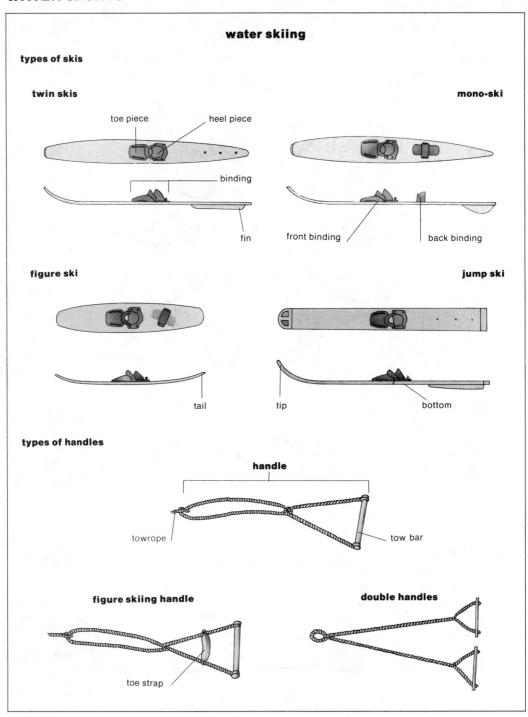

water skiing

types of skis

twin skis

toe piece

heel piece

binding

fin

mono-ski

front binding

back binding

figure ski

tail

jump ski

tip

bottom

types of handles

handle

towrope

tow bar

figure skiing handle

toe strap

double handles

rowing and sculling

types of boat

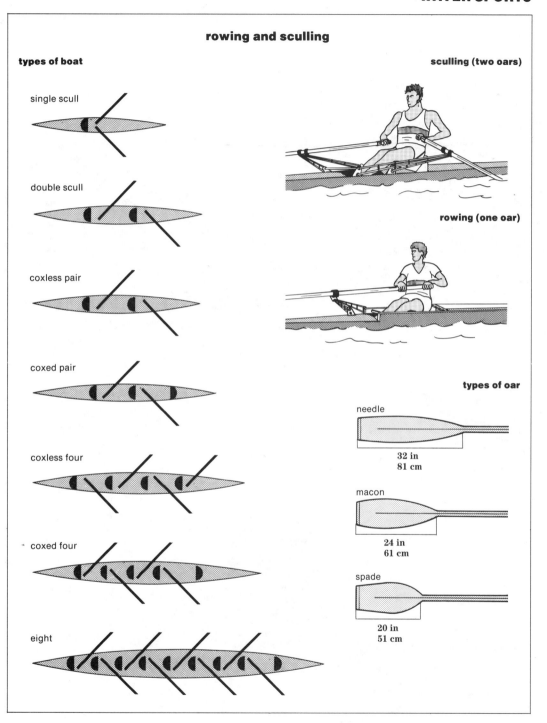

single scull

double scull

coxless pair

coxed pair

coxless four

coxed four

eight

sculling (two oars)

rowing (one oar)

types of oar

needle

32 in
81 cm

macon

24 in
61 cm

spade

20 in
51 cm

gliding

glider

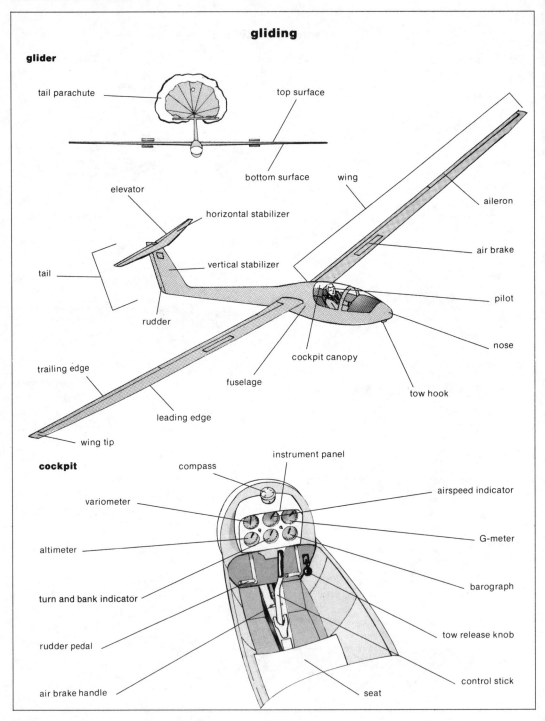

tail parachute

top surface

bottom surface

wing

aileron

air brake

elevator

horizontal stabilizer

vertical stabilizer

tail

pilot

rudder

nose

trailing edge

cockpit canopy

fuselage

tow hook

leading edge

wing tip

cockpit

instrument panel

compass

airspeed indicator

variometer

G-meter

altimeter

barograph

turn and bank indicator

tow release knob

rudder pedal

control stick

air brake handle

seat

hang gliding

hang glider

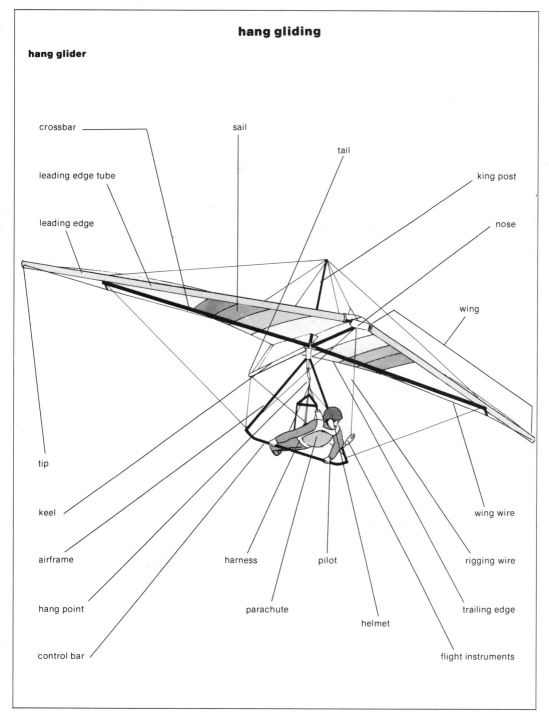

crossbar

sail

tail

king post

leading edge tube

nose

leading edge

wing

tip

keel

wing wire

airframe

harness

pilot

rigging wire

hang point

parachute

trailing edge

helmet

control bar

flight instruments

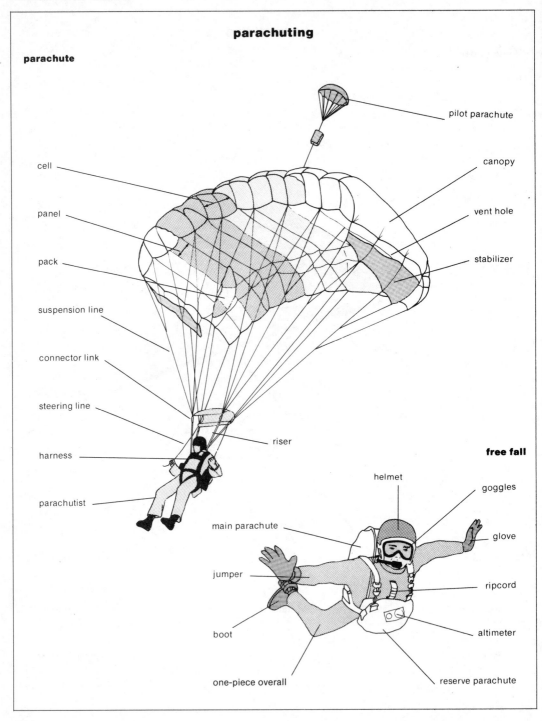

parachuting

parachute

pilot parachute

cell

canopy

panel

vent hole

pack

stabilizer

suspension line

connector link

steering line

riser

free fall

harness

helmet

goggles

parachutist

glove

main parachute

jumper

ripcord

boot

altimeter

one-piece overall

reserve parachute

skiing

skier

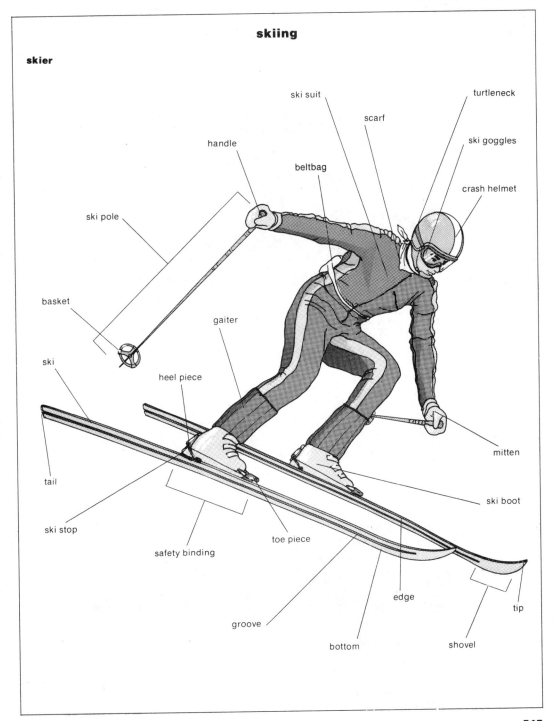

ski suit

turtleneck

scarf

handle

ski goggles

beltbag

crash helmet

ski pole

basket

gaiter

ski

heel piece

mitten

tail

ski boot

ski stop

safety binding

toe piece

edge

tip

groove

bottom

shovel

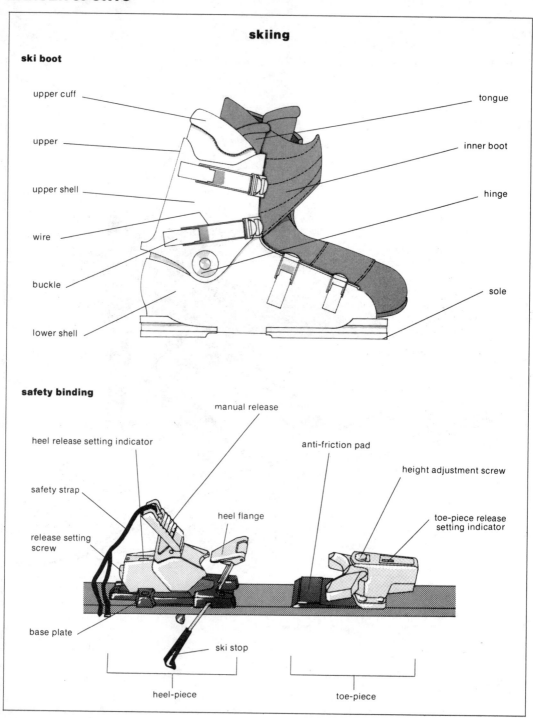

skiing

ski boot

upper cuff

tongue

upper

inner boot

upper shell

hinge

wire

buckle

sole

lower shell

safety binding

manual release

heel release setting indicator

anti-friction pad

height adjustment screw

safety strap

heel flange

toe-piece release setting indicator

release setting screw

base plate

ski stop

heel-piece

toe-piece

skiing

ski resort

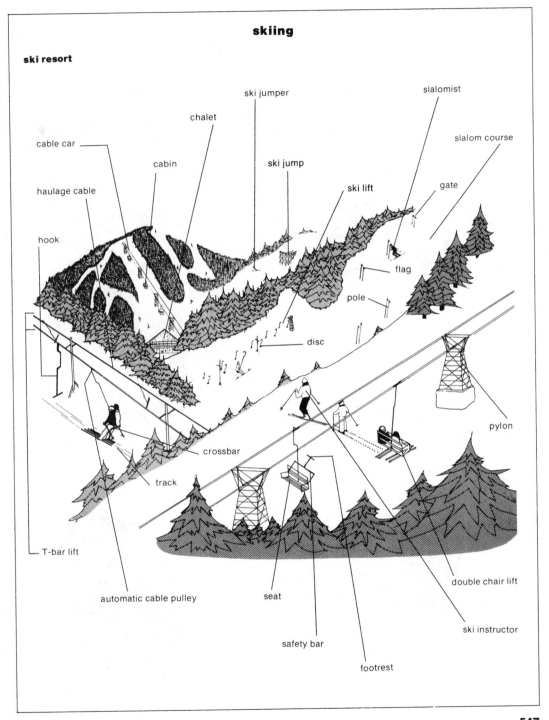

- ski jumper
- slalomist
- chalet
- slalom course
- cable car
- cabin
- ski jump
- gate
- haulage cable
- ski lift
- hook
- flag
- pole
- disc
- pylon
- crossbar
- track
- T-bar lift
- double chair lift
- automatic cable pulley
- seat
- ski instructor
- safety bar
- footrest

547

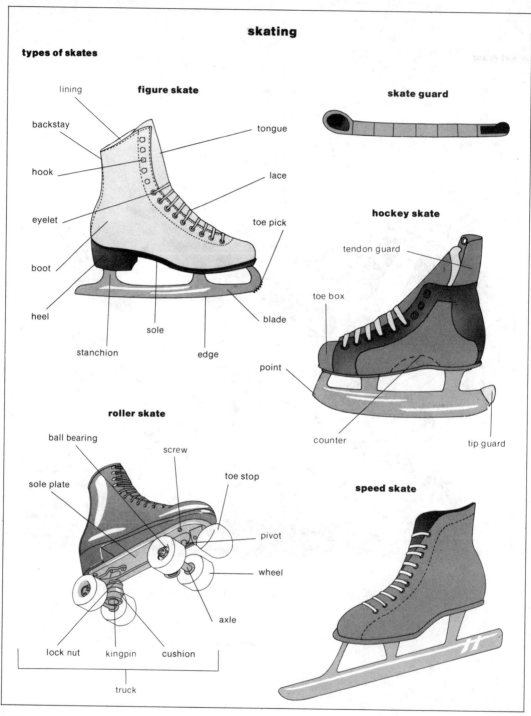

skating

types of skates

figure skate

lining

backstay

hook

eyelet

boot

heel

stanchion

sole

edge

tongue

lace

toe pick

blade

skate guard

hockey skate

tendon guard

toe box

point

counter

tip guard

roller skate

ball bearing

screw

toe stop

sole plate

pivot

wheel

axle

lock nut

kingpin

cushion

truck

speed skate

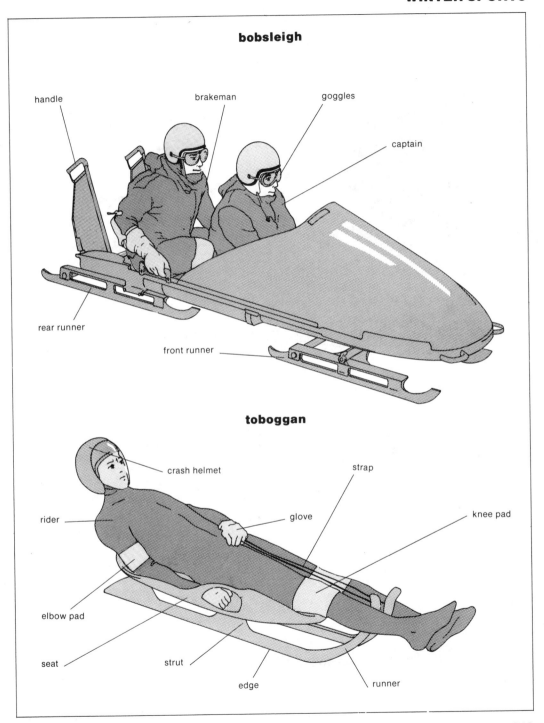

bobsleigh

handle

brakeman

goggles

captain

rear runner

front runner

toboggan

crash helmet

strap

rider

glove

knee pad

elbow pad

seat

strut

edge

runner

darts

dartboard

scoring areas

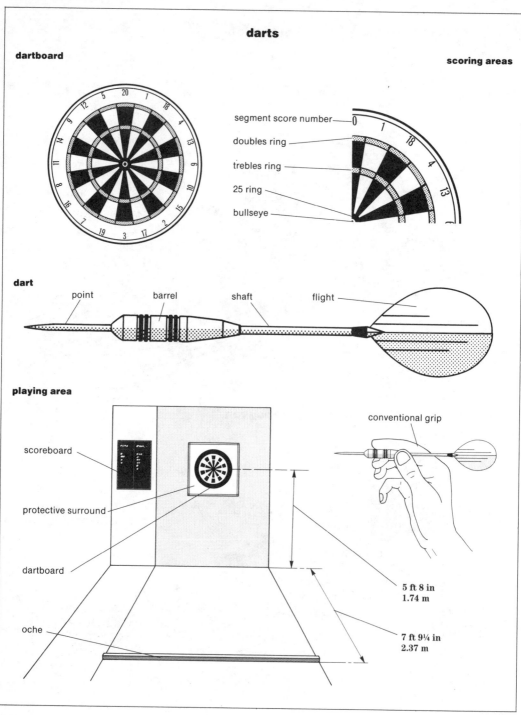

segment score number

doubles ring

trebles ring

25 ring

bullseye

dart

point

barrel

shaft

flight

playing area

conventional grip

scoreboard

protective surround

dartboard

oche

5 ft 8 in
1.74 m

7 ft 9¼ in
2.37 m

riding

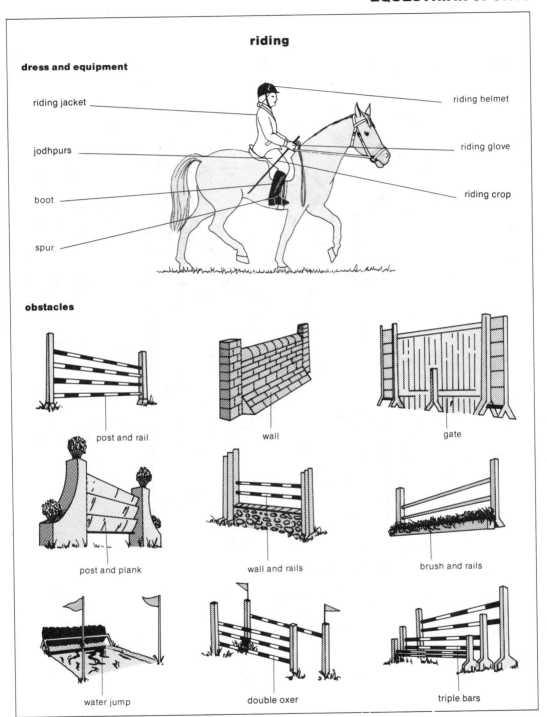

dress and equipment

riding jacket

jodhpurs

boot

spur

riding helmet

riding glove

riding crop

obstacles

post and rail

wall

gate

post and plank

wall and rails

brush and rails

water jump

double oxer

triple bars

551

riding

competition ring

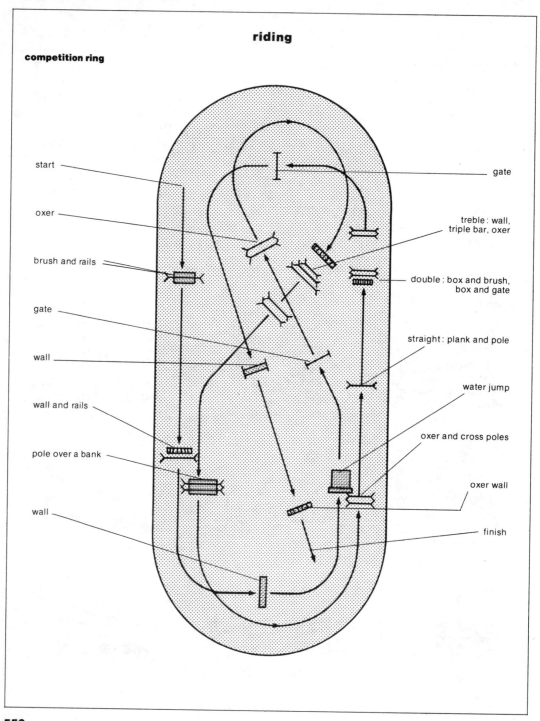

start

oxer

brush and rails

gate

wall

wall and rails

pole over a bank

wall

gate

treble : wall,
triple bar, oxer

double : box and brush,
box and gate

straight : plank and pole

water jump

oxer and cross poles

oxer wall

finish

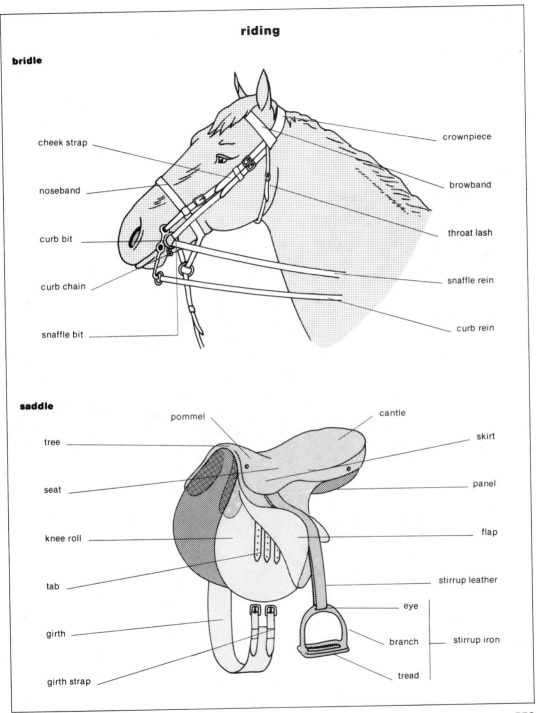

riding

bridle

cheek strap

noseband

curb bit

curb chain

snaffle bit

crownpiece

browband

throat lash

snaffle rein

curb rein

saddle

pommel

cantle

tree

seat

knee roll

tab

girth

girth strap

skirt

panel

flap

stirrup leather

eye

branch — stirrup iron

tread

553

horse racing

horse and jockey

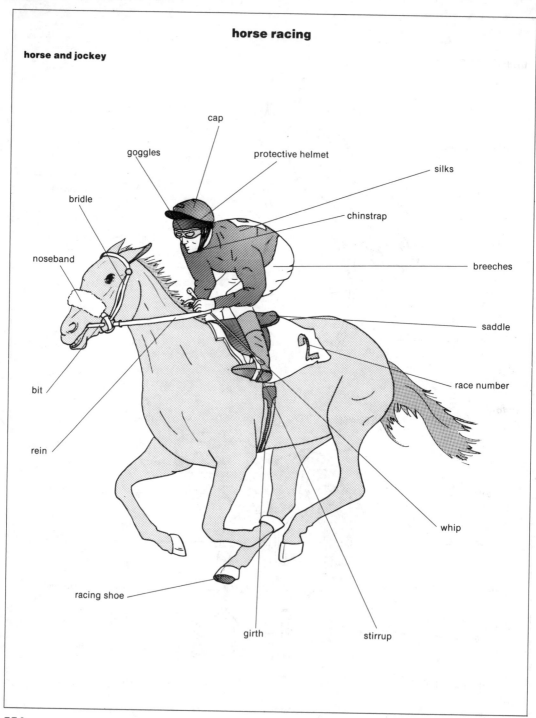

cap

goggles

protective helmet

silks

bridle

chinstrap

noseband

breeches

saddle

bit

race number

rein

whip

racing shoe

girth

stirrup

horse racing

racing programme

racecourse name

tipster's choices

race programme

state of course

race name

race time

race number

six-figure form

name of horse

blinkers

form details

prize money

distance

number of runners

starting price

jockey's name

owner's name

trainer's name

handicapper's rating

age and weight

result of last meeting

tipster's choice

NOTTINGHAM

Selections
By Mandarin

12.30 Don Sabreur.
1.00 Happy Breed.
1.30 Against The Grain.

2.00 Fourth Tudor.
2.30 Planet Man.
3.00 Croix De Guerre.

Going: good to soft (chase course) ; soft (hurdles)

12.30 DALESIDE CONDITIONAL JOCKEYS HANDICAP CHASE(£1,255 : 2m 6f)
(7 runners)

1	2P-PP	DON SABREUR (Exors D Pearman) Mrs S Pearman 10-11-10	J Hurst	—	9-1
2	401423	MORNING BREAKS (J Upson) T Casey 10-11-1	E Buckley	96	5-2
4	23030/P-	TRUST THE KING (N Delamain) C Vernon Miller 10-10-6	B Dowling		9-1
5	21B2-01	MANNA REEF (K Al-Said) J Edwards 9-10-9 (5ex)	G Landau	99	F9-4
7	4124U4	CORKER (W A Stephenson) W A Stephenson 11-10-0	NON-RUNNER		
9	443-0F4	HIGH RIDGE (B) (E Lodge) J Perrett 8-10-0	L Harvey	86	10-1
12	U32-40P	WOODLAND GENERATOR (Miss M Preece) P Pritchard 8-10-0	M Bowlby	87	10-1

1986 : Meeting abandoned - frost

FORM DON SABREUR yet to show his form at his best he will go close, last time completed (10-1) 2nd beaten 31 to Elmboy (11-1) at Cheltenham (3m, £4184, firm, Nov 6, 6 ran). **MORNING BREAKS** (11-6) 3rd, never a serious threat, beaten 381 to Whiskey Eyes (11-10) at Kempton (2m, 4f, £2001, good to soft, Nov 20, 7 ran). **MANNA REEF** (9-12) was left clear at the last to win on his own at Leicester (2m, 4f, £4,518, soft, Dec 31, 4 ran). **CORKER** latest unseated rider, earlier (9-7) 4th beaten over 351 to Be Free (9-7) at Ayr (3m 110yd, £1956, soft, 6 ran). **HIGH RIDGE** (10-5) 4th beaten 6l to Prince Moon (10-4) at Folkestone (2m 4f, £948, soft, 8 ran).
Selection : DON SABREUR

race course

home straight

far turn

pole

back straight

stable

judge's stand

grandstand

club house

finishing post

club house turn

tote board

furlong chute

paddock

track and field athletics

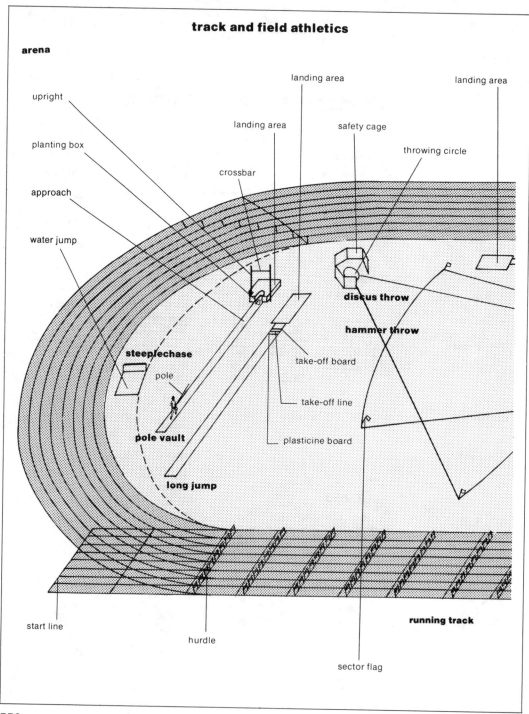

arena

upright

planting box

approach

water jump

landing area

landing area

landing area

safety cage

throwing circle

crossbar

steeplechase

pole

pole vault

long jump

take-off board

take-off line

plasticine board

discus throw

hammer throw

start line

hurdle

running track

sector flag

556

track and field athletics

arena

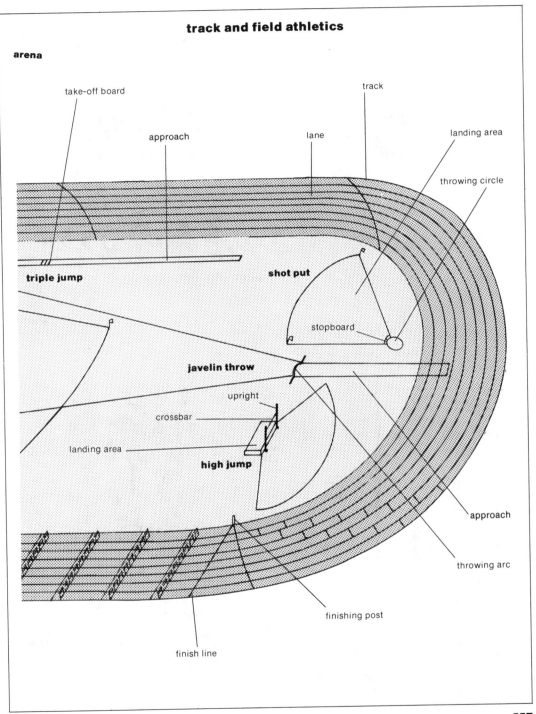

take-off board

approach

track

lane

landing area

throwing circle

triple jump

shot put

stopboard

javelin throw

upright

crossbar

landing area

high jump

approach

throwing arc

finishing post

finish line

field events

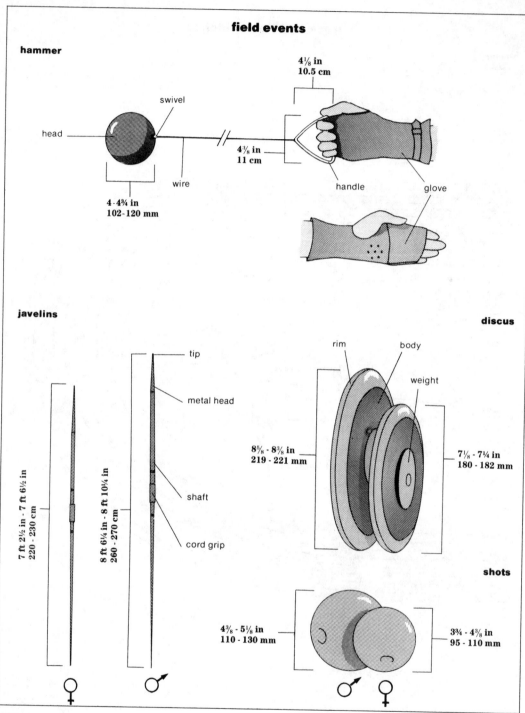

hammer

swivel

head

wire

4 - 4¾ in
102 - 120 mm

4⅛ in
10.5 cm

4⅜ in
11 cm

handle

glove

javelins

tip

metal head

shaft

cord grip

7 ft 2½ in - 7 ft 6½ in
220 - 230 cm

8 ft 6¼ in - 8 ft 10¼ in
260 - 270 cm

discus

rim

body

weight

8⅝ - 8⅜ in
219 - 221 mm

7⅛ - 7¼ in
180 - 182 mm

shots

4⅜ - 5⅛ in
110 - 130 mm

3¾ - 4⅜ in
95 - 110 mm

gymnastics

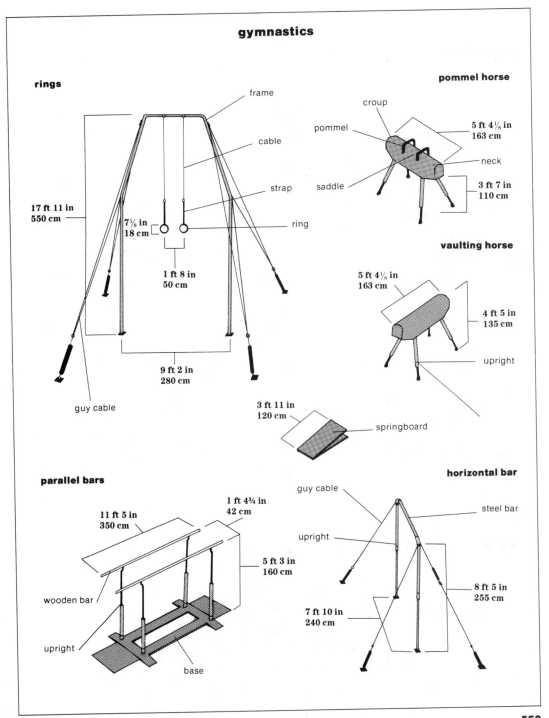

rings

frame

cable

strap

17 ft 11 in
550 cm

7⅛ in
18 cm

ring

1 ft 8 in
50 cm

9 ft 2 in
280 cm

guy cable

pommel horse

croup

pommel

5 ft 4⅛ in
163 cm

neck

saddle

3 ft 7 in
110 cm

vaulting horse

5 ft 4⅛ in
163 cm

4 ft 5 in
135 cm

upright

3 ft 11 in
120 cm

springboard

parallel bars

11 ft 5 in
350 cm

1 ft 4¾ in
42 cm

5 ft 3 in
160 cm

wooden bar

upright

base

horizontal bar

guy cable

steel bar

upright

8 ft 5 in
255 cm

7 ft 10 in
240 cm

559

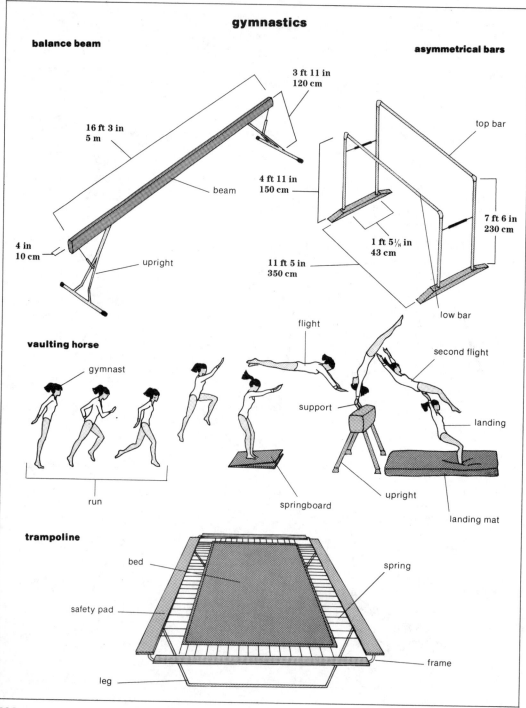

gymnastics

balance beam

asymmetrical bars

3 ft 11 in
120 cm

16 ft 3 in
5 m

top bar

4 ft 11 in
150 cm

beam

7 ft 6 in
230 cm

4 in
10 cm

1 ft 5⅛ in
43 cm

upright

11 ft 5 in
350 cm

low bar

flight

second flight

vaulting horse

gymnast

support

landing

run

springboard

upright

landing mat

trampoline

bed

spring

safety pad

frame

leg

560

weightlifting

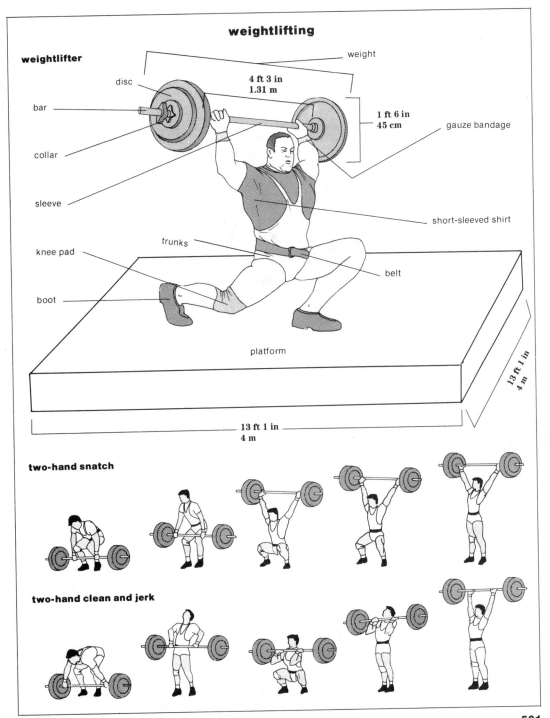

weightlifter

weight

disc

4 ft 3 in
1.31 m

bar

1 ft 6 in
45 cm

gauze bandage

collar

sleeve

short-sleeved shirt

trunks

knee pad

belt

boot

platform

13 ft 1 in
4 m

13 ft 1 in
4 m

two-hand snatch

two-hand clean and jerk

COMBAT SPORTS

fencing

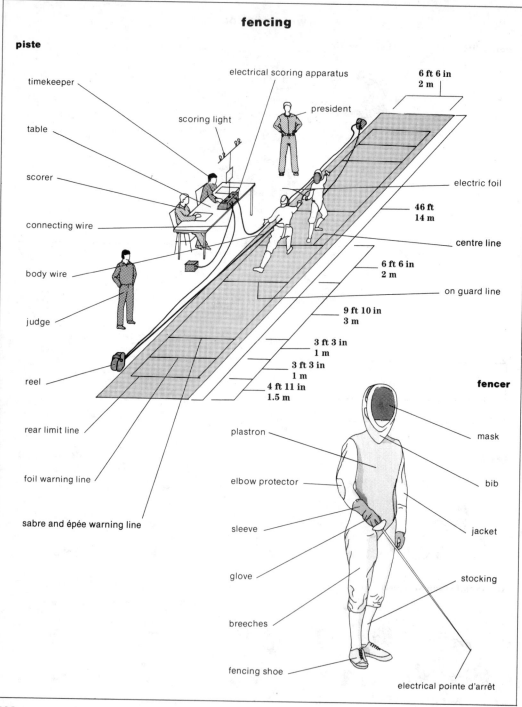

piste

timekeeper

electrical scoring apparatus

president

6 ft 6 in
2 m

scoring light

table

scorer

electric foil

46 ft
14 m

connecting wire

centre line

6 ft 6 in
2 m

body wire

on guard line

9 ft 10 in
3 m

judge

3 ft 3 in
1 m

3 ft 3 in
1 m

4 ft 11 in
1.5 m

reel

fencer

rear limit line

plastron

mask

foil warning line

elbow protector

bib

sabre and épée warning line

sleeve

jacket

glove

stocking

breeches

fencing shoe

electrical pointe d'arrêt

fencing

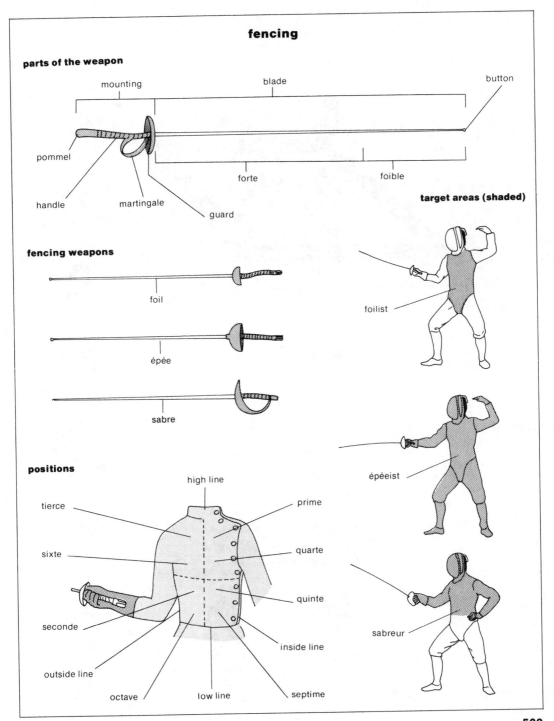

parts of the weapon

mounting · blade · button

pommel · handle · martingale · guard · forte · foible

fencing weapons

foil

épée

sabre

target areas (shaded)

foilist

épéeist

sabreur

positions

high line · tierce · prime · sixte · quarte · quinte · seconde · outside line · inside line · octave · low line · septime

COMBAT SPORTS

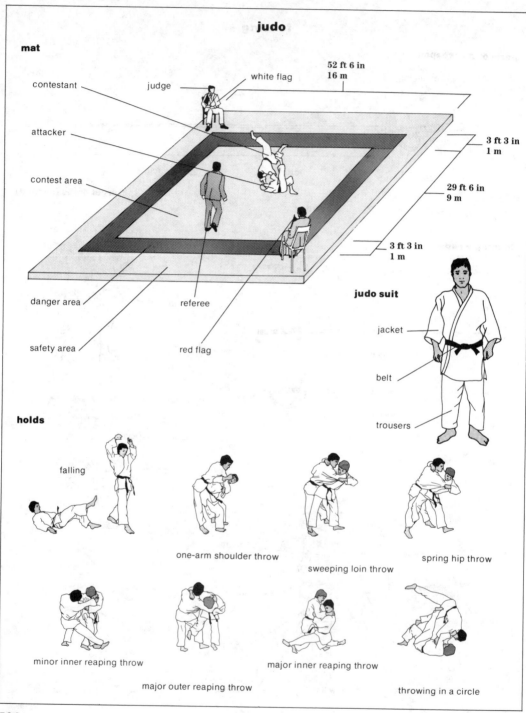

judo

mat

52 ft 6 in
16 m

contestant — judge — white flag

attacker

3 ft 3 in
1 m

contest area

29 ft 6 in
9 m

3 ft 3 in
1 m

danger area — referee

safety area — red flag

judo suit

jacket

belt

trousers

holds

falling

one-arm shoulder throw

sweeping loin throw

spring hip throw

minor inner reaping throw

major inner reaping throw

major outer reaping throw

throwing in a circle

boxing

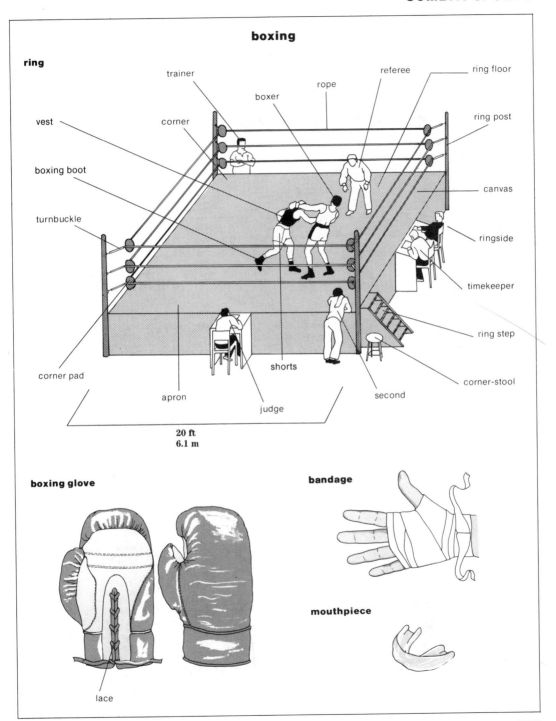

ring

trainer

referee

ring floor

rope

boxer

ring post

vest

corner

boxing boot

canvas

turnbuckle

ringside

timekeeper

ring step

corner pad

corner-stool

apron

shorts

second

judge

20 ft
6.1 m

boxing glove

bandage

mouthpiece

lace

LEISURE SPORTS

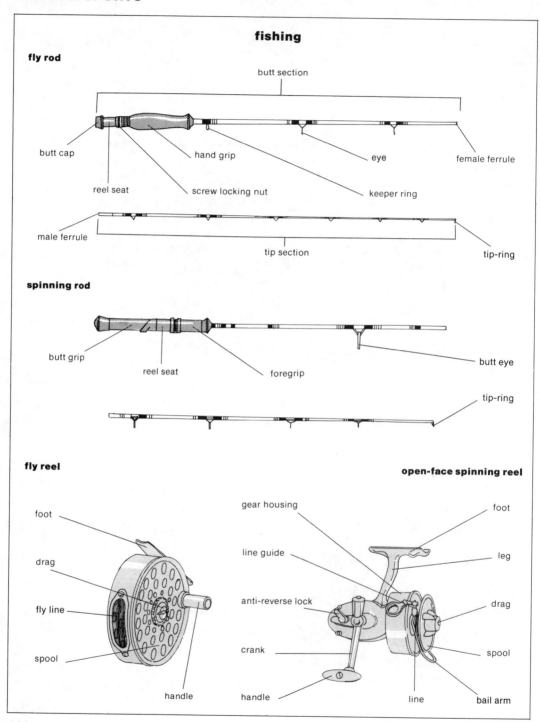

fishing

fly rod

butt section

butt cap

hand grip

eye

female ferrule

reel seat

screw locking nut

keeper ring

male ferrule

tip section

tip-ring

spinning rod

butt grip

butt eye

reel seat

foregrip

tip-ring

fly reel

open-face spinning reel

foot

gear housing

foot

drag

line guide

leg

fly line

anti-reverse lock

drag

spool

spool

handle

crank

line

bail arm

handle

handle

fishing

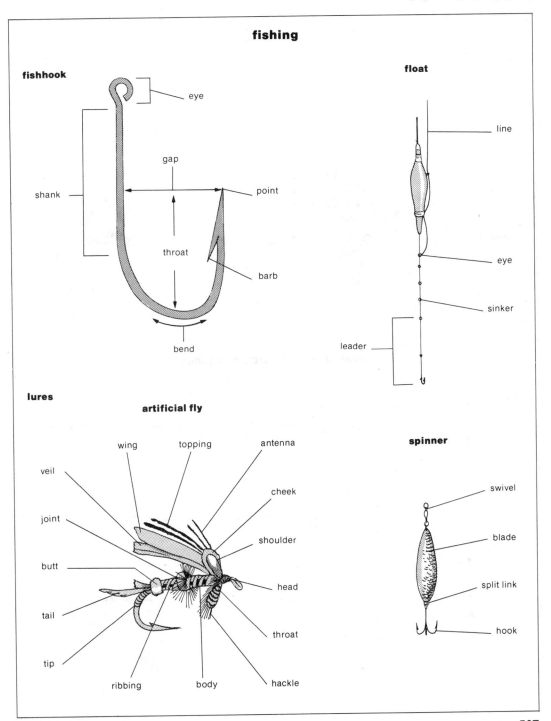

fishhook

eye

gap

shank

point

throat

barb

bend

float

line

eye

sinker

leader

lures

artificial fly

wing topping antenna

veil

cheek

joint

shoulder

butt

head

tail

throat

tip

ribbing body hackle

spinner

swivel

blade

split link

hook

567

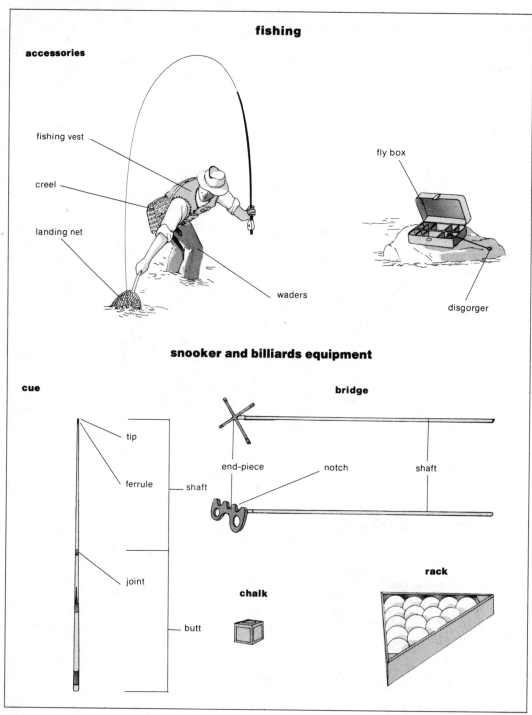

fishing

accessories

fishing vest

creel

landing net

waders

fly box

disgorger

snooker and billiards equipment

cue

tip

ferrule

shaft

joint

butt

bridge

end-piece

notch

shaft

chalk

rack

snooker and billiards

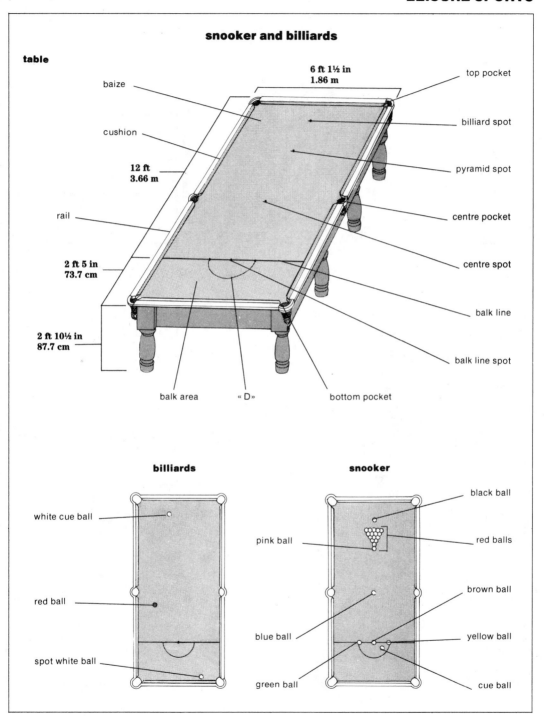

table

baize

cushion

12 ft
3.66 m

rail

2 ft 5 in
73.7 cm

2 ft 10½ in
87.7 cm

6 ft 1½ in
1.86 m

top pocket

billiard spot

pyramid spot

centre pocket

centre spot

balk line

balk line spot

balk area

« D »

bottom pocket

billiards

white cue ball

red ball

spot white ball

snooker

black ball

pink ball

red balls

brown ball

blue ball

yellow ball

green ball

cue ball

LEISURE SPORTS

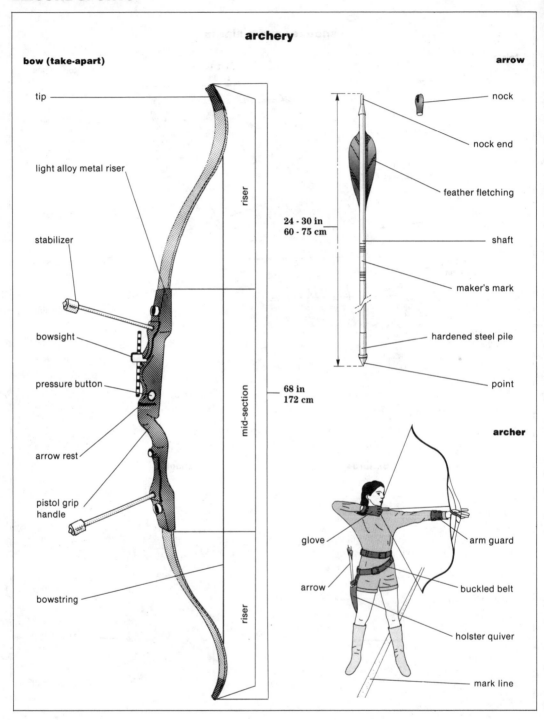

archery

bow (take-apart)

tip

light alloy metal riser

stabilizer

bowsight

pressure button

arrow rest

pistol grip
handle

bowstring

riser

mid-section

riser

68 in
172 cm

arrow

nock

nock end

feather fletching

24 - 30 in
60 - 75 cm

shaft

maker's mark

hardened steel pile

point

archer

glove

arrow

arm guard

buckled belt

holster quiver

mark line

golf

course

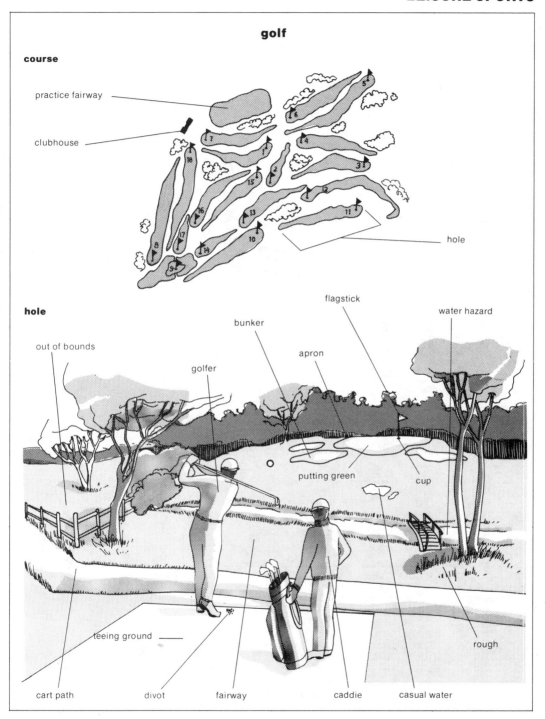

practice fairway

clubhouse

hole

hole

flagstick

water hazard

bunker

out of bounds

apron

golfer

putting green

cup

teeing ground

rough

cart path

divot

fairway

caddie

casual water

golf

types of golf clubs

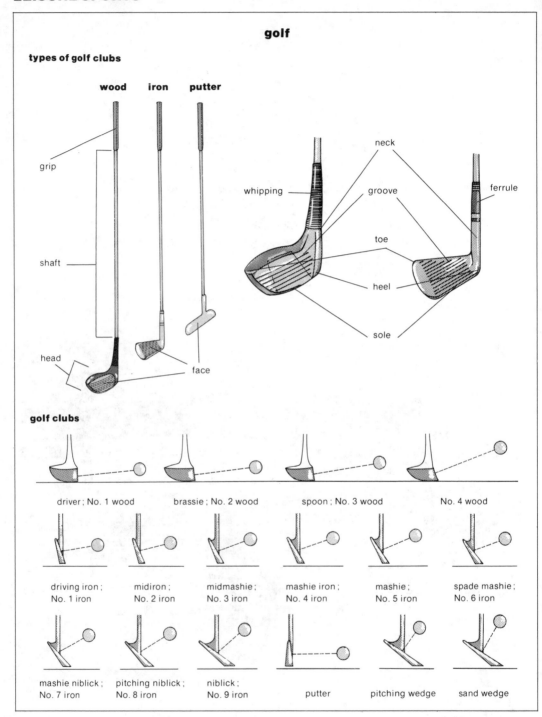

wood iron putter

grip

shaft

head

face

whipping

neck

groove

toe

heel

sole

ferrule

golf clubs

driver ; No. 1 wood

brassie ; No. 2 wood

spoon ; No. 3 wood

No. 4 wood

driving iron ;
No. 1 iron

midiron ;
No. 2 iron

midmashie ;
No. 3 iron

mashie iron ;
No. 4 iron

mashie ;
No. 5 iron

spade mashie ;
No. 6 iron

mashie niblick ;
No. 7 iron

pitching niblick ;
No. 8 iron

niblick ;
No. 9 iron

putter

pitching wedge

sand wedge

golf

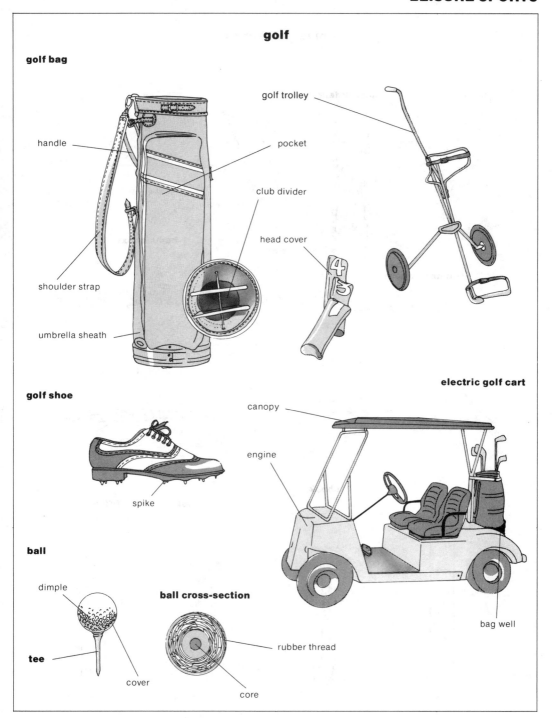

golf bag

golf trolley

handle

pocket

club divider

head cover

shoulder strap

umbrella sheath

electric golf cart

golf shoe

canopy

engine

spike

ball

dimple

ball cross-section

tee

rubber thread

cover

core

bag well

573

mountaineering

equipment

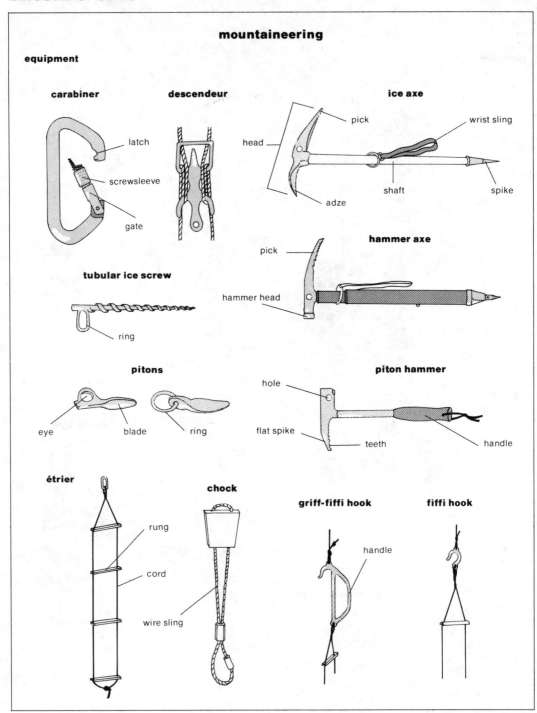

carabiner

latch

screwsleeve

gate

descendeur

ice axe

pick

head

wrist sling

shaft

spike

adze

hammer axe

pick

hammer head

tubular ice screw

ring

pitons

eye

blade

ring

piton hammer

hole

flat spike

teeth

handle

étrier

rung

cord

wire sling

chock

griff-fiffi hook

handle

fiffi hook

mountaineering

mountaineer

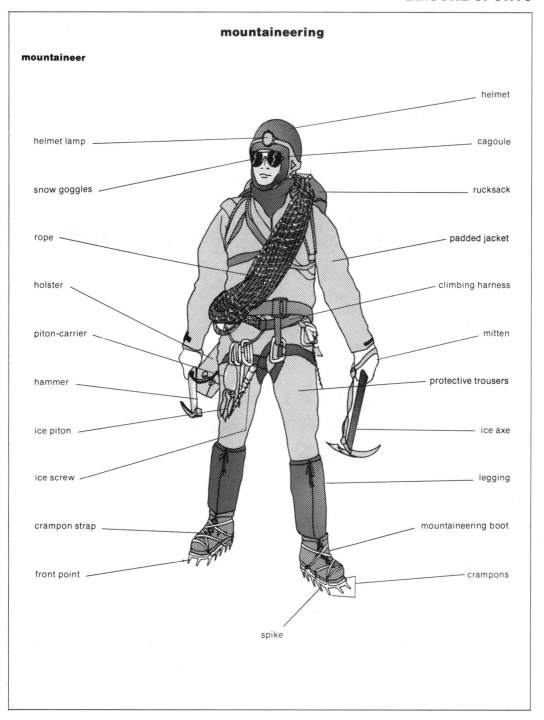

helmet

helmet lamp

cagoule

snow goggles

rucksack

rope

padded jacket

holster

climbing harness

piton-carrier

mitten

hammer

protective trousers

ice piton

ice axe

ice screw

legging

crampon strap

mountaineering boot

front point

crampons

spike

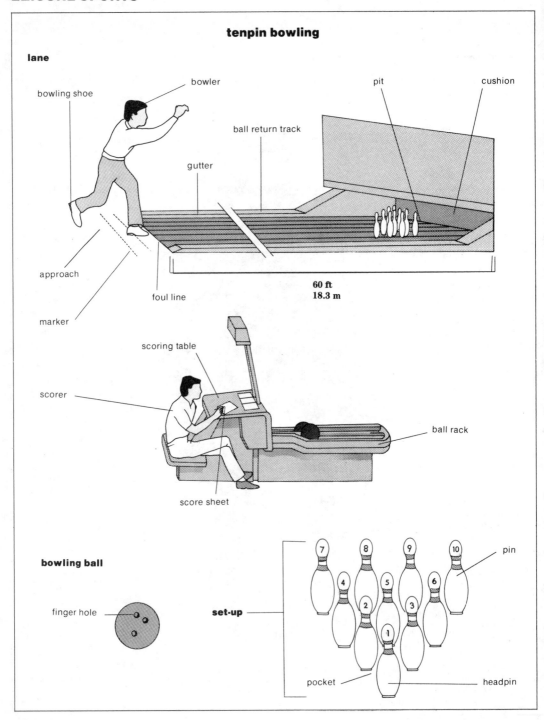

tenpin bowling

lane

bowling shoe

bowler

pit

cushion

ball return track

gutter

approach

foul line

marker

60 ft
18.3 m

scoring table

scorer

ball rack

score sheet

bowling ball

finger hole

set-up

pin

pocket

headpin

chess

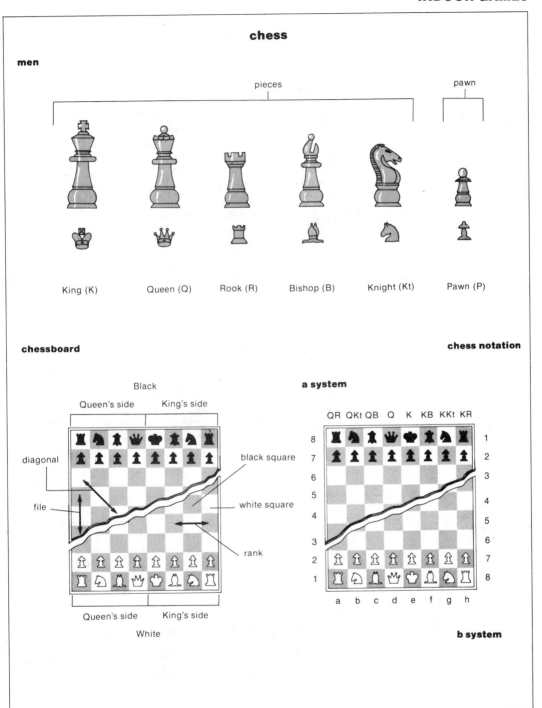

men

pieces — pawn

King (K) Queen (Q) Rook (R) Bishop (B) Knight (Kt) Pawn (P)

chessboard

chess notation

Black

Queen's side King's side

diagonal

file

black square

white square

rank

Queen's side King's side

White

a system

QR QKt QB Q K KB KKt KR

8 7 6 5 4 3 2 1

1 2 3 4 5 6 7 8

a b c d e f g h

b system

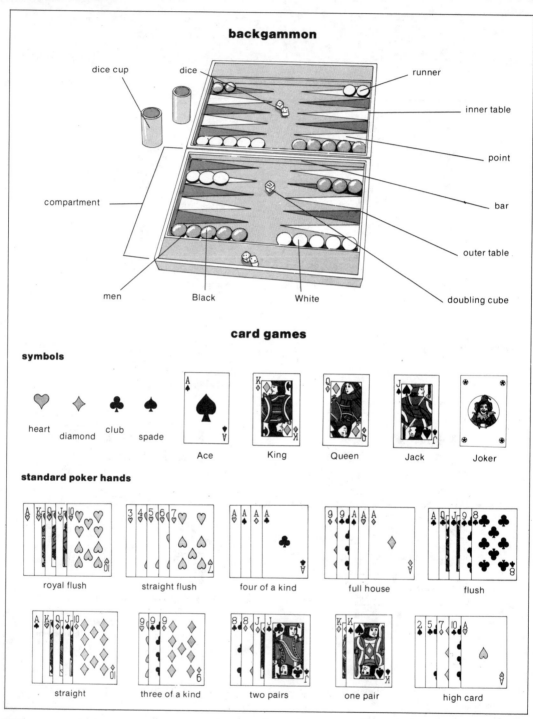

backgammon

dice cup

dice

runner

inner table

point

bar

compartment

outer table

men

Black

White

doubling cube

card games

symbols

heart

diamond

club

spade

Ace

King

Queen

Jack

Joker

standard poker hands

royal flush

straight flush

four of a kind

full house

flush

straight

three of a kind

two pairs

one pair

high card

578

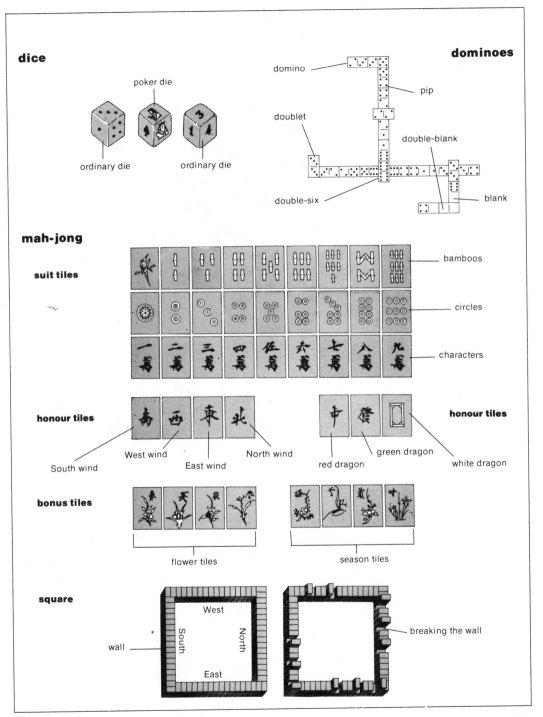

dice

poker die

ordinary die

ordinary die

dominoes

domino

pip

doublet

double-blank

double-six

blank

mah-jong

suit tiles

bamboos

circles

characters

honour tiles

West wind

East wind

North wind

South wind

honour tiles

red dragon

green dragon

white dragon

bonus tiles

flower tiles

season tiles

square

West

South

North

East

wall

breaking the wall

roulette table

French roulette wheel

betting layout (French)

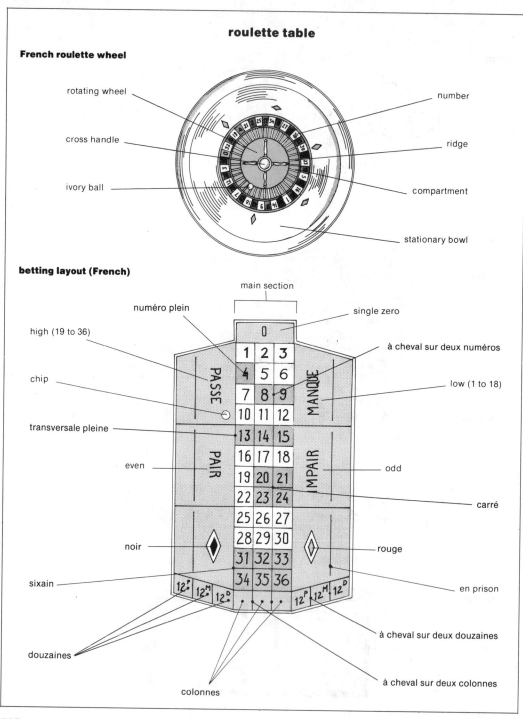

rotating wheel

number

cross handle

ridge

ivory ball

compartment

stationary bowl

main section

numéro plein

single zero

high (19 to 36)

à cheval sur deux numéros

chip

low (1 to 18)

transversale pleine

even

odd

carré

noir

rouge

sixain

en prison

douzaines

à cheval sur deux douzaines

colonnes

à cheval sur deux colonnes

PASSE

MANQUE

PAIR

IMPAIR

caravan

4-berth caravan

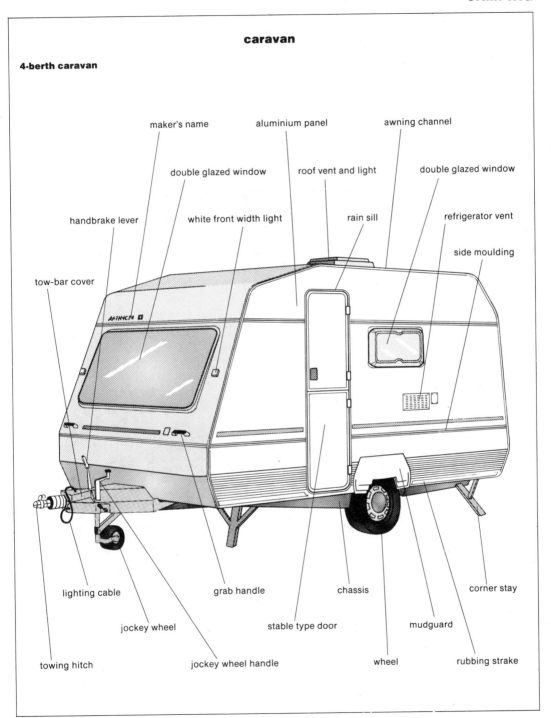

maker's name

aluminium panel

awning channel

double glazed window

roof vent and light

double glazed window

handbrake lever

white front width light

rain sill

refrigerator vent

tow-bar cover

side moulding

lighting cable

grab handle

chassis

corner stay

jockey wheel

stable type door

mudguard

towing hitch

jockey wheel handle

wheel

rubbing strake

CAMPING

tents

family tents

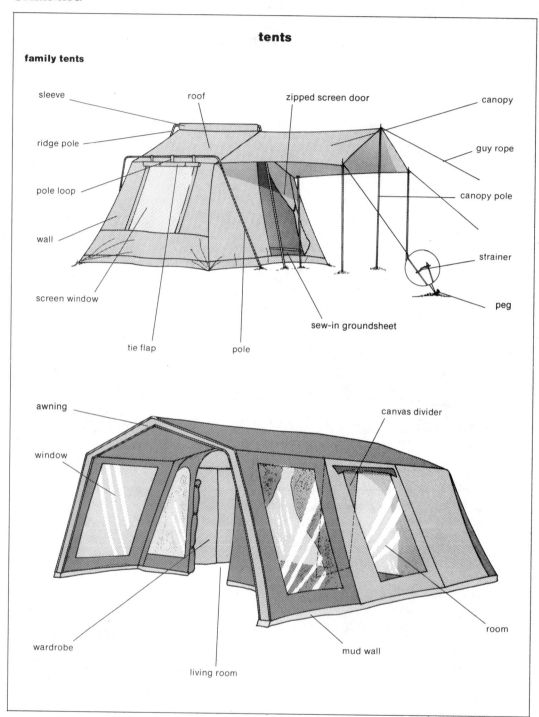

sleeve

roof

zipped screen door

canopy

ridge pole

guy rope

pole loop

canopy pole

wall

strainer

screen window

peg

sew-in groundsheet

tie flap

pole

awning

canvas divider

window

wardrobe

living room

mud wall

room

tents

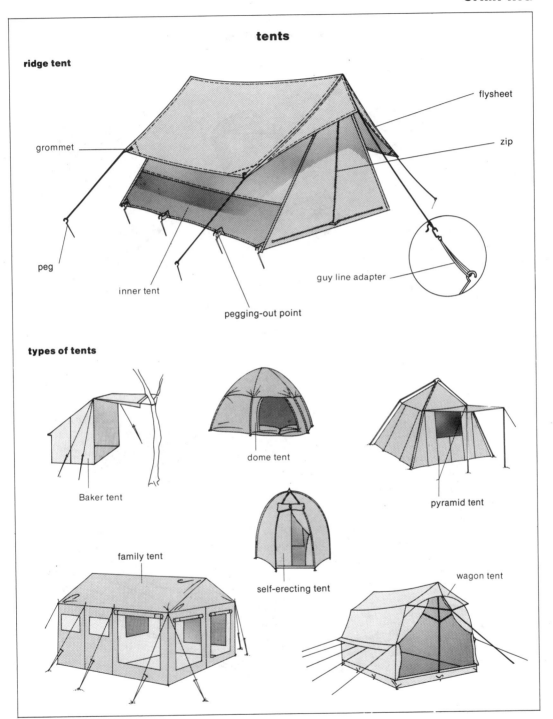

ridge tent

flysheet

zip

grommet

peg

inner tent

pegging-out point

guy line adapter

types of tents

Baker tent

dome tent

pyramid tent

family tent

self-erecting tent

wagon tent

583

CAMPING

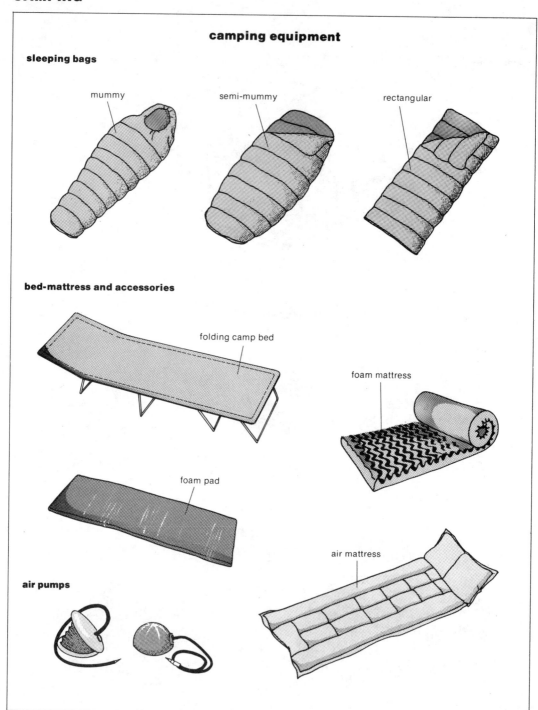

camping equipment

sleeping bags

mummy

semi-mummy

rectangular

bed-mattress and accessories

folding camp bed

foam mattress

foam pad

air mattress

air pumps

camping equipment

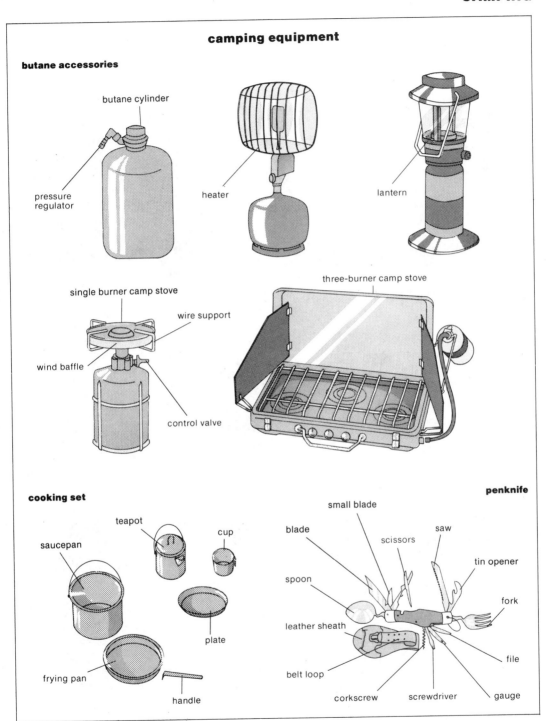

butane accessories

butane cylinder

pressure regulator

heater

lantern

single burner camp stove

wire support

wind baffle

control valve

three-burner camp stove

cooking set

penknife

teapot

cup

saucepan

small blade

blade

scissors

saw

tin opener

spoon

fork

leather sheath

plate

file

frying pan

belt loop

corkscrew

screwdriver

gauge

handle

585

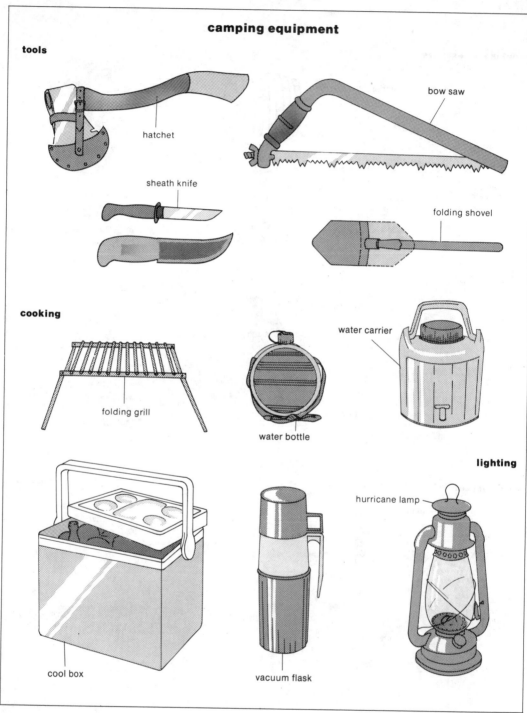

camping equipment

tools

hatchet

bow saw

sheath knife

folding shovel

cooking

folding grill

water carrier

water bottle

lighting

hurricane lamp

cool box

vacuum flask

knots

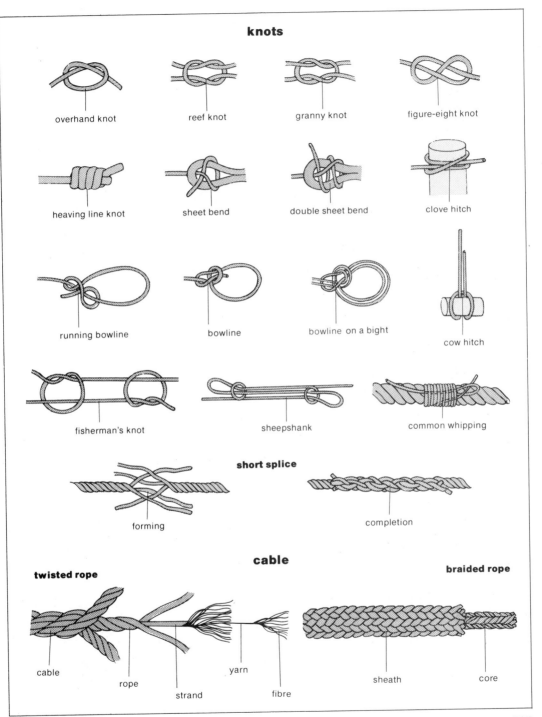

overhand knot

reef knot

granny knot

figure-eight knot

heaving line knot

sheet bend

double sheet bend

clove hitch

running bowline

bowline

bowline on a bight

cow hitch

fisherman's knot

sheepshank

common whipping

short splice

forming

completion

cable

twisted rope

braided rope

cable

rope

strand

yarn

fibre

sheath

core

MEASURING DEVICES

measure of time

mechanical watch

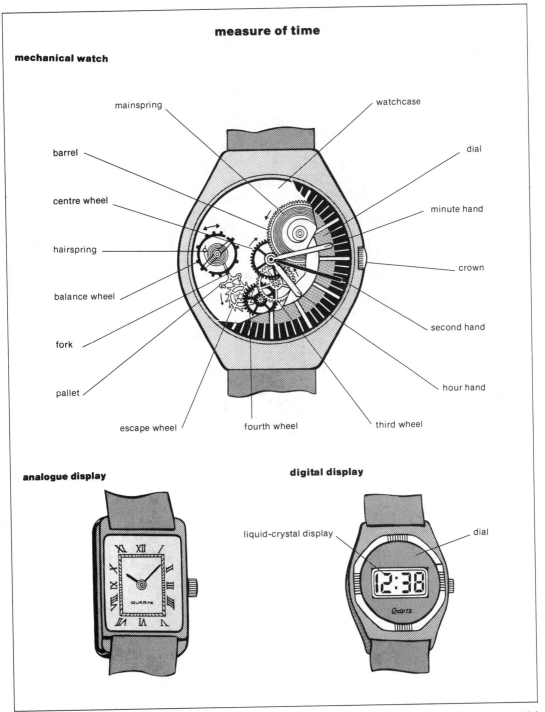

mainspring

watchcase

barrel

dial

centre wheel

minute hand

hairspring

crown

balance wheel

fork

second hand

pallet

hour hand

escape wheel

fourth wheel

third wheel

analogue display

digital display

liquid-crystal display

dial

MEASURING DEVICES

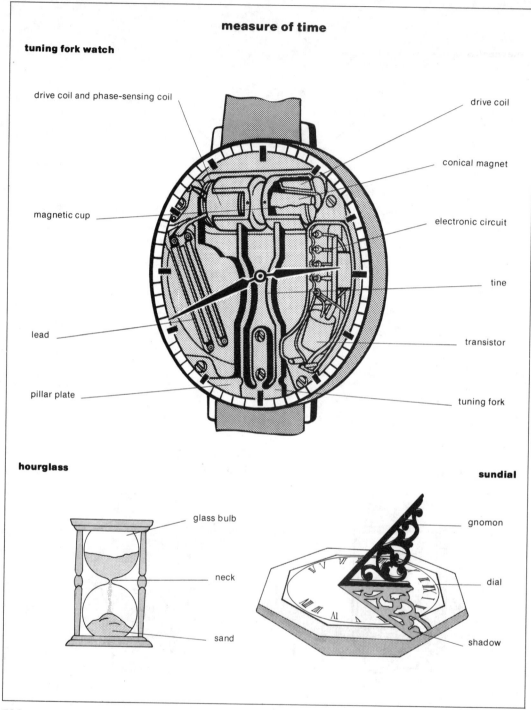

measure of time

tuning fork watch

drive coil and phase-sensing coil

drive coil

conical magnet

magnetic cup

electronic circuit

tine

lead

transistor

pillar plate

tuning fork

hourglass

sundial

glass bulb

gnomon

neck

dial

sand

shadow

measure of time

weight-driven clock mechanism

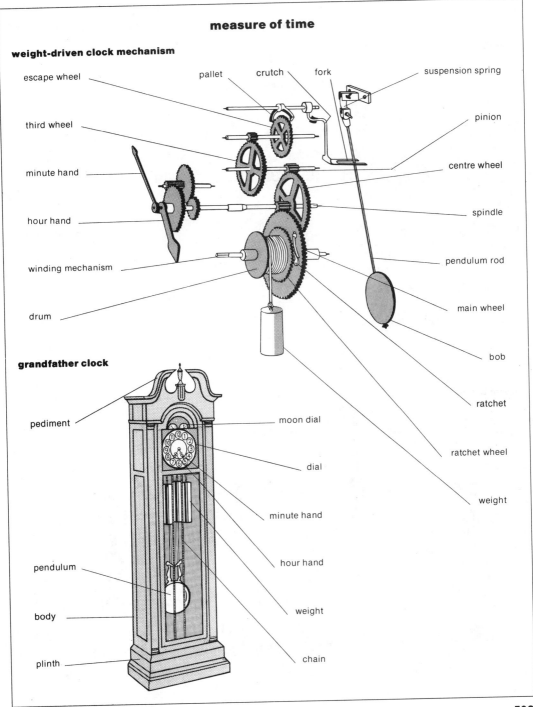

escape wheel

pallet

crutch

fork

suspension spring

third wheel

pinion

minute hand

centre wheel

hour hand

spindle

winding mechanism

pendulum rod

drum

main wheel

bob

ratchet

ratchet wheel

weight

grandfather clock

pediment

moon dial

dial

minute hand

hour hand

pendulum

weight

body

plinth

chain

593

MEASURING DEVICES

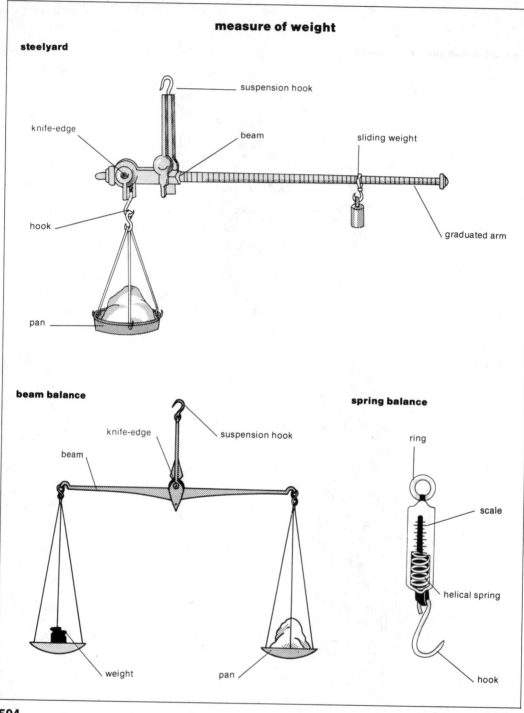

measure of weight

steelyard

suspension hook

knife-edge

beam

sliding weight

hook

graduated arm

pan

beam balance

knife-edge

suspension hook

beam

weight

pan

spring balance

ring

scale

helical spring

hook

measure of weight

Roberval's balance

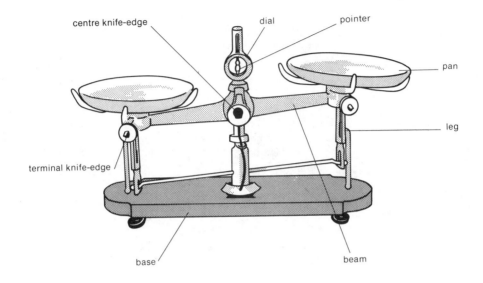

centre knife-edge

dial

pointer

pan

leg

terminal knife-edge

base

beam

analytical balance

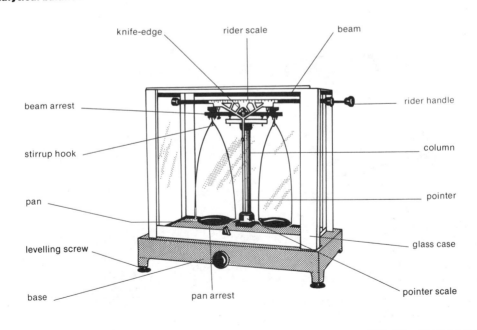

knife-edge

rider scale

beam

rider handle

beam arrest

stirrup hook

column

pan

pointer

levelling screw

glass case

base

pan arrest

pointer scale

MEASURING DEVICES

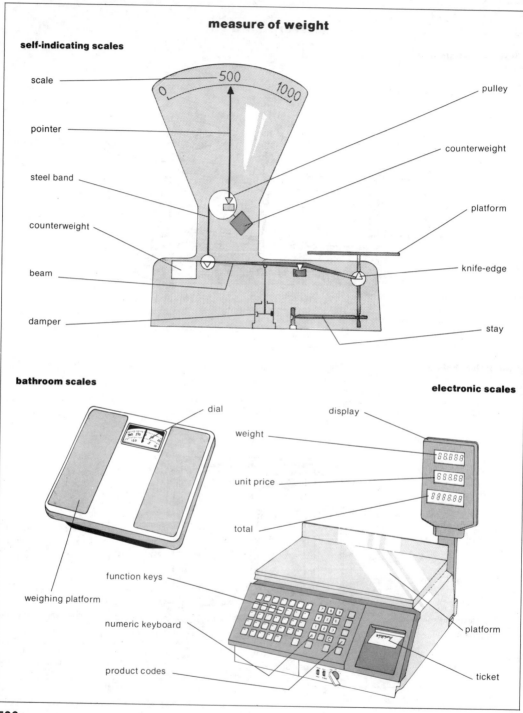

measure of weight

self-indicating scales

scale

pointer

steel band

counterweight

beam

damper

pulley

counterweight

platform

knife-edge

stay

bathroom scales

dial

weighing platform

electronic scales

display

weight

unit price

total

function keys

numeric keyboard

product codes

platform

ticket

596

mesure of temperature

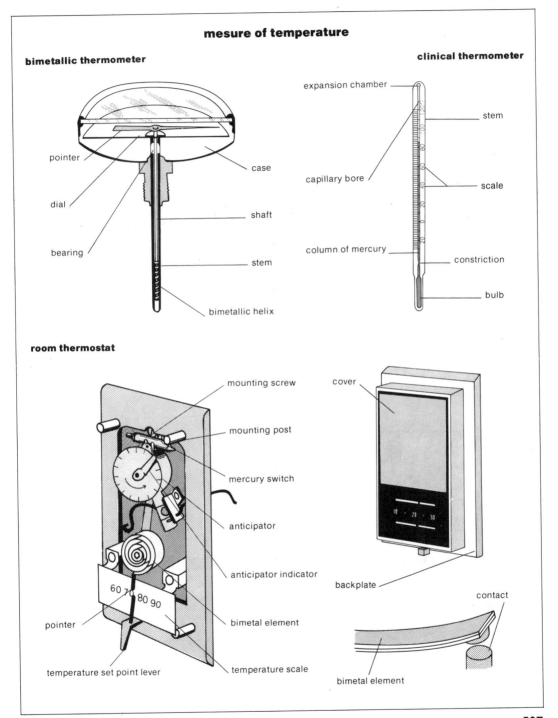

bimetallic thermometer

pointer

dial

bearing

case

shaft

stem

bimetallic helix

clinical thermometer

expansion chamber

stem

capillary bore

scale

column of mercury

constriction

bulb

room thermostat

mounting screw

mounting post

mercury switch

anticipator

anticipator indicator

bimetal element

temperature scale

pointer

temperature set point lever

cover

backplate

contact

bimetal element

60 70 80 90

MEASURING DEVICES

measure of pressure

aneroid barometer

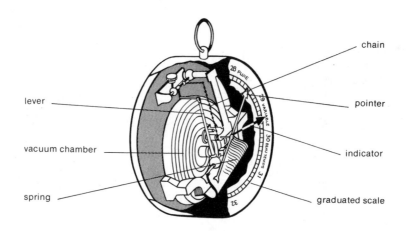

chain

pointer

indicator

graduated scale

lever

vacuum chamber

spring

sphygmomanometer

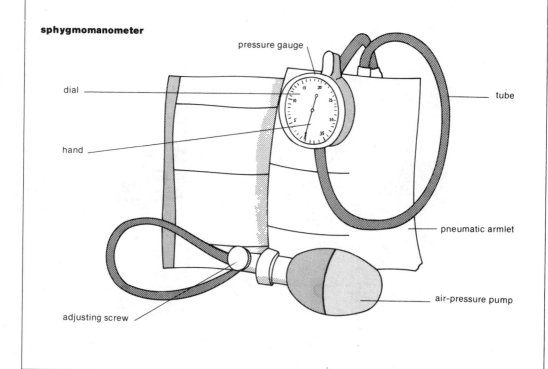

pressure gauge

dial

tube

hand

pneumatic armlet

air-pressure pump

adjusting screw

measure of length and width

tape measure

pedometer

case

tape lock

pointer

step setting

dial

scale

30

5

25

10

20

15

tape

hook

case

micrometer

anvil

spindle

lock nut

sleeve

spindle screw

adjusting nut

frame

thimble

ratchet knob

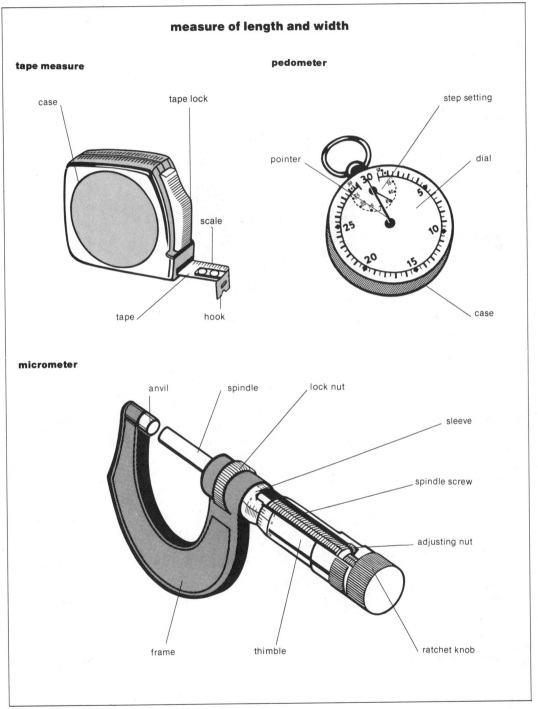

theodolite

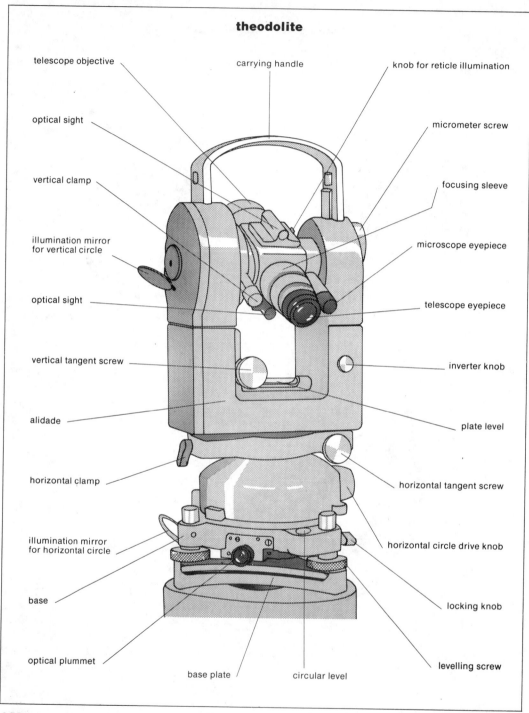

telescope objective

carrying handle

knob for reticle illumination

optical sight

micrometer screw

vertical clamp

focusing sleeve

illumination mirror
for vertical circle

microscope eyepiece

optical sight

telescope eyepiece

vertical tangent screw

inverter knob

alidade

plate level

horizontal clamp

horizontal tangent screw

illumination mirror
for horizontal circle

horizontal circle drive knob

base

locking knob

optical plummet

levelling screw

base plate

circular level

watt-hour meter

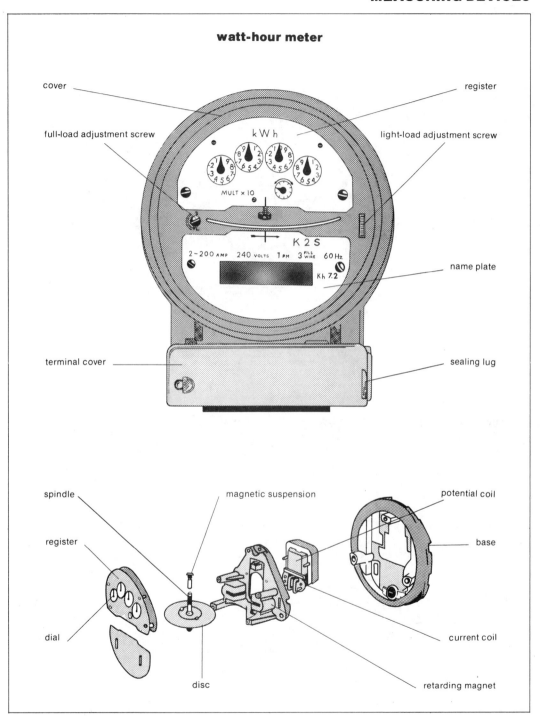

cover

register

full-load adjustment screw

light-load adjustment screw

kWh

MULT × 10

K 2 S

2~200 AMP 240 VOLTS 1 PM 3 PHS WIRE 60 Hz

Kh 7.2

name plate

terminal cover

sealing lug

spindle

magnetic suspension

potential coil

register

base

dial

current coil

disc

retarding magnet

MEASURING DEVICES

seismographs

horizontal seismograph

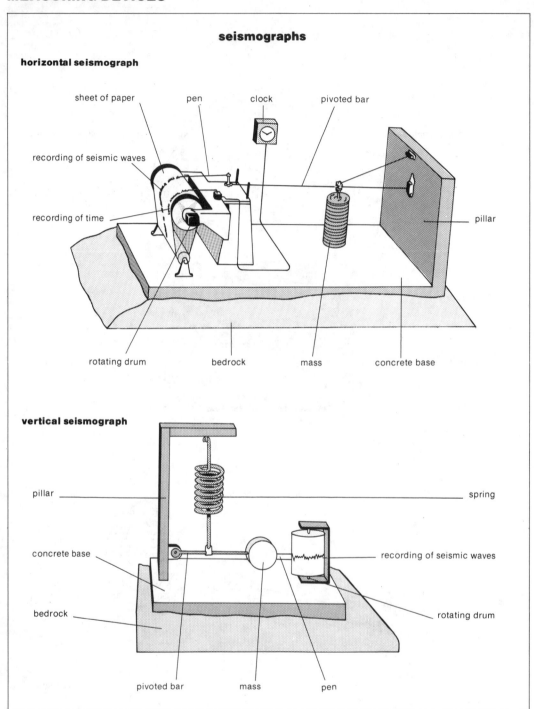

sheet of paper · pen · clock · pivoted bar

recording of seismic waves

recording of time

pillar

rotating drum · bedrock · mass · concrete base

vertical seismograph

pillar · spring

concrete base · recording of seismic waves

bedrock · rotating drum

pivoted bar · mass · pen

OPTICAL INSTRUMENTS

binocular microscope

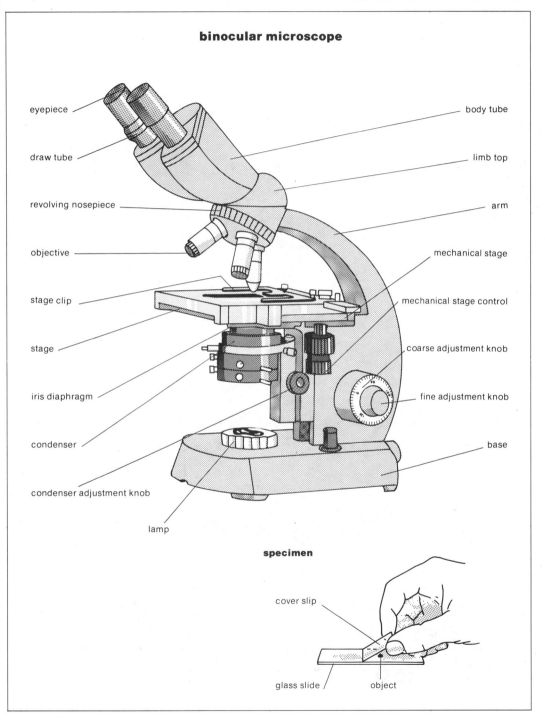

eyepiece

body tube

draw tube

limb top

revolving nosepiece

arm

objective

mechanical stage

stage clip

mechanical stage control

stage

coarse adjustment knob

iris diaphragm

fine adjustment knob

condenser

base

condenser adjustment knob

lamp

specimen

cover slip

glass slide

object

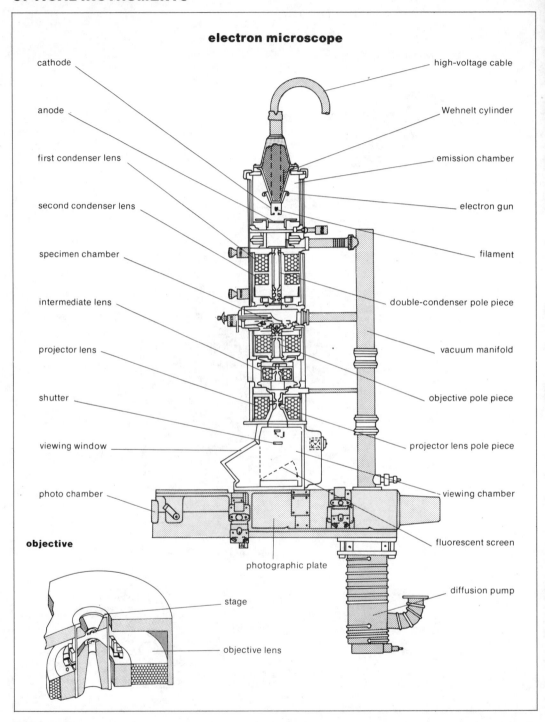

electron microscope

cathode

anode

first condenser lens

second condenser lens

specimen chamber

intermediate lens

projector lens

shutter

viewing window

photo chamber

objective

high-voltage cable

Wehnelt cylinder

emission chamber

electron gun

filament

double-condenser pole piece

vacuum manifold

objective pole piece

projector lens pole piece

viewing chamber

fluorescent screen

photographic plate

diffusion pump

stage

objective lens

prism binoculars

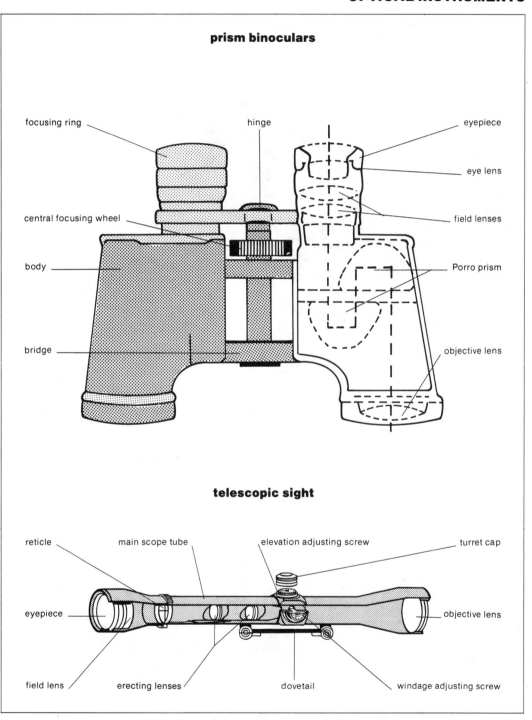

focusing ring

hinge

eyepiece

eye lens

central focusing wheel

field lenses

body

Porro prism

bridge

objective lens

telescopic sight

reticle

main scope tube

elevation adjusting screw

turret cap

eyepiece

objective lens

field lens

erecting lenses

dovetail

windage adjusting screw

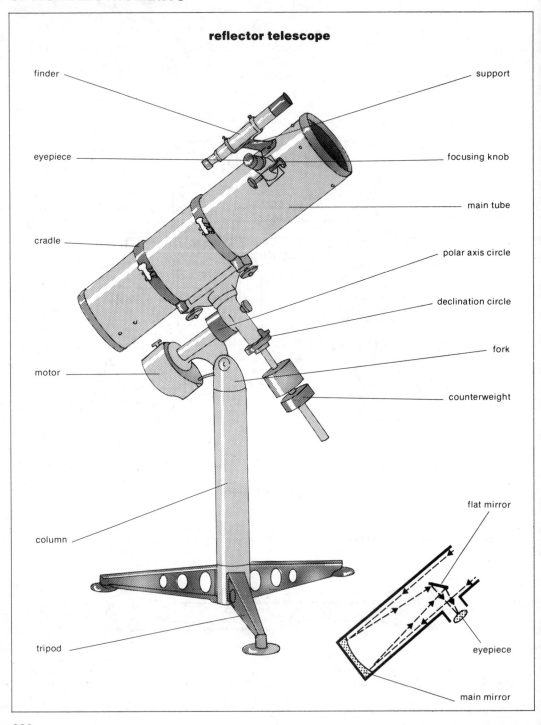

reflector telescope

finder

support

eyepiece

focusing knob

main tube

cradle

polar axis circle

declination circle

motor

fork

counterweight

column

flat mirror

eyepiece

tripod

main mirror

refractor telescope

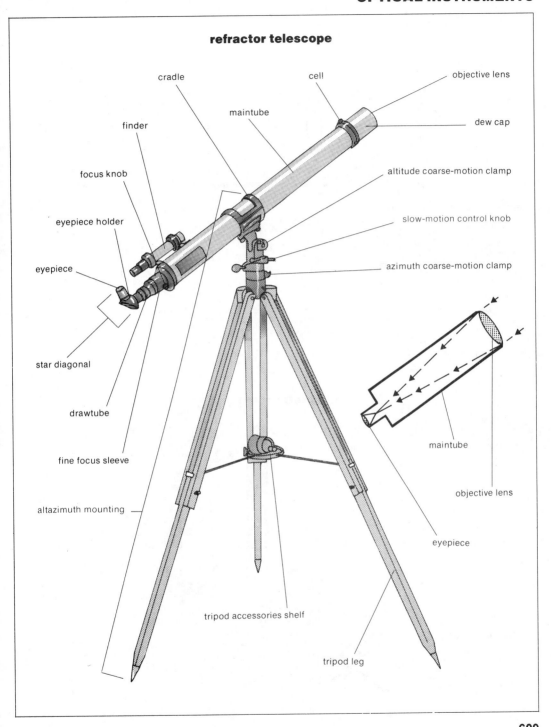

cradle

cell

objective lens

maintube

dew cap

finder

altitude coarse-motion clamp

focus knob

slow-motion control knob

eyepiece holder

azimuth coarse-motion clamp

eyepiece

star diagonal

drawtube

maintube

fine focus sleeve

objective lens

altazimuth mounting

eyepiece

tripod accessories shelf

tripod leg

OPTICAL INSTRUMENTS

lens

converging lens

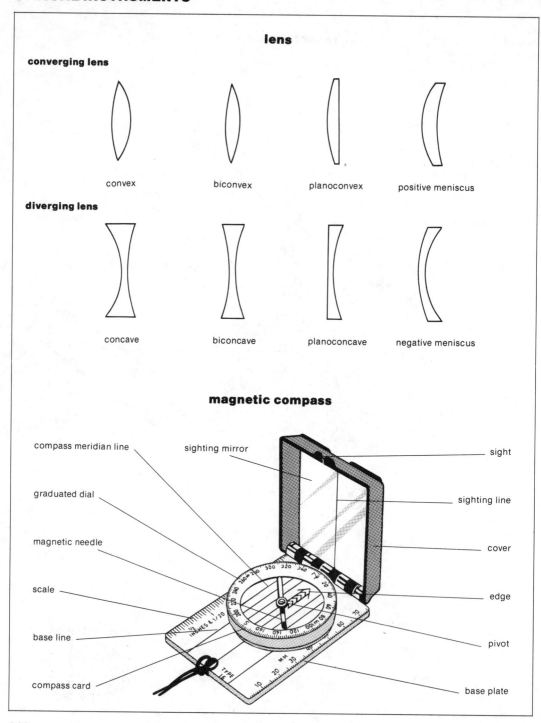

convex

biconvex

planoconvex

positive meniscus

diverging lens

concave

biconcave

planoconcave

negative meniscus

magnetic compass

compass meridian line

sighting mirror

sight

graduated dial

sighting line

magnetic needle

cover

scale

edge

base line

pivot

compass card

base plate

radar

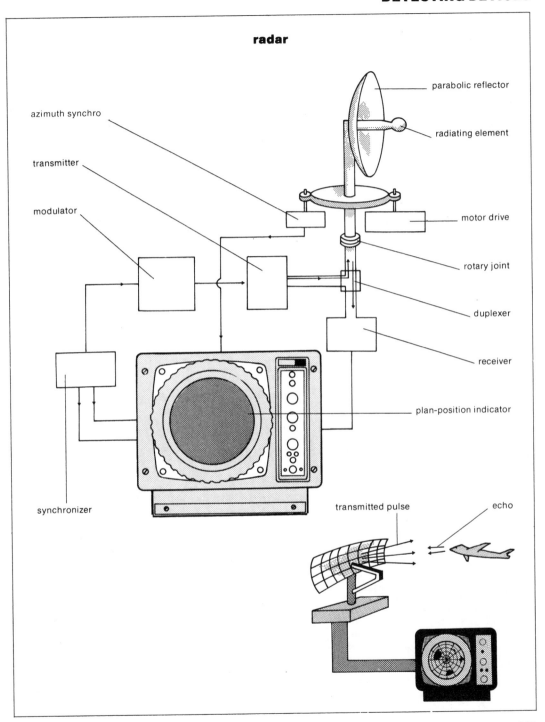

parabolic reflector

radiating element

azimuth synchro

transmitter

modulator

motor drive

rotary joint

duplexer

receiver

plan-position indicator

synchronizer

transmitted pulse

echo

HEALTH

first aid kit

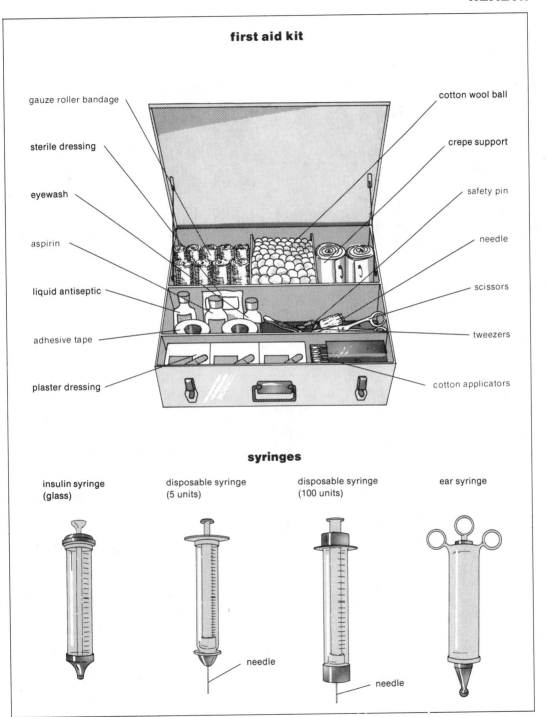

gauze roller bandage

sterile dressing

eyewash

aspirin

liquid antiseptic

adhesive tape

plaster dressing

cotton wool ball

crepe support

safety pin

needle

scissors

tweezers

cotton applicators

syringes

insulin syringe
(glass)

disposable syringe
(5 units)

disposable syringe
(100 units)

ear syringe

needle

needle

walking aids

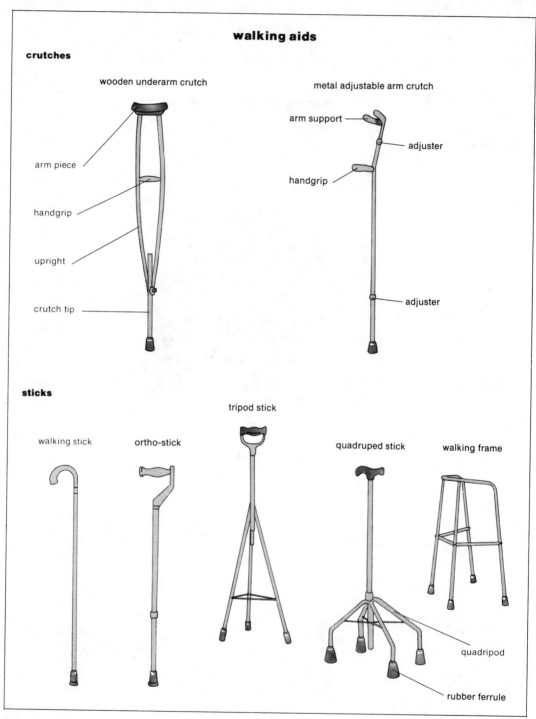

crutches

wooden underarm crutch

metal adjustable arm crutch

arm piece

handgrip

upright

crutch tip

arm support

adjuster

handgrip

adjuster

sticks

tripod stick

walking stick

ortho-stick

quadruped stick

walking frame

quadripod

rubber ferrule

wheelchair

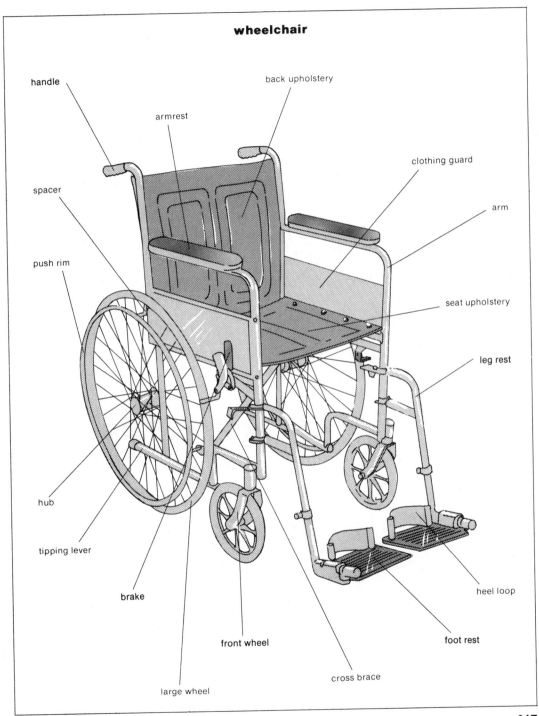

handle

back upholstery

armrest

clothing guard

spacer

arm

push rim

seat upholstery

leg rest

hub

tipping lever

heel loop

brake

foot rest

front wheel

cross brace

large wheel

ENERGY

coal mine

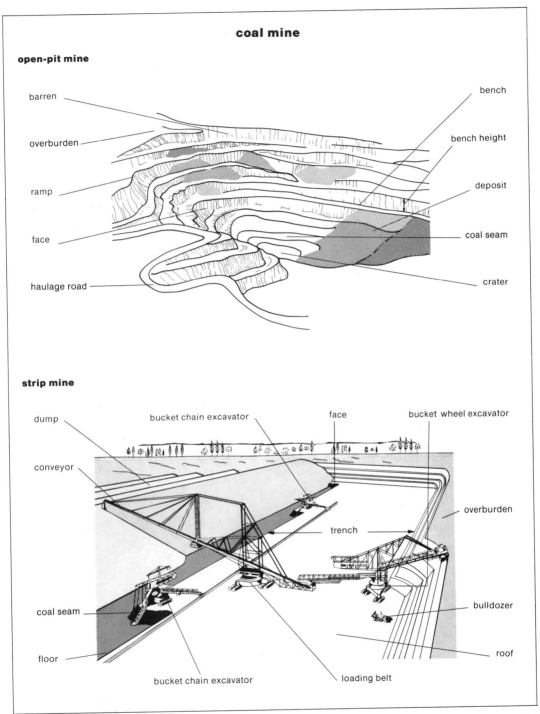

open-pit mine

barren

overburden

ramp

face

haulage road

bench

bench height

deposit

coal seam

crater

strip mine

dump

conveyor

coal seam

floor

bucket chain excavator

bucket chain excavator

face

trench

loading belt

bucket wheel excavator

overburden

bulldozer

roof

621

metalliferous mine

mining

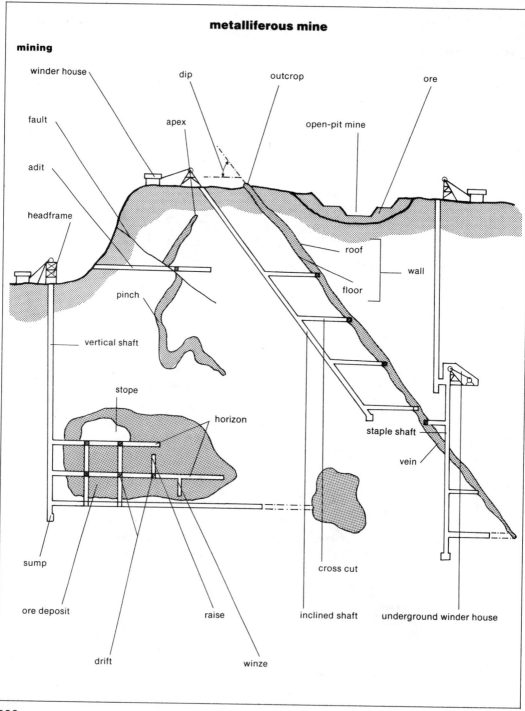

winder house

dip

outcrop

ore

fault

apex

open-pit mine

adit

headframe

roof

wall

floor

pinch

vertical shaft

stope

horizon

staple shaft

vein

sump

cross cut

ore deposit

raise

inclined shaft

underground winder house

drift

winze

coal mine

underground mine

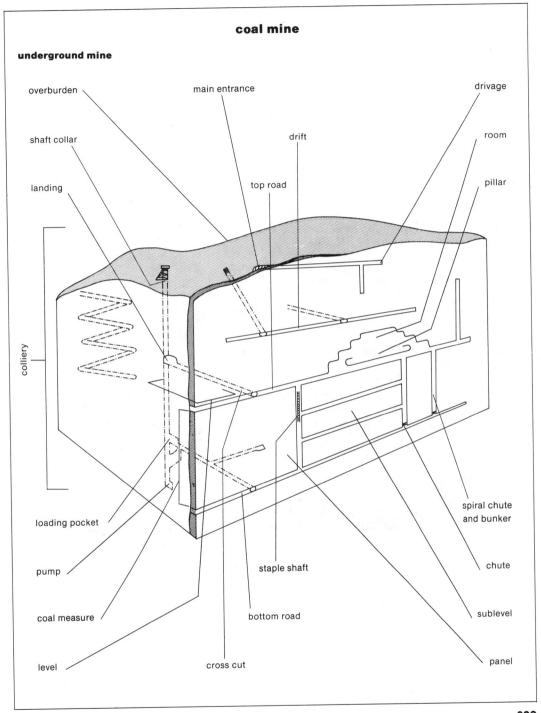

overburden

main entrance

drivage

shaft collar

drift

room

landing

top road

pillar

colliery

loading pocket

spiral chute and bunker

pump

chute

coal measure

staple shaft

sublevel

level

bottom road

cross cut

panel

coal mine

pithead

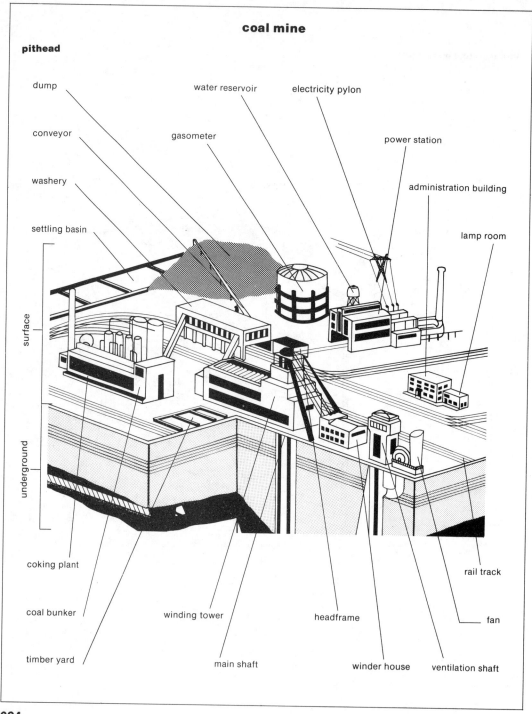

dump

water reservoir

electricity pylon

conveyor

gasometer

power station

washery

administration building

settling basin

lamp room

surface

underground

coking plant

rail track

coal bunker

winding tower

headframe

fan

timber yard

main shaft

winder house

ventilation shaft

624

coal mine

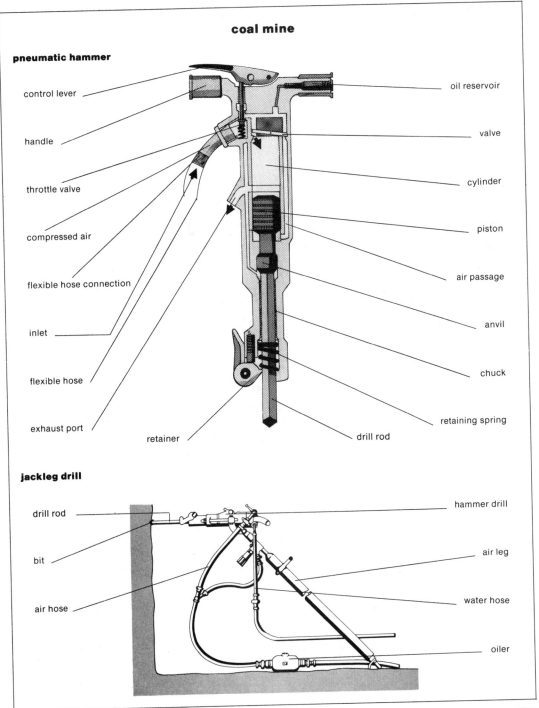

pneumatic hammer

- control lever
- handle
- throttle valve
- compressed air
- flexible hose connection
- inlet
- flexible hose
- exhaust port
- retainer
- drill rod

- oil reservoir
- valve
- cylinder
- piston
- air passage
- anvil
- chuck
- retaining spring

jackleg drill

- drill rod
- bit
- air hose

- hammer drill
- air leg
- water hose
- oiler

oil

drilling rig

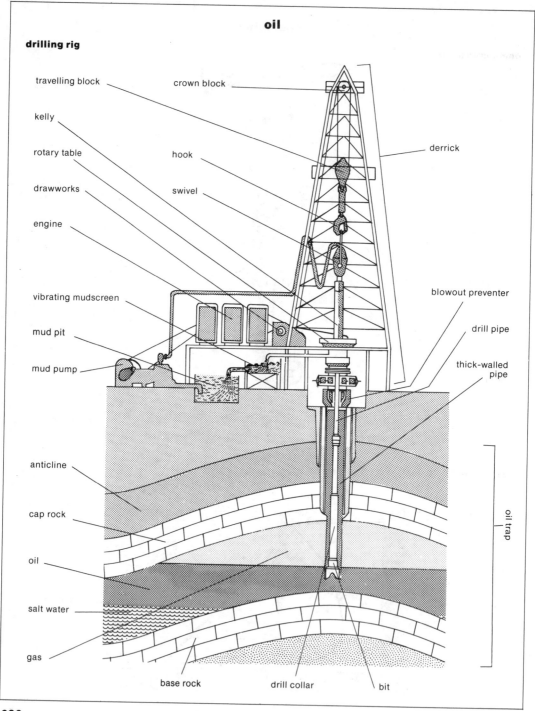

travelling block

crown block

kelly

rotary table

hook

drawworks

swivel

engine

derrick

vibrating mudscreen

blowout preventer

mud pit

drill pipe

mud pump

thick-walled pipe

anticline

cap rock

oil

salt water

gas

oil trap

base rock

drill collar

bit

oil

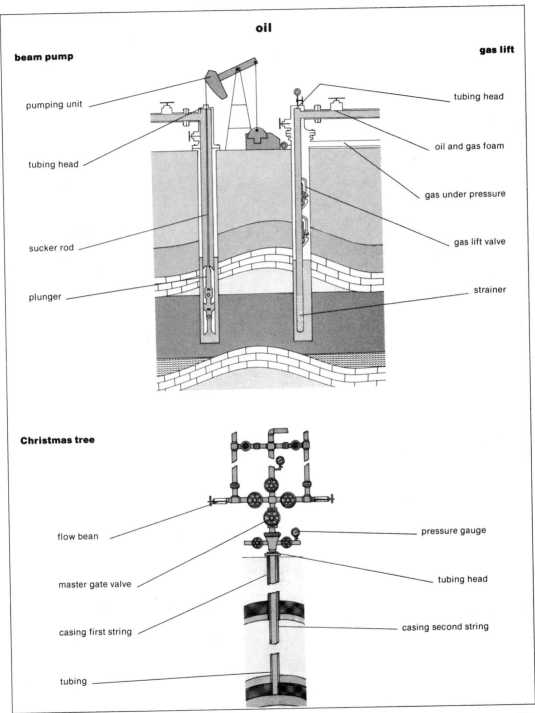

beam pump

gas lift

pumping unit

tubing head

tubing head

oil and gas foam

sucker rod

gas under pressure

gas lift valve

plunger

strainer

Christmas tree

flow bean

pressure gauge

master gate valve

tubing head

casing first string

casing second string

tubing

oil

offshore drilling and rigs

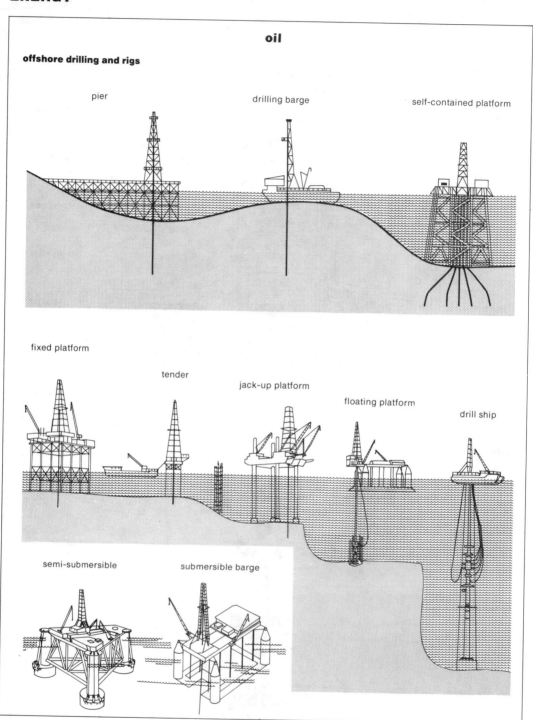

pier

drilling barge

self-contained platform

fixed platform

tender

jack-up platform

floating platform

drill ship

semi-submersible

submersible barge

oil

production platform

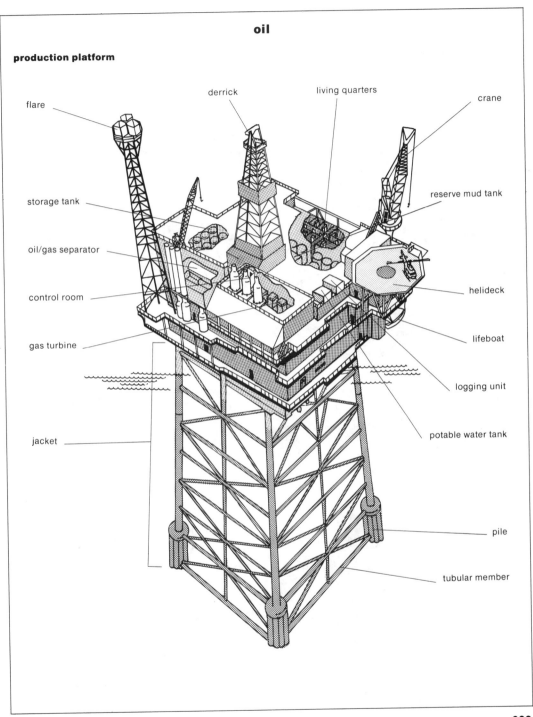

flare

derrick

living quarters

crane

storage tank

oil/gas separator

control room

gas turbine

jacket

reserve mud tank

helideck

lifeboat

logging unit

potable water tank

pile

tubular member

oil

crude oil pipeline

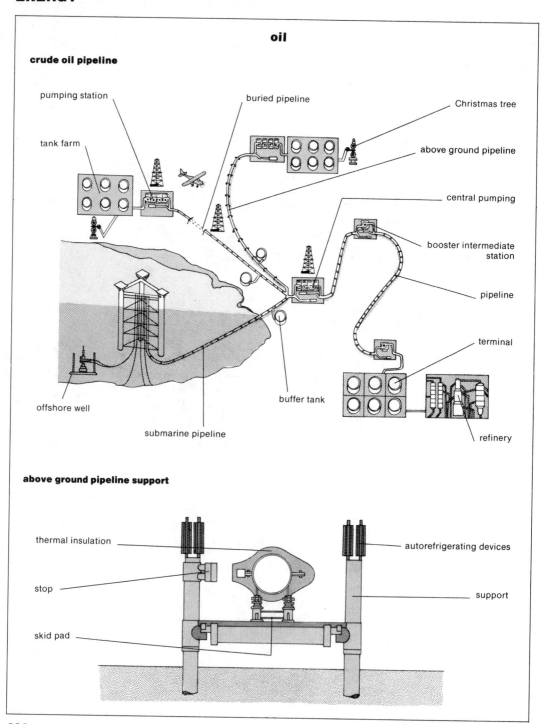

pumping station

buried pipeline

Christmas tree

tank farm

above ground pipeline

central pumping

booster intermediate station

pipeline

terminal

offshore well

buffer tank

submarine pipeline

refinery

above ground pipeline support

thermal insulation

autorefrigerating devices

stop

support

skid pad

oil

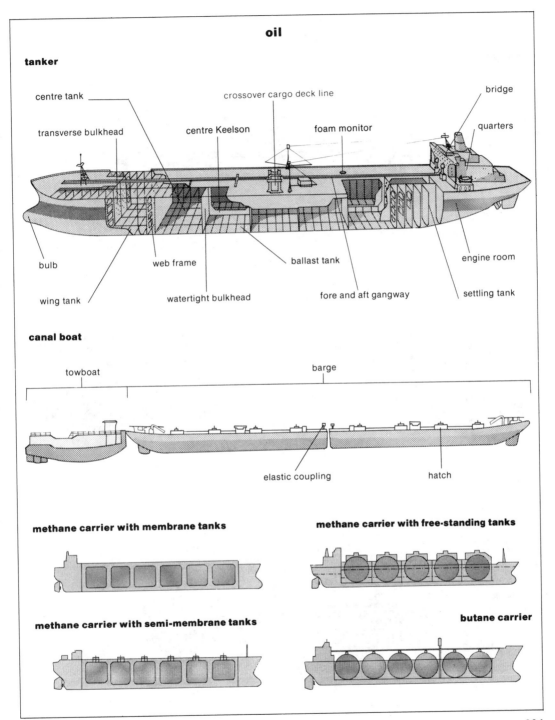

tanker

centre tank

transverse bulkhead

crossover cargo deck line

centre Keelson

foam monitor

bridge

quarters

bulb

wing tank

web frame

watertight bulkhead

ballast tank

fore and aft gangway

engine room

settling tank

canal boat

towboat

barge

elastic coupling

hatch

methane carrier with membrane tanks

methane carrier with free-standing tanks

methane carrier with semi-membrane tanks

butane carrier

oil transport

rail tank

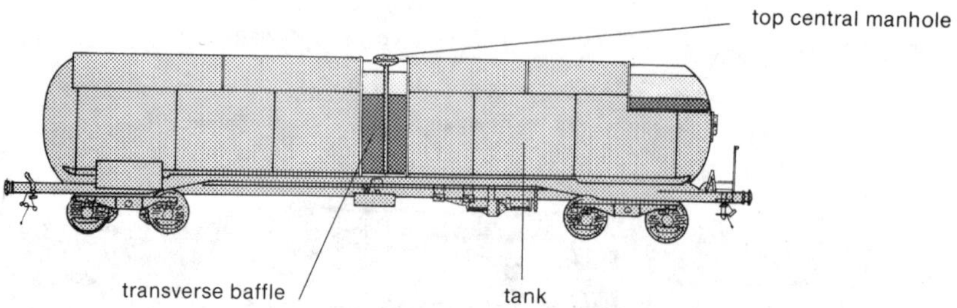

top central manhole

transverse baffle

tank

road tankers

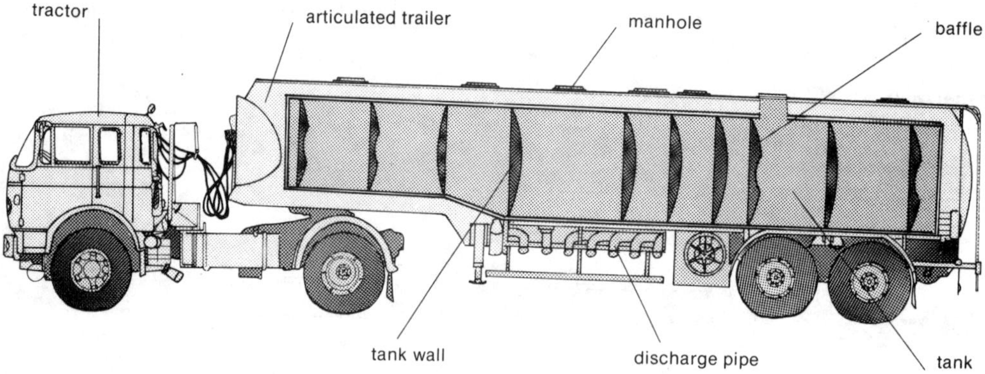

tractor

articulated trailer

manhole

baffle

tank wall

discharge pipe

tank

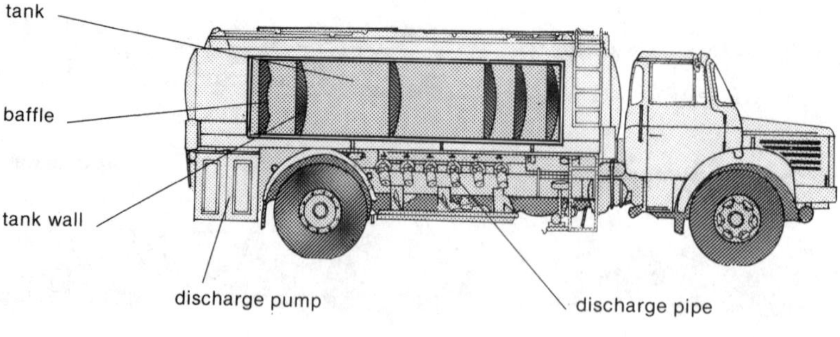

tank

baffle

tank wall

discharge pump

discharge pipe

oil storage

floating-roof tank

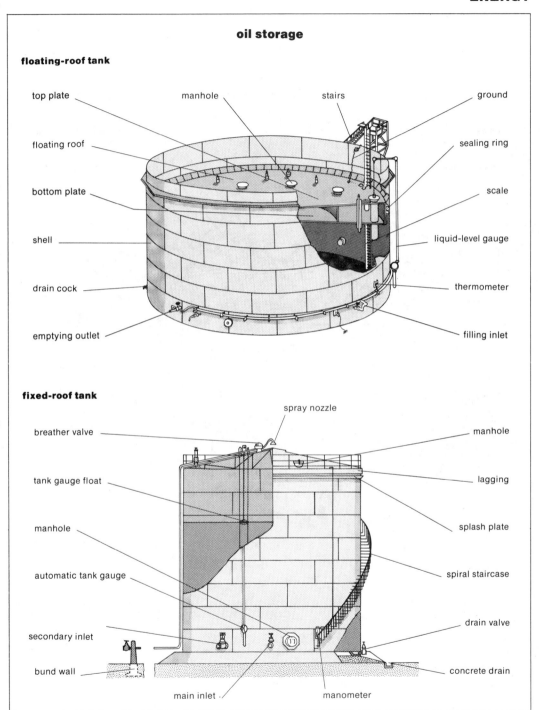

top plate

floating roof

bottom plate

shell

drain cock

emptying outlet

manhole

stairs

ground

sealing ring

scale

liquid-level gauge

thermometer

filling inlet

fixed-roof tank

spray nozzle

breather valve

tank gauge float

manhole

automatic tank gauge

secondary inlet

bund wall

manhole

lagging

splash plate

spiral staircase

drain valve

concrete drain

main inlet

manometer

oil refinery

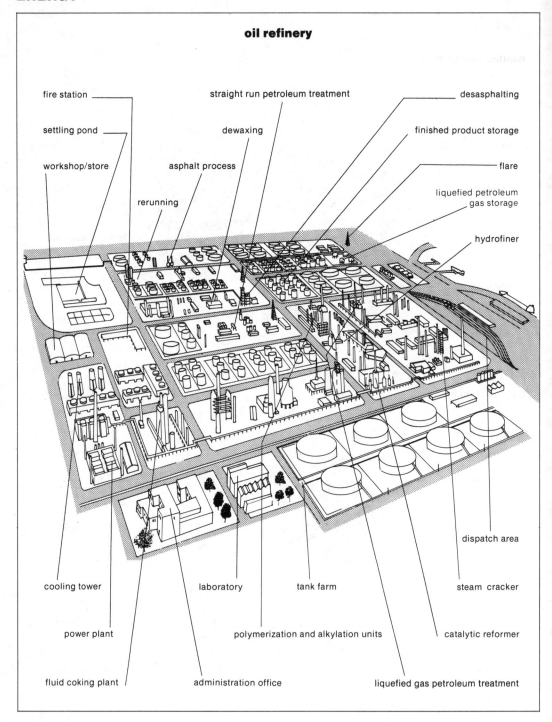

fire station

settling pond

workshop/store

rerunning

straight run petroleum treatment

dewaxing

asphalt process

desasphalting

finished product storage

flare

liquefied petroleum gas storage

hydrofiner

cooling tower

laboratory

tank farm

steam cracker

power plant

polymerization and alkylation units

catalytic reformer

fluid coking plant

administration office

liquefied gas petroleum treatment

dispatch area

634

oil

refinery products

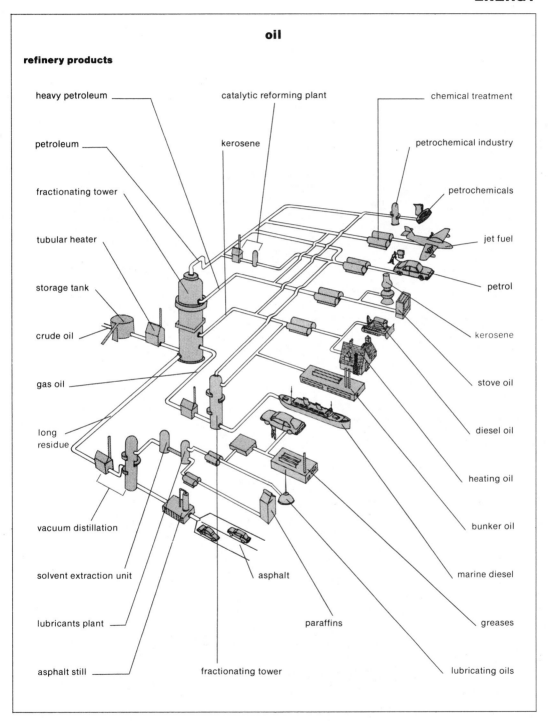

heavy petroleum

catalytic reforming plant

chemical treatment

petroleum

kerosene

petrochemical industry

petrochemicals

fractionating tower

jet fuel

tubular heater

petrol

storage tank

kerosene

crude oil

stove oil

gas oil

diesel oil

long residue

heating oil

vacuum distillation

bunker oil

solvent extraction unit

asphalt

marine diesel

lubricants plant

paraffins

greases

asphalt still

fractionating tower

lubricating oils

oil

oil sands mining plant

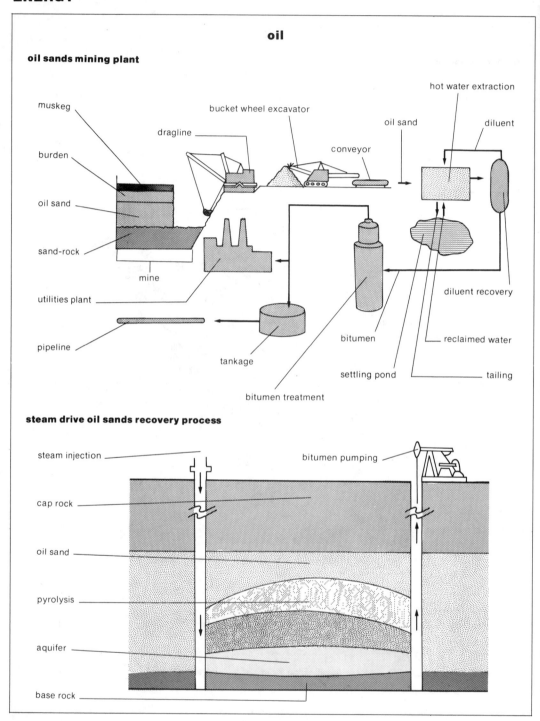

hot water extraction

oil sand

diluent

muskeg

dragline

bucket wheel excavator

conveyor

burden

oil sand

sand-rock

mine

utilities plant

diluent recovery

pipeline

bitumen

reclaimed water

tankage

settling pond

tailing

bitumen treatment

steam drive oil sands recovery process

steam injection

bitumen pumping

cap rock

oil sand

pyrolysis

aquifer

base rock

electricity

hydroelectric complex

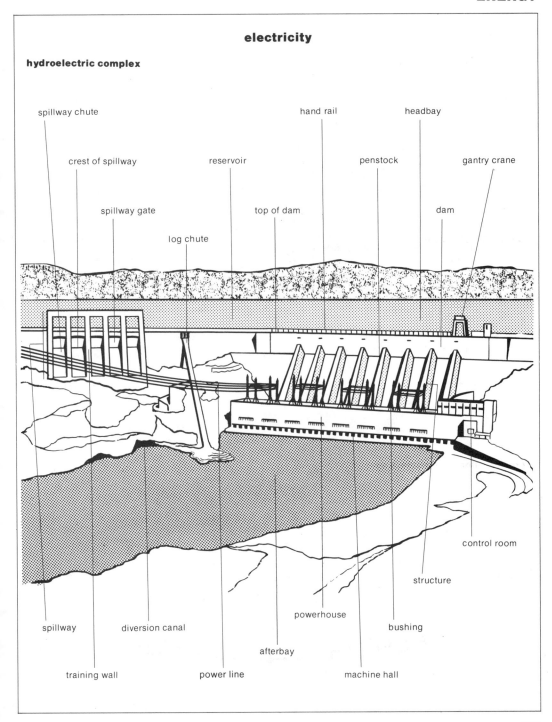

spillway chute

hand rail

headbay

crest of spillway

reservoir

penstock

gantry crane

spillway gate

top of dam

dam

log chute

control room

structure

spillway

diversion canal

powerhouse

bushing

training wall

power line

afterbay

machine hall

electricity

cross section of an embankment dam

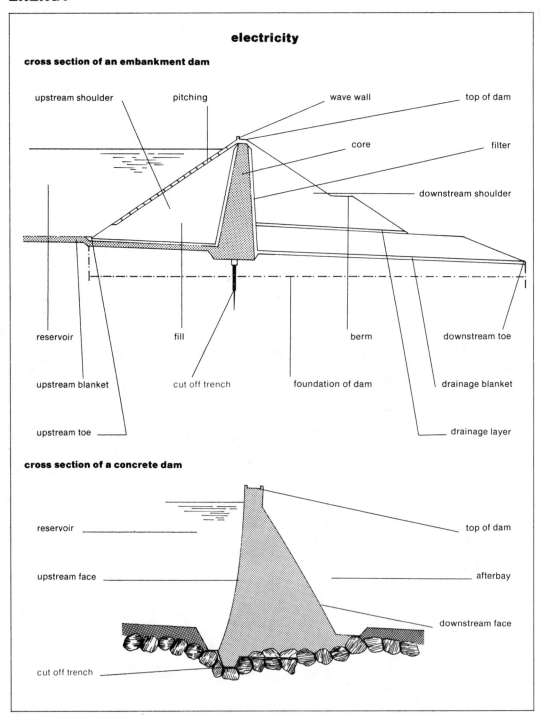

upstream shoulder   pitching   wave wall   top of dam

core   filter

downstream shoulder

reservoir   fill   berm   downstream toe

upstream blanket   cut off trench   foundation of dam   drainage blanket

upstream toe   drainage layer

cross section of a concrete dam

reservoir   top of dam

upstream face   afterbay

downstream face

cut off trench

electricity

major types of dams

embankment dam

cross section of an embankment dam

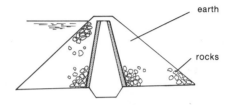

earth

rocks

gravity dam

cross section of a gravity dam

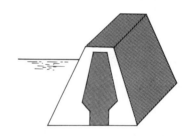

arch dam

cross section of an arch dam

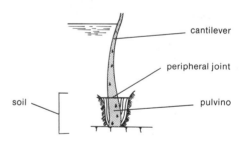

cantilever

peripheral joint

pulvino

soil

buttress dam

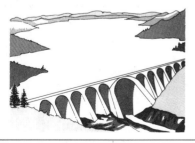

cross section of a buttress dam

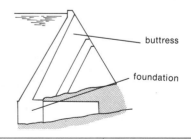

buttress

foundation

electricity

steps in production of electricity

rotation of the rotor in the stator

energy transmission at the alternator voltage

voltage induction

energy integration to the transmission network

water under pressure

high-tension energy transmission to consumers

supply of water

head of water

voltage increase

force of the water on the blades

creation of a magnetic field

rotation of the turbine

transformation of mechanical work into electrical energy

transmission of the rotative movement to the rotor

turbined water draining

electricity

cross section of a hydroelectric power station

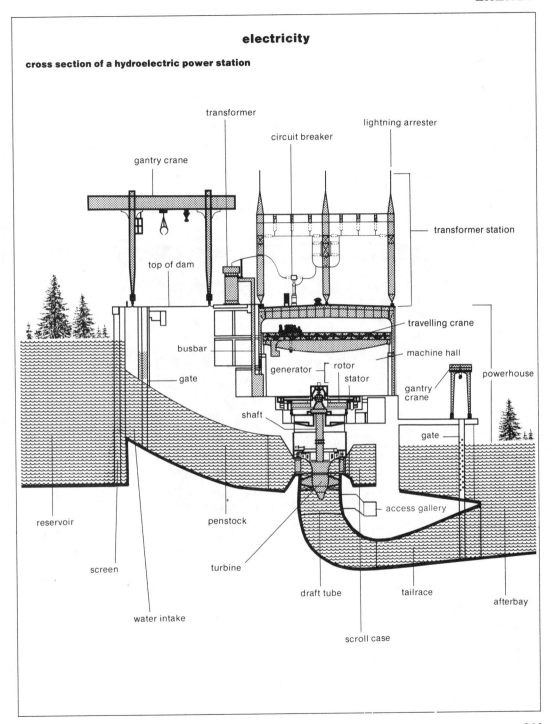

electricity

generator

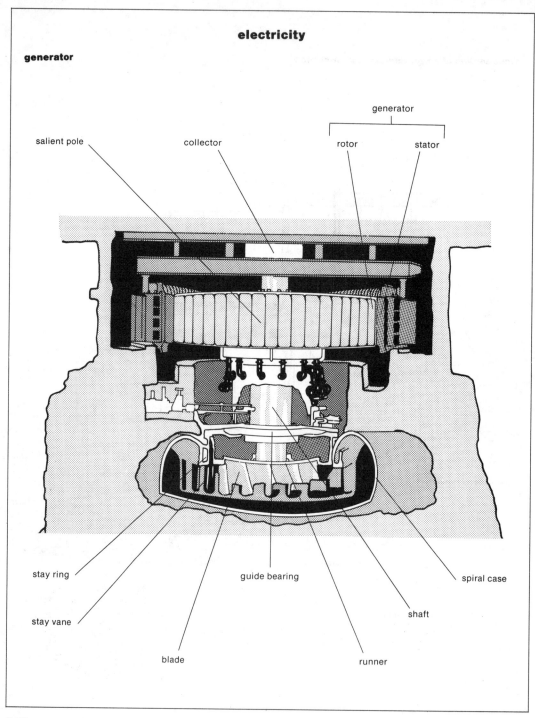

generator

salient pole   collector   rotor   stator

stay ring

stay vane

blade

guide bearing

runner

shaft

spiral case

electricity

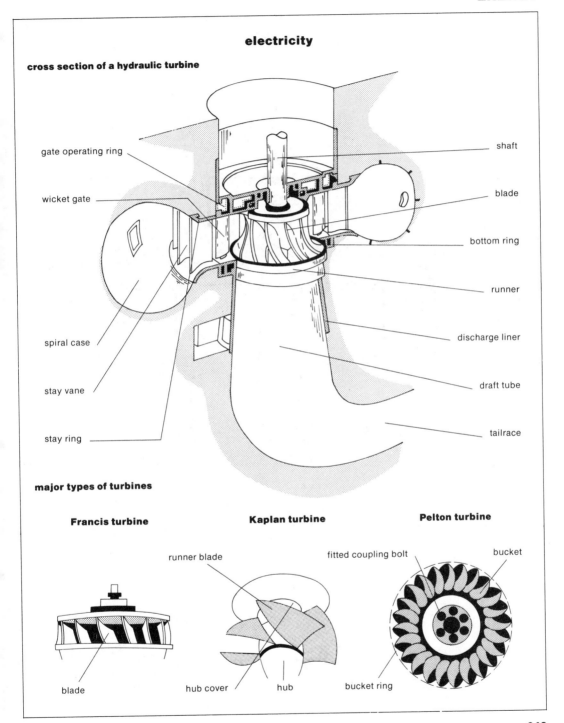

cross section of a hydraulic turbine

gate operating ring

wicket gate

spiral case

stay vane

stay ring

shaft

blade

bottom ring

runner

discharge liner

draft tube

tailrace

major types of turbines

Francis turbine

Kaplan turbine

Pelton turbine

runner blade

fitted coupling bolt

bucket

blade

hub cover

hub

bucket ring

electricity

suspension tower

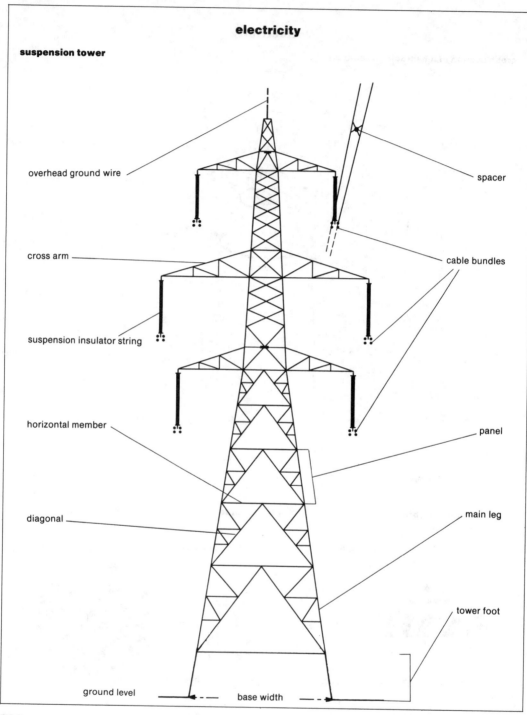

overhead ground wire

spacer

cross arm

cable bundles

suspension insulator string

horizontal member

panel

diagonal

main leg

tower foot

ground level — base width

electricity

overhead connection

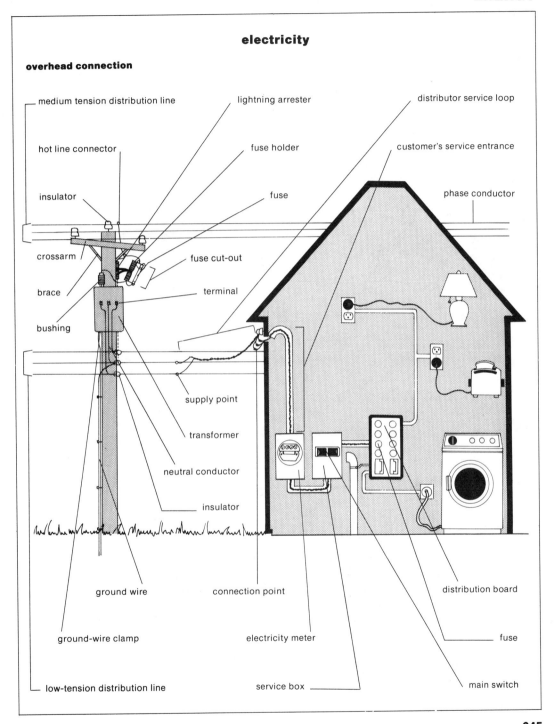

medium tension distribution line

lightning arrester

distributor service loop

hot line connector

fuse holder

customer's service entrance

insulator

fuse

phase conductor

crossarm

fuse cut-out

brace

terminal

bushing

supply point

transformer

neutral conductor

insulator

ground wire

connection point

distribution board

ground-wire clamp

electricity meter

fuse

low-tension distribution line

service box

main switch

electricity

tidal power plant

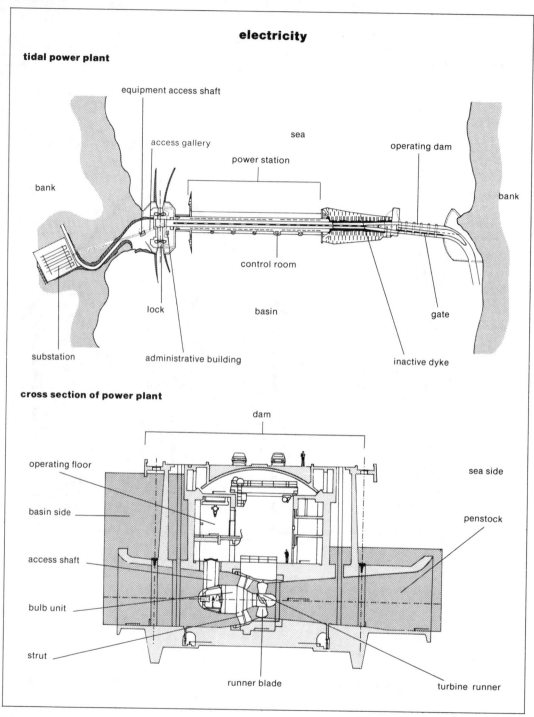

equipment access shaft

access gallery

sea

operating dam

power station

bank

bank

bank

control room

lock

basin

gate

substation

administrative building

inactive dyke

cross section of power plant

dam

operating floor

sea side

basin side

penstock

access shaft

bulb unit

strut

runner blade

turbine runner

coal fired power station

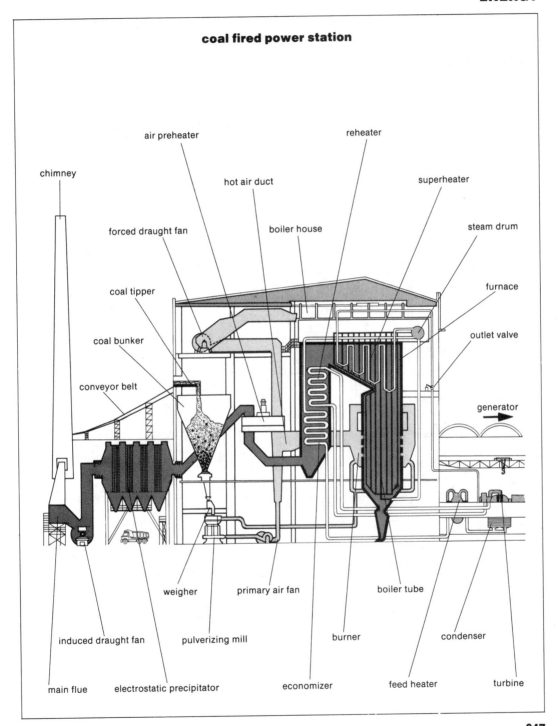

air preheater

reheater

chimney

hot air duct

superheater

forced draught fan

boiler house

steam drum

coal tipper

furnace

coal bunker

outlet valve

conveyor belt

generator

weigher

primary air fan

boiler tube

induced draught fan

pulverizing mill

burner

condenser

main flue

electrostatic precipitator

economizer

feed heater

turbine

nuclear power station

advanced gas-cooled reactor

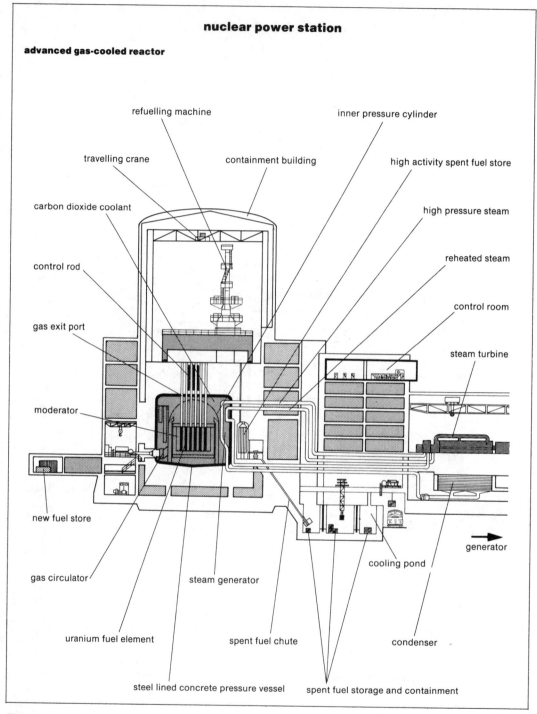

refuelling machine

inner pressure cylinder

travelling crane

containment building

high activity spent fuel store

carbon dioxide coolant

high pressure steam

control rod

reheated steam

gas exit port

control room

steam turbine

moderator

new fuel store

generator

gas circulator

cooling pond

steam generator

uranium fuel element

spent fuel chute

condenser

steel lined concrete pressure vessel

spent fuel storage and containment

power station

turbo-generator

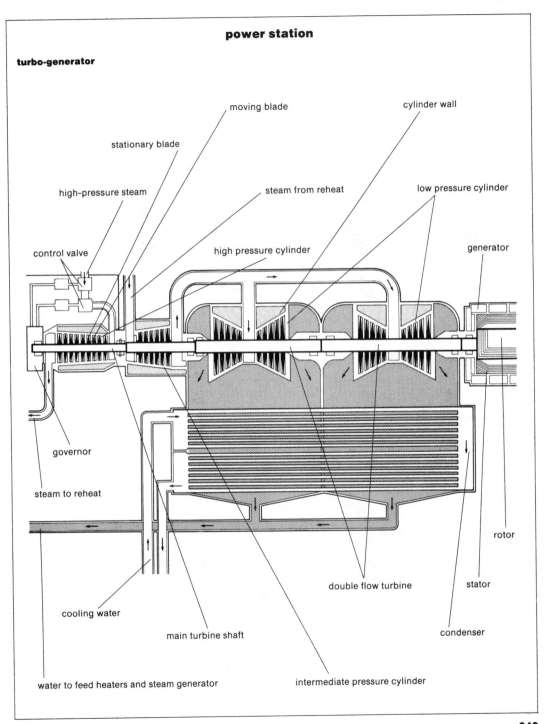

moving blade

cylinder wall

stationary blade

high-pressure steam

steam from reheat

low pressure cylinder

control valve

high pressure cylinder

generator

governor

steam to reheat

rotor

cooling water

double flow turbine

stator

main turbine shaft

condenser

water to feed heaters and steam generator

intermediate pressure cylinder

nuclear energy

Magnox reactor

- concrete shield
- graphite moderator
- control rod
- steam generator
- fuel element
- carbon dioxide gas coolant
- steel pressure vessel
- turbo-generator

advance gas-cooled reactor

- control rod
- graphite moderator
- steam generator
- fuel element
- carbon dioxide gas coolant
- concrete pressure vessel
- turbo-generator

nuclear energy

pressurized water reactor

fast reactor

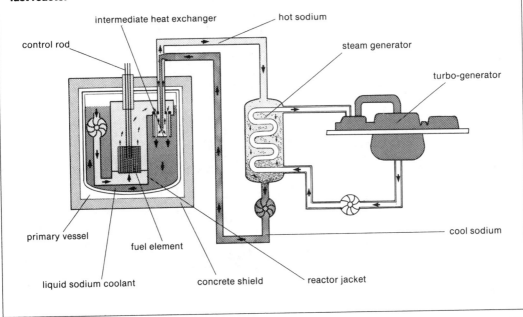

nuclear energy

control room

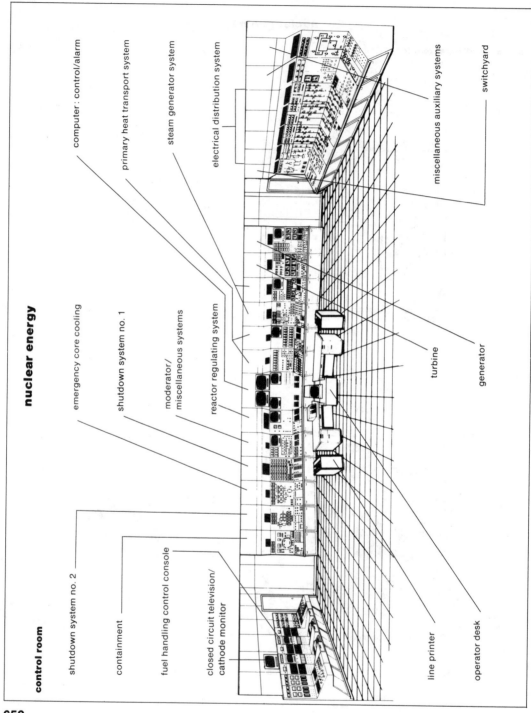

- computer : control/alarm
- primary heat transport system
- steam generator system
- electrical distribution system
- miscellaneous auxiliary systems
- switchyard
- emergency core cooling
- shutdown system no. 1
- moderator/ miscellaneous systems
- reactor regulating system
- turbine
- generator
- shutdown system no. 2
- containment
- fuel handling control console
- closed circuit television/ cathode monitor
- line printer
- operator desk

nuclear energy

production of electricity from nuclear energy

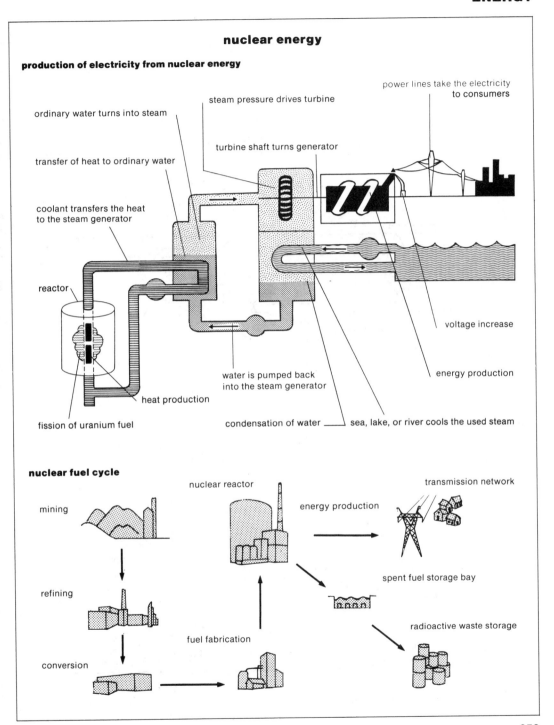

ordinary water turns into steam

steam pressure drives turbine

power lines take the electricity to consumers

transfer of heat to ordinary water

turbine shaft turns generator

coolant transfers the heat to the steam generator

reactor

voltage increase

energy production

water is pumped back into the steam generator

heat production

fission of uranium fuel

condensation of water

sea, lake, or river cools the used steam

nuclear fuel cycle

mining

nuclear reactor

transmission network

energy production

refining

spent fuel storage bay

conversion

fuel fabrication

radioactive waste storage

653

solar energy

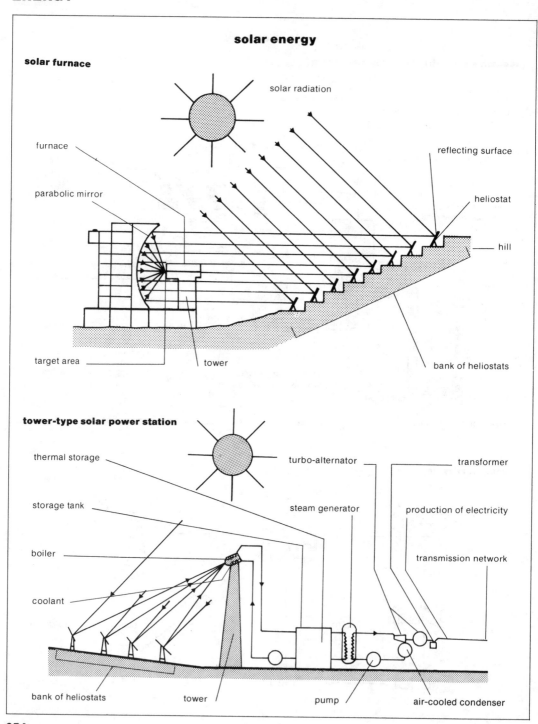

solar furnace

solar radiation

furnace

reflecting surface

parabolic mirror

heliostat

hill

target area

tower

bank of heliostats

tower-type solar power station

thermal storage

turbo-alternator

transformer

storage tank

steam generator

production of electricity

boiler

transmission network

coolant

bank of heliostats

tower

pump

air-cooled condenser

654

solar energy

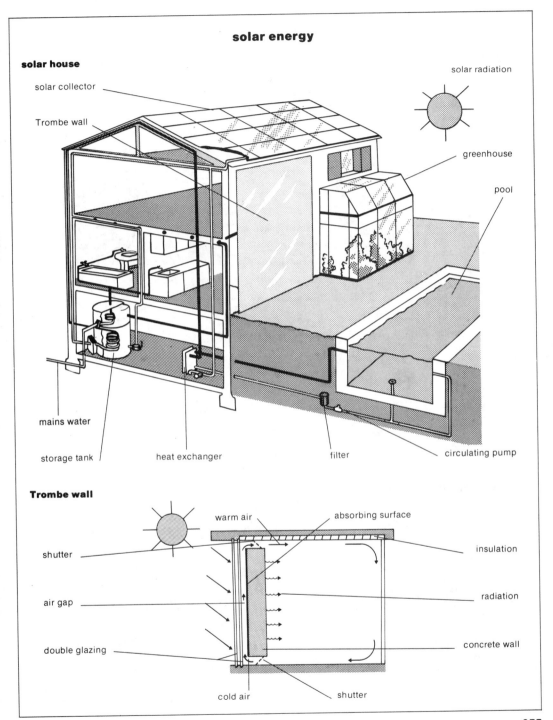

solar house

- solar collector
- Trombe wall
- solar radiation
- greenhouse
- pool
- mains water
- storage tank
- heat exchanger
- filter
- circulating pump

Trombe wall

- shutter
- air gap
- double glazing
- warm air
- absorbing surface
- cold air
- shutter
- insulation
- radiation
- concrete wall

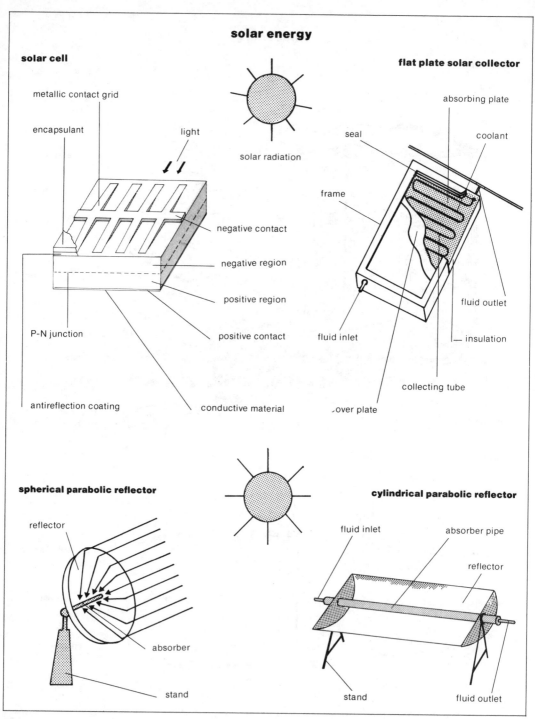

solar energy

solar cell

metallic contact grid

encapsulant

light

solar radiation

negative contact

negative region

positive region

P-N junction

positive contact

antireflection coating

conductive material

flat plate solar collector

absorbing plate

seal

coolant

frame

fluid outlet

fluid inlet

insulation

collecting tube

cover plate

spherical parabolic reflector

reflector

absorber

stand

cylindrical parabolic reflector

fluid inlet

absorber pipe

reflector

stand

fluid outlet

windmill

tower mill

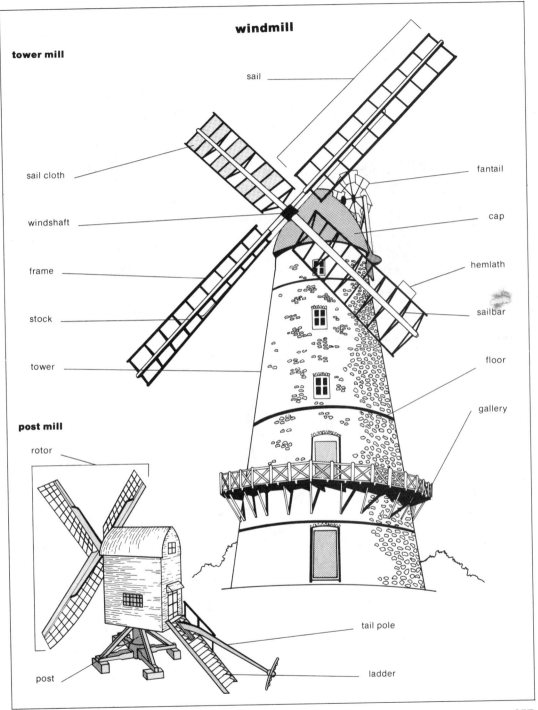

sail

sail cloth

windshaft

frame

stock

tower

fantail

cap

hemlath

sailbar

floor

gallery

post mill

rotor

tail pole

ladder

post

wind turbine

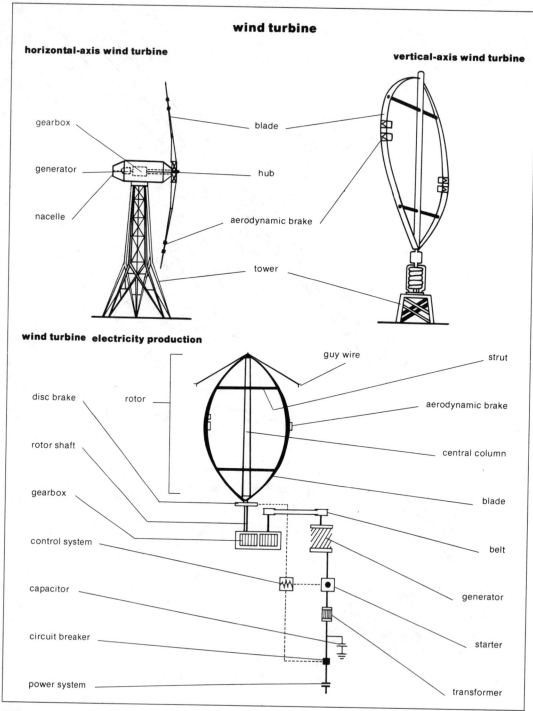

horizontal-axis wind turbine

gearbox

generator

nacelle

blade

hub

aerodynamic brake

tower

vertical-axis wind turbine

wind turbine electricity production

disc brake

rotor shaft

gearbox

control system

capacitor

circuit breaker

power system

rotor

guy wire

strut

aerodynamic brake

central column

blade

belt

generator

starter

transformer

HEAVY MACHINERY
AND PLANT

dragline

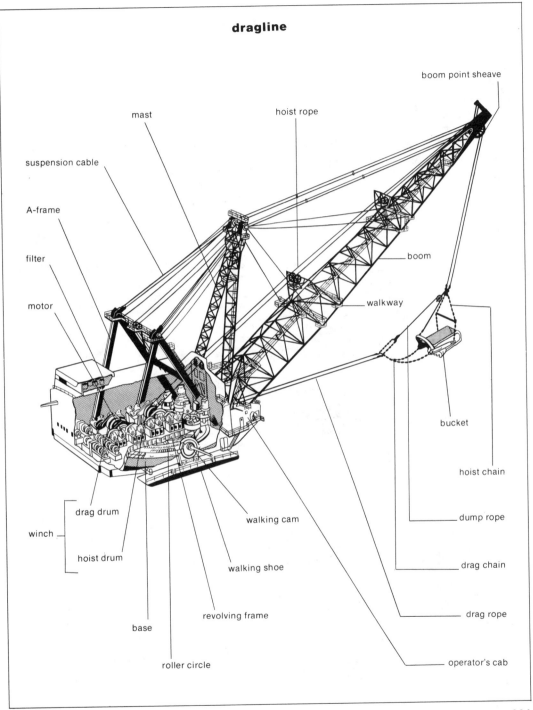

boom point sheave

mast

hoist rope

suspension cable

A-frame

filter

motor

boom

walkway

bucket

drag drum

winch

hoist drum

hoist chain

walking cam

dump rope

walking shoe

drag chain

revolving frame

base

drag rope

roller circle

operator's cab

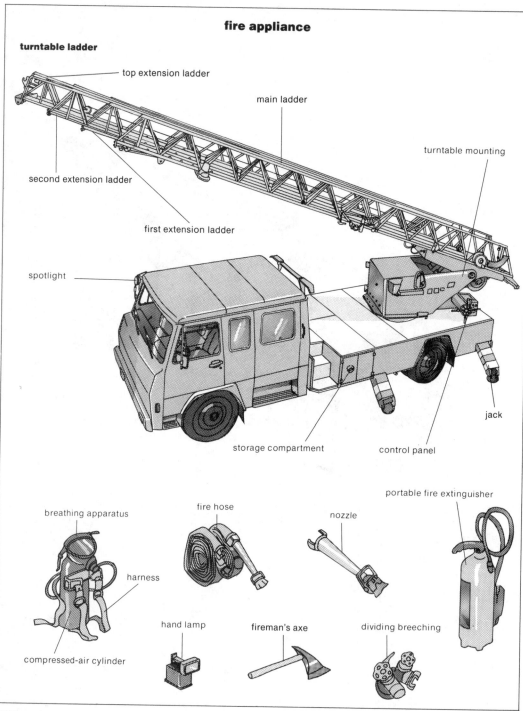

fire appliance

turntable ladder

top extension ladder

main ladder

second extension ladder

turntable mounting

first extension ladder

spotlight

jack

storage compartment

control panel

portable fire extinguisher

breathing apparatus

fire hose

nozzle

harness

hand lamp

fireman's axe

dividing breeching

compressed-air cylinder

fire appliance

water-tender

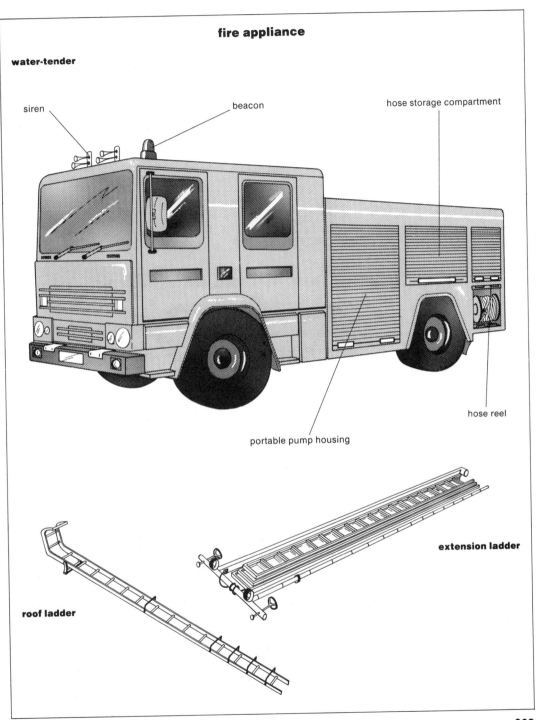

siren

beacon

hose storage compartment

hose reel

portable pump housing

extension ladder

roof ladder

bulldozer

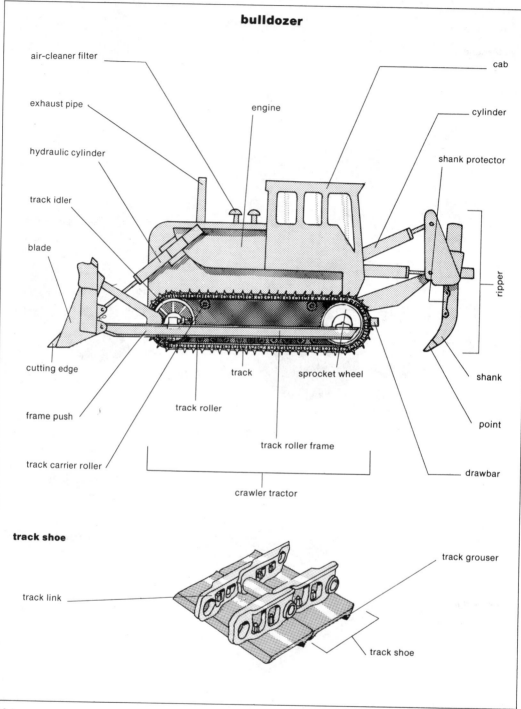

air-cleaner filter

cab

exhaust pipe

engine

cylinder

hydraulic cylinder

shank protector

track idler

blade

ripper

cutting edge

track

sprocket wheel

shank

frame push

track roller

point

track roller frame

track carrier roller

drawbar

crawler tractor

track shoe

track grouser

track link

track shoe

wheel loader

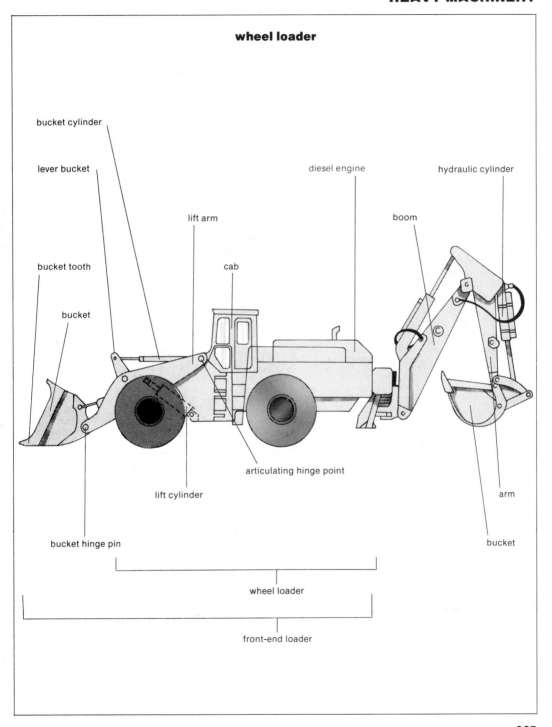

bucket cylinder

lever bucket

diesel engine

hydraulic cylinder

lift arm

boom

bucket tooth

cab

bucket

articulating hinge point

lift cylinder

arm

bucket hinge pin

bucket

wheel loader

front-end loader

grader

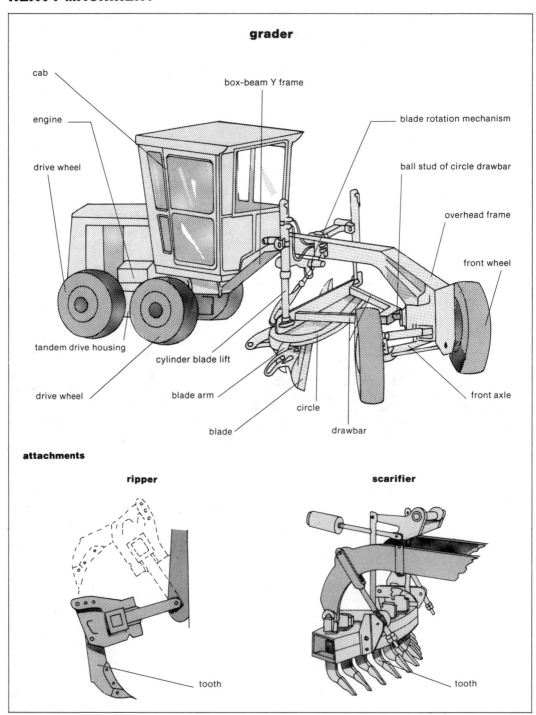

cab

box-beam Y frame

blade rotation mechanism

engine

ball stud of circle drawbar

drive wheel

overhead frame

front wheel

tandem drive housing

cylinder blade lift

drive wheel

blade arm

front axle

circle

blade

drawbar

attachments

ripper

scarifier

tooth

tooth

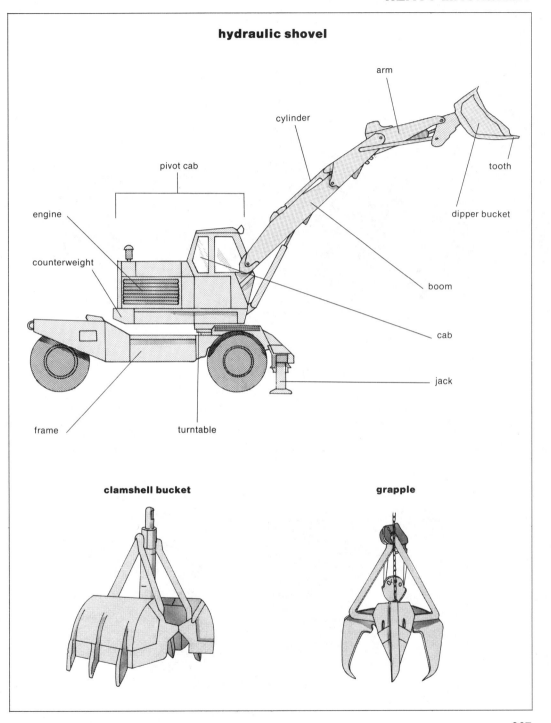

hydraulic shovel

arm

cylinder

tooth

pivot cab

dipper bucket

engine

counterweight

boom

cab

jack

frame

turntable

clamshell bucket

grapple

HEAVY MACHINERY

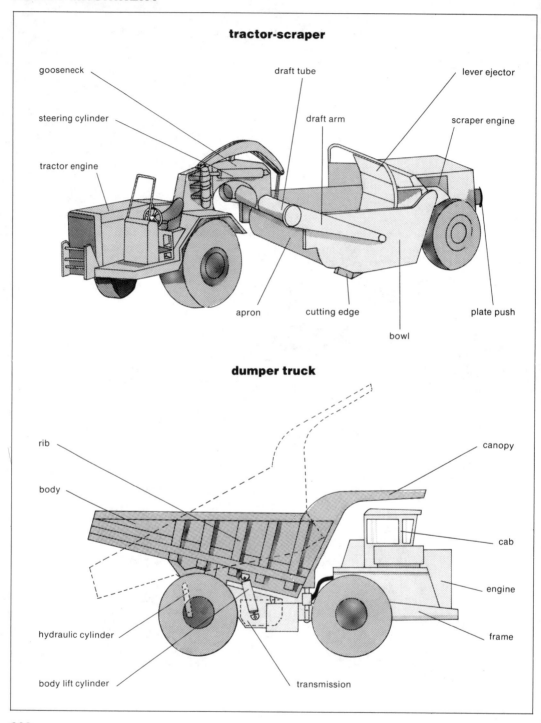

tractor-scraper

gooseneck

draft tube

lever ejector

steering cylinder

draft arm

scraper engine

tractor engine

apron

cutting edge

plate push

bowl

dumper truck

rib

canopy

body

cab

engine

hydraulic cylinder

frame

body lift cylinder

transmission

668

crane

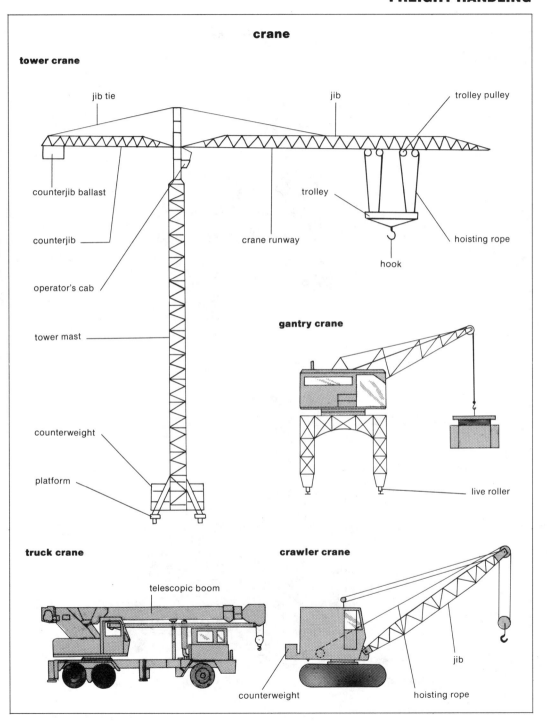

tower crane

jib tie

jib

trolley pulley

counterjib ballast

trolley

counterjib

crane runway

hoisting rope

hook

operator's cab

gantry crane

tower mast

counterweight

platform

live roller

truck crane

crawler crane

telescopic boom

jib

counterweight

hoisting rope

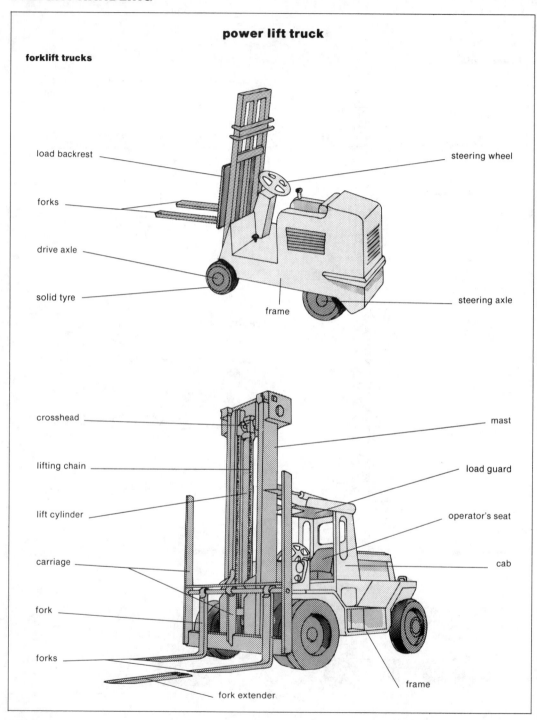

power lift truck

forklift trucks

load backrest

steering wheel

forks

drive axle

solid tyre

steering axle

frame

crosshead

mast

lifting chain

load guard

lift cylinder

operator's seat

carriage

cab

fork

forks

frame

fork extender

handling appliances

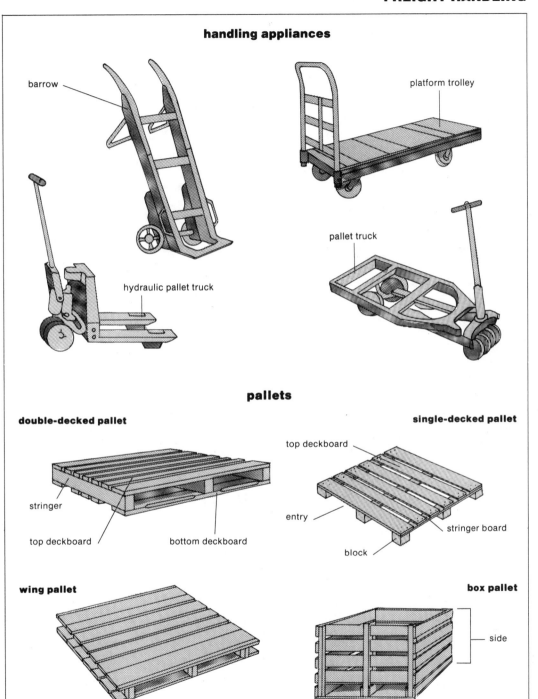

barrow

platform trolley

pallet truck

hydraulic pallet truck

pallets

double-decked pallet

single-decked pallet

stringer

top deckboard

top deckboard

entry

bottom deckboard

stringer board

block

wing pallet

box pallet

side

WEAPONS

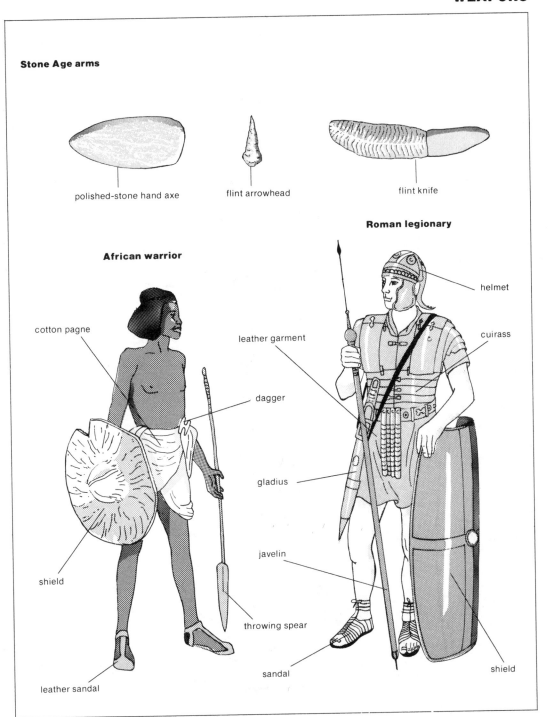

Stone Age arms

polished-stone hand axe

flint arrowhead

flint knife

Roman legionary

African warrior

cotton pagne

leather garment

helmet

cuirass

dagger

gladius

shield

javelin

throwing spear

sandal

shield

leather sandal

armour

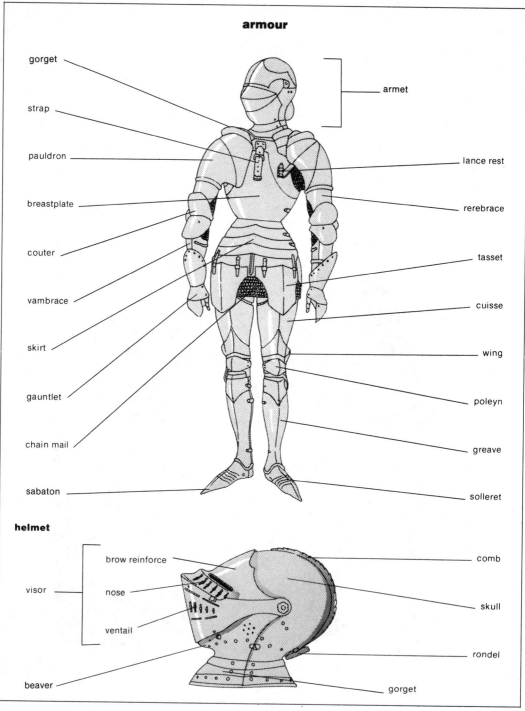

gorget

strap

pauldron

breastplate

couter

vambrace

skirt

gauntlet

chain mail

sabaton

armet

lance rest

rerebrace

tasset

cuisse

wing

poleyn

greave

solleret

helmet

visor

brow reinforce

nose

ventail

beaver

comb

skull

rondel

gorget

bows and crossbow

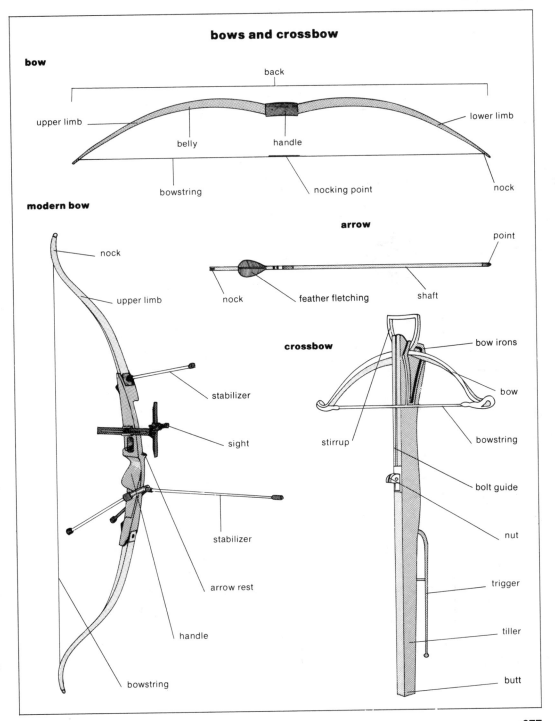

bow

back

upper limb

lower limb

belly

handle

bowstring

nocking point

nock

modern bow

nock

upper limb

arrow

point

nock

feather fletching

shaft

crossbow

stabilizer

sight

stirrup

bow irons

bow

bowstring

bolt guide

nut

stabilizer

arrow rest

trigger

tiller

handle

butt

bowstring

WEAPONS

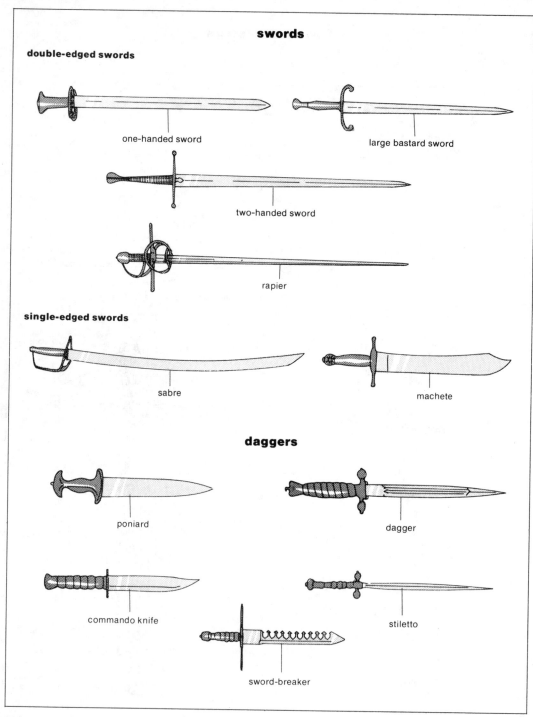

swords

double-edged swords

one-handed sword

large bastard sword

two-handed sword

rapier

single-edged swords

sabre

machete

daggers

poniard

dagger

commando knife

stiletto

sword-breaker

678

bayonets

major types of bayonets

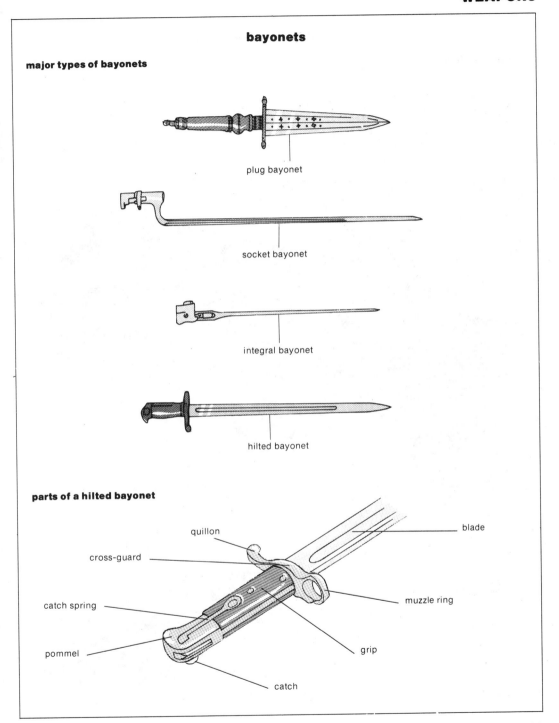

plug bayonet

socket bayonet

integral bayonet

hilted bayonet

parts of a hilted bayonet

quillon

cross-guard

catch spring

pommel

catch

blade

muzzle ring

grip

679

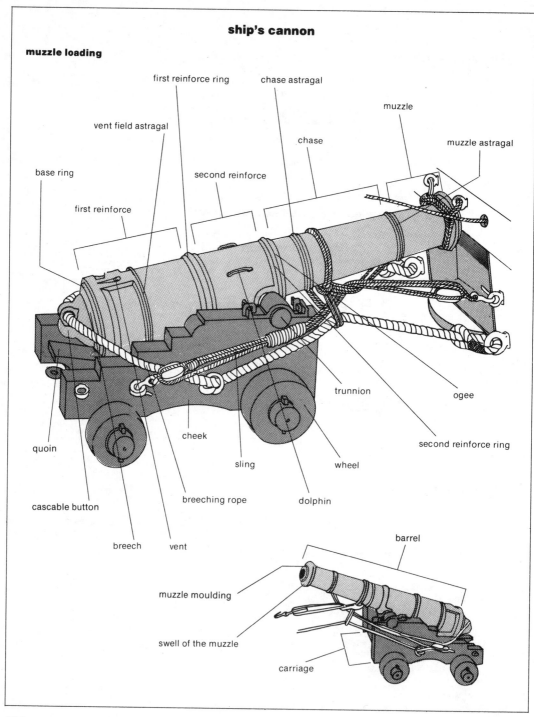

ship's cannon

muzzle loading

first reinforce ring

chase astragal

muzzle

vent field astragal

chase

muzzle astragal

base ring

second reinforce

first reinforce

trunnion

ogee

quoin

cheek

second reinforce ring

sling

wheel

cascable button

breeching rope

dolphin

breech

vent

barrel

muzzle moulding

swell of the muzzle

carriage

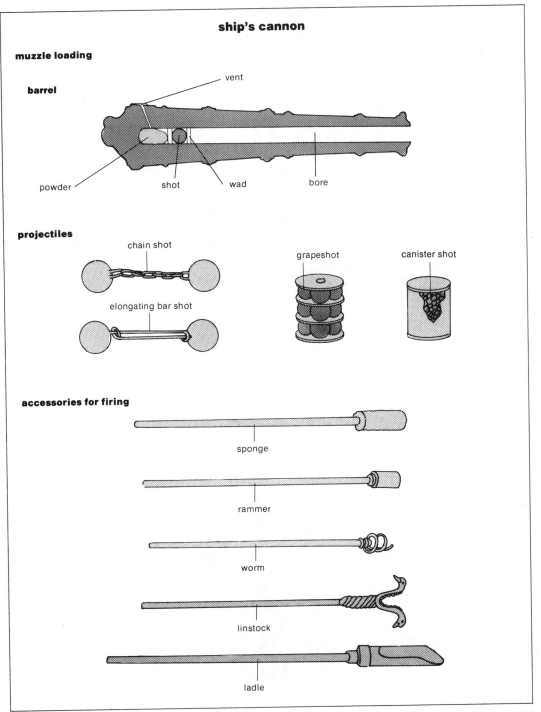

ship's cannon

muzzle loading

barrel

vent

powder · shot · wad · bore

projectiles

chain shot

elongating bar shot

grapeshot

canister shot

accessories for firing

sponge

rammer

worm

linstock

ladle

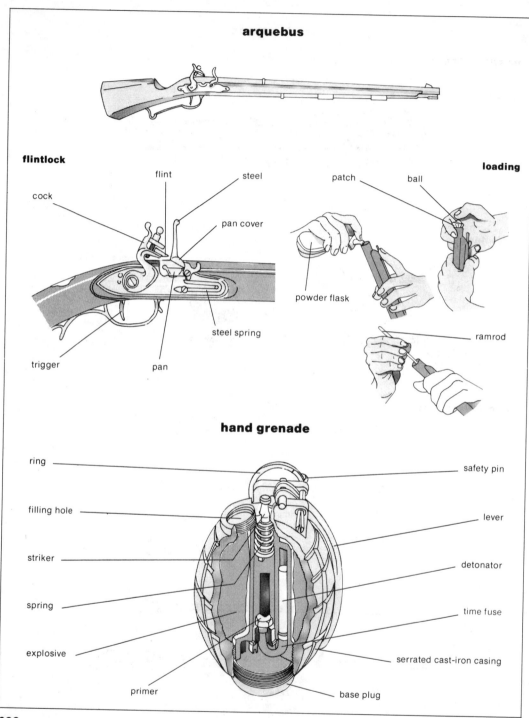

arquebus

flintlock

cock

flint

steel

pan cover

steel spring

trigger

pan

loading

patch

ball

powder flask

ramrod

hand grenade

ring

safety pin

filling hole

lever

striker

detonator

spring

time fuse

explosive

serrated cast-iron casing

primer

base plug

mortar

modern

early

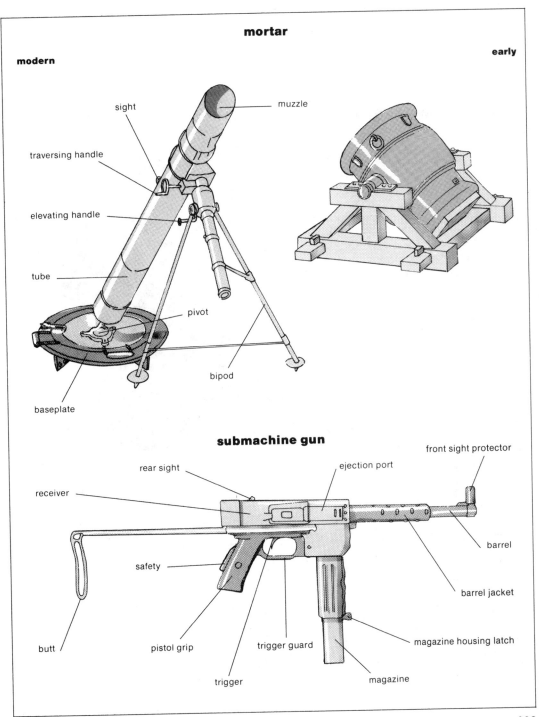

sight

muzzle

traversing handle

elevating handle

tube

pivot

bipod

baseplate

submachine gun

front sight protector

rear sight

ejection port

receiver

barrel

safety

barrel jacket

butt

magazine housing latch

pistol grip

trigger guard

trigger

magazine

modern howitzer

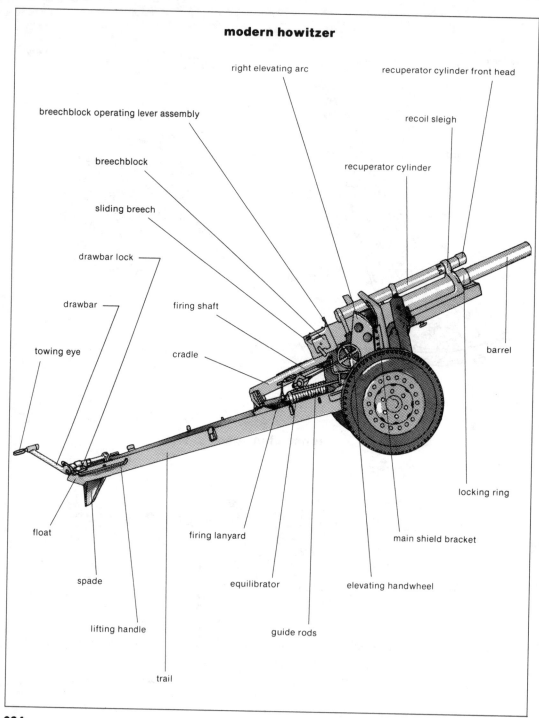

right elevating arc

recuperator cylinder front head

breechblock operating lever assembly

recoil sleigh

breechblock

recuperator cylinder

sliding breech

drawbar lock

drawbar

firing shaft

towing eye

cradle

barrel

locking ring

float

firing lanyard

main shield bracket

spade

equilibrator

elevating handwheel

lifting handle

guide rods

trail

automatic rifle

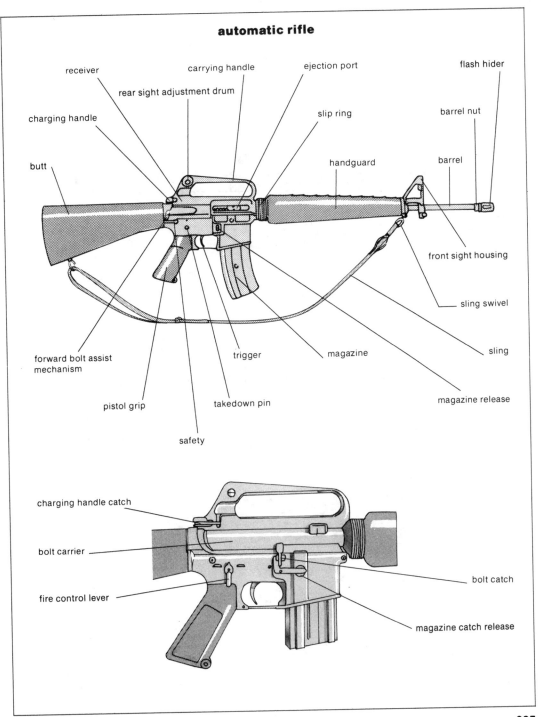

receiver

carrying handle

ejection port

flash hider

rear sight adjustment drum

slip ring

barrel nut

charging handle

handguard

barrel

butt

front sight housing

sling swivel

sling

forward bolt assist mechanism

trigger

magazine

pistol grip

takedown pin

magazine release

safety

charging handle catch

bolt carrier

bolt catch

fire control lever

magazine catch release

WEAPONS

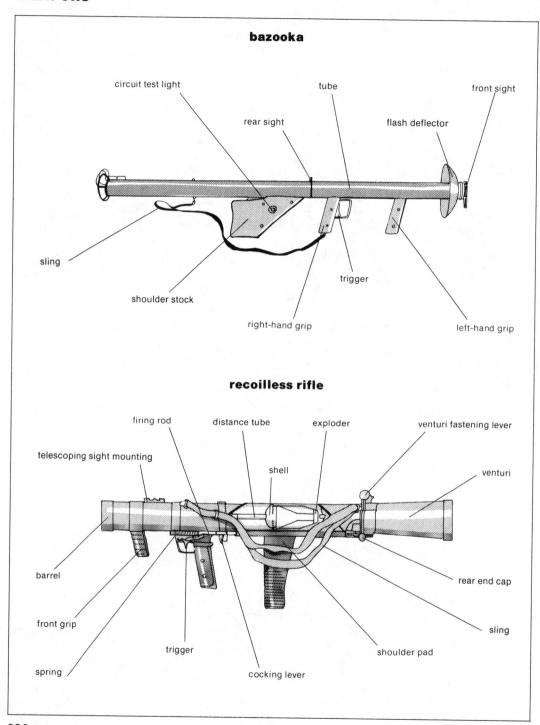

bazooka

circuit test light

rear sight

tube

front sight

flash deflector

sling

shoulder stock

trigger

right-hand grip

left-hand grip

recoilless rifle

firing rod

distance tube

exploder

venturi fastening lever

telescoping sight mounting

shell

venturi

barrel

rear end cap

front grip

sling

trigger

shoulder pad

spring

cocking lever

heavy machine gun

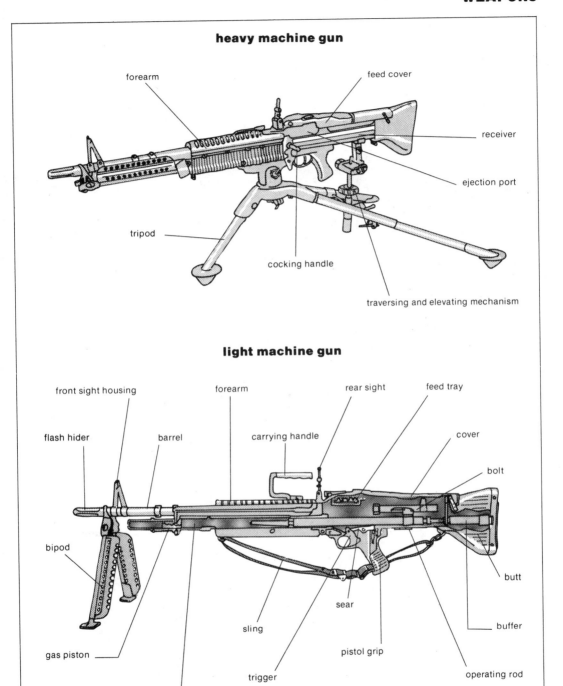

forearm

feed cover

receiver

ejection port

tripod

cocking handle

traversing and elevating mechanism

light machine gun

front sight housing

forearm

rear sight

feed tray

flash hider

barrel

carrying handle

cover

bolt

bipod

butt

gas piston

sear

buffer

sling

pistol grip

operating rod

trigger

gas cylinder

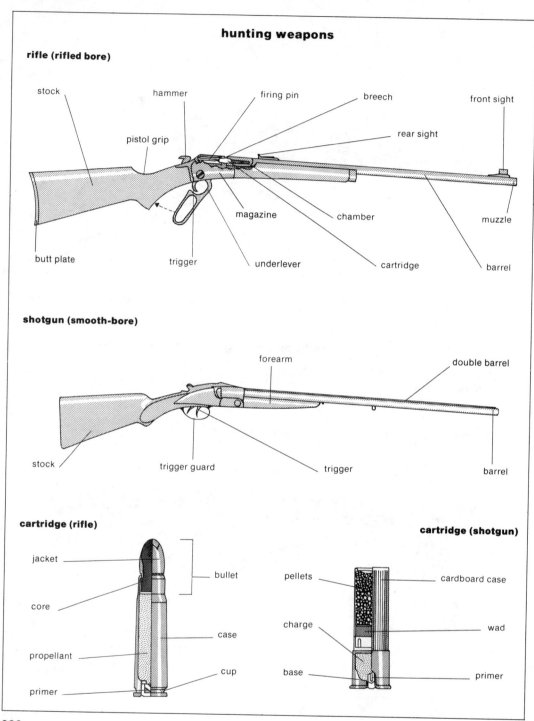

hunting weapons

rifle (rifled bore)

stock · hammer · firing pin · breech · front sight · rear sight · pistol grip · magazine · chamber · muzzle · butt plate · trigger · underlever · cartridge · barrel

shotgun (smooth-bore)

forearm · double barrel · stock · trigger guard · trigger · barrel

cartridge (rifle)

jacket · bullet · core · case · propellant · cup · primer

cartridge (shotgun)

pellets · cardboard case · charge · wad · base · primer

pistol

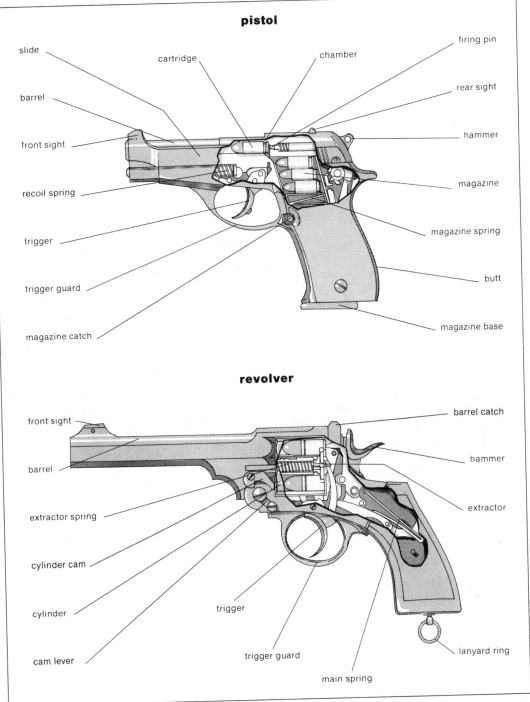

slide

cartridge

chamber

firing pin

barrel

rear sight

front sight

hammer

recoil spring

magazine

trigger

magazine spring

trigger guard

butt

magazine catch

magazine base

revolver

front sight

barrel catch

barrel

hammer

extractor spring

extractor

cylinder cam

cylinder

trigger

cam lever

trigger guard

lanyard ring

main spring

tank

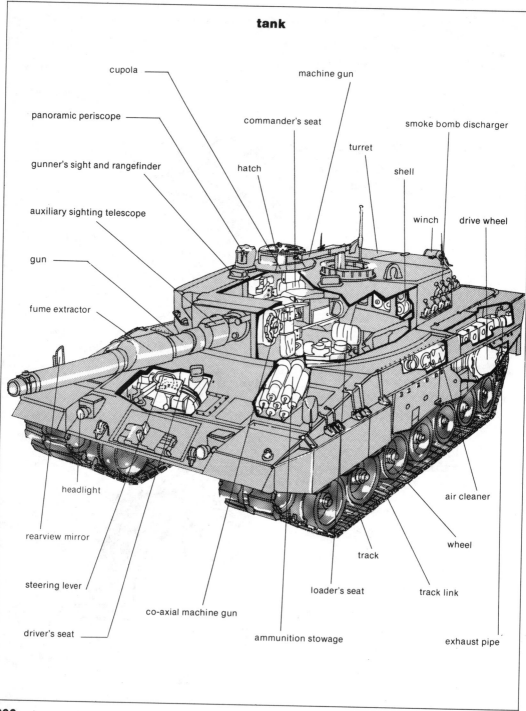

cupola

machine gun

panoramic periscope

commander's seat

smoke bomb discharger

gunner's sight and rangefinder

turret

hatch

shell

auxiliary sighting telescope

winch

drive wheel

gun

fume extractor

headlight

air cleaner

rearview mirror

wheel

track

steering lever

track link

co-axial machine gun

loader's seat

driver's seat

ammunition stowage

exhaust pipe

690

combat aircraft

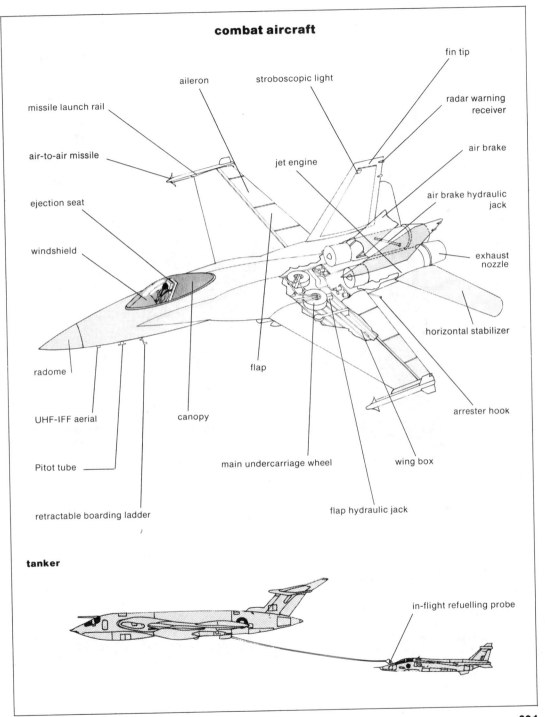

fin tip

aileron

stroboscopic light

radar warning receiver

missile launch rail

air brake

jet engine

air-to-air missile

air brake hydraulic jack

ejection seat

exhaust nozzle

windshield

horizontal stabilizer

radome

flap

arrester hook

UHF-IFF aerial

canopy

Pitot tube

main undercarriage wheel

wing box

retractable boarding ladder

flap hydraulic jack

tanker

in-flight refuelling probe

691

WEAPONS

missiles

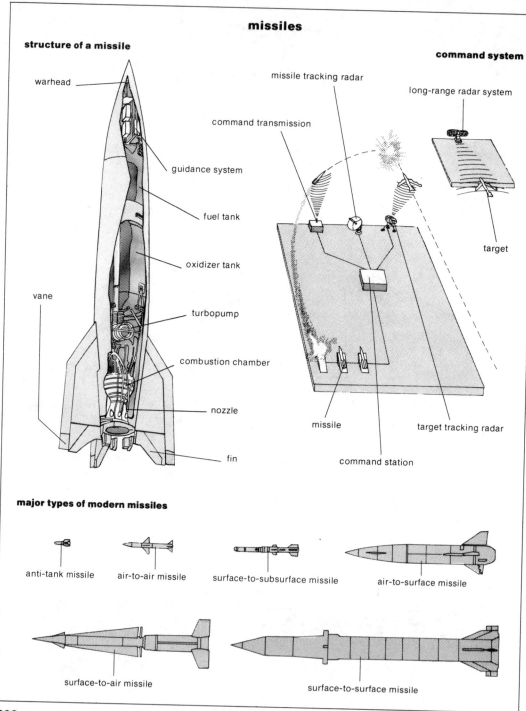

structure of a missile

- warhead
- guidance system
- fuel tank
- oxidizer tank
- vane
- turbopump
- combustion chamber
- nozzle
- fin

command system

- missile tracking radar
- command transmission
- long-range radar system
- target
- missile
- target tracking radar
- command station

major types of modern missiles

- anti-tank missile
- air-to-air missile
- surface-to-subsurface missile
- air-to-surface missile
- surface-to-air missile
- surface-to-surface missile

692

SYMBOLS

flag and shield

parts of a flag

shield

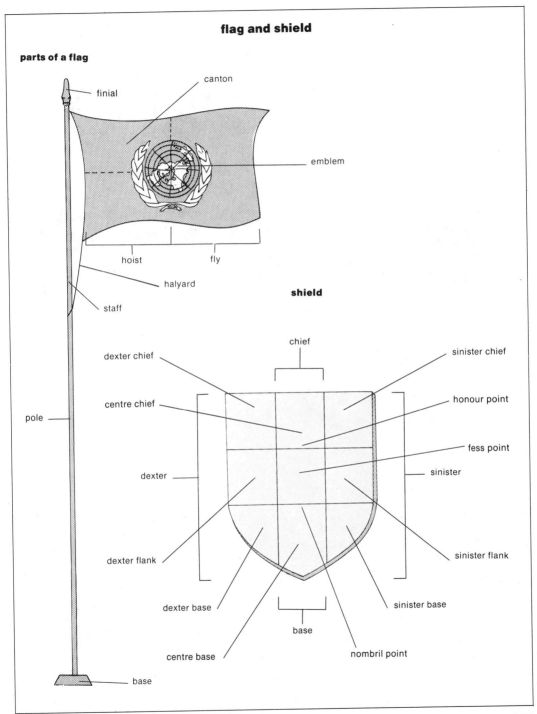

HERALDRY

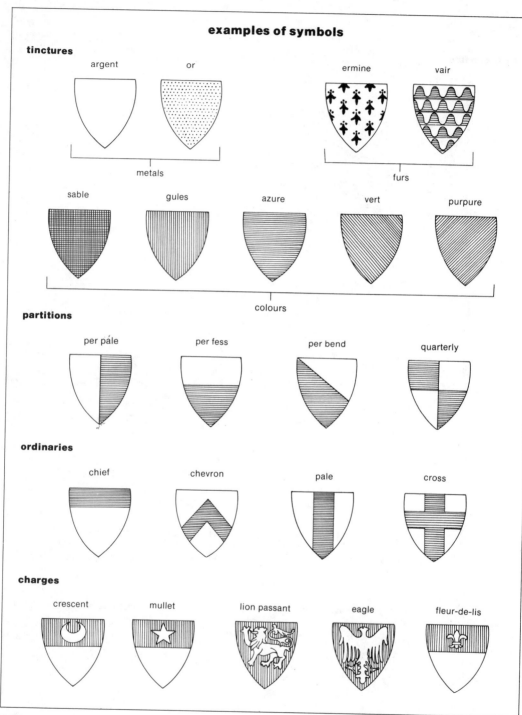

examples of symbols

tinctures

argent | or | ermine | vair

metals | furs

sable | gules | azure | vert | purpure

colours

partitions

per pale | per fess | per bend | quarterly

ordinaries

chief | chevron | pale | cross

charges

crescent | mullet | lion passant | eagle | fleur-de-lis

flag shapes

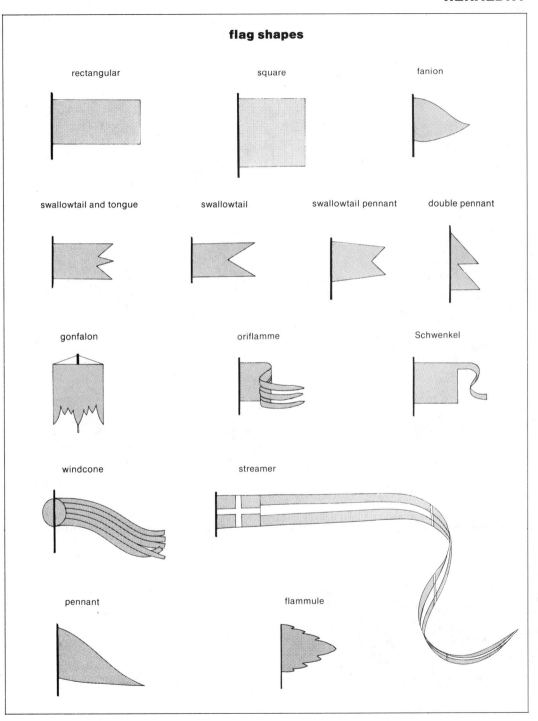

rectangular

square

fanion

swallowtail and tongue

swallowtail

swallowtail pennant

double pennant

gonfalon

oriflamme

Schwenkel

windcone

streamer

pennant

flammule

SIGNS OF THE ZODIAC

constellations

ancient and modern signs

Aries, the Ram
(21 March–20 April)

Taurus, the Bull
(21 April–21 May)

Gemini, the Twins
(22 May–21 June)

Cancer, the Crab
(22 June–23 July)

Leo, the Lion
(24 July–23 August)

Virgo, the Virgin
(24 August–23 September)

Libra, the Balance
(24 September–23 October)

Scorpio, the Scorpion
(24 October–22 November)

Sagittarius, the Archer
(23 November–21 December)

Capricorn, the Goat
(22 December–20 January)

Aquarius, the Water Bearer
(21 January–19 February)

Pisces, the Fishes
(20 February–20 March)

graphic elements for symbols

colours

red = danger, no... or do not...

examples

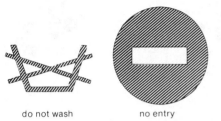

do not wash   no entry

blue = regulation, indication

examples

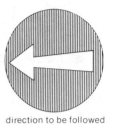

hospital   direction to be followed

yellow = be careful

examples

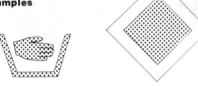

hand wash in luke warm water   priority road

green = permission, indication

example

medium machine wash
in hand hot water

graphic elements

 or  = do not... no...

= danger, be careful

examples

no left turn   no stopping

examples

flammable   pedestrian crossing

INFORMATION SYMBOLS

international road signs

danger warning signs

right bend

double bend

dangerous bend

dangerous descent

steep hill

road narrows

uneven surface

ramp

slippery road

loose chippings

falling rocks

schoolchildren

pedestrian crossing

international road signs

danger warning signs (cont.)

cyclists

cattle

wild animals

road works

traffic lights

two-way traffic

other danger

roundabout

priority junction

level crossing with barrier or gate

signs showing priority at junctions

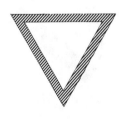
give way

stop

priority

end of priority

INFORMATION SYMBOLS

international road signs

prohibitory or regulatory signs

no entry

no vehicles

no cycling

no motorcycles

no goods vehicles

no pedestrians

no motor vehicles

width clearance

height limit

weight limit

no left turn

no U-turn

no overtaking

give priority to vehicles
from opposite direction

maximum speed limit

national speed limit applies

international road signs

mandatory signs

direction to be followed

direction to be followed

direction to be followed

direction to be followed

roundabout

informative signs

one-way traffic

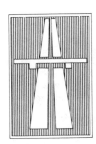

motorway

end of motorway

parking and stopping signs

parking prohibited or restricted

no stopping

parking

INFORMATION SYMBOLS

common symbols

information

first aid

hospital

police

telephone

do not enter

no dogs

fire hose

fire extinguisher

caution,
pedestrian crossing

caution, slippery floor

radioactive material

danger, electrical hazard

danger, poison

danger, flammable

common symbols

access for physically
handicapped

do not use for wheelchairs

smoking permitted

smoking prohibited

toilet for men

toilet for women

toilet for men and women

passenger lift

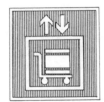

goods lift

escalator, up

escalator, down

stairs

restaurant

buffet

INFORMATION SYMBOLS

common symbols

taxis

waiting room

way in

way out

duty-free shop

post office

currency exchange

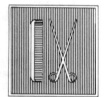

hairdresser

luggage trolleys

do not use luggage trolleys

luggage lockers

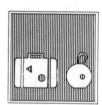

luggage claim

luggage registration

car rental

buses and taxis

706

common symbols

airport

helicopters

trains

service station

camping and caravan site

picnic area

camping area

camping prohibited

crosses

Latin

patriarchal

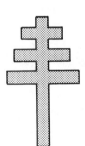

papal

Celtic

Greek

Lorraine

Maltese

Saint Andrew's

ankh

SCIENTIFIC SYMBOLS

biology

♂ male

♀ female

† death

✳ birth

mathematics

+ addition

− subtraction

× multiplication

÷ division

± plus or minus

= is equal to

≠ is not equal to

≡ is identical with

≢ is not identical with

≈ is approximately equal to

≋ is equivalent to

> is greater than

≥ is equal to or greater than

< is less than

≤ is equal to or less than

√ square root of

∞ infinity

% per cent

∪ union

∩ intersection

⊂ is contained in

∈ is a member of

∅ empty set

miscellaneous

℞ prescription

& ampersand

© copyright

® registered trademark

$ dollar

¢ cent

£ pound

→ reaction direction

⇄ reversible reaction

+ positive charge

− negative charge

GENERAL INDEX

1

10 yard line. 513.
15 yard line. 513.

2

25 ring. 550.
25 yard line. 516.

3

3-point line. 523.

4

4-berth caravan. 581.

5

5 yard line. 513.

A

à cheval sur deux colonnes. 580.
à cheval sur deux douzaines. 580.
à cheval sur deux numéros. 580.
A-frame. 661.
abacus. 160.
abdomen. 92, 95, 98, 106.
abdominal aorta. 117, 120.
abdominal rectus. 110.
abdominal segment. 92.
above ground pipeline. 630.
above ground pipeline support. 630.
abruptly pinnate. 62.
absorbent sock. 522.
absorber. 656.
absorber pipe. 656.
absorbing plate. 656.
absorbing surface. 655.
abutment. 165, 400, 401, 402.
abyssal deposits. 42.
abyssal plain. 42.
acanthus leaf. 160, 200.
accelerator pedal. 386.
accent mark. 462.
access for physically handicapped. 705.
access gallery. 641, 646.
access panel. 195, 263.
access shaft. 646.
accidentals. 462.
accommodation ladder. 420.
accordion. 475.
accordion pleat. 294.
account book. 450.
Ace. 578.
acetylene cylinder. 271.
acetylene valve. 272.
achene. 66, 70.
acorn nut. 254.

acoustic baffle. 421.
acoustic ceiling. 169.
acoustic coupler. 457.
acoustic coupler. 454, 455.
acoustic echo. 428.
acoustic resistance. 372.
acromion. 113.
acroterion. 161.
acrylic window. 423.
action of wind. 50.
acute accent. 347.
Adam's apple. 106.
adapter. 275.
addition. 708.
addressee. 349.
adductor muscle. 94.
adhesive tape. 615.
adipose tissue. 109, 128.
adit. 622.
adjustable channel. 249.
adjustable foot. 368.
adjustable frame. 252.
adjustable pedestal. 195.
adjustable seat. 407.
adjustable spanner. 248.
adjustable waist tab. 283.
adjuster. 616.
adjusting knob. 247.
adjusting lever. 478.
adjusting nut. 599.
adjusting ring. 250.
adjusting screw. 249, 272, 598.
adjustment slide. 284.
adjustment wheel. 277.
administration building. 624.
administration office. 634.
administrative building. 646.
adrenal gland. 120.
advance and retard capsule. 391.
advance gas-cooled reactor. 650.
advanced gas-cooled reactor. 648.
advertising sign. 414.
adze. 574.
aerated filter. 267.
aerial. 383.
aerodynamic brake. 658.
affricate consonants. 348.
Africa. 41.
African warrior. 675.
Afro. 321.
Afro comb. 328.
aft stabilizer fin. 419.
after hydroplane. 424.
afterbay. 637, 638, 641.
afterfeather. 88.
aftermast. 416.
aftermast topgallant staysail. 417.
age and weight. 555.
agnolotti. 137.
agricultural machinery. 152, 153, 154.
aiguillette de gîte à la noix. 141.
aiguillette de romsteck. 141.
aileron. 434, 542, 691.

air brake. 542, 691.
air brake handle. 542.
air brake hydraulic jack. 691.
air cap. 270.
air chamber. 262.
air-circulating fan. 196.
air cleaner. 690.
air-cleaner filter. 664.
air conditioning. 196.
air conditioning. 407.
air-cooled condenser. 654.
air diffuser. 415.
air fan. 155.
air filter. 243, 391.
air gap. 655.
air hole. 99, 335, 352.
air hose. 536, 625.
air inlet. 436.
air inlet control. 191.
air inlet grille. 330.
air intake. 34, 404, 422, 441.
air leg. 625.
air-line. 387.
air mattress. 584.
air outlet grille. 330.
air passage. 625.
air preheater. 647.
air pressure adjusting screw. 270.
air-pressure pump. 598.
air pumps. 584.
air sealing gland. 468.
air shutter release. 359.
air space. 34, 89.
air temperature. 54, 55.
air-to-air missile. 691, 692.
air-to-surface missile. 692.
air transport. 434.
air tube. 195.
air valve. 270.
air vent. 232.
air warning radar. 425.
airbrick. 177.
aircraft gate. 438.
airframe. 543.
airlock. 34.
airport. 438, 439.
airport. 707.
airspeed indicator. 542.
aisle. 164.
ala. 125.
albumen. 89.
alidade. 600.
alighting board. 99.
align horizontally. 350.
align vertically. 350.
all-in-one vest. 305.
almond. 67, 70.
alphabet. 371.
alphabet. 137.
alphanumeric keyboard. 456.
Alsace glass. 212.
Altar. 33.
altazimuth mounting. 609.
alteration line. 489.
alternator. 391, 404.
alternator indicator. 385.

altimeter. 542, 544.
altitude coarse-motion clamp. 609.
altitude control system. 57.
altitude scales. 39.
altocumulus. 44.
altostratus. 44.
alula. 88.
aluminium panel. 581.
alveolar bone. 115.
Amanita virosa. 65.
ambulatory. 164.
American corn bread. 138.
American football. 518, 519.
ammunition stowage. 690.
ampersand. 708.
amphibian. 97.
amplifier. 374.
amplifier-tuner. 364.
ampulla. 128.
ampulla of fallopian tube. 109.
anal canal. 119.
anal fin. 90.
anal proleg. 92.
analogue display. 591.
analogue frequency meter. 364.
analytical balance. 595.
anchor. 433.
anchor cable. 433.
anchor-windlass room. 419.
anchorage block. 402.
anchors, types of. 433.
anconeus. 111.
Andromeda. 32.
anemometer. 55.
aneroid barometer. 598.
angle brace. 180.
angle scale. 253.
angle valve. 193.
anglepoise lamp. 211.
Anik. 378.
animal cell. 105.
animal kingdom. 79.
ankh. 707.
ankle. 106.
ankle length. 287.
ankle sock. 301.
ankle-strap sandal. 309.
annular combustion chamber. 436.
annular eclipse. 29.
annulet. 160.
anode. 263, 606.
Antarctic Circle. 27.
Antarctic Ocean. 41.
antenna. 92, 95, 98, 434, 567.
antennule. 95.
anterior chamber. 123.
anterior commissure. 122.
anterior end. 93.
anterior notch. 124.
anterior pulmonary plexus. 118.
anterior root. 122.
anterior tibial. 110.
anther. 64.
anti-aircraft gun. 425.
anti-collision light. 434.
anti-friction pad. 546.

The terms in **bold type** indicate the title of an illustration.

anti-reverse lock. 566.
anti-skating device. 365.
anti-slip shoe. 268.
anti-submarine mortar. 425.
anti-syphon vent. 257.
anti-tank missile. 692.
anticipator. 597.
anticipator indicator. 597.
anticline. 626.
antifixa. 161.
antihelix. 124.
antireflection coating. 656.
antitragus. 124.
antivibration handle. 243.
anus. 91, 94, 96, 108, 109, 119.
anvil. 599, 625.
aorta. 118.
aperture. 93.
aperture scale. 357.
apex. 93, 96, 115, 126, 622.
apical foramen. 115.
apocrine sweat gland. 128.
apostrophe. 347, 350.
apple. 68.
apple. 68.
appoggiatura. 462.
appointment book. 450.
approach. 556, 557, 576.
approach ramp. 402.
approach span. 401.
apricot. 67.
apron. 199, 200, 203, 438, 565,
    571, 668.
apse. 164.
apsidiole. 164.
Aquarius, the Water Bearer. 698.
aquatic bird. 89.
aquatic bird. 89.
aqueous humour. 123.
aquifer. 636.
Arabic writing style. 345.
arbor. 237.
arc. 429.
arc tube. 274.
arc tube mount structure. 274.
arc welding. 271.
arc welding machine. 271.
arcade. 164.
arch. 34, 165, 401.
arch bridge. 401.
arch bridges, types of. 401.
arch dam. 639.
**arch dam, cross section of an.
639.**
arch of the aorta. 116.
archboard. 450.
archer. 570.
Archer. 33.
archery. 570.
arches. 162.
arches, types of. 162, 401.
architectural styles. 160.
architecture. 157.
architrave. 160.
architrave rail. 188.
archivolt. 165.
Arctic Circle. 27.
arctic continental. 54.
arctic maritime. 54.
Arctic Ocean. 41.
arena. 556, 557.
Arenberg parquet. 186.
areola. 109.
argent. 696.
Aries, the Ram. 698.
arm. 83, 107, 200, 211, 433, 473,
    485, 605, 617, 665, 667.
arm elevator. 365.
arm guard. 519, 570.
arm nut. 492.
arm piece. 616.
arm position. 535.
arm rest. 365, 386.
arm slit. 291.
arm stump. 200.
arm support. 616.

armchair. 200.
**armchairs, principal types of.
200.**
Armenian writing style. 345.
armet. 676.
armet. 676.
armhole. 287, 296.
armoire. 205.
armour. 676.
armpit. 106.
armrest. 617.
armstand. 534.
armstand dive. 535.
arpeggio. 462.
arquebus. 682.
array elevation and tensioning
    mechanism. 378.
arrester hook. 691.
arrivals concourse. 440.
arrivals timetable. 412.
arrow. 570, 677.
Arrow. 32, 570.
arrow rest. 570, 677.
arteries. 117.
artichoke. 73.
articulated trailer. 632.
articulated vehicle. 389.
articulating hinge point. 665.
articulation. 384.
artificial fly. 567.
artificial satellite. 39.
ASA/DIN dial. 353.
ASA/DIN exposure index. 357.
asbestos shingle. 185.
ascending aorta. 116.
ascending colon. 119.
ash. 334.
ash layer. 45.
ash lid. 191.
ashtray. 334.
Asia. 41.
asparagus. 77.
asphalt. 635.
asphalt process. 634.
asphalt shingle. 185.
asphalt still. 635.
aspirin. 615.
assembly process. 507.
assistant timer. 531.
asterisk. 347.
asteroids. 28.
asthenosphere. 39.
astragal. 160, 431.
astrakhan. 288.
astronomical observatory. 34.
astronomy. 45.
asymmetrical bars. 560.
at least. 530.
atenna. 529.
Atlantic Ocean. 41.
atlas. 113.
atmosphere. 39.
atrium. 163.
attaché case. 340.
attached curtain. 207.
attack line. 529.
attack zone. 529.
attacker. 564.
attacking zone. 517.
attitude acquisition. 379.
aubergine. 73.
audio input. 367.
audio output. 367.
auditorium. 35.
auditory ossicles. 124.
auger bit. 250.
aunt by marriage. 130.
auricle. 98, 124.
auricular. 87.
Australia. 41.
auto/manual aperture (iris) control.
    369.
auto-manual focusing switch. 369.
automatic air vent. 194.
automatic answer indicator. 373.
automatic cable pulley. 547.

automatic circulating pump. 194.
automatic control system. 422.
automatic fade control. 369.
automatic flex reel. 234.
automatic frequency control. 364.
automatic relief valve. 194.
automatic rifle. 685.
automatic shut-off. 196.
automatic tank gauge. 633.
automatic tweezers. 332.
automatically-controlled door. 440.
autopilot control. 437.
autorefrigerating devices. 630.
autumn. 27.
autumn squash. 73.
autumnal equinox. 27.
auxiliary handle. 251.
auxiliary projector. 35.
auxiliary sighting telescope. 690.
auxiliary tank. 388.
avocado. 72.
awning. 582.
awning channel. 581.
axial-flow compressor. 436.
axial rib. 93.
axillary artery. 117.
axillary bud. 61, 62.
axillary nerve. 121.
axillary vein. 117.
axis. 113.
axle. 404, 548.
axon. 127.
azimuth coarse-motion clamp. 609.
azimuth synchro. 611.
azure. 696.

B

baby doll. 301.
Babybel (French). 145.
babygro. 305.
back. 83, 87, 107, 203, 214, 215,
    216, 217, 252, 255, 283, 294,
    463, 481, 677.
back beam. 494.
back belt. 290.
back binding. 540.
back board. 498.
back boundary line. 526.
back brace. 481.
back cornering. 498.
back court. 524.
back inlay. 481.
back judge. 518.
back pocket. 284.
back straight. 555.
back upholstery. 617.
back wall. 527.
back zone. 529.
backboard. 523.
backboard support. 523.
backdrop. 170.
backgammon. 578.
background. 359.
backguard. 228, 231.
backing. 500.
backing board. 500.
backing hammer. 500.
backplate. 597.
backspace key. 453, 456.
backstay. 416, 548.
backstop. 520.
backstroke. 533.
backstroke start. 533.
backstroke swimmer. 533.
backstroke turn indicator. 532.
backward. 534.
backward dive. 535.
backward point. 514.
badminton. 526.
badminton racquet. 526.
badminton shoe. 526.
baffle. 191, 632.
bag. 474, 520.
bag well. 573.

baggage check-in counter. 440.
baggage claim area. 440.
baggage compartment. 441.
baggage conveyor. 439.
baggage racks. 421.
baggage trailer. 439.
baggage trolley. 440.
bagpipes. 474.
baguette cut. 317.
bail. 515.
bail arm. 566.
bailey. 167.
Bailey bridge. 403.
baize. 569.
Baker tent. 583.
baking sheet. 220.
baking utensils. 220.
balaclava. 288, 304.
balalaika. 473.
Balance. 33.
balance beam. 560.
balance beam. 426.
balance control. 364.
balance hammer. 466.
balance rail. 466.
balance wheel. 591.
balcony. 178.
balk area. 569.
balk line. 569.
balk line spot. 569.
ball. 515, 516, 521, 573.
ball. 488, 496, 528, 531, 682.
ball (rugby). 512.
ball assembly. 261.
ball bearing. 352, 548.
ball boy. 524.
ball-cock supply valve. 258.
ball cross-section. 573.
ball-end. 507.
ball of clay. 505.
ball pein. 247.
ball pein hammer. 247.
ball rack. 576.
ball return track. 576.
ball stud of circle drawbar. 666.
ball winder. 496.
ballast. 408.
ballast tank. 631.
ballerina. 311.
ballet shoes. 311.
**ballistic missile nuclear
    submarine. 424.**
ballpoint pen. 352.
baluster. 187.
balustrade. 172, 178.
bamboos. 579.
banana. 72.
band. 365.
band ring. 315.
band selectors. 364.
bandage. 565.
banding wheel. 505.
banjo. 473.
bank. 530, 646.
bank of heliostats. 654.
banquette. 202.
bar. 85, 471, 478, 561, 578.
bar frame. 211.
bar line. 462.
bar nose. 243.
barb. 53, 88, 567.
barber comb. 328.
barbette. 166.
barbican. 167.
baren. 501.
barge. 631.
bark. 63.
barn. 151.
barn doors. 358.
barograph. 55, 542.
barometric pressure. 54.
barometric tendency. 54.
barred spiral galaxy. 31.
barrel. 681.

barrel. 330, 331, 352, 475, 550, 591, 680, 683, 684, 685, 686, 687, 688, 689.
barrel bag. 337, 338.
barrel catch. 689.
barrel cuff. 296.
barrel jacket. 683.
barrel nut. 685.
barrel organ. 475.
barren. 621.
barrow. 413, 671.
bartizan. 167.
basaltic layer. 40.
base. 160, 190, 204, 210, 232, 233, 250, 251, 330, 365, 377, 409, 500, 559, 595, 600, 601, 605, 661, 688, 695.
base elbow. 265.
base line. 610.
base of lamp. 357.
base of splat. 200.
base plate. 56, 182, 253, 365, 546, 600, 610.
base plug. 682.
base ring. 680.
base rock. 626, 636.
base width. 644.
baseball. 520, 521.
baseboard. 361.
basecourse. 399.
baseline. 524.
basement. 179.
basement membrane. 127.
baseplate. 683.
basic weaves. 497.
basil. 135.
basilic vein. 117.
basin. 646.
basin side. 646.
basket. 523.
basket. 223, 523, 545.
basket-handle. 162.
basketball. 523.
basketball. 523.
basketball shoe. 523.
bass drum. 472.
bass drum. 477, 479.
bass pick-up. 480.
bass register. 475.
bass string. 465.
bass tone control. 364.
basses. 475.
bassoon. 469, 476, 477.
bassoons. 479.
baster. 221.
bastion. 166.
bat. 100, 515, 521, 528.
bat. 521.
bath. 259.
bathing trunks. 531.
bathroom. 259.
bathroom. 179.
bathroom scales. 596.
batsman. 514, 515.
batt insulation. 185.
batten. 170, 537, 538.
batten pocket. 537, 538.
batter. 520.
batter head. 472.
batter's box. 520.
batter's helmet. 521.
battery. 357, 392.
battery. 57, 356.
battery box. 388.
battery case. 392.
battery check meter. 368.
battery cover. 392.
battery pod. 423.
battery pod release hand pump. 423.
battery pod release lever. 423.
batting glove. 521.
battlement. 167.
batwing sleeve. 296.
bavette. 141.
bay. 30.

bay antler. 81.
bay window. 177.
bayonet mount. 353, 355.
bayonets. 679.
bayonets, major types of. 679.
bazooka. 686.
beach. 40, 43.
beach bag. 338.
beacon. 663.
Beacon antenna. 57.
bead. 393.
beam. 81, 153, 182, 560, 594, 595, 596.
beam arrest. 595.
beam balance. 594.
beam bridge. 400.
beam bridges, types of. 400.
beam pump. 627.
beam reach. 539.
bean bag chair. 202.
bean sprouts. 77.
bear away (to). 537.
bearer. 468.
bearing. 401, 597.
beater. 155, 225, 472, 494.
beater ejector. 225.
beater handtree. 494.
beater sley. 494.
beaters. 225.
Beatle cut. 321.
beaver. 82.
beaver. 676.
bed. 204.
bed. 499, 502, 503, 504, 560.
bed handle. 503.
bed-mattress. 584.
bedrock. 602.
bedroom. 179, 431.
bedside lamp. 210.
beef. 140, 141.
beehive. 151.
beer mug. 212.
beetroot. 76.
begin a new paragraph. 350.
Bel Paese (Italian). 145.
belfry. 164.
Belisha beacon. 168.
bell. 469, 470.
bell bottoms. 300.
bell brace. 469.
bell buoy. 430.
bell roof. 181.
bell tower. 165.
bellows. 361, 475.
bellows strap. 475.
bellowslike joint. 444.
belly. 83, 87, 142, 463, 677.
below-stage. 170.
belt. 284.
belt. 251, 281, 561, 564, 658.
belt buckle. 281.
belt carrier. 284, 306.
belt loop. 281, 585.
beltbag. 545.
belted radial tyre. 393.
bench. 202, 414, 621.
bench height. 621.
bench saw. 252.
bend. 318, 567.
Berenice's Hair. 32.
beret. 304.
bergère. 200.
bergschrund. 48.
Bering Sea. 41.
berm. 638.
Bermuda rigged ketch. 418.
Bermuda shorts. 300.
berries, major types of. 66.
berry, section of a. 66.
bertha collar. 298.
best end. 139, 143.
betting layout (French). 580.
between-the-lens shutter. 356.
bevel. 525.
bezel. 315.
bezel facet. 317.

bias. 488.
bib. 305.
bib. 300, 306, 562.
bib tap. 261.
biceps of arm. 110.
biceps of thigh. 111.
bichord. 465.
biconcave. 610.
biconvex. 610.
bicycle. 397, 398.
bicycle horn. 398.
bifocal. 318.
bikini. 303.
bikini briefs. 287.
bill. 433.
billhook. 242.
billiard spot. 569.
billiards. 569.
billiards. 568.
bills, principal types of. 89.
bimetal element. 597.
bimetallic helix. 597.
bimetallic thermometer. 597.
binding. 288, 540.
binocular microscope. 605.
biology. 708.
bipod. 683, 687.
bird. 87, 88, 89.
Bird of Paradise. 33.
bird of prey. 89.
bird of prey. 89.
birth. 708.
biscuit. 147.
biscuit cutters. 220.
biscuit press. 220.
Bishop (B). 577.
bishop sleeve. 296.
bit. 250, 554, 625, 626.
bite. 335.
bitumen. 636.
bitumen pumping. 636.
bitumen treatment. 636.
bivalve shell. 93.
Black. 577, 578.
black ball. 569.
black currant. 66.
black rye bread. 138.
black salsify. 76.
Black Sea. 41.
black square. 577.
blackhead remover. 333.
blade. 62, 196, 214, 224, 226, 242, 247, 248, 252, 253, 277, 327, 328, 486, 487, 516, 528, 536, 548, 563, 567, 574, 585, 642, 643, 658, 664, 666, 679.
blade arm. 666.
blade close stop. 328.
blade guard. 252, 270.
blade height adjustment. 252.
blade injector. 327.
blade lever. 499.
blade lift fan. 421.
blade-locking bolt. 253.
blade rotation mechanism. 666.
blade tilt lock. 253.
blade tilting mechanism. 252.
blank. 579.
blanket. 204, 502.
blanket insulation. 185.
blastodisc. 89.
blazer. 297.
bleeder valve. 193.
blender. 225.
blending attachment. 225.
blind cloth. 209.
blinkers. 555.
block. 468, 539, 671.
blockboard. 255.
blood circulation. 116, 117.
blood vessel. 115, 128, 129.
blood vessels. 100.
blouse. 522, 525.
blouses. 295.
blouson. 291.
blow pipe. 474.

blower. 194, 195, 196, 467.
blower motor. 195.
blowing snow. 52.
blowlamp. 271.
blowout preventer. 626.
blue ball. 569.
blue cap. 531.
blue beam. 377.
blue flag. 531.
blue line. 517.
blueberry. 66.
blusher brush. 322.
boa. 299.
board. 255.
board. 537.
board cutter. 499.
boarding joist. 186.
boarding step. 441.
boards. 517.
boat, types of. 541.
boat deck. 419.
boater. 288, 304.
bob. 321, 593.
bobbin. 492.
bobbin. 486, 495, 496.
bobbin case. 486.
bobbin lace. 492.
bobbin winder. 496.
bobbin winder. 485.
bobsleigh. 549.
bobstay. 416.
body. 126, 233, 250, 349, 387, 407, 430, 468, 469, 558, 567, 593, 667, 668.
body, types of. 384.
body lift cylinder. 668.
body of nail. 129.
body shaper. 302.
body shirt. 295.
body tube. 605.
body whorl. 93.
body wire. 562.
bogie. 415.
bogie. 404, 407.
bogie car-carrying wagon. 406.
bogie flat wagon. 406.
bogie frame. 404.
bogie open wagon. 406.
bogie tank wagon. 406.
bogie van. 406.
bogie wagon. 405.
bogie well wagon. 406.
boiler. 194.
boiler. 193, 654.
boiler house. 647.
boiler room. 179, 419, 425.
boiler tube. 647.
bold. 351.
bold capitals. 351.
bole. 63.
bolero. 297.
bollard. 426.
bolster. 204, 214, 217.
bolster pillow. 204.
bolt. 254.
bolt. 249, 687.
bolt carrier. 685.
bolt catch. 685.
bolt follower. 256.
bolt guide. 677.
bone folder. 498.
boning knife. 217.
bonnet. 305, 383, 389.
bonus tiles. 579.
book end. 448.
bookbinding leather. 500.
booking hall. 412.
boom. 538, 661, 665, 667.
boom arm. 359.
boom operator. 375.
boom point sheave. 661.
boom vang. 538.
booster intermediate station. 630.
booster parachute. 443.
boot. 383, 468, 536, 544, 548, 551, 561.

The terms in **bold type** indicate the title of an illustration.

boot jack. 310.
borage. 135.
bordeaux. 212.
bore. 468, 681.
bottle cart. 271.
bottle opener. 219, 233.
bottom. 540, 545.
bottom bracket axle. 398.
bottom cylinder. 502, 504.
bottom deckboard. 671.
bottom-end transverse member. 411.
bottom of collar. 295.
bottom of the pool. 531, 534.
bottom plate. 633.
bottom pocket. 569.
bottom rail. 188, 205.
bottom retainer. 405.
bottom ring. 643.
bottom road. 623.
bottom side rail. 411.
bottom surface. 542.
bottomboard. 468.
bouffant. 320.
bound book. 498.
boundary line. 514.
Boursin au Poivre (French). 145.
bow. 464, 677.
bow. 288, 537, 538, 677.
bow (take-apart). 570.
bow collar. 298.
bow door ramp. 421.
bow horizontal thruster. 423.
bow irons. 677.
bow plane. 423.
bow rudder. 420.
bow saw. 586.
bow tie. 285.
bowl. 530.
bowl. 216, 226, 335, 429, 668.
bowl lid. 335.
bowl with serving spout. 226.
bowler. 514, 576.
bowler hat. 288.
bowline. 587.
bowline on a bight. 587.
bowling ball. 576.
bowling crease. 514.
bowling shoe. 576.
bowls. 530.
bows. 677.
bowsight. 570.
bowsprit. 416.
bowstring. 570, 677.
bowstring girder bridge. 401.
box. 169.
box and brush. 552.
box and gate. 552.
box bag. 338.
box-beam Y frame. 666.
box front lights. 169.
box jacket. 297.
box pallet. 671.
box pleat. 207, 294.
boxer. 565.
boxer shorts. 287.
boxing. 565.
boxing boot. 565.
boxing glove. 565.
bra. 303.
brace. 250.
brace. 182, 269, 417, 645.
brace clip. 284.
bracelet with curb chain. 315.
bracelets. 315.
braces. 284.
brachial. 110.
brachial artery. 117.
brachial plexus. 121.
brachioradial. 110.
brachioradialis. 111.
bracket. 208, 329, 428, 481.
bracket base. 205.
bracket slot. 209.
brackets. 347.
bract. 70.

bradawl. 248.
braided rope. 587.
braids. 320.
brail. 417.
Braille. 346.
brain. 91.
brake. 617.
brake cable. 397.
brake lever. 397.
brake line. 393.
brake lining. 393.
brake pad. 393.
brake pedal. 386.
brake shoe. 393.
brake van. 406.
brakeman. 549.
brakes. 393.
branch. 63, 77, 85, 257, 553.
branch duct. 192.
branch return pipe. 193.
branch supply pipe. 193.
branches. 63.
branching, examples of. 262.
brandy. 212.
brass family. 470.
brassie. 572.
brassiere cup. 303.
brattice. 167.
Brazil nut. 70.
bread. 138.
bread guide. 227.
bread knife. 217.
break line. 298.
breaker. 43.
breaking pliers. 507.
breaking the wall. 579.
breast. 109.
breast. 87, 106, 139, 143.
breast beam. 494.
breast dart. 282.
breast pocket. 282, 285, 295.
breast welt pocket. 283.
breastplate. 676.
breaststroke. 533.
breaststroke kick. 533.
breaststroke swimmer. 533.
breaststroke turn. 533.
breather valve. 633.
breathing apparatus. 662.
breathing in. 533.
breathing out. 533.
breech. 680, 688.
breechblock. 684.
breechblock operating lever assembly. 684.
breeches. 300, 311, 554, 562.
breeching rope. 680.
breve. 461.
breve rest. 461.
brick. 183.
brick pattern half bond. 186.
bridge. 568.
bridge. 208, 318, 420, 424, 463, 465, 475, 607, 631.
bridge fin. 424.
bridge of nose. 125.
bridge unit. 480.
bridle. 553.
bridle tape. 466.
Brie (French). 145.
briefcase. 340.
briefs. 287.
briefs. 303.
brig. 418.
brigantine. 418.
bright star projector. 35.
brightness control. 377.
brilliant cut facets. 317.
brilliant full cut. 317.
brim. 288, 304.
brioche. 146.
briolette cut. 317.
brisket. 140.
bristle. 327, 328, 329, 331.
bristles. 270.
British cheeses. 144.

British cut. 139, 140, 142, 143.
British model. 349.
broad beans. 77.
broad-leaved endive. 74.
broad ligament of uterus. 109.
broad reach. 539.
broad welt. 290.
broad welt side pocket. 281, 294.
broccoli. 73.
brooch. 315.
brood cell. 99.
brood chamber. 99.
brother. 130.
brow brush. 323.
brow reinforce. 676.
brow tine. 81.
browband. 553.
brown ball. 569.
brush. 270.
brush. 71, 329, 501.
brush and rails. 551, 552.
Brussels sprouts. 74.
buck shots. 137.
bucket. 643, 661, 665.
bucket chain excavator. 621.
bucket cylinder. 665.
bucket hinge pin. 665.
bucket ring. 643.
bucket seat. 386.
bucket tooth. 665.
bucket wheel excavator. 621, 636.
buckle. 488.
buckle. 284, 339, 386, 546.
buckled belt. 570.
bud. 75.
buffer. 404, 687.
buffer tank. 630.
bufferstop. 410.
buffet. 705.
bugle. 470.
building line. 178.
building materials. 183, 184, 185.
building sewer. 257.
buildings. 151.
built-in microphone. 369.
bulb. 77, 85, 274, 597, 631.
bulb, section of a. 75.
bulb planter. 239.
bulb unit. 646.
bulb vegetables. 75.
bulbil. 75.
bulk carrier. 427.
bulkhead deck. 420.
bulkhead flat wagon. 406.
Bull. 32.
bulldozer. 664.
bulldozer. 621.
bullet. 688.
bullfighter. 311.
bullion stitch. 493.
bullseye. 432, 550.
bulwark. 416.
bumper. 234, 383, 389.
bun. 320, 321.
bunch. 334.
bund wall. 633.
bundle. 77.
bung. 506.
bungalow. 173.
bunk. 424.
bunker. 571, 623.
bunker oil. 635.
buoyancy compensator. 536.
buoys. 430.
burden. 636.
bureau. 206.
burgundy. 212.
buried pipeline. 630.
burin. 502.
burner. 223, 647.
burner ring. 223.
burnisher. 501.
burr. 81.
bus stop. 168.
busbar. 641.
buses and taxis. 707.

bush. 237.
bushing. 637, 645.
butane accessories. 585.
butane carrier. 631.
butane cylinder. 585.
butane tank. 334.
butt. 334, 492, 567, 568, 677, 683, 685, 687, 689.
butt cap. 566.
butt eye. 566.
butt grip. 566.
butt hinge. 199.
butt plate. 688.
butt section. 566.
butt-strap. 318.
butt welding. 272.
butte. 47.
butter compartment. 229.
butter curler. 217.
butter dish. 213.
butter knife. 214.
butterfly. 92.
butterfly kick. 533.
butterfly stroke. 533.
butterfly swimmer. 533.
butterfly turn. 533.
buttock. 107.
button. 274, 285, 475, 563.
button loop. 284.
button notch. 233.
button strap. 306.
button-through smock. 295.
buttondown collar. 285.
buttoned placket. 285, 291, 295.
buttonhole. 281, 285, 286.
buttress. 164, 165, 639.
buttress dam. 639.
buttress dam, cross section of a. 639.
by-pass taxiway. 438.
bypass. 400.
bypass contact. 370.

C

c clef. 461.
cab. 664, 665, 666, 667, 668, 670.
cabbage lettuce. 74.
cabin. 420, 441, 547.
cabinet. 196, 231, 259, 363, 377.
cable. 587.
cable. 251, 369, 428, 559, 587.
cable bundles. 644.
cable car. 547.
cable release. 359.
cable sleeve. 251.
cable stay anchorage. 402.
cable-stayed bridge. 402.
cable stitch. 490.
cabochon cut. 317.
cabriole leg. 200.
cabriolet. 200.
cactus. 47.
caddie. 571.
caecum. 119.
Caerphilly. 144.
café curtain. 207.
cage. 211, 430.
cagoule. 575.
cairel. 311.
caisson. 427.
cake mascara. 323.
cake tin. 220.
calamus. 88.
calcaneus. 113.
calcar. 100.
calculator. 341, 357.
calculator/cheque book holder. 341.
calculator dial. 357.
calendar pad. 450.
calf. 107.
calf-lenght jeans. 300.
caliper. 393.
calipers. 503.

The terms in **bold type** indicate the title of an illustration.

Callisto. 28.
calls indicator. 373.
callus. 93.
calm. 53.
calyx. 64, 66, 68, 71, 120.
cam. 492.
cam lever. 492, 689.
cam ring. 250.
cambium. 63.
Camembert (French). 145.
camera. 376.
camera battery. 368.
camera body. 353.
camera crane. 375.
camera pedestal. 375.
camera platform. 359.
camera screw. 359.
cameraman. 375.
camisole. 302.
camping and caravan site. 707.
camping equipment. 584, 585, 586.
camping prohibited. 707.
camshaft. 391, 503.
can. 430.
can buoy. 430.
Canadian elk. 81.
canal boat. 631.
canal lock. 426.
canal lock. 427.
Cancer, the Crab. 698.
cane. 336.
cane pen. 352.
canine. 82, 115.
canister shot. 681.
canister vacuum cleaner. 234.
cannelloni. 137.
cannon. 83.
canopy. 336, 544, 573, 582, 668, 691.
canopy pole. 582.
cantaloupe. 73.
cantilever. 639.
cantilever bridge. 400.
cantilever span. 400.
cantle. 553.
canton. 695.
canvas. 565.
canvas divider. 582.
canvas shoe. 522.
cap. 65, 187, 265, 271, 274, 304, 554, 657.
cap iron. 247.
cap rock. 626, 636.
cap sleeve. 296.
capacitor. 658.
cape. 291.
cape. 311.
capillary bore. 597.
capital. 160.
capitals. 351.
capitulum. 64.
capless wig. 321.
caponiere. 166.
capped column. 49.
capped inspection tee. 192.
cappelletti. 137.
Capricorn, the Goat. 698.
capstan. 425, 502.
capsule. 71.
capsule, section of a. 71.
captain. 549.
captain's quarters. 419.
captain's seat. 437.
car. 383, 384, 385, 386.
car anchor. 433.
car coat. 290.
car deck. 421.
car parking. 178.
car rental. 707.
carabiner. 574.
carafe. 224.
carapace. 95, 101.
caravan. 581.
caraway seeded rye bread. 138.
carbon. 507.

carbon copy. 349.
carbon dioxide gas coolant. 650.
carbon droxide coolant. 648.
carbon granules. 372.
carburettor. 390, 391, 395.
card and photo case. 341.
card games. 578.
card holder. 452.
card index cabinet. 450.
card punch. 458.
card reader. 458.
card support. 56.
cardboard case. 688.
cardiac plexus. 118.
cardiac sphincter. 119.
cardigan. 286, 297.
cardinal system of marking. 430.
cardoon. 77.
cards. 450.
cargo-bay access hatch. 443.
cargo-bay door. 443.
cargo boom. 420.
cargo hatch. 419.
cargo hold. 419.
cargo terminal. 438.
Caribbean Sea. 41.
carnassial. 82.
carnivore's jaw. 82.
carousel. 440.
carpal pad. 86.
carpentry. 255.
carpentry: fasteners. 254.
carpentry: tools. 247, 248, 249, 250, 251, 252, 253.
carpet nozzle. 234.
carpus. 84, 112.
carré. 142, 580.
carré raccourci. 139.
carriage. 492.
carriage. 453, 491, 492, 670, 680.
carriage release lever. 453.
carriage return. 453.
carriageway. 399.
carrier. 208, 281, 284, 397.
carrier bag. 338.
carrot. 76.
carry handle. 331, 337.
carrying handle. 600, 685, 687.
cart path. 571.
carton. 334.
cartoon. 507.
cartridge. 352, 356, 688, 689.
cartridge (rifle). 688.
cartridge (shotgun). 688.
cartridge fuse. 275.
cartridge stem. 261.
cartwheel hat. 304.
carved Queen Anne leg. 200.
carving fork. 217.
carving knife. 217.
cascable button. 680.
case. 232, 233, 234, 327, 331, 332, 475, 478, 597, 599, 688.
casement. 189.
casement window. 189.
cash readout. 387.
cashew. 70.
casing. 193, 196.
casing first string. 627.
casing second string. 627.
Caspian Sea. 41.
cassette. 356, 455.
cassette deck. 363.
cassette holder. 366.
cassette loading slot. 367.
cassette recorder. 455.
Cassiopeia. 32.
cast-on stitches. 490.
castanets. 471.
caster. 196, 234, 472.
castle. 167.
casual water. 571.
cat. 86.
catadioptric ring. 432.
catalytic reformer. 634.
catalytic reforming plant. 635.

catch. 339, 341, 679.
catch spring. 679.
catcher. 521.
catcher. 520.
catcher's box. 520.
catcher's glove. 521.
catering vehicle. 439.
caterpillar. 92.
cathedral. 164.
cathode. 606.
cattle. 701.
catwalk. 375.
caudal fin. 90.
caudal vertebrae. 84.
cauliflower. 73.
caution. 704.
caution, pedestrian crossing. 704.
caution, slippery floor. 704.
cave. 46.
cave. 43.
cedilla. 347.
ceiling. 527.
ceiling collar. 192.
ceiling fan. 196.
ceiling fitting. 210.
ceiling grille. 192.
ceiling joist. 182.
celeriac. 76.
celery. 77.
celesta. 479.
celestial co-ordinate system. 27.
celestial equator. 27.
celestial meridian. 27.
celestial sphere. 27.
cell. 92, 544, 609.
cell body. 127.
cell body of sensory neuron. 127.
cell connector. 392.
cell membrane. 105.
cell wall. 105.
cello. 463, 476.
cellophane wrapped packet. 334.
cellos. 479.
Celtic. 707.
cement. 115.
cement screed. 186.
cent. 708.
Centaur. 33.
Central America. 41.
central column. 658.
central compartment. 339.
central console. 437.
central focusing wheel. 607.
central incisor. 115.
central instrument panel. 437.
central nervous system. 122.
central ply. 255.
central processing unit. 454, 455, 458.
central pumping. 630.
central screw. 500.
centre. 350, 517, 518, 523.
centre-aisle. 407.
centre-back. 511, 529.
centre back vent. 283.
centre base. 695.
centre bearing. 436.
centre chief. 695.
centre circle. 511, 522, 523.
centre console. 385.
centre electrode. 392.
centre face-off circle. 517.
centre field. 520.
centre fielder. 520.
centre flag. 511.
centre forward. 511, 516, 529.
centre half. 516.
centre hole. 365.
centre Keelson. 631.
centre knife-edge. 595.
centre line. 516, 517, 519, 523, 526, 528, 529, 562.
centre line of rink. 530.
centre mark. 524.
centre midfield. 511.
centre pocket. 569.

centre post. 205.
centre service line. 524.
centre span. 402.
centre spot. 511, 569.
centre stand. 395.
centre strap. 524.
centre tank. 631.
centre third. 522.
centre wheel. 591, 593.
centreboard. 538.
centriole. 105.
cep. 65.
cephalic vein. 117.
cephalothorax. 95.
Cepheus. 32.
cereal bowl. 213.
cerebellum. 122.
cerebrospinal axis. 122.
cerebrum. 122.
cervical plexus. 121.
cervical vertebra. 113.
cervical vertebrae. 84.
chaffer sieve. 155.
chain. 210, 398, 593, 598.
chain brake. 243.
chain guide. 398.
chain mail. 676.
chain of dunes. 47.
chain pipe wrench. 266.
chain shot. 681.
chain stay. 397.
chain stitch. 493.
chain wheel. 397, 398.
chainsaw. 243.
chainsaw chain. 243.
chairs. 201.
chairs, types of. 203.
chalaza. 89.
chaleco. 311.
chalet. 547.
chalet bungalow. 173.
chalk. 568.
chamber. 689.
Chameleon. 33.
champagne flute. 212.
champagne glass. 212.
chandelier. 210.
change dial. 491.
change machine. 412.
channel. 409, 499, 507.
channel selector control. 367.
chanter. 474.
chanterelle. 65.
Chantilly parquet. 186.
chapel. 419.
character. 452.
characters. 579.
chard. 74.
charge. 688.
charges. 696.
charging handle. 685.
charging handle catch. 685.
charging light. 327.
Charioteer. 32.
charlotte. 146.
charm bracelet. 315.
charms. 315.
charting device. 491.
chase. 680.
chase astragal. 680.
chassis. 389, 581.
check. 466.
check-in area. 440.
check nut. 56.
check-rail. 408.
check valve. 267, 272.
cheek. 83, 106, 247, 567, 680.
cheek strap. 553.
cheese knife. 214.
chela. 95.
chemical treatment. 635.
chemise. 167.
cheque book cover. 341.
cheque book holder. 341.
cherimoya. 72.
cherry. 67.

The terms in **bold type** indicate the title of an illustration.

cherry-picker truck. 439.
chervil. 135.
Cheshire. 144.
chess. 577.
chess notation. 577.
chessboard. 577.
chest. 83, 106.
chest of drawers. 206.
chest protector. 519, 521.
chesterfield. 201.
chestnut. 70, 83.
chevron. 696.
chevron stitch. 493.
chick peas. 77.
chicory. 74.
chief. 695, 696.
chief timekeeper. 532.
children. 130, 131.
children's clothing. 305, 306, 307.
chilli pepper. 73.
chimney. 192.
chimney. 190, 647.
chimney connection. 191.
chimney flue. 190.
chimney pot. 177.
chimney stack. 177.
chin. 87, 106.
chin strap. 519.
China Sea. 41.
Chinese cabbage. 74.
Chinese writing style. 345.
chinstrap. 554.
chip. 580.
chipboard. 255.
chisel. 248.
chisel. 502.
chive. 75.
chloroplast. 105.
chock. 574.
choir. 164.
choir organ manual. 467.
choker. 316.
chopsticks. 223.
chord. 462.
choroid. 123.
choux bun. 147.
christening set. 305.
Christmas tree. 627.
Christmas tree. 630.
chromatin. 105.
chromosphere. 29.
chrysalis. 92.
chuck. 248, 250, 251, 625.
chuck key. 251.
chuck rib. 140.
chukka. 310.
chump end. 143.
chute. 623.
cigar. 334.
cigar band. 334.
cigar box. 334.
cigarette. 334.
cigarette holder. 334.
ciliary body. 123.
ciliate. 62.
cine scale. 357.
cinema. 168.
cinematography. 368.
circle. 666.
circles. 579.
circuit breaker. 641, 658.
circuit test light. 686.
circular level. 600.
circular needle. 490.
circular saw. 253.
circular saw blade. 253.
circulating pump. 193, 655.
circulation, schema of. 116.
circumflex accent. 347.
cirque. 30.
cirrocumulus. 44.
cirrostratus. 44.
cirrus. 44.
citrus fruit, section of a. 69.
citrus fruits, major types of. 69.

citrus juicer. 226.
citrus juicer. 218.
clam. 94.
clam-cleat. 537, 539.
clamp. 211, 267, 331, 491, 496, 499.
clamp binder. 449.
clamp lever. 331.
clamping handle. 226.
clamping nut. 226.
clamshell bucket. 667.
clapper. 372.
clarinet. 469, 476, 477.
clarinets. 479.
clasp. 339, 340.
class ring. 315.
classic. 295.
classic bag. 339.
classical guitar. 481.
classification yard. 411.
clavicle. 112.
claw. 86, 87, 89, 92, 95, 98, 100, 247, 315, 500.
claw grip. 530.
claw hammer. 247.
claw weight. 491.
cleaning brush. 327.
cleaning plug. 260.
cleaning tools. 234.
cleaning tools. 234.
cleansing sponge. 323.
clear sky. 53.
clear space. 529.
clearance light. 388.
cleared ground. 55.
cleat. 538, 539.
cleated shoe. 519.
cleaver. 217.
clefs. 461.
clew. 537.
clew line. 417.
cliff. 30, 40, 43.
climates of the world. 51.
climbing harness. 575.
climbing iron. 310.
climbing plant. 237.
clinical thermometer. 597.
clint. 46.
clip. 208, 284, 331, 352.
clip earring. 315.
clip spot. 210.
clipboard. 450.
clippers. 328.
clitoris. 109.
cloche. 304.
clock. 376, 385, 602.
clock operator. 523.
clock timer. 227, 228.
clog. 309.
close hauled. 539.
close reach. 539.
close up. 350.
close-up lens. 355.
closed circuit television/cathode monitor. 652.
closed expansion tank. 194.
closeness setting. 327.
closing salutation. 349.
closure rail. 408.
cloth cap. 288.
cloth roller. 494.
clothing. 279.
clothing guard. 617.
cloud amount. 53.
cloud amount. 54.
cloud of volcanic ash. 45.
clouds. 44.
clouds of vertical development. 44.
cloudy sky. 53.
clove hitch. 587.
club. 578.
club chair. 201.
club divider. 573.
clubhouse. 571.
clutch bag. 338.

clutch lever. 396.
clutch pedal. 386.
co-axial machine gun. 690.
coach's box. 520.
coal bunker. 624, 647.
coal fired power station. 647.
coal measure. 623.
coal mine. 621, 623, 624, 625.
coal seam. 621.
coal upper. 647.
coarse adjustment knob. 605.
coast. 40.
coat dress. 292.
coat hook. 451.
coat rack. 451.
coats. 290, 291.
cob. 77.
coccygeal nerve. 121.
coccyx. 112.
cochlea. 124.
cochlear nerve. 124.
cock. 682.
cocking handle. 687.
cocking lever. 686.
cockle. 94.
cockleshell. 200.
cockpit. 542.
cockpit. 538.
cockpit canopy. 542.
cocktail. 212.
cocktail cabinet. 206.
coconut. 70.
coeliac trunk. 116, 120.
coffee makers. 224.
coffee mill. 224.
coffee mug. 213.
coffee spoon. 216.
coil. 372.
coil spring. 209.
coiling. 505.
coin purse. 341.
coin slot. 373.
coinbox telephone. 373.
coking plant. 624.
colander. 218.
cold air. 655.
cold room. 179.
cold-water riser. 257.
cold-water supply. 258, 262, 263.
collagenous fibre. 128.
collar. 298.
collar. 35, 61, 281, 283, 285, 327, 561.
collar bar. 316.
collar point. 285, 298.
collar stay. 285.
collars, types of. 298.
collateral. 127.
collecting funnel. 56.
collecting tube. 656.
collector. 642.
collet. 139, 143, 250, 359.
collet nut. 250.
colliery. 623.
colon. 347, 350, 371.
colonnes. 580.
colour analyser. 360.
colour filter. 355.
colour filter set. 358.
colour temperature switch. 369.
coloured sweatshirt. 516.
colours. 696.
columella. 93.
columella fold. 93.
column. 46, 49, 193, 210, 251, 359, 361, 401, 485, 595, 608.
column base. 160.
column crank. 359.
column lock. 359.
column of mercury. 597.
column radiator. 193.
coma. 31.
comb. 495.
comb. 676.
comb foundation. 99.
comb plate. 172.

combat aircraft. 691.
combination. 287.
combination lock. 340.
combination pliers. 277.
combination spanner. 248.
combine harvester. 155.
combs. 328.
combustion chamber. 390, 436, 692.
comet. 31.
comfort contoured handle. 331.
comma. 347, 350, 371.
command antenna. 57, 378.
command module. 442.
command station. 692.
command system. 692.
command transmission. 692.
commander's seat. 690.
commando knife. 678.
commissure of lips of mouth. 126.
common coastal features. 43.
common extensor of fingers. 111.
common hepatic artery. 117.
common iliac artery. 117, 120.
common iliac vein. 120.
common mussel. 94.
common periwinkle. 96.
common peroneal nerve. 121.
common symbols. 704, 705, 706, 707.
common whipping. 587.
communicating rami. 122.
communications. 343.
company number. 349.
compartment. 340, 578, 580.
Compass. 33, 536, 542.
compass card. 429, 610.
compass meridian line. 610.
compensating cables. 171.
competition ring. 552.
competitive course. 532.
competitor. 532.
completion. 587.
complex dune. 47.
complexus. 111.
compluvium. 163.
composite topmark. 430.
composite window. 189.
compound eye. 92, 98.
compound fleshy fruits. 66.
compound leaves. 62.
compressed air. 625.
compressed-air cylinder. 536, 662.
compression coupling. 260.
compression fitting. 264.
compressor. 194, 229, 390, 450.
compressor turbine. 390.
computer:control/alarm. 652.
computer room. 458.
concave. 155, 610.
concha. 124.
conchigliette. 137.
Concorde. 39.
concrete. 184.
concrete base. 602.
concrete block. 183.
concrete dam, cross section of a. 638.
concrete drain. 633.
concrete pressure vessel. 650.
concrete shield. 650, 651.
concrete wall. 655.
condensation. 50.
condenser. 196, 361, 362, 605, 647, 648, 649.
condenser adjustment knob. 605.
condenser coil. 196, 229.
condensor. 194.
conductive material. 656.
conductor. 211.
conductor's podium. 479.
cone. 45, 363, 430.
configuration keys. 456.
conical broach roof. 181.
conical buoy. 430.

conical magnet. 592.
conical snoot. 358.
conical washer. 258.
conjunctiva. 123.
connecting cable. 363.
connecting wire. 562.
connection and concentration equipment network. 379.
connection cable. 363.
connection point. 645.
connective tissue. 127, 128.
connector link. 544.
conning tower. 423.
console. 467.
constellations. 698.
constellations of the northern hemisphere. 32.
constellations of the southern hemisphere. 33.
constriction. 597.
contact. 597.
contact printer. 360.
container. 411.
container. 56, 225, 270, 420.
container flat wagon. 406.
container hold. 420.
container-loading bridge. 427.
container ship. 420.
container ship. 427.
container terminal. 427.
containment. 652.
containment building. 648.
contest area. 564.
contestant. 564.
Continental cheeses. 145.
continental climates. 51.
continental margin. 42.
continental mass. 42.
continental plate. 42.
continental rise. 42.
continental shelf. 40, 42.
continental slope. 40, 42.
continents, configuration of the. 41.
continuity tester. 276.
continuous beam. 400.
continuous drizzle. 52.
continuous rain. 52.
continuous snow. 52.
contour feather. 88.
contrabassoon. 479.
contrast control. 377.
contre-filet. 141.
control bar. 543.
control cable. 398.
control column. 437, 441.
control console. 35, 458.
control key. 456.
control knob. 228, 457, 506.
control lever. 625.
control panel. 196, 227, 228, 231, 232, 374, 375, 376, 457, 662.
control rod. 648, 650, 651.
control room. 35.
control room. 35, 424, 431, 629, 637, 646, 648.
control stand. 404.
control stick. 542.
control system. 658.
control tower. 438.
control valve. 585, 649.
controller. 171, 172.
controls. 371.
convection zone. 29.
convector. 193.
conventional grip. 550.
converging lens. 610.
convertible. 384.
convex. 610.
conveyor. 621, 624, 636.
conveyor belt. 647.
cook's knife. 217.
cooking. 586.
cooking set. 585.
cooking surface. 227.
cooking utensils. 222, 223.

cool box. 586.
cool sodium. 651.
cool tip. 331.
coolant. 654, 656.
cooling air. 444.
cooling fan. 362, 390, 391, 392.
cooling/heating coils. 194.
cooling liquid pump. 444.
cooling pond. 648.
cooling tower. 634.
cooling water. 649.
copper foil. 507.
copper pipe. 264.
copper to plastic. 265.
copper to steel. 265.
copperplate. 501.
copy holder. 371.
copyright. 708.
cor anglais. 469, 479.
corbel. 167.
corbel piece. 190.
cord. 372, 499, 574.
cord grip. 558.
cord tieback. 207.
cordate. 62.
cordless shoe care kit. 310.
cordless telephone. 373.
core. 29, 68, 573, 587, 638, 688.
corer. 221.
corinthian order. 160.
cork tip. 526.
corkscrew. 585.
corn cutter. 332.
corn salad. 74.
cornea. 123.
corner. 498, 565.
corner arc. 511.
corner cap. 405.
corner cupboard. 206.
corner display cabinet. 206.
corner fitting. 411.
corner flag. 511, 516.
corner lighting. 210.
corner pad. 565.
corner pin. 530.
corner stay. 581.
corner-stool. 565.
corner structure. 411.
corner stud. 182.
corner tower. 167.
cornet. 470, 477.
cornets. 479.
cornice. 161, 177, 188, 205.
corolla. 64.
corona. 29.
coronal suture. 114.
coronet. 83, 85.
corpus callosum. 122.
corpus cavernosum. 108.
correct a letter. 350.
correct a word. 350.
correcting tape. 452.
correction fluid. 447.
correction paper. 447.
corrections of diacritic symbols. 350.
corrections of errors. 350.
corrections of punctuation marks. 350.
corrections of type. 350.
corridor. 407.
corridor connection. 407.
corrugation. 363.
corselette. 302.
corset. 303.
corssbar. 473.
cortex. 120, 129.
corymb. 64.
cos lettuce. 74.
cosmetic sponge. 323.
cosmetic tray. 337.
costal shield. 101.
costumes. 311.
côtelettes découvertes. 143.
côtelettes premières et secondes. 143.

côtes. 142.
côtes découvertes. 139.
cottage. 173.
Cottage cheese. 144.
cottage curtain. 207.
cottage loaf. 138.
cotton applicators. 615.
cotton pads. 675.
cotton wool ball. 615.
cotyledon. 61, 67, 71.
couched stitches. 493.
couches. 201.
coulter. 153.
counter. 308, 548.
counter memory button. 367.
counter reset button. 366.
counterguard. 166.
counterjib. 669.
counterjib ballast. 669.
counterscarp. 166.
countersink. 250.
countersunk. 254.
counterweight. 171, 365, 403, 408, 409, 596, 608, 667, 669.
counterweight guide rail. 171.
coupé. 384.
coupler head. 405.
coupler knuckle. 405.
coupler knuckle pin. 405.
courgette. 73.
course (golf). 571.
court. 309.
court (badminton). 526.
court (basketball). 523.
court (netball). 522.
court (squash). 527.
court (tennis). 524.
court (volleyball). 529.
couscous kettle. 222.
cousins. 130.
couter. 676.
cover. 336.
cover. 226, 259, 261, 335, 341, 521, 573, 597, 601, 610, 687.
cover plate. 656.
cover point. 514.
cover slip. 605.
covered parapet walk. 167.
covered postern. 166.
covered way. 166.
covering. 500.
covering. 528.
covering disc. 154.
cow hitch. 587.
cowl. 192.
cowl collar. 298.
Cowper's gland. 108.
cowshed. 151.
coxa. 92, 98.
coxed four. 541.
coxed pair. 541.
coxless four. 541.
coxless pair. 541.
Crab. 32, 95.
cradle. 209, 372, 608, 609, 684.
crak rye bread. 138.
crampon strap. 575.
crampons. 575.
cranberry. 66.
crane. 669.
Crane. 33, 34, 629.
crane runway. 669.
cranial nerves. 121.
crank. 250, 398, 426, 566.
crank handle. 503.
crankcase. 395.
crash helmet. 545, 549.
crater. 30, 45, 621.
cravat. 285.
crawl swimmer. 533.
crawler crane. 669.
crawler tractor. 664.
crayfish. 95.
crazy paving. 237.
cream blush. 322.
cream jug. 213.

cream lipstick. 322.
crease. 284, 515.
creative leisure activities. 483.
credit card wallet. 341.
creel. 568.
cremaster. 92.
crenate. 62.
crenel. 167.
crenulate margin. 93.
crepe support. 615.
crepidoma. 161.
crescent. 696.
crescentic dune. 47.
crest. 43, 46.
crest of spillway. 637.
crest-to-crest wave length. 43.
crevasse. 48.
crevice tool. 234.
crew cut. 321.
crew neck. 305.
crew neck sweater. 286.
crew quarters. 419.
crew sweater. 297.
cribriform plate of ethmoid. 125.
cricket. 514, 515.
cricket player. 515.
crimper. 277.
crinoline stretcher. 203.
crisper. 229.
crisscross curtains. 207.
crochet hook. 490.
croissant. 138.
crook. 469, 474.
crop elevator. 155.
cross. 696.
cross arm. 644.
cross brace. 617.
cross cut. 622, 623.
cross-guard. 679.
cross handle. 580.
cross head (Phillips). 254.
cross-ply tyre. 393.
cross poles. 552.
cross rail. 203.
cross stitches group. 493.
cross stretcher. 203.
crossarm. 645.
crossbar. 152, 397, 495, 499, 512, 531, 543, 547, 556, 557.
crossbeam. 494.
crossbow. 677.
crossbow. 677.
crosse. 139, 141, 142.
crosses. 707.
crosshead. 670.
crossing. 164, 413.
crossing gate mechanism. 409.
crossover. 410.
crossover back straps dungarees. 306.
crossover cargo deck line. 631.
crosspiece. 199, 494.
crosstree. 538.
crosswise grain. 488.
crotch. 287.
crotch piece. 295.
crotchet. 461.
crotchet rest. 461.
croup. 83, 559.
Crow. 33.
crown. 63, 87, 115, 288, 304, 317, 433, 506, 591.
crown block. 626.
crown tine. 81.
crownpiece. 553.
crude oil. 635.
crude oil pipeline. 630.
crus of helix. 124.
crustaceans. 95.
crutch. 593.
crutch tip. 616.
crutches. 616.
crystal button. 210.
crystal drop. 210.
cubiculum. 163.

The terms in **bold type** indicate the title of an illustration.

cubital vein. 117.
cucumber. 73.
cue. 568.
cue ball. 569.
cue screen. 376.
cuff. 285, 308.
cuirass. 675.
cuisse. 676.
cuisseau. 139.
culet. 317.
culotte. 141, 293.
cultivated mushroom. 65.
cultivator. 153.
cumulonimbus. 44.
cumulus. 44.
Cup. 33, 213, 372, 571, 585, 688.
cup conveyor. 154.
cupboard. 178, 206.
cupola. 431, 690.
cupule. 70.
curb bit. 553.
curb chain. 553.
curb rein. 553.
curled endive. 74.
curled kale. 74.
curling brush. 331.
curling iron. 331.
curly hair. 320.
curly lasagna. 136.
currant. 66.
currency exchange. 706.
currency exchange counter. 440.
current coil. 601.
cursor. 457.
cursor movement keys. 456.
curtain. 207.
curtain. 166.
curtain pole. 208.
curtain track. 208.
curved handrail. 187.
curved jaw. 249.
cushion. 548, 569, 576.
custard tart. 155.
customer's service entrance. 645.
customs control. 440.
customs house. 427.
cut. 170.
cut off trench. 638.
cut-out button. 396.
cut ribbed macaroni. 137.
cut-throat razor. 327.
cutaway armhole. 296.
cuticle. 129.
cuticle knife. 332.
cuticle pliers. 332.
cuticle pusher. 332.
cuticle scissors. 332.
cutlery basket. 232.
cutter bar. 155.
cutter link. 243.
cutting blade. 225, 499.
cutting cylinder. 242.
cutting edge. 214, 217, 328, 664, 668.
cutting guide. 499.
cutting line. 489.
cutting nozzle. 272.
cutting oxygen handle. 272.
cutting torch. 272.
cutting wheel. 233.
cyclists. 701.
cyclorama. 375.
cylinder. 256, 395, 504, 625, 667, 689.
cylinder blade lift. 666.
cylinder cam. 689.
cylinder-head. 395.
cylinder hole. 256.
cylinder lock. 256.
cylinder pressure gauge. 272.
cylinder wall. 649.
cylindrical parabolic reflector. 656.
cymbals. 471.
cymbals. 477.
cymbals, triangle, castanets. 479.

cytoplasm. 105.

D

[D]. 569.
dabber. 502.
dado rail. 187.
dagger. 675, 678.
daggerboard. 537.
daggerboard well. 537.
daggers. 678.
dairy. 151.
dairy compartment. 229.
dam. 637, 646.
damp proof course. 177.
damp proof membrane. 186.
damper. 190, 192, 466, 596.
damper lever. 466.
damper rail. 466.
dams, major types of. 639.
dandelion. 74.
danger, electrical hazard. 704.
danger, flammable. 704.
danger, poison. 704.
danger area. 564.
danger warning signs. 700, 701.
dangerous bend. 700.
dangerous descent. 700.
Danish Blue (Denmark). 145.
Danish rye bread. 138.
Danish writing style. 345.
darkroom. 360.
dart. 550.
dart. 489.
dartboard. 550.
darts. 550.
dash. 347, 371.
dashboard. 385.
dasher. 226.
data acquisition. 454.
data display. 454.
data processing. 454.
data processing devices. 454.
data recording on RAM* memory. 454.
data storage. 454.
date. 67.
dateline. 349.
dater. 448.
dating nail. 408.
daughter. 130.
daughter-in-law. 131.
davit. 416.
daylight filter control. 368.
dead ball line. 512.
dead bolt. 256.
dead bowl area. 530.
deadly mushroom. 65.
deaf-mute alphabet. 347.
death. 708.
decanter. 212.
deck. 400, 401, 402.
deck arch bridge. 401.
declination. 27.
declination axis. 34.
declination circle. 608.
decorative sheet. 255.
deep-fat fryer. 223.
deep fine leg. 514.
deep peroneal nerve. 121.
deep-sea floor. 40.
deer, kinds of. 81.
deer antlers. 81.
deer family. 81.
deerstalker. 288.
defending zone. 517.
defensive. 518.
defrost heater. 229.
defrost timer. 229.
dehumidifier. 196.
dehumidifier. 444.
Deimos. 37.
delay indicator. 413.
delete. 350.
delicious lactarius. 65.

delivery. 530.
delivery. 530.
delta wing. 435.
deltoid. 110.
deluxe suite. 419.
demi-semi-quaver. 461.
demi-semi-quaver rest. 461.
demi-tasse. 213.
demilune. 166.
denominations. 49.
dental alveolus. 115.
dental floss. 329.
dentate. 62.
dentil. 160.
dentine. 115.
department store. 168.
departure time indicator. 413.
departures concourse. 440.
departures room. 440.
departures timetable. 412.
deposit. 621.
depth gauge. 423, 536.
depth-of-field scale. 355.
depth of focus. 45.
depth stop. 251.
deputy sound supervisor. 374.
Derby. 144.
dermal papilla. 127, 128.
dermis. 127, 128, 129.
derrick. 626, 629.
desasphalting. 634.
descendeur. 574.
descending aorta. 116.
descending colon. 119.
desert. 47.
desert. 51.
desk lamp. 211.
desk pad. 450.
desk tray. 448.
despin. 379.
dessert fork. 215.
dessert knife. 214.
dessert spoon. 216.
desserts. 146, 147.
dessus de côtes. 139, 141.
destination indicator. 413.
detachable control. 227.
detachable handle. 191.
detached house. 173.
detergent dispenser. 232.
detonator. 682.
developer bath. 360.
developing film. 356.
developing tank. 360.
dew cap. 609.
dew claw. 86.
dew pad. 86.
dewaxing. 634.
dexter. 695.
dexter base. 695.
dexter chief. 695.
dexter flank. 695.
diacritic symbols. 347.
diagonal. 577, 644.
diagonal buttress. 165.
diagram of a circuit. 370.
dial. 371, 372, 591, 592, 593, 595, 596, 597, 598, 599, 601.
dial-type display. 428.
diamond. 578.
diamond head. 507.
diamond mesh expanded metal lath. 184.
diamond point. 205.
diaphragm. 118, 119, 353, 363, 369, 372.
diaphram. 372.
diastema. 82.
dibber. 239.
dice. 579.
dice. 578.
dice cup. 578.
diesel-electric locomotive. 404.
diesel engine. 390.
diesel engine. 404, 422, 665.

diesel oil. 635.
diesel shop. 410.
diffuser. 358.
diffuser filter set. 358.
diffusion pump. 606.
digestive gland. 94.
digestive system. 119.
digging fork. 238.
digit. 86, 97.
digital clock. 367.
digital display. 591.
digital frequency display. 364.
digital nerve. 121.
digital pad. 86.
digital pulp. 129.
dill. 135.
diluent. 636.
diluent recovery. 636.
dimple. 573.
dinghy. 538.
dining car. 407.
dining room. 179, 419, 420.
dining section. 407.
dinner fork. 215.
dinner knife. 214.
dinner plate. 213.
dinnerware. 213.
dioptric ring. 432.
dip. 622.
dip switch. 386, 396.
diphthongs. 348.
dipper bucket. 667.
direct-reading rain gauge. 56.
direction in orbit. 57.
direction to be followed. 703.
directional sign. 414.
director/producer. 376.
director's chair. 201.
disc. 356, 393, 503, 547, 561, 601.
disc brake. 393.
disc brake. 395, 658.
disc camera. 354.
disc seat. 261.
disc seat ring. 261.
discharge line. 267.
discharge liner. 643.
discharge pipe. 632.
discharge pump. 632.
discharge spout. 152, 153.
discs. 226.
discus. 558.
discus throw. 556.
disgorger. 568.
dishwasher. 232.
disk. 458.
disk. 455.
disk control unit. 458.
disk drive. 455, 458.
disk storage. 458.
dispatch area. 634.
display. 596.
display cabinet. 451.
disposable gas cylinder. 271.
disposable razor. 327.
disposable syringe. 615.
distal phalanx. 86, 112, 113, 129.
distal sesamoid. 84.
distance. 318, 555.
distance scale. 355.
distance tube. 686.
distribution board. 645.
distribution field. 267.
distributor. 391.
distributor service loop. 645.
ditali. 137.
ditch. 530.
diver. 535.
diver lockout compartment. 423.
diverging lens. 610.
diversion canal. 637.
diversity of jewellery. 315.
diverter valve. 259.
dives, groups of. 535.
divider. 155, 337, 340, 449.
dividing breeching. 662.
diving. 534.

The terms in **bold type** indicate the title of an illustration.

diving goggles. 319.
diving installations. 534.
division. 708.
divot. 571.
do not enter. 704.
do not use for wheelchairs. 705.
do not use luggage trolleys. 706.
document folder. 449.
dog ear collar. 298.
dog tag. 315.
Dolby noise reduction switch. 366.
dollar. 708.
Dolphin. 32, 680.
dome roof. 181.
dome shutter. 34.
dome tent. 583.
domestic appliances. 225, 226, 227, 228, 229, 230, 231, 232, 233, 234.
domestic sink. 262.
domino. 579.
dominoes. 579.
door. 188, 386.
door. 205, 227, 230, 231, 383, 527.
door for driver and courier. 394.
door gasket. 230.
door handle. 383.
door hasp. 405.
door hasp fastener. 405.
door lock. 383.
door mirror. 383, 389.
door operator. 171.
door panel. 205, 415.
door pillar. 383.
door shelf. 229.
door stop. 229, 405.
door switch. 231.
doorknob. 188.
doors, types of. 188.
doorstep. 177.
doric order. 160.
dormant volcano. 45.
dorsal aorta. 91.
dorsal view. 93.
dorsum of nose. 125.
dorsum of tongue. 126.
dot. 371.
dot matrix printer. 457.
double. 552.
double barrel. 688.
double bass. 463, 477.
double basses. 479.
double bend. 700.
double-blank. 579.
double boiler. 222.
double-bowl kitchen sink. 257.
double-breasted buttoning. 281, 291.
double-breasted jacket. 283.
double chair lift. 547.
double-condenser pole piece. 606.
double cuff. 296.
double curtain rod. 208.
double-decked pallet. 671.
double-edge blade. 327.
double-edge razor. 327.
double-edged swords. 678.
double flat. 462.
double flow turbine. 649.
double fluked anchor. 433.
double glazed window. 581.
double glazing. 655.
Double Gloucester. 144.
double handles. 540.
double-leaf bascule bridge. 403.
double oxer. 551, 552.
double pennant. 697.
double reed. 469, 474.
double scull. 541.
double seat. 415.
double sharp. 462.
double sheet bend. 587.
double-six. 579.
double-twist auger bit. 250.
doubles pole. 524.

doubles ring. 550.
doubles service court. 526.
doubles sideline. 524, 526.
doublet. 579.
doubling cube. 578.
doubly dentate. 62.
dough hook. 225.
doughnut. 146.
douzaines. 580.
Dove. 33.
dovetail. 607.
dowel hole. 318.
down. 178.
down tube. 397.
down wind. 539.
downhaul. 537.
downstream face. 638.
downstream shoulder. 638.
downstream toe. 638.
draft arm. 668.
draft pipe. 668.
draft tube. 641, 643, 668.
drag. 566.
drag chain. 661.
drag drum. 661.
drag rope. 661.
dragline. 661.
dragline. 636.
Dragon. 32.
drain. 168, 262.
drain cock. 633.
drain filter. 230.
drain hose. 232, 262.
drain line. 194.
drain pan. 229.
drain pump. 230.
drain trap. 260.
drain valve. 194, 263, 633.
drainage blanket. 638.
drainage layer. 638.
draining spoon. 219.
draped neck. 299.
draped neckline. 299.
draw curtain. 207.
draw hoe. 238.
draw tube. 605.
drawbar. 664, 666, 684.
drawbar lock. 684.
drawbridge. 167.
drawer. 199, 206, 450.
drawstring. 282, 311, 339.
drawstring bag. 339.
drawstring hood. 307.
drawtube. 609.
drawworks. 626.
dress. 305.
dresses. 292.
dressing gown. 301.
dressing table. 206.
dressmaker's model. 487.
drift. 622, 623.
drifting snow. 52.
drill. 250.
drill collar. 626.
drill pipe. 626.
drill rod. 625.
drill ship. 628.
drilling barge. 628.
drilling rig. 626.
drip bowl. 229.
drip moulding. 383.
drivage. 623.
drive axle. 670.
drive belt. 231, 365.
drive chain. 397.
drive coil. 592.
drive coil and phase-sensing coil. 592.
drive mechanism. 432.
drive shaft. 152, 441.
drive sheave. 171.
drive wheel. 233, 250, 666, 690.
driver. 572.
driver's cab. 404.
driver's seat. 690.
driveway. 178.
driving glove. 289.

driving iron. 572.
driving turbine. 390.
driving wheel. 496.
drone. 98.
drone. 474.
drop earring. 315.
drop-leaf. 199.
drop light. 211.
drop waist dress. 292.
drum. 160, 209, 226, 230, 231, 393, 593.
drum brake. 393.
drum kit. 477.
drum motor. 230.
druplet. 66.
dry-cell water alarm. 423.
dry continental - arid. 51.
dry continental - semiarid. 51.
dry dock. 427.
dry fruits. 70, 71.
dry gallery pot hole. 46.
dry mounting press. 360.
dry-point. 501, 503.
dry snow. 49.
dry subtropical. 51.
dual seat. 395.
dual swivel mirror. 330.
dual voltage selector switch. 330.
duct. 128.
duct deferens. 108.
duffle coat. 282.
dump. 621, 624.
dump rope. 661.
dumper truck. 668.
dune. 43.
dungarees. 300.
Dunlop. 144.
duo. 476.
duodenum. 119.
duplexer. 611.
dura mater of spinal cord. 122.
dural cul-de-sac. 122.
dust cover. 365.
dust storm. 52.
dust tail. 31.
dusting brush. 234.
Dutch hoe. 238.
Dutch oven. 222.
Dutch writing style. 345.
duty-free counter. 440.
duty-free shop. 706.
dyke. 45.
dynamic microphone. 369.
dynamics propeller. 421.
dynamo. 397.

E

Eagle. 32, 33, 696.
ear. 100, 106, 107, 203, 468.
ear cushion. 363.
ear drum. 97, 124.
ear loaf. 138.
ear syringe. 615.
earphone jack. 377.
earpiece. 318, 372.
Earth. 28, 29, 30, 370, 378, 639.
Earth, structure of the. 39.
earth clamp. 271.
Earth co-ordinate system. 27.
earth green and yellow wire. 275.
earth lead. 365.
Earth's atmosphere, profile of the. 39.
Earth's crust. 39, 45.
Earth's crust, section of the. 40.
earth sensor. 378.
earthquake. 45.
easel. 361.
easel. 360.
east. 430, 579.
east-west axis. 35.
East wind. 579.
eaves. 177.
eccrine sweat gland. 128.

échine. 142.
echinus. 160.
echo. 611.
echo sounder. 428.
economizer. 647.
Edam (Dutch). 145.
edge. 255, 487, 545, 548, 549, 610.
edging. 237.
edible gyromitra. 65.
edible mushrooms. 65.
egg. 89.
egg. 99.
egg beater. 220.
egg poacher. 223.
egg slicer. 221.
egg timer. 219.
egg tray. 229.
eggs. 91, 97.
eiderdown. 204.
eight. 541.
eight cut. 317.
ejaculatory duct. 108.
eject. 367.
eject button. 366.
ejection port. 683, 685, 687.
ejection seat. 691.
elastic. 204.
elastic ankle. 307.
elastic coupling. 631.
elastic leg opening. 305.
elastic ligament. 86, 94.
elastic waistband. 305.
elastic webbing. 284.
elastic wristband. 307.
elasticized leg opening. 287.
elbow. 83, 100, 107, 191, 192, 193, 265.
elbow macaroni. 137.
elbow pad. 519, 549.
elbow protector. 562.
electric arc. 271.
electric cooker. 228.
electric current source. 370.
electric drill. 251.
electric element. 228.
electric foil. 562.
electric golf cart. 573.
electric grill. 227.
electric guitar. 480.
electric heating unit. 195.
electric kiln. 506.
electric motor. 172, 195, 356.
electric razor. 327.
electric supply. 194, 263.
electric tin-opener. 233.
electric toothbrush. 329.
electric water-heater tank. 263.
electrical connection. 388.
electrical distribution system. 652.
electrical pointe d'arrêt. 562.
electrical power unit. 439.
electrical scoring apparatus. 562.
electrically illuminated point signal. 409.
electrician's tools. 276, 277.
electricity. 274, 275, 276, 277, 637, 638, 639, 640, 641, 642, 643, 644, 645, 646.
electricity, steps in production of. 640.
electricity cable. 399.
electricity meter. 645.
electricity pylon. 624.
electrified fence. 151.
electrode. 271, 274, 372.
electrode assembly. 195.
electrode holder. 271.
electrode lead. 271.
electromagnet. 370.
electron beam. 377.
electron gun. 377, 606.
electron microscope. 606.
electronic circuit. 592.
electronic flash. 357.
electronic scales. 596.

The terms in **bold type** indicate the title of an illustration.

electronic viewfinder. 369.
electronic viewfinder display control. 369.
electrostatic precipitator. 647.
element. 392.
elevating handle. 683.
elevating handwheel. 684.
elevation adjusting screw. 607.
elevator. 152, 434, 542.
elevon. 443.
ellipsis. 347.
elliptical galaxy. 31.
elongating bar shot. 681.
embankment dam. 639.
embankment dam, cross section of an. 638, 639.
emblem. 383, 695.
embrasure. 166.
embroidery. 493.
embryo. 67.
emerald cut. 317.
emergency brake lever. 415.
emergency core cooling. 652.
emergency oxygen supply. 444.
emery board. 333.
emission chamber. 606.
Emmental (Swiss). 145.
empty set. 708.
emptying outlet. 633.
en prison. 580.
enamel. 115.
enamelled hardboard. 184.
encapsulant. 656.
end block. 481.
end bracket. 208, 209.
end cap. 208.
end door. 411.
end grain. 255.
end joist. 182.
end ladder. 405.
end line. 519, 523, 528, 529.
end of motorway. 703.
end of priority. 701.
end of the lap. 533.
end panel. 227.
end piece. 108, 568.
end pin. 463.
end stop. 208.
end wall. 532.
end zone. 519.
endocarp. 67, 68.
endoplasmic reticulum. 105.
endpaper. 498.
energy. 619.
engagement ring. 315.
engine. 391.
engine. 155, 573, 626, 664, 666, 667, 668.
engine air intake. 421.
engine block. 391.
engine housing. 243.
engine instruments. 437.
engine mounting pylon. 435.
engine room. 424, 425, 631.
engines. 390.
engines. 443.
English Cheddar. 144.
engraving tools. 501.
enlarger. 361.
enlarger. 360.
enlarger timer. 360.
enlarging lens. 361.
entablature. 160, 188.
entame de romsteck. 141.
enter key. 456.
entire. 62.
entrance. 99.
entrance slide. 99.
entrance turnstile. 414.
entrecôtes couvertes. 141.
entrecôtes découvertes. 141.
entries. 534.
entry. 535, 671.
épaule. 139, 143.
epaulet. 281, 311.
epaulet sleeve. 296.

épée. 563.
épéeist. 563.
epicalyx. 66.
epicentre. 45.
epicondyle. 113.
epidermicula. 129.
epidermis. 127, 128, 129.
epiglottis. 118, 126.
epitrochlea. 113.
eponychium. 129.
equalizer. 363.
equalizing buckle. 209.
equator. 27.
equilateral. 162.
equilibrator. 684.
equipment. 568.
equipment access shaft. 646.
erase button. 373.
eraser. 447.
erecting lenses. 607.
ermine. 696.
escalator. 172.
escalator. 414.
escalator, down. 705.
escalator, up. 705.
escape key. 456.
escape tower. 424.
escape wheel. 591, 593.
escapement mechanism. 478.
escutcheon. 93, 256, 260.
espadrille. 309.
espresso coffee maker. 224.
estate car. 384.
etching tools. 501.
étrier. 574.
euphonium. 470.
Europa. 28.
Europe. 41.
Eustachian tube. 124, 125.
euthynteria. 161.
evaporation. 50.
evaporator. 196.
evaporator coil. 229.
evaporator coils. 196.
even. 580.
evening glove. 289.
exclamation mark. 347.
executive chair. 451.
executive desk. 451.
exhaust cone. 436.
exhaust duct. 231, 436.
exhaust gas inlet pipe. 390.
exhaust gas outlet pipe. 390.
exhaust hose. 231.
exhaust manifold. 390, 391, 392.
exhaust nozzle. 436, 691.
exhaust pipe. 390, 436, 441, 664, 690.
exhaust port. 625.
exhaust stack. 389.
exhaust system. 392.
exhaust tube. 274.
exhaust valve. 390.
exit turnstile. 414.
exocarp. 66, 67, 68.
exosphere. 37.
expanding file. 449.
expansion bolt. 254.
expansion chamber. 429, 597.
expansion space. 408.
expansion tank. 193.
exploder. 686.
explosive. 682.
exposure control. 356.
exposure meter. 357.
exposure-time scale. 357.
exposure value. 357.
exposure value scale. 357.
extendable solar array. 378.
extended character keys. 456.
extended claw. 86.
extension ladder. 663.
extension ladder. 268.
extension pipe. 234.
extension table. 199.
exterior dome shell. 34.

exterior door. 188.
exterior pocket. 337, 340.
exterior sign. 414.
external acoustic meatus. 124.
external auditory meatus. 114.
external conductive coating. 377.
external ear. 124.
external ear. 124.
external gills. 97.
external iliac artery. 117.
external nose. 125.
external oblique. 110, 111.
external tank. 443.
external tooth lock washer. 254.
extra cover. 514.
extractor. 689.
extractor fan. 360.
extractor spring. 689.
extrados. 162.
eye. 123.
eye. 96, 97, 101, 106, 247, 486, 487, 495, 553, 566, 567, 574.
eye lens. 607.
eye ring. 87.
eye shield protector. 507.
eye-socket. 83.
eye stripe. 87.
eyeball. 123.
eyebrow. 123.
eyebrow pencil. 323.
eyebrow tweezers. 332.
eyecup. 368, 369.
eyecups. 355.
eyeglasses. 318, 319.
eyeglasses, principal types of. 319.
eyelash. 123.
eyelash curler. 323.
eyelashes. 86.
eyelet. 284, 308, 491, 548.
eyelet tab. 308.
eyelid. 101.
eyeliner. 322.
eyepiece. 356, 357, 605, 607, 608, 609.
eyepiece holder. 609.
eyepiece magnifier. 355.
eyeshadow. 322.
eyestalk. 96.
eyewash. 615.

F

F-1 engine. 442.
f clef. 461.
fabric guide. 233.
fabric structure. 488.
façade. 165.
face. 106, 166, 247, 341, 500, 507, 528, 572, 621.
face-off circle. 517.
face-off spot. 517.
face pipes. 467.
face ply. 255.
face-shield. 273.
face side. 255.
faceplate. 256, 377.
faces. 247.
facial nerve. 124.
facility telephone system. 373.
facing. 283.
faculae. 29.
fairlead. 539.
fairway. 571.
fall. 298.
falling. 564.
falling rocks. 700.
fallopian tube. 109.
false rib (3). 113.
false start rope. 532.
false tuck. 305.
family relationships. 130, 131.
family tent. 583.
family tents. 582.

fan. 194, 195, 196, 229, 231, 415, 436, 624.
fan belt. 391, 392.
fan blade. 436.
fan brush. 323.
fan cable stays. 402.
fan control. 196.
fan housing. 330.
fan motor. 196.
fan stout. 481.
fan trellis. 237.
fang. 101.
fanion. 697.
fantail. 657.
far side. 30.
farfalline. 137.
farmhouse. 151.
farming. 149.
farmyard. 151.
fascia. 160.
fast forward. 367.
fast-forward button. 366, 373.
fast reactor. 651.
fastener binder. 449.
fasteners. 488.
fastening screw. 357.
father. 130, 131.
father-in-law. 131.
fault. 40, 45, 622.
fax machine. 379.
feather crown. 526.
feather fletching. 570, 677.
feather stitch. 493.
fedelini. 136.
feed cover. 687.
feed dog. 486.
feed heater. 647.
feed lever. 251.
feed pin. 457.
feed tray. 687.
feed tube. 226, 352.
feeding dial. 491.
feet. 464, 500.
feet, principal types of. 89.
feet-first entry. 534.
felt hat. 288.
female. 708.
female ferrule. 566.
female genital organs. 109.
femoral artery. 117.
femoral nerve. 121.
femoral vein. 117.
femur. 84, 92, 97, 98, 100, 112.
fencer. 562.
fencing. 562, 563.
fencing shoe. 562.
fencing weapons. 563.
fennel. 77.
ferrule. 214, 270, 328, 336, 568, 572.
ferryboat. 427.
fertilizer distributor. 154.
fess point. 695.
Feta (Greek). 145.
fetlock. 83.
fetlock joint. 83.
fettling knife. 505.
fibre. 587.
fibula. 112.
field (American football). 519.
field (baseball). 520.
field (cricket). 514.
field (hockey). 516.
field (rugby). 512.
field events. 558.
field heap spreader. 154.
field lens. 607.
field lenses. 607.
fielder. 515.
fiffi hook. 574.
fifth. 462.
fifth wheel. 389.
figure-eight knot. 587.
figure skate. 548.
figure ski. 540.
figure skiing handle. 540.

The terms in **bold type** indicate the title of an illustration.

filament. 29, 64, 274, 606.
file. 577, 585.
file guides. 449.
filet. 142, 143.
filing box. 448.
fill. 638.
fill opening. 233.
filler. 334.
filler hole. 391.
filler neck. 389.
filler plug. 429.
filler rod. 272.
filler tube. 258.
fillet. 140, 160.
filleting knife. 217.
filling hole. 682.
filling inlet. 633.
film advance lever. 353.
film drying cabinet. 360.
film footage counter. 368.
film leader. 356.
film-pack. 356.
film path. 368.
film take-up spool. 353.
film transport sprocket. 353.
filming trigger. 369.
films. 356.
filter. 194, 195, 223, 224, 335, 638, 655, 661.
filter basket. 224.
filter coffee maker. 224.
filter drawer. 361.
filter tip. 334.
fin. 421, 434, 441, 536, 540, 692.
fin-mounted tail unit. 435.
fin tip. 691.
final limit cam. 171.
final limit switch. 171.
finder. 608, 609.
fine adjustment knob. 605.
fine bookbinding. 498, 499, 500.
fine focus sleeve. 609.
fine tuning knob. 377.
finger. 152, 521.
finger button. 470.
finger hole. 576.
finger stop. 372.
fingerboard. 463, 473, 480, 481.
fingerless mitt. 289.
fingerwaves. 320.
finial. 409, 695.
finish. 552.
finish line. 557.
finished product storage. 634.
finishing post. 555, 557.
finned tube. 193.
Finnish writing style. 345.
fire appliance. 662, 663.
fire control lever. 685.
fire-dog. 191.
fire extinguisher. 704.
fire hose. 662, 704.
fire irons. 191.
fire station. 634.
firebox. 191.
firebrick. 195.
firebrick back. 190.
fireman's axe. 662.
fireplace. 190.
fireplace. 178.
firestopping. 182.
firing. 506.
firing, accessories for. 681.
firing chamber. 688.
firing lanyard. 684.
firing pin. 688.
firing pine. 689.
firing rod. 686.
firing shaft. 684.
firn. 48.
first aid. 704.
first aid kit. 615.
first base. 520.
first baseman. 520.
first condenser lens. 606.
first dorsal fin. 90.

first extension ladder. 662.
first floor. 178, 179.
first molar. 115.
first officer's seat. 437.
first premolar. 115.
first quarter. 30.
first reinforce. 680.
first reinforce ring. 680.
first slip. 514.
first space. 523.
first stage. 442.
first violins. 479.
fish. 90, 91.
fish-eye lens. 35, 355.
fish fork. 215.
fish kettle. 222.
fish knife. 214.
fish platter. 213.
fish slice. 219.
fishbone stitch. 493.
fisherman's knot. 587.
Fishes. 32.
fishhook. 567.
fishing. 566, 567, 568.
fishing vest. 568.
fishnet tights. 301.
fishplate. 408.
fishplate bolt. 408.
fitted coupling bolt. 643.
fitted sheet. 204.
fitting. 264.
fittings. 265.
fittings. 337.
fixed arch. 401.
fixed blade. 499.
fixed bridges. 400, 401, 402.
fixed distance marking. 438.
fixed jaw. 248, 249.
fixed platform. 628.
fixed-roof tank. 633.
fixed stairs. 414.
fixed weight. 478.
fixing bath. 360.
fixtures. 539.
flag. 695.
flag. 512, 529, 547.
flag, parts of a. 695.
flag shapes. 697.
flagstick. 571.
flame adjustment wheel. 334.
flame spreader tip. 271.
flammule. 697.
flan tin. 220.
flanchet. 141.
flange. 258.
flange bolt. 258.
flange nut. 264.
flank. 83, 87, 166, 500.
flanker. 513.
flanking tower. 167.
flap. 339, 341, 553, 691.
flap guide rail. 435.
flap hydraulic jack. 691.
flap pocket. 282, 283, 294.
flap servo actuator. 422.
flap side pocket. 283.
flapover bag. 338.
flare. 29, 629, 634.
flare joint. 264.
flare nut. 264.
flash. 358.
flash bracket. 357.
flash deflector. 686.
flash hider. 685, 687.
flash lamp. 357.
flash meter. 358.
flash outlet. 357.
flash sensor. 357.
flash socket. 368.
flash synchronization terminal. 353.
flash umbrella. 358.
flash unit. 357.
flashbar socket. 356.
flashcube. 357.
flashing. 177, 192.
flashing light. 409.

flat. 462.
flat-back brush. 328.
flat-bed. 485.
flat end pin. 209.
flat mirror. 34, 608.
flat part. 490.
flat plate solar collector. 656.
flat pleat. 207.
flat roof. 180.
flat sheet. 204.
flat side of the grip. 525.
flat spike. 574.
flat stitches group. 493.
flat washer. 254.
flesh. 66, 67, 68.
fleshy fruits: berry fruits. 66.
fleshy fruits: citrus fruits. 69.
fleur-de-lis. 696.
flex. 210, 211, 233, 275.
flexible hose. 234, 259, 625.
flexible hose connection. 625.
flexible rubber hose. 262.
flexible skirt. 421.
flies. 170.
flight. 165, 535, 550, 560.
flight bag. 337.
flight deck. 437.
flight deck. 434, 441, 443.
flight engineer's panel. 437.
flight engineer's seat. 437.
flight information board. 440.
flight instruments. 543.
flight of stairs. 187.
flights. 534.
flint. 273, 682.
flint arrowhead. 675.
flint knife. 675.
flintlock. 682.
flip-flop. 309.
flip turn. 533.
float. 567.
float. 258, 267, 429, 684.
float clamp. 267.
floating bridge. 403.
floating crane. 427.
floating dock. 427.
floating head. 327.
floating platform. 628.
floating rib. 112.
floating roof. 633.
floating-roof tank. 633.
floodlight. 375.
floor. 182, 527, 621, 622, 657.
floor board. 186.
floor brush. 234.
floor crew. 375.
floor joist. 182.
floor manager. 375.
floor selector. 171.
floor tile. 185.
floorboard. 186.
flow bean. 627.
flower. 61.
flower, structure of a. 64.
flower bed. 237.
flower bud. 61.
flower tiles. 579.
flue. 468.
flue collar. 191.
flue damper. 191.
flue pipe. 468.
flue pipe. 191.
fluff trap. 231.
fluid adjustment screw. 270.
fluid coking plant. 634.
fluid inlet. 656.
fluid outlet. 656.
fluke. 433.
fluorescent screen. 606.
fluorescent tube. 274.
flush. 578.
flush bushing. 265.
flush door. 178.
flush handle. 259.
flute. 250, 469, 476.
fluted land. 250.

fluted pole. 208.
flutes. 479.
fluting. 160.
flux. 507.
flux brush. 507.
Fly. 33, 284, 287, 695.
fly agaric. 65.
fly box. 568.
fly front closing. 290.
fly half. 512.
fly line. 566.
fly reel. 566.
fly rod. 566.
flying buttress. 164, 165.
Flying Fish. 33.
flying instruments. 437.
flying jib. 417.
flyleaf. 498.
flysheet. 583.
flywheel. 390, 391, 505.
FM mode selector. 364.
FM stereo indicator. 364.
foam. 43.
foam insulation. 185.
foam mattress. 584.
foam monitor. 631.
foam pad. 584.
foam rubber insulation. 185.
foam windscreen. 369.
focal plane shutter. 353.
focus. 45.
focus knob. 609.
focus magnifier. 361.
focus setting ring. 369.
focusing. 654.
focusing control. 368.
focusing knob. 361, 362, 608.
focusing magnifier. 360.
focusing ring. 355, 368, 607.
focusing sleeve. 600.
fog. 52.
fog light. 389.
foible. 563.
foil. 563.
foil warning line. 562.
foilist. 563.
fold line. 294, 489.
fold-out table. 407.
foldback clip. 447.
folder. 449.
folding. 188.
folding camera. 354.
folding camp bed. 584.
folding chair. 203.
folding grill. 586.
folding nail file. 333.
folding shovel. 586.
folding sliding door. 178.
foliage. 63.
follicle. 71.
follicle, section of a. 71.
follow-through. 530.
fondue fork. 215.
fondue pot. 223.
fondue set. 223.
food. 133.
food processor. 226.
foot. 87, 96, 100, 107, 205, 305, 306, 408, 468, 481, 537, 566.
foot brake pedal. 396.
foot control. 485.
foot fault judge. 524.
foot hole. 468.
foot pocket. 536.
foot rest. 505, 617.
foot rope. 416.
footboard. 204.
footbridge. 410, 414.
footing. 182.
footlights. 170.
footrest. 396, 547.
footstool. 202.
footstrap. 300.
footway. 399.
foramen caecum. 126.
foramen ovale. 114.

The terms in **bold type** indicate the title of an illustration.

forced draught fan. 647.
forced warm-air system. 192.
fore and aft gangway. 631.
fore court. 524.
fore edge. 498.
fore leg. 92, 98.
fore rib. 140.
fore royal sail. 417.
fore topmast staysail. 417.
fore wing. 92, 98.
forearm. 107, 687, 688.
forecourt. 387.
foregrip. 566.
forehead. 87, 106.
foreleg. 86.
forelimb. 97.
forelock. 83.
foremast. 416.
foresail. 417.
forestay. 538.
fork. 215.
fork. 81, 397, 585, 591, 593, 608,
    670.
fork extender. 670.
fork pocket. 411.
forked tongue. 101.
forklift trucks. 670.
forks. 670.
forks, major types of. 215.
form details. 555.
formation level. 399.
formeret. 165.
forming. 587.
forms. 49.
forte. 563.
forward. 534.
forward bolt assist mechanism.
    685.
forward dive. 535.
forward/reverse switch. 368.
forward short leg. 514.
forward swing. 530.
foul line. 520, 576.
foundation. 182, 639.
foundation of dam. 638.
foundation of tower. 402.
foundation slip. 302.
foundations. 182.
fountain pen. 352.
four blade beater. 225.
four-door saloon. 384.
four-foot. 415.
four-four time. 462.
four-masted bark. 416, 417.
four of a kind. 578.
fourchette. 289.
fourth. 462.
fourth wheel. 591.
fovea. 123.
fractionating tower. 635.
frame. 182, 493.
frame. 99, 249, 269, 336, 337,
    340, 395, 429, 471, 474, 494,
    503, 525, 527, 559, 560, 599,
    656, 657, 667, 668, 670.
frame counter. 353.
frame push. 664.
frame stile. 205.
framework. 432.
framing control. 368.
Francis turbine. 643.
franzipan. 146.
free fall. 544.
free margin. 129.
free-standing tanks. 631.
free throw lane. 523.
free throw line. 523.
freezer bucket. 226.
freezer compartment. 229.
freezer door. 229.
freezing rain. 52.
freight hold. 434.
freight station. 410.
freight wagons, types of. 406.
French cut. 317.
French horn. 470, 476, 477.

French horns. 479.
French knot stitch. 493.
French pleat. 321.
French roulette wheel. 580.
French sticks. 138.
French window. 189.
French writing style. 345.
fresh air inlet. 190.
fret. 473, 480, 481.
fricative consonants. 348.
friction strip. 335.
fridge-freezer. 229.
frieze. 160, 205.
frigate. 425.
frilly pants. 305.
fringe. 321.
fringe trimming. 207.
frog. 97.
frog. 85, 153, 282, 298, 408, 464.
frog, life cycle of the. 97.
front. 283, 285, 388.
front apron. 285.
front axle. 666.
front bearing. 436.
front binding. 540.
front board. 498.
front brake. 397.
front brake lever. 396.
front bumper. 383.
front crawl stroke. 533.
front derailleur. 397, 398.
front door. 177.
front-end loader. 665.
front flap. 335.
front foil. 422.
front footrest. 395.
front grip. 686.
front hose. 247.
front knob. 247.
front leg. 203.
front mudguard. 395.
front pipe. 392.
front point. 575.
front runner. 549.
front sight. 686, 688, 689.
front sight housing. 685, 687.
front sight protector. 683.
front spar. 435.
front tip. 233.
front top pocket. 300.
front wall. 527.
front wheel. 617, 666.
frontal. 110, 112.
frontal bone. 114.
frontal sinus. 125.
fronts. 53.
fruit flan. 147.
fruit loaf. 147.
fruit-picking ladder. 269.
fruit vegetables. 73.
frying pan. 223.
frying pan. 585.
fuel element. 650, 651.
fuel handling control console. 652.
fuel indicator. 385.
fuel injector pump. 390.
fuel pump belt. 390.
fuel spray manifold. 436.
fuel tank. 243, 389, 395, 422, 431,
    441, 692.
fuel tanker. 439.
fuel transfer pipe. 442.
fulcrum. 534.
full and by. 539.
full back. 512, 513.
full house. 578.
full-load adjustment screw. 601.
full Moon. 30.
full stop. 347, 350, 371.
fullback. 518.
fumarole. 45.
fume extractor. 690.
function keys. 456, 596.
function lever. 365.
function selector. 196.
funiculus. 66, 71.
funnel. 218, 377, 420.

funnel aileron. 419.
fur hood. 304.
Furnace. 33, 647, 654.
furs. 696.
fuse. 195, 275, 645.
fuse carrier. 275.
fuse cut-out. 645.
fuse holder. 645.
fuse pullers. 276.
fuselage. 434, 542.
fuselage mounted tail unit. 435.

G

G-clamp. 249.
g clef. 461.
G-meter. 542.
gable. 165.
gable-and-valley roof. 181.
gable roof. 180.
gaff sail. 418.
gaff topsail. 417.
gaiter. 545.
galaxy. 31.
gall bladder. 91, 119.
gallery. 165, 169, 431, 657.
galley. 434.
galosh. 310.
game timekeeper. 517.
gantry crane. 669.
gantry crane. 637, 641.
Ganymede. 28.
gap. 567.
garage. 177, 179, 419, 420.
garden. 237.
garden. 163, 178.
garden hose. 240.
garden light. 237.
garden line. 239.
garden sorrel. 74.
gardening. 235.
garlic. 75.
garlic press. 218.
garment bag. 337.
garment fabric. 488.
garment strap. 337.
garter. 302.
garter stitch. 490.
gas. 274, 626.
gas circulator. 648.
gas cylinder. 687.
gas exit port. 648.
gas inlet. 444.
gas lift. 627.
gas lift valve. 627.
gas lighter. 334.
gas main. 399.
gas oil. 635.
gas outlet. 444.
gas piston. 687.
gas tail. 31.
gas turbine. 421, 629.
gas under pressure. 627.
gasket. 228, 232, 261, 264.
gaskin. 83.
gasometer. 624.
gastrocnemius. 110, 111.
gastropods. 96.
gate. 547, 551, 552, 574, 641,
    646.
gate arm. 409.
gate arm lamp. 409.
gate arm support. 409.
gate-leg. 199.
gate-leg table. 199.
gate operating ring. 643.
gateau. 146.
gather. 295.
gather skirt. 293.
gathered heading. 207.
gathering. 498.
gauge. 499, 585.
gauntlet. 273, 289, 676.
gauze bandage. 561.
gauze roller bandage. 615.

gear. 496.
gear housing. 566.
gear selector. 397, 398.
gear train. 356.
gearbox. 422, 503, 658.
gearchange lever. 385.
gearchange pedal. 395, 396.
Gemini, the Twins. 698.
gemstones, cuts for. 317.
generator. 642.
generator. 641, 642, 647, 648,
    649, 652, 658.
genital pore. 96.
gentry bag. 339.
geography. 37.
geostationary orbit. 379.
geostationary orbit injection. 379.
germ. 71.
German rye bread. 138.
German writing style. 345.
geyser. 45.
gigot. 143.
gill. 65.
gill cover. 90.
gill filament. 90.
gill raker. 90.
gills. 90.
gills. 91, 94.
gimbal ring. 429.
Giraffe. 32.
girder. 34.
girdle. 303, 317.
girth. 553, 554.
girth strap. 553.
gîte à la noix. 141.
gîte de derrière. 141.
gîte de devant. 141.
give priority to vehicles from
    opposite direction. 702.
give way. 701.
glacial cirque. 48.
glacier. 48.
glacier tongue. 48.
glacis. 166.
gladius. 675.
glans penis. 108.
glass. 230, 517, 527.
glass bulb. 357, 592.
glass case. 595.
glass cover. 229.
glass curtain. 207.
glass cutter. 507.
glass cutting. 507.
glass dome. 429.
glass-fibre cloth. 444.
glass-fronted display cabinet. 206.
glass grinder. 507.
glass slide. 605.
glass sphere. 56.
glassware. 212.
glazed frost. 49.
glider. 542.
glides. 348.
gliding. 542.
globe. 210.
glove. 289, 521.
glove. 444, 515, 536, 544, 549,
    558, 562, 570.
glove compartment. 385.
glove finger. 289.
gloves, types of. 289.
glue. 186.
glue stick. 447.
gluteal nerve. 121.
gluteus maximus. 111.
gnomon. 592.
goal. 531.
goal. 511, 512, 517, 531.
goal area. 511.
goal circle. 522.
goal crease. 517.
goal judge. 531.
goal judge's box. 517.
goal line. 511, 512, 516, 517, 519,
    522, 531.
goal post. 512, 519.

The terms in **bold type** indicate the title of an illustration.

goal third. 522.
goalkeeper. 516.
goalkeeper. 511, 516, 517, 531.
goalpost. 522.
goalpost. 522.
goggles. 273, 544, 549.
going. 187.
golf. 571, 572, 573.
golf bag. 573.
golf clubs. 572.
golf clubs, types of. 572.
golf shoe. 573.
golf trolley. 573.
golfball element. 452.
golfball release lever. 452.
golfer. 571.
Golgi body. 105.
gonfalon. 697.
gong. 471.
gong. 372, 479.
goods lift. 705.
gooseberry. 66.
gooseneck. 668.
gored skirt. 293.
gorge. 46, 142, 166.
gorget. 676.
Gorgonzola (Italian). 145.
Gothic. 162.
gothic cathedral. 164, 165.
Gouda (Dutch). 145.
gouge. 332.
gouged section. 504.
gour. 46.
governor. 171, 649.
grab handle. 389, 581.
gracile. 111.
grader. 666.
graduated arm. 594.
graduated dial. 610.
graduated scale. 598.
grafting knife. 242.
grain. 255.
grain auger. 155.
grain of wheat, section of a. 71.
grain pan. 155.
grain sieve. 155.
grain tank. 155.
grain unloading auger. 155.
granddaughter. 131.
grandfather. 131.
grandfather clock. 593.
grandmother. 131.
grandson. 131.
granitic layer. 40.
granivorous bird. 89.
granny knot. 587.
granulation. 29.
grape. 66.
grape. 66.
grapefruit. 69.
grapefruit knife. 217.
grapeshot. 681.
graphic elements for symbols. 699.
graphic symbols. 49.
graphite moderator. 650.
grapnel. 433.
grapple. 667.
grass catcher. 242.
grass ley. 151.
grater. 218.
grater disc. 226.
grave accent. 347.
gravel. 182, 267.
gravity band. 433.
gravity dam. 639.
gravity dam, cross section of a. 639.
gravity shackle. 433.
gravure printing, diagram of. 504.
gravy boat and stand. 213.
grease trap. 267.
grease well. 227.
greases. 635.
great adductor. 111.

Great Bear. 32.
great foramen. 114.
great-granddaughter. 131.
great-grandfather. 131.
great-grandmother. 131.
great-grandson. 131.
great organ manual. 467.
great saphenous vein. 117.
great scallop. 94.
greater alar cartilage. 125.
greater covert. 88.
Greater Dog. 33.
greater pectoral. 110.
greater trochanter. 113.
greave. 676.
Greek. 707.
Greek temple. 161.
Greek temple, basic plan of the. 161.
Greek writing style. 345.
green. 530.
green ball. 569.
green beam. 377.
green bean. 73.
green cabbage. 74.
green dragon. 579.
green peas. 77.
green russula. 65.
green walnut. 70.
greenhouse. 151, 655.
grid. 170.
griddle. 227.
griff-fiffi hook. 574.
grike. 46.
grill. 161.
grill elements. 228.
grille. 196, 363, 383, 475.
grip. 357, 527, 572, 679.
grips, types of. 528.
groin. 106.
grommet. 583.
groove. 227, 365, 486, 545, 572.
grooved sleeve. 261.
gros bout de poitrine. 141.
ground. 633.
ground airport equipment. 439.
ground electrode. 392.
ground floor. 178, 179.
ground level. 515, 644.
ground moraine. 48.
ground sill. 166.
ground wire. 645.
ground-wire clamp. 645.
group retarders. 411.
groups of stitches. 493.
growth line. 93, 96.
grozzing teeth. 507.
grubber hoe. 238.
Gruyere (Swiss). 145.
guard. 187, 217, 251, 563.
guard rail. 229.
guardhouse. 167.
guava. 72.
guidance system. 692.
guide bar. 243.
guide bar and live rail. 415.
guide bearing. 642.
guide post. 452.
guide rods. 684.
guiding tower. 403.
guillotine trimmer. 360.
gules. 696.
gully. 514.
gum. 115.
gun. 690.
gun body. 270.
gun flap. 281.
gun mounting. 425.
gunner's sight. 690.
gunter rig whale boat. 418.
gusset. 338.
gusset pocket. 294, 297.
gusseted pocket. 341.
Gutenberg discontinuity. 39.
guttae. 160.
gutter. 81, 177, 399, 576.

guy cable. 559.
guy line adapter. 583.
guy rope. 582.
guy wire. 658.
guyot. 42.
gymnast. 560.
gymnastics. 559, 560.
gyro repeater. 423.

H

H stretcher. 203.
hackle. 567.
hacksaw. 252.
hacksaw. 266.
hail. 49.
hail shower. 52.
hair. 129.
hair. 107, 128, 464.
hair, kinds of. 320.
hair bulb. 129.
hair clip. 333.
hair dryer. 330.
hair follicle. 129.
hair grip. 333.
hair roller. 333.
hair shaft. 129.
hair slide. 333.
hair styles. 320, 321.
hair styles, components of. 320, 321.
hairbrushes. 328.
haircutting scissors. 328.
hairdresser. 706.
hairpieces. 321.
hairpieces. 321.
hairpin. 333.
hairsetter. 331.
hairspring. 591.
hairstyling implements. 333.
half barb. 53.
half court line. 527.
half-distance line. 531.
half-glasses. 319.
half handle. 217.
half hoe. 287.
half-slip. 303.
half-through arch bridge. 401.
half way line. 511.
halfway line. 512.
hall. 169.
hall. 179, 419.
halyard. 417, 695.
ham knife. 217.
hammer. 558.
hammer. 277, 466, 575, 688, 689.
hammer axe. 574.
hammer beam. 180.
hammer butt. 466.
hammer drill. 625.
hammer head. 466, 574.
hammer rail. 466.
hammer shank. 466.
hammer throw. 556.
hampe. 141.
hand. 107, 598.
hand blender. 225.
hand brake gear housing. 405.
hand brake wheel. 405.
hand brake winding chain. 405.
hand drill. 250.
hand fork. 239.
hand grenade. 682.
hand grip. 566.
hand guard. 519.
hand lamp. 662.
hand mixer. 225.
hand mower. 242.
hand rail. 637.
hand shears. 239.
hand shield. 273.
hand vice. 501.
hand warmer pocket. 291.
hand warmer pouch. 294.
hand wheel. 485, 500.

handbags. 338, 339.
handbrake lever. 385, 581.
handgrip. 368, 369, 616.
handguard. 685.
handicapper's rating. 555.
handle. 540.
handle. 204, 211, 214, 215, 216, 225, 226, 227, 228, 229, 233, 234, 243, 247, 248, 249, 250, 252, 253, 261, 270, 272, 327, 329, 330, 331, 336, 337, 339, 340, 370, 464, 475, 487, 492, 494, 503, 507, 521, 525, 528, 545, 549, 558, 566, 573, 574, 585, 617, 625, 677.
handle post. 340.
handlebars. 397.
handles, types of. 540.
handling appliances. 671.
handrail. 172, 187, 415.
handrail drive. 172.
hands-free telephone. 373.
handsaw. 252.
handset. 372, 373, 457.
handset cord. 372.
hang glider. 543.
hang gliding. 543.
hang point. 543.
hang-up ring. 330.
hanger. 337, 362.
hanger loop. 286.
hanging basket. 237.
hanging glacier. 48.
hanging pendant. 210.
hanging stile. 188, 189, 205.
hank. 538, 539.
harbour. 427.
harbour station. 427.
hard palate. 114, 126.
hard shell clam. 94.
hardboard. 255.
hardboards. 184.
hardened steel pile. 570.
Hare. 33.
harmonica. 474.
harness. 494, 536, 543, 544, 662.
harnesses. 494.
harp. 464.
Harp. 32, 479.
harp cable stays. 402.
harpsichord. 476.
harrow. 152.
harth bread. 138.
hasp. 337.
hat stand. 451.
hat veil. 304.
hatband. 288.
hatch. 631, 690.
hatchback. 384.
hatchet. 586.
hatching. 497.
haulage cable. 547.
haulage road. 621.
haunch. 83.
haut de côtelettes. 143.
haut de côtes. 139.
hay turner. 154.
hazelnut. 70.
hazelnut, section of a. 70.
head. 86.
head. 31, 77, 92, 96, 98, 107, 108, 116, 142, 250, 254, 327, 329, 334, 335, 408, 464, 472, 473, 480, 481, 485, 490, 492, 498, 500, 525, 558, 567, 572, 574.
head band. 304.
head binder. 182.
head board. 388.
head cover. 573.
head-first entry. 534.
head linesman. 518.
head nut. 480.
head of femur. 113.
head of frame. 189.
head of humerus. 113.
head of sail. 537.

The terms in **bold type** indicate the title of an illustration.

head rotation lock. 361.
head tube. 272, 397.
headband. 363, 498, 525.
headbay. 637.
headboard. 204.
headcap. 498.
header. 190.
header joist. 182.
headframe. 622, 624.
headgear. 288, 304.
headgear, types of. 288.
headlamp bezel. 384.
headland. 43.
headlight. 384.
headlight. 383, 389, 395, 413, 690.
headlight housing shell. 384.
headphone. 363.
headphone. 363.
headphone jack. 364, 366.
headpin. 576.
headrail. 209.
headrest. 386, 407.
headwind. 539.
health. 613.
hearing. 124.
heart. 116.
heart. 91, 94, 507, 578.
hearth. 506.
hearth-brush. 191.
heartwood. 63.
heat comfort control. 331.
heat deflecting disc. 274.
heat exchanger. 655.
heat pipe radiator. 378.
heat ready indicator dot. 331.
heat shield. 443.
heat/speed selector switch. 330.
heater. 585.
heater control. 385.
heating. 190, 191, 192, 193, 194, 195.
heating duct. 231.
heating element. 194, 195, 230, 231, 232, 506.
heating elements indicator. 194.
heating oil. 635.
heating unit. 193.
heating unit. 192, 194.
heaving line knot. 587.
heavy duty boot. 310.
heavy machine gun. 687.
heavy machinery. 659.
heavy petroleum. 635.
heavy thunderstorm. 52.
Hebrew writing style. 345.
heddle. 494, 495.
heddle rod. 495.
heddles. 495.
hedge. 237.
hedge trimmer. 242.
heel. 85, 107, 153, 217, 247, 252, 287, 308, 464, 481, 521, 548, 572.
heel calk. 85.
heel flange. 546.
heel grip. 308.
heel loop. 617.
heel piece. 540, 545, 546.
heel release setting indicator. 546.
heel rest. 225, 233.
height. 534, 581.
height adjustment screw. 546.
height control. 361.
height limit. 702.
height of the dive. 535.
height scale. 361.
helical spring. 594.
helicopter. 441.
helicopter. 425.
helicopter hangar and flight deck. 425.
helicopters. 707.
helideck. 629.
heliostat. 654.
helium sphere. 442.
helix. 124.

helm roof. 181.
helmet. 444, 543, 544, 575, 675.
helmet lamp. 575.
hem. 209.
hemi-demi-semi-quave. 461.
hemi-demi-semi-quaver rest. 461.
hemibranch. 90.
hemispherical dome. 35.
hemlath. 657.
hemline. 489.
hepatic vein. 116, 117.
herbivore's jaw. 82.
herbs. 135.
herbs. 135.
Hercules. 32.
Herdsman. 32.
Hermes satellite. 378.
herringbone pattern. 186.
herringbone stitch. 493.
herringbone strutting. 182.
hex nut. 392.
hexagon bushing. 265.
hidden pocket. 341.
high activity spent fuel store. 648.
high-back dungarees. 306.
high card. 578.
high clouds. 44.
high focal plane buoy. 430.
high jump. 557.
high line. 563.
high-power light bulb. 35.
high pressure centre. 54.
high pressure cylinder. 649.
high pressure steam. 648, 649.
high-rise block. 173.
high-rise office building. 168.
high-speed exit taxiway. 438.
high street. 168.
high-temperature cutoff. 263.
high tension lead. 391.
high-voltage cable. 606.
high-voltage tester. 276.
highland climates. 51.
highway crossing bell. 409.
hill. 46, 654.
hilted bayonet. 679.
hilted bayonet, parts of a. 679.
hilus of kidney. 120.
hind leg. 92, 98, 100.
hind limb. 97.
hind toe. 87, 89.
hind wing. 92, 98.
Hindi writing style. 345.
hindlimb, skeleton of the. 97.
hinge. 188, 189, 205, 227, 228, 232, 337, 339, 365, 498, 546, 607.
hinge tooth. 93.
hinged presser foot. 485, 486.
hip. 107.
hip pad. 519.
hip roof. 180.
hitting area. 521.
hive. 99.
hive body. 99.
hoarding. 167, 168.
hob. 228.
hock. 83, 142.
hockey. 516.
hockey skate. 548.
hoist. 170, 375, 695.
hoist ropes. 171.
hoisting chain. 661.
hoisting drum. 661.
hoisting rope. 268, 661, 669.
hold-up stocking. 301.
hold yard. 411.
holdall. 337.
holdback. 207.
holder. 507.
holding area marking. 438.
holds. 564.
hole. 571.
hole. 463, 503, 571, 574.
hollow-wood construction. 255.
holster. 575.

holster quiver. 570.
home key. 456.
home plate. 520.
home straight. 555.
honey cell. 99.
honeybee. 98, 99.
honeycomb diffuser. 358.
honeycomb section. 99.
honour point. 695.
honour tiles. 579.
hood. 190, 282, 536.
hood cover. 330.
hooded towelling robe. 305.
hoof. 85.
hoof. 83.
hook. 189, 208, 211, 341, 486, 488, 490, 492, 547, 548, 567, 594, 599, 626, 669.
hook and eyes. 488.
hook ladder. 268.
hooker. 512, 513.
hoop. 493.
hoop earring. 315.
hopper. 154.
hopper ore wagon. 406.
hopper wagon. 406.
horizon. 622.
horizon mirror. 429.
horizon mirror shades. 429.
horizon scanner. 57.
horizontal-axis wind turbine. 658.
horizontal bar. 559.
horizontal circle drive knob. 600.
horizontal clamp. 600.
horizontal end handhold. 405.
horizontal floor loom. 494.
horizontal member. 644.
horizontal pivoting. 189.
horizontal seismograph. 602.
horizontal stabilizer. 542, 691.
horizontal tangent screw. 600.
horn. 315, 385, 404.
horn button. 396.
horns. 96.
horny beak. 101.
hors d'oeuvre dish. 213.
horse. 82, 83, 84, 85.
horse racing. 554, 555.
horseradish. 76.
horseshoe. 212, 315.
horseshoe. 85.
horseshoe mount. 34.
hose. 301.
hose. 271.
hose nozzle. 240.
hose reel. 240, 663.
hose storage compartment. 663.
hospital. 704.
hot air duct. 647.
hot-air register. 192.
hot line connector. 645.
hot pepper. 73.
hot shoe. 357.
hot sodium. 651.
hot water extraction. 636.
hot-water heater. 257.
hot-water main. 194.
hot-water riser. 257.
hot-water supply. 262, 263.
hot-water supply line. 262.
hotel reservation desk. 440.
hour angle gear. 34.
hour hand. 591, 593.
hourglass. 592.
house. 251, 178.
house, exterior of a. 177.
house furniture. 197.
house styles. 173.
housing. 251, 327, 329, 330, 369, 372, 428.
hovercraft. 421.
hub. 397, 617, 643, 658.
hub cover. 643.
Hubble's classification. 31.
hubcap. 383.

huckleberry. 66.
hull. 71.
human being. 103.
human body. 106, 107.
human denture. 115.
humerus. 84, 100, 112.
humid subtropical. 51.
humid temperate - long summer. 51.
humid temperate - short summer. 51.
humidifier. 194.
humidity. 55.
hump. 411.
hump area. 411.
Hungarian writing style. 345.
Hunting Dogs. 32.
hunting weapons. 688.
hurdle. 556.
hurricane. 52.
hurricane deck. 420.
hurricane lamp. 586.
husband. 130, 131.
husk. 70, 77.
hut. 159.
hydraulic cylinder. 664, 665, 668.
hydraulic pallet truck. 671.
hydraulic shovel. 667.
hydraulic turbine, cross section of a. 643.
hydroelectric complex. 637.
hydroelectric power station, cross section of a. 641.
hydrofiner. 634.
hydrofoil. 422.
hydrofoil boat. 422.
hydrologic cycle. 50.
hydrostatic pad. 34.
hygrograph. 55.
hypha. 65.
hyphen. 347, 350, 371.
hypogastric artery. 120.
hyssop. 135.

I

ice. 50.
ice axe. 574.
ice axe. 575.
ice cream. 147.
ice-cream can. 226.
ice-cream freezer. 226.
ice cream scoop. 221.
ice cube tray. 229.
ice hockey. 517.
ice piton. 575.
ice screw. 575.
icing syringe. 220.
idler pulley. 231.
igloo. 159.
igneous rocks. 40.
ignition switch. 396.
ignition transformer. 195.
ileum. 119.
iliohypogastric nerve. 121.
ilioinguinal nerve. 121.
ilium. 112.
illumination mirror for horizontal circle. 600.
illumination mirror for vertical circle. 600.
image dissector camera. 57.
immigration control. 440.
impeller. 232.
imperial roof. 181.
implement bar. 152.
impluvium. 163.
impost. 162.
impression control. 452.
in-flight refuelling probe. 691.
in goal. 512.
in km. 39.
in thousands of feet. 39.
inactive dyke. 646.
inbound line. 519.

The terms in **bold type** indicate the title of an illustration.

incandescent lamp. 432.
incident-light measuring diffuser. 357.
incisor. 82.
inclined shaft. 622.
incoming message cassette. 373.
index bar. 429.
index mirror. 429.
index shades. 429.
Indian. 33.
Indian chapati bread. 138.
Indian fig. 72.
Indian naan bread. 138.
Indian Ocean. 41.
indication of types. 351.
indicator. 232, 388, 506, 598.
indicator board. 413.
indicator lamp. 395.
indicator light. 383, 457.
indicator needle. 357.
indicator switch. 386.
indifferent cells. 129.
individual bun tin. 220.
indoor/outdoor position. 369.
induced draught fan. 647.
inert gas. 274.
inferior dental arch. 126.
inferior mesenteric artery. 120.
inferior nasal concha. 125.
inferior umbilicus. 88.
inferior vena cava. 116, 117, 120.
infield. 520.
infiltration. 50.
infinity. 708.
inflated carrying tyre. 415.
inflated guiding tyre. 415.
inflorescences, types of. 64.
inflorescent vegetables. 73.
information. 704.
information counter. 440.
information office. 412.
informative signs. 703.
infra-red spectrometer. 57.
infraorbital foramen. 114.
infrared transmitter. 358.
infraspiatus. 111.
infundibulum of fallopian tube. 109.
inhaul. 537.
injector. 390.
injector pipe. 390.
ink. 352, 502.
ink roller. 502.
inked roller. 370.
inking slab. 502.
inlaid parquet. 186.
inlet. 625.
inlet guide vanes. 436.
inlet hose. 232.
inlet valve. 390, 391.
inner boot. 546.
inner core. 39.
inner edge. 85.
inner hearth. 190.
inner jib. 417.
inner lining. 393.
inner lip. 93.
inner lockout hatch. 423.
inner ply. 255.
inner pressure cylinder. 648.
inner rail. 172.
inner root sheath. 129.
inner table. 578.
inner tent. 583.
inner toe. 87.
input devices. 454.
input selectors. 364.
insectivorous bird. 89.
insert here. 350.
insert space. 350.
inset pocket. 294.
inside. 216.
inside knob. 256.
inside-leg snap-fastening. 306.
inside line. 563.
inside linebacker. 518.
insole. 308, 310.

inspection chamber. 267.
inspection cover. 267.
instep. 287.
instrument panel. 385.
instrument panel. 385, 542.
instrument unit. 442.
**instrumental groups, examples
    of. 476, 477.**
insulated blade. 276.
insulated handle. 276, 277.
insulation. 263, 655, 656.
insulator. 392, 645.
insulin syringe. 615.
intaglio press. 502.
intaglio printing. 502.
integral bayonet. 679.
Intelsat. 378.
inter-island ferry. 420.
interchangeable end assembly. 34.
interchangeable lens. 353.
interchangeable lenses. 355.
interconnecting truss. 57.
intercostal nerve. 121.
interfacing. 285, 488.
interfemoral membrane. 100.
interior dome shell. 34.
interior door handle. 386.
interior door lock button. 386.
interior pocket. 337, 341.
interlining. 488.
interlock. 497.
intermediate heat exchanger. 651.
intermediate lens. 606.
intermediate pressure cylinder. 649.
intermittent drizzle. 52.
intermittent rain. 52.
intermittent snow. 52.
internal and middle ear. 124.
internal ear. 124.
internal iliac artery. 116, 117.
internal iliac vein. 116.
internal jugular vein. 117.
internal tooth lock washer. 254.
**international phonetic alphabet.
    348.**
**international road signs. 700,
    701, 702, 703.**
**international weather symbols.
    52, 53.**
internode. 61.
interplanetary space. 39.
interrogation recording and
    location system antenna. 57.
intersection. 708.
intertragic notch. 124.
intervals. 462.
intervertebral foramen. 122.
intestine. 91, 94, 116.
intrados. 162.
intrusive rocks. 40.
Inuktitut writing style. 345.
inverness cape. 282.
inverted pleat. 207, 294.
inverter knob. 600.
inward dive. 535.
Io. 28.
Ionic order. 160.
ionosphere. 39.
Iranian writing style. 345.
iris. 123.
iris diaphragm. 605.
iron. 572.
iron curtain. 170.
iron frame. 465.
irregular crystal. 49.
irregular galaxy. 31.
is a member of. 708.
is approximately equal to. 708.
is contained in. 708.
is equal to. 708.
is equal to or greater than. 708.
is equal to or less than. 708.
is equivalent to. 708.
is greater than. 708.
is identical with. 708.

is less than. 708.
is not equal to. 708.
is not identical with. 708.
isba. 159.
ischium. 113.
isobar. 54.
isoseismal line. 45.
isthmus of fallopian tube. 109.
isthmus of fauces. 126.
ital. bold. 351.
Italian writing style. 345.
italic. 351.
italic capitals. 351.
ivory ball. 580.

J

J-2 engine. 442.
jabot. 298.
jack. 530.
jack. 363, 466, 530, 578, 662, 667.
jack socket. 480.
jack spring. 466.
jack staff. 425.
jack-up platform. 628.
jacket. 562, 564, 629, 688.
jackleg drill. 625.
jalousie. 189.
jamb. 188, 189, 190.
jambon. 142.
jambonneau arrière. 142.
jambonneau avant. 142.
Japan plum. 68.
Japanese persimmon. 72.
Japanese writing style. 345.
japonaise fancy. 146.
jar. 335.
jarret arrière. 139.
jarret avant. 139.
javelin. 675.
javelin throw. 557.
javelins. 558.
jaw. 248, 250, 251, 277, 333.
jaws, types of. 82.
jazz band. 477.
jeans. 300.
jejunum. 119.
Jerusalem artichoke. 76.
jet deflector. 242.
jet engine. 691.
jet fuel. 635.
jet tip. 329.
jetfoil. 422.
Jew's harp. 474.
jewel cap. 429.
jewellery. 315, 316, 317.
Jewish chollar. 138.
jib. 538, 669.
jib halyard. 538.
jib tie. 669.
jibsheet. 538.
jingle. 472.
job title. 349.
jockey. 554.
jockey roller. 398.
jockey's name. 555.
jockey wheel. 581.
jockey wheel handle. 581.
jodhpurs. 551.
joint. 352, 567, 568.
joist. 186.
Joker. 578.
journal box. 404.
joystick. 457.
joystick. 455.
judge. 562, 564, 565.
judo. 564.
judo suit. 564.
juice extractor. 226.
juice sac. 69.
jumeaux. 141.
jump ski. 540.
jumper. 544.
jumpsuit. 306.
jumpsuit. 300.

junction box. 409.
Jupiter. 28.

K

Kaplan turbine. 643.
keel. 543.
keep. 167.
keep-left sign. 168.
keeper ring. 566.
kelly. 626.
kerb. 399.
kerb weir. 399.
kernel. 70, 77.
kerosene. 442, 635.
ketch. 418.
kettle. 233.
kettledrum. 472.
key. 256, 370, 453, 466, 469, 475, 478.
key case. 341.
key finger button. 469.
key lock. 340.
key signature. 462.
keybed. 465.
keyboard. 456.
keyboard. 371, 453, 455, 465, 475.
keyboard instruments. 465, 466.
keystone. 162, 165.
keyway. 256.
kick. 533.
kick wheel. 505.
kickplate. 229.
kickstart pedal. 396.
kidney. 91, 116.
kilt. 293.
kimono. 301.
kimono sleeve. 296.
King. 578.
King (K). 577.
king pin. 404.
king post. 543.
King's side. 577.
kingpin. 388, 548.
kitchen. 163, 179, 407.
kitchen knife. 217.
kitchen knives, types of. 217.
kitchen scales. 219.
kitchen timer. 219.
**kitchen utensils. 217, 218, 219,
    220, 221.**
kiwi. 72.
knee. 83, 100, 106.
knee brace. 180.
knee pad. 519, 521, 549, 561.
knee roll. 553.
knife. 214.
knife. 155, 502, 536.
knife-edge. 594, 595, 596.
knife pleat. 294.
knife sharpener. 221.
Knight (Kt). 577.
knit shirt. 286.
knitting. 490.
knitting machine. 491, 492.
knitting measure. 490.
knitting needles. 490.
knives, major types of. 214.
knob. 199, 256, 521.
knob for reticle illumination. 600.
knob handle. 253.
knot. 497.
knot stitches group. 493.
knots. 587.
knuckel. 139.
knuckle. 139.
knurled bolt. 270.
knurled button. 428.
kohl pencil. 322.
kohlrabi. 76.
kraft paper. 255.
kumquat. 69.

The terms in **bold type** indicate the title of an illustration.

L

label. 334, 365.
label maker. 447.
labia major. 109.
labia minora. 109.
labial palp. 92, 94.
laboratory. 634.
laccolith. 45.
lace. 305, 521, 548, 565.
lace-up. 310.
lacrimal duct. 123.
lactiferous duct. 109.
ladder. 209, 657.
ladders. 269.
ladders and stepladders. 268.
ladle. 219, 681.
Lady chapel. 164.
lagging. 633.
lagoon. 43.
lake. 30.
lam. 494.
lamb. 143.
lambdoid suture. 114.
lamina cribrosa. 125.
laminate board. 255.
laminboard. 255.
lamp. 361, 368, 605.
lamp-post. 211.
lamp-post. 168.
lamp room. 624.
lamphouse. 361.
Lancashire. 144.
lance rest. 676.
lanceolate. 62.
land. 250.
land drain. 182.
landing. 179, 187, 560, 623.
landing area. 556, 557.
landing light. 441.
landing mat. 560.
landing net. 568.
landside. 153.
lane. 576.
lane. 532, 557.
lane number. 532.
lane rope. 532.
lane timekeeper. 532.
languid. 468.
lantern. 431, 585.
lantern of lighthouse. 432.
lantern pane. 431.
lanyard ring. 689.
lapel. 283, 298.
large bastard sword. 678.
large intestine. 119.
large wheel. 617.
larva. 99.
larynx. 118.
lasagna. 136.
lasagna verde. 136.
lash comb. 323.
LASH ship. 427.
last quarter. 30.
latch. 227, 228, 232, 256, 492, 574.
latch bolt. 256.
latch follower. 256.
latch lever. 256, 486.
latch needle. 492.
lateen sail. 418.
lateral adjusting lever. 247.
lateral condyle of femur. 113.
lateral cutaneous nerve of thigh. 121.
lateral filing cabinet. 451.
lateral great. 111.
lateral groove. 85.
lateral incisor. 115.
lateral line. 90.
lateral moraine. 48.
lateral root. 61.
lateral semicircular canal. 124.
lateral system of marking. 430.
Latin. 707.
latissimus dorsi. 111.

latitude. 27.
latitude scale. 56.
launch escape system. 442.
launching orbit. 379.
laundry room. 179.
lava flow. 45.
lava layer. 45.
lava plateau. 45.
lawn. 178, 237.
lawn aerator. 241.
lawn edger. 238.
lawn mowers. 242.
lawn rake. 238.
lay edge. 499.
layout. 507.
layout paper. 507.
lead. 592.
lead came. 507.
lead-in wire. 274, 357.
lead knife. 507.
lead pencil. 352.
lead screw. 250.
lead stretcher. 507.
leader. 567.
leading edge. 298, 434, 542, 543.
leading edge flap. 434.
leading edge tube. 543.
leaf. 62.
leaf. 61, 77, 199.
leaf axil. 61, 62.
leaf margin. 62.
leaf vegetables. 74.
lean-to roof. 180.
leash rod. 494, 495.
leather end. 284.
leather garment. 665.
leather goods. 340, 341.
leather sandal. 675.
leather sheath. 585.
leather skin. 515.
leaves, types of. 62.
LED peak level meter. 366.
ledger line. 461.
leech. 537.
leek. 75.
left atrium. 116.
left back. 516, 529.
left bronchus. 118.
left centre. 512, 513.
left cornerback. 518.
left defence. 517.
left defensive end. 518.
left defensive tackle. 518.
left field. 520.
left fielder. 520.
left forward. 523, 529.
left fullback. 517.
left guard. 518, 523.
left half. 516.
left halfback. 518.
left-hand grip. 686.
left inner. 516.
left kidney. 120.
left-luggage office. 412.
left lung. 116, 118.
left midfield. 511.
left safety. 518.
left service court. 524, 527.
left tackle. 518.
left valve. 93.
left ventricle. 116.
left wing. 511, 512, 513, 516, 517.
leg. 101, 107, 139, 142, 143, 153, 199, 204, 287, 472, 528, 560, 566, 595.
leg-of-mutton sleeve. 296.
leg position. 535.
leg rest. 617.
leg stump. 515.
legging. 575.
legume, section of a. 71.
leisure. 509.
lemon. 69.
lenghtwise grain. 489.
length. 534, 581.
length, measure of. 599.

lengthwise grain. 488.
lens. 610.
lens. 123, 356, 357, 362.
lens aperture ring. 355.
lens cap. 355.
lens carriage. 432.
lens hood. 355.
lens mount. 353.
lenticular galaxy. 31.
lentils. 77.
Leo, the Lion. 698.
leopard. 82.
leotard. 307.
lesser covert. 88.
Lesser Dog. 32.
let is stand. 350.
letter opener. 447.
letter scales. 447.
letterhead. 349.
letterpress printing, diagram of. 504.
letters. 346, 347.
leucoplast. 105.
level. 623.
level controls. 363.
level crossing. 409.
level crossing sign. 409.
level crossing with automatic gates. 410.
level crossing with barrier or gate. 701.
levelling foot. 362.
levelling screw. 56, 595, 600.
lever. 227, 249, 260, 261, 333, 370, 387, 457, 503, 598, 682.
lever bucket. 665.
lever corkscrew. 219.
lever cover. 261.
lever ejector. 668.
lever tap. 261.
levigator. 503.
Libra, the Balance. 698.
lid. 222, 223, 224, 226, 227, 331.
lid latch. 331.
life buoy. 422.
life raft. 421, 425.
lifeboat. 416, 629.
lift. 171.
lift. 171.
lift arm. 665.
lift bridge. 403.
lift buffer. 171.
lift cord. 209.
lift cord lock. 209.
lift cylinder. 665, 670.
lift-fan air intake. 421.
lift guide rail. 171.
lift safety device. 171.
lift span. 403.
lifting chain. 670.
lifting handle. 684.
lifting lever. 405.
ligament, position of the. 93.
ligature. 469.
light. 415, 430, 536, 656.
light alloy metal riser. 570.
light bar. 330.
light bulb. 274.
light from Sun. 30.
light-load adjustment screw. 601.
light machine gun. 687.
light pen. 455.
light-reading scale. 357.
lightbox. 360.
lighted mirror. 330.
lighthouse. 431.
lighting. 586.
lighting and vision assistant. 374.
lighting and vision control room. 374.
lighting cable. 581.
lighting control panel. 374.
lighting director. 374.
lightning arrester. 641, 645.
lights. 210, 211.
lighttight box. 353.

lightweight building block. 183.
limb. 63.
limb top. 605.
limousine. 384.
limpet. 96.
line. 370, 461, 566, 567.
line guide. 371, 566.
line judge. 518.
line map. 414.
line of scrimmage. 518.
line of touch. 513.
line out. 513.
line out plan. 513.
line printer. 652.
line space regulator. 453.
linear. 62.
linen. 204.
linen chest. 206.
lines. 370.
linesman. 511, 517, 524, 526, 529.
lingual papillae. 126.
lingual tonsil. 126.
lining. 283, 308, 338, 340, 481, 488, 548.
linstock. 681.
lintel. 165, 190.
Lion. 32.
lion passant. 696.
lip. 86, 256, 507.
lipbrush. 323.
lipid droplet. 105.
lipliner. 323.
lipstick. 323.
liquefied gas petroleum treatment. 634.
liquefied petroleum gas storage. 634.
liqueur. 212.
liquid antiseptic. 615.
liquid compass. 429.
liquid consonants. 348.
liquid-cooled garment. 444.
liquid-crystal display. 591.
liquid foundation. 322.
liquid hydrogen (fuel). 442.
liquid-level gauge. 633.
liquid oxygen (lox). 442.
liquid oxygen (lox) transfer pipe. 442.
liquid sodium coolant. 651.
litchi. 72.
litho crayon. 503.
litho pencil. 503.
litho press. 503.
lithographic printing, diagram of. 504.
lithographic stone. 503, 504.
lithographic tusche. 503.
lithography. 503.
lithosphere. 39.
litter bin. 168, 414.
Little Bear. 32.
little finger hook. 470.
Little Horse. 32.
Little Lion. 32.
live brown wire. 275.
live roller. 669.
liver. 91, 116, 119.
livestock van. 406.
living quarters. 431, 443, 629.
living room. 179, 582.
Lizard. 32.
load backrest. 670.
load guard. 670.
loader's seat. 690.
loading. 682.
loading belt. 621.
loading door. 191.
loading pocket. 623.
lobate web. 89.
lobe. 89, 109.
lobed. 62.
lobster. 95.
lobule. 124.
lock. 256.
lock. 188, 205, 337, 398, 646.

lock-chamber. 426.
lock forward. 512, 513.
lock keeper's building. 427.
lock nut. 56, 548, 599.
lock rail. 188.
lock ring. 362.
locked groove. 365.
locker. 451.
lockers. 412.
locket pendant. 316.
locking device. 268.
locking knob. 600.
locking nut. 258.
locking ring. 248, 684.
locknut. 260.
loculus. 68.
loft ladder. 268.
log carrier. 191.
log chute. 637.
logging unit. 629.
loin. 83, 107, 139, 142.
long adductor. 110.
long and short stitch. 493.
long cardigan. 297.
long-distance coach. 394.
long extensor of toes. 110.
long johns. 287.
long jump. 556.
long leg. 514.
long-nose pliers. 277.
long-off. 514.
long-on. 514.
long palmar. 110.
long peroneal. 110.
long radial extensor of wrist. 111.
long-range aircraft. 434.
long-range radar system. 692.
long residue. 635.
long service line (doubler). 526.
long service line (singler). 526.
longe. 139.
longitude. 27.
longitudinal dunes. 47.
lookout tower. 167.
loop. 285.
loop stitches group. 493.
loophole. 167.
loose boxes. 151.
loose chippings. 700.
loose curtain. 207.
loose fill insulation. 185.
loose-head prop. 513.
loose powder. 322.
loose powder brush. 322.
loosely tied bow. 299.
lopping shears. 239.
lore. 87.
lorgnette. 319.
Lorraine. 707.
loud pedal. 465.
loudness switch. 364.
loudspeaker. 363, 375, 415, 457.
lounge. 419.
louvre. 196, 211.
louvre-board. 165.
louvred window. 189.
lovage. 135.
low bar. 560.
low clouds. 44.
low line. 563.
low pressure centre. 54.
low pressure cylinder. 649.
low-rise apartments. 173.
low-tension distribution line. 645.
lower berth. 407.
lower blade guard. 253.
lower bout. 481.
lower bowl. 224.
lower chord. 401.
lower deck. 394.
lower eyelid. 86, 97, 123.
lower fore topgallant sail. 417.
lower fore topsail. 417.
lower gill arch. 90.
lower girdle facet. 317.
lower guard retracting lever. 253.

lower heating element. 263.
lower landing plate. 172.
lower level. 426.
lower limb. 677.
lower lip. 126, 468.
lower lobe. 118.
lower mandible. 87.
lower mantle. 39.
lower mast. 416.
lower pan-head mounting screw. 359.
lower shell. 546.
lower side-rail. 388.
lower sphere clamp. 56.
lower support screw. 56.
lower thermostat. 263.
lox tank baffles. 442.
lubber's line. 429.
lubber's-line disk. 429.
lubricants plant. 635.
lubricating oils. 635.
luff. 537.
luff (to). 537.
lug. 318, 472.
luggage. 337.
luggage claim. 706.
luggage label. 337.
luggage lockers. 706.
luggage rack. 384.
luggage registration. 706.
luggage trolley. 337.
luggage trolleys. 706.
lumache. 137.
lumbar plexus. 121.
lumbar vertebra. 113.
lumbar vertebra, cross section of. 122.
lumbar vertebrae. 84.
lunar boot. 444.
lunar eclipse. 30.
lunar features. 30.
lunar module. 442.
lungs. 118.
lunula. 129.
lunule. 93.
lures. 567.
lying press. 500.
Lymeswold. 144.
Lynx. 32.
lyre. 473.
lysosome. 105.

M

machete. 678.
machicolation. 167.
machine gun. 690.
machine hall. 637, 641.
machine head. 480.
machinery. 155.
machinery store. 151.
macon. 541.
macreuse. 141.
macro focusing knob. 368.
mafalde. 136.
magazine. 683, 685, 688, 689.
magazine base. 689.
magazine catch. 685, 689.
magazine housing latch. 683.
magazine release. 685.
magazine spring. 689.
magma. 45.
magma chamber. 45.
magnesium wire. 357.
magnet. 487.
magnet. 429.
magnetic compass. 610.
magnetic cup. 592.
magnetic gasket. 229.
magnetic lid holder. 233.
magnetic needle. 610.
magnetic suspension. 601.
magnetic tape controller. 458.
magnetic tape drive. 458.
magnetic tape storage. 458.

magnifying mirror. 330.
Magnox reactor. 650.
mah-jong. 579.
main beam warning light. 396.
main drive chain. 172.
main drive shaft. 172.
main duct. 192.
main electrode. 274.
main engines. 443.
main entrance. 178.
main flue. 647.
main generator. 404.
main halyard. 538.
main handle. 250.
main inlet. 633.
main inspection eye. 257.
main ladder. 662.
main leg. 644.
main line. 410.
main lower topgallant sail. 417.
main lower topsail. 417.
main mirror. 608.
main parachute. 544.
main passenger entrance door. 394.
main petrol tap. 396.
main return pipe. 193.
main royal sail. 417.
main running track. 411.
main sail. 417.
main scope tube. 607.
main section. 580.
main sewer. 399.
main shaft. 624.
main shield bracket. 684.
main spar. 435.
main spring. 689.
main supply pipe. 193.
main switch. 645.
main tube. 608.
main turbine shaft. 649.
main undercarriage. 434.
main undercarriage mounting beam. 435.
main undercarriage wheel. 691.
main upper topgallant sail. 417.
main upper topsail. 417.
main wheel. 593.
mainmast. 416.
mains lead. 362.
mains water. 655.
mainsail. 538.
mainsheet. 538.
mainspring. 591.
maintenance hangar. 438.
maintube. 609.
maisonette. 173.
major inner reaping throw. 564.
major outer reaping throw. 564.
make-up. 322, 323.
make-up, products for. 323.
make-up kit. 322.
make-up products. 322.
make-up sponges. 323.
maker's mark. 570.
maker's name. 581.
malar bone. 112.
malar region. 87.
male. 708.
male ferrule. 566.
male genital organs. 108.
male urethra. 108.
mallet. 247.
mallet. 502.
mallets. 471.
Malpighi's pyramid. 120.
Maltese. 707.
mammary gland. 109.
mandarin. 69.
mandarin collar. 298.
mandatory signs. 703.
mandible. 84, 90, 92, 95, 98, 112, 114, 115.
mandolin. 473.
mane. 83.
mangetout. 77.

mango. 67.
manhole. 399, 632, 633.
manicotti. 137.
manicure set. 332.
manicure stick. 332.
manicuring instruments. 333.
manoeuvring engine. 443.
manometer. 194, 633.
mansard roof. 181.
mantel. 190.
mantel shelf. 190.
mantle. 96.
mantle edge. 94.
manual. 468.
manual aperture control. 368.
manual release. 546.
manual zoom ring. 368, 369.
manually-operated points. 408.
manuals. 467.
manure spreader. 153.
manure spreader box. 153.
margin. 62.
margin release. 453.
margin stop. 453.
marginal shield. 101.
marine diesel. 635.
maritime signals. 430, 431, 432.
maritime transport. 416.
marjoram. 135.
mark line. 570.
marker. 352, 576.
marker bib. 522.
marking dot. 489.
marrow. 73.
Mars. 28.
martingale. 563.
mascara. 322.
mascara brush. 323.
mashie. 572.
mashie iron. 572.
mashie niblick. 572.
mask. 521, 536, 562.
mass. 602.
masseter. 110.
mast. 409, 410, 441, 537, 538, 661, 670.
mast foot. 537.
mast sleeve. 537.
master bedroom. 179.
master carrier. 208.
master gate valve. 627.
master retarders. 411.
masthead. 416, 537.
masthead light. 420.
masting and standing rigging. 416.
mastoid process. 114.
mat. 564.
mat. 530.
mat position on green. 530.
matchbook. 335.
matchbox. 335.
matchstick. 335.
maternal aunt. 130.
maternal uncle. 130.
maternity dress. 292.
mathematical symbols. 346.
mathematics. 708.
maths symbol sign. 346.
matinee length necklace. 316.
mattress. 204.
mattress cover. 204.
maxilla. 90, 95, 112, 114, 115, 125.
maxilliped. 95.
maximum and minimum thermometers. 55.
maximum speed limit. 702.
measuring cap. 225.
measuring cup. 331.
measuring cups. 219.
measuring devices. 589.
measuring drawtape. 277.
measuring spoons. 219.
measuring tube. 56.
meat keeper. 229.

The terms in **bold type** indicate the title of an illustration.

meat thermometer. 219.
mechanical connectors. 264.
mechanical pencil. 352.
mechanical stage. 605.
mechanical stage control. 605.
mechanical watch. 591.
medial condyle of femur. 113.
medial moraine. 48.
median groove. 85.
median lingual sulcus. 126.
median nerve. 121.
median vein of forearm. 117.
medical injection disc. 444.
Mediterranean Sea. 41.
medium format SLR (6 x 6). 354.
medium tension distribution line. 645.
medulla. 120, 129.
medulla oblongata. 122.
Meissner's corpuscle. 128.
melanocyte. 128.
melody string. 473.
melting snow. 49.
meltwater. 48.
membrane tanks. 631.
memo pad. 450.
memory button. 364.
men. 577.
men. 578.
men's clothing. 281, 282, 283, 284, 285, 286, 287, 288.
men's pompadour. 321.
mental foramen. 114.
Mercury. 28, 274.
mercury bath. 432.
Mercury capsule (USA). 39.
mercury switch. 597.
mercury-vapour lamp. 274.
meridian. 27.
méridienne. 201.
meringue gateau. 146.
merlon. 167.
mesa. 47.
mesh. 528.
mesocarp. 66, 67, 68, 69.
mesosphere. 39.
mesothorax. 92.
metacarpal. 100.
metacarpus. 84, 86, 112.
metal adjustable arm crutch. 616.
metal bench top. 271.
metal counterhoop. 472.
metal head. 558.
metal heat reflector. 190.
metal plate. 318, 504.
metal rod. 471.
metal washer. 260.
metallic contact grid. 656.
metalliferous mine. 622.
metals. 696.
metamorphic rocks. 40.
metatarsus. 84, 97, 112.
metathorax. 92.
meteorological ground. 55.
meteorological measuring instruments. 56.
meteorological satellite. 57.
meteorological symbols. 44.
meteorology. 54, 55.
methane carrier. 631.
metope. 160.
metopic suture. 114.
metronome. 478.
mezzani. 136.
mezzanine. 169, 414.
microcomputer. 454, 455, 456, 457.
micrometer. 599.
micrometer screw. 429, 600.
microphone. 363, 373, 457.
microphone boom. 375.
microphone jack. 366.
microprocessor. 455.
microscope eyepiece. 600.
microwave oven. 227.
mid-off. 514.

mid-on. 514.
mid range pick-up. 480.
mid-section. 570.
mid-wicket. 514.
middle clouds. 44.
middle covert. 88.
middle ear. 124.
middle leg. 92, 98.
middle linebacker. 518.
middle lobe. 118.
middle nasal concha. 125.
middle neck. 143.
middle panel. 188.
middle phalanx. 86, 112, 113.
middle piece. 108.
middle primary covert. 88.
middle rail. 205.
middle rib. 140.
middle sole. 308.
middle stump. 515.
middle toe. 87.
midiron. 572.
midmashie. 572.
midrange. 363.
midrib. 62, 71.
midriff band. 303.
milieu de poitrine. 141.
milieu de sous-noix. 139.
milk bread. 138.
milking parlour. 151.
Milky Way. 32.
Milky Way projector. 35.
minaudiere. 339.
mincer. 218.
mine. 636.
mine entrance. 623.
minim. 461.
minim rest. 461.
mining. 622.
minor inner reaping throw. 564.
mint. 135.
minute hand. 591, 593.
mirror. 322, 337, 353, 395.
miscellaneous auxiliary systems. 652.
missile. 424, 692.
missile, structure of a. 692.
missile director. 425.
missile launch rail. 691.
missile launcher. 692.
missile tracking radar. 692.
missile tube. 424.
missiles. 692.
missiles, major types of modern. 692.
mist. 52.
mist sprayer. 240.
mitochondrion. 105.
mitral valve. 116.
mitre gauge. 252.
mitre gauge slot. 252.
mitten. 273, 289, 307, 545, 575.
mixed gas sphere. 423.
mixer. 225.
mixing bowl. 225.
mixing bowls. 220.
mixing chamber. 272.
mizzen course. 417.
mizzenmast. 416.
moat. 166, 167.
mob-cap. 304.
mobile passenger stairs. 439.
mobile septum of nose. 125.
moccasin. 309.
mock pocket. 291.
moderator. 648.
moderator/miscellaneous systems. 652.
modern bow. 677.
modern howitzer. 684.
modesty. 298.
modillion. 160.
modulator. 611.
Mohorovicic discontinuity. 39, 40.
moistener. 448.
moisture activated thermostat. 196.

molar. 82.
molar, cross section of a. 115.
mole wrench. 249.
molluscs. 94.
money clip. 341.
monitor. 376.
monitor button. 373.
monitor indicator. 364.
monitor pusher. 375.
monitor roof. 181.
monitor speaker. 376.
monitor stack. 376.
monkey wrench. 266.
mono-ski. 540.
monocle. 319.
mons pubis. 109.
montera. 311.
Moon. 30.
Moon. 28, 29, 30.
Moon, phases of the. 30.
moon dial. 593.
Moon's orbit. 30.
moose. 81.
mordent. 462.
morel. 65.
Morse code. 371.
mortar. 683.
mortar. 183, 218.
mortise. 335, 493.
mortise lock. 256.
mother. 130, 131.
mother-in-law. 131.
motor. 196, 231, 234, 250, 251, 253, 362, 485, 608, 661.
motor car. 415.
motor cell. 127.
motor compartment. 423.
motor-compressor unit. 196.
motor drive. 611.
motor end plate. 127.
motor generator. 171.
motor generator set. 171.
motor mower. 242.
motor neuron. 127.
motor pulley. 365.
motor unit. 224, 225, 226.
motorcycle. 395, 396.
motorway. 703.
mouldboard. 153.
moulded plywood. 255.
mound. 520.
mountain. 46.
mountain range. 30, 40.
mountain slope. 46.
mountain torrent. 46.
mountaineer. 575.
mountaineering. 574, 575.
mountaineering boot. 575.
mounting. 563.
mounting post. 597.
mounting screw. 597.
mouse. 455.
mousse. 147.
mouth. 126.
mouth. 94, 96, 97, 106, 468.
mouthparts. 98.
mouthpiece. 565.
mouthpiece. 372, 469, 470, 536.
mouthpiece receiver. 470.
mouthpipe. 470.
movable bridges. 403.
movable condenser. 361.
movable jaw. 248, 249.
movable maxillary. 101.
move to left. 350.
move to right. 350.
moving blade. 649.
moving coil. 369.
Mt Everest. 39.
mud flap. 383, 388, 389.
mud pit. 626.
mud pump. 626.
mud wall. 582.
mudgard. 397.
mudguard. 581.
muff. 339.

muffle. 506.
mule. 309.
mullet. 696.
multi-pliers. 249.
multi-ply plywood. 255.
multimeter. 276.
multiple access station. 379.
multiple copy control. 453.
multiple-span beam bridge. 400.
multiplexing equipment. 379.
multiplication. 708.
multipurpose ladder. 268.
multipurpose tool. 277.
mummy. 584.
muntin. 188, 189.
murette. 431.
muscle arrector pili. 128, 129.
muscle fibre. 127.
muscle scar. 93.
muscle segment. 91.
muscles. 110, 111.
musculocutaneous nerve. 121.
mushroom, structure of a. 65.
mushroom anchor. 433.
mushrooms. 65.
music. 459.
music rest. 478.
music stand. 478.
musical accessories. 478.
musical notation. 461, 462.
muskeg. 636.
muskmelon. 73.
muslin. 501.
mustard. 71.
mute. 470.
mutule. 160.
muzzle. 86, 680, 683, 688.
muzzle astragal. 680.
muzzle loading. 680, 681.
muzzle moulding. 680.
muzzle ring. 679.
mycelium. 65.
myelin sheath. 127.

N

nacelle. 658.
nacreous cloud. 39.
nail. 129, 254.
nail. 101.
nail bed. 129.
nail brush. 332.
nail buffer. 332.
nail cleaner. 333.
nail clippers. 333.
nail file. 332.
nail hole. 85.
nail matrix. 129.
nail pliers. 332.
nail scissors. 332.
nail shaper. 332.
nail whitener pencil. 333.
nails. 495.
name of horse. 555.
name of sender. 349.
name plate. 251, 601.
naos. 161.
nape. 87, 107.
nappy. 305.
naris. 125.
narrow cuff. 296.
narthex. 164.
nasal bone. 114, 125.
nasal cavity. 118.
nasal fossa. 114.
nasal fossae. 125.
nasopharynx. 125.
national speed limit applies. 702.
natural. 462.
natural arch. 43.
natural sponge. 323.
nave. 164.
navel. 106.
navette cut. 317.
navigating bridge. 420.

navigation aids. 428, 429.
navigation light. 434.
navigational radar. 425.
Neapolitan coffee maker. 224.
near side. 30.
neck. 83, 101, 106, 108, 115, 139, 140, 215, 216, 377, 463, 464, 473, 480, 481, 500, 559, 572, 592.
neck end. 139, 285.
neck of femur. 113.
neck of uterus. 109.
neck ring. 444.
neck-scrag end. 143.
neckhole. 287.
necklaces. 316.
necklines. 299.
neckroll. 204.
necks. 299.
necks. 299.
neckstrap lug. 353, 369.
necktie. 285.
nectarine. 67.
needle. 486.
needle. 49, 485, 486, 487, 541, 615.
needle bar. 486.
needle bed. 491.
needle bed. 491.
needle bed groove. 491.
needle clamp. 486.
needle clamp screw. 486.
needle plate. 485.
needle threader. 487.
needle threader. 486.
needle tool. 505.
negative carrier. 361.
negative charge. 708.
negative contact. 656.
negative meniscus. 610.
negative plate. 392.
negative plate group. 392.
negative region. 656.
negative terminal. 392.
negligee. 301.
neon lamp. 276.
neon screwdriver. 276.
neon sign. 168.
nephew. 130.
Neptune. 28.
nerve. 129.
nerve fibre. 127.
nerve termination. 127.
nerveux de gîte à la noix. 141.
nerveux de sous-noix. 139.
nervous system. 121, 122.
nest of tables. 199.
Net. 33, 517, 523, 524, 526, 528, 529.
net band. 524.
net judge. 524.
net support. 528.
netball. 522.
netball player. 522.
network management centre. 379.
neural spine. 91, 113.
neuron. 127.
neutral blue wire. 275.
neutral conductor. 645.
neutral zone. 517, 518.
new fuel store. 648.
new Moon. 30.
newel post. 187.
newspaper vendor. 168.
nib. 352.
niblick. 572.
nictitating membrane. 86.
niece. 130.
nightdress. 301.
nightwear. 301.
nimbostratus. 44.
nipple. 106, 109, 265.
Nissl bodies. 127.
nitrogen. 274.
no. 1 iron. 572.
no. 1 wood. 572.

no. 2 iron. 572.
no. 2 wood. 572.
no. 3 iron. 572.
no. 3 wood. 572.
no. 4 iron. 572.
no. 4 wood. 572.
no. 5 iron. 572.
no. 6 iron. 572.
no. 7 iron. 572.
no. 8 forward. 512.
no. 8 iron. 572.
no. 9 iron. 572.
no cycling. 702.
no dogs. 704.
no entry. 702.
no goods vehicles. 702.
no left turn. 702.
no motor vehicles. 702.
no motorcycles. 702.
no overtakin. 702.
no pedestrians. 702.
no stopping. 703.
no U-turn. 702.
no vehicles. 702.
nock. 570, 677.
nock end. 570.
nocking point. 677.
noctilucent cloud. 39.
node. 61.
node of Ranvier. 127.
noir. 580.
noix. 139.
noix de hachage. 142.
noix pâtissière. 139.
nombril point. 695.
non-return air vent. 267.
non-skid spaghetti. 136.
noodles. 136.
normal mode acquisition. 379.
normal mode satellite. 379.
north. 430, 579.
North America. 41.
North American reindeer. 81.
North celestial pole. 27.
North pole. 27.
North Sea. 41.
North wind. 579.
Northern Crown. 32.
northern hemisphere. 27.
Norwegian writing style. 345.
nose. 83, 106, 434, 542, 543, 676.
nose cone. 436.
nose leaf. 100.
nose leather. 86.
nose pad. 318.
nose wheel. 434.
noseband. 553.
nosepad. 318.
nosing. 187.
nostril. 83, 87, 90, 97, 101.
notch. 283, 489, 568.
notched double-edged thinning scissors. 328.
notched lapel. 281, 291, 298.
notched single-edged thinning scissors. 328.
note symbols. 461.
notepad. 341.
nozzle. 195, 270, 272, 330, 442, 662, 692.
nuchal shield. 101.
nuclear energy. 650, 651, 652, 653.
nuclear fuel cycle. 653.
nuclear membrane. 105.
nuclear power station. 648.
nuclear whorl. 93.
nucleolus. 105.
nucleus. 31, 105, 127.
number. 580.
number of runners. 555.
number of tracks sign. 409.
numbering machine. 448.
numbers. 347.
numerals. 346, 371.
numeric keyboard. 596.

numeric keypad. 456.
numéro plein. 580.
nut. 70, 254, 408, 428, 463, 481, 677.
nut and bolt. 249.
nutcracker. 218.
nuts, major types of. 70.
nylon frilly tights. 305.

O

o-ring. 261.
oar, types of. 541.
oasis. 47.
object. 605.
objective. 606.
objective. 605.
objective lens. 357, 606, 607, 609.
objective pole piece. 606.
oboe. 469, 476.
oboes. 479.
obscured sky. 53.
observation deck. 440.
observation window. 443.
observer's seat. 437.
obstacles. 551.
obturator nerve. 121.
occipital. 111, 113.
occipital bone. 114.
occipital condyle. 114.
occluded front. 53.
ocean. 50.
ocean. 30.
ocean floor. 42.
Oceania. 41.
oceanic trench. 42.
ocelli. 92.
oche. 550.
Octant. 33.
octave. 462, 563.
octave mechanism. 469.
odd. 580.
odometer. 385.
oesophagus. 91, 94, 119.
off-on knob. 377.
off stump. 515.
offensive. 518.
office furniture. 451.
office supplies and equipment. 445.
offset. 265.
offshore drilling. 628.
offshore well. 630.
ogee. 162, 680.
ogee roof. 181.
oil. 626, 627, 628, 629, 630, 631, 635, 636.
oil. 626.
oil and gas foam. 627.
oil burner. 195.
oil-dip stick. 391.
oil drain plug. 391.
oil filter. 391.
oil/gas separator. 629.
oil indicator. 385.
oil pressure. 396.
oil pump. 195.
oil refinery. 634.
oil reservoir. 625.
oil sand. 636.
oil sands mining plant. 636.
oil storage. 633.
oil sump. 243.
oil supply line. 195.
oil tank cap. 396.
oil transport. 632.
oil trap. 626.
oiler. 625.
oilstone. 501.
okra. 73.
Olde English writing style. 345.
olecranon. 113.
olfactory bulb. 91, 125.
olfactory centre. 125.
olfactory membrane. 125.

olfactory nerve. 91, 125.
olive. 67.
on-deck circle. 520.
on guard line. 562.
on light. 331.
on-off indicator. 228.
on-off switch. 211, 234, 267, 327, 329, 330, 331, 368, 369, 428.
on/play button. 373.
on the wind. 539.
one-arm shoulder throw. 564.
one-bar shoe. 309.
one-handed sword. 678.
one pair. 578.
one-piece overall. 544.
one-piece sleepsuit. 307.
one way head. 254.
one-way traffic. 703.
onglet. 139, 141.
open end spanner. 248.
open-face spinning reel. 566.
open flat semi-trailer. 388.
open housing. 151.
open-pit mine. 621.
open-pit mine. 622.
open string. 187, 473.
opening. 289.
opening salutation. 349.
opening vent. 394.
opera glasses. 319.
opera length necklace. 316.
operating cord. 208.
operating dam. 646.
operating floor. 646.
operating rod. 687.
operator. 458.
operator desk. 652.
operator's cab. 661, 669.
operator's seat. 670.
operculum. 90, 97.
opisthodomos. 161.
optic chiasm. 122.
optic nerve. 123.
optical axis. 35.
optical instruments. 603.
optical plummet. 600.
optical sight. 600.
or. 696.
oral cavity. 118, 119.
orange. 69.
orange. 69.
orbicular. 62.
orbicularis oculi. 110.
orbital cavity. 114.
orbiter. 443.
orchard. 151.
orchestra pit. 170.
orchestra seat. 169.
order. 165.
ordinaries. 696.
ordinary die. 579.
ore. 622.
ore deposit. 622.
oregano. 135.
organ. 467, 468.
organ, mechanism of the. 468.
organ pipes. 468.
Oriental couching stitch. 493.
oriflamme. 697.
Orion. 32, 33.
ornaments. 462.
ortho-stick. 616.
oscalcis. 84.
oscillating sprinkler. 240.
osteology of skull. 114.
ostium. 129.
other danger. 701.
otolith. 91.
out of bounds. 571.
outbound. 411.
outcrop. 622.
outdoor condensing unit. 194.
outdoor drain cock. 257.
outer boundary line. 527.
outer core. 39.
outer edge. 85.

The terms in **bold type** indicate the title of an illustration.

729

outer hearth. 190.
outer jib. 417.
outer lip. 93.
outer lockout hatch. 423.
outer rail. 172.
outer root sheath. 129.
outer table. 578.
outer toe. 87.
outfield. 520.
outgoing announcement cassette. 373.
outhaul. 537.
outlet grille. 193.
outlet valve. 647.
output devices. 454.
output lead. 365.
outside counter. 308.
outside-half. 513.
outside knob. 256.
outside line. 563.
outside linebacker. 518.
outside ticket pocket. 283.
outsole. 308.
outwash plain. 48.
oval cut. 317.
ovary. 64, 91, 109.
ovate. 62.
oven. 228.
oven lamp. 227, 228.
over read ground wire. 644.
overbridge. 400.
overburden. 621, 623.
overcast sky. 53.
overcoat. 282.
overcurtain. 207.
overflow. 259.
overflow bend. 257.
overflow pipe. 263.
overflow protection switch. 232.
overflow tube. 258.
overhand knot. 587.
overhead connection. 645.
overhead electric wire. 413.
overhead frame. 666.
overhead switch panel. 437.
overlap carrier. 208.
overlay flooring. 186.
overrider. 383.
overshirt. 295.
overshoe. 310.
ovule. 64.
owner's name. 555.
oxer. 552.
oxer wall. 552.
oxidizer tank. 692.
oxyacetylene welding. 271.
oxygen cylinder. 271.
oxygen supply pressure gauge. 444.
oxygen valve. 272.
oyster. 94.
oyster fork. 215.
oyster knife. 217.
oyster mushroom. 65.
ozone. 39.

P

[P] trap. 257.
P-N junction. 656.
Pacific Ocean. 41.
Pacinian corpuscle. 128.
pack. 544.
packet of cigarette papers. 334.
packing. 261.
packing material. 504.
packing nut. 261.
packing retainer ring. 261.
pad. 318, 515, 516.
pad arm. 318.
padded jacket. 575.
paddle valve. 426.
padlock. 337.
page boy. 320.
pagoda sleeve. 296.

paint roller. 270.
painting upkeep. 268, 269, 270.
palate. 125.
palatine tonsil. 126.
palato-pharyngeal arch. 126.
palatoglossal arch. 126.
pale. 696.
paleron. 141.
palette. 142.
paling fence. 237.
pallet. 468, 475, 591, 593.
pallet and container transporter. 439.
pallet spring. 468.
pallet truck. 671.
pallets. 671.
pallial line. 93.
pallial sinus. 93.
palm. 81, 289, 433, 521.
palm grove. 47.
palmar pad. 86.
palmate. 62.
palmette. 200.
pan. 594, 595, 682.
pan arrest. 595.
pan cover. 682.
pan handle. 359.
pancake. 147.
pancake pan. 223.
pancreas. 119.
pane. 189.
panel. 188, 207, 284, 303, 544, 553, 623, 644.
panoramic and tilting head. 359.
panoramic periscope. 690.
panoramic window. 407.
panpipe. 474.
pantee corselette. 302.
pantograph. 413.
pantry. 179.
pants. 521.
panty girdle. 303.
papal. 707.
papaya. 72.
paper. 334, 504.
paper bail. 453.
paper centring scale. 453.
paper clips. 447.
paper fasteners. 447.
paper guide. 453.
paper guide roller. 457.
paper punch. 448.
paper release lever. 453.
paper safe. 360.
paper tape. 370, 371.
paper tape start button. 371.
papilla. 123, 129.
papillary muscle. 116.
parabolic antenna. 379.
parabolic dune. 47.
parabolic mirror. 654.
parabolic reflector. 358, 611.
parachute. 544.
parachute. 543.
parachuting. 544.
parachutist. 544.
parade ground. 166.
paraffins. 635.
parallel bars. 559.
parapet. 400.
parapet walk. 167.
parcels office. 412.
parentheses. 347, 350.
parents. 130, 131.
parents-in-law. 131.
parietal. 113.
parietal bone. 114.
parietal foramen. 114.
parietal pleura. 118.
paring knife. 217.
Parisian cut. 139, 141, 142, 143.
parka. 282.
parking. 703.
parking and stopping signs. 703.
parking area. 438.
parking meter. 168.

parking prohibited or restricted. 703.
Parmesan (Italian). 145.
parsley. 135.
parsnip. 76.
parterre. 169.
partial eclipse. 29, 30.
particle board. 184.
partition. 70, 451.
partitions. 696.
partriachal. 707.
pass. 46.
passenger cabin. 421, 434.
passenger car. 415.
passenger car interior. 415.
passenger coaches, types of. 407.
passenger lift. 705.
passenger liner. 419.
passenger platform. 413.
passenger seating. 422.
passenger station. 410.
passenger terminal. 440.
passenger terminal. 438.
passenger transfer vehicle. 439, 440.
passenger walkway. 438.
passport control. 440.
passport holder. 341.
pasta. 136, 137.
pasta maker. 218.
pastern. 83.
pastry brush. 220.
pastry cutting wheel. 220.
patch. 682.
patch pocket. 290, 294, 306.
patch pocket with turn-down flap. 290.
patella. 84, 112.
patera. 200.
paternal aunt. 130.
paternal uncle. 130.
path. 237.
patio. 178, 237.
patio door. 178.
pattern. 489.
pattern. 492, 507.
pattern scissors. 507.
pauldron. 676.
pause. 462.
pause button. 366.
pause/still. 367.
pavement. 399.
pavilion. 317.
pavilion facet. 317.
pavilion roof. 180.
pawl. 209, 250.
pawn. 577.
Pawn (P). 577.
payload. 442.
pea. 71.
pea. 71.
pea jacket. 291.
peach. 67.
peach. 67.
Peacock. 33.
peak. 46.
peaked cap. 288.
peaked lapel. 282, 283.
peanut. 70.
pear. 68.
pear-shaped cut. 317.
pearl. 81.
pearl screen. 362.
pecan nut. 70.
pecten. 98.
pectoral fin. 90.
pectoral limb. 116.
pedal. 397, 398, 464, 472.
pedal board. 467.
pedal key. 467.
pedal pusher. 300.
pedestal. 387, 464.
pedestal drill. 251.
pedestal type sump pump. 267.
pedestrian crossing. 168, 700.

pedestrian precinct. 168.
pedicel. 64, 66, 68.
pedicle. 81.
pediment. 161, 593.
pedometer. 599.
peeled veneer. 255.
peeler. 217.
peep hole. 409.
peg. 205, 335, 463, 493, 496, 582, 583.
peg box. 463.
Pegasus. 32.
pegging-out point. 583.
pelerine. 290.
pelerine. 290.
pellets. 688.
pelmet. 207.
pelmet lighting. 210.
peltate. 62.
Pelton turbine. 643.
pelvic fin. 90.
pelvic girdle. 97.
pelvic limb. 116.
pelvis. 84, 120.
pen. 370, 602.
pen holder. 341.
penalty arc. 511.
penalty area. 511.
penalty bench. 517.
penalty spot. 511.
penalty timekeeper. 517.
pencil point tip. 271.
pencil sharpeners. 448.
pendant. 316.
pendulum. 593.
pendulum rod. 593.
penholder grip. 528.
penis. 106, 108.
penknife. 585.
pennant. 53, 697.
penne. 137.
pennine. 137.
penstock. 637, 641, 646.
pentaprism. 353.
penumbra. 30.
penumbra shadow. 29.
pepperpot. 213.
per bend. 696.
per cent. 708.
per fess. 696.
per pale. 696.
perching bird. 89.
percolator. 224.
percussion instruments. 471, 472.
perforated gypsum lath. 184.
perforated hardboard. 184.
perforated pipe. 267.
perforated toe cap. 308.
perforation. 289, 356.
perforator. 371.
pergola. 237.
pericardium. 118.
pericarp. 69, 70.
periodontal ligament. 115.
periople. 85.
peripheral equipment. 457.
peripheral joint. 639.
peripheral nervous system. 121.
periscope. 424.
peristyle. 161, 163.
peritoneum. 108.
permanent magnet. 372.
permanent pasture. 151.
permanent wiring. 372.
Perseus. 32.
personal adornment. 313.
personal articles. 325.
pestle. 218.
petals. 64.
Peter Pan collar. 298.
petiole. 64.
petits fours. 146.
petrochemical industry. 635.
petrochemicals. 635.
petrol. 635.

The terms in **bold type** indicate the title of an illustration.

petrol engine. 391.
petrol flap. 383.
petrol pump. 387.
petrol pump. 387, 391.
petrol pump hose. 387.
petrol tank cap. 396.
petroleum. 635.
phalange. 84.
phalanges. 97.
pharynx. 118, 119.
phase conductor. 645.
Phillips tip. 248.
philtrum. 125.
phloem. 63.
Phobos. 28.
Phoenix. 33.
phosphor coating. 274.
phosphor dot. 377.
photo chamber. 606.
photoelectric cell. 356.
photographic accessories. 359.
photographic plate. 606.
photography. 353, 354, 355, 356,
  357, 358, 359, 360, 361, 362.
photosphere. 29.
phrenic nerve. 118.
piano. 476, 477, 479.
piccolo. 469, 479.
pick. 238, 335, 574.
pick-up. 152.
pick-up automatic baler. 152.
pick-up loader. 152.
pick-up selector. 480.
pickguard. 480.
pickling onion. 75.
pickup reel. 155.
picnic area. 707.
picture tube. 377.
pie. 146.
pie tin. 220.
pieces. 577.
pied. 142.
piedmont glacier. 48.
pier. 162, 400, 401, 628.
pier foundation. 400.
pierce lever. 233.
pierced earring. 315.
piers. 165.
piggery. 151.
piggyback flat wagon. 406.
pigtail. 311.
pike position. 534.
pile. 629.
pillar. 165, 464, 602, 623.
pillar plate. 592.
pillbox hat. 304.
pillion footrest. 395.
pillow. 492.
pillow. 204.
pillow protector. 204.
pilot. 466, 542, 543.
pilot light. 331.
pilot parachute. 544.
pilots control consolette. 423.
pilots control station. 423.
pin. 199, 256, 274, 475, 487, 576.
pin cushion. 487.
pinafore. 292.
pince-nez. 319.
pinch. 622.
pinch pleat. 207.
pine kernel. 70.
pineal body. 122.
pineapple. 72.
pinion. 250, 593.
pink ball. 569.
pink stocking. 311.
pinking shears. 487.
pinnacle. 164, 165.
pinnate. 62.
pinnatifid. 62.
pinocytic vesicle. 105.
pip. 68, 69, 579.
pipe. 335.
pipe. 234, 264, 468, 475.

pipe cleaner. 335.
pipe coupling. 265.
pipe cross section. 335.
pipe-lagging insulation. 185.
pipe rack. 335.
pipe section. 192.
pipe threader. 266.
pipe tools. 335.
pipe-wrapping insulation. 185.
pipe wrench. 266.
pipeline. 630, 636.
pipework. 467.
Pisces, the Fishes. 698.
pistachio nut. 70.
piste (fencing). 562.
pistil. 64.
pistol. 689.
pistol grip. 683, 685, 687, 688.
pistol grip handle. 251, 252, 570.
pistol spray. 240.
piston. 390, 391, 393, 625.
pit. 576.
pitch. 514.
pitch axis. 378.
pitch link. 441.
pitch nozzle. 57.
pitched roof. 180.
pitcher. 520.
pitcher's plate. 520.
pitchfork comb. 328.
pitching. 638.
pitching niblick. 572.
pitching wedge. 572.
pith. 63.
pithead. 624.
piton-carrier. 575.
piton hammer. 574.
pitons. 574.
Pitot tube. 691.
pituitary gland. 122.
pivot. 277, 327, 328, 429, 478,
  487, 548, 610, 683.
pivot cab. 667.
pivot spindle. 384.
pivoted bar. 602.
placard board. 405.
placing judge. 532.
placket. 298.
plain gypsum lath. 184.
plain pole. 208.
plain weave. 497.
plaits. 320.
plan. 164, 178.
plan-position indicator. 611.
plan symbols. 188.
plane. 247.
planet projection system. 35.
planetarium. 35.
planetarium projector. 35.
planets, symbols of the. 28.
planets of the solar system. 28.
plank and pole. 552.
planoconcave. 610.
planoconvex. 610.
plant, structure of a. 61, 62.
plant cell. 105.
plantar. 111.
plantar interosseous. 110.
plantar surface of the hoof. 85.
planting box. 556.
plasmodesmata. 105.
plaster. 184.
plaster bat. 505.
plaster dressing. 615.
plasterboard. 184.
plastic-laminated hardboard. 184.
plastic pants. 305.
plasticine board. 556.
plastron. 101, 562.
plat de côte couvert. 141.
plat de côte découvert. 141.
plate. 140, 227, 318, 585.
plate crystal. 49.
plate grid. 392.

plate level. 600.
plate push. 668.
plateau. 46.
platen. 453, 500.
platen knob. 453, 457.
platform. 269, 388, 403, 534, 561,
  596, 669.
platform diver. 534.
platform edge. 413, 414.
platform ladder. 269.
platform number. 413.
platform shelter. 410.
platform trolley. 413, 671.
platter. 213, 365.
play. 367.
play button. 366.
player. 521.
player. 531.
players' bench. 517, 520, 523,
  529.
players' rotation. 529.
playing area. 550.
playing area (water polo). 531.
playing field (soccer). 511.
playing surface. 528.
playroom. 179, 419.
pleat skirts. 294.
pleated heading. 207.
plectrum. 473.
plenum. 192.
pleural cavity. 118.
plinth. 593.
plotter. 455.
ploughed land. 151.
plug. 275, 369.
plug bayonet. 679.
plum. 67.
plumbing. 257, 258, 259, 260,
  261, 262, 263, 264, 265, 266,
  267.
plumbing system. 257.
plumbing tools. 266.
plumbing wrench. 266.
plunger. 224.
plunger. 266, 372, 627.
plunging neckline. 299.
plus or minus. 708.
Pluto. 28.
plywood. 255.
plywood. 184.
pneumatic armlet. 598.
pneumatic hammer. 625.
pneumostome. 96.
pocket. 339, 340, 341, 573, 576.
pocket handkerchief. 283.
pocket instamatic camera. 354.
pockets. 294.
point. 215, 217, 352, 464, 486,
  490, 548, 550, 567, 570, 578,
  664, 677.
point lever. 408.
point lock. 409.
point motor. 409.
point signal. 408.
point wire. 409.
pointed tab end. 285, 296.
pointer. 595, 596, 597, 598, 599.
pointer scale. 595.
points. 410.
points of sailing. 539.
poisonous mushroom. 65.
poitrine. 139, 142, 143.
poker. 191.
poker die. 579.
polar axis. 34.
polar axis circle. 608.
polar climates. 51.
polar ice cap. 51.
polar lights. 39.
polar tundra. 51.
polarizing filter. 355.
Polaroid Land camera. 356.
pole. 208, 416, 547, 556, 582, 695.
pole beacon. 430.
pole loop. 582.
pole over a bank. 552.

pole piece. 372.
Pole Star. 32.
pole vault. 556.
poleyn. 676.
police. 704.
Polish writing style. 345.
polished-stone hand axe. 675.
pollen brush. 98.
pollen cell. 99.
pollen packer. 98.
pollen press. 98.
polymerization and alkylation units.
  634.
pome fleshy fruits. 68.
pome fruit, section of a. 68.
pome fruits, principal types of.
  68.
pomegranate. 72.
pommel. 553, 559, 563, 679.
pommel horse. 559.
pompom. 304.
poncho. 291.
pond. 237.
poniard. 678.
pons. 122.
pontoon. 403.
pony tail. 320.
poodle cut. 321.
pool. 655.
poop. 416.
pop sock. 301.
popping crease. 514.
poppy. 71.
porch. 164.
pore. 71, 105, 128.
pork. 142.
Porro prism. 607.
port. 212.
Port-Salut (French). 145.
port tack. 539.
portable fire extinguisher. 662.
portable life support system. 444.
portable life support system
  control unit. 444.
portable pump housing. 663.
portable shower head. 259.
portal. 165.
portal bridge. 401.
portal vein. 116, 117.
porter. 413.
portfolios. 340.
Portuguese writing style. 345.
position marker. 480.
positions. 563.
positive charge. 708.
positive contact. 656.
positive meniscus. 610.
positive plate. 392.
positive plate group. 392.
positive region. 656.
positive terminal. 392.
post. 494, 526, 529, 531, 657.
post and plank. 551.
post and rail. 551.
post binder. 449.
post-hole digger. 238.
post mill. 657.
post office. 706.
posterior chamber. 123.
posterior commissure. 122.
posterior cutaneous nerve of thigh.
  121.
posterior end. 93.
posterior root. 122.
posterior rugae. 107.
posterior semicircular canal. 124.
postern. 167.
postscript. 349.
potable water tank. 629.
potable water truck. 439.
potato. 76.
potato masher. 219.
potato planter. 154.
potential coil. 601.
pothole lid. 191.
pottery. 505, 506.

The terms in **bold type** indicate the title of an illustration.

pouch. 339.
pouch of Douglas. 109.
pouf. 202.
poultry house. 151.
poultry shears. 221.
pound. 708.
powder. 681.
powder flask. 682.
powder puff. 322.
power cord. 363, 365.
power generators. 431.
power lift truck. 670.
power line. 637.
power plant. 634.
power plant, cross section of. 646.
power relay. 195.
power station. 649.
power station. 624, 646.
power supply cord. 330.
power switch. 364, 366, 367.
power system. 658.
power take off. 152.
power/timer off switch. 367.
power train. 398.
power zoom control. 369.
powerhouse. 637, 641.
practice fairway. 571.
pre-tuning control. 367.
preamplifier. 363.
precipice. 46.
precipitation. 50.
precipitation, kinds of. 49.
precipitation area. 54.
premaxilla. 90.
premolar. 82.
prepuce. 108.
prescription. 708.
present state of weather. 54.
presenter. 375.
preset tuning button. 364.
president. 562.
press. 525.
press camera. 354.
press-stud. 488.
press-stud. 338.
pressed powder compact. 322.
presser bar. 486.
presser foot. 486.
presser foot lifter. 485.
pressing. 500.
pressing board. 500.
pressstud. 341.
pressure. 55.
pressure, measure of. 598.
pressure button. 570.
pressure change. 54.
pressure cooker. 222.
pressure gauge. 444, 598, 627.
pressure regulator. 272.
pressure regulator. 222, 271, 585.
pressure relief valve. 263, 444.
pressure screw. 502, 503.
pressure suit. 444.
pressure switch. 230.
pressure tight hatch. 423.
pressuriser. 651.
pressurized water reactor. 651.
prestressed concrete. 183.
preview monitor. 376.
price per litre/gallon. 387.
pricker. 492.
primaries. 88.
primary air fan. 647.
primary covert. 88.
primary heat transport system. 652.
primary mirror. 34.
primary power distribution panel. 423.
primary root. 61.
primary vessel. 651.
prime. 563.
prime focus. 34.
prime focus observing capsule. 34.
primer. 682, 688.

princess dress. 292.
princess seaming. 302.
principal rafter. 180.
print drying rack. 360.
print head. 457.
print washer. 360.
printed circuit. 356.
printed image. 504.
printer. 455, 458.
printing. 504.
printing image. 504.
priority. 701.
priority junction. 701.
prism binoculars. 607.
prismatic section. 432.
prize money. 555.
probe receptacle. 227.
proboscis. 92.
processing rollers. 356.
product codes. 596.
production assistant. 376.
production control room. 376.
production control room. 374.
production of electricity. 654.
production platform. 629.
profiterole. 146.
programmable timer. 367.
programmer. 228, 231, 232.
progressive wave. 43.
prohibitory signs. 702.
projectiles. 681.
projection gallery. 35.
projection lamp. 362.
projection room. 35.
projection screen. 362.
projector lens. 606.
projector lens pole piece. 606.
projector zoom lens. 368.
proleg. 92.
prominence. 29.
prompt box. 170.
pronaos. 161.
prong. 215, 284.
proofreading. 350, 351.
prop. 506.
prop forward. 512.
prop stand. 395.
propellant. 688.
propeller. 419, 422, 424.
propeller gearbox. 421.
propeller shaft. 419, 420, 422.
propman. 375.
proscenium. 170.
prostate. 108.
protected cable. 373.
protective clothing. 273.
protective cup. 519.
protective equipment. 519.
protective helmet. 554.
protective relay. 195.
protective sheet. 255.
protective surround. 550.
protective trousers. 575.
protective window. 377.
prothorax. 92.
proximal phalanx. 86, 112, 113.
proximal sesamoid. 84.
pruning hook. 239.
pruning knife. 242.
pruning saw. 242.
psychrometer. 55.
pubis. 106.
puff pastry. 147.
puff sleeve. 296.
pull bail. 362.
pull rod. 408.
pull strap. 337.
pulley. 251, 268, 391, 596.
pulley safety guard. 251.
pullover. 297.
pullovers. 286, 297.
pulmonary artery. 117, 118.
pulmonary trunk. 116.
pulmonary vein. 116, 117.
pulp. 69, 115.
pulp canal. 115.

pulp cavity. 115.
pulse button. 225.
pulse of sound. 428.
pulverizing mill. 647.
pulvino. 639.
pumice correcting pencil. 503.
pump. 232, 309, 623, 654.
pump attendant. 387.
pump motor. 267.
pump nozzle. 387.
pump suction head. 267.
pumpernickel bread. 138.
pumping station. 630.
pumping unit. 627.
pumpkin. 73.
punch card. 458.
punch card. 491.
punch card feeding dial. 491.
punch card feeding mechanism. 491.
punch card reader. 491.
punch hole. 308.
punched paper tape reader. 371.
punctuation. 371.
punctuation marks. 346, 347.
pupil. 86, 123.
purfling. 463.
purge valve. 536.
purlin. 180.
purlin cleat. 180.
purpure. 696.
purse. 341.
push-button. 256, 336, 352, 362, 457.
push-button control. 232.
push-button release. 327.
push-button telephone. 373.
push buttons. 373.
push rim. 617.
pushback tractor. 439.
pusher. 226.
putter. 572.
putter. 572.
putting green. 571.
pygal shield. 101.
pyjamas. 301.
pylon. 421, 547.
pyloric caecum. 91.
pyloric sphincter. 119.
pylorus. 119.
pyramid spot. 569.
pyramid tent. 583.
pyrolysis. 636.
pyrometer. 506.
pyrometric cone. 506.

Q

quadripod. 616.
quadruped stick. 616.
quarte. 563.
quarter. 85, 308.
quarter window. 383.
quarterback. 518.
quarterly. 696.
quarters. 631.
quartet. 476.
quasi. 139.
quasi-stationary front. 53.
quaver. 461.
quaver rest. 461.
quayside crane. 427.
quayside railway. 427.
queen. 98.
Queen. 578.
Queen (Q). 577.
queen cell. 99.
queen excluder. 99.
Queen's side. 577.
question mark. 347, 371.
quiche tin. 220.
quill. 250, 251, 352.
quill brush. 328.
quill lock. 251.
quillon. 679.

quince. 68.
quinte. 563.
quintet. 476.
quizzing glass. 319.
quoin. 680.
quotation marks. 347, 350.
quotation marks ((*csp*)). 371.

R

race course. 555.
race name. 555.
race number. 554, 555.
race programme. 555.
race time. 555.
racecourse name. 555.
raceme. 64.
rachis. 88.
racing car. 384.
racing programme. 555.
racing shoe. 554.
rack. 568.
rack. 222, 228, 232, 432.
rackboard. 468.
racks. 223.
radar. 611.
radar. 421.
radar mast. 424.
radar warning receiver. 691.
radial artery. 117.
radial nerve. 121.
radial passenger loading area. 438.
radial ply. 393.
radial tyre. 393.
radial vein. 117.
radiating element. 611.
radiation. 655.
radiation zone. 29.
radiator. 392.
radiator. 392, 404.
radiator hose. 392.
radiator pressure cap. 392.
radicle. 63.
radio antenna. 444.
radio mast. 424.
radioactive material. 704.
radish. 76.
radius. 84, 100, 112.
radome. 691.
rafter. 180, 182.
raglan. 290.
raglan sleeve. 281, 290, 296, 306.
rail. 408, 491, 536, 569.
rail anchor. 408.
rail joint. 408.
rail tank. 632.
rail track. 624.
rail transport. 404.
railway map. 412.
railway station. 410.
railway track. 408, 409.
rain. 49.
rain gauge. 55.
rain shower. 52.
rain sill. 581.
raincoat. 281.
rainfall. 55.
raise. 622.
raised band. 498.
raised head. 254.
rake. 238.
rake comb. 328.
Ram. 32.
RAM: Random Access Memory. 454.
ramekin. 213.
rammer. 681.
ramp. 161, 177, 178, 410, 621, 700.
rampart. 166, 167.
ramrod. 683.
rangefinder. 354, 690.
rank. 577.
rapier. 678.
raspberry. 66.

ratchet. 209, 248, 250, 494, 593.
ratchet knob. 599.
ratchet wheel. 494, 593.
ravioli. 137.
razor clam. 94.
razors. 327.
reaction control thruster. 378.
reaction direction. 708.
reactor. 424.
reactor compartment. 424.
reactor jacket. 651.
reactor regulating system. 652.
reading. 318.
reamer. 226.
rear apron. 285.
rear brake. 397.
rear derailleur. 397.
rear end cap. 686.
rear foil. 422.
rear leg. 203.
rear light. 383, 388, 395, 397.
rear limit line. 562.
rear load area. 384.
rear-mounted engine. 394.
rear of estate car. 384.
rear runner. 549.
rear seat. 386.
rear sight. 683, 686, 687, 688,
 689.
rear sight adjustment drum. 685.
rear suspension unit. 395.
rear window. 383.
rear window frame. 383.
rearview mirror. 385, 690.
récamier. 201.
receiver. 370, 372.
receiver. 372, 524, 526, 527, 528,
 611, 683, 685, 687.
receiver-indicator. 428.
receiving station. 370.
receiving yard. 411.
receptacle. 64, 66.
receptor. 127.
recess area. 504.
reciprocating knife mower. 152.
reclaimed water. 636.
recoil sleigh. 684.
recoil spring. 689.
recoilless rifle. 686.
record. 365.
record. 367.
record announcement button. 373.
record button. 366.
record muting button. 366.
recorder. 532.
recording level button. 366.
recording of seismic waves. 602.
recording of time. 602.
recording reproducing head. 368.
recording switch. 368.
recovery vehicle. 387.
rectangular. 584, 697.
rectum. 108, 119, 120.
rectus femoris. 110.
recuperator cylinder. 684.
recuperator cylinder front head.
 684.
red ball. 569.
red balls. 569.
red beam. 377.
red cap. 531.
red dragon. 579.
red flag. 531, 564.
Red Leicester. 144.
red marker light. 388.
red ochre pencil. 503.
red safelight filter. 361.
Red Sea. 41.
redan. 166.
redoubt. 166.
reduce space. 350.
reducing coupling. 265.
reed. 494.
reed hook. 496.
reed panicle. 352.
reed pipe. 468.

reeds. 469.
reef band. 417.
reef knot. 587.
reef point. 417.
reel. 154, 360, 562.
reel seat. 566.
referee. 511, 512, 517, 518, 523,
 528, 529, 531, 532, 564, 565.
reference station. 379.
refill. 352.
refill tube. 258.
refinery. 634.
refinery. 630.
refinery products. 635.
reflecting screen. 358.
reflecting surface. 654.
reflector. 211, 274, 359, 388, 656.
reflector telescope. 608.
refractor telescope. 609.
refractory brick. 506.
refractory fire pot. 195.
refrigerant tubing. 194.
refrigeration unit. 388.
refrigerator compartment. 229.
refrigerator van. 406.
refrigerator vent. 581.
refuelling machine. 648.
register. 601.
registered office address. 349.
registered trademark. 708.
regulatory signs. 702.
reheated steam. 648.
reheater. 647.
rein. 554.
reinforced concrete. 183.
reject chute. 373.
relay. 196.
release bar. 389.
release button. 353.
release handle. 386.
release lever. 249.
release setting screw. 546.
release treadle. 494.
relief printing process. 502.
relief track. 410.
remote control. 362.
remote-control arm. 443.
remote control socket. 368.
remote-controlled points. 409.
removable blade. 270.
renal artery. 117, 120.
renal papilla. 120.
renal vein. 117, 120.
reniform. 62.
repeat mark. 462.
reptile. 101.
rerebrace. 676.
rerunning. 634.
reserve mud tank. 629.
reserve parachute. 544.
reserve petrol tap. 396.
reservoir. 224, 467, 637, 638, 641.
reset button. 367.
reset key. 456.
resin-coated paper dryer. 360.
resonator. 392, 468, 471.
respiratory system. 118.
rest symbols. 461.
restaurant. 705.
restricted area. 523.
result of last meeting. 555.
resurgence. 46.
retainer. 625.
retainer nut. 261.
retaining ring. 384.
retaining spring. 625.
retarding magnet. 601.
reticle. 607.
retina. 123.
retractable boarding ladder. 691.
retractable flex. 234.
retractable handle. 340.
retracted claw. 86.
retrenchment. 166.
return. 451.
return air. 195.

return crease. 514.
return duct. 194.
return elevator. 155.
return key. 456.
return main. 194.
return spring. 370, 393.
reverse dive. 535.
reversible reaction. 708.
reversing light. 152, 383.
revolution counter. 385.
revolver. 689.
revolving cylinder. 492.
revolving frame. 661.
revolving nosepiece. 605.
revolving sprinkler. 240.
rewind. 367.
rewind button. 366, 373.
rewind crank. 353.
rhomboideus. 111.
rhubarb. 77.
rib. 77, 336, 463, 668.
rib pad. 519.
rib stitch. 490.
ribbing. 286, 291, 305, 306, 307,
 567.
ribbing plough. 153.
ribbon. 311, 452, 453.
ribbon cartridge. 452.
ribbon end indicator. 452.
ribbon guide. 452.
ribbon load lever. 452.
ribosome. 105.
ribs. 84, 112, 505.
Ricotta (Italian). 145.
rider. 549.
rider handle. 595.
rider scale. 595.
ridge. 42, 294, 580.
ridge beam. 180.
ridge pole. 582.
ridge tent. 583.
ridge tile. 177.
ridging hoe. 238.
riding. 551, 552, 553.
riding crop. 551.
riding glove. 551.
riding helmet. 551.
riding jacket. 551.
rifle (rifled bore). 688.
rift. 42.
rigatoni. 137.
rigging wire. 543.
right angle finder. 355.
right ascension. 27.
right atrium. 116.
right back. 516, 529.
right bend. 700.
right bronchus. 118.
right centre. 512, 513.
right cornerback. 518.
right defence. 517.
right defensive end. 518.
right defensive tackle. 518.
right elevating arc. 684.
right field. 520.
right fielder. 520.
right forward. 523, 529.
right fullback. 511.
right guard. 518, 523.
right half. 516.
right halfback. 518.
right-hand grip. 686.
right inner. 516.
right kidney (sagittal section). 120.
right lung. 116, 118.
right midfield. 511.
right safety. 518.
right service court. 524, 527.
right side. 294.
right tackle. 518.
right ventricle. 116.
right wing. 511, 512, 513, 516,
 517.
rigid board insulation. 185.
rigid frame. 35.
rigs. 628.

rigs, types of. 418.
rim. 318, 393, 395, 397, 558.
rim flange. 393.
rinceau. 200.
rind. 69.
ring. 63, 65, 208, 336, 433, 470,
 488, 523, 559, 574, 594, 682.
ring (boxing). 565.
ring binder. 449.
ring floor. 565.
ring nut. 264.
ring post. 565.
ring spanner. 248.
ring step. 565.
ringer coil. 372.
ringlets. 320.
rings. 315, 559.
rings. 137.
ringside. 565.
rink. 517.
rink. 530.
rink corner. 517.
rink number. 530.
rinse-aid dispenser. 232.
rip fence. 252, 253.
rip fence adjustment. 252.
rip fence guide. 252.
rip fence lock. 252.
ripcord. 544.
ripper. 666.
ripper. 664.
ripper cylinder. 664.
rise. 187.
riser. 35, 187, 544, 570.
rising main. 257.
River Eridanus. 33.
rivet. 217, 249, 318.
road, cross section of a. 399.
road base. 399.
road tankers. 632.
road transport. 383.
road works. 701.
roadway narrows. 700.
roast sensor probe. 228.
roasting pans. 222.
Roberval's balance. 595.
rock basin. 48.
rock garden. 237.
rock sample pocket. 444.
rock step. 48.
rocker cover. 391.
rocket. 442.
rocket. 39.
rocking chair. 201, 203.
rocking tool. 501.
rocks. 639.
rocky desert. 47.
rod. 196, 478, 495.
rodent's jaw. 82.
roe deer. 81.
roll. 298.
roll axis. 378.
roll line. 298.
roll nozzle. 57.
roll of paper. 371.
roll-on roll-off ramp. 427.
roll-up blind. 209.
roller. 208, 209, 232, 241, 331,
 432, 452, 501.
roller blind. 209.
roller board and arms. 468.
roller circle. 661.
roller cover. 270.
roller frame. 270.
roller guides. 171.
roller pins. 333.
roller skate. 548.
rolling ladder. 269.
rolling pin. 220.
ROM* memory. 454.
ROM: Read Only Memory. 454.
Roman house. 163.
Roman legionary. 675.
Roman metal pen. 352.
Romanian couching stitch. 493.
Romanian writing style. 345.

The terms in **bold type** indicate the title of an illustration.

733

romsteck. 141.
rond de gîte à la noix. 141.
rondel. 676.
roof. 99, 177, 383, 388, 411, 582, 621, 622.
roof flashing. 257.
roof ladder. 663.
roof structure. 180.
roof vent. 265.
roof vent and light. 581.
roofs, types of. 180, 181.
Rook (R). 577.
room. 582, 623.
room air conditioner. 196.
room thermostat. 597.
rooms of the house. 179.
root. 61.
root. 61, 75, 115, 126, 215.
root cap. 61.
root-hair zone. 63.
root hairs. 61.
root of hair. 129.
root of nail. 129.
root rib. 435.
root vegetables. 76.
rope. 316, 565, 575, 587.
rope belt. 306.
rope ladder. 268.
Roquefort (French). 145.
rose. 240, 256.
rose cut. 317.
rose window. 165.
rosemary. 135.
rosette. 160.
rostrum. 95.
rotary file. 450.
rotary hoe. 153.
rotary joint. 611.
rotary table. 626.
rotating auger. 155.
rotating dome. 34.
rotating dome truck. 34.
rotating drum. 602.
rotating wheel. 580.
rotisserie. 228.
rotor. 256, 641, 642, 649, 657, 658.
rotor blade. 436, 441.
rotor head. 441.
rotor hub. 441.
rotor shaft. 658.
rotovator. 241.
rotunda roof. 181.
rouelle. 139.
rouge. 580.
rough. 571.
roulette. 501.
roulette table. 580.
round brush. 328.
round end pin. 209.
round eye. 488.
round head. 254.
round ligament of uterus. 109.
round loaf. 138.
round neck. 299.
round pronator. 110.
round trefoil. 162.
roundabout. 701, 703.
router. 250.
routing cardboard. 405.
row. 329.
row indicator. 491.
rowing. 541.
rowing (one oar). 541.
rowing (two oars). 541.
royal flush. 578.
royal mast. 416.
rub rail. 388.
rubber base. 328.
rubber ferrule. 616.
rubber gasket. 260.
rubber mat. 365.
rubber stamp. 448.
rubber thread. 573.
rubber wall. 393.
rubber washer. 260.

rubbing strake. 581.
rubbing strip. 393.
rucksack. 575.
rudder. 419, 421, 424, 434, 443, 538, 542.
rudder pedal. 437, 542.
ruff. 298.
ruffle. 207.
rugby. 512.
rugby union. 512, 513.
rump. 87, 139, 140.
run. 560.
run on. 350.
rung. 268, 574.
runner. 199, 232, 549, 578, 642, 643.
runner blade. 643, 646.
running bowline. 587.
running rail. 415.
running track. 556.
running track. 411.
runway. 415, 438.
runway centre line markings. 438.
runway designation marking. 438.
runway end lights. 438.
runway side markings. 438.
runway threshold markings. 438.
runway touchdown zone marking. 438.
Russian pumpernickel. 138.
Russian writing style. 345.
rye crispbread. 138.

S

s-band antenna. 57.
sabaton. 676.
sable. 696.
sabre. 563, 678.
sabre and épée warning line. 562.
sabreur. 563.
sacral plexus. 121.
sacral vertebrae. 84.
sacrum. 112.
saddle. 553.
saddle. 143, 335, 362, 397, 554, 559.
safari jacket. 297.
safe and arm device. 378.
safelight. 360.
safety. 683, 685.
safety area. 564.
safety bar. 388, 547.
safety binding. 546.
safety binding. 545.
safety cage. 556.
safety glasses. 319.
safety line. 414.
safety match. 335.
safety pad. 560.
safety pin. 615, 682.
safety pins. 487.
safety rail. 269.
safety scissors. 333.
safety strap. 546.
safety thermostat. 231.
safety valve. 222.
sage. 135.
saggar. 506.
sagittal suture. 114.
Sagittarius, the Archer. 698.
sagittate. 62.
sail. 537, 543, 657.
sail cloth. 657.
sail panel. 538.
sail plan. 417.
sailbar. 657.
sailboard. 537.
sailor collar. 298.
sailor tunic. 295.
sails, types of. 418.
Saint Andrew's. 707.
salad bowl. 213.
salad fork. 215.
salad plate. 213.

salad shaker. 218.
salad spinner. 218.
salient angle. 166.
salient pole. 642.
saline lake. 47.
salivary glands. 119.
salon-style hair dryer. 330.
saloon open coach. 407.
salsify. 76.
salt marsh. 43.
salt water. 626.
saltcellar. 213.
sample. 490.
sand. 592.
sand bar. 43.
sand island. 43.
sand-rock. 636.
sand wedge. 572.
sandal. 309, 675.
sandstorm. 52.
sandy desert. 47.
saphenous nerve. 121.
sapwood. 63.
sarong. 293.
sartorius. 110.
sash. 311.
sash-frame. 189.
sash window. 189.
satellites, examples of. 378.
satin weave. 497.
Saturn. 28.
saucepan. 222.
saucepan. 585.
saucer. 213.
sauté pan. 223.
savarin. 146.
savory. 135.
savoy bag and nozzles. 220.
saw. 585.
sawing-in. 499.
sawtooth roof. 181.
saxophone. 469.
saxophone. 469, 477.
scale. 65, 89, 90, 101, 594, 596, 597, 599, 610, 633.
scale (music). 461.
scale leaf. 75.
scale of speeds. 478.
scallop. 94.
scampi. 95.
scapula. 84, 112.
scapular. 88.
scarf. 545.
scarf turban. 304.
scarifier. 666.
scarp. 166, 167.
scatter cushion. 204.
scattered sky. 53.
schoolchildren. 700.
Schwenkel. 697.
sciatic nerve. 121.
scissor-lift truck. 439.
scissors. 487.
scissors. 485, 615.
scissors cut. 317.
scissors-glasses. 319.
sclera. 123.
sconce. 210.
scoop. 335.
score sheet. 576.
scoreboard. 550.
scorer. 517, 523, 529, 562, 576.
scoring areas. 550.
scoring light. 562.
scoring table. 576.
Scorpio, the Scorpion. 698.
Scorpion. 33.
scotia. 160.
scraper. 270.
scraper. 501, 503.
scraper bar. 504.
scraper bar holder. 503.
scraper engine. 668.
screen. 327, 369, 377, 641.
screen case. 362.

screen front. 305.
screen print. 306.
screen window. 582.
screen wiper. 394.
screw. 254.
screw. 256, 464, 548.
screw base. 274.
screw earring. 315.
screw eye. 494.
screw locking nut. 566.
screwdriver. 248.
screwdriver. 585.
screwsleeve. 574.
scrimmage. 518.
scroll. 463.
scroll case. 641.
scrotum. 106, 108.
scrubber. 423.
scrum. 512.
scrum. 512.
scrum half. 512, 513.
scuba diver. 536.
sculling. 541.
Sculptor. 33.
scum. 267.
scuttle panel. 383.
scythe. 242.
sea. 30, 646.
sea anchor. 433.
Sea Goat. 33.
sea level. 40, 42.
sea-level pressure. 54.
Sea Serpent. 33.
sea side. 646.
seal. 258, 263, 656.
sealed-beam mounting ring. 384.
sealed cell. 99.
sealing lug. 601.
sealing ring. 633.
seam. 289, 334, 515.
seam allowance. 489.
seam line. 489.
seam pocket. 290, 294.
seaming. 290.
seamount. 42.
sear. 687.
season tiles. 579.
seasons of the year. 27.
seat. 169, 200, 203, 259, 505, 542, 547, 549, 553.
seat belt. 386.
seat post. 397.
seat stay. 397.
seat tube. 397.
seat upholstery. 617.
seats. 202, 386.
sebaceous gland. 128, 129.
secateurs. 239.
second. 462, 565.
second balcony. 169.
second base. 520.
second baseman. 520.
second condenser lens. 606.
second dorsal fin. 90.
second extension ladder. 662.
second flight. 560.
second hand. 591.
second linesman. 529.
second molar. 115.
second premolar. 115.
second reinforce. 680.
second reinforce ring. 680.
second slip. 514.
second space. 523.
second stage. 442.
second violins. 479.
secondaries. 88.
secondary inlet. 633.
secondary root. 61.
secondary sheave. 171.
seconde. 563.
secretarial desk. 451.
secretary. 531.
sector. 458.
sector flag. 556.
security check. 440.

The terms in **bold type** indicate the title of an illustration.

sediment chamber. 392.
sedimentary rocks. 40.
see-through windows. 341.
seed. 66, 67, 68, 69, 70, 71.
seed coat. 67, 71.
seed drill. 154.
seed vegetables. 77.
seeder. 239, 241.
seeds. 137.
segment. 69.
segment score number. 550.
seismic wave. 45.
seismographs. 602.
self-adhesive labels. 448.
self-contained platform. 628.
self-erecting tent. 583.
self-indicating scales. 596.
self timer. 353.
selle. 143.
selvage. 488.
semaphore. 410.
semi-breve. 461.
semi-breve rest. 461.
semi-detached house. 173.
semi-fish-eye lens. 355.
semi-membrane tanks. 631.
semi-mummy. 584.
semi-quaver. 461.
semi-quaver rest. 461.
semi-submersible. 628.
semi-trailer. 388.
semi-trailer. 389.
semicircular arch. 162.
semicolon. 347, 350, 371.
semimembranosus. 111.
seminal vesicle. 108.
semitendinosus. 111.
sender's reference. 349.
sending station. 370.
sense organs. 123, 124, 125, 126,
127.
sense receptor. 127.
senses of smell and taste. 125.
sensor probe. 227.
sensory impulse. 127.
sensory neuron. 127.
sepal. 66.
sepals. 64.
separator. 392.
separator wire. 452.
separators. 491.
septal cartilage of nose. 125.
septic tank. 267.
septic tank first compartment. 267.
septic tank second compartment.
267.
septime. 563.
septum. 71.
septum of scrotum. 108.
septum pellucidum. 122.
serac. 48.
Serpent. 32, 33.
Serpent Bearer. 32, 33.
serrated cast-iron casing. 682.
server. 524, 526, 527, 528, 529.
service area. 529.
service box. 527, 645.
service judge. 526.
service line. 524, 527.
service module. 442.
service room. 431.
service station. 387.
service station. 707.
serving bowl. 213.
serving trolley. 199.
sesame seeded pita. 138.
set in boldface. 350.
set in capitals. 350.
set in italic. 350.
set in lower case. 350.
set in roman. 350.
set-in-sleeve. 281, 285, 286, 296.
set in small capitals. 350.
set of utensils. 219.
set-off button. 466.
set-up. 576.

setting. 315.
settling basin. 624.
settling pond. 634, 636.
settling tank. 631.
seventh. 462.
sew-through buttons. 488.
sewing. 485, 486, 487, 488, 489.
sewing frame. 499.
sewing machine. 485, 486.
sewing spool. 485.
sewn-in groundsheet. 582.
sextant. 429.
sextet. 477.
shackle. 539.
shade. 210, 211.
shadow. 592.
shadow mask. 377.
shaft. 53, 160, 318, 496, 505, 525,
527, 550, 558, 568, 570, 572,
574, 597, 641, 642, 643, 677.
shaft collar. 623.
shag. 321.
shag-carpet-rake. 234.
shake-hands grip. 528.
shaker. 221.
shallot. 75, 468.
shallow root. 63.
shank. 140, 248, 250, 254, 308,
328, 335, 336, 433, 486, 487,
490, 492, 567, 664.
shank button. 488.
shank protector. 664.
share. 153.
sharp. 462.
sharpening steel. 217.
shaving brush. 327.
shaving mug. 327.
shawl collar. 298.
shawm. 474.
sheath. 62, 83, 587.
sheath dress. 292.
sheath knife. 586.
sheath of Schwann. 127.
sheath skirt. 293.
shed. 237.
shed stick. 495.
sheepshank. 587.
sheepskin jacket. 282.
sheer curtain. 207.
sheet. 417, 498.
sheet bend. 587.
sheet lead. 539.
sheet of paper. 602.
shelf. 206, 229, 269, 506.
shelf channel. 229.
shell. 70, 89, 94, 96, 101, 337,
472, 633, 686, 690.
shell membrane. 89.
shells. 137.
SHF antenna. 378.
SHF beacon antenna. 378.
shield. 695.
Shield. 33, 675, 695.
shift key. 453.
shift keys. 456.
shift lock key. 453, 456.
shin. 140.
shin guard. 519, 521.
ship's anchor. 433.
ship's cannon. 680, 681.
Ship's Keel. 33.
ship's motor boat. 425.
Ship's Sails. 33.
ship's side. 416.
Ship's Stern. 33.
shirt. 285.
shirt. 311, 525.
shirt collar. 295, 298.
shirt sleeve. 295.
shirt-tail. 295.
shirttail. 285.
shirtwaist dress. 292.
shirtwaist sleeve. 296.
shock absorber. 230.
shoe. 362.
shoe, parts of a. 308.

shoe horn. 310.
shoe rack. 310.
shoe tree. 310.
shoelace. 308.
shoes. 308, 309, 310.
shoes, principal types of. 309,
310.
shoeshine kit. 310.
shoot. 61, 63.
shooting star. 39.
shop. 163.
shop sign. 168.
shop window. 168.
shopping bag. 338.
short. 287.
short extensor of toes. 110.
short extra cover. 514.
short fine leg. 514.
short glove. 289.
short line. 527.
short palmar. 110.
short peroneal. 111.
short radial extensor of wrist. 111.
short service line. 526.
short-sleeved shirt. 561.
short sock. 301.
shortbread. 146.
shorts. 300.
shorts. 300, 525, 565.
shortstop. 520.
shot. 681.
shot put. 557.
shot splice. 587.
shotgun (smooth-bore). 688.
shots. 558.
shoulder. 46, 83, 106, 139, 142,
143, 254, 525, 567.
shoulder bag. 339.
shoulder blade. 107.
shoulder bolt. 254.
shoulder pad. 519, 686.
shoulder stock. 686.
shoulder-strap. 303, 336, 337, 339,
573.
shovel. 191, 238, 545.
shower and bath fixture. 257.
shower head. 259.
showerproof hat. 304.
shrimp. 95.
shroud. 416, 538.
shunting engine. 411.
shutdown system. 652.
shutoff valve. 260, 262.
shutter. 189, 606, 655.
shutter button. 356.
shutter release. 353.
shutter speed dial. 353.
shutters. 209.
shuttle. 486.
shuttlecock. 526.
sickle. 242.
side. 214, 481, 671.
side back vent. 283.
side chair. 203.
side chapel. 164.
side door. 411.
side entrance. 178.
side handle. 250.
side handrail. 415.
side ladder. 405.
side ladder tread. 405.
side lever. 492.
side line. 516, 522, 528.
side mirror. 330.
side moulding. 581.
side panel. 383.
side plate. 213.
side platform. 414.
side pocket. 281.
side post. 180.
side rail. 205.
side span. 402.
side-tilt lock. 359.
side wall. 85, 411, 426, 527, 532.
side wall line. 527.
side window. 389.

sideboard. 206.
sidelight. 413.
sideline. 519.
sideline. 523, 529.
sidestroke. 533.
sidewall. 388.
sieve. 218.
sifter. 220.
sight. 123, 610, 677, 683.
sight-glass tube. 233.
sighting line. 610.
sighting mirror. 610.
sigmoid colon. 119.
signal background plate. 409.
signal box. 410.
signal gantry. 410.
signalbox and yard office. 411.
signals. 409.
signature. 498.
signature of sender. 349.
signet ring. 315.
signs showing priority at
junctions. 701.
silage bunker. 151.
silage harvester. 153.
silencer. 243, 392, 395.
silique, section of a. 71.
silk. 77.
silks. 554.
sill. 45, 182.
sill of frame. 189.
sill plate. 182.
sill step. 405.
silly mid-off. 514.
silverside. 140.
silverware. 214, 215, 216.
sima. 160.
simple leaves. 62.
simple-span beam bridge. 400.
simple topmarks. 430.
single-breasted coat. 283.
single burner camp stove. 585.
single curtain rod. 208.
single-decked pallet. 671.
single-edged swords. 678.
single-handle kitchen tap. 261.
single-handle kitchen tap. 260.
single herringbone parquet. 186.
single-leaf bascule bridge. 403.
single-lens reflex camera. 353.
single pipe heating system. 193.
single quotation marks. 347.
single reed. 469.
single scull. 541.
single seat. 415.
single spring washer. 254.
single string. 465.
single twist. 250.
single zero. 580.
singles pole. 524.
singles service court. 526.
singles sideline. 524, 526.
Sinhalese writing style. 345.
sinister. 695.
sinister base. 695.
sinister chief. 695.
sinister flank. 695.
sink. 260.
sink. 259, 360.
sink hole. 46.
sink strainer. 260.
sinker. 567.
sinker plate. 491, 492.
sinus of kidney. 120.
siphon. 46.
siphonal canal. 93.
siren. 422, 663.
sirloin. 140.
sister. 130.
site plan. 178.
six-figure form. 555.
sixain. 580.
sixte. 563.
sixth. 462.
skate guard. 548.
skates, types of. 548.

The terms in **bold type** indicate the title of an illustration.

735

skating. 548.
skeg. 537.
skeleton. 112, 113.
sketch. 507.
ski. 545.
ski boot. 546.
ski boot. 546.
ski goggles. 319, 545.
ski instructor. 547.
ski jump. 547.
ski jumper. 547.
ski lift. 547.
ski pants. 300.
ski pole. 545.
ski resort. 547.
ski shuttle. 495.
ski stop. 545, 546.
ski suit. 545.
skid. 441.
skid pad. 630.
skid ramp. 389.
skier. 545.
skiing. 545, 546, 547.
skimmer. 153, 219.
skin. 127, 128.
skin. 66, 67, 68, 97, 127.
skin diving. 536.
skin surface. 127, 128.
skirt. 516, 522, 525, 553, 676.
skirt finger. 421.
skirt marker. 487.
skirting board. 187.
skirting convector. 193.
skirting grille. 192.
skirts. 293.
skis, types of. 540.
skull. 84, 91, 106, 676.
skull cap. 288.
skylight. 177.
slab building. 505.
slalom course. 547.
slalomist. 547.
slash. 347, 371.
slash neck. 299.
slat. 209, 426, 493.
sleeper. 408.
sleeping bag. 306.
sleeping bags. 584.
sleeping car. 407.
sleepsuit. 305, 306.
sleet. 49, 52.
sleeve. 283, 561, 562, 582, 599.
sleeve protector. 473.
sleeve strap. 281.
sleeve strap loop. 281.
sleeves. 296.
sliced white bread. 138.
slide. 362.
slide. 488, 689.
slide-bar. 491.
slide chair. 408.
slide changer. 362.
slide mount. 362.
slide plate. 485.
slide projector. 362.
slide selector. 227, 233.
slide tray. 362.
slider. 468.
sliding. 188, 189.
sliding breech. 684.
sliding door. 178.
sliding folding. 188, 189.
sliding weight. 478, 594.
sliding window. 407.
slightly covered sky. 53.
sling. 680, 685, 686, 687.
sling swivel. 685.
slip. 170, 302.
slip joint. 249.
slip joint pliers. 249.
slip-on. 310.
slip ring. 685.
slip-stitched seam. 285.
slipover. 286, 297.
slippers. 311.
slippery road. 700.

slit. 497.
slit pocket. 284.
sloped turret. 181.
sloping cornice. 161.
slot. 170, 215, 227, 254, 499.
slotted bit. 248.
slotted bracket. 209.
slotted wall bracket. 259.
slow-motion control knob. 609.
sludge. 267.
sluice hole. 426.
small blade. 585.
small capitals. 351.
small hand cultivator. 239.
small intestine. 119.
smell. 125.
smock. 292, 295.
smoke. 52.
smoke bomb discharger. 690.
smoke dome. 190.
smoke filter. 419.
smoking accessories. 334, 335.
smoking permitted. 705.
smoking prohibited. 705.
snaffle bit. 553.
snaffle rein. 553.
snail. 96.
snail dish. 221.
snail tongs. 221.
snap fastener. 289.
snap-fastening adjustable strap. 306.
snap-fastening front. 306.
snap-fastening shoulder strap. 306.
snap-fastening side. 305.
snap-fastening waist. 305.
snap shackle. 539.
snare. 472.
snare drum. 472.
snare drum. 477, 479.
snare head. 472.
snare strainer. 472.
sneaker. 309.
snooker. 568, 569.
snorkel. 536.
snort exhaust. 424.
snort induction. 424.
snout. 97.
snow. 50.
snow crystals, classification of. 49.
snow goggles. 575.
snow pellet. 49.
snow shower. 52.
snow tyre. 393.
snowsuit. 307.
soap dish. 259.
soccer. 511.
soccer ball. 511.
sock. 287.
sock. 301, 516, 525.
sock lining. 308.
socket. 275, 488.
socket bayonet. 679.
soda bread. 138.
soft cup bra. 303.
soft keys. 456.
soft palate. 126.
soft pedal. 465.
soft ray. 90.
soft shell clam. 94.
softlight reflector. 358.
soil. 639.
soil drain. 257.
soil-or-waste stack. 257.
soil vent. 257.
solar cell. 656.
solar cell. 378.
solar collector. 655.
solar eclipse. 29.
solar energy. 654, 655, 656.
solar furnace. 654.
solar house. 655.
solar panel. 57.
solar panel deployment. 379.
solar radiation. 654, 655, 656.

solder. 273, 507.
soldering. 271, 272, 273.
soldering gun. 271.
soldering iron. 271.
soldering iron. 507.
soldering process. 507.
sole. 85, 129, 287, 311, 546, 548, 572.
sole plate. 548.
soleplate. 233, 408.
soleus. 110.
solid body. 480.
solid-rocket booster. 443.
solid rubber tyre. 670.
solitaire ring. 315.
solleret. 676.
solvent extraction unit. 635.
something omitted. 350.
son. 130.
son-in-law. 131.
sonar display and control. 423.
sonar housing. 423.
sonic height sensor. 422.
sorbet. 147.
sou'wester. 288, 304.
soufflé. 147.
sound-board. 464.
sound box. 464.
sound camera. 368.
sound control room. 374.
sound desk. 374.
sound-on-sound control. 368.
sound-post. 464.
sound projector. 368.
sound reproducing system. 363, 364, 365, 366.
sound supervisor. 374.
soundboard. 465, 481.
soundbox. 473.
soundhole. 481.
sounding balloon. 39, 55.
soup bowl. 213.
soup spoon. 216.
soup tureen. 213.
south. 430, 579.
South America. 41.
South celestial pole. 27.
South pole. 27.
South wind. 579.
Southern Cross. 33.
Southern Crown. 33.
Southern Fish. 33.
southern hemisphere. 27.
Southern Triangle. 33.
soybeans. 77.
space. 461.
space achievements. 39.
space bar. 453, 456.
space probe. 39.
space shuttle. 443.
space shuttle at take-off. 443.
space shuttle in orbit. 443.
space travel. 442.
spacelab. 443.
spacer. 617, 644.
spacesuit. 444.
spade. 238, 541, 578, 684.
spade mashie. 572.
spadix. 64.
spaghetti. 136.
spaghetti tongs. 221.
spandrel. 162.
Spanish onion. 75.
Spanish writing style. 345.
spanker. 417.
spanker boom. 416.
spanker gaff. 416.
spanners. 248.
spark plug. 392.
spark plug. 243.
spark plug body. 392.
spark plug gap. 392.
spark plug gasket. 392.
spark plug terminal. 392.
spathulate. 62.
spatial dendrite. 49.

spatula. 219, 502.
speaker. 363.
speaker. 35, 368, 377.
speaker selector. 364.
speaking window membrane. 412.
spear. 77.
speargun. 536.
special effects. 376.
specific data processing program. 454.
specimen. 605.
specimen chamber. 606.
spectacles. 319.
speed control. 225.
speed selector. 226.
speed selector lever. 365.
speed skate. 548.
speedometer. 385, 396.
spent fuel chute. 648.
spent fuel storage and containment. 648.
spermatozoon. 108.
sphenoid bone. 114.
sphenoidal sinus. 125.
sphere. 430.
sphere support. 56.
spherical parabolic reflector. 656.
sphincter muscle of anus. 119.
sphygmomanometer. 598.
spicule. 29.
spider. 153.
spider (cross-piece). 230.
spike. 64, 408, 573, 574, 575.
spike file. 447.
spike-tooth. 152.
spiked shoe. 521.
spillway. 637.
spillway chute. 637.
spillway gate. 637.
spinach. 74.
spinach noodles. 136.
spinal column. 112.
spinal cord. 91, 122, 127.
spinal ganglion. 127.
spinal nerve. 122, 127.
spindle. 203, 226, 256, 261, 365, 593, 599, 601.
spindle hole. 256.
spindle screw. 599.
spine. 93, 498, 500.
spine of scapula. 113.
spine of the book. 500.
spinnaker boom. 538.
spinnaker sheet lead. 538.
spinner. 567.
spinning rod. 566.
spiny lobster. 95.
spiny ray. 90.
spiracle. 92.
spiral. 137, 248, 365.
spiral arms. 31.
spiral beater. 225.
spiral binding. 449.
spiral case. 642, 643.
spiral chute. 623.
spiral galaxy. 31.
spiral-in groove. 365.
spiral ratchet screwdriver. 248.
spiral rib. 93.
spiral staircase. 633.
spire. 93, 96, 164.
spirit level. 248.
spit. 43.
splash plate. 633.
splat. 200.
splay. 165.
splayed leg. 199.
splaying. 190.
spleen. 91, 116.
sleeping compartment. 407.
splenic artery. 117.
splenic vein. 117.
splenius muscle of head. 111.
spline. 392.
split end. 518.

split link. 567.
split system heating pump. 194.
spoiler. 434.
spoke. 397.
sponge. 681.
sponge-tipped applicator. 322.
spongy body. 108.
spool. 492, 566.
spool pin. 485.
spool rack. 496.
spoon. 216.
spoon. 572, 585.
spoons, major types of. 216.
spores. 65.
sports. 509.
spot. 211.
spot projector attachment. 358.
spot white ball. 569.
spotlight. 375, 422, 662.
spotmeter. 357.
spouse. 130.
spout. 224, 233, 261.
spout assembly. 260.
spray. 233.
spray arm. 232.
spray button. 233.
spray head. 260.
spray hose. 260.
spray nozzle. 633.
spray paint gun. 270.
spread collar. 285.
spreader. 241, 336.
spreader adjustment valve. 270.
spreading fork. 238.
spreading rotor. 153.
spring. 27, 211, 249, 256, 261,
    352, 404, 560, 598, 602, 682,
    686.
spring balance. 594.
spring binder. 449.
spring hip throw. 564.
spring onion. 75.
spring washer. 408.
spring wing. 254.
springboard. 534, 559, 560.
springboard diver. 534.
springer. 162.
sprinkler hose. 240.
sprocket. 180.
sprocket cluster. 398.
sprocket wheel. 664.
spur. 46, 250, 472, 551.
spy hole. 506.
squab. 386.
squall. 52.
squamous suture. 114.
square. 579.
square. 498, 697.
square basket weave pattern. 186.
square head plug. 265.
square leg. 514.
square neck. 299.
square root of. 708.
square sail. 418.
squash. 527.
squash ball. 527.
squash racquet. 527.
St George's cross. 430.
stabilizer. 420, 544, 677.
stabilizer foot. 232.
stabilizing fin. 442.
stabilizing plane. 423.
stable type door. 581.
stack. 43.
stacking chairs. 203.
staff. 461.
staff. 695.
stage. 35, 170, 605, 606.
stage, cross section of a. 170.
stage clip. 605.
stage curtain. 170.
stage-house. 170.
stained glass. 507.
stairs. 187.
stairs. 178, 633, 705.
stairwell. 179.

stake. 237.
stalactite. 46.
stalagmite. 46.
stalk. 66, 68, 77.
stalk vegetables. 77.
stalked eye. 95.
stamen. 64, 68.
stamp pad. 448.
stamp pocket. 341.
stamp rack. 448.
stanchion. 548.
stand. 210, 223, 225, 298, 331,
    337, 358, 359, 656.
stand-up collar. 298.
standard hardboard. 184.
standard lamp. 210.
standard lens. 355.
standard poker hands. 578.
standing press. 500.
standpipe. 262.
staple remover. 447.
staple shaft. 622, 623.
stapler. 447.
staples. 447.
star anise. 71.
star diagonal. 609.
star facet. 317.
star projection condenser. 35.
star projection lens. 35.
star sphere. 35.
starch. 71.
starch granule. 105.
stars. 137.
start. 552.
start line. 556.
start switch. 231.
start wall. 532.
startboard tack. 539.
starter. 391, 532, 658.
starter handle. 243.
starting block. 532.
starting dive. 532.
starting electrode. 274.
starting grip. 532.
starting position. 535.
starting position (swimming).
    532.
starting positions (diving). 534.
starting price. 555.
starting resistor. 274.
starting signal. 413.
state of course. 555.
state of ground. 55.
station circle. 53, 54.
station concourse. 412.
station model. 54.
station name. 414.
station platform. 413.
station platform. 410.
station sign. 413.
stationary bowl. 580.
stationery. 447, 448, 449, 450.
stationery blade. 649.
stationery cabinet. 451.
stator. 641, 642, 649.
stator vane. 436.
statue. 161.
stay. 416, 596.
stay ring. 642, 643.
stay vane. 642, 643.
staysail-stay. 416.
steak knife. 214.
steam button. 233.
steam cracker. 634.
steam drive oil sands recovery
    process. 636.
steam drum. 647.
steam from reheat. 649.
steam generator. 424, 648, 650,
    651, 654.
steam generator system. 652.
steam injection. 636.
steam iron. 233.
steam to reheat. 649.
steam turbine. 420, 648.
steel. 303, 682.

steel band. 596.
steel bar. 559.
steel beam. 183.
steel lined concrete pressure
    vessel. 648.
steel pen. 352.
steel pressure vessel. 650, 651.
steel safety wheel. 415.
steel spring. 682.
steel to plastic. 265.
steelyard. 594.
steep hill. 700.
steeplechase. 556.
steering. 386.
steering axle. 670.
steering column. 386.
steering cylinder. 668.
steering damper. 396.
steering lever. 690.
steering line. 544.
steering lock. 396.
steering wheel. 155, 385, 386,
    670.
stellar crystal. 49.
stem. 61.
stem. 61, 65, 75, 224, 274, 335,
    397, 416, 597.
step. 172, 269, 389.
step chain. 172.
step chair. 202.
step cut. 317.
step groove. 187.
step setting. 599.
step stool. 269.
stepladder. 269.
stepladders. 269.
steppe. 51.
stereo camera. 354.
sterile dressing. 615.
stern. 537.
stern horizontal thruster. 423.
stern loading door. 420.
stern vertical thruster. 423.
sternomastoid. 110.
sternum. 84, 112.
Stevenson's screen. 55.
stick. 516.
stick. 464.
stick shuttle. 495.
stick umbrella. 336.
sticker. 475.
stickpin. 315.
sticks. 471, 616.
stiffening girder. 402.
stifle. 83.
stigma. 64, 70.
stile. 188, 203.
stile groove of sash. 189.
stile tongue of sash. 189.
stiletto. 678.
still cameras. 354.
stilt. 506.
stilted Norman. 162.
Stilton. 144.
sting. 98.
stipule. 62.
stirrup. 554, 677.
stirrup hook. 595.
stirrup iron. 553.
stirrup leather. 553.
stirrup sock. 521.
stitch. 308.
stitch length regulator. 485.
stitch patterns. 490.
stitch selector. 485.
stitched pleat. 294.
stitches. 521.
stitching. 289.
stock. 433, 474, 657, 688.
stock pot. 222.
stockade. 167.
stocked anchor. 433.
stocking. 301, 562.
stocking cap. 304.
stocking stitch. 490.
stockless anchor. 433.

stomach. 91, 94, 116, 119.
stone. 66, 67, 183.
Stone Age arms. 675.
stone fleshy fruits. 67.
stone fruit, section of a. 67.
stone fruits, major types of. 67.
stoner. 221.
stool. 202.
stop. 367, 467, 488, 630, 701.
stop bath. 360.
stop button. 243, 366, 373, 478.
stop consonants. 348.
stop knob. 468.
stop motion knob. 485.
stop rod. 468.
stopboard. 557.
stopcock. 257, 258, 262, 263.
stope. 622.
storage compartment. 662.
storage door. 229.
storage furniture. 205, 206.
storage space. 179.
storage tank. 629, 635, 654, 655.
storm collar. 192.
stove oil. 635.
straight. 552, 578.
straight eye. 488.
straight flush. 578.
straight hair. 320.
straight jaw. 249.
straight ladder. 268.
straight position. 534.
straight run petroleum treatment.
    634.
straight skirt. 293.
straight-up ribbed top. 287.
straight wing. 435.
strainer. 226, 261, 582, 627.
strainer body. 260.
strainer coupling. 260.
strainer plug. 261.
strainer sleeve. 260.
strand. 587.
strap. 337, 339, 341, 521, 549,
    559, 676.
strap handle. 336.
strap wrench. 266.
strapless brassiere. 303.
stratocumulus. 44.
stratosphere. 39.
stratum basale. 128.
stratum corneum. 128.
stratum granular. 128.
stratum lucidum. 128.
stratum spinosum. 128.
stratus. 44.
straw walker. 155.
strawberry, section of a. 66.
streamer. 697.
street, cross section of a. 399.
street café. 168.
street light. 168.
street sign. 168.
stretcher. 199.
stretcher bar. 409.
stretchers. 203.
strike plate. 256.
striker. 273, 682.
striker wheel. 334.
striking circle. 516.
strimmer. 242.
string. 77, 304, 463, 464, 466.
stringed instruments. 463, 464.
stringer. 435, 671.
stringer board. 671.
stringing. 525.
strings. 527.
strip light. 211.
strip light. 375.
strip loin. 140.
strip mine. 621.
stripper beater. 155.
stirrer cover. 227.
stroboscopic light. 691.
stroke judge. 532.
strokes, types of. 533.

The terms in **bold type** indicate the title of an illustration.

structure. 637.
strut. 180, 422, 549, 646, 658.
stud. 182, 339, 393, 428.
studded boot. 516.
studio. 374.
studio accessories. 359.
studio and control rooms. 374.
studio floor. 375.
studio lighting. 358.
study. 179.
stummel. 335.
stump. 63.
stump. 514, 515.
style. 64, 66, 67, 68, 71.
stylobate. 161.
stylus. 352.
stylus cartridge. 365.
sub-base. 56, 399.
subarctic climates. 51.
subclavian artery. 117.
subclavian vein. 117.
subcutaneous tissue. 128.
subgrade. 399.
subject. 349.
sublevel. 623.
sublimation. 50.
submachine gun. 683.
submarine canyon. 42.
submarine pipeline. 630.
submerged foils. 422.
submersible. 423.
submersible barge. 628.
submersible watch. 536.
subminiature camera. 354.
subpapillary network. 128.
subscript. 350.
subsoil plough. 154.
substation. 646.
substitute. 523, 529, 531.
subterranean cavern. 46.
subterranean stream. 46.
subtraction. 708.
subtropical climates. 51.
suburban commuter railway. 410.
subway entrance. 168.
subway to platforms. 412.
sucker rod. 627.
suction regulator. 234.
sugar bowl. 213.
sugar spoon. 216.
suit tiles. 579.
suitcase. 337.
sulcus terminalis. 126.
summer. 27.
summer solstice. 27.
summit. 46.
sump. 267, 391, 622.
Sun. 29.
Sun. 27, 28, 29, 30, 57.
Sun, structure of the. 29.
sun direction. 379.
sun roof. 383.
sun sensor. 57, 378.
sun visor. 385.
sundae spoon. 216.
sundeck. 419.
sundial. 592.
sundress. 292.
sunshine. 55.
sunshine recorder. 56.
sunshine recorder. 55.
sunspot. 29.
super. 99.
superciliary arch. 114.
superficial peroneal nerve. 121.
superheater. 647.
superior dental arch. 126.
superior longitudinal sinus. 122.
superior mesenteric artery. 117, 120.
superior nasal concha. 125.
superior semicircular canal. 124.
superior umbilicus. 88.
superior vena cava. 116, 117.
superscript. 350.
supertweeter. 363.

supply duct. 194.
supply point. 645.
supply reel. 368.
supply spool. 452.
supply tube. 260.
support. 56, 203, 208, 274, 495, 560, 608, 630.
support wheel. 231.
supraorbital foramen. 114.
suprascapular nerve. 121.
sural nerve. 121.
surface. 624.
surface cold front. 53.
surface element. 228.
surface of the water. 534.
surface-piercing foils. 422.
surface runoff. 50.
surface-to-air missile. 692.
surface-to-subsurface missile. 692.
surface-to-surface missile. 692.
surface warm front. 53.
surface water drain. 399.
surlonge. 141.
surroyal antler. 81.
suspended span. 400.
suspender. 303, 402.
suspender belt. 303.
suspension bridge. 402.
suspension cable. 402, 661.
suspension file. 449.
suspension hook. 594.
suspension insulator string. 644.
suspension line. 544.
suspension spring. 593.
suspension tower. 644.
suspensory ligament. 123.
sustaining pedal. 465.
suture. 71, 93.
swallow-hole. 46.
swallowtail. 697.
swallowtail and tongue. 697.
swallowtail pennant. 697.
Swan. 32.
swede. 76.
Swedish writing style. 345.
sweeper. 511.
sweeping loin throw. 564.
sweet bay. 135.
sweet corn. 77.
sweet pepper. 73.
sweet potato. 76.
sweetheart neckline. 299.
swell of the muzzle. 680.
swell organ manual. 467.
swell pedal. 467.
swept-back wing. 435.
swift. 496.
swim bladder. 91.
swimmer. 532.
swimmeret. 95.
swimming. 532.
swimming competition. 532.
swimming pool. 419, 531.
swing. 188.
swing bridge. 403.
Swiss chard. 77.
Swiss roll. 147.
switch. 228, 229, 250, 251, 357, 453, 457.
switch rail. 408.
switchboard. 379.
switchhook. 372.
switchyard. 652.
swivel. 558, 567, 626.
swivel arm wall bracket lamp. 210.
swivel base. 249.
swivel head. 249.
swivel lock. 249.
swivelling power supply cord. 331.
sword-breaker. 678.
Swordfish. 33.
swords. 678.
symbols. 693.
Symphony. 378.
symphony orchestra. 479.

symphysis pubis. 108, 109.
synapse. 127.
sync cable. 358.
synchro cord. 357.
synchronizer. 611.
synthetic sponge. 323.
syringes. 615.
system elements. 363.

T

T-bar lift. 547.
T-shirt. 295.
T-shirt collar. 298.
T-shirt dress. 292.
T-strap shoe. 309.
T-tail unit. 435.
tab. 336, 340, 449, 488, 553.
tab-key. 456.
table. 199, 528, 569.
table. 251, 252, 317, 468, 562.
table cut. 317.
table extension. 252.
table lamp. 210.
table-locking clamp. 251.
table tennis. 528.
table tennis player. 528.
table tennis shoe. 528.
tables, types of. 199.
tablespoon. 216.
tablinum. 163.
tabulator. 453.
tabulator clear key. 453.
tabulator set key. 453.
tachometer. 396.
tack. 537.
tag. 308.
tagliatelle. 136.
tail. 95, 100, 101, 108, 434, 498, 500, 540, 542, 543, 545, 567.
tail assembly. 434.
tail boom. 441.
tail comb. 328.
tail feather. 87.
tail of helix. 124.
tail-out groove. 365.
tail parachute. 542.
tail pipe. 392.
tail pipe extension. 392.
tail plane. 434, 441.
tail pole. 657.
tail rotor. 441.
tail shape. 435.
tailgate. 384.
tailing. 636.
tailored collar. 291, 298.
tailored sleeve. 296.
tailpiece. 260, 463.
tailrace. 641, 643.
take back to previous line. 350.
take-off board. 556, 557.
take-off line. 556.
take over to next line. 350.
take-up handle. 494.
take-up knob. 452.
take-up reel. 368.
take-up spool. 452.
takedown pin. 685.
taking mirror. 356.
tall tumbler. 212.
talus. 113.
tam- o'-shanter. 304.
tam-o'-shanter. 288.
tambourine. 472.
tamper. 335.
tandem disc harrow. 154.
tandem drive housing. 666.
tang. 214, 217.
tangent clamp. 429.
tank. 690.
tank. 632.
tank farm. 630, 634.
tank gauge float. 633.
tank lid. 259.
tank sprayer. 240.

tank valve. 258.
tank wall. 632.
tankage. 636.
tanker. 631, 691.
tanks. 443.
tap body. 261.
tape. 447, 488, 493, 521, 529, 599.
tape counter. 366, 367.
tape deck. 366.
tape dispenser. 447.
tape load lever. 452.
tape lock. 599.
tape measure. 487, 599.
tape monitor switch. 364.
tape selector. 366.
tape speed selector. 367.
tape-type indicator. 366.
taped handle. 516.
taper. 501.
tapered wing. 435.
tapestry bobbin. 495.
taproot. 63.
target. 692.
target area. 654.
target areas. 563.
target tracking radar. 692.
tarpaulin covered open wagon. 406.
tarragon. 135.
tarsus. 84, 87, 92, 97, 98, 112.
tassel. 207, 311.
tasset. 676.
taste. 126.
Taurus, the Bull. 698.
taxi rank. 168.
taxi telephone. 168.
taxis. 706.
taxiway. 438.
tea infuser. 221.
team bench. 531.
team playing positions. 513.
team shirt. 516, 521.
teapot. 213, 585.
tear-off calendar. 450.
tear tape. 334.
teaser comb. 328.
teaspoon. 216.
technical co-ordinator. 376.
tee. 573.
tee. 262, 265.
teeing ground. 571.
teeth. 115.
teeth. 252, 488, 574.
tele-converter. 355.
Telecom 1 satellite. 379.
telecommunication satellites. 378, 379.
telecommunications network. 379.
telecomputer. 379.
teleconference. 379.
telegraph. 370, 371.
telemetry antenna. 378.
telephone. 704.
telephone answering machine. 373.
telephone box. 168.
telephone cable. 399.
telephone cord. 373.
telephone index. 450.
telephone set. 372.
telephones, types of. 373.
telephoto lens. 355.
teleprompter. 375.
Telescope. 33, 429.
telescope base. 34.
telescope control room. 34.
telescope eyepiece. 600.
telescope objective. 600.
telescopic aerial. 377.
telescopic boom. 669.
telescopic corridor. 438.
telescopic front fork. 395.
telescopic sight. 607.
telescopic sight mounting. 686.

The terms in **bold type** indicate the title of an illustration.

telescopic umbrella. 336.
telescoping leg. 359.
telescoping uncoupling rod. 405.
teletex. 379.
television. 374, 375, 376, 377.
television set. 377.
telex: teleprinter. 371.
telltale. 527, 538.
telson. 95.
temperate climates. 51.
temperate marine. 51.
temperature, measure of. 597.
temperature control. 227, 331.
temperature dial. 233.
temperature indicator. 385.
temperature of dew point. 54.
temperature of the soil surface. 55.
temperature scale. 597.
temperature selector. 231.
temperature sensing bulb. 228.
temperature set point lever. 597.
template. 457.
temple. 318, 496.
temple. 106, 499.
temporal. 112.
temporal bone. 114.
temporal fossa. 114.
tenaille. 166.
tender. 628.
tenderloin. 140.
tendon. 86.
tendon guard. 548.
tendron. 139, 141.
tennis. 524, 525.
tennis ball. 525.
tennis players. 525.
tennis racquet. 525.
tennis shoe. 309, 525.
tenon saw. 499.
tenor drum. 472.
tenor drum. 477.
tenpin bowling. 576.
tension block. 491.
tension controller. 491.
tension dial. 486.
tension dial. 485, 486, 491, 492.
tension disc. 486, 491.
tension guide. 491.
tension pulley set. 208.
tension pulley wheel. 208.
tension rod. 472.
tension roller. 398.
tension screw. 472.
tension spring. 384, 486, 491.
tensor of fascia lata. 110.
tentacle. 96.
tents. 582, 583.
tents, types of. 583.
tepee. 159.
teres major. 111.
teres minor. 111.
terminal. 228, 458, 630, 645.
terminal arborization. 127.
terminal bronchiole. 118.
terminal bud. 61.
terminal connections. 194.
terminal cover. 601.
terminal filament. 122.
terminal knife-edge. 595.
terminal moraine. 48.
terminal stopping switch. 171.
terminal stopping switch cam. 171.
terrace. 168.
terraced house. 173.
terreplein. 166.
terrestrial sphere. 27.
tertial. 88.
test-lamp. 276.
test pattern. 376.
tester probe. 276.
testicle. 108.
theatre. 169, 170.
theatre. 419.
theodolite. 600.
theodolite. 55.
thermal control shutter. 57.

thermal insulation. 630.
thermal storage. 654.
thermometer. 633.
thermosphere. 39.
thermostat. 194, 195, 196, 230.
thermostat control. 229.
thick flank. 140.
thick-walled pipe. 626.
thigh. 87, 107.
thigh pad. 519.
thimble. 487.
thimble. 599.
thin flank. 140.
thin macaroni. 136.
thin spring-metal insulation. 185.
thinning razor. 328.
third. 462.
third base. 520.
third baseman. 520.
third molar. 115.
third stage. 442.
third wheel. 591, 593.
thoracic leg. 92.
thoracic vertebra. 113.
thoracic vertebrae. 84.
thorax. 92, 98, 106.
thread. 254, 261.
thread guide. 485, 486, 496.
thread take-up lever. 485.
thread trimmer. 486.
threaded cap. 265.
threaded rod. 254.
threading hook. 496.
three-burner camp stove. 585.
three-four time. 462.
three-hinged arch. 401.
three of a kind. 578.
three-pin plug. 275.
three-quarter coat. 282.
three-quarter sleeve. 296.
three-seater settee. 201.
threequarter backs. 512.
threshold. 188.
throat. 87, 190, 249, 433, 525, 567.
throat lash. 553.
throat protector. 521.
throttle. 243.
throttle valve. 625.
throttles. 437.
thrower-in. 513.
throwing arc. 557.
throwing circle. 556, 557.
throwing in a circle. 564.
throwing spear. 675.
thrust device. 352.
thrust tube. 352.
thumb. 100, 289, 521.
thumb hook. 470.
thumb piston. 467.
thumb rest. 233, 469.
thumb string. 473.
thumb string peg. 473.
thumbscrew. 248.
thunderstorm. 52.
thyme. 135.
tibia. 84, 92, 98, 100, 112.
tibial nerve. 121.
tibiofibula. 97.
ticket. 596.
ticket collector's booth. 414.
ticket counter. 412, 440.
ticket office. 412.
ticket pocket. 341.
tidal power plant. 646.
tie. 311, 336, 462.
tie beam. 180.
tie closure. 336.
tie flap. 582.
tie slide. 316.
tie tack. 316.
tieback. 207.
tieback hook. 207.
tierce. 563.
tiered necklace. 316.
tiered skirt. 293.

tight end. 518.
tight-head prop. 513.
tightening band. 56.
tights. 301, 311.
tile. 161, 185.
tiller. 538, 677.
tilt-back head. 225.
tilt cord. 209.
tilt tube. 209.
timber. 161.
timber yard. 624.
time, measure of. 591, 592, 593.
time fuse. 682.
time signatures. 462.
timekeeper. 523, 531, 562, 565.
timer. 230, 360.
timer on switch. 367.
timetables. 412.
timpani. 479.
tin opener. 219, 585.
tinctures. 696.
tine. 592.
tip. 62, 77, 214, 216, 248, 253, 254, 271, 284, 333, 336, 507, 540, 543, 545, 558, 567, 568, 570.
tip cleaner. 507.
tip cleaners. 273.
tip guard. 548.
tip of nose. 125.
tip-ring. 566.
tip section. 566.
tipping lever. 617.
tipping valve tap. 261.
tipster's choices. 555.
tipter's choice. 555.
tissue holder. 259.
Titan. 28.
toaster. 227.
tobacco. 334.
tobacco hole. 335.
tobacco pouch. 335.
toboggan. 574.
toe. 85, 89, 106, 247, 252, 287, 311, 572.
toe box. 548.
toe clip. 85, 397.
toe pick. 548.
toe piece. 540, 545, 546.
toe-piece release setting indicator. 546.
toe piston. 467.
toe stop. 548.
toe-strap. 309, 540.
toenail scissors. 333.
toggle bolt. 254.
toggle fastening. 282.
toilet. 258.
toilet. 179, 259, 407.
toilet bowl. 258, 259.
toilet cistern. 259.
toilet for men. 705.
toilet for men and women. 705.
toilet for women. 705.
toilet truck. 439.
tomato. 1.
tombolo. 43.
tone arm. 365.
tone control. 368, 480.
tongs. 191, 221.
tongue. 91, 119, 125, 126, 308, 339, 468, 474, 488, 546, 548.
tongue sheath. 101.
tool tray. 269.
tools. 586.
tooth. 101, 154, 253, 328, 666, 667.
toothbrush. 329.
toothbrush shaft. 329.
toothbrush well. 329.
toothed jaw. 249.
toothed rotor. 154.
toothpaste. 329.
top. 63, 416, 525.
top bar. 560.
top central manhole. 632.

top coat. 290.
top collar. 283.
top cylinder. 502, 504.
top deckboard. 671.
top-end transverse member. 411.
top extension ladder. 662.
top hat. 288.
top lift. 308.
top of dam. 637, 638, 641.
top plate. 180, 453, 633.
top plate of wall frame. 182.
top pocket. 569.
top rail. 188, 203, 205.
top rail of sash. 189.
top road. 623.
top roller. 494.
top stitched pleat. 294.
top stitching. 284, 306.
top surface. 542.
topgallant mast. 416.
topmark. 430.
topmast. 416.
topping. 567.
topping lift. 416.
topside. 140.
toque. 304.
torch. 211.
torch. 266.
torero. 311.
torpedo. 424.
torpedo storage compartment. 424.
tortellini. 137.
torus. 160.
total. 596.
total eclipse. 29, 30.
tote bag. 338.
Toucan. 33.
touch. 127.
touch in goal line. 512.
touch line. 511, 512, 513.
toupee. 321.
tourist-class cabin. 419.
tow bar. 540.
tow-bar cover. 581.
tow hook. 542.
tow release knob. 542.
tow tractor. 439.
towboat. 631.
towel rail. 259.
tower. 164, 402, 654, 657, 658.
tower crane. 669.
tower crane. 427.
tower foot. 644.
tower mast. 669.
tower mill. 657.
tower scaffold. 269.
tower silo. 151.
tower-type solar power station. 654.
towing eye. 684.
towing hitch. 581.
towing hook. 152.
towing truck. 387.
towrope. 540.
town house. 173.
tracery. 165.
trachea. 118.
tracing wheel. 487.
track. 208, 413, 414, 415, 458, 547, 557, 664, 690.
track and field athletics. 556, 557.
track carrier roller. 664.
track grouser. 664.
track idler. 664.
track lighting. 211.
track link. 664, 690.
track roller. 664.
track roller frame. 664.
track shoe. 664.
track shoe. 664.
tracker. 468.
tracking control. 367.
traction motor. 404.
traction motor ventilator. 404.
tractor. 152.

The terms in **bold type** indicate the title of an illustration.

tractor. 632.
tractor engine. 668.
tractor-scraper. 668.
tractor unit. 389.
tractor unit. 389.
traditional houses. 159.
traditional musical instruments. 473, 474, 475.
traffic island. 168.
traffic lights. 168, 701.
tragus. 100, 124.
trail. 684.
trailer leg. 388.
trailer leg foot. 388.
trailer leg winding gear. 388.
trailing edge. 434, 542, 543.
trailing edge flap. 434.
train delays notice board. 412.
train set. 410.
trainer. 565.
trainer's name. 555.
training shoe. 309.
training wall. 637.
trains. 707.
trajectory of a satellite. 379.
trampoline. 560.
tranche grasse. 141.
transceiver. 444.
transducer. 428.
transept. 164.
transfer. 379.
transfer orbit satellite. 379.
transfer orbit solar cell. 378.
transfer scale. 357.
transform fault. 42.
transformer. 195, 358, 641, 645, 654, 658.
transformer station. 641.
transistor. 592.
transit shed. 427.
transition fittings. 265.
translation wave. 43.
transmission. 668.
transmission-line contact. 370.
transmission monitor. 376.
transmission network. 654.
transmission of telegraph signals. 370.
transmitted pulse. 611.
transmitter. 370, 372.
transmitter. 372, 611.
transmitter-receiver. 379.
transmitter-receiver terminal. 379.
transparent line indicator. 453.
transpiration. 50.
transport. 381.
transporter bridge. 403.
transpose lines. 350.
transpose two letters. 350.
transpose two words. 350.
transversale pleine. 580.
transverse baffle. 632.
transverse bulkhead. 631.
transverse colon. 119.
transverse dunes. 47.
transverse process of vertebrae. 113.
transverse strut. 481.
trap. 260, 265.
trap and drain auger. 266.
trap coupling. 260.
trapezius. 110.
traveller. 539.
travelling block. 626.
travelling cables. 171.
travelling crane. 641, 648.
traverse arch. 165.
traverse rod. 208.
traversing and elevating mechanism. 687.
traversing handle. 683.
tray. 270.
tray. 223, 337.
tray tine. 81.
tread. 187, 553.
tread bracing layer. 393.

tread design. 393.
treadle. 494.
treadle cord. 494.
treble. 552.
treble pick-up. 480.
treble register. 475.
treble tone control. 364.
trebles ring. 550.
tree. 63.
tree. 553.
tree, structure of a. 63.
tree pruner. 239.
trefoil. 165.
trench. 621.
trench coat. 281.
triangle. 471.
Triangle. 32.
triangular body. 473.
triangular fossa. 124.
triceps of arm. 111.
trichord. 465.
triclinium. 163.
tricuspid valve. 116.
trifoliolate. 62.
triforium. 164, 165.
trigger. 243, 270, 368, 677, 682, 683, 685, 686, 687, 688, 689.
trigger guard. 683, 688, 689.
trigger switch. 253.
triglyph. 160.
trilby. 288, 304.
trill. 462.
trim. 337.
trim collar. 191.
trim ring. 228.
trim system control valve. 423.
trimmer. 327.
trimming. 499.
trimming. 339, 341.
trimming tool. 505.
trio. 476.
trip lever. 258.
triple bars. 551, 552.
triple jump. 557.
triple tail unit. 435.
tripod. 359.
tripod. 362, 478, 608, 687.
tripod accessories shelf. 609.
tripod leg. 609.
tripod stand. 472.
tripod stick. 616.
Triton. 28.
trochanter. 92, 98.
trolley. 403, 669.
trolley pulley. 669.
Trombe wall. 655.
Trombe wall. 655.
trombone. 470, 477.
trombones. 479.
tropic of Cancer. 27.
tropic of Capricorn. 27.
tropical climates. 51.
tropical fruits. 72.
tropical fruits, major types of. 72.
tropical maritime. 54.
tropical rain forest. 51.
tropical savanna. 51.
tropical storm. 52.
troposphere. 39.
trotter. 142.
trough. 43, 54, 409.
trough-to-trough wave lenght. 43.
trousers. 284, 300.
trousers. 516, 564.
trowel. 239.
truck. 548.
truck crane. 669.
truck trailer. 389.
truffle. 65.
trumpet. 470.
trumpet. 470, 477.
trumpets. 479.
trunk. 337.
trunk. 63, 107.
trunk, cross section of a. 63.

trunks. 561.
trunnion. 680.
truss. 172, 180.
truss rod adjustment. 480.
trussed arch. 401.
TT & C belt antenna. 378.
tub. 230, 232, 237.
tuba. 470, 479.
tube. 362, 598, 683, 686.
tube bangle. 315.
tube cutter. 266.
tube end. 264.
tube flaring tool. 266.
tuber vegetables. 76.
tubercles. 93.
tubing. 627.
tubing head. 627.
tubular bells. 471.
tubular bells. 479.
tubular element. 228.
tubular heater. 635.
tubular ice screw. 574.
tubular lock. 256.
tubular member. 629.
tuck. 334.
tuck brush. 492.
tuck position. 534.
Tudor. 162.
tumble dryer. 231.
tumbler. 212.
tumbler holder. 259.
tuner. 363.
tunic. 292, 295.
tuning buttons. 364.
tuning control. 428.
tuning fork. 478.
tuning fork. 592.
tuning fork watch. 592.
tuning hammer. 478.
tuning machine. 481.
tuning peg. 464.
tuning pin. 465.
tuning screw. 472.
tuning slide. 470.
tuning spring. 468.
turban. 304.
turbine. 424, 436, 641, 647, 652.
turbine blade. 436.
turbine-compressor shaft. 436.
turbine guide vane. 436.
turbine runner. 646.
turbines, major types of. 643.
turbo-alternator. 654.
turbo-charged engine. 390.
turbo-generator. 649.
turbo-generator. 650, 651.
turbo-jet engine. 436.
turbocharger. 404.
turbofan engine. 436.
turbofan jet engine. 434.
turbopump. 692.
turn. 462.
turn and bank indicator. 542.
turn-up. 284, 300.
turnbuckle. 409, 539, 565.
turning handle. 250.
turning judge. 532.
turnip. 76.
turntable. 365.
turntable. 225, 363, 403, 667.
turntable ladder. 662.
turntable mounting. 662.
turret. 167, 690.
turret cap. 607.
turtle. 101.
turtleneck. 286, 297, 298, 545.
tutu. 311.
tweeter. 363.
tweezers. 333, 615.
twig. 61, 63.
twill weave. 497.
twin-lens reflex camera. 354.
twin-set. 297.
twin skis. 540.
twin turret. 425.
Twins. 32.

twist dive. 535.
twist drill. 250.
twist grip throttle. 396.
twisted macaroni. 136.
twisted rope. 587.
two-door saloon. 384.
two-hand clean and jerk. 561.
two-hand snatch. 561.
two-handed sword. 678.
two-hinged arch. 401.
two-masted staysail schooner. 418.
two pairs. 578.
two-piece long-sleeved pyjamas. 307.
two-seater settee. 201.
two-two time. 462.
two-way collar. 281.
two-way traffic. 701.
tympan. 503, 504.
tympanum. 101, 161, 165.
type forme. 504.
type of fuel. 387.
type of high cloud. 54.
type of low cloud. 54.
type of middle cloud. 54.
type of the air mass. 54.
typestyle. 452.
typewriter. 452, 453.
typical letter. 349.
typist's chair. 451.
tyre. 389, 397.
tyre pump. 397.
tyre rack. 387.
tyre valve. 397.
tyres. 393.

U

U-bend. 265.
U-shaped gouge. 502.
UHF channel selector. 377.
UHF-IFF aerial. 691.
Ukrainian writing style. 345.
ulna. 112.
ulnar artery. 117.
ulnar extensor of wrist. 111.
ulnar flexor of wrist. 110, 111.
ulnar nerve. 121.
umbel. 64.
umbilicus. 93.
umbo. 93.
umbra. 30.
umbra shadow. 29.
umbrella. 336.
umbrella sheath. 573.
umbrella stand. 336.
umlaut. 347.
umpire. 514, 518, 524, 526, 528, 529.
umpire-in-chief. 520.
umpire position. 522.
umpire's stand. 526.
uncle by marriage. 130.
under tail covert. 87.
underground. 624.
underground flow. 50.
underground map. 414, 415.
underground mine. 623.
underground railway. 415.
underground station. 414.
underground train. 415.
underground winder house. 622.
underlever. 688.
underlining. 488.
underlying fabrics. 488.
undershirt. 521.
underwater communications set. 423.
underwear. 287, 302, 303.
underwired bra. 303.
underwiring. 303.
uneven surface. 700.
Unicorn. 33.
union. 264.
union. 264, 708.

The terms in **bold type** indicate the title of an illustration.

union nut. 264.
unison. 462.
unit price. 596.
univalve shell. 93.
universal step. 439.
unleavened bread. 138.
unmounted sleeve. 296.
uphaul. 537.
upholstery nozzle. 234.
upper. 546.
upper berth. 407.
upper blade guard. 253.
upper bout. 481.
upper bowl. 224.
upper chord. 401.
upper cold front. 53.
upper cuff. 546.
upper deck. 394, 420.
upper edge. 528.
upper eyelid. 86, 97, 123.
upper fore topgallant sail. 417.
upper fore topsail. 417.
upper gill arch. 90.
upper girdle facet. 317.
upper heating element. 263.
upper level. 426.
upper limb. 677.
upper lip. 126, 468.
upper lobe. 118.
upper mandible. 87.
upper mantle. 39.
upper shell. 546.
upper side-rail. 388.
upper sphere clamp. 56.
upper support screw. 56.
upper tail covert. 87.
upper thermostat. 263.
upper warm front. 53.
upperboard. 468.
upright. 494, 495, 499, 500, 556, 557, 559, 560, 616.
upright floor loom. 495.
upright piano. 465.
upright piano action. 466.
upstage. 169, 170.
upstream blanket. 638.
upstream face. 638.
upstream gate. 426.
upstream level. 426.
upstream shoulder. 638.
upstream toe. 638.
uranium fuel element. 648.
Uranus. 28.
urban scene. 168.
ureter. 120.
urethra. 109, 120.
urinary bladder. 91, 108, 109, 120.
urinary meatus. 108.
urinary system. 120.
urine transfer fitting. 444.
urogenital aperture. 91.
uropod. 95.
urostyle. 97.
user station. 379.
uterovesical pouch. 109.
uterus. 109.
utilities plant. 636.
utility case. 337.
utility speaker. 376.
uvula. 125, 126.

V

V-neck. 283, 286.
V-neck cardigan. 286.
V-shaped gouge. 502.
V-shaped neck. 299.
V-shaped row. 126.
vacherin. 146.
vacuole. 105.
vacuum chamber. 598.
vacuum coffee maker. 224.
vacuum distillation. 635.
vacuum flask. 586.
vacuum manifold. 606.

vagina. 109.
vagus nerve. 118.
vair. 696.
valance. 204, 207.
valley. 46, 177.
valve. 71, 93, 334, 470, 625.
valve casing. 470.
valve seat. 261.
valve seat shaft. 258.
valve slide. 470.
valve spring. 390, 391.
valve stem. 261.
vambrace. 676.
vamp. 308.
vane. 88, 231, 692.
vanity case. 337.
vanity mirror. 385.
vapour discharge outlet. 230.
variable depth sonar. 425.
variable geometry wing. 435.
variable pitch space. 453.
variable spacer. 453.
variometer. 542.
varistor. 372.
vas deferens. 108.
vastus lateralis. 110.
vastus medialis. 110.
Vauban fortification. 166.
vault. 165.
vaulting horse. 559, 560.
VCR pause switch. 369.
veal. 139.
vegetable bowl. 213.
vegetable brush. 221.
vegetable garden. 151, 178.
vegetable kingdom. 59.
vegetable steamer. 222.
vegetables. 73, 74, 75, 76, 77.
veil. 567.
vein. 62, 622.
veins. 117.
velum. 98.
velvet band chocker. 316.
Venetian blind. 209.
venom canal. 101.
venom-conducting tube. 101.
venom gland. 101.
venomous snake's head. 101.
vent. 45, 196, 385, 680, 681.
vent brush. 328.
vent cap. 392.
vent door. 388.
vent field astragal. 680.
vent hole. 270, 544.
vent line. 265.
ventail. 676.
ventilating fan. 404.
ventilation shaft. 624.
ventral aorta. 91.
ventricular septum. 116.
venturi. 686.
venturi fastening lever. 686.
Venus. 28.
vermicelli. 136.
vermiform appendix. 119.
vernal equinox. 27.
Versailles parquet. 186.
vert. 696.
vertebral column. 91, 97.
vertebral shield. 101.
vertical-axis wind turbine. 658.
vertical clamp. 600.
vertical flex support. 233.
vertical frame. 495.
vertical pivoting. 189.
vertical pupil. 101.
vertical seismograph. 602.
vertical shaft. 622.
vertical side band. 529.
vertical stabilizer. 542.
vertical tangent screw. 600.
very cloudy sky. 53.
vest. 287, 305.
vest. 306, 565.
vestibular nerve. 124.
vestibule. 124, 163, 407.

vestibule door. 407.
VHF aerial. 435.
VHF channel selector. 377.
viaduct. 400.
vibrating mudscreen. 626.
vibrola arm. 480.
vice. 249.
video camera. 369.
video input. 367.
video operator. 374.
video output. 367.
video tape recorder. 367.
video tape recorder. 374.
video/TV selector. 367.
Vienna bread. 138.
Vietnamese writing style. 345.
view camera. 354.
viewfinder. 353, 368.
viewing chamber. 606.
viewing window. 606.
vine leaf. 74.
vinyl grip sole. 305, 306.
vinyl insulation. 185.
viola. 463, 476.
violas. 479.
violin. 463, 464.
violin. 463, 476.
violin family. 463.
Virgin. 32, 33.
Virgo, the Virgin. 698.
vision mixer. 376.
visor. 409, 444, 676.
visual display unit. 455.
vitelline membrane. 89.
vitreous humour. 123.
vocal cord. 118.
volcano. 45.
volcano. 40.
volcano during eruption. 45.
volleyball. 529.
volleyball. 529.
voltage stabilizer. 361.
volume control. 363, 364, 368, 373, 480.
volume readout. 387.
volute. 160, 200.
volva. 65.
voussoir. 162.
vowels. 348.
voyager bag. 339.
vulva. 109.

W

wad. 681, 688.
waders. 568.
wading bird. 89.
waffle. 147.
wagon. 411.
wagon tent. 583.
waist. 107, 463, 481.
waistband. 284, 287, 291.
waistband extension. 284.
waistcoat. 283.
waistcoat. 297.
waistcoats. 297.
waiter's friend. 219.
waiting room. 412, 706.
walking aids. 616.
walking cam. 661.
walking frame. 616.
walking leg. 95.
walking shoe. 661.
walking stick. 336.
walking stick. 616.
walkway. 661.
wall. 30, 69, 85, 551, 552, 579, 582, 622.
wall bracket. 210.
wall grille. 192.
wall lantern. 211.
wall stack duct. 192.
wall string. 187.

wall stud. 182.
wallet. 341.
wallet section. 341.
walnut. 70.
walnut, section of a. 70.
waning crescent. 30.
waning gibbous. 30.
wardrobe. 179, 206, 582.
warhead. 692.
warm air. 655.
warm-air comb. 328.
warm temperate Western margin. 51.
warming plate. 224.
warning light. 396.
warning plate. 251.
warp. 494, 495.
warp roller. 494.
warp thread. 497.
warping mill. 496.
wash tower. 232.
washer. 261.
washery. 624.
washing machine. 230, 262.
washroom and toilet. 394.
Wassily chair. 200.
waste. 257.
waste container bin. 371.
waste disposal sink. 260.
waste disposal unit. 260.
waste pipe. 258.
waste tee. 262.
watch pocket. 283.
watchcase. 591.
water authority main. 257.
Water Bearer. 33.
water bottle. 397, 586.
water bottle clip. 397.
water carrier. 586.
water collection pan. 196.
water coolant and moderator. 651.
water cress. 74.
water ditch. 556.
water forms. 49.
water goblet. 212.
water hazard. 571.
water hose. 625.
water inlet valve. 230.
water intake. 641.
water jug. 213.
water jump. 551, 552.
water key. 470.
water main. 399.
water meter. 257.
Water Monster. 32, 33.
water polo. 531.
water pump. 392.
water reservoir. 624.
water service pipe. 257.
water skiing. 540.
water table. 46.
water tank. 404, 407.
water temperature thermostat. 194.
water-tender. 663.
water to feed heaters and steam generator. 649.
waterfall. 46.
watering can. 240.
waterline. 425.
watermelon. 73.
waterproof pants. 305.
waterproofed electrical supply. 267.
watertight bulkhead. 631.
watt-hour meter. 601.
wave. 43.
wave base. 43.
wave clip. 333.
wave height. 43.
wave wall. 638.
wavy hair. 320.
wavy lasagna. 136, 137.
wax plate. 98.
waxing crescent. 30.
waxing gibbous. 30.
way in. 706.

The terms in **bold type** indicate the title of an illustration.

way out. 706.
WC pedestal. 257.
weapon, parts of the. 563.
weapons. 673.
wearing course. 399.
weather map. 54.
weather radar. 434.
weatherboard. 188, 189.
weaving. 494, 495, 496, 497.
weaving brush. 492.
weaving principle, diagram of. 497.
web. 89, 408, 521.
web frame. 631.
web member. 180.
webbed foot. 97.
webbing. 493.
wedding ring. 315.
wedge. 468.
wedge iron. 247.
wedge lever. 247.
weeder. 239.
weeding hoe. 238.
weekender. 337.
weft. 494.
weft thread. 497.
Wehnelt cylinder. 606.
weigher. 647.
weighing platform. 596.
weight. 558, 561, 593, 594, 596.
weight, measure of. 594, 595, 596.
weight belt. 536.
weight-driven clock mechanism. 593.
weight limit. 702.
weightlifter. 561.
weightlifting. 561.
weld bead. 271, 272.
welding. 271, 272, 273.
welding curtain. 273.
welding torch. 272.
welding torch. 271.
welding torch nozzle. 272.
well. 151.
Welsh writing style. 345.
welt. 308.
welt pocket. 286, 294, 297.
west. 430, 579.
West wind. 579.
wet snow. 49.
wet suit. 536.
Whale. 32, 33.
wheat. 151.
wheel. 393.
wheel. 337, 383, 389, 487, 507, 548, 581, 680, 690.
wheel chock. 439.
wheel cylinder. 393.
wheel head. 505.
wheel loader. 665.
wheel loader. 665.
wheelbarrow. 241.
wheelchair. 617.
wheelhouse. 421, 422.
wheels. 137.
whelk. 96.
whip. 554.
whipping. 572.
whisk. 220.
whiskers. 86.
whistle buoy. 430.
White. 577, 578.
white balance control. 369.
white cabbage. 74.
white cap. 531.
white cue ball. 569.
white dragon. 579.
white flag. 531, 564.
white front width light. 581.
white line. 85.
white square. 577.
white tape. 526, 528.
white wine. 212.
whole wheat bread. 138.
wholemeal bread. 138.

whorl. 93.
wicket. 515.
wicket gate. 643.
wicket keeper. 514, 515.
wide angle adapter. 357.
wide-angle lens. 355.
width. 534, 581.
width, measure of. 599.
width clearance. 702.
wife. 130, 131.
wigs. 321.
wigwam. 159.
wild animals. 701.
wild blackberry, section of a. 66.
willow. 515.
winch. 420, 425, 539, 661, 690.
wind. 53.
wind. 47, 539.
wind abeam. 539.
wind arrow. 53.
wind baffle. 585.
wind chest. 467.
wind deflector. 389.
wind direction. 54.
wind direction and speed. 54.
wind duct. 467.
wind indicator. 538.
wind instruments. 469, 470.
wind scale. 53.
wind speed. 54, 55.
wind speed in knots. 53.
wind trunk. 467, 468.
wind turbine. 658.
wind turbine electricity production. 658.
wind vane. 55.
windage adjusting screw. 607.
windcheater. 291.
windcone. 697.
winder house. 622, 624.
winding mechanism. 209.
winding mechanism. 593.
winding tower. 624.
windlass. 422.
windmill. 657.
window. 189.
window. 178, 227, 228, 341, 383, 415, 434, 537, 582.
window accessories. 207, 208, 209.
window frame. 177.
window sill. 177.
window tab. 449.
window winder handle. 386.
windows, types of. 189.
windscreen. 34, 383, 389, 691.
windscreen wiper. 384.
windscreen wiper blade. 384.
windshaft. 657.
windshield. 434, 437.
wine cellar. 419.
wing. 88.
wing. 87, 92, 100, 383, 389, 434, 443, 542, 543, 567, 676.
wing box. 691.
wing covert. 87.
wing forward. 512.
wing membrane. 100.
wing nut. 254.
wing nut. 252.
wing pallet. 671.
wing rib. 140, 435.
wing shape. 435.
wing structure. 435.
wing tank. 631.
wing tip. 435, 542.
wing vein. 92.
wing wire. 543.
wings. 169.
wings. 169.
winter. 27.
winter solstice. 27.
winze. 622.
wiper arm. 384.
wiper blade rubber. 384.
wiper switch. 386.

wippen. 466.
wire. 546, 558.
wire beater. 225.
wire brushes. 471.
wire cutter. 249, 277, 505.
wire cutters. 277.
wire sling. 574.
wire stripper. 277.
wire support. 585.
wishbone boom. 537.
withers. 83.
wok. 223.
wok set. 223.
Wolf. 33.
women's clothing. 290, 291, 292, 293, 294, 295, 296, 297, 298, 299, 300, 301, 302, 303, 304.
women's pompadour. 321.
wood. 572.
wood. 184.
wood block. 502.
wood burning stove. 191.
wood flooring. 186.
wood flooring. 186.
wood flooring arrangements. 186.
wood flooring on cement screed. 186.
wood flooring on wooden structure. 186.
wood ray. 63.
wood shingle. 185.
woodcut. 502.
wooden bar. 559.
wooden modelling tools. 505.
wooden underarm crutch. 616.
woodwind family. 469.
woofer. 363.
word processing keys. 456.
work lead. 271.
worker. 98.
working area. 35.
working pressure gauge. 272.
workshop. 179, 387.
workshop/store. 634.
worktop surface. 232.
worm. 475, 496, 681.
worm gear. 209.
wrap-over dress. 292.
wrap-over skirt. 293.
wrap-over top. 295.
wrapper. 334.
wrest plant. 465.
wrist. 100, 107.
wrist-length glove. 289.
wrist pad. 519.
wrist sling. 574.
wrist strap. 339, 340, 369.
wristband. 525.
writing brush. 352.
writing case. 340.
writing instruments. 352.
writing styles of the world. 345.

X

X-15 (USA). 39.
xylophone. 471.
xylophone. 479.

Y

Y-branch. 265.
yard. 411.
yard. 416.
yard line. 519.
yarn. 587.
yarn clip. 491.
yarn feeder. 492.
yarn rod. 491.
yaw axis. 378.
yaw nozzle. 57.
yellow ball. 569.
yoke. 208, 285, 295.
yoke skirt. 293.

yolk. 89.
yurt. 159.

Z

Z-bed. 203.
zenith. 35.
zest. 69.
zester. 217.
zip. 305, 306, 307, 332, 336, 337, 338, 583.
zip fastener. 488.
zip line. 489.
zip pocket. 340.
zipped screen door. 582.
zither. 473.
ziti. 136, 137.
zoom lens. 355, 369.
zoom-speed selector. 369.
zygomatic arch. 114.
zygomatic bone. 114.
zygomaticofacial foramen. 114.

The terms in **bold type** indicate the title of an illustration.

THEMATIC INDEXES

ANIMAL KINGDOM

abdomen. 92, 95, 98.
abdominal segment. 92.
adductor muscle. 94.
afterfeather. 88.
air hole. 99.
air space. 89.
albumen. 89.
alighting board. 99.
alula. 88.
amphibian. 97.
anal fin. 90.
anal proleg. 92.
animal kingdom. 79.
antenna. 92, 95, 98.
antennule. 95.
anterior end. 93.
anus. 91, 94, 96.
aperture. 93.
apex. 93, 96.
aquatic bird. 89.
aquatic bird. 89.
arm. 83.
auricle. 98.
auricular. 87.
axial rib. 93.
back. 83, 87.
bar. 85.
barb. 88.
bat. 100.
bay antler. 81.
beam. 81.
beaver. 82.
belly. 83, 87.
bills, principal types of. 89.
bird. 87, 88, 89.
bird of prey. 89.
bird of prey. 89.
bivalve shell. 93.
blastodisc. 89.
blood vessels. 100.
body whorl. 93.
brain. 91.
branch. 85.
breast. 87.
brood cell. 99.
brood chamber. 99.
brow tine. 81.
bulb. 85.
burr. 81.
butterfly. 92.
calamus. 88.
calcar. 100.
callus. 93.
Canadian elk. 81.
canine. 82.
cannon. 83.
carapace. 95, 101.
carnassial. 82.
carnivore's jaw. 82.
carpal pad. 86.
carpus. 84.
cat. 86.
caterpillar. 92.
caudal fin. 90.

caudal vertebrae. 84.
cell. 92.
cephalothorax. 95.
cervical vertebrae. 84.
chalaza. 89.
cheek. 83.
chela. 95.
chest. 83.
chestnut. 83.
chin. 87.
chrysalis. 92.
clam. 94.
claw. 86, 87, 89, 92, 95, 98, 100.
cockle. 94.
columella. 93.
columella fold. 93.
comb foundation. 99.
common mussel. 94.
common periwinkle. 96.
compound eye. 92, 98.
contour feather. 88.
coronet. 83, 85.
costal shield. 101.
coxa. 92, 98.
crab. 95.
crayfish. 95.
cremaster. 92.
crenulate margin. 93.
croup. 83.
crown. 87.
crown tine. 81.
crustaceans. 95.
deer, kinds of. 81.
deer antlers. 81.
deer family. 81.
dew claw. 86.
dew pad. 86.
diastema. 82.
digestive gland. 94.
digit. 86, 97.
digital pad. 86.
distal phalanx. 86.
distal sesamoid. 84.
dorsal aorta. 91.
dorsal view. 93.
drone. 98.
ear. 100.
ear drum. 97.
egg. 89.
egg. 99.
eggs. 91, 97.
elastic ligament. 86, 94.
elbow. 83, 100.
entrance. 99.
entrance slide. 99.
escutcheon. 93.
extended claw. 86.
external gills. 97.
eye. 96, 97, 101.
eye ring. 87.
eye-socket. 83.
eye stripe. 87.
eyelashes. 86.
eyelid. 101.
eyestalk. 96.
fang. 101.

feet, principal types of. 89.
femur. 84, 92, 97, 98, 100.
fetlock. 83.
fetlock joint. 83.
first dorsal fin. 90.
fish. 90, 91.
flank. 83, 87.
foot. 87, 96, 100.
fore leg. 92, 98.
fore wing. 92, 98.
forehead. 87.
foreleg. 86.
forelimb. 97.
forelock. 83.
fork. 81.
forked tongue. 101.
frame. 99.
frog. 97.
frog. 85.
frog, life cycle of the. 97.
gall bladder. 91.
gaskin. 83.
gastropods. 96.
genital pore. 96.
gill cover. 90.
gill filament. 90.
gill raker. 90.
gills. 90.
gills. 91, 94.
granivorous bird. 89.
great scallop. 94.
greater covert. 88.
growth line. 93, 96.
gutter. 81.
hard shell clam. 94.
haunch. 83.
head. 86.
head. 92, 96, 98.
heart. 91, 94.
heel. 85.
heel calk. 85.
hemibranch. 90.
herbivore's jaw. 82.
hind leg. 92, 98, 100.
hind legs of the worker. 98.
hind limb. 97.
hind toe. 87, 89.
hind wing. 92, 98.
hindlimb, skeleton of the. 97.
hinge tooth. 93.
hive. 99.
hive body. 99.
hock. 83.
honey cell. 99.
honeybee. 98, 99.
honeycomb section. 99.
hoof. 85.
hoof. 83.
horns. 96.
horny beak. 101.
horse. 82, 83, 84, 85.
horseshoe. 85.
humerus. 84, 100.
incisor. 82.
inferior umbilicus. 88.
inner edge. 85.

inner lip. 93.
inner toe. 87.
insectivorous bird. 89.
interfemoral membrane. 100.
intestine. 91, 94.
jaws, types of. 82.
kidney. 91.
knee. 83, 100.
labial palp. 92, 94.
larva. 99.
lateral groove. 85.
lateral line. 90.
left valve. 93.
leg. 101.
leopard. 82.
lesser covert. 88.
ligament, position of the. 93.
limpet. 96.
lip. 86.
liver. 91.
lobate web. 89.
lobe. 89.
lobster. 95.
loin. 83.
lore. 87.
lower eyelid. 86, 97.
lower gill arch. 90.
lower mandible. 87.
lumbar vertebrae. 84.
lunule. 93.
malar region. 87.
mandible. 84, 90, 92, 95, 98.
mane. 83.
mantle. 96.
mantle edge. 94.
marginal shield. 101.
maxilla. 90, 95.
maxilliped. 95.
median groove. 85.
mesothorax. 92.
metacarpal. 100.
metacarpus. 84, 86.
metatarsus. 84, 97.
metathorax. 92.
middle covert. 88.
middle leg. 92, 98.
middle phalanx. 86.
middle primary covert. 88.
middle toe. 87.
molar. 82.
molluscs. 94.
moose. 81.
mouth. 94, 96, 97.
mouthparts. 98.
movable maxillary. 101.
muscle scar. 93.
muscle segment. 91.
muzzle. 86.
nail. 101.
nail hole. 85.
nape. 87.
neck. 83, 101.
neural spine. 91.
nictitating membrane. 86.
North American reindeer. 81.
nose. 83.

The terms in **bold type** indicate the title of an illustration.

nose leaf. 100.
nose leather. 86.
nostril. 83, 87, 90, 97, 101.
nuchal shield. 101.
nuclear whorl. 93.
ocelli. 92.
oesophagus. 91, 94.
olfactory bulb. 91.
olfactory nerve. 91.
operculum. 90, 97.
oscalcis. 84.
otolith. 91.
outer edge. 85.
outer lip. 93.
outer toe. 87.
ovary. 91.
oyster. 94.
pallial line. 93.
pallial sinus. 93.
palm. 81.
palmar pad. 86.
pastern. 83.
patella. 84.
pearl. 81.
pecten. 98.
pectoral fin. 90.
pedicle. 81.
pelvic fin. 90.
pelvic girdle. 97.
pelvis. 84.
perching bird. 89.
periople. 85.
phalange. 84.
phalanges. 97.
plantar surface of the hoof. 85.
plastron. 101.
pneumostome. 96.
pollen brush. 98.
pollen cell. 99.
pollen packer. 98.
pollen press. 98.
posterior end. 93.
premaxilla. 90.
premolar. 82.
primaries. 88.
primary covert. 88.
proboscis. 92.
proleg. 92.
prothorax. 92.
proximal phalanx. 86.
proximal sesamoid. 84.
pupil. 86.
pygal shield. 101.
pyloric caecum. 91.
quarter. 85.
queen. 98.
queen cell. 99.
queen excluder. 99.
rachis. 88.
radius. 84, 100.
razor clam. 94.
reptile. 101.
retracted claw. 86.
ribs. 84.
rodent's jaw. 82.
roe deer. 81.
roof. 99.
rostrum. 95.
rump. 87.
sacral vertebrae. 84.
scale. 89, 90, 101.
scallop. 94.
scampi. 95.
scapula. 84.
scapular. 88.
sealed cell. 99.
second dorsal fin. 90.
secondaries. 88.
sheath. 83.
shell. 89, 94, 96, 101.
shell membrane. 89.
shoulder. 83.
shrimp. 95.
side wall. 85.
siphonal canal. 93.
skin. 97.

skull. 84, 91.
snail. 96.
snout. 97.
soft ray. 90.
soft shell clam. 94.
sole. 85.
spinal cord. 91.
spine. 93.
spiny lobster. 95.
spiny ray. 90.
spiracle. 92.
spiral rib. 93.
spire. 93, 96.
spleen. 91.
stalked eye. 95.
sternum. 84.
stifle. 83.
sting. 98.
stomach. 91, 94.
super. 99.
superior umbilicus. 88.
surroyal antler. 81.
suture. 93.
swim bladder. 91.
swimmeret. 95.
tail. 95, 100, 101.
tail feather. 87.
tarsus. 84, 87, 92, 97, 98.
telson. 95.
tendon. 86.
tentacle. 96.
tertial. 88.
thigh. 87.
thoracic leg. 92.
thoracic vertebrae. 84.
thorax. 92, 98.
throat. 87.
thumb. 100.
tibia. 84, 92, 98, 100.
tibiofibula. 97.
toe. 85, 89.
toe clip. 85.
tongue. 91.
tongue sheath. 101.
tooth. 101.
tragus. 100.
tray tine. 81.
trochanter. 92, 98.
tubercles. 93.
turtle. 101.
tympanum. 101.
umbilicus. 93.
umbo. 93.
under tail covert. 87.
univalve shell. 93.
upper eyelid. 86, 97.
upper gill arch. 90.
upper mandible. 87.
upper tail covert. 87.
urinary bladder. 91.
urogenital aperture. 91.
uropod. 95.
urostyle. 97.
valve. 93.
vane. 88.
velum. 98.
venom canal. 101.
venom-conducting tube. 101.
venom gland. 101.
venomous snake's head. 101.
ventral aorta. 91.
vertebral column. 91, 97.
vertebral shield. 101.
vertical pupil. 101.
vitelline membrane. 89.
wading bird. 89.
walking leg. 95.
wall. 85.
wax plate. 98.
web. 89.
webbed foot. 97.
whelk. 96.
whiskers. 86.
white line. 85.
whorl. 93.
wing. 88.

wing. 87, 92, 100.
wing covert. 87.
wing membrane. 100.
wing vein. 92.
withers. 83.
worker. 98.
wrist. 100.
yolk. 89.

ARCHITECTURE

abacus. 160.
abutment. 165.
acanthus leaf. 160.
acoustic ceiling. 169.
acroterion. 161.
aisle. 164.
ambulatory. 164.
annulet. 160.
antifixa. 161.
apse. 164.
apsidiole. 164.
arcade. 164.
arch. 165.
arches. 162.
arches, types of. 162.
architectural styles. 160.
architecture. 157.
architrave. 160.
archivolt. 165.
astragal. 160.
atrium. 163.
backdrop. 170.
bailey. 167.
balustrade. 172.
barbette. 166.
barbican. 167.
bartizan. 167.
base. 160.
basket-handle. 162.
bastion. 166.
batten. 170.
battlement. 167.
belfry. 164.
Belisha beacon. 168.
bell tower. 165.
below-stage. 170.
box. 169.
box front lights. 169.
brattice. 167.
bungalow. 173.
bus stop. 168.
buttress. 164, 165.
capital. 160.
caponiere. 166.
castle. 167.
cathedral. 164.
chalet bungalow. 173.
chemise. 167.
choir. 164.
cinema. 168.
column base. 160.
comb plate. 172.
compensating cables. 171.
compluvium. 163.
controller. 171, 172.
corbel. 167.
corinthian order. 160.
corner tower. 167.
cornice. 161.
cottage. 173.
counterguard. 166.
counterscarp. 166.
counterweight. 171.
counterweight guide rail. 171.
covered parapet walk. 167.
covered postern. 166.
covered way. 166.
crenel. 167.
crepidoma. 161.
crossing. 164.
cubiculum. 163.
curtain. 166.
cut. 170.
demilune. 166.

dentil. 160.
department store. 168.
detached house. 173.
diagonal buttress. 165.
door operator. 171.
doric order. 160.
drain. 168.
drawbridge. 167.
drive sheave. 171.
drum. 160.
echinus. 160.
electric motor. 172.
embrasure. 166.
entablature. 160.
equilateral. 162.
escalator. 172.
euthynteria. 161.
extrados. 162.
façade. 165.
face. 166.
fascia. 160.
fillet. 160.
final limit cam. 171.
final limit switch. 171.
flank. 166.
flanking tower. 167.
flies. 170.
flight. 165.
floor selector. 171.
fluting. 160.
flying buttress. 164, 165.
footlights. 170.
formeret. 165.
frieze. 160.
gable. 165.
gallery. 165, 169.
garden. 163.
glacis. 166.
gorge. 166.
Gothic. 162.
gothic cathedral. 164, 165.
governor. 171.
Greek temple. 161.
Greek temple, basic plan of the. 161.
grid. 170.
grill. 161.
ground sill. 166.
guardhouse. 167.
guttae. 160.
hall. 169.
handrail. 172.
handrail drive. 172.
high-rise block. 173.
high-rise office building. 168.
high street. 168.
hoarding. 167, 168.
hoist. 170.
hoist ropes. 171.
horseshoe. 162.
house styles. 173.
hut. 159.
igloo. 159.
impluvium. 163.
impost. 162.
inner rail. 172.
intrados. 162.
ionic order. 160.
iron curtain. 170.
isba. 159.
keep. 167.
keep-left sign. 168.
keystone. 162, 165.
kitchen. 163.
Lady chapel. 164.
lamp-post. 168.
lift. 171.
lift. 171.
lift buffer. 171.
lift guide rail. 171.
lift safety device. 171.
lintel. 165.
litter bin. 168.
lookout tower. 167.
loophole. 167.
louvre-board. 165.

The terms in **bold type** indicate the title of an illustration.

low-rise apartments. 173.
lower landing plate. 172.
machicolation. 167.
main drive chain. 172.
main drive shaft. 172.
maisonette. 173.
merlon. 167.
metope. 160.
mezzanine. 169.
moat. 166, 167.
modillion. 160.
motor generator. 171.
motor generator set. 171.
mutule. 160.
naos. 161.
narthex. 164.
nave. 164.
neon sign. 168.
newspaper vendor. 168.
ogee. 162.
opisthodomos. 161.
orchestra pit. 170.
orchestra seat. 169.
order. 165.
outer rail. 172.
parade ground. 166.
parapet walk. 167.
parking meter. 168.
parterre. 169.
pedestrian crossing. 168.
pedestrian precinct. 168.
pediment. 161.
peristyle. 161, 163.
pier. 162.
piers. 165.
pillar. 165.
pinnacle. 164, 165.
plan. 164.
porch. 164.
portal. 165.
postern. 167.
prompt box. 170.
pronaos. 161.
proscenium. 170.
ramp. 161.
rampart. 166, 167.
redan. 166.
redoubt. 166.
retrenchment. 166.
roller guides. 171.
Roman house. 163.
rose window. 165.
rosette. 160.
round trefoil. 162.
salient angle. 166.
scarp. 166, 167.
scotia. 160.
seat. 169.
second balcony. 169.
secondary sheave. 171.
semi-detached house. 173.
semicircular arch. 162.
shaft. 160.
shop. 163.
shop sign. 168.
shop window. 168.
side chapel. 164.
sima. 160.
slip. 170.
sloping cornice. 161.
slot. 170.
spandrel. 162.
spire. 164.
splay. 165.
springer. 162.
stage. 170.
stage, cross section of a. 170.
stage curtain. 170.
stage-house. 170.
statue. 161.
step. 172.
step chain. 172.
stilted Norman. 162.
stockade. 167.
street café. 168.
street light. 168.

street sign. 168.
stylobate. 161.
subway entrance. 168.
tablinum. 163.
taxi rank. 168.
taxi telephone. 168.
telephone box. 168.
tenaille. 166.
tepee. 159.
terminal stopping switch. 171.
terminal stopping switch cam. 171.
terrace. 168.
terraced house. 173.
terreplein. 166.
theatre. 169, 170.
tile. 161.
timber. 161.
torus. 160.
tower. 164.
town house. 173.
tracery. 165.
traditional houses. 159.
traffic island. 168.
traffic lights. 168.
transept. 164.
travelling cables. 171.
traverse arch. 165.
trefoil. 165.
triclinium. 163.
triforium. 164, 165.
triglyph. 160.
truss. 172.
Tudor. 162.
turret. 167.
tympanum. 161, 165.
upstage. 169, 170.
urban scene. 168.
Vauban fortification. 166.
vault. 165.
vestibule. 163.
volute. 160.
voussoir. 162.
wigwam. 159.
wings. 169.
wings. 169.
yurt. 159.

ASTRONOMY

air intake. 34.
air space. 34.
airlock. 34.
Altar. 33.
Andromeda. 32.
annular eclipse. 29.
Antarctic Circle. 27.
arch. 34.
Archer. 33.
Arctic Circle. 27.
Arrow. 32.
asteroids. 28.
astronomical observatory. 34.
auditorium. 35.
autumn. 27.
autumnal equinox. 27.
auxiliary projector. 35.
Balance. 33.
barred spiral galaxy. 31.
bay. 30.
Berenice's Hair. 32.
Bird of Paradise. 33.
bright star projector. 35.
Bull. 32.
Callisto. 28.
Cassiopeia. 32.
celestial co-ordinate system. 27.
celestial equator. 27.
celestial meridian. 27.
celestial sphere. 27.
Centaur. 33.
Cepheus. 32.
Chameleon. 33.
Charioteer. 32.
chromosphere. 29.
cirque. 30.

cliff. 30.
collar. 35.
coma. 31.
comet. 31.
Compass. 33.
constellations of the northern hemisphere. 32.
constellations of the southern hemisphere. 33.
control console. 35.
control room. 35.
convection zone. 29.
core. 29.
corona. 29.
Crab. 32.
Crane. 33, 34.
crater. 30.
Crow. 33.
Cup. 33.
declination. 27.
declination axis. 34.
Deimos. 28.
Dolphin. 32.
dome shutter. 34.
Dove. 33.
Dragon. 32.
dust tail. 31.
Eagle. 32, 33.
Earth. 28, 29, 30.
Earth co-ordinate system. 27.
east-west axis. 35.
elliptical galaxy. 31.
equator. 27.
Europa. 28.
exterior dome shell. 34.
faculae. 29.
far side. 30.
filament. 29.
first quarter. 30.
fish-eye lens. 35.
Fishes. 32.
flare. 29.
flat mirror. 34.
Fly. 33.
Flying Fish. 33.
full Moon. 30.
Furnace. 33.
galaxy. 31.
Ganymede. 28.
gas tail. 31.
Giraffe. 32.
girder. 34.
granulation. 29.
Great Bear. 32.
Greater Dog. 33.
Hare. 33.
Harp. 32.
head. 31.
hemispherical dome. 35.
Hercules. 32.
Herdsman. 32.
high-power light bulb. 35.
horseshoe mount. 34.
hour angle gear. 34.
Hubble's classification. 31.
Hunting Dogs. 32.
hydrostatic pad. 34.
Indian. 33.
interchangeable end assembly. 34.
interior dome shell. 34.
Io. 28.
irregular galaxy. 31.
Jupiter. 28.
lake. 30.
last quarter. 30.
latitude. 27.
lenticular galaxy. 31.
Lesser Dog. 33.
light from Sun. 30.
Lion. 32.
Little Bear. 32.
Little Horse. 32.
Little Lion. 32.
Lizard. 32.
longitude. 27.
lunar eclipse. 30.

lunar features. 30.
Lynx. 32.
Mars. 28.
Mercury. 28.
meridian. 27.
Milky Way. 32.
Milky Way projector. 35.
Moon. 30.
Moon. 28, 29, 30.
Moon, phases of the. 30.
Moon's orbit. 30.
mountain range. 30.
near side. 30.
Neptune. 28.
Net. 33.
new Moon. 30.
North celestial pole. 27.
North pole. 27.
Northern Crown. 32.
northern hemisphere. 27.
nucleus. 31.
ocean. 30.
Octant. 33.
optical axis. 35.
Orion. 32, 33.
partial eclipse. 29, 30.
Peacock. 33.
Pegasus. 32.
penumbra. 30.
penumbra shadow. 29.
Perseus. 32.
Phobos. 28.
Phoenix. 33.
photosphere. 29.
planet projection system. 35.
planetarium. 35.
planetarium projector. 35.
planetarium projector. 35.
planets, symbols of the. 28.
planets of the solar system. 28.
Pluto. 28.
polar axis. 34.
Pole Star. 32.
primary mirror. 34.
prime focus. 34.
prime focus observing capsule. 34.
projection gallery. 35.
projection room. 35.
prominence. 29.
radiation zone. 29.
Ram. 32.
right ascension. 27.
rigid frame. 35.
riser. 35.
River Eridanus. 33.
rotating dome. 34.
rotating dome truck. 34.
Saturn. 28.
Scorpion. 33.
Sculptor. 33.
sea. 30.
Sea Goat. 33.
Sea Serpent. 33.
seasons of the year. 27.
Serpent. 32, 33.
Serpent Bearer. 32, 33.
Shield. 33.
Ship's Keel. 33.
Ship's Sails. 33.
Ship's Stern. 33.
solar eclipse. 29.
South celestial pole. 27.
South pole. 27.
Southern Cross. 33.
Southern Crown. 33.
Southern Fish. 33.
southern hemisphere. 27.
Southern Triangle. 33.
speaker. 35.
spicule. 29.
spiral arms. 31.
spiral galaxy. 31.
spring. 27.
stage. 35.
star projection condenser. 35.
star projection lens. 35.

The terms in **bold type** indicate the title of an illustration.

star sphere. 35.
summer. 27.
summer solstice. 27.
Sun. 29.
Sun. 27, 28, 29, 30.
Sun, structure of the. 29.
sunspot. 29.
Swan. 32.
Swordfish. 33.
Telescope. 33.
telescope base. 34.
telescope control room. 34.
terrestrial sphere. 27.
Titan. 28.
total eclipse. 29, 30.
Toucan. 33.
Triangle. 32.
Triton. 28.
tropic of Cancer. 27.
tropic of Capricorn. 27.
Twins. 32.
umbra. 30.
umbra shadow. 29.
Unicorn. 33.
Uranus. 28.
Venus. 28.
vernal equinox. 27.
Virgin. 32, 33.
wall. 30.
waning crescent. 30.
waning gibbous. 30.
Water Bearer. 33.
Water Monster. 32, 33.
waxing crescent. 30.
waxing gibbous. 30.
Whale. 32, 33.
windscreen. 34.
winter. 27.
winter solstice. 27.
Wolf. 33.
working area. 35.
zenith. 35.

CLOTHING

accordion pleat. 294.
adjustable waist tab. 283.
adjustment slide. 284.
all-in-one vest. 305.
ankle length. 287.
ankle sock. 301.
ankle-strap sandal. 309.
arm slit. 291.
armhole. 287, 296.
astrakhan. 288.
baby doll. 301.
babygro. 305.
back. 283, 294.
back belt. 290.
back pocket. 284.
balaclava. 288, 304.
ballerina. 311.
ballet shoes. 311.
barrel cuff. 296.
batwing sleeve. 296.
bell bottoms. 300.
belt. 284.
belt. 281.
belt buckle. 281.
belt carrier. 284, 306.
belt loop. 281.
beret. 304.
Bermuda shorts. 300.
bertha collar. 298.
bib. 305.
bib. 300, 306.
bikini. 303.
bikini briefs. 287.
binding. 288.
bishop sleeve. 296.
blazer. 297.
blouses. 295.
blouson. 291.
boa. 299.
boater. 288, 304.

body shaper. 302.
body shirt. 295.
bolero. 297.
bonnet. 305.
boot jack. 310.
bottom of collar. 295.
bow. 288.
bow collar. 298.
bow tie. 285.
bowler hat. 288.
box jacket. 297.
box pleat. 294.
boxer shorts. 287.
bra. 303.
brace clip. 284.
braces. 284.
brassiere cup. 303.
break line. 298.
breast dart. 282.
breast pocket. 282, 285, 295.
breast welt pocket. 283.
breeches. 300, 311.
briefs. 287.
briefs. 303.
brim. 288, 304.
broad welt. 290.
broad welt side pocket. 281, 294.
buckle. 284.
bullfighter. 311.
button. 285.
button loop. 284.
button strap. 306.
button-through smock. 295.
buttondown collar. 285.
buttoned placket. 285, 291, 295.
buttonhole. 281, 285, 286.
cairel. 311.
calf-lenght jeans. 300.
camisole. 302.
cap. 304.
cap sleeve. 296.
cape. 291.
cape. 311.
car coat. 290.
cardigan. 286, 297.
carrier. 281, 284.
cartwheel hat. 304.
centre back vent. 283.
chaleco. 311.
children's clothing. 305, 306, 307.
christening set. 305.
chukka. 310.
classic. 295.
climbing iron. 310.
clip. 284.
cloche. 304.
clog. 309.
cloth cap. 288.
clothing. 279.
coat dress. 292.
coats. 290, 291.
collar. 298.
collar. 281, 283, 285.
collar point. 285, 298.
collar stay. 285.
collars, types of. 298.
combination. 287.
cordless shoe care kit. 310.
corselette. 302.
corset. 303.
costumes. 311.
counter. 308.
court. 309.
cowl collar. 298.
cravat. 285.
crease. 284.
crew neck. 305.
crew neck sweater. 286.
crew sweater. 297.
crossover back straps dungarees. 306.
crotch. 287.
crotch piece. 295.
crown. 288, 304.
cuff. 285, 308.

culotte. 293.
cutaway armhole. 296.
deerstalker. 288.
dog ear collar. 298.
double-breasted buttoning. 281, 291.
double-breasted jacket. 283.
double cuff. 296.
draped neck. 299.
draped neckline. 299.
drawstring. 282, 311.
drawstring hood. 307.
dress. 305.
dresses. 292.
dressing gown. 301.
driving glove. 289.
drop waist dress. 292.
duffle coat. 282.
dungarees. 300.
elastic ankle. 307.
elastic leg opening. 305.
elastic waistband. 305.
elastic webbing. 284.
elastic wristband. 307.
elasticized leg opening. 287.
epaulet. 281, 311.
epaulet sleeve. 296.
espadrille. 309.
evening glove. 289.
eyelet. 284, 308.
eyelet tab. 308.
facing. 283.
fall. 298.
false tuck. 305.
felt hat. 288.
fingerless mitt. 289.
fishnet tights. 301.
flap pocket. 282, 283, 294.
flap side pocket. 283.
flip-flop. 309.
fly. 284, 287.
fly front closing. 290.
fold line. 294.
foot. 305, 306.
footstrap. 300.
foundation slip. 302.
fourchette. 289.
frilly pants. 305.
frog. 282, 298.
front. 283, 285.
front apron. 285.
front top pocket. 300.
fur hood. 304.
galosh. 310.
garter. 302.
gather. 295.
gather skirt. 293.
gauntlet. 289.
girdle. 303.
glove. 289.
glove finger. 289.
gloves, types of. 289.
gored skirt. 293.
gun flap. 281.
gusset pocket. 294, 297.
half hoe. 287.
half-slip. 303.
hand warmer pocket. 291.
hand warmer pouch. 294.
hanger loop. 286.
hat veil. 304.
hatband. 288.
head band. 304.
headgear. 288, 304.
headgear, types of. 288.
heavy duty boot. 310.
heel. 287, 308.
heel grip. 308.
high-back dungarees. 306.
hold-up stocking. 301.
hood. 282.
hooded towelling robe. 305.
hose. 301.
inset pocket. 294.
inside-leg snap-fastening. 306.
insole. 308, 310.

instep. 287.
interfacing. 285.
inverness cape. 282.
inverted pleat. 294.
jabot. 298.
jeans. 300.
jumpsuit. 306.
jumpsuit. 300.
kick pleat. 294.
kilt. 293.
kimono. 301.
kimono sleeve. 296.
knife pleat. 294.
knit shirt. 286.
lace. 305.
lace-up. 310.
lapel. 283, 298.
leading edge. 298.
leather end. 284.
leg. 287.
leg-of-mutton sleeve. 296.
leotard. 307.
lining. 283, 308.
long cardigan. 297.
long johns. 287.
loop. 285.
loosely tied bow. 299.
mandarin collar. 298.
maternity dress. 292.
men's clothing. 281, 282, 283, 284, 285, 286, 287, 288.
middle sole. 308.
midriff band. 303.
mitten. 289, 307.
mob-cap. 304.
moccasin. 309.
mock pocket. 291.
modesty. 298.
montera. 311.
mule. 309.
nappy. 305.
narrow cuff. 296.
neck end. 285.
neckhole. 287.
necklines. 299.
necks. 299.
necks. 299.
necktie. 285.
negligee. 301.
nightdress. 301.
nightwear. 301.
notch. 283.
notched lapel. 281, 291, 298.
nylon frilly tights. 305.
one-bar shoe. 309.
one-piece sleepsuit. 307.
opening. 289.
outside counter. 308.
outside ticket pocket. 283.
outsole. 308.
overcoat. 282.
overshirt. 295.
overshoe. 310.
pagoda sleeve. 296.
palm. 289.
panel. 284, 303.
pantee corselette. 302.
panty girdle. 303.
parka. 282.
patch pocket. 290, 294, 306.
patch pocket with turn-down flap. 290.
pea jacket. 291.
peaked cap. 288.
peaked lapel. 282, 283.
pedal pusher. 300.
pelerine. 290.
pelerine. 290.
perforated toe cap. 308.
perforation. 289.
Peter Pan collar. 298.
pigtail. 311.
pillbox hat. 304.
pinafore. 307.
pinafore. 292.
pink stocking. 311.

The terms in **bold type** indicate the title of an illustration.

placket. 298.
plastic pants. 305.
pleat skirts. 294.
plunging neckline. 299.
pocket handkerchief. 283.
pockets. 294.
pointed tab end. 285, 296.
pompom. 304.
poncho. 291.
pop sock. 301.
princess dress. 292.
princess seaming. 302.
prong. 284.
puff sleeve. 296.
pullover. 297.
pullovers. 286, 297.
pump. 309.
punch hole. 308.
pyjamas. 301.
quarter. 308.
raglan. 290.
raglan sleeve. 281, 290, 296, 306.
raincoat. 281.
rear apron. 285.
ribbing. 286, 291, 305, 306, 307.
ribbon. 311.
ridge. 294.
right side. 294.
roll. 298.
roll line. 298.
rope belt. 306.
round neck. 299.
ruff. 298.
safari jacket. 297.
sailor collar. 298.
sailor tunic. 295.
sandal. 309.
sarong. 293.
sash. 311.
scarf turban. 304.
screen front. 305.
screen print. 306.
seam. 289.
seam pocket. 290, 294.
seaming. 290.
set-in-sleeve. 281, 285, 286, 296.
shank. 308.
shawl collar. 298.
sheath dress. 292.
sheath skirt. 293.
sheepskin jacket. 282.
shirt. 285.
shirt. 311.
shirt collar. 295, 298.
shirt sleeve. 295.
shirt-tail. 295.
shirttail. 285.
shirtwaist dress. 292.
shirtwaist sleeve. 296.
shoe, parts of a. 308.
shoe horn. 310.
shoe rack. 310.
shoe tree. 310.
shoelace. 308.
shoes. 308, 309, 310.
**shoes, principal types of. 309,
310.**
shoeshine kit. 310.
short. 287.
short glove. 289.
short sock. 301.
shorts. 300.
shorts. 300.
shoulder-strap. 303.
showerproof hat. 304.
side back vent. 283.
side pocket. 281.
single-breasted coat. 283.
ski pants. 300.
skirts. 293.
skull cap. 288.
slash neck. 299.
sleeping bag. 306.
sleepsuit. 305, 306.
sleeve. 283.
sleeve strap. 281.

sleeve strap loop. 281.
sleeves. 296.
slip. 302.
slip-on. 310.
slip-stitched seam. 285.
slipover. 286, 297.
slippers. 311.
slit pocket. 284.
smock. 292, 295.
snap fastener. 289.
snap-fastening adjustable strap.
306.
snap-fastening front. 306.
snap-fastening shoulder strap. 306.
snap-fastening side. 305.
snap-fastening waist. 305.
sneaker. 309.
snowsuit. 307.
sock. 287.
sock. 301.
sock lining. 308.
soft cup bra. 303.
sole. 287, 311.
sou'wester. 288, 304.
spread collar. 285.
square neck. 299.
stand. 298.
stand-up collar. 298.
steel. 303.
stitch. 308.
stitched pleat. 294.
stitching. 289.
stocking. 301.
stocking cap. 304.
straight skirt. 293.
straight-up ribbed top. 287.
strapless brassiere. 303.
string. 304.
sundress. 292.
suspender. 303.
suspender belt. 303.
sweetheart neckline. 299.
T-shirt. 295.
T-shirt collar. 298.
T-shirt dress. 292.
T-strap shoe. 309.
tag. 308.
tailored collar. 291, 298.
tailored sleeve. 296.
tam- o'-shanter. 304.
tam-o'-shanter. 288.
tassel. 311.
tennis shoe. 309.
three-quarter coat. 282.
three-quarter sleeve. 296.
thumb. 289.
tie. 311.
tiered skirt. 293.
tights. 301, 311.
tip. 284.
toe. 287, 311.
toe-strap. 309.
toggle fastening. 282.
tongue. 308.
top coat. 290.
top collar. 283.
top hat. 288.
top lift. 308.
top stitched pleat. 294.
top stitching. 284, 306.
toque. 304.
torero. 311.
training shoe. 309.
trench coat. 281.
trilby. 288, 304.
trousers. 284, 300.
tunic. 292, 295.
turban. 304.
turn-up. 284, 300.
turtleneck. 286, 297, 298.
tutu. 311.
twin-set. 297.
**two-piece long-sleeved pyjamas.
307.**
two-way collar. 281.
underwear. 287, 302, 303.

underwired bra. 303.
underwiring. 303.
unmounted sleeve. 296.
V-neck. 283, 286.
V-neck cardigan. 286.
V-shaped neck. 299.
vamp. 308.
vest. 287, 305.
vest. 306.
vinyl grip sole. 305, 306.
waistband. 284, 287, 291.
waistband extension. 284.
waistcoat. 283.
waistcoat. 297.
waistcoats. 297.
watch pocket. 283.
waterproof pants. 305.
welt. 308.
welt pocket. 286, 294, 297.
windcheater. 291.
**women's clothing. 290, 291, 292,
293, 294, 295, 296, 297, 298,
299, 300, 301, 302, 303, 304.**
wrap-over dress. 292.
wrap-over skirt. 293.
wrap-over top. 295.
wrist-length glove. 289.
yoke. 285, 295.
yoke skirt. 293.
zip. 305, 306, 307.

COMMUNICATIONS

acoustic resistance. 372.
acute accent. 347.
addressee. 349.
adjustable foot. 368.
affricate consonants. 348.
air hole. 352.
air shutter release. 359.
align horizontally. 350.
align vertically. 350.
alphabet. 371.
amplifier. 374.
amplifier-tuner. 364.
analogue frequency meter. 364.
Anik. 378.
anti-skating device. 365.
aperture scale. 357.
apostrophe. 347, 350.
Arabic writing style. 345.
arm elevator. 365.
arm rest. 365.
Armenian writing style. 345.
array elevation and tensioning
mechanism. 378.
ASA/DIN dial. 353.
ASA/DIN exposure index. 357.
asterisk. 347.
attitude acquisition. 379.
audio input. 367.
audio output. 367.
auto/manual aperture (iris) control.
369.
auto-manual focusing switch. 369.
automatic answer indicator. 373.
automatic fade control. 369.
automatic frequency control. 364.
background. 359.
balance control. 364.
ball bearing. 352.
ballpoint pen. 352.
band. 365.
band selectors. 364.
barn doors. 358.
barrel. 352.
base. 365, 377.
base of lamp. 357.
base plate. 365.
baseboard. 361.
bass tone control. 364.
battery. 357.
battery. 356.
battery check meter. 368.
bayonet mount. 353, 355.

begin a new paragraph. 350.
bellows. 361.
between-the-lens shutter. 356.
blue beam. 377.
body. 349.
bold. 351.
bold capitals. 351.
boom arm. 359.
boom operator. 375.
brackets. 347.
Braille. 346.
brightness control. 377.
British model. 349.
built-in microphone. 369.
bypass contact. 370.
cabinet. 363, 377.
cable. 369.
cable release. 359.
calculator. 357.
calculator dial. 357.
calls indicator. 373.
camera. 376.
camera battery. 368.
camera body. 353.
camera crane. 375.
camera pedestal. 375.
camera platform. 359.
camera screw. 359.
cameraman. 375.
cane pen. 352.
capitals. 351.
carbon copy. 349.
carbon granules. 372.
cartridge. 352, 356.
cassette. 356.
cassette deck. 363.
cassette holder. 366.
cassette loading slot. 367.
catwalk. 375.
cedilla. 347.
centre. 350.
centre hole. 365.
channel selector control. 367.
Chinese writing style. 345.
cine scale. 357.
cinematography. 368.
circumflex accent. 347.
clapper. 372.
clip. 352.
clock. 376.
close up. 350.
close-up lens. 355.
closing salutation. 349.
coil. 372.
coin slot. 373.
coinbox telephone. 373.
collet. 359.
colon. 347, 350, 371.
colour analyser. 360.
colour filter. 355.
colour filter set. 358.
colour temperature switch. 369.
column. 359, 361.
column crank. 359.
column lock. 359.
comma. 347, 350, 371.
command antenna. 378.
communications. 343.
company number. 349.
condenser. 361, 362.
cone. 363.
conical snoot. 358.
connecting cable. 363.
connection and concentration
equipment network. 379.
contact printer. 360.
contrast control. 377.
control panel. 374, 375, 376.
controls. 371.
cooling fan. 362.
copy holder. 371.
cord. 372.
cordless telephone. 373.
correct a letter. 350.
correct a word. 350.

The terms in **bold type** indicate the title of an illustration.

corrections of diacritic symbols. **350.**
corrections of errors. 350.
corrections of punctuation marks. 350.
corrections of type. 350.
corrugation. 363.
counter memory button. 367.
counter reset button. 366.
counterweight. 365.
cradle. 372.
cue screen. 376.
cup. 372.
cyclorama. 375.
Danish writing style. 345.
darkroom. 360.
dash. 347, 371.
dateline. 349.
daylight filter control. 368.
deaf-mute alphabet. 347.
delete. 350.
depth-of-field scale. 355.
deputy sound supervisor. 374.
despin. 379.
developer bath. 360.
developing film. 356.
developing tank. 360.
diacritic symbols. 347.
diagram of a circuit. 370.
dial. 371, 372.
diaphragm. 353, 363, 369, 372.
diaphram. 372.
diffuser. 358.
diffuser filter set. 358.
digital clock. 367.
digital frequency display. 364.
diphthongs. 348.
director/producer. 376.
disc. 356.
disc camera. 354.
distance scale. 355.
Dolby noise reduction switch. 366.
dot. 371.
drive belt. 365.
dry mounting press. 360.
dust cover. 365.
Dutch writing style. 345.
dynamic microphone. 369.
ear cushion. 363.
earphone jack. 377.
earpiece. 372.
earth. 370, 378.
earth lead. 365.
earth sensor. 378.
easel. 361.
easel. 360.
eject. 367.
eject button. 366.
electric current source. 370.
electric motor. 356.
electrode. 372.
electromagnet. 370.
electron beam. 377.
electron gun. 377.
electronic flash. 357.
electronic viewfinder. 369.
electronic viewfinder display control. 369.
ellipsis. 347.
enlarger. 361.
enlarger. 360.
enlarger timer. 360.
enlarging lens. 361.
equalizer. 363.
erase button. 363.
exclamation mark. 347.
exposure control. 356.
exposure meter. 357.
exposure-time scale. 357.
exposure value. 357.
exposure value scale. 357.
extendable solar array. 378.
external conductive coating. 377.
extractor fan. 360.
eyecup. 368, 369.
eyecups. 355.

eyepiece. 356, 357.
eyepiece magnifier. 355.
faceplate. 377.
facility telephone system. 373.
fast forward. 367.
fast-forward button. 366, 373.
fastening screw. 357.
fax machine. 379.
feed tube. 352.
film advance lever. 353.
film drying cabinet. 360.
film footage counter. 368.
film leader. 356.
film-pack. 356.
film path. 368.
film take-up spool. 353.
film transport sprocket. 353.
filming trigger. 369.
films. 356.
filter drawer. 361.
fine tuning knob. 377.
finger stop. 372.
Finnish writing style. 345.
fish-eye lens. 355.
fixing bath. 360.
flash. 358.
flash bracket. 357.
flash lamp. 357.
flash meter. 358.
flash outlet. 357.
flash sensor. 357.
flash socket. 368.
flash synchronization terminal. 353.
flash umbrella. 358.
flash unit. 357.
flashbar socket. 356.
flashcube. 357.
floodlight. 375.
floor crew. 375.
floor manager. 375.
FM mode selector. 364.
FM stereo indicator. 364.
foam windscreen. 369.
focal plane shutter. 353.
focus magnifier. 361.
focus setting ring. 369.
focusing control. 368.
focusing knob. 361, 362.
focusing magnifier. 360.
focusing ring. 355, 368.
folding camera. 354.
forward/reverse switch. 368.
fountain pen. 352.
frame counter. 353.
framing control. 368.
French writing style. 345.
fricative consonants. 348.
full stop. 347, 350, 371.
function lever. 365.
funnel. 377.
gear train. 356.
geostationary orbit. 379.
geostationary orbit injection. 379.
German writing style. 345.
glass bulb. 357.
glides. 348.
gong. 372.
grave accent. 347.
Greek writing style. 345.
green beam. 377.
grille. 363.
grip. 357.
groove. 365.
guillotine trimmer. 360.
handgrip. 368, 369.
handle. 370.
hands-free telephone. 373.
handset. 372, 373.
handset cord. 372.
hanger. 362.
head rotation lock. 361.
headband. 363.
headphone. 363.
headphone. 363.
headphone jack. 364, 366.
heat pipe radiator. 378.

Hebrew writing style. 345.
height control. 361.
height scale. 361.
Hermes satellite. 378.
Hindi writing style. 345.
hinge. 365.
hoist. 375.
honeycomb diffuser. 358.
hot shoe. 357.
housing. 369, 372.
Hungarian writing style. 345.
hyphen. 347, 350, 371.
incident-light measuring diffuser. 357.
incoming message cassette. 373.
indication of types. 351.
indicator needle. 357.
indoor/outdoor position. 369.
infrared transmitter. 358.
ink. 352.
inked roller. 370.
input selectors. 364.
insert here. 350.
insert space. 350.
Intelsat. 378.
interchangeable lens. 353.
interchangeable lenses. 355.
international phonetic alphabet. 348.
Inuktitut writing style. 345.
Iranian writing style. 345.
ital. bold. 351.
Italian writing style. 345.
italic. 351.
italic capitals. 351.
jack. 363.
Japanese writing style. 345.
job title. 349.
joint. 352.
key. 370.
keyboard. 371.
label. 365.
lamp. 361, 368.
lamphouse. 361.
launching orbit. 379.
lead-in wire. 357.
lead pencil. 352.
LED peak level meter. 366.
lens. 356, 357, 362.
lens aperture ring. 355.
lens cap. 355.
lens hood. 355.
lens mount. 353.
let is stand. 350.
letterhead. 349.
letters. 346, 347.
level controls. 350.
levelling foot. 362.
lever. 370.
light-reading scale. 357.
lightbox. 360.
lighting and vision assistant. 374.
lighting and vision control room. 374.
lighting control panel. 374.
lighting director. 374.
lighttight box. 353.
line. 370.
line guide. 371.
lines. 370.
liquid consonants. 348.
lock ring. 362.
locked groove. 365.
loudness switch. 364.
loudspeaker. 363, 375.
lower pan-head mounting screw. 359.
macro focusing knob. 368.
magnesium wire. 357.
mains lead. 362.
manual aperture control. 368.
manual zoom ring. 368, 369.
marker. 352.
mathematical symbols. 346.
maths symbol sign. 346.
mechanical pencil. 352.

medium format SLR (6 x 6). 354.
memory button. 364.
microphone. 363, 373.
microphone boom. 375.
microphone jack. 366.
midrange. 363.
mirror. 353.
monitor. 376.
monitor button. 373.
monitor indicator. 364.
monitor pusher. 375.
monitor speaker. 376.
monitor stack. 376.
Morse code. 371.
motor. 362.
motor pulley. 365.
mouthpiece. 372.
movable condenser. 361.
move to left. 350.
move to right. 350.
moving coil. 369.
multiple access station. 379.
multiplexing equipment. 379.
name of sender. 349.
neck. 377.
neckstrap lug. 353, 369.
negative carrier. 361.
network management centre. 379.
nib. 352.
normal mode acquisition. 379.
normal mode satellite. 379.
Norwegian writing style. 345.
numbers. 347.
numerals. 346, 371.
objective lens. 357.
off-on knob. 377.
Olde English writing style. 345.
on/off switch. 368, 369.
on/play button. 373.
opening salutation. 349.
outgoing announcement cassette. 373.
output lead. 365.
pan handle. 359.
panoramic and tilting head. 359.
paper safe. 360.
paper tape. 370, 371.
paper tape start button. 371.
parabolic antenna. 379.
parabolic reflector. 358.
parentheses. 347, 350.
pause button. 366.
pause/still. 367.
pearl screen. 362.
pen. 370.
pentaprism. 353.
perforation. 356.
perforator. 371.
permanent magnet. 372.
permanent wiring. 372.
phosphor dot. 377.
photoelectric cell. 356.
photographic accessories. 359.
photography. 353, 354, 355, 356, 357, 358, 359, 360, 361, 362.
picture tube. 377.
pitch axis. 378.
platter. 365.
play. 367.
play button. 366.
plug. 369.
plunger. 372.
pocket instamatic camera. 354.
point. 352.
polarizing filter. 355.
Polaroid Land camera. 356.
pole piece. 372.
Polish writing style. 345.
Portuguese writing style. 345.
postscript. 349.
power cord. 363, 365.
power switch. 364, 366, 367.
power/timer off switch. 367.
power zoom control. 369.
pre-tuning control. 367.
preamplifier. 363.

The terms in **bold type** indicate the title of an illustration.

presenter. 375.
preset tuning button. 364.
press camera. 354.
preview monitor. 376.
print drying rack. 360.
print washer. 360.
printed circuit. 356.
processing rollers. 356.
production assistant. 376.
production control room. 376.
production control room. 374.
programmable timer. 367.
projection lamp. 362.
projection screen. 362.
projector zoom lens. 368.
proofreading. 350, 351.
propman. 375.
protected cable. 373.
protective window. 377.
pull bail. 362.
punched paper tape reader. 371.
punctuation. 371.
punctuation marks. 346, 347.
push-button. 352, 362.
push-button telephone. 373.
push buttons. 373.
question mark. 347, 371.
quill. 352.
quotation marks. 347, 350.
quotation marks ((*csp*)). 371.
rangefinder. 354.
reaction control thruster. 378.
receiver. 370, 372.
receiver. 372.
receiving station. 370.
record. 365.
record. 367.
record announcement button. 373.
record button. 366.
record muting button. 366.
recording level button. 366.
recording reproducing head. 368.
recording switch. 368.
red beam. 377.
red safelight filter. 361.
reduce space. 350.
reed panicle. 352.
reel. 360.
reference station. 379.
refill. 352.
reflecting screen. 358.
reflector. 359.
registered office address. 349.
reject chute. 373.
release button. 353.
remote control. 362.
remote control socket. 368.
reset button. 367.
resin-coated paper dryer. 360.
return spring. 370.
rewind. 367.
rewind button. 366, 373.
rewind crank. 353.
right angle finder. 355.
ringer coil. 372.
roll axis. 378.
roll of paper. 371.
Roman metal pen. 352.
Romanian writing style. 345.
rubber mat. 365.
run on. 350.
Russian writing style. 345.
saddle. 362.
safe and arm device. 378.
safelight. 360.
satellite launcher separation. 379.
satellites, examples of. 378.
screen. 369, 377.
screen case. 362.
self timer. 353.
semi-fish-eye lens. 355.
semicolon. 347, 350, 371.
sender's reference. 349.
sending station. 370.
set in boldface. 350.
set in capitals. 350.

set in italic. 350.
set in lower case. 350.
set in roman. 350.
set in small capitals. 350.
shadow mask. 377.
SHF antenna. 378.
SHF beacon antenna. 378.
shoe. 362.
shutter button. 356.
shutter release. 353.
shutter speed dial. 353.
side-tilt lock. 359.
signature of sender. 349.
single-lens reflex camera. 353.
single quotation marks. 347.
Sinhalese writing style. 345.
sink. 360.
slash. 347, 371.
slide. 362.
slide changer. 362.
slide mount. 362.
slide projector. 362.
slide tray. 362.
small capitals. 351.
softlight reflector. 358.
solar cell. 378.
solar panel deployment. 379.
something omitted. 350.
sound camera. 368.
sound control room. 374.
sound desk. 374.
sound projector. 368.
sound-on-sound control. 368.
sound reproducing system. 363, 364, 365, 366.
sound supervisor. 374.
Spanish writing style. 345.
speaker. 363.
speaker. 368, 377.
speaker selector. 364.
special effects. 376.
speed selector lever. 365.
spindle. 365.
spiral. 365.
spiral-in groove. 365.
spot projector attachment. 358.
spotlight. 375.
spotmeter. 357.
spring. 352.
stand. 358, 359.
standard lens. 355.
steel pen. 352.
stereo camera. 354.
still cameras. 354.
stop. 367.
stop bath. 360.
stop button. 366, 373.
stop consonants. 348.
strip light. 375.
studio. 374.
studio accessories. 359.
studio and control rooms. 374.
studio floor. 375.
studio lighting. 358.
stylus. 352.
stylus cartridge. 365.
subject. 349.
subminiature camera. 354.
subscript. 350.
sun direction. 379.
sun sensor. 378.
superscript. 350.
supertweeter. 363.
supply reel. 368.
Swedish writing style. 345.
switch. 357.
switchboard. 379.
switchhook. 372.
Symphony. 378.
sync cable. 358.
synchro cord. 357.
system elements. 363.
tail-out groove. 365.
take back to previous line. 350.
take over to next line. 350.
take-up reel. 368.

taking mirror. 356.
tape counter. 366, 367.
tape deck. 366.
tape monitor switch. 364.
tape selector. 366.
tape speed selector. 367.
tape-type indicator. 366.
technical co-ordinator. 376.
tele-converter. 355.
Telecom 1 satellite. 379.
telecommunication satellites. 378, 379.
telecommunications network. 379.
telecomputer. 379.
teleconference. 379.
telegraph. 370, 371.
telemetry antenna. 378.
telephone answering machine. 373.
telephone cord. 373.
telephone set. 372.
telephones, types of. 373.
telephoto lens. 355.
teleprompter. 375.
telescopic aerial. 377.
telescoping leg. 359.
teletex. 379.
television. 374, 375, 376, 377.
television set. 377.
telex: teleprinter. 371.
test pattern. 376.
thrust device. 352.
thrust tube. 352.
timer. 360.
timer on switch. 367.
tone arm. 365.
tone control. 368.
tracking control. 367.
trajectory of a satellite. 379.
transfer. 379.
transfer orbit satellite. 379.
transfer orbit solar cell. 378.
transfer scale. 357.
transformer. 358.
transmission-line contact. 370.
transmission monitor. 376.
transmission of telegraph signals. 370.
transmitter. 370, 372.
transmitter. 372.
transmitter-receiver. 379.
transmitter-receiver terminal. 379.
transpose lines. 350.
transpose two letters. 350.
transpose two words. 350.
treble tone control. 364.
trigger. 368.
tripod. 359.
tripod. 362.
TT & C belt antenna. 378.
tube. 362.
tuner. 362.
tuning buttons. 364.
turntable. 365.
turntable. 363.
tweeter. 363.
twin-lens reflex camera. 354.
typical letter. 349.
UHF channel selector. 377.
Ukrainian writing style. 345.
umlaut. 347.
user station. 379.
utility speaker. 376.
varistor. 372.
VCR pause switch. 369.
VHF channel selector. 377.
video camera. 369.
video input. 367.
video operator. 374.
video output. 367.
video tape recorder. 367.
video tape recorder. 374.
video/TV selector. 367.
Vietnamese writing style. 345.
view camera. 354.

viewfinder. 353, 368.
vision mixer. 376.
voltage stabilizer. 361.
volume control. 363, 364, 368, 373.
vowels. 348.
waste container bin. 371.
Welsh writing style. 345.
white balance control. 369.
wide angle adapter. 357.
wide-angle lens. 355.
woofer. 363.
wrist strap. 369.
writing brush. 352.
writing instruments. 352.
writing styles of the world. 345.
yaw axis. 378.
zoom lens. 355, 369.
zoom-speed selector. 369.

CREATIVE LEISURE ACTIVITIES

alteration line. 489.
arm. 485.
arm nut. 492.
assembly process. 507.
back beam. 494.
back board. 498.
back cornering. 498.
backing. 500.
backing board. 500.
backing hammer. 500.
ball. 488, 496.
ball-end. 507.
ball of clay. 505.
ball winder. 496.
banding wheel. 505.
baren. 501.
base. 500.
basic weaves. 497.
beater. 494.
beater handtree. 494.
beater sley. 494.
bed. 499, 502, 503, 504.
bed handle. 503.
bias. 488.
blade. 486, 487.
blade lever. 499.
blanket. 502.
board cutter. 499.
bobbin. 492.
bobbin. 486, 495, 496.
bobbin case. 486.
bobbin lace. 492.
bobbin winder. 496.
bobbin winder. 485.
bone folder. 498.
bookbinding leather. 500.
bottom cylinder. 502, 504.
bound book. 498.
breaking pliers. 507.
breast beam. 494.
brush. 501.
buckle. 488.
bullion stitch. 493.
bung. 506.
burin. 502.
burnisher. 501.
butt. 492.
cable stitch. 490.
calipers. 503.
cam. 492.
cam lever. 492.
camshaft. 503.
capstan. 502.
carbon. 507.
carriage. 492.
carriage. 491, 492.
cartoon. 507.
cast-on stitches. 490.
central screw. 500.
chain stitch. 493.
change dial. 491.
channel. 499, 507.

charting device. 491.
chevron stitch. 493.
chisel. 502.
circular needle. 490.
clamp. 491, 496, 499.
claw. 500.
claw weight. 491.
cloth roller. 494.
coiling. 505.
column. 485.
comb. 495.
control knob. 506.
copper foil. 507.
copperplate. 501.
cord. 499.
corner. 498.
couched stitches. 493.
covering. 500.
crank handle. 503.
creative leisure activities. 483.
crochet hook. 490.
cross stitches group. 493.
crossbar. 495, 499.
crossbeam. 494.
crosspiece. 494.
crosswise grain. 488.
crown. 507.
cutting blade. 499.
cutting guide. 489.
cutting line. 489.
cylinder. 504.
dabber. 502.
dart. 489.
diamond head. 507.
disc. 503.
dressmaker's model. 487.
driving wheel. 496.
dry-point. 501, 503.
edge. 487.
electric kiln. 506.
embroidery. 493.
endpaper. 498.
engraving tools. 501.
etching tools. 501.
eye. 486, 487, 495.
eye shield protector. 507.
eyelet. 491.
fabric structure. 488.
face. 500, 507.
fasteners. 488.
feather stitch. 493.
feed dog. 486.
feeding dial. 491.
feet. 500.
fettling knife. 505.
fine bookbinding. 498, 499, 500.
firing. 506.
fishbone stitch. 493.
fixed blade. 499.
flank. 500.
flat-bed. 485.
flat part. 490.
flat stitches group. 493.
flux. 507.
flux brush. 507.
flyleaf. 498.
flywheel. 505.
fold line. 489.
foot control. 485.
foot rest. 505.
fore edge. 498.
frame. 493.
frame. 494, 503.
French knot stitch. 493.
front board. 498.
garment fabric. 488.
garter stitch. 490.
gathering. 498.
gauge. 499.
gear. 496.
gearbox. 503.
glass cutter. 507.
glass cutting. 507.
glass grinder. 507.
gouged section. 504.

gravure printing, diagram of. 504.
groove. 486.
groups of stitches. 493.
grozzing teeth. 507.
hand vice. 501.
hand wheel. 485, 500.
handle. 487, 492, 494, 503, 507.
harness. 494.
harnesses. 494.
hatching. 497.
head. 485, 490, 492, 498, 500.
headband. 498.
headcap. 498.
heart. 507.
hearth. 506.
heating element. 506.
heddle. 494, 495.
heddle rod. 495.
heddles. 495.
hemline. 489.
herringbone stitch. 493.
hinge. 498.
hinged presser foot. 485, 486.
holder. 507.
hole. 503.
hook. 486, 488, 490, 492.
hook and eyes. 488.
hoop. 493.
horizontal floor loom. 494.
indicator. 506.
ink. 502.
ink roller. 502.
inking slab. 502.
intaglio press. 502.
intaglio printing. 502.
interfacing. 488.
interlining. 488.
interlock. 497.
kick wheel. 505.
knife. 502.
knitting. 490.
knitting machine. 491, 492.
knitting measure. 490.
knitting needles. 490.
knot. 497.
knot stitches group. 493.
lam. 494.
latch. 492.
latch lever. 486.
latch needle. 492.
lay edge. 499.
layout. 507.
layout paper. 507.
lead came. 507.
lead knife. 507.
lead stretcher. 507.
leash rod. 494, 495.
lenghtwise grain. 489.
lengthwise grain. 488.
letterpress printing, diagram of. 504.
lever. 503.
levigator. 503.
lining. 488.
lip. 507.
litho crayon. 503.
litho pencil. 503.
litho press. 503.
lithographic printing, diagram of. 504.
lithographic stone. 503, 504.
lithographic tusche. 503.
lithography. 503.
long and short stitch. 493.
loop stitches group. 493.
lying press. 500.
magnet. 487.
mallet. 502.
marking dot. 489.
metal plate. 504.
mortise. 493.
motor. 485.
muffle. 506.
muslin. 501.
nails. 495.

neck. 500.
needle. 486.
needle. 485, 486, 487.
needle bar. 486.
needle bed. 491.
needle bed. 491.
needle bed groove. 491.
needle clamp. 486.
needle clamp screw. 486.
needle plate. 485.
needle threader. 487.
needle threader. 486.
needle tool. 505.
notch. 489.
oilstone. 501.
Oriental couching stitch. 493.
packing material. 504.
paper. 504.
pattern. 489.
pattern. 492, 507.
pattern scissors. 507.
peg. 493, 496.
pillow. 492.
pin. 487.
pin cushion. 487.
pinking shears. 487.
pivot. 487.
plain weave. 497.
plaster bat. 505.
platen. 500.
point. 486, 490.
post. 494.
pottery. 505, 506.
press-stud. 488.
presser bar. 486.
presser foot. 486.
presser foot lifter. 485.
pressing. 500.
pressing board. 500.
pressure screw. 502, 503.
pricker. 492.
printed image. 504.
printing. 504.
printing image. 504.
prop. 506.
pumice correcting pencil. 503.
punch card. 491.
punch card feeding dial. 491.
punch card feeding mechanism. 491.
punch card reader. 491.
pyrometer. 506.
pyrometric cone. 506.
rail. 491.
raised band. 498.
ratchet. 494.
ratchet wheel. 494.
recess area. 504.
red ochre pencil. 503.
reed. 494.
reed hook. 496.
refractory brick. 506.
release treadle. 494.
relief printing process. 502.
revolving cylinder. 492.
rib stitch. 490.
ribs. 505.
ring. 488.
rocking tool. 501.
rod. 495.
roller. 501.
Romanian couching stitch. 493.
roulette. 501.
round eye. 488.
row indicator. 491.
safety pins. 487.
saggar. 506.
sample. 490.
satin weave. 497.
sawing-in. 499.
scissors. 487.
scraper. 501, 503.
scraper bar. 504.
scraper bar holder. 503.
screw eye. 494.
seam allowance. 489.

seam line. 489.
seat. 505.
selvage. 488.
separators. 491.
sew-through buttons. 488.
sewing. 485, 486, 487, 488, 489.
sewing frame. 499.
sewing machine. 485, 486.
sewing spool. 485.
shaft. 496, 505.
shank. 486, 487, 490, 492.
shank button. 488.
shed stick. 495.
sheet. 498.
shelf. 506.
shuttle. 486.
side lever. 492.
signature. 498.
sinker plate. 491, 492.
sketch. 507.
ski shuttle. 495.
skirt marker. 487.
slab building. 505.
slat. 493.
slide. 488.
slide-bar. 491.
slide plate. 485.
slit. 497.
slot. 499.
socket. 488.
solder. 507.
soldering iron. 507.
soldering process. 507.
spatula. 502.
spine. 498, 500.
spine of the book. 500.
spool. 492.
spool pin. 485.
spool rack. 496.
spy hole. 506.
square. 499.
stained glass. 507.
standing press. 500.
stick shuttle. 495.
stilt. 506.
stitch length regulator. 485.
stitch patterns. 490.
stitch selector. 485.
stocking stitch. 490.
stop. 488.
stop motion knob. 485.
straight eye. 488.
support. 495.
swift. 496.
tab. 488.
tail. 498, 500.
take-up handle. 494.
tape. 488, 493.
tape measure. 487.
taper. 501.
tapestry bobbin. 495.
teeth. 488.
temple. 496.
temple. 499.
tenon saw. 499.
tension block. 491.
tension controller. 491.
tension dial. 486.
tension dial. 485, 486, 491, 492.
tension disc. 486, 491.
tension guide. 491.
tension spring. 486, 491.
thimble. 487.
thread guide. 485, 486, 496.
thread take-up lever. 485.
thread trimmer. 486.
threading hook. 496.
tip. 507.
tip cleaner. 507.
tongue. 488.
top cylinder. 502, 504.
top roller. 494.
tracing wheel. 487.
treadle. 494.
treadle cord. 494.
trimming. 499.

The terms in **bold type** indicate the title of an illustration.

trimming tool. 505.
tuck brush. 492.
twill weave. 497.
tympan. 503, 504.
type forme. 504.
U-shaped gouge. 502.
underlining. 488.
underlying fabrics. 488.
upright. 494, 495, 499, 500.
upright floor loom. 495.
V-shaped gouge. 502.
vertical frame. 495.
warp. 494, 495.
warp roller. 494.
warp thread. 497.
warping mill. 496.
weaving. 494, 495, 496, 497.
weaving brush. 492.
weaving principle, diagram of. 497.
webbing. 493.
weft. 494.
weft thread. 497.
wheel. 487, 507.
wheel head. 505.
wire cutter. 505.
wood block. 502.
woodcut. 502.
wooden modelling tools. 505.
worm. 496.
yarn clip. 491.
yarn feeder. 492.
yarn rod. 491.
zip fastener. 488.
zip line. 489.

ENERGY

above ground pipeline. 630.
above ground pipeline support. 630.
absorber. 656.
absorber pipe. 656.
absorbing plate. 656.
absorbing surface. 655.
access gallery. 641, 646.
access shaft. 646.
adit. 622.
administration building. 624.
administration office. 634.
administrative building. 646.
advance gas-cooled reactor. 650.
advanced gas-cooled reactor. 648.
aerodynamic brake. 658.
afterbay. 637, 638, 641.
air-cooled condenser. 654.
air gap. 655.
air hose. 625.
air leg. 625.
air passage. 625.
air preheater. 647.
anticline. 626.
antireflection coating. 656.
anvil. 625.
apex. 622.
aquifer. 636.
arch dam. 639.
arch dam, cross section of an. 639.
articulated trailer. 632.
asphalt. 635.
asphalt process. 634.
asphalt still. 635.
automatic tank gauge. 633.
autorefrigerating devices. 630.
baffle. 632.
ballast tank. 631.
bank. 646.
bank of heliostats. 654.
barge. 631.
barren. 621.
base rock. 626, 636.
base width. 644.

basin. 646.
basin side. 646.
beam pump. 627.
belt. 658.
bench. 621.
bench height. 621.
berm. 638.
bit. 625, 626.
bitumen. 636.
bitumen pumping. 636.
bitumen treatment. 636.
blade. 642, 643, 658.
blowout preventer. 626.
boiler. 654.
boiler house. 647.
boiler tube. 647.
booster intermediate station. 630.
bottom plate. 633.
bottom ring. 643.
bottom road. 623.
brace. 645.
breather valve. 633.
bridge. 631.
bucket. 643.
bucket chain excavator. 621.
bucket ring. 643.
bucket wheel excavator. 621, 636.
buffer tank. 630.
bulb. 631.
bulb unit. 646.
bulldozer. 621.
bund wall. 633.
bunker. 623.
bunker oil. 635.
burden. 636.
buried pipeline. 630.
burner. 647.
busbar. 641.
bushing. 637, 645.
butane carrier. 631.
buttress. 639.
buttress dam. 639.
buttress dam, cross section of a. 639.
cable bundles. 644.
canal boat. 631.
cantilever. 639.
cap. 657.
cap rock. 626, 636.
capacitor. 658.
carbon dioxide gas coolant. 650.
carbon droxide coolant. 648.
casing first string. 627.
casing second string. 627.
catalytic reformer. 634.
catalytic reforming plant. 635.
central column. 658.
central pumping. 630.
centre Keelson. 631.
centre tank. 631.
chemical treatment. 635.
chimney. 647.
Christmas tree. 627.
Christmas tree. 630.
chuck. 625.
chute. 623.
circuit breaker. 641, 658.
circulating pump. 655.
closed circuit television/cathode monitor. 652.
coal bunker. 624, 647.
coal fired power station. 647.
coal measure. 623.
coal mine. 621, 623, 624, 625.
coal seam. 621.
coal upper. 647.
coking plant. 624.
cold air. 655.
collecting tube. 656.
collector. 642.
colliery. 623.
compressed air. 625.
computer:control/alarm. 652.
concrete dam, cross section of a. 638.
concrete drain. 633.

concrete pressure vessel. 650.
concrete shield. 650, 651.
concrete wall. 655.
condenser. 647, 648, 649.
conductive material. 656.
connection point. 645.
containment. 652.
containment building. 648.
control lever. 625.
control rod. 648, 650, 651.
control room. 652.
control room. 629, 637, 646, 648.
control system. 658.
control valve. 649.
conveyor. 621, 624, 636.
conveyor belt. 647.
cool sodium. 651.
coolant. 654, 656.
cooling pond. 648.
cooling tower. 634.
cooling water. 649.
core. 638.
cover plate. 656.
crane. 629.
crater. 621.
crest of spillway. 637.
cross arm. 644.
cross cut. 622, 623.
crossarm. 645.
crossover cargo deck line. 631.
crown block. 626.
crude oil. 635.
crude oil pipeline. 630.
customer's service entrance. 645.
cut off trench. 638.
cylinder. 625.
cylinder wall. 649.
cylindrical parabolic reflector. 656.
dam. 637, 646.
dams, major types of. 639.
deposit. 621.
derrick. 626, 629.
desasphalting. 634.
dewaxing. 634.
diagonal. 644.
diesel oil. 635.
diluent. 636.
diluent recovery. 636.
dip. 622.
disc brake. 658.
discharge liner. 643.
discharge pipe. 632.
discharge pump. 632.
dispatch area. 634.
distribution board. 645.
distributor service loop. 645.
diversion canal. 637.
double flow turbine. 649.
double glazing. 655.
downstream face. 638.
downstream shoulder. 638.
downstream toe. 638.
draft tube. 641, 643.
dragline. 636.
drain cock. 633.
drain valve. 633.
drainage blanket. 638.
drainage layer. 638.
drawworks. 626.
drift. 622, 623.
drill collar. 626.
drill pipe. 626.
drill rod. 625.
drill ship. 628.
drilling barge. 628.
drilling rig. 626.
drivage. 623.
dump. 621, 624.
earth. 639.
economizer. 647.
elastic coupling. 631.
electrical distribution system. 652.
electricity. 637, 638, 639, 640, 641, 642, 643, 644, 645, 646.

electricity, steps in production of. 640.
electricity meter. 645.
electricity pylon. 624.
electrostatic precipitator. 647.
embankment dam. 639.
embankment dam, cross section of an. 638, 639.
emergency core cooling. 652.
emptying outlet. 633.
encapsulant. 656.
energy. 619.
engine. 626.
engine room. 631.
equipment access shaft. 646.
exhaust port. 625.
face. 621.
fan. 624.
fantail. 657.
fast reactor. 651.
fault. 622.
feed heater. 647.
fill. 638.
filling inlet. 633.
filter. 638, 655.
finished product storage. 634.
fire station. 634.
fitted coupling bolt. 643.
fixed platform. 628.
fixed-roof tank. 633.
flare. 629, 634.
flat plate solar collector. 656.
flexible hose. 625.
flexible hose connection. 625.
floating platform. 628.
floating roof. 633.
floating-roof tank. 633.
floor. 621, 622, 657.
flow bean. 627.
fluid coking plant. 634.
fluid inlet. 656.
fluid outlet. 656.
foam monitor. 631.
focusing. 654.
forced draught fan. 647.
fore and aft gangway. 631.
foundation. 639.
foundation of dam. 638.
fractionating tower. 635.
frame. 656, 657.
Francis turbine. 643.
free-standing tanks. 631.
fuel element. 650, 651.
fuel handling control console. 652.
furnace. 647, 654.
fuse. 645.
fuse cut-out. 645.
fuse holder. 645.
gallery. 657.
gantry crane. 637, 641.
gas. 626.
gas circulator. 648.
gas exit port. 648.
gas lift. 627.
gas lift valve. 627.
gas oil. 635.
gas turbine. 629.
gas under pressure. 627.
gasometer. 624.
gate. 641, 646.
gate operating ring. 643.
gearbox. 658.
generator. 642.
generator. 641, 642, 647, 648, 649, 652, 658.
governor. 649.
graphite moderator. 650.
gravity dam. 639.
gravity dam, cross section of a. 639.
greases. 635.
greenhouse. 655.
ground. 633.
ground level. 644.
ground wire. 645.
ground-wire clamp. 645.

The terms in **bold type** indicate the title of an illustration.

guide bearing. 642.
guy wire. 658.
hammer drill. 625.
hand rail. 637.
handle. 625.
hatch. 631.
haulage road. 621.
headbay. 637.
headframe. 622, 624.
heat exchanger. 655.
heating oil. 635.
heavy petroleum. 635.
helideck. 629.
heliostat. 654.
hemlath. 657.
high activity spent fuel store. 648.
high pressure cylinder. 649.
high pressure steam. 648, 649.
hill. 654.
hook. 626.
horizon. 622.
horizontal-axis wind turbine. 658.
horizontal member. 644.
hot air duct. 647.
hot line connector. 645.
hot sodium. 651.
hot water extraction. 636.
hub. 643, 658.
hub cover. 643.
hydraulic turbine, cross section of a. 643.
hydroelectric complex. 637.
hydroelectric power station, cross section of a. 641.
hydrofiner. 634.
inactive dyke. 646.
inclined shaft. 622.
induced draught fan. 647.
inlet. 625.
inner pressure cylinder. 648.
insulation. 655, 656.
insulator. 645.
intermediate heat exchanger. 651.
intermediate pressure cylinder. 649.
jack-up platform. 628.
jacket. 629.
jackleg drill. 625.
jet fuel. 635.
Kaplan turbine. 643.
kelly. 626.
kerosene. 635.
laboratory. 634.
ladder. 657.
lagging. 633.
lamp room. 624.
landing. 623.
level. 623.
lifeboat. 629.
light. 656.
lightning arrester. 641, 645.
line printer. 652.
liquefied gas petroleum treatment. 634.
liquefied petroleum gas storage. 634.
liquid-level gauge. 633.
liquid sodium coolant. 651.
living quarters. 629.
loading belt. 621.
loading pocket. 623.
lock. 646.
log chute. 637.
logging unit. 629.
long residue. 635.
low pressure cylinder. 649.
low-tension distribution line. 645.
lubricants plant. 635.
lubricating oils. 635.
machine hall. 637, 641.
Magnox reactor. 650.
main flue. 647.
main inlet. 633.
main leg. 644.
main shaft. 624.

main switch. 645.
main turbine shaft. 649.
mains water. 655.
manhole. 632, 633.
manometer. 633.
marine diesel. 635.
master gate valve. 627.
medium tension distribution line. 645.
membrane tanks. 631.
metallic contact grid. 656.
metalliferous mine. 622.
methane carrier. 631.
mine. 636.
mine entrance. 623.
mining. 622.
miscellaneous auxiliary systems. 652.
moderator. 648.
moderator/miscellaneous systems. 652.
moving blade. 649.
mud pit. 626.
mud pump. 626.
muskeg. 636.
nacelle. 658.
negative contact. 656.
negative region. 656.
neutral conductor. 645.
new fuel store. 648.
nuclear energy. 650, 651, 652, 653.
nuclear fuel cycle. 653.
nuclear power station. 648.
offshore drilling. 628.
offshore well. 630.
oil. 626, 627, 628, 629, 630, 631, 635, 636.
oil. 626.
oil and gas foam. 627.
oil/gas separator. 629.
oil refinery. 634.
oil reservoir. 625.
oil sand. 636.
oil sands mining plant. 636.
oil storage. 633.
oil transport. 632.
oil trap. 626.
oiler. 625.
open-pit mine. 621.
open-pit mine. 622.
operating dam. 646.
operating floor. 646.
operator desk. 652.
ore. 622.
ore deposit. 622.
outcrop. 622.
outlet valve. 647.
over read ground wire. 644.
overburden. 621, 623.
overhead connection. 645.
P-N junction. 656.
panel. 623, 644.
parabolic mirror. 654.
paraffins. 635.
Pelton turbine. 643.
penstock. 637, 641, 646.
peripheral joint. 639.
petrochemical industry. 635.
petrochemicals. 635.
petrol. 635.
petroleum. 635.
phase conductor. 645.
pier. 628.
pile. 629.
pillar. 623.
pinch. 622.
pipeline. 630, 636.
piston. 625.
pitching. 637.
pithead. 624.
plunger. 627.
pneumatic hammer. 625.
polymerization and alkylation units. 634.
pool. 655.

positive contact. 656.
positive region. 656.
post. 657.
post mill. 657.
potable water tank. 629.
power line. 637.
power plant. 634.
power plant, cross section of. 646.
power station. 649.
power station. 624, 646.
power system. 658.
powerhouse. 637, 641.
pressure gauge. 627.
pressuriser. 651.
pressurized water reactor. 651.
primary air fan. 647.
primary heat transport system. 652.
primary vessel. 651.
production of electricity. 654.
production platform. 629.
pulverizing mill. 647.
pulvino. 639.
pump. 623, 654.
pumping station. 630.
pumping unit. 627.
pyrolysis. 636.
quarters. 631.
radiation. 655.
rail tank. 632.
rail track. 624.
raise. 622.
ramp. 621.
reactor jacket. 651.
reactor regulating system. 652.
reclaimed water. 636.
refinery. 634.
refinery. 630.
refinery products. 635.
reflecting surface. 654.
reflector. 656.
refuelling machine. 648.
reheated steam. 648.
reheater. 647.
rerunning. 634.
reserve mud tank. 629.
reservoir. 637, 638, 641.
retainer. 625.
retaining spring. 625.
rigs. 628.
road tankers. 632.
rocks. 639.
roof. 621, 622.
room. 623.
rotary table. 626.
rotor. 641, 642, 649, 657, 658.
rotor shaft. 658.
runner. 642, 643.
runner blade. 643, 646.
sail. 657.
sail cloth. 657.
sailbar. 657.
salient pole. 642.
salt water. 626.
sand-rock. 636.
scale. 633.
screen. 641.
scroll case. 641.
sea. 646.
sea side. 646.
seal. 656.
sealing ring. 633.
secondary inlet. 633.
self-contained platform. 628.
semi-membrane tanks. 631.
semi-submersible. 628.
service box. 645.
settling basin. 624.
settling pond. 634, 636.
settling tank. 631.
shaft. 641, 642, 643.
shaft collar. 623.
shell. 633.
shutdown system. 652.
shutter. 655.

skid pad. 630.
soil. 639.
solar cell. 656.
solar collector. 655.
solar energy. 654, 655, 656.
solar furnace. 654.
solar house. 655.
solar radiation. 654, 655, 656.
solvent extraction unit. 635.
spacer. 644.
spent fuel chute. 648.
spent fuel storage and containment. 648.
spherical parabolic reflector. 656.
spillway. 637.
spillway chute. 637.
spillway gate. 637.
spiral case. 642, 643.
spiral chute. 623.
spiral staircase. 633.
splash plate. 633.
spray nozzle. 633.
stairs. 633.
stand. 656.
staple shaft. 622, 623.
starter. 658.
stationery blade. 649.
stator. 641, 642, 649.
stay ring. 642, 643.
stay vane. 642, 643.
steam cracker. 634.
steam drive oil sands recovery process. 636.
steam drum. 647.
steam from reheat. 649.
steam generator. 648, 650, 651, 654.
steam generator system. 652.
steam injection. 636.
steam to reheat. 649.
steam turbine. 648.
steel lined concrete pressure vessel. 648.
steel pressure vessel. 650, 651.
stock. 657.
stop. 630.
stope. 622.
storage tank. 629, 635, 654, 655.
stove oil. 635.
straight run petroleum treatment. 634.
strainer. 627.
strip mine. 621.
structure. 637.
strut. 646, 658.
sublevel. 623.
submarine pipeline. 630.
submersible barge. 628.
substation. 646.
sucker rod. 627.
sump. 622.
superheater. 647.
supply point. 645.
support. 630.
surface. 624.
suspension insulator string. 644.
suspension tower. 644.
switchyard. 652.
swivel. 626.
tail pole. 657.
tailing. 636.
tailrace. 641, 643.
tank. 632.
tank farm. 630, 634.
tank gauge float. 633.
tank wall. 632.
tankage. 636.
tanker. 631.
target area. 654.
tender. 628.
terminal. 630, 645.
thermal insulation. 630.
thermal storage. 654.
thermometer. 633.
thick-walled pipe. 626.

The terms in **bold type** indicate the title of an illustration.

throttle valve. 625.
tidal power plant. 646.
timber yard. 624.
top central manhole. 632.
top of dam. 637, 638, 641.
top plate. 633.
top road. 623.
towboat. 631.
tower. 654, 657, 658.
tower foot. 644.
tower mill. 657.
tower-type solar power station. 654.
tractor. 632.
training wall. 637.
transformer. 641, 645, 654, 658.
transformer station. 641.
transmission network. 654.
transverse baffle. 632.
transverse bulkhead. 631.
travelling block. 626.
travelling crane. 641, 648.
trench. 621.
Trombe wall. 655.
Trombe wall. 655.
tubing. 627.
tubing head. 627.
tubular heater. 635.
tubular member. 629.
turbine. 641, 647, 652.
turbine runner. 646.
turbines, major types of. 643.
turbo-alternator. 654.
turbo-generator. 649.
turbo-generator. 650, 651.
underground. 624.
underground mine. 623.
underground winder house. 622.
upstream blanket. 638.
upstream face. 638.
upstream shoulder. 638.
upstream toe. 638.
uranium fuel element. 648.
utilities plant. 636.
vacuum distillation. 635.
valve. 625.
vein. 622.
ventilation shaft. 624.
vertical-axis wind turbine. 658.
vertical shaft. 622.
vibrating mudscreen. 626.
wall. 622.
warm air. 655.
washery. 624.
water coolant and moderator. 651.
water hose. 625.
water intake. 641.
water reservoir. 624.
water to feed heaters and steam generator. 649.
watertight bulkhead. 631.
wave wall. 638.
web frame. 631.
weigher. 647.
wicket gate. 643.
wind turbine. 658.
wind turbine electricity production. 658.
winder house. 622, 624.
winding tower. 624.
windmill. 657.
windshaft. 657.
wing tank. 631.
winze. 622.
workshop/store. 634.

FARMING

agricultural machinery. 152, 153, 154.
air fan. 155.
barn. 151.
beam. 153.
beater. 155.
beehive. 151.

buildings. 151.
chaffer sieve. 155.
combine harvester. 155.
concave. 155.
coulter. 153.
covering disc. 154.
cowshed. 151.
crop elevator. 155.
crossbar. 152.
cultivator. 153.
cup conveyor. 154.
cutter bar. 155.
dairy. 151.
discharge spout. 152, 153.
divider. 155.
drive shaft. 152.
electrified fence. 151.
elevator. 152.
engine. 155.
farmhouse. 151.
farming. 149.
farmyard. 151.
fertilizer distributor. 154.
field heap spreader. 154.
finger. 152.
frog. 153.
grain auger. 155.
grain pan. 155.
grain sieve. 155.
grain tank. 155.
grain unloading auger. 155.
grass ley. 151.
greenhouse. 151.
harrow. 152.
hay turner. 154.
heel. 153.
hopper. 154.
implement bar. 152.
knife. 155.
landside. 153.
leg. 153.
loose boxes. 151.
machinery. 155.
machinery store. 151.
manure spreader. 153.
manure spreader box. 153.
milking parlour. 151.
mouldboard. 153.
open housing. 151.
orchard. 151.
permanent pasture. 151.
pick-up. 152.
pick-up automatic baler. 152.
pick-up loader. 152.
pickup reel. 155.
piggery. 151.
ploughed land. 151.
potato planter. 154.
poultry house. 151.
power take off. 152.
reciprocating knife mower. 152.
reel. 154.
return elevator. 155.
reversing light. 152.
ribbing plough. 153.
rotary hoe. 153.
rotating auger. 155.
seed drill. 154.
share. 153.
silage bunker. 151.
silage harvester. 153.
skimmer. 153.
spider. 153.
spike-tooth. 152.
spreading rotor. 155.
steering wheel. 155.
straw walker. 155.
stripper beater. 155.
subsoil plough. 154.
tandem disc harrow. 154.
tooth. 154.
toothed rotor. 154.
tower silo. 151.
towing hook. 152.
tractor. 152.
vegetable garden. 151.

well. 151.
wheat. 151.

FOOD

agnolotti. 137.
aiguillette de gîte à la noix. 141.
aiguillette de romsteck. 141.
alphabet. 137.
American corn bread. 138.
Babybel (French). 145.
basil. 135.
bavette. 141.
beef. 140, 141.
Bel Paese (Italian). 145.
belly. 142.
best end. 139, 143.
biscuit. 138.
black rye bread. 138.
borage. 135.
Boursin au Poivre (French). 145.
bread. 138.
breast. 139, 143.
Brie (French). 145.
brioche. 146.
brisket. 140.
British cheeses. 144.
British cut. 139, 140, 142, 143.
buck shots. 137.
Caerphilly. 144.
Camembert (French). 145.
cannelloni. 137.
cappelletti. 137.
caraway seeded rye bread. 138.
carré. 142.
carré raccourci. 139.
charlotte. 146.
chervil. 135.
Cheshire. 144.
choux bun. 147.
chuck rib. 140.
chump end. 143.
collet. 139, 143.
conchigliette. 137.
Continental cheeses. 145.
contre-filet. 141.
côtelettes découvertes. 143.
côtelettes premières et secondes. 143.
côtes. 142.
côtes découvertes. 139.
Cottage cheese. 144.
cottage loaf. 138.
crak rye bread. 138.
croissant. 138.
crosse. 139, 141, 142.
cuisseau. 139.
culotte. 141.
curly lasagna. 136.
custard tart. 147.
cut ribbed macaroni. 137.
Danish Blue (Denmark). 145.
Danish rye bread. 138.
Derby. 144.
desserts. 146, 147.
dessus de côtes. 139, 141.
dill. 135.
ditali. 137.
Double Gloucester. 144.
doughnut. 146.
Dunlop. 144.
ear loaf. 138.
échine. 142.
Edam (Dutch). 145.
elbow macaroni. 137.
Emmental (Swiss). 145.
English Cheddar. 144.
entame de romsteck. 141.
entrecôtes couvertes. 141.
entrecôtes découvertes. 141.
épaule. 139, 143.
farfalline. 137.
fedelini. 136.
Feta (Greek). 145.
filet. 142, 143.

fillet. 140.
flanchet. 141.
food. 133.
fore rib. 140.
franzipan. 146.
French sticks. 138.
fruit flan. 147.
fruit loaf. 147.
gateau. 146.
German rye bread. 138.
gigot. 143.
gîte à la noix. 141.
gîte de derrière. 141.
gîte de devant. 141.
gorge. 142.
Gorgonzola (Italian). 145.
Gouda (Dutch). 145.
gros bout de poitrine. 141.
Gruyere (Swiss). 145.
hampe. 141.
harth bread. 138.
haut de côtelettes. 143.
haut de côtes. 139.
head. 142.
herbs. 135.
hock. 142.
hyssop. 135.
ice cream. 147.
Indian chapati bread. 138.
Indian naan bread. 138.
jambon. 142.
jambonneau arrière. 142.
jambonneau avant. 142.
japonaise fancy. 146.
jarret arrière. 139.
jarret avant. 139.
Jewish chollar. 138.
jumeaux. 141.
knuckel. 139.
knuckle. 139.
lamb. 143.
Lancashire. 144.
lasagna. 136.
lasagna verde. 136.
leg. 139, 142, 143.
loin. 139, 142.
longe. 139.
lovage. 135.
lumache. 137.
Lymeswold. 144.
macreuse. 141.
mafalde. 136.
manicotti. 137.
marjoram. 135.
meringue gateau. 146.
mezzani. 136.
middle neck. 143.
middle rib. 140.
milieu de poitrine. 141.
milieu de sous-noix. 139.
milk bread. 138.
mint. 135.
mousse. 147.
neck. 139, 140.
neck end. 139.
neck-scrag end. 143.
nerveux de gîte à la noix. 141.
nerveux de sous-noix. 139.
noix. 139.
noix de hachage. 142.
noix pâtissière. 139.
non-skid spaghetti. 136.
noodles. 136.
onglet. 139, 141.
oregano. 135.
paleron. 141.
palette. 142.
pancake. 147.
Parisian cut. 139, 141, 142, 143.
Parmesan (Italian). 145.
parsley. 135.
pasta. 136, 137.
penne. 137.
pennine. 137.
petits fours. 146.
pie. 146.

The terms in **bold type** indicate the title of an illustration.

pied. 142.
pita bread. 138.
plat de côte couvert. 141.
plat de côte découvert. 141.
plate. 140.
poitrine. 139, 142, 143.
pork. 142.
Port-Salut (French). 145.
profiterole. 146.
puff pastry. 147.
pumpernickel bread. 138.
quasi. 139.
ravioli. 137.
Red Leicester. 144.
Ricotta (Italian). 145.
rigatoni. 137.
rings. 137.
romsteck. 141.
rond de gîte à la noix. 141.
Roquefort (French). 145.
rosemary. 135.
rouelle. 139.
round loaf. 138.
rump. 139, 140.
Russian pumpernickel. 138.
rye crispbread. 138.
saddle. 143.
sage. 135.
savarin. 146.
savory. 135.
seeds. 137.
selle. 143.
sesame seeded pita. 138.
shank. 140.
shells. 137.
shin. 140.
shortbread. 146.
shoulder. 139, 142, 143.
silverside. 140.
sirloin. 140.
sliced white bread. 138.
soda bread. 138.
sorbet. 147.
soufflé. 147.
spaghetti. 136.
spinach noodles. 136.
spiral. 137.
stars. 137.
Stilton. 144.
strip loin. 140.
surlonge. 141.
sweet bay. 135.
Swiss roll. 147.
tagliatelle. 136.
tarragon. 135.
tenderloin. 140.
tendron. 139, 141.
thick flank. 140.
thin flank. 140.
thin macaroni. 136.
thyme. 135.
topside. 140.
tortellini. 137.
tranche grasse. 141.
trotter. 142.
twisted macaroni. 136.
unleavened bread. 138.
vacherin. 146.
veal. 139.
vermicelli. 136.
Vienna bread. 138.
waffle. 147.
wavy lasagna. 136, 137.
wheels. 137.
whole wheat bread. 138.
wholemeal bread. 138.
wing rib. 140.
ziti. 136, 137.

GARDENING

air filter. 243.
antivibration handle. 243.
arbor. 237.
bar nose. 243.

billhook. 242.
blade. 242.
bulb planter. 239.
bush. 237.
chain brake. 243.
chainsaw. 243.
chainsaw chain. 243.
climbing plant. 237.
crazy paving. 237.
cutter link. 243.
cutting cylinder. 242.
dibber. 239.
digging fork. 238.
draw hoe. 238.
Dutch hoe. 238.
edging. 237.
engine housing. 243.
fan trellis. 237.
flower bed. 237.
fuel tank. 243.
garden. 237.
garden hose. 240.
garden light. 237.
garden line. 239.
gardening. 235.
grafting knife. 242.
grass catcher. 242.
grubber hoe. 238.
guide bar. 243.
hand fork. 239.
hand mower. 242.
hand shears. 239.
handle. 243.
hanging basket. 237.
hedge. 237.
hedge trimmer. 242.
hose nozzle. 240.
hose reel. 240.
jet deflector. 242.
lawn. 237.
lawn aerator. 241.
lawn edger. 238.
lawn mowers. 242.
lawn rake. 238.
lopping shears. 239.
mist sprayer. 240.
motor mower. 242.
oil sump. 243.
oscillating sprinkler. 240.
paling fence. 237.
path. 237.
patio. 237.
pergola. 237.
pick. 238.
pistol spray. 240.
pond. 237.
post-hole digger. 238.
pruning hook. 239.
pruning knife. 242.
pruning saw. 242.
rake. 238.
revolving sprinkler. 240.
ridging hoe. 238.
rock garden. 237.
roller. 241.
rose. 240.
rotovator. 241.
scythe. 242.
secateurs. 239.
seeder. 239, 241.
shed. 237.
shovel. 238.
sickle. 242.
silencer. 243.
small hand cultivator. 239.
spade. 238.
spark plug. 243.
spreader. 241.
spreading fork. 238.
sprinkler hose. 240.
stake. 237.
starter handle. 243.
stop button. 243.
strimmer. 242.
tank sprayer. 240.
throttle. 243.

tree pruner. 239.
trigger. 243.
trowel. 239.
tub. 237.
watering can. 240.
weeder. 239.
weeding hoe. 238.
wheelbarrow. 241.

GEOGRAPHY

abyssal deposits. 42.
abyssal plain. 42.
action of wind. 50.
Africa. 41.
air temperature. 54, 55.
altitude control system. 57.
altitude scales. 39.
altocumulus. 44.
altostratus. 44.
anemometer. 55.
Antarctic Ocean. 41.
arctic continental. 54.
arctic maritime. 54.
Arctic Ocean. 41.
artificial satellite. 39.
ash layer. 45.
Asia. 41.
asthenosphere. 39.
astronomy. 45.
Atlantic Ocean. 41.
atmosphere. 39.
Australia. 41.
barb. 53.
barograph. 55.
barometric pressure. 54.
barometric tendency. 54.
basaltic layer. 40.
base plate. 56.
battery. 57.
beach. 40, 43.
Beacon antenna. 57.
bergschrund. 48.
Bering Sea. 41.
Black Sea. 41.
blowing snow. 52.
breaker. 43.
butte. 47.
cactus. 47.
calm. 53.
capped column. 49.
card support. 56.
Caribbean Sea. 41.
Caspian Sea. 41.
cave. 46.
cave. 43.
Central America. 41.
chain of dunes. 47.
check nut. 56.
China Sea. 41.
cirrocumulus. 44.
cirrostratus. 44.
cirrus. 44.
clear sky. 53.
cleared ground. 55.
cliff. 40, 43.
climates of the world. 51.
clint. 46.
cloud amount. 53.
cloud amount. 54.
cloud of volcanic ash. 45.
clouds. 44.
clouds of vertical development. 44.
cloudy sky. 53.
coast. 40.
collecting funnel. 56.
column. 46, 49.
command antenna. 57.
common coastal features. 43.
complex dune. 47.
Concorde. 39.
condensation. 50.
cone. 45.
container. 56.

continental climates. 51.
continental margin. 42.
continental mass. 42.
continental plate. 42.
continental rise. 42.
continental shelf. 40, 42.
continental slope. 40, 42.
continents, configuration of the. 41.
continuous drizzle. 52.
continuous rain. 52.
continuous snow. 52.
crater. 45.
crescentic dune. 47.
crest. 43, 46.
crest-to-crest wave length. 43.
crevasse. 48.
cumulonimbus. 44.
cumulus. 44.
deep-sea floor. 40.
denominations. 49.
depth of focus. 45.
desert. 47.
desert. 51.
direct-reading rain gauge. 56.
direction in orbit. 57.
dormant volcano. 45.
drifting snow. 52.
dry continental - arid. 51.
dry continental - semiarid. 51.
dry gallery pot hole. 46.
dry snow. 49.
dry subtropical. 51.
dune. 43.
dust storm. 52.
dyke. 45.
Earth, structure of the. 39.
Earth's atmosphere, profile of the. 39.
Earth's crust. 39, 45.
Earth's crust, section of the. 40.
earthquake. 45.
epicentre. 45.
Europe. 41.
evaporation. 50.
exosphere. 39.
fault. 40, 45.
firn. 48.
foam. 43.
focus. 45.
fog. 52.
forms. 49.
freezing rain. 52.
fronts. 53.
fumarole. 45.
geography. 37.
geyser. 45.
glacial cirque. 48.
glacier. 48.
glacier tongue. 48.
glass sphere. 56.
glazed frost. 49.
gorge. 46.
gour. 46.
granitic layer. 40.
graphic symbols. 49.
grike. 46.
ground moraine. 48.
Gutenberg discontinuity. 39.
guyot. 42.
hail. 49.
hail shower. 52.
half barb. 53.
hanging glacier. 48.
headland. 43.
heavy thunderstorm. 52.
high clouds. 44.
high pressure centre. 54.
highland climates. 51.
hill. 46.
horizon scanner. 57.
humid subtropical. 51.
humid temperate - long summer. 51.
humid temperate - short summer. 51.

The terms in **bold type** indicate the title of an illustration.

humidity. 55.
hurricane. 52.
hydrologic cycle. 50.
hygrograph. 55.
ice. 50.
igneous rocks. 40.
image dissector camera. 57.
in km. 39.
in thousands of feet. 39.
Indian Ocean. 41.
infiltration. 50.
infra-red spectrometer. 57.
inner core. 39.
interconnecting truss. 57.
intermittent drizzle. 52.
intermittent rain. 52.
intermittent snow. 52.
**international weather symbols.
52, 53.**
interplanetary space. 39.
interrogation recording and
location system antenna. 57.
intrusive rocks. 40.
ionosphere. 39.
irregular crystal. 49.
isobar. 54.
isoseismal line. 45.
laccolith. 45.
lagoon. 43.
lateral moraine. 48.
latitude scale. 56.
lava flow. 45.
lava layer. 45.
lava plateau. 45.
levelling screw. 56.
lithosphere. 39.
lock nut. 56.
longitudinal dunes. 47.
low clouds. 44.
low pressure centre. 54.
lower mantle. 39.
lower sphere clamp. 56.
lower support screw. 56.
magma. 45.
magma chamber. 45.
maximum and minimum
thermometers. 55.
measuring tube. 56.
medial moraine. 48.
Mediterranean Sea. 41.
melting snow. 49.
meltwater. 48.
Mercury capsule (USA). 39.
mesa. 47.
mesosphere. 39.
metamorphic rocks. 40.
meteorological ground. 55.
**meteorological measuring
instruments. 56.**
meteorological satellite. 57.
meteorological symbols. 44.
meteorology. 54, 55.
middle clouds. 44.
mist. 52.
Mohorovicic discontinuity. 39, 40.
mountain. 46.
mountain range. 40.
mountain slope. 46.
mountain torrent. 46.
Mt Everest. 39.
nacreous cloud. 39.
natural arch. 43.
needle. 49.
nimbostratus. 44.
noctilucent cloud. 39.
North America. 41.
North Sea. 41.
oasis. 47.
obscured sky. 53.
occluded front. 53.
ocean. 50.
ocean floor. 42.
Oceania. 41.
oceanic trench. 42.
outer core. 39.
outwash plain. 48.

overcast sky. 53.
ozone. 39.
Pacific Ocean. 41.
palm grove. 47.
parabolic dune. 47.
pass. 46.
peak. 46.
pennant. 53.
piedmont glacier. 48.
pitch nozzle. 57.
plate crystal. 49.
plateau. 46.
polar climates. 51.
polar ice cap. 51.
polar lights. 39.
polar tundra. 51.
precipice. 46.
precipitation. 50.
precipitation, kinds of. 49.
precipitation area. 54.
present state of weather. 54.
pressure. 55.
pressure change. 54.
progressive wave. 43.
psychrometer. 55.
quasi-stationary front. 53.
rain. 49.
rain gauge. 55.
rain shower. 52.
rainfall. 55.
Red Sea. 41.
resurgence. 46.
ridge. 42.
rift. 42.
rock basin. 48.
rock step. 48.
rocket. 39.
rocky desert. 47.
roll nozzle. 57.
s-band antenna. 57.
saline lake. 47.
salt marsh. 43.
sand bar. 43.
sand island. 43.
sandstorm. 52.
sandy desert. 47.
scattered sky. 53.
sea level. 40, 42.
sea-level pressure. 54.
seamount. 42.
sedimentary rocks. 40.
seismic wave. 45.
serac. 48.
shaft. 53.
shooting star. 39.
shoulder. 46.
sill. 45.
sink hole. 46.
siphon. 46.
sleet. 49, 52.
slightly covered sky. 53.
smoke. 52.
snow. 50.
**snow crystals, classification of.
49.**
snow pellet. 49.
snow shower. 52.
solar panel. 57.
sounding balloon. 39, 55.
South America. 41.
space achievements. 39.
space probe. 39.
spatial dendrite. 49.
sphere support. 56.
spit. 43.
spur. 46.
squall. 52.
stack. 43.
stalactite. 46.
stalagmite. 46.
state of ground. 55.
station circle. 53, 54.
station model. 54.
stellar crystal. 49.
steppe. 51.
Stevenson's screen. 55.

stratocumulus. 44.
stratosphere. 39.
stratus. 44.
sub-base. 56.
subarctic climates. 51.
sublimation. 50.
submarine canyon. 42.
subterranean cavern. 46.
subterranean stream. 46.
subtropical climates. 51.
summit. 46.
sun. 57.
sun sensor. 57.
sunshine. 55.
sunshine recorder. 56.
sunshine recorder. 55.
support. 56.
surface cold front. 53.
surface runoff. 50.
surface warm front. 53.
swallow-hole. 46.
temperate climates. 51.
temperate marine. 51.
temperature of dew point. 54.
temperature of the soil surface. 55.
terminal moraine. 48.
theodolite. 55.
thermal control shutter. 57.
thermosphere. 39.
thunderstorm. 52.
tightening band. 56.
tombolo. 43.
transform fault. 42.
translation wave. 43.
transpiration. 50.
transverse dunes. 47.
tropical climates. 51.
tropical maritime. 51.
tropical rain forest. 51.
tropical savanna. 51.
tropical storm. 52.
troposphere. 39.
trough. 43, 54.
trough-to-trough wave lenght. 43.
type of high cloud. 54.
type of low cloud. 54.
type of middle cloud. 54.
type of the air mass. 54.
underground flow. 50.
upper cold front. 53.
upper mantle. 39.
upper sphere clamp. 56.
upper support screw. 56.
upper warm front. 53.
valley. 46.
vent. 45.
very cloudy sky. 53.
volcanic island. 42.
volcano. 45.
volcano. 40.
volcano during eruption. 45.
warm temperate Western margin.
51.
water forms. 49.
water table. 46.
waterfall. 46.
wave. 43.
wave base. 43.
wave height. 43.
weather map. 54.
wet snow. 49.
wind. 53.
wind. 41.
wind arrow. 53.
wind direction. 54.
wind direction and speed. 54.
wind scale. 53.
wind speed. 54, 55.
wind speed in knots. 53.
wind vane. 55.
X-15 (USA). 39.
yaw nozzle. 57.

HEALTH

adhesive tape. 615.
adjuster. 616.
arm. 617.
arm piece. 616.
arm support. 616.
armrest. 617.
aspirin. 615.
back upholstery. 617.
brake. 617.
clothing guard. 617.
cotton applicators. 615.
cotton wool ball. 615.
crepe support. 615.
cross brace. 617.
crutch tip. 616.
crutches. 616.
disposable syringe. 615.
ear syringe. 615.
eyewash. 615.
first aid kit. 615.
foot rest. 617.
front wheel. 617.
gauze roller bandage. 615.
handgrip. 616.
handle. 617.
health. 613.
heel loop. 617.
hub. 617.
insulin syringe. 615.
large wheel. 617.
leg rest. 617.
liquid antiseptic. 615.
metal adjustable arm crutch. 616.
needle. 615.
ortho-stick. 616.
plaster dressing. 615.
push rim. 617.
quadripod. 616.
quadruped stick. 616.
rubber ferrule. 616.
safety pin. 615.
scissors. 615.
seat upholstery. 617.
spacer. 617.
sterile dressing. 615.
sticks. 616.
syringes. 615.
tipping lever. 617.
tripod stick. 616.
tweezers. 615.
upright. 616.
walking aids. 616.
walking frame. 616.
walking stick. 616.
wheelchair. 617.
wooden underarm crutch. 616.

HEAVY MACHINERY

A-frame. 661.
air-cleaner filter. 664.
apron. 668.
arm. 665, 667.
articulating hinge point. 665.
ball stud of circle drawbar. 666.
barrow. 671.
base. 661.
beacon. 663.
blade. 664, 666.
blade arm. 666.
blade rotation mechanism. 666.
block. 671.
body. 668.
body lift cylinder. 668.
boom. 661, 665, 667.
boom point sheave. 661.
bottom deckboard. 671.
bowl. 668.
box-beam Y frame. 666.
box pallet. 671.
breathing apparatus. 662.
bucket. 661, 665.
bucket cylinder. 665.

The terms in **bold type** indicate the title of an illustration.

bucket hinge pin. 665.
bucket tooth. 665.
bulldozer. 664.
cab. 664, 665, 666, 667, 668, 670.
canopy. 668.
carriage. 670.
circle. 666.
clamshell bucket. 667.
compressed-air cylinder. 662.
control panel. 662.
counterjib. 669.
counterjib ballast. 669.
counterweight. 667, 669.
crane. 669.
crane runway. 669.
crawler crane. 669.
crawler tractor. 664.
crosshead. 670.
cutting edge. 664, 668.
cylinder. 667.
cylinder blade lift. 666.
diesel engine. 665.
dipper bucket. 667.
dividing breeching. 662.
double-decked pallet. 671.
draft arm. 668.
draft tube. 668.
drag chain. 661.
drag drum. 661.
drag rope. 661.
dragline. 661.
drawbar. 664, 666.
drive axle. 670.
drive wheel. 666.
dump rope. 661.
dumper truck. 668.
engine. 664, 666, 667, 668.
entry. 671.
exhaust pipe. 664.
extension ladder. 663.
filter. 661.
fire appliance. 662, 663.
fire hose. 662.
fireman's axe. 662.
first extension ladder. 662.
fork. 670.
fork extender. 670.
forklift trucks. 670.
forks. 670.
frame. 667, 668, 670.
frame push. 664.
front axle. 666.
front-end loader. 665.
front wheel. 666.
gantry crane. 669.
gooseneck. 668.
grader. 666.
grapple. 666.
handling appliances. 671.
harness. 662.
heavy machinery. 659.
hoisting chain. 661.
hoisting drum. 661.
hoisting rope. 661, 669.
hook. 669.
hose reel. 663.
hose storage compartment. 663.
hydraulic cylinder. 664, 665, 668.
hydraulic pallet truck. 671.
hydraulic shovel. 667.
jack. 662, 667.
jib. 669.
jib tie. 669.
lever bucket. 665.
lever ejector. 668.
lift arm. 665.
lift cylinder. 665, 670.
lifting chain. 670.
live roller. 669.
load backrest. 670.
load guard. 670.
main ladder. 662.
mast. 661, 670.
motor. 661.
nozzle. 662.

operator's cab. 661, 669.
operator's seat. 670.
overhead frame. 666.
pallet truck. 671.
pallets. 671.
pivot cab. 667.
plate push. 668.
platform. 669.
platform trolley. 671.
point. 664.
portable fire extinguisher. 662.
portable pump housing. 663.
power lift truck. 670.
revolving frame. 661.
rib. 668.
ripper. 666.
ripper. 664.
ripper cylinder. 664.
roller circle. 661.
roof ladder. 663.
scarifier. 666.
scraper engine. 668.
second extension ladder. 662.
shank. 664.
shank protector. 664.
side. 671.
single-decked pallet. 671.
siren. 663.
solid rubber tyre. 670.
spotlight. 662.
sprocket wheel. 664.
steering axle. 670.
steering cylinder. 668.
steering wheel. 670.
storage compartment. 662.
stringer. 671.
stringer board. 671.
suspension cable. 661.
tandem drive housing. 666.
telescopic boom. 669.
tooth. 666, 667.
top deckboard. 671.
top extension ladder. 662.
tower crane. 669.
tower mast. 669.
track. 664.
track carrier roller. 664.
track grouser. 664.
track idler. 664.
track link. 664.
track roller. 664.
track roller frame. 664.
track shoe. 664.
track shoe. 664.
tractor engine. 668.
tractor-scraper. 668.
transmission. 668.
trolley. 669.
trolley pulley. 669.
truck crane. 669.
turntable. 667.
turntable ladder. 662.
turntable mounting. 662.
walking cam. 661.
walking shoe. 661.
walkway. 661.
water-tender. 663.
wheel loader. 665.
wheel loader. 665.
winch. 661.
wing pallet. 671.

HOUSE

access panel. 195.
adjustable pedestal. 195.
air-circulating fan. 196.
air conditioning. 196.
air inlet control. 191.
air tube. 195.
airbrick. 177.
angle brace. 180.
angle valve. 193.
architrave rail. 188.
Arenberg parquet. 186.

asbestos shingle. 185.
ash lid. 191.
asphalt shingle. 185.
automatic air vent. 194.
automatic circulating pump. 194.
automatic relief valve. 194.
automatic shut-off. 196.
baffle. 191.
balcony. 178.
baluster. 187.
balustrade. 178.
base. 190.
base plate. 182.
basement. 179.
bathroom. 179.
batt insulation. 185.
bay window. 177.
beam. 182.
bedroom. 179.
bell roof. 181.
blade. 196.
blanket insulation. 185.
bleeder valve. 193.
blower. 194, 195, 196.
blower motor. 195.
boarding joist. 186.
boiler. 194.
boiler. 193.
boiler room. 179.
bottom rail. 188.
brace. 182.
branch duct. 192.
branch return pipe. 193.
branch supply pipe. 193.
brick. 183.
brick pattern half bond. 186.
building line. 178.
building materials. 183, 184, 185.
cabinet. 196.
cap. 187.
capped inspection tee. 192.
car parking. 178.
casement. 189.
casement window. 189.
casing. 193, 196.
caster. 196.
ceiling collar. 192.
ceiling fan. 196.
ceiling grille. 192.
ceiling joist. 182.
cement screed. 186.
Chantilly parquet. 186.
chimney. 192.
chimney. 190.
chimney connection. 191.
chimney flue. 190.
chimney pot. 177.
chimney stack. 177.
circulating pump. 193.
closed expansion tank. 194.
cold room. 179.
column. 193.
column radiator. 193.
composite window. 189.
compressor. 194.
concrete. 196.
concrete block. 183.
condenser. 196.
condenser coil. 196.
condensor. 194.
conical broach roof. 181.
control panel. 196.
convector. 193.
cooling/heating coils. 194.
corbel piece. 190.
corner stud. 182.
cornice. 177, 188.
cowl. 192.
cupboard. 178.
curved handrail. 187.
dado rail. 187.
damp proof course. 177.
damp proof membrane. 186.
damper. 190, 192.
dehumidifier. 196.
detachable handle. 191.

diamond mesh expanded metal
lath. 184.
dining room. 179.
dome roof. 181.
door. 188.
doorknob. 188.
doors, types of. 188.
doorstep. 177.
down. 178.
drain line. 194.
drain valve. 194.
driveway. 178.
eaves. 177.
elbow. 191, 192, 193.
electric heating unit. 195.
electric motor. 195.
electric supply. 194.
electrode assembly. 195.
enamelled hardboard. 184.
end joist. 182.
entablature. 188.
evaporator. 196.
evaporator coils. 196.
expansion tank. 193.
exterior door. 188.
fan. 194, 195, 196.
fan control. 196.
fan motor. 196.
filter. 194, 195.
finned tube. 193.
fire-dog. 191.
fire irons. 191.
firebox. 191.
firebrick. 195.
firebrick back. 190.
fireplace. 190.
fireplace. 178.
firestopping. 182.
first floor. 178, 179.
flashing. 177, 192.
flat roof. 180.
flight of stairs. 187.
floor. 182.
floor board. 186.
floor joist. 182.
floor tile. 185.
floorboard. 186.
flue collar. 191.
flue damper. 191.
flue pipe. 191.
flush door. 178.
foam insulation. 185.
foam rubber insulation. 185.
folding. 188.
folding sliding door. 178.
footing. 182.
forced warm-air system. 192.
foundation. 182.
foundations. 182.
frame. 182.
French window. 189.
fresh air inlet. 190.
front door. 177.
function selector. 196.
fuse. 195.
gable-and-valley roof. 181.
gable roof. 180.
garage. 177, 179.
garden. 178.
glue. 186.
going. 187.
gravel. 182.
grille. 196.
ground floor. 178, 179.
guard. 187.
gutter. 177.
hall. 179.
hammer beam. 180.
handrail. 187.
hanging stile. 188, 189.
hardboards. 184.
head binder. 182.
head of frame. 189.
header. 190.
header joist. 182.
hearth-brush. 191.

The terms in **bold type** indicate the title of an illustration.

heating. 190, 191, 192, 193, 194, 195.
heating element. 194, 195.
heating elements indicator. 194.
heating unit. 193.
heating unit. 192, 194.
helm roof. 181.
herringbone pattern. 186.
herringbone strutting. 182.
hinge. 188, 189.
hip roof. 180.
hood. 190.
hook. 189.
horizontal pivoting. 189.
hot-air register. 192.
hot-water main. 194.
house. 175, 178.
house, exterior of a. 177.
humidifier. 194.
ignition transformer. 195.
imperial roof. 181.
inlaid parquet. 186.
inner hearth. 190.
jalousie. 189.
jamb. 188, 189, 190.
joist. 186.
kitchen. 179.
knee brace. 180.
land drain. 182.
landing. 179, 187.
laundry room. 179.
lawn. 178.
lean-to roof. 180.
lightweight building block. 183.
lintel. 190.
living room. 179.
loading door. 191.
lock. 188.
lock rail. 188.
log carrier. 191.
loose fill insulation. 185.
louvre. 196.
louvred window. 189.
main duct. 192.
main entrance. 178.
main return pipe. 193.
main supply pipe. 193.
manometer. 194.
mansard roof. 181.
mantel. 190.
mantel shelf. 190.
master bedroom. 179.
metal heat reflector. 190.
middle panel. 188.
moisture activated thermostat. 196.
monitor roof. 181.
mortar. 183.
motor. 196.
motor-compressor unit. 196.
muntin. 188, 189.
newel post. 187.
nosing. 187.
nozzle. 195.
ogee roof. 181.
oil burner. 195.
oil pump. 195.
oil supply line. 195.
open string. 187.
outdoor condensing unit. 194.
outer hearth. 190.
outlet grille. 193.
overlay flooring. 186.
pane. 189.
panel. 188.
pantry. 179.
particle board. 184.
patio. 178.
patio door. 178.
pavilion roof. 180.
perforated gypsum lath. 184.
perforated hardboard. 184.
pipe-lagging insulation. 185.
pipe section. 192.
pipe-wrapping insulation. 185.
pitched roof. 180.
plain gypsum lath. 184.

plan. 178.
plan symbols. 188.
plaster. 184.
plasterboard. 184.
plastic-laminated hardboard. 184.
playroom. 179.
plenum. 192.
plywood. 184.
poker. 191.
pothole lid. 191.
power relay. 195.
prestressed concrete. 183.
principal rafter. 180.
protective relay. 195.
purlin. 180.
purlin cleat. 180.
rafter. 180, 182.
ramp. 177, 178.
refractory fire pot. 195.
refrigerant tubing. 194.
reinforced concrete. 183.
relay. 196.
return air. 195.
return duct. 194.
return main. 194.
ridge beam. 180.
ridge tile. 177.
rigid board insulation. 185.
rise. 187.
riser. 187.
rod. 196.
roof. 177.
roof structure. 180.
roofs, types of. 180, 181.
room air conditioner. 196.
rooms of the house. 179.
rotunda roof. 181.
sash-frame. 189.
sash window. 189.
sawtooth roof. 181.
shovel. 191.
shutter. 189.
side entrance. 178.
side post. 180.
sill. 182.
sill of frame. 189.
sill plate. 182.
single herringbone parquet. 186.
single pipe heating system. 193.
site plan. 178.
skirting board. 187.
skirting convector. 193.
skirting grille. 192.
skylight. 177.
sliding. 188, 189.
sliding door. 178.
sliding folding. 188, 189.
sloped turret. 181.
smoke dome. 190.
splaying. 190.
split system heating pump. 194.
sprocket. 180.
square basket weave pattern. 186.
stairs. 187.
stairs. 178.
stairwell. 179.
standard hardboard. 184.
steel beam. 183.
step groove. 187.
stile. 188.
stile groove of sash. 189.
stile tongue of sash. 189.
stone. 183.
storage space. 179.
storm collar. 192.
strut. 180.
stud. 182.
study. 179.
supply duct. 194.
swing. 188.
terminal connections. 194.
thermostat. 194, 195, 196.
thin spring-metal insulation. 185.
threshold. 188.
throat. 190.
tie beam. 180.

tile. 185.
toilet. 179.
tongs. 191.
top plate. 180.
top plate of wall frame. 182.
top rail. 188.
top rail of sash. 189.
transformer. 195.
tread. 187.
trim collar. 191.
truss. 180.
valley. 177.
vegetable garden. 178.
vent. 196.
Versailles parquet. 186.
vertical pivoting. 189.
vinyl insulation. 185.
wall grille. 192.
wall stack duct. 192.
wall string. 187.
wall stud. 182.
wardrobe. 179.
water collection pan. 196.
water temperature thermostat. 194.
weatherboard. 188, 189.
web member. 180.
window. 189.
window. 178.
window frame. 177.
window sill. 177.
windows, types of. 189.
wood. 184.
wood burning stove. 191.
wood flooring. 186.
wood flooring. 186.
wood flooring arrangements. 186.
wood flooring on cement screed. 186.
wood flooring on wooden structure. 186.
wood shingle. 185.
workshop. 179.

HOUSE FURNITURE

acanthus leaf. 200.
air vent. 232.
Alsace glass. 212.
anglepoise lamp. 211.
apron. 199, 200, 203.
arm. 200, 211.
arm stump. 200.
armchair. 200.
armchairs, principal types of. 200.
armoire. 205.
attached curtain. 207.
automatic flex reel. 234.
back. 203, 214, 215, 216, 217.
backguard. 228, 231.
baking sheet. 220.
banquette. 202.
bar frame. 211.
base. 204, 210, 232, 233.
base of splat. 200.
basket. 223.
baster. 221.
bean bag chair. 202.
beater. 225.
beater ejector. 225.
beaters. 225.
bed. 204.
bedside lamp. 210.
beer mug. 212.
bench. 202.
bergère. 200.
biscuit cutters. 220.
biscuit press. 220.
blade. 214, 217, 224, 226.
blanket. 204.
blender. 225.
blending attachment. 225.
blind cloth. 209.

body. 233.
bolster. 204, 214, 217.
bolster pillow. 204.
boning knife. 217.
bordeaux. 212.
bottle opener. 219, 233.
bottom rail. 205.
bowl. 216, 226.
bowl with serving spout. 226.
box pleat. 207.
bracket. 208.
bracket base. 205.
bracket slot. 209.
brandy. 212.
bread guide. 227.
bread knife. 217.
bridge. 208.
bumper. 234.
bureau. 206.
burgundy. 212.
burner. 223.
burner ring. 223.
butt hinge. 199.
butter compartment. 229.
butter curler. 217.
butter dish. 213.
butter knife. 214.
button notch. 233.
cabinet. 231.
cabriole leg. 200.
cabriolet. 200.
café curtain. 207.
cage. 211.
cake tin. 220.
canister vacuum cleaner. 234.
carafe. 224.
carpet nozzle. 234.
carrier. 208.
carved Queen Anne leg. 200.
carving fork. 217.
carving knife. 217.
case. 232, 233, 234.
caster. 234.
ceiling fitting. 210.
centre post. 205.
cereal bowl. 213.
chain. 210.
chairs. 201.
chairs, types of. 203.
champagne flute. 212.
champagne glass. 212.
chandelier. 210.
cheese knife. 214.
chest of drawers. 206.
chesterfield. 201.
chopsticks. 223.
citrus juicer. 226.
citrus juicer. 218.
clamp. 211.
clamping handle. 226.
clamping nut. 226.
cleaning tools. 234.
cleaning tools. 234.
cleaver. 217.
clip. 208.
clip spot. 210.
clock timer. 227, 228.
club chair. 201.
cockleshell. 200.
cocktail. 212.
cocktail cabinet. 206.
coffee makers. 224.
coffee mill. 224.
coffee mug. 213.
coffee spoon. 216.
coil spring. 209.
colander. 218.
column. 210.
compressor. 229.
condenser coil. 229.
conductor. 211.
container. 225.
control knob. 228.
control panel. 227, 228, 231, 232.
cook's knife. 217.
cooking surface. 227.

The terms in **bold type** indicate the title of an illustration.

cooking utensils. 222, 223.
cord tieback. 207.
corer. 221.
corner cupboard. 206.
corner display cabinet. 206.
corner lighting. 210.
cornice. 205.
cottage curtain. 207.
couches. 201.
couscous kettle. 222.
cover. 226.
cradle. 209.
cream jug. 213.
crevice tool. 234.
crinoline stretcher. 203.
crisper. 229.
crisscross curtains. 207.
cross rail. 203.
cross stretcher. 203.
crosspiece. 199.
crystal button. 210.
crystal drop. 210.
cup. 213.
cupboard. 206.
curtain. 207.
curtain pole. 208.
curtain track. 208.
cutlery basket. 232.
cutting blade. 214.
cutting edge. 214, 217.
cutting wheel. 233.
dairy compartment. 229.
dasher. 226.
decanter. 212.
deep-fat fryer. 223.
defrost heater. 229.
defrost timer. 229.
demi-tasse. 213.
desk lamp. 211.
dessert fork. 215.
dessert knife. 214.
dessert spoon. 216.
detachable control. 227.
detergent dispenser. 232.
diamond point. 205.
dinner fork. 215.
dinner knife. 214.
dinner plate. 213.
dinnerware. 213.
director's chair. 201.
discs. 226.
dishwasher. 232.
domestic appliances. 225, 226,
227, 228, 229, 230, 231, 232,
233, 234.
door. 205, 227, 230, 231.
door gasket. 230.
door panel. 205.
door shelf. 229.
door stop. 229.
door switch. 231.
double boiler. 222.
double curtain rod. 208.
dough hook. 225.
drain filter. 230.
drain hose. 231.
drain pan. 229.
drain pump. 230.
draining spoon. 219.
draw curtain. 207.
drawer. 199, 206.
dressing table. 206.
drip bowl. 228.
drive belt. 231.
drive wheel. 233.
drop-leaf. 199.
drop light. 211.
drum. 209, 226, 230, 231.
drum motor. 230.
dusting brush. 234.
Dutch oven. 222.
ear. 203.
egg beater. 220.
egg poacher. 223.
egg slicer. 221.
egg timer. 219.

egg tray. 229.
eiderdown. 204.
elastic. 204.
electric cooker. 228.
electric element. 228.
electric grill. 227.
electric tin-opener. 233.
end bracket. 208, 209.
end cap. 208.
end panel. 227.
end stop. 208.
equalizing buckle. 209.
espresso coffee maker. 224.
evaporator coil. 229.
exhaust duct. 231.
exhaust hose. 231.
extension pipe. 234.
extension table. 199.
fabric guide. 233.
fan. 229, 231.
feed tube. 226.
ferrule. 214.
fill opening. 233.
filleting knife. 217.
filter. 223, 224.
filter basket. 224.
filter coffee maker. 224.
fish fork. 215.
fish kettle. 222.
fish knife. 214.
fish platter. 213.
fish slice. 219.
fitted sheet. 204.
flan tin. 220.
flat end pin. 209.
flat pleat. 207.
flat sheet. 204.
flex. 210, 211, 233.
flexible hose. 234.
floor brush. 234.
fluff trap. 231.
fluted pole. 208.
folding chair. 203.
fondue fork. 215.
fondue pot. 223.
fondue set. 223.
food processor. 226.
foot. 205.
footboard. 204.
footstool. 202.
fork. 215.
forks, major types of. 215.
four blade beater. 225.
frame stile. 205.
freezer bucket. 226.
freezer compartment. 229.
freezer door. 229.
fridge-freezer. 229.
frieze. 205.
fringe trimming. 207.
front leg. 203.
front tip. 233.
frying pan. 223.
funnel. 218.
garlic press. 218.
gasket. 228, 232.
gate-leg. 199.
gate-leg table. 199.
gathered heading. 207.
glass. 230.
glass cover. 204.
glass curtain. 207.
glass-fronted display cabinet. 206.
glassware. 212.
globe. 210.
grapefruit knife. 217.
grater. 218.
grater disc. 226.
gravy boat and stand. 213.
grease well. 227.
griddle. 227.
grill element. 228.
groove. 227.
guard. 217.
guard rail. 229.
H stretcher. 203.

half handle. 217.
ham knife. 217.
hand blender. 225.
hand mixer. 225.
handle. 204, 211, 214, 215, 216,
225, 226, 227, 228, 229, 233,
234.
hanging pendant. 210.
hanging stile. 205.
headboard. 204.
headrail. 209.
heating duct. 231.
heating element. 230, 231, 232.
heel. 217.
heel rest. 225, 233.
hem. 209.
hinge. 205, 227, 228, 232.
hob. 228.
holdback. 207.
hook. 208, 211.
hors d'oeuvre dish. 213.
house furniture. 197.
ice-cream can. 226.
ice-cream freezer. 226.
ice cream scoop. 221.
ice cube tray. 229.
icing syringe. 220.
idler pulley. 231.
impeller. 232.
indicator. 232.
individual bun tin. 220.
inlet hose. 232.
inside. 216.
inverted pleat. 207.
juice extractor. 226.
kettle. 233.
kickplate. 229.
kitchen knife. 217.
kitchen knives, types of. 217.
kitchen scales. 219.
kitchen timer. 219.
kitchen utensils. 217, 218, 219,
220, 221.
knife. 214.
knife sharpener. 221.
knives, major types of. 214.
knob. 199.
ladder. 209.
ladle. 219.
lamp-post. 211.
latch. 227, 228, 232.
leaf. 199.
leg. 199, 204.
lever. 227.
lever corkscrew. 219.
lid. 222, 223, 224, 226, 227.
lift cord. 209.
lift cord lock. 209.
lights. 210, 211.
linen. 204.
linen chest. 206.
liqueur. 212.
lock. 205.
loose curtain. 207.
louvre. 211.
lower bowl. 224.
magnetic gasket. 229.
magnetic lid holder. 233.
master carrier. 208.
mattress. 204.
mattress cover. 204.
measuring cap. 225.
measuring cups. 219.
measuring spoons. 219.
meat keeper. 229.
meat thermometer. 219.
méridienne. 201.
microwave oven. 227.
middle rail. 205.
mincer. 218.
mixer. 225.
mixing bowl. 225.
mixing bowls. 220.
mortar. 218.
motor. 231, 234.
motor unit. 224, 225, 226.

Neapolitan coffee maker. 224.
neck. 215, 216.
neckroll. 204.
nest of tables. 199.
nutcracker. 218.
on-off indicator. 228.
on-off switch. 211, 234.
operating cord. 208.
oven. 228.
oven lamp. 227, 228.
overcurtain. 207.
overflow protection switch. 232.
overlap carrier. 208.
oyster fork. 215.
oyster knife. 217.
palmette. 200.
pancake pan. 223.
panel. 207.
paring knife. 217.
pasta maker. 218.
pastry brush. 220.
pastry cutting wheel. 220.
patera. 200.
pawl. 209.
peeler. 217.
peg. 205.
pelmet. 207.
pelmet lighting. 210.
pepperpot. 213.
percolator. 224.
pestle. 218.
pie tin. 220.
pierce lever. 233.
pillow. 204.
pillow protector. 204.
pin. 199.
pinch pleat. 207.
pipe. 234.
plain pole. 208.
plate. 227.
platter. 213.
pleated heading. 207.
plunger. 224.
point. 215, 217.
pole. 208.
port. 212.
potato masher. 219.
pouf. 202.
poultry shears. 221.
pressure cooker. 222.
pressure regulator. 222.
pressure switch. 230.
probe receptacle. 227.
programmer. 228, 231, 232.
prong. 215.
pulse button. 225.
pump. 232.
push-button control. 232.
pusher. 226.
quiche tin. 220.
rack. 222, 228, 232.
racks. 223.
ramekin. 213.
ratchet. 209.
reamer. 226.
rear leg. 203.
récamier. 201.
reflector. 211.
refrigerator compartment. 229.
reservoir. 224.
retractable flex. 234.
rinceau. 200.
ring. 208.
rinse-aid dispenser. 232.
rivet. 217.
roast sensor probe. 228.
roasting pans. 222.
rocking chair. 201, 203.
roll-up blind. 209.
roller. 208, 209, 232.
roller blind. 209.
rolling pin. 220.
root. 215.
rotisserie. 228.
round end pin. 209.
ruffle. 207.

The terms in **bold type** indicate the title of an illustration.

runner. 199, 232.
safety thermostat. 231.
safety valve. 222.
salad bowl. 213.
salad fork. 215.
salad plate. 213.
salad shaker. 218.
salad spinner. 218.
saltcellar. 213.
saucepan. 222.
saucer. 213.
sauté pan. 223.
savoy bag and nozzles. 220.
scatter cushion. 204.
sconce. 210.
seat. 200, 203.
seats. 202.
sensor probe. 227.
serving bowl. 213.
serving trolley. 199.
set of utensils. 219.
shade. 210, 211.
shag-carpet-rake. 234.
shaker. 221.
sharpening steel. 217.
sheer curtain. 207.
shelf. 206, 229.
shelf channel. 229.
shock absorber. 230.
shutters. 209.
side. 214.
side chair. 203.
side plate. 213.
sideboard. 206.
sieve. 218.
sifter. 220.
sight-glass tube. 233.
silverware. 214, 215, 216.
single curtain rod. 208.
skimmer. 219.
slat. 209.
slide selector. 227, 233.
slot. 215, 227.
slotted bracket. 209.
snail dish. 221.
snail tongs. 221.
soleplate. 233.
soup bowl. 213.
soup spoon. 216.
soup tureen. 213.
spaghetti tongs. 221.
spatula. 219.
speed control. 225.
speed selector. 226.
spider (cross-piece). 230.
spindle. 203, 226.
spiral beater. 225.
splat. 200.
splayed leg. 199.
spoon. 216.
spoons, major types of. 216.
spot. 211.
spout. 224, 233.
spray. 233.
spray arm. 232.
spray button. 233.
spring. 211.
stabilizer foot. 232.
stacking chairs. 203.
stand. 210, 223, 225.
standard lamp. 210.
start switch. 231.
steak knife. 214.
steam button. 233.
steam iron. 233.
stem. 224.
step chair. 202.
stile. 203.
stock pot. 222.
stoner. 221.
stool. 202.
storage door. 229.
storage furniture. 205, 206.
strainer. 226.
stretcher. 199.
stretchers. 203.

strip light. 211.
strirrer cover. 227.
suction regulator. 234.
sugar bowl. 213.
sugar spoon. 216.
sundae spoon. 216.
support. 203, 208.
support wheel. 231.
surface element. 228.
switch. 228, 229.
swivel arm wall bracket lamp.
210.
table. 199.
table lamp. 210.
tables, types of. 199.
tablespoon. 216.
tall tumbler. 212.
tang. 214, 217.
tassel. 207.
tea infuser. 221.
teapot. 213.
teaspoon. 216.
temperature control. 227.
temperature dial. 233.
temperature selector. 231.
temperature sensing bulb. 228.
tension pulley set. 208.
tension pulley wheel. 208.
terminal. 228.
thermostat. 230.
thermostat control. 229.
three-seater settee. 201.
thumb rest. 233.
tieback. 207.
tieback hook. 207.
tilt-back head. 225.
tilt cord. 209.
tilt tube. 209.
timer. 230.
tin opener. 219.
tip. 214, 216.
toaster. 227.
tongs. 221.
top rail. 203, 205.
torch. 211.
track. 208.
track lighting. 211.
traverse rod. 208.
tray. 223.
trim ring. 228.
tub. 230, 232.
tubular element. 228.
tumble dryer. 231.
tumbler. 212.
turntable. 225.
two-seater settee. 201.
upholstery nozzle. 234.
upper bowl. 224.
vacuum coffee maker. 224.
valance. 204, 207.
vane. 231.
vapour discharge outlet. 230.
vegetable bowl. 213.
vegetable brush. 221.
vegetable steamer. 222.
Venetian blind. 209.
vertical flex support. 233.
volute. 200.
waiter's friend. 219.
wall bracket. 210.
wall lantern. 211.
wardrobe. 206.
warming plate. 224.
wash tower. 232.
washing machine. 230.
Wassily chair. 200.
water goblet. 212.
water inlet valve. 230.
water jug. 213.
whisk. 220.
white wine. 212.
winding mechanism. 209.
window. 227, 228.
window accessories. 207, 208,
209.
wire beater. 225.

wok. 223.
wok set. 223.
worktop surface. 232.
worm gear. 209.
yoke. 208.
Z-bed. 203.
zester. 217.

HUMAN BEING

abdomen. 106.
abdominal aorta. 117, 120.
abdominal rectus. 110.
acromion. 113.
Adam's apple. 106.
adipose tissue. 109, 128.
adrenal gland. 120.
ala. 125.
alveolar bone. 115.
ampulla. 128.
ampulla of fallopian tube. 109.
anal canal. 119.
anconeus. 111.
animal cell. 105.
ankle. 106.
anterior chamber. 123.
anterior commissure. 122.
anterior notch. 124.
anterior pulmonary plexus. 118.
anterior root. 122.
anterior tibial. 110.
antihelix. 124.
antitragus. 124.
anus. 108, 109, 119.
aorta. 118.
apex. 115, 126.
apical foramen. 115.
apocrine sweat gland. 128.
aqueous humour. 123.
arch of the aorta. 116.
areola. 109.
arm. 107.
armpit. 106.
arteries. 117.
ascending aorta. 116.
ascending colon. 119.
atlas. 113.
auditory ossicles. 124.
aunt by marriage. 130.
auricle. 124.
axillary artery. 117.
axillary nerve. 121.
axillary vein. 117.
axis. 113.
axon. 127.
back. 107.
basement membrane. 127.
basilic vein. 117.
biceps of arm. 110.
biceps of thigh. 111.
blood circulation. 116, 117.
blood vessel. 115, 128, 129.
body. 126.
body of nail. 129.
brachial. 110.
brachial artery. 117.
brachial plexus. 121.
brachioradial. 111.
brachioradialis. 111.
breast. 109.
breast. 106.
bridge of nose. 125.
broad ligament of uterus. 109.
brother. 130.
buttock. 107.
caecum. 119.
calcaneus. 113.
calf. 107.
calyx. 120.
canine. 115.
cardiac plexus. 118.
cardiac sphincter. 119.
carpus. 113.
cell body. 127.
cell body of sensory neuron. 127.

cell membrane. 105.
cell wall. 105.
cement. 115.
central incisor. 115.
central nervous system. 122.
centriole. 105.
cephalic vein. 117.
cerebellum. 122.
cerebrospinal axis. 122.
cerebrum. 122.
cervical plexus. 121.
cervical vertebra. 113.
cheek. 106.
chest. 106.
children. 130, 131.
chin. 106.
chloroplast. 105.
choroid. 123.
chromatin. 105.
ciliary body. 123.
circulation, schema of. 116.
clavicle. 112.
clitoris. 109.
coccygeal nerve. 121.
coccyx. 112.
cochlea. 124.
cochlear nerve. 124.
coeliac trunk. 116, 120.
collagenous fibre. 128.
collateral. 127.
commissure of lips of mouth. 126.
common carotid artery. 117.
common extensor of fingers. 111.
common hepatic artery. 117.
common iliac artery. 117, 120.
common iliac vein. 120.
common peroneal nerve. 121.
communicating rami. 122.
complexus. 111.
concha. 124.
conjunctiva. 123.
connective tissue. 127, 128.
cornea. 123.
coronal suture. 114.
corpus callosum. 122.
corpus cavernosum. 108.
cortex. 120, 129.
cousins. 130.
Cowper's gland. 108.
cranial nerves. 121.
cribriform plate of ethmoid. 125.
crown. 115.
crus of helix. 124.
cubital vein. 117.
cuticle. 129.
cytoplasm. 105.
daughter. 130.
daughter-in-law. 131.
deep peroneal nerve. 121.
deltoid. 110.
dendrite. 127.
dental alveolus. 115.
dentine. 115.
dermal papilla. 127, 128.
dermis. 127, 128, 129.
descending aorta. 116.
descending colon. 119.
diaphragm. 118, 119.
digestive system. 119.
digital nerve. 121.
digital pulp. 129.
distal phalanx. 112, 113, 129.
dorsum of nose. 125.
dorsum of tongue. 126.
duct. 128.
duct deferens. 108.
duodenum. 119.
dura mater of spinal cord. 122.
dural cul-de-sac. 122.
ear. 106, 107.
ear drum. 124.
eccrine sweat gland. 128.
ejaculatory duct. 108.
elbow. 107.
enamel. 115.
end piece. 108.

The terms in **bold type** indicate the title of an illustration.

endoplasmic reticulum. 105.
epicondyle. 113.
epidermicula. 129.
epidermis. 127, 128, 129.
epiglottis. 118, 126.
epitrochlea. 113.
eponychium. 129.
Eustachian tube. 124, 125.
external acoustic meatus. 124.
external auditory meatus. 114.
external ear. 124.
external ear. 124.
external iliac artery. 117.
external nose. 125.
external oblique. 110, 111.
eye. 123.
eye. 106.
eyeball. 123.
eyebrow. 123.
eyelash. 123.
face. 106.
facial nerve. 124.
fallopian tube. 109.
false rib (3). 113.
family relationships. 130, 131.
father. 130, 131.
father-in-law. 131.
female genital organs. 109.
femoral artery. 117.
femoral nerve. 117.
femoral vein. 117.
femur. 112.
fibula. 112.
first molar. 115.
first premolar. 115.
floating rib. 112.
foot. 107.
foramen caecum. 126.
foramen ovale. 114.
forearm. 107.
forehead. 106.
fovea. 123.
free margin. 129.
frontal. 110, 112.
frontal bone. 114.
frontal sinus. 125.
gall-bladder. 119.
gastrocnemius. 110, 111.
glans penis. 108.
gluteal nerve. 121.
gluteus maximus. 111.
Golgi body. 105.
gracile. 111.
granddaughter. 131.
grandfather. 131.
grandmother. 131.
grandson. 131.
great adductor. 111.
great foramen. 114.
great-granddaughter. 131.
great-grandfather. 131.
great-grandmother. 131.
great-grandson. 131.
great saphenous vein. 117.
greater alar cartilage. 125.
greater pectoral. 110.
greater trochanter. 113.
groin. 106.
gum. 115.
hair. 129.
hair. 107, 128.
hair bulb. 129.
hair follicle. 129.
hair shaft. 129.
hand. 107.
hard palate. 114, 126.
head. 107, 108, 116.
head of femur. 113.
head of humerus. 113.
hearing. 124.
heart. 116.
heel. 107.
helix. 124.
hepatic vein. 116, 117.
hilus of kidney. 120.
hip. 107.

human being. 103.
human body. 106, 107.
human denture. 115.
humerus. 112.
husband. 130, 131.
hypogastric artery. 120.
ileum. 119.
iliohypogastric nerve. 121.
ilioinguinal nerve. 121.
ilium. 112.
indifferent cells. 129.
inferior dental arch. 126.
inferior mesenteric artery. 120.
inferior nasal concha. 125.
inferior vena cava. 116, 117, 120.
infraorbital foramen. 114.
infraspiatus. 111.
infundibulum of fallopian tube. 109.
inner root sheath. 129.
intercostal nerve. 121.
internal and middle ear. 124.
internal ear. 124.
internal iliac artery. 116, 117.
internal iliac vein. 116.
internal jugular vein. 117.
intertragic notch. 124.
intervertebral foramen. 122.
intestine. 116.
iris. 123.
ischium. 113.
isthmus of fallopian tube. 109.
isthmus of fauces. 126.
jejunum. 119.
kidney. 116.
knee. 106.
labia major. 109.
labia minora. 109.
lacrimal duct. 123.
lactiferous duct. 109.
lambdoid suture. 114.
lamina cribrosa. 125.
large intestine. 119.
larynx. 118.
lateral condyle of femur. 113.
lateral cutaneous nerve of thigh. 121.
lateral great. 111.
lateral incisor. 115.
lateral semicircular canal. 124.
latissimus dorsi. 111.
left atrium. 116.
left bronchus. 118.
left kidney. 120.
left lung. 116, 118.
left ventricle. 116.
leg. 107.
lens. 123.
leucoplast. 105.
lingual papillae. 126.
lingual tonsil. 126.
lipid droplet. 105.
liver. 116, 119.
lobe. 109.
lobule. 124.
loin. 107.
long adductor. 110.
long extensor of toes. 110.
long palmar. 110.
long peroneal. 110.
long radial extensor of wrist. 111.
lower eyelid. 123.
lower lip. 126.
lower lobe. 118.
lumbar plexus. 121.
lumbar vertebra. 113.
lumbar vertebra, cross section of. 122.
lungs. 118.
lunula. 129.
lysosome. 105.
malar bone. 112.
male genital organs. 108.
male urethra. 108.
Malpighi's pyramid. 120.
mammary gland. 109.
mandible. 112, 114, 115.

masseter. 110.
mastoid process. 114.
maternal aunt. 130.
maternal uncle. 130.
maxilla. 112, 114, 115, 125.
medial condyle of femur. 113.
median lingual sulcus. 126.
median nerve. 121.
median vein of forearm. 117.
medulla. 120, 129.
medulla oblongata. 122.
Meissner's corpuscle. 128.
melanocyte. 128.
mental foramen. 114.
metacarpus. 112.
metatarsus. 112.
metopic suture. 114.
middle ear. 124.
middle lobe. 118.
middle nasal concha. 125.
middle phalanx. 112, 113.
middle piece. 108.
mitochondrion. 105.
mitral valve. 116.
mobile septum of nose. 125.
molar, cross section of a. 115.
mons pubis. 109.
mother. 130, 131.
mother-in-law. 131.
motor cell. 127.
motor end plate. 127.
motor neuron. 127.
mouth. 126.
mouth. 106.
muscle arrector pili. 128, 129.
muscle fibre. 127.
muscles. 110, 111.
musculocutaneous nerve. 121.
myelin sheath. 127.
nail. 129.
nail bed. 129.
nail matrix. 129.
nape. 107.
naris. 125.
nasal bone. 114, 125.
nasal cavity. 118.
nasal fossa. 114.
nasal fossae. 125.
nasopharynx. 125.
navel. 106.
neck. 106, 108, 115.
neck of femur. 113.
neck of uterus. 109.
nephew. 130.
nerve. 129.
nerve fibre. 127.
nerve termination. 127.
nervous system. 121, 122.
neural spine. 113.
neuron. 127.
niece. 130.
nipple. 106, 109.
Nissl bodies. 127.
node of Ranvier. 127.
nose. 106.
nuclear membrane. 105.
nucleolus. 105.
nucleus. 105, 127.
obturator nerve. 121.
occipital. 111, 113.
occipital bone. 114.
occipital condyle. 114.
oesophagus. 119.
olecranon. 111.
olfactory bulb. 125.
olfactory centre. 125.
olfactory membrane. 125.
olfactory nerve. 125.
optic chiasm. 122.
optic nerve. 123.
oral cavity. 118, 119.
orbicularis oculi. 110.
orbital cavity. 114.
osteology of skull. 114.
ostium. 129.
outer root sheath. 129.

ovary. 109.
Pacinian corpuscle. 128.
palate. 125.
palatine tonsil. 126.
palato-pharyngeal arch. 126.
palatoglossal arch. 126.
pancreas. 119.
papilla. 123, 129.
papillary muscle. 116.
parents. 130, 131.
parents-in-law. 131.
parietal. 113.
parietal bone. 114.
parietal foramen. 114.
parietal pleura. 118.
patella. 112.
paternal aunt. 130.
paternal uncle. 130.
pectoral limb. 116.
pelvic limb. 116.
pelvis. 120.
penis. 106, 108.
pericardium. 118.
periodontal ligament. 115.
peripheral nervous system. 121.
peritoneum. 108.
pharynx. 118, 119.
philtrum. 125.
phrenic nerve. 118.
pineal body. 122.
pinocytic vesicle. 105.
pituitary gland. 122.
plant cell. 105.
plantar. 111.
plantar interosseous. 110.
plasmodesmata. 105.
pleural cavity. 118.
pons. 122.
pore. 105, 128.
portal vein. 116, 117.
posterior chamber. 123.
posterior commissure. 122.
posterior cutaneous nerve of thigh. 121.
posterior root. 122.
posterior rugae. 107.
posterior semicircular canal. 124.
pouch of Douglas. 109.
prepuce. 108.
prostate. 108.
proximal phalanx. 112, 113.
pubis. 106.
pulmonary artery. 117, 118.
pulmonary trunk. 116.
pulmonary vein. 116, 117.
pulp. 115.
pulp canal. 115.
pulp cavity. 115.
pupil. 123.
pyloric sphincter. 119.
pylorus. 119.
radial artery. 117.
radial nerve. 121.
radial vein. 117.
radius. 112.
receptor. 127.
rectum. 108, 119, 120.
rectus femoris. 110.
renal artery. 117, 120.
renal papilla. 120.
renal vein. 117, 120.
respiratory system. 118.
retina. 123.
rhomboideus. 111.
ribosome. 105.
ribs. 112.
right atrium. 116.
right bronchus. 118.
right kidney (sagittal section). 120.
right lung. 116, 118.
right ventricle. 116.
root. 115, 126.
root of hair. 129.
root of nail. 129.
round ligament of uterus. 109.
round pronator. 110.

The terms in **bold type** indicate the title of an illustration.

sacral plexus. 121.
sacrum. 112.
sagittal suture. 114.
salivary glands. 119.
saphenous nerve. 121.
sartorius. 110.
scapula. 112.
sciatic nerve. 121.
sclera. 123.
scrotum. 106, 108.
sebaceous gland. 128, 129.
second molar. 115.
second premolar. 115.
semimembranosus. 111.
seminal vesicle. 108.
semitendinosus. 111.
sense organs. 123, 124, 125, 126, 127.
sense receptor. 127.
senses of smell and taste. 125.
sensory impulse. 127.
sensory neuron. 127.
septal cartilage of nose. 125.
septum of scrotum. 108.
septum pellucidum. 122.
sheath of Schwann. 127.
short extensor of toes. 110.
short palmar. 110.
short peroneal. 111.
short radial extensor of wrist. 111.
shoulder. 106.
shoulder blade. 107.
sight. 123.
sigmoid colon. 119.
sinus of kidney. 120.
sister. 130.
skeleton. 112, 113.
skin. 127, 128.
skin. 127.
skin surface. 127, 128.
skull. 106.
small intestine. 119.
smell. 125.
soft palate. 126.
sole. 129.
soleus. 110.
son. 130.
son-in-law. 131.
spermatozoon. 108.
sphenoid bone. 114.
sphenoidal sinus. 125.
sphincter muscle of anus. 119.
spinal column. 112.
spinal cord. 122, 127.
spinal ganglion. 127.
spinal nerve. 122, 127.
spine of scapula. 113.
spleen. 116.
splenic artery. 117.
splenic vein. 117.
splenius muscle of head. 111.
spongy body. 108.
spouse. 130.
squamous suture. 114.
starch granule. 105.
sternomastoid. 110.
sternum. 112.
stomach. 116, 119.
stratum basale. 128.
stratum corneum. 128.
stratum granular. 128.
stratum lucidum. 128.
stratum spinosum. 128.
subclavian artery. 117.
subclavian vein. 117.
subcutaneous tissue. 128.
subpapillary network. 128.
sulcus terminalis. 126.
superciliary arch. 114.
superficial peroneal nerve. 121.
superior dental arch. 126.
superior longitudinal sinus. 122.
superior mesenteric artery. 117, 120.
superior nasal concha. 125.
superior semicircular canal. 124.

superior vena cava. 116, 117.
supraorbital foramen. 114.
suprascapular nerve. 121.
sural nerve. 121.
suspensory ligament. 123.
symphysis pubis. 108, 109.
synapse. 127.
tail. 108.
tail of helix. 124.
talus. 113.
tarsus. 112.
taste. 126.
teeth. 115.
temple. 106.
temporal. 112.
temporal bone. 114.
temporal fossa. 114.
tensor of fascia lata. 110.
teres major. 111.
teres minor. 111.
terminal arborization. 127.
terminal bronchiole. 118.
terminal filament. 122.
testicle. 108.
thigh. 107.
third molar. 115.
thoracic vertebra. 113.
thorax. 106.
tibia. 112.
tibial nerve. 121.
tip of nose. 125.
toe. 106.
tongue. 119, 125, 126.
touch. 127.
trachea. 118.
tragus. 124.
transverse colon. 119.
transverse process of vertebrae. 113.
trapezius. 110.
triangular fossa. 124.
triceps of arm. 111.
tricuspid valve. 116.
trunk. 107.
ulna. 112.
ulnar artery. 117.
ulnar extensor of wrist. 111.
ulnar flexor of wrist. 110, 111.
ulnar nerve. 121.
uncle by marriage. 130.
upper eyelid. 123.
upper lip. 126.
upper lobe. 118.
ureter. 120.
urethra. 109, 120.
urinary bladder. 108, 109, 120.
urinary meatus. 108.
urinary system. 120.
uterovesical pouch. 109.
uterus. 109.
uvula. 125, 126.
V-shaped row. 126.
vacuole. 105.
vagina. 109.
vagus nerve. 118.
vas deferens. 108.
vastus lateralis. 110.
vastus medialis. 110.
veins. 117.
ventricular septum. 116.
vermiform appendix. 119.
vestibular nerve. 124.
vestibule. 124.
vitreous humour. 123.
vocal cord. 118.
vulva. 109.
waist. 107.
wife. 130, 131.
wrist. 107.
zygomatic arch. 114.
zygomatic bone. 114.
zygomaticofacial foramen. 114.

MEASURING DEVICES

adjusting nut. 599.
adjusting screw. 598.
air-pressure pump. 598.
alidade. 600.
analogue display. 591.
analytical balance. 595.
aneroid barometer. 598.
anticipator. 597.
anticipator indicator. 597.
anvil. 599.
backplate. 597.
balance wheel. 591.
barrel. 591.
base. 595, 600, 601.
base plate. 600.
bathroom scales. 596.
beam. 594, 595, 596.
beam arrest. 595.
beam balance. 594.
bearing. 597.
bedrock. 602.
bimetal element. 597.
bimetallic helix. 597.
bimetallic thermometer. 597.
bob. 593.
body. 593.
bulb. 597.
capillary bore. 597.
carrying handle. 600.
case. 597, 599.
centre knife-edge. 595.
centre wheel. 591, 593.
chain. 593, 598.
circular level. 600.
clinical thermometer. 597.
clock. 602.
column. 595.
column of mercury. 597.
concrete base. 602.
conical magnet. 592.
constriction. 597.
contact. 597.
counterweight. 596.
cover. 597, 601.
crown. 591.
crutch. 593.
current coil. 601.
damper. 596.
dial. 591, 592, 593, 595, 596, 597, 598, 599, 601.
digital display. 591.
disc. 601.
display. 596.
drive coil. 592.
drive coil and phase-sensing coil. 592.
drum. 593.
electronic circuit. 592.
electronic scales. 596.
escape wheel. 591, 593.
expansion chamber. 597.
focusing sleeve. 600.
fork. 591, 593.
fourth wheel. 591.
frame. 599.
full-load adjustment screw. 601.
function keys. 596.
glass bulb. 592.
glass case. 595.
gnomon. 602.
graduated arm. 594.
graduated scale. 598.
grandfather clock. 593.
hairspring. 591.
hand. 598.
helical spring. 594.
hook. 594, 599.
horizontal circle drive knob. 600.
horizontal clamp. 600.
horizontal seismograph. 602.
horizontal tangent screw. 600.
hour hand. 591, 593.
hourglass. 592.

illumination mirror for horizontal circle. 600.
illumination mirror for vertical circle. 600.
indicator. 598.
inverter knob. 600.
knife-edge. 594, 595, 596.
knob for reticle illumination. 600.
lead. 592.
leg. 595.
length, measure of. 599.
levelling screw. 595, 600.
lever. 598.
light-load adjustment screw. 601.
liquid-crystal display. 591.
lock nut. 599.
locking knob. 600.
magnetic cup. 592.
magnetic suspension. 601.
main wheel. 593.
mainspring. 591.
mass. 602.
measuring devices. 589.
mechanical watch. 591.
mercury switch. 597.
micrometer. 599.
micrometer screw. 600.
microscope eyepiece. 600.
minute hand. 591, 593.
moon dial. 593.
mounting post. 597.
mounting screw. 597.
name plate. 601.
neck. 592.
numeric keyboard. 596.
optical plummet. 600.
optical sight. 600.
pallet. 591, 593.
pan. 594, 595.
pan arrest. 595.
pediment. 593.
pedometer. 599.
pen. 602.
pendulum. 593.
pendulum rod. 593.
pillar. 602.
pillar plate. 592.
pinion. 593.
pivoted bar. 602.
plate level. 600.
platform. 596.
plinth. 593.
pneumatic armlet. 598.
pointer. 595, 596, 597, 598, 599.
pointer scale. 595.
potential coil. 601.
pressure, measure of. 598.
pressure gauge. 598.
product codes. 596.
pulley. 596.
ratchet. 593.
ratchet knob. 599.
ratchet wheel. 593.
recording of seismic waves. 602.
recording of time. 602.
register. 601.
retarding magnet. 601.
rider handle. 595.
rider scale. 595.
ring. 594.
Roberval's balance. 595.
room thermostat. 597.
rotating drum. 602.
sand. 592.
scale. 594, 596, 597, 599.
sealing lug. 601.
second hand. 591.
seismographs. 602.
self-indicating scales. 596.
shadow. 592.
shaft. 597.
sheet of paper. 602.
sleeve. 599.
sliding weight. 594.
sphygmomanometer. 598.
spindle. 593, 599, 601.

The terms in **bold type** indicate the title of an illustration.

761

spindle screw. 599.
spring. 598, 602.
spring balance. 594.
stay. 596.
steel band. 596.
steelyard. 594.
stem. 597.
step setting. 599.
stirrup hook. 595.
sundial. 592.
suspension hook. 594.
suspension spring. 593.
tape. 599.
tape lock. 599.
tape measure. 599.
telescope eyepiece. 600.
telescope objective. 600.
temperature, measure of. 597.
temperature scale. 597.
temperature set point lever. 597.
terminal cover. 601.
terminal knife-edge. 595.
theodolite. 600.
thimble. 599.
third wheel. 591, 593.
ticket. 596.
time, measure of. 591, 592, 593.
tine. 592.
total. 596.
transistor. 592.
tube. 598.
tuning fork. 592.
tuning fork watch. 592.
unit price. 596.
vacuum chamber. 598.
vertical clamp. 600.
vertical seismograph. 602.
vertical tangent screw. 600.
watchcase. 591.
watt-hour meter. 601.
weighing platform. 596.
weight. 593, 594, 596.
weight, measure of. 594, 595, 596.
weight-driven clock mechanism. 593.
width, measure of. 599.
winding mechanism. 593.

MUSIC

accent mark. 462.
accidentals. 462.
accordion. 475.
adjusting lever. 478.
air sealing gland. 468.
appoggiatura. 462.
arm. 473.
arpeggio. 462.
back. 463, 481.
back brace. 481.
back inlay. 481.
bag. 474.
bagpipes. 474.
balalaika. 473.
balance hammer. 466.
balance rail. 466.
banjo. 473.
bar. 471, 478.
bar line. 462.
barrel. 475.
barrel organ. 475.
bass drum. 472.
bass drum. 477, 479.
bass pick-up. 480.
bass register. 475.
bass string. 465.
basses. 475.
bassoon. 469, 476, 477.
bassoons. 479.
batter head. 472.
bearer. 468.
beater. 472.
bell. 469, 470.
bell brace. 469.

bellows. 475.
bellows strap. 475.
belly. 463.
bichord. 465.
block. 468.
blow pipe. 474.
blower. 467.
body. 468, 469.
boot. 468.
bore. 468.
bottomboard. 468.
bow. 464.
bracket. 481.
brass family. 470.
breve. 461.
breve rest. 461.
bridge. 463, 465, 475.
bridge unit. 480.
bridle tape. 466.
bugle. 470.
button. 475.
c clef. 461.
case. 475, 478.
castanets. 471.
caster. 472.
celesta. 479.
cello. 463, 476.
cellos. 479.
chanter. 474.
check. 466.
choir organ manual. 467.
chord. 462.
clarinet. 469, 476, 477.
clarinets. 479.
classical guitar. 481.
clefs. 461.
conductor's podium. 479.
console. 467.
contrabassoon. 479.
cor anglais. 469, 479.
cornet. 470, 477.
cornets. 479.
corssbar. 473.
crook. 469, 474.
crotchet. 461.
crotchet rest. 461.
cymbals. 471.
cymbals. 479.
cymbals, triangle, castanets. 479.
damper. 466.
damper lever. 466.
damper rail. 466.
demi-semi-quaver. 461.
demi-semi-quaver rest. 461.
double bass. 463, 477.
double basses. 479.
double flat. 462.
double reed. 469, 474.
double sharp. 462.
drone. 474.
drum kit. 477.
duo. 476.
ear. 468.
electric guitar. 480.
end block. 481.
end pin. 463.
escapement mechanism. 478.
euphonium. 470.
f clef. 461.
face pipes. 467.
fan stout. 481.
feet. 464.
fifth. 462.
finger button. 470.
fingerboard. 463, 473, 480, 481.
first violins. 479.
fixed weight. 478.
flat. 462.
flue. 468.
flue pipe. 468.
flute. 469, 476.
flutes. 479.
foot. 468, 481.
foot hole. 468.
four-four time. 462.
fourth. 462.

frame. 471, 474.
French horn. 470, 476, 477.
French horns. 479.
fret. 473, 480, 481.
frog. 464.
g clef. 461.
gong. 471.
gong. 479.
great organ manual. 467.
grille. 475.
hair. 464.
hammer. 466.
hammer butt. 466.
hammer head. 466.
hammer rail. 466.
hammer shank. 466.
handle. 464, 475.
harmonica. 474.
harp. 464.
harp. 479.
harpsichord. 476.
head. 464, 472, 473, 480, 481.
head nut. 480.
heel. 464, 481.
hemi-demi-semi-quave. 461.
hemi-demi-semi-quaver rest. 461.
hole. 463.
instrumental groups, examples of. 476, 477.
intervals. 462.
iron frame. 465.
jack. 466.
jack socket. 480.
jack spring. 466.
jazz band. 477.
Jew's harp. 474.
jingle. 472.
kettledrum. 472.
key. 466, 469, 475, 478.
key finger button. 469.
key signature. 462.
keybed. 465.
keyboard. 465, 475.
keyboard instruments. 465, 466.
languid. 468.
ledger line. 461.
leg. 472.
ligature. 469.
line. 461.
lining. 481.
little finger hook. 470.
loud pedal. 465.
lower boot. 481.
lower lip. 468.
lug. 472.
lyre. 473.
machine head. 480.
mallets. 471.
mandolin. 473.
manual. 468.
manuals. 467.
melody string. 473.
metal counterhoop. 472.
metal rod. 471.
metronome. 478.
mid range pick-up. 480.
minim. 461.
minim rest. 461.
mordent. 462.
mouth. 468.
mouthpiece. 469, 470.
mouthpiece receiver. 470.
mouthpipe. 470.
music. 459.
music rest. 478.
music stand. 478.
musical accessories. 478.
musical notation. 461, 462.
mute. 470.
natural. 462.
neck. 463, 464, 473, 480, 481.
note symbols. 461.
nut. 463, 481.
oboe. 469, 476.
oboes. 479.
octave. 462.

octave mechanism. 469.
open string. 473.
organ. 467, 468.
organ, mechanism of the. 468.
organ pipes. 468.
ornaments. 462.
pallet. 468, 475.
pallet spring. 468.
panpipe. 474.
pause. 462.
pedal. 464, 472.
pedal board. 467.
pedal key. 467.
pedestal. 464.
peg. 463.
peg box. 463.
percussion instruments. 471, 472.
piano. 476, 477, 479.
piccolo. 469, 479.
pick-up selector. 480.
pickguard. 480.
pillar. 464.
pilot. 466.
pin. 475.
pipe. 468, 475.
pipework. 467.
pivot. 478.
plectrum. 473.
point. 464.
position marker. 480.
purfling. 463.
quartet. 476.
quaver. 461.
quaver rest. 461.
quintet. 476.
rackboard. 468.
reed pipe. 468.
reeds. 469.
repeat mark. 462.
reservoir. 467.
resonator. 468, 471.
rest symbols. 461.
rib. 463.
ring. 470.
rod. 478.
roller board and arms. 468.
saxophone. 469.
saxophone. 469, 477.
scale (music). 461.
scale of speeds. 478.
screw. 464.
scroll. 463.
second. 462.
second violins. 479.
semi-breve. 461.
semi-breve rest. 461.
semi-quaver. 461.
semi-quaver rest. 461.
set-off button. 466.
seventh. 462.
sextet. 477.
shallot. 468.
sharp. 462.
shawm. 474.
shell. 472.
side. 481.
single reed. 469.
single string. 465.
sixth. 462.
sleeve protector. 473.
slider. 468.
sliding weight. 478.
snare. 472.
snare drum. 472.
snare drum. 477, 479.
snare head. 472.
snare strainer. 472.
soft pedal. 465.
solid body. 480.
sound-board. 464.
sound box. 464.
sound-post. 464.
soundboard. 465, 481.
soundbox. 473.
soundhole. 481.

The terms in **bold type** indicate the title of an illustration.

space. 461.
spur. 472.
staff. 461.
stick. 464.
sticker. 475.
sticks. 471.
stock. 474.
stop. 467.
stop button. 478.
stop knob. 468.
stop rod. 468.
string. 463, 464, 466.
stringed instruments. 463, 464.
sustaining pedal. 465.
swell organ manual. 467.
swell pedal. 467.
symphony orchestra. 479.
table. 466.
tailpiece. 463.
tambourine. 472.
tenor drum. 472.
tenor drum. 477.
tension rod. 472.
tension screw. 472.
third. 462.
three-four time. 462.
thumb hook. 470.
thumb piston. 467.
thumb rest. 469.
thumb string. 473.
thumb string peg. 473.
tie. 462.
time signatures. 462.
timpani. 479.
toe piston. 467.
tone control. 480.
tongue. 468, 474.
tracker. 468.
traditional musical instruments. 473, 474, 475.
transverse strut. 481.
treble pick-up. 480.
treble register. 475.
triangle. 471.
triangular body. 473.
trichord. 465.
trill. 462.
trio. 476.
tripod. 478.
tripod stand. 472.
trombone. 470, 477.
trombones. 479.
trumpet. 470.
trumpet. 470, 477.
trumpets. 479.
truss rod adjustment. 480.
tuba. 470, 479.
tubular bells. 471.
tubular bells. 479.
tuning fork. 478.
tuning hammer. 478.
tuning machine. 481.
tuning peg. 464.
tuning pin. 465.
tuning screw. 472.
tuning slide. 470.
tuning slide. 468.
turn. 462.
two-two time. 462.
unison. 462.
upper bout. 481.
upper lip. 468.
upperboard. 468.
upright piano. 465.
upright piano action. 466.
valve. 470.
valve casing. 470.
valve slide. 470.
vibrola arm. 480.
viola. 463, 476.
violas. 479.
violin. 463, 464.
violin. 463, 476.
violin family. 463.
volume control. 480.
waist. 463, 481.

water key. 470.
wedge. 468.
wind chest. 467.
wind duct. 467.
wind instruments. 469, 470.
wind trunk. 467, 468.
wippen. 466.
wire brushes. 471.
woodwind family. 469.
worm. 475.
wrest plant. 465.
xylophone. 471.
xylophone. 479.
zither. 473.

OFFICE SUPPLIES AND EQUIPMENT

account book. 450.
acoustic coupler. 457.
acoustic coupler. 454, 455.
alphanumeric keyboard. 456.
appointment book. 450.
archboard. 450.
backspace key. 453, 456.
book end. 448.
calendar pad. 450.
card holder. 452.
card index cabinet. 450.
card punch. 458.
card reader. 458.
cards. 450.
carriage. 453.
carriage release lever. 453.
carriage return. 453.
cassette. 455.
cassette recorder. 455.
central processing unit. 454, 455, 458.
character. 452.
clamp binder. 449.
clipboard. 450.
coat hook. 451.
coat rack. 451.
compressor. 450.
computer room. 458.
configuration keys. 456.
connection cable. 457.
control console. 458.
control key. 456.
control knob. 457.
control panel. 457.
correcting tape. 452.
correction fluid. 447.
correction paper. 447.
credenza. 451.
cursor. 457.
cursor movement keys. 456.
data acquisition. 454.
data display. 454.
data processing. 454.
data processing devices. 454.
data recording on RAM* memory. 454.
data storage. 454.
dater. 448.
desk pad. 450.
desk tray. 448.
disk. 458.
disk. 455.
disk control unit. 458.
disk drive. 455, 458.
disk storage. 458.
display cabinet. 451.
divider. 449.
document folder. 449.
dot matrix printer. 457.
drawer. 450.
enter key. 456.
eraser. 447.
escape key. 456.
executive chair. 451.
executive desk. 451.
expanding file. 449.
extended character keys. 456.

fastener binder. 449.
feed pin. 457.
file guides. 449.
filing box. 448.
foldback clip. 447.
folder. 449.
function keys. 456.
glue stick. 447.
golfball element. 452.
golfball release lever. 452.
guide post. 452.
handset. 457.
hat stand. 451.
home key. 456.
impression control. 452.
indicator light. 457.
input devices. 454.
joystick. 457.
joystick. 455.
key. 453.
keyboard. 456.
keyboard. 453, 455.
label maker. 447.
lateral filing cabinet. 451.
letter opener. 447.
letter scales. 447.
lever. 457.
light pen. 455.
line space regulator. 453.
locker. 451.
loudspeaker. 457.
magnetic tape controller. 458.
magnetic tape drive. 458.
magnetic tape storage. 458.
margin release. 453.
margin stop. 453.
memo pad. 450.
microcomputer. 454, 455, 456, 457.
microphone. 457.
microprocessor. 455.
moistener. 448.
mouse. 455.
multiple copy control. 453.
numbering machine. 448.
numeric keypad. 456.
office furniture. 451.
office supplies and equipment. 445.
operator. 458.
output devices. 454.
paper bail. 453.
paper centring scale. 453.
paper clips. 447.
paper fasteners. 447.
paper guide. 453.
paper guide roller. 457.
paper punch. 448.
paper release lever. 453.
partition. 451.
pencil sharpeners. 448.
peripheral equipment. 457.
platen. 453.
platen knob. 453, 457.
plotter. 455.
post binder. 449.
print head. 457.
printer. 455, 458.
punch card. 458.
push button. 457.
RAM: Random Access Memory. 454.
reset key. 456.
return. 451.
return key. 456.
ribbon. 452, 453.
ribbon cartridge. 452.
ribbon end indicator. 452.
ribbon guide. 452.
ribbon load lever. 452.
ring binder. 449.
roller. 452.
ROM* memory. 454.
ROM: Read Only Memory. 454.
rotary file. 450.
rubber stamp. 448.

secretarial desk. 451.
sector. 458.
self-adhesive labels. 448.
separator wire. 452.
shift key. 453.
shift keys. 456.
shift lock key. 453, 456.
soft keys. 456.
space bar. 453, 456.
specific data processing program. 454.
spike file. 447.
spiral binding. 449.
spring binder. 449.
stamp pad. 448.
stamp rack. 448.
staple remover. 447.
stapler. 447.
staples. 447.
stationery. 447, 448, 449, 450.
stationery cabinet. 451.
supply spool. 452.
suspension file. 449.
switch. 453, 457.
tab. 449.
tab-key. 456.
tabulator. 453.
tabulator clear key. 453.
tabulator set key. 453.
take-up knob. 452.
take-up spool. 452.
tape. 447.
tape dispenser. 447.
tape load lever. 452.
tear-off calendar. 450.
telephone index. 450.
template. 457.
terminal. 458.
top plate. 453.
track. 458.
transparent line indicator. 453.
typestyle. 452.
typewriter. 452, 453.
typist's chair. 451.
variable pitch space. 453.
variable spacer. 453.
visual display unit. 455.
window tab. 449.
word processing keys. 456.

OPTICAL INSTRUMENTS

altazimuth mounting. 609.
altitude coarse-motion clamp. 609.
anode. 606.
arm. 605.
azimuth coarse-motion clamp. 609.
azimuth synchro. 611.
base. 605.
base line. 610.
base plate. 610.
biconcave. 610.
biconvex. 610.
binocular microscope. 605.
body. 607.
body tube. 605.
bridge. 607.
cathode. 606.
cell. 609.
central focusing wheel. 607.
coarse adjustment knob. 605.
column. 608.
compass card. 610.
compass meridian line. 610.
concave. 610.
condenser. 605.
condenser adjustment knob. 605.
converging lens. 610.
convex. 610.
counterweight. 608.
cover. 610.
cover slip. 605.
cradle. 608, 609.
declination circle. 608.
dew cap. 609.

The terms in **bold type** indicate the title of an illustration.

763

diffusion pump. 606.
diverging lens. 610.
double-condenser pole piece. 606.
dovetail. 607.
draw tube. 605.
drawtube. 605.
duplexer. 611.
echo. 611.
edge. 611.
electron gun. 606.
electron microscope. 606.
elevation adjusting screw. 607.
emission chamber. 606.
erecting lenses. 607.
eye lens. 607.
eyepiece. 605, 607, 608, 609.
eyepiece holder. 609.
field lens. 607.
field lenses. 607.
filament. 606.
fine adjustment knob. 605.
fine focus sleeve. 609.
first condenser lens. 606.
flat mirror. 608.
fluorescent screen. 606.
focus knob. 609.
focusing knob. 608.
focusing ring. 607.
fork. 608.
glass slide. 605.
graduated dial. 610.
high-voltage cable. 606.
hinge. 607.
intermediate lens. 606.
iris diaphragm. 605.
lamp. 605.
lens. 610.
limb top. 605.
magnetic compass. 610.
magnetic needle. 610.
main mirror. 608.
main scope tube. 607.
main tube. 608.
maintube. 609.
mechanical stage. 605.
mechanical stage control. 605.
modulator. 611.
motor. 608.
motor drive. 611.
negative meniscus. 610.
object. 605.
objective. 606.
objective. 605.
objective lens. 606, 607, 609.
objective pole piece. 606.
optical instruments. 603.
parabolic reflector. 611.
photo chamber. 606.
photographic plate. 606.
pivot. 610.
plan-position indicator. 611.
planoconcave. 610.
planoconvex. 610.
polar axis circle. 608.
Porro prism. 607.
positive meniscus. 610.
prism binoculars. 607.
projector lens. 606.
projector lens pole piece. 606.
radar. 611.
radiating element. 611.
receiver. 611.
reflector telescope. 608.
refractor telescope. 609.
reticle. 607.
revolving nosepiece. 605.
rotary joint. 611.
scale. 610.
second condenser lens. 606.
shutter. 606.
sight. 610.
sighting line. 610.
sighting mirror. 610.
slow-motion control knob. 609.
specimen. 605.

specimen chamber. 606.
stage. 605, 606.
stage clip. 605.
star diagonal. 609.
support. 608.
synchronizer. 611.
telescopic sight. 607.
transmitted pulse. 611.
transmitter. 611.
tripod. 608.
tripod accessories shelf. 609.
tripod leg. 609.
turret cap. 607.
vacuum manifold. 606.
viewing chamber. 606.
viewing window. 606.
Wehnelt cylinder. 606.
windage adjusting screw. 607.

PERSONAL ADORNMENT

Afro. 321.
baguette cut. 317.
band ring. 315.
Beatle cut. 321.
bend. 318.
bezel. 315.
bezel facet. 317.
bifocal. 318.
blusher brush. 322.
bob. 321.
bouffant. 320.
bracelet with curb chain. 315.
bracelets. 315.
braids. 320.
bridge. 318.
brilliant cut facets. 317.
brilliant full cut. 317.
briolette cut. 317.
brooch. 315.
brow brush. 323.
bun. 320, 321.
butt-strap. 318.
cabochon cut. 317.
cake mascara. 323.
capless wig. 321.
charm bracelet. 315.
charms. 315.
choker. 316.
class ring. 315.
claw. 315.
cleansing sponge. 323.
clip earring. 315.
collar bar. 316.
cosmetic sponge. 323.
cream blush. 322.
cream lipstick. 322.
crew cut. 321.
crown. 317.
culet. 317.
curly hair. 320.
distance. 318.
diversity of jewellery. 315.
diving goggles. 319.
dog tag. 315.
dowel hole. 318.
drop earring. 315.
earpiece. 318.
eight cut. 317.
emerald cut. 317.
engagement ring. 315.
eyebrow pencil. 323.
eyeglasses. 318, 319.
eyeglasses, principal types of. 319.
eyelash curler. 323.
eyeliner. 322.
eyeshadow. 322.
fan brush. 323.
fingerwaves. 320.
French cut. 317.
French pleat. 321.
fringe. 321.
gemstones, cuts for. 317.

girdle. 317.
hair, kinds of. 320.
hair styles. 320, 321.
hair styles, components of. 320, 321.
hairpieces. 321.
hairpieces. 321.
half-glasses. 319.
hoop earring. 315.
horn. 315.
horseshoe. 315.
jewellery. 315, 316, 317.
kohl pencil. 322.
lash comb. 323.
lipbrush. 323.
lipliner. 323.
lipstick. 323.
liquid foundation. 322.
locket pendant. 316.
loose powder. 322.
loose powder brush. 322.
lorgnette. 319.
lower girdle facet. 317.
lug. 318.
make-up. 322, 323.
make-up, products for. 323.
make-up kit. 322.
make-up products. 322.
make-up sponges. 323.
mascara. 322.
mascara brush. 323.
matinee length necklace. 316.
men's pompadour. 321.
metal plate. 318.
mirror. 322.
monocle. 319.
navette cut. 317.
necklaces. 316.
nose pad. 318.
nosepad. 318.
opera glasses. 319.
opera length necklace. 316.
oval cut. 317.
pad. 318.
pad arm. 318.
page boy. 320.
pavilion. 317.
pavilion facet. 317.
pear-shaped cut. 317.
pendant. 316.
personal adornment. 313.
pierced earring. 315.
pince-nez. 319.
plaits. 320.
plate. 318.
pony tail. 320.
poodle cut. 321.
powder puff. 322.
pressed powder compact. 322.
quizzing glass. 319.
reading. 318.
rim. 318.
ringlets. 320.
rings. 315.
rivet. 318.
rope. 316.
rose cut. 317.
safety glasses. 319.
scissors cut. 317.
scissors-glasses. 319.
screw earring. 315.
setting. 315.
shaft. 318.
shag. 321.
signet ring. 315.
ski goggles. 319.
solitaire ring. 315.
spectacles. 319.
sponge-tipped applicator. 322.
star facet. 317.
step cut. 317.
stickpin. 315.
straight hair. 320.
synthetic sponge. 323.
table. 317.

table cut. 317.
temple. 318.
tie slide. 316.
tie tack. 316.
tiered necklace. 316.
toupee. 321.
tube bangle. 315.
upper girdle facet. 317.
velvet band chocker. 316.
wavy hair. 320.
wedding ring. 315.
wigs. 321.
women's pompadour. 321.

PERSONAL ARTICLES

Afro comb. 328.
air hole. 335.
air inlet grille. 330.
air outlet grille. 330.
ash. 334.
ashtray. 334.
attaché case. 340.
automatic tweezers. 332.
barber comb. 328.
barrel. 330, 331.
barrel bag. 337, 338.
base. 330.
beach bag. 338.
bite. 335.
blackhead remover. 333.
blade. 327, 328.
blade close stop. 328.
blade injector. 327.
bowl. 335.
bowl lid. 335.
box bag. 338.
bracket. 329.
briefcase. 340.
bristle. 327, 328, 329, 331.
brush. 329.
buckle. 339.
bunch. 334.
butane tank. 334.
butt. 334.
calculator. 341.
calculator/cheque book holder. 341.
cane. 336.
canopy. 336.
card and photo case. 341.
carry handle. 331, 337.
carrier bag. 338.
carton. 334.
case. 327, 331, 332.
catch. 339, 341.
cellophane wrapped packet. 334.
central compartment. 339.
charging light. 327.
cheque book cover. 341.
cheque book holder. 341.
cigar. 334.
cigar band. 334.
cigar box. 334.
cigarette. 334.
cigarette holder. 334.
clamp. 331.
clamp lever. 331.
clasp. 339, 340.
classic bag. 339.
cleaning brush. 327.
clip. 331.
clippers. 328.
closeness setting. 327.
clutch bag. 338.
coin purse. 341.
collar. 327.
combination lock. 340.
combs. 328.
comfort contoured handle. 331.
compartment. 340.
cool tip. 331.
corn cutter. 332.
cosmetic tray. 337.
cover. 336.

The terms in **bold type** indicate the title of an illustration.

cover. 335, 341.
credit card wallet. 341.
curling brush. 331.
curling iron. 331.
cut-throat razor. 327.
cuticle knife. 332.
cuticle pliers. 332.
cuticle pusher. 332.
cuticle scissors. 332.
cutting edge. 328.
dental floss. 329.
disposable razor. 327.
divider. 337, 340.
double-edge blade. 327.
double-edge razor. 327.
drawstring. 339.
drawstring bag. 339.
dual swivel mirror. 330.
dual voltage selector switch. 330.
electric razor. 327.
electric toothbrush. 329.
emery board. 333.
exterior pocket. 337, 340.
eyebrow tweezers. 332.
face. 341.
fan housing. 330.
ferrule. 328, 336.
filler. 334.
filter. 335.
filter tip. 334.
fittings. 337.
flame adjustment wheel. 334.
flap. 339, 341.
flapover bag. 338.
flat-back brush. 328.
flight bag. 337.
floating head. 327.
folding nail file. 333.
frame. 336, 337, 340.
friction strip. 335.
front flap. 335.
garment bag. 337.
garment strap. 337.
gas lighter. 334.
gentry bag. 339.
gouge. 332.
gusset. 338.
gusseted pocket. 341.
hair clip. 333.
hair dryer. 330.
hair grip. 333.
hair roller. 333.
hair slide. 333.
hairbrushes. 328.
haircutting scissors. 328.
hairpin. 333.
hairsetter. 331.
hairstyling implements. 333.
handbags. 338, 339.
handle. 327, 329, 330, 331, 336, 337, 339, 340.
handle post. 340.
hang-up ring. 330.
hanger. 337.
hasp. 337.
head. 327, 329, 334, 335.
heat comfort control. 331.
heat ready indicator dot. 331.
heat/speed selector switch. 330.
hidden pocket. 341.
hinge. 337, 339.
holdall. 337.
hood cover. 330.
hook. 341.
housing. 327, 329, 330.
interior pocket. 337, 341.
jar. 335.
jaw. 333.
jet tip. 329.
key case. 341.
key lock. 340.
label. 334.
leather goods. 340, 341.
lever. 333.
lid. 331.
lid latch. 331.

light bar. 330.
lighted mirror. 330.
lining. 338, 340.
lock. 337.
luggage. 337.
luggage label. 337.
luggage trolley. 337.
magnifying mirror. 330.
manicure set. 332.
manicure stick. 332.
manicuring instruments. 333.
matchbook. 335.
matchbox. 335.
matchstick. 335.
measuring cup. 331.
minaudiere. 339.
mirror. 337.
money clip. 341.
mortise. 335.
muff. 339.
nail brush. 332.
nail buffer. 332.
nail cleaner. 333.
nail clippers. 333.
nail file. 332.
nail pliers. 332.
nail scissors. 332.
nail shaper. 332.
nail whitener pencil. 333.
notched double-edged thinning scissors. 328.
notepad. 341.
nozzle. 330.
on light. 331.
on-off switch. 327, 329, 330, 331.
packet of cigarette papers. 334.
padlock. 337.
paper. 334.
passport holder. 341.
peg. 335.
pen holder. 341.
personal articles. 325.
pick. 335.
pilot light. 331.
pipe. 335.
pipe cleaner. 335.
pipe cross section. 335.
pipe rack. 335.
pipe tools. 335.
pitchfork comb. 328.
pivot. 327, 328.
pocket. 339, 340, 341.
portfolios. 340.
pouch. 339.
power supply cord. 330.
press-stud. 338.
pressstud. 341.
pull strap. 337.
purse. 341.
push button. 336.
push-button release. 327.
quill brush. 328.
rake comb. 328.
razors. 327.
retractable handle. 340.
rib. 336.
ring. 336.
roller. 331.
roller pins. 333.
round brush. 328.
row. 329.
rubber base. 328.
saddle. 335.
safety match. 335.
safety scissors. 333.
salon-style hair dryer. 330.
scoop. 335.
screen. 327.
seam. 334.
see-through windows. 341.
shank. 328, 335, 336.
shaving brush. 327.
shaving mug. 327.
shell. 337.

shopping bag. 338.
shoulder bag. 339.
shoulder strap. 336, 337, 339.
side mirror. 330.
smoking accessories. 334, 335.
spreader. 336.
stamp pocket. 341.
stand. 331, 337.
stem. 335.
stick umbrella. 336.
strap. 337, 339, 341.
strap handle. 336.
striker wheel. 334.
stud. 339.
stummel. 335.
suitcase. 337.
swivelling power supply cord. 331.
tab. 336, 340.
tail comb. 328.
tamper. 335.
tear tape. 334.
teaser comb. 328.
telescopic umbrella. 336.
temperature control. 331.
thinning razor. 328.
ticket pocket. 341.
tie. 336.
tie closure. 336.
tip. 333, 336.
tobacco. 334.
tobacco hole. 335.
tobacco pouch. 335.
toenail scissors. 333.
tongue. 339.
tooth. 328.
toothbrush. 329.
toothbrush shaft. 329.
toothbrush well. 329.
toothpaste. 329.
tote bag. 338.
tray. 337.
trim. 337.
trimmer. 327.
trimming. 339, 341.
trunk. 337.
tuck. 334.
tweezers. 333.
umbrella. 336.
umbrella stand. 336.
utility case. 337.
valve. 334.
vanity case. 337.
vent brush. 328.
voyager bag. 339.
walking stick. 336.
wallet. 341.
wallet section. 341.
warm-air comb. 328.
wave clip. 333.
weekender. 337.
wheel. 337.
window. 341.
wrapper. 334.
wrist strap. 339, 340.
writing case. 340.
zip. 332, 336, 337, 338.
zip pocket. 340.

SPORTS

10 yard line. 513.
15 yard line. 513.
25 ring. 550.
25 yard line. 516.
3-point line. 523.
4-berth caravan. 581.
5 yard line. 513.
à cheval sur deux colonnes. 580.
à cheval sur deux douzaines. 580.
à cheval sur deux numéros. 580.
absorbent sock. 522.
Ace. 578.
adze. 574.
age and weight. 555.
aileron. 542.

air brake. 542.
air brake handle. 542.
air hose. 536.
air mattress. 584.
air pumps. 584.
airframe. 543.
airspeed indicator. 542.
altimeter. 542, 544.
aluminium panel. 581.
American football. 518, 519.
antenna. 567.
anti-friction pad. 546.
anti-reverse lock. 566.
approach. 556, 557, 576.
apron. 565, 571.
archer. 570.
archery. 570.
arena. 556, 557.
arm guard. 519, 570.
arm position. 535.
armstand. 534.
armstand dive. 535.
arrow. 570.
arrow. 570.
arrow rest. 570.
artificial fly. 567.
assistant timer. 531.
asymmetrical bars. 560.
at least. 530.
atenna. 529.
attack line. 529.
attack zone. 529.
attacker. 564.
attacking zone. 517.
automatic cable pulley. 547.
awning. 582.
awning channel. 581.
axle. 548.
back binding. 540.
back boundary line. 526.
back court. 524.
back judge. 518.
back straight. 555.
back wall. 527.
back zone. 529.
backboard. 523.
backboard support. 523.
backgammon. 578.
backstay. 548.
backstop. 520.
backstroke. 533.
backstroke start. 533.
backstroke swimmer. 533.
backstroke turn indicator. 532.
backward. 534.
backward dive. 535.
backward point. 514.
badminton. 526.
badminton racquet. 526.
badminton shoe. 526.
bag. 520.
bag well. 573.
bail. 515.
bail arm. 566.
baize. 569.
Baker tent. 583.
balance beam. 560.
balk area. 569.
balk line. 569.
balk line spot. 569.
ball. 515, 516, 521, 573.
ball. 528, 531.
ball (rugby). 512.
ball bearing. 548.
ball boy. 524.
ball cross-section. 573.
ball rack. 576.
ball return track. 576.
bamboos. 579.
bandage. 565.
bank. 530.
bar. 561, 578.
barb. 567.
barograph. 542.
barrel. 550.
base. 559.

The terms in **bold type** indicate the title of an illustration.

base plate. 546.
baseball. 520, 521.
baseline. 524.
basket. 523.
basket. 523, 545.
basketball. 523.
basketball. 523.
basketball shoe. 523.
bat. 515, 521, 528.
bat. 521.
bathing trunks. 531.
batsman. 514, 515.
batten. 537, 538.
batten pocket. 537, 538.
batter. 520.
batter's box. 520.
batter's helmet. 521.
batting glove. 521.
beam. 560.
beam reach. 539.
bear away (to). 537.
bed. 560.
bed-mattress. 584.
belt. 561, 564.
belt loop. 585.
beltbag. 545.
bend. 567.
betting layout (French). 580.
bevel. 525.
bib. 562.
billiard spot. 569.
billiards. 569.
billiards. 568.
binding. 540.
Bishop (B). 577.
bit. 554.
Black. 577, 578.
black ball. 569.
black square. 577.
blade. 516, 528, 536, 548, 563,
    567, 574, 585.
blank. 579.
blinkers. 555.
block. 539.
blouse. 522, 525.
blue ball. 569.
blue cap. 531.
blue flag. 531.
blue line. 517.
board. 537.
boards. 517.
boat, types of. 541.
bobsleigh. 549.
body. 558, 567.
body wire. 562.
bonus tiles. 579.
boom. 538.
boom vang. 538.
boot. 536, 544, 548, 551, 561.
bottom. 540, 545.
bottom of the pool. 531, 534.
bottom pocket. 569.
bottom surface. 542.
boundary line. 514.
bow. 537, 538.
bow (take-apart). 570.
bow saw. 586.
bowl. 530.
bowler. 514, 576.
bowline. 587.
bowline on a bight. 587.
bowling ball. 576.
bowling crease. 514.
bowling shoe. 576.
bowls. 530.
bowsight. 570.
bowstring. 570.
box and brush. 552.
box and gate. 552.
boxer. 565.
boxing. 565.
boxing boot. 565.
boxing glove. 565.
braided rope. 587.
brakeman. 549.
branch. 553.

brassie. 572.
breaking the wall. 579.
breaststroke. 533.
breaststroke kick. 533.
breaststroke swimmer. 533.
breaststroke turn. 533.
breathing in. 533.
breathing out. 533.
breeches. 554, 562.
bridge. 568.
bridle. 553.
broad reach. 539.
browband. 553.
brown ball. 569.
brush and rails. 551, 552.
buckle. 546.
buckled belt. 570.
bullseye. 550.
bunker. 571.
buoyancy compensator. 536.
butane accessories. 585.
butane cylinder. 585.
butt. 567, 568.
butt cap. 566.
butt eye. 566.
butt grip. 566.
butt section. 566.
butterfly kick. 533.
butterfly stroke. 533.
butterfly swimmer. 533.
butterfly turn. 533.
button. 563.
cabin. 547.
cable. 587.
cable. 559, 587.
cable car. 547.
caddie. 571.
cagoule. 575.
**camping equipment. 584, 585,
    586.**
canopy. 544, 573, 582.
canopy pole. 582.
cantle. 553.
canvas. 565.
canvas divider. 582.
canvas shoe. 522.
cap. 554.
captain. 549.
carabiner. 574.
caravan. 581.
card games. 578.
carré. 580.
cart path. 571.
catcher. 521.
catcher. 520.
catcher's box. 520.
catcher's glove. 521.
ceiling. 527.
cell. 544.
centre. 517, 518, 523.
centre-back. 511, 529.
centre circle. 511, 522, 523.
centre face-off circle. 517.
centre field. 520.
centre fielder. 520.
centre flag. 511.
centre forward. 511, 516, 529.
centre half. 516.
centre line. 516, 517, 519, 523,
    526, 528, 529, 562.
centre line of rink. 530.
centre mark. 524.
centre midfield. 511.
centre pocket. 569.
centre service line. 524.
centre spot. 511, 569.
centre strap. 524.
centre third. 522.
centreboard. 538.
chalet. 547.
chalk. 568.
characters. 579.
chassis. 581.
cheek. 567.
cheek strap. 553.

chess. 577.
chess notation. 577.
chessboard. 577.
chest protector. 519, 521.
chief timekeeper. 532.
chin strap. 519.
chinstrap. 554.
chip. 580.
chock. 574.
circles. 579.
clam-cleat. 537, 539.
claw grip. 530.
clear space. 529.
cleat. 538, 539.
cleated shoe. 519.
clew. 537.
climbing harness. 575.
clock operator. 523.
close hauled. 539.
close reach. 539.
clove hitch. 587.
club. 578.
club divider. 573.
clubhouse. 571.
coach's box. 520.
cockpit. 542.
cockpit. 538.
cockpit canopy. 542.
collar. 561.
colonnes. 580.
coloured sweatshirt. 516.
common whipping. 587.
compartment. 578, 580.
compass. 536, 542.
competition ring. 552.
competitive course. 532.
competitor. 532.
completion. 587.
compressed-air cylinder. 536.
connecting wire. 562.
connector link. 544.
contest area. 564.
contestant. 564.
control bar. 543.
control stick. 542.
control valve. 585.
conventional grip. 550.
cooking. 586.
cooking set. 585.
cool box. 586.
cord. 559.
cord grip. 558.
core. 573, 587.
cork tip. 526.
corkscrew. 585.
corner. 565.
corner arc. 511.
corner flag. 511, 516.
corner pad. 565.
corner pin. 530.
corner stay. 581.
corner-stool. 565.
counter. 548.
course (golf). 571.
court (badminton). 526.
court (basketball). 523.
court (netball). 522.
court (squash). 527.
court (tennis). 524.
court (volleyball). 529.
cover. 521, 573.
cover point. 514.
covering. 528.
cow hitch. 587.
coxed four. 541.
coxed pair. 541.
coxless four. 541.
coxless pair. 541.
crampon strap. 575.
crampons. 575.
crank. 566.
crash helmet. 545, 549.
crawl swimmer. 533.
crease. 515.
creel. 568.
cricket. 514, 515.

cricket player. 515.
cross handle. 580.
cross poles. 552.
crossbar. 512, 531, 543, 547, 556,
    557.
crosstree. 538.
croup. 559.
crownpiece. 553.
cue. 568.
cue ball. 569.
cup. 571, 585.
curb bit. 553.
curb chain. 553.
curb rein. 553.
cushion. 548, 569, 576.
[D]. 569.
daggerboard. 537.
daggerboard well. 537.
danger area. 564.
dart. 550.
dartboard. 550.
darts. 550.
dead ball line. 512.
dead bowl area. 530.
deep fine leg. 514.
defending zone. 517.
defensive. 518.
delivery. 530.
delivery. 530.
depth gauge. 536.
descendeur. 574.
diagonal. 577.
diamond. 578.
dice. 579.
dice. 578.
dice cup. 578.
dimple. 573.
dinghy. 538.
disc. 547, 561.
discus. 558.
discus throw. 556.
disgorger. 568.
distance. 555.
ditch. 530.
diver. 535.
dives, groups of. 535.
diving. 534.
diving installations. 534.
divot. 571.
dome tent. 583.
domino. 579.
dominoes. 579.
door. 527.
double. 552.
double-blank. 579.
double chair lift. 547.
double glazed window. 581.
double handles. 540.
double oxer. 551, 552.
double scull. 541.
double sheet bend. 587.
double-six. 579.
doubles pole. 524.
doubles ring. 550.
doubles service court. 526.
doubles sideline. 524, 526.
doublet. 579.
doubling cube. 578.
douzaines. 580.
down wind. 539.
downhaul. 537.
drag. 566.
driver. 572.
driving iron. 572.
East. 579.
East wind. 579.
edge. 545, 548, 549.
eight. 541.
elbow pad. 519, 549.
elbow protector. 562.
electric foil. 562.
electric golf cart. 573.
electrical pointe d'arrêt. 562.
electrical scoring apparatus. 562.
elevator. 542.
en prison. 580.

The terms in **bold type** indicate the title of an illustration.

end line. 519, 523, 528, 529.
end of the lap. 533.
end-piece. 568.
end wall. 532.
end zone. 519.
engine. 573.
entries. 534.
entry. 535.
épée. 563.
épéeist. 563.
equipment. 568.
étrier. 574.
even. 580.
extra cover. 514.
eye. 553, 566, 567, 574.
eyelet. 548.
face. 528, 572.
face-off circle. 517.
face-off spot. 517.
fairlead. 539.
fairway. 571.
falling. 564.
false start rope. 532.
family tent. 583.
family tents. 582.
feather crown. 526.
feather fletching. 570.
feet-first entry. 534.
female ferrule. 566.
fencer. 562.
fencing. 562, 563.
fencing shoe. 562.
fencing weapons. 563.
ferrule. 568, 572.
fibre. 587.
field (American football). 519.
field (baseball). 520.
field (cricket). 514.
field (hockey). 516.
field (rugby). 512.
field events. 558.
fielder. 515.
fiffi hook. 574.
figure-eight knot. 587.
figure skate. 548.
figure ski. 540.
figure skiing handle. 540.
file. 577, 585.
fin. 536, 540.
finger. 521.
finger hole. 576.
finish. 552.
finish line. 557.
finishing post. 555, 557.
first base. 520.
first baseman. 520.
first slip. 514.
first space. 523.
fisherman's knot. 587.
fishhook. 567.
fishing. 566, 567, 568.
fishing vest. 568.
fixtures. 539.
flag. 512, 529, 547.
flagstick. 571.
flanker. 513.
flap. 553.
flat side of the grip. 525.
flat spike. 574.
flight. 535, 550, 560.
flight instruments. 543.
flights. 534.
flip turn. 533.
float. 567.
floor. 527.
flower tiles. 579.
flush. 578.
fly box. 568.
fly half. 512.
fly line. 566.
fly reel. 566.
fly rod. 566.
flysheet. 583.
foam mattress. 584.
foam pad. 584.
foible. 563.

foil. 563.
foil warning line. 562.
foilist. 563.
folding camp bed. 584.
folding grill. 586.
folding shovel. 586.
follow-through. 530.
foot. 537, 566.
foot fault judge. 524.
foot pocket. 536.
footrest. 547.
fore court. 524.
foregrip. 566.
forestay. 538.
fork. 585.
form details. 555.
forming. 587.
forte. 563.
forward. 534.
forward dive. 535.
forward short leg. 514.
forward swing. 530.
foul line. 520, 576.
four of a kind. 578.
frame. 525, 527, 559, 560.
free fall. 544.
free throw lane. 523.
free throw line. 523.
French roulette wheel. 580.
front binding. 540.
front crawl stroke. 533.
front point. 575.
front runner. 549.
front wall. 527.
frying pan. 585.
fulcrum. 534.
full and by. 539.
full back. 512, 513.
full house. 578.
fullback. 518.
fuselage. 542.
G-meter. 542.
gaiter. 545.
game timekeeper. 517.
gap. 567.
gate. 547, 551, 552, 574.
gauge. 585.
gauze bandage. 561.
gear housing. 566.
girth. 553, 554.
girth strap. 553.
glass. 517, 527.
glider. 542.
gliding. 542.
glove. 521.
glove. 515, 536, 544, 549, 558,
562, 570.
goal. 531.
goal. 511, 512, 517, 531.
goal area. 511.
goal circle. 522.
goal crease. 517.
goal judge. 531.
goal judge's box. 517.
goal line. 511, 512, 516, 517, 519,
522, 531.
goal post. 512, 519.
goal third. 522.
goalkeeper. 516.
goalkeeper. 511, 516, 517, 531.
goalpost. 522.
goalpost. 522.
goggles. 544, 549.
golf. 571, 572, 573.
golf bag. 573.
golf clubs. 572.
golf clubs, types of. 572.
golf shoe. 573.
golf trolley. 573.
golfer. 571.
grab handle. 581.
granny knot. 587.
green. 530.
green ball. 569.
green dragon. 579.
griff-fiffi hook. 574.

grip. 527, 572.
grips, types of. 528.
grommet. 583.
groove. 545, 572.
ground level. 515.
guard. 563.
gully. 514.
gutter. 576.
guy cable. 559.
guy line adapter. 583.
guy rope. 582.
gymnast. 560.
gymnastics. 559, 560.
hackle. 567.
half court line. 527.
half-distance line. 531.
half way line. 511.
halfway line. 512.
hammer. 558.
hammer. 575.
hammer axe. 574.
hammer head. 574.
hammer throw. 556.
hand grip. 566.
hand guard. 519.
handbrake lever. 581.
handcapper's rating. 555.
handle. 540.
handle. 521, 525, 528, 545, 549,
558, 563, 566, 573, 574, 585.
handles, types of. 540.
hang glider. 543.
hang gliding. 543.
hang point. 543.
hank. 538, 539.
hardened steel pile. 570.
harness. 536, 543, 544.
hatchet. 586.
haulage cable. 547.
head. 525, 558, 567, 572, 574.
head cover. 573.
head-first entry. 534.
head linesman. 518.
head of sail. 537.
headband. 525.
headpin. 576.
headwind. 539.
heart. 578.
heater. 585.
heaving line knot. 587.
heel. 521, 548, 572.
heel flange. 546.
heel piece. 540, 545, 546.
heel release setting indicator. 546.
height. 581, 581.
height adjustment screw. 546.
height of the dive. 535.
helmet. 543, 544, 575.
helmet lamp. 575.
high card. 578.
high jump. 557.
high line. 563.
hinge. 546.
hip pad. 519.
hitting area. 521.
hockey. 516.
hockey skate. 548.
holds. 564.
hole. 571.
hole. 571, 574.
holster. 570.
holster quiver. 570.
home plate. 520.
home straight. 555.
honour tiles. 579.
hood. 536.
hook. 547, 548, 567.
hooker. 512, 513.
horizontal bar. 559.
horizontal stabilizer. 542.
horse racing. 554, 555.
hurdle. 557.
hurricane lamp. 586.
ice axe. 574.
ice axe. 575.
ice hockey. 517.

ice piton. 575.
ice screw. 575.
in goal. 512.
inbound line. 519.
infield. 520.
inhaul. 537.
inner boot. 546.
inner table. 578.
inner tent. 583.
inside line. 563.
inside linebacker. 518.
instrument panel. 542.
inward dive. 535.
iron. 572.
ivory ball. 580.
jack. 530.
jack. 530, 578.
jacket. 562, 564.
javelin throw. 557.
javelins. 558.
jib. 538.
jib halyard. 538.
jibsheet. 538.
jockey. 554.
jockey's name. 555.
jockey wheel. 581.
jockey wheel handle. 581.
jodhpurs. 551.
joint. 567, 568.
Joker. 578.
judge. 562, 564, 565.
judo. 564.
judo suit. 564.
jump ski. 540.
jumper. 544.
keel. 543.
keeper ring. 566.
kick. 533.
King. 578.
King (K). 577.
king post. 543.
King's side. 577.
kingpin. 581.
knee pad. 519, 521, 549, 561.
knee roll. 553.
knife. 536.
Knight (Kt). 577.
knob. 521.
knots. 587.
lace. 521, 548, 565.
landing. 560.
landing area. 556, 557.
landing mat. 560.
landing net. 568.
lane. 576.
lane. 532, 557.
lane number. 532.
lane rope. 532.
lane timekeeper. 532.
lantern. 585.
latch. 574.
leader. 567.
leading edge. 542, 543.
leading edge tube. 543.
leather sheath. 585.
leather skin. 515.
leech. 537.
left back. 516, 529.
left centre. 512, 513.
left cornerback. 518.
left defence. 517.
left defensive end. 518.
left defensive tackle. 518.
left field. 520.
left fielder. 520.
left forward. 523, 529.
left fullback. 511.
left guard. 518, 523.
left half. 516.
left halfback. 518.
left inner. 516.
left midfield. 511.
left safety. 518.
left service court. 524, 527.
left tackle. 518.
left wing. 511, 512, 513, 516, 517.

The terms in **bold type** indicate the title of an illustration.

767

leg. 528, 560, 566.
leg position. 535.
leg stump. 515.
legging. 575.
leisure. 509.
length. 534, 581.
light. 536.
light alloy metal riser. 570.
lighting. 586.
lighting cable. 581.
line. 566, 567.
line guide. 566.
line judge. 518.
line of scrimmage. 518.
line of touch. 513.
line out. 513.
line out plan. 513.
linesman. 511, 517, 524, 526, 529.
lining. 548.
living room. 582.
lock forward. 512, 513.
lock nut. 548.
long jump. 556.
long leg. 514.
long-off. 514.
long-on. 514.
long service line (doubler). 526.
long service line (singler). 526.
loose-head prop. 513.
low bar. 560.
low line. 563.
lower shell. 546.
luff. 537.
luff (to). 537.
lures. 567.
macon. 541.
mah-jong. 579.
main halyard. 538.
main parachute. 544.
main section. 580.
mainsail. 538.
mainsheet. 538.
major inner reaping throw. 564.
major outer reaping throw. 564.
maker's mark. 570.
maker's name. 581.
male ferrule. 566.
manual release. 546.
mark line. 570.
marker. 576.
marker bib. 522.
martingale. 563.
mashie. 572.
mashie iron. 572.
mashie niblick. 572.
mask. 521, 536, 562.
mast. 537, 538.
mast foot. 537.
mast sleeve. 537.
masthead. 537.
mat. 564.
mat. 530.
mat position on green. 530.
men. 577.
men. 578.
mesh. 528.
metal head. 558.
mid-off. 514.
mid-on. 514.
mid-section. 570.
mid-wicket. 514.
middle linebacker. 518.
middle stump. 515.
midiron. 572.
midmashie. 572.
minor inner reaping throw. 564.
mitten. 545, 575.
mono-ski. 540.
mound. 520.
mountaineer. 575.
mountaineering. 574, 575.
mountaineering boot. 575.
mounting. 563.
mouthpiece. 565.
mouthpiece. 536.
mud wall. 582.

mudguard. 581.
mummy. 584.
name of horse. 555.
neck. 559, 572.
needle. 541.
net. 517, 523, 524, 526, 528, 529.
net band. 524.
net judge. 524.
net support. 528.
netball. 522.
netball player. 522.
neutral zone. 517, 518.
niblick. 572.
no. 1 iron. 572.
no. 1 wood. 572.
no. 2 iron. 572.
no. 2 wood. 572.
no. 3 iron. 572.
no. 3 wood. 572.
no. 4 iron. 572.
no. 4 wood. 572.
no. 5 iron. 572.
no. 6 iron. 572.
no. 7 iron. 572.
no. 8 forward. 512.
no. 8 iron. 572.
no. 9 iron. 572.
nock. 570.
nock end. 570.
noir. 580.
North. 579.
North wind. 579.
nose. 542, 543.
noseband. 553.
notch. 568.
number. 580.
number of runners. 555.
numéro plein. 580.
oar, types of. 541.
obstacles. 551.
oche. 550.
octave. 563.
odd. 580.
off stump. 515.
offensive. 518.
on-deck circle. 520.
on guard line. 562.
on the wind. 539.
one-arm shoulder throw. 564.
one pair. 578.
one-piece overall. 544.
open-face spinning reel. 566.
ordinary die. 579.
out of bounds. 571.
outer boundary line. 527.
outer table. 578.
outfield. 520.
outhaul. 537.
outside-half. 513.
outside line. 563.
outside linebacker. 518.
overhand knot. 587.
owner's name. 555.
oxer. 552.
oxer wall. 552.
pack. 544.
pad. 515, 516.
padded jacket. 575.
palm. 521.
panel. 544, 553.
pants. 521.
parachute. 544.
parachute. 543.
parachuting. 544.
parachutist. 544.
parallel bars. 559.
pawn. 577.
Pawn (P). 577.
peg. 582, 583.
pegging-out point. 583.
penalty arc. 511.
penalty area. 511.
penalty bench. 517.
penalty spot. 511.
penalty timekeeper. 517.
penholder grip. 528.

penknife. 585.
pick. 574.
pieces. 577.
pike position. 534.
pilot. 542, 543.
pilot parachute. 544.
pin. 576.
pink ball. 569.
pip. 579.
piste (fencing). 562.
pistol grip handle. 570.
pit. 576.
pitch. 514.
pitcher. 520.
pitcher's plate. 520.
pitching niblick. 572.
pitching wedge. 572.
piton-carrier. 575.
piton hammer. 574.
pitons. 574.
pivot. 548.
placing judge. 532.
plank and pole. 552.
planting box. 556.
plasticine board. 556.
plastron. 562.
plate. 585.
platform. 534, 561.
platform diver. 534.
player. 521.
player. 531.
players' bench. 517, 520, 523, 529.
players' rotation. 529.
playing area. 550.
playing area (water polo). 531.
playing field (soccer). 511.
playing surface. 528.
pocket. 573, 576.
point. 548, 550, 567, 570, 578.
points of sailing. 539.
poker die. 579.
pole. 547, 556, 582.
pole loop. 582.
pole over a bank. 552.
pole vault. 556.
pommel. 553, 559, 563.
pommel horse. 559.
popping crease. 514.
port tack. 539.
positions. 563.
post. 526, 529, 531.
post and plank. 551.
post and rail. 551.
practice fairway. 571.
president. 562.
press. 525.
pressure button. 570.
pressure regulator. 585.
prime. 563.
prize money. 555.
prop forward. 512.
protective cup. 519.
protective equipment. 519.
protective helmet. 554.
protective surround. 550.
protective trousers. 575.
purge valve. 536.
putter. 572.
putter. 572.
putting green. 571.
pylon. 547.
pyramid spot. 569.
pyramid tent. 583.
quarte. 563.
quarterback. 518.
Queen. 578.
Queen (Q). 577.
Queen's side. 577.
quinte. 563.
race course. 555.
race name. 555.
race number. 554, 555.
race programme. 555.
race time. 555.
racecourse name. 555.

racing programme. 555.
racing shoe. 554.
rack. 568.
rail. 536, 569.
rain sill. 581.
rank. 577.
rear limit line. 562.
rear runner. 549.
receiver. 524, 526, 527, 528.
recorder. 532.
rectangular. 584.
red ball. 569.
red balls. 569.
red cap. 531.
red dragon. 579.
red flag. 531, 564.
reef knot. 587.
reel. 562.
reel seat. 566.
referee. 511, 512, 517, 518, 523, 528, 529, 531, 532, 564, 565.
refrigerator vent. 581.
rein. 554.
release setting screw. 546.
reserve parachute. 544.
restricted area. 523.
result of last meeting. 555.
return crease. 514.
reverse dive. 535.
rib pad. 519.
ribbing. 567.
rider. 549.
ridge. 580.
ridge pole. 582.
ridge tent. 583.
riding. 551, 552, 553.
riding crop. 551.
riding glove. 551.
riding helmet. 551.
riding jacket. 551.
rigging wire. 543.
right back. 516, 529.
right centre. 512, 513.
right cornerback. 518.
right defence. 517.
right defensive end. 518.
right defensive tackle. 518.
right field. 520.
right fielder. 520.
right forward. 523, 529.
right fullback. 511.
right guard. 518, 523.
right half. 516.
right halfback. 518.
right inner. 516.
right midfield. 511.
right safety. 518.
right service court. 524, 527.
right tackle. 518.
right wing. 511, 512, 513, 516, 517.
rim. 558.
ring. 523, 559, 574.
ring (boxing). 565.
ring floor. 565.
ring post. 565.
ring step. 565.
rings. 559.
ringside. 565.
rink. 517.
rink. 530.
rink corner. 517.
rink number. 530.
ripcord. 544.
riser. 544, 570.
roller skate. 548.
roof. 582.
roof vent and light. 581.
Rook (R). 577.
room. 582.
rope. 565, 575, 587.
rotating wheel. 580.
rouge. 580.
rough. 571.
roulette table. 580.
rowing. 541.

The terms in **bold type** indicate the title of an illustration.

rowing (one oar). 541.
rowing (two oars). 541.
royal flush. 578.
rubber thread. 573.
rubbing strake. 581.
rucksack. 575.
rudder. 538, 542.
rudder pedal. 542.
rugby. 512.
rugby union. 512, 513.
run. 560.
rung. 574.
runner. 549, 578.
running bowline. 587.
running track. 556.
sabre. 563.
sabre and épée warning line. 562.
sabreur. 563.
saddle. 553.
saddle. 554, 559.
safety area. 564.
safety bar. 547.
safety binding. 546.
safety binding. 545.
safety cage. 556.
safety pad. 560.
safety strap. 546.
sail. 537, 543.
sail panel. 538.
sailboard. 537.
sand wedge. 572.
saucepan. 585.
saw. 585.
scarf. 545.
scissors. 585.
score sheet. 576.
scoreboard. 550.
scorer. 517, 523, 529, 562, 576.
scoring areas. 550.
scoring light. 562.
scoring table. 576.
screen window. 582.
screw. 548.
screw locking nut. 566.
screwdriver. 585.
screwsleeve. 574.
scrimmage. 518.
scrum. 512.
scrum. 512.
scrum half. 512, 513.
scuba diver. 536.
sculling. 541.
seam. 515.
season tiles. 579.
seat. 542, 547, 549, 553.
second. 565.
second base. 520.
second baseman. 520.
second flight. 560.
second linesman. 529.
second slip. 514.
second space. 523.
seconde. 563.
secretary. 531.
sector flag. 556.
segment score number. 550.
self-erecting tent. 583.
semi-mummy. 584.
septime. 563.
server. 524, 526, 527, 528, 529.
service area. 529.
service box. 527.
service judge. 526.
service line. 524, 527.
set-up. 576.
sewn-in groundsheet. 582.
shackle. 539.
shaft. 525, 527, 550, 558, 568, 570, 572, 574.
shake-hands grip. 528.
shank. 567.
sheath. 587.
sheath knife. 586.
sheepshank. 587.
sheet bend. 587.
sheet lead. 539.

shin guard. 519, 521.
shirt. 525.
short extra cover. 514.
short fine leg. 514.
short line. 527.
short service line. 526.
short-sleeved shirt. 561.
shorts. 525, 565.
shortstop. 520.
shot put. 557.
shot splice. 587.
shots. 558.
shoulder. 525, 567.
shoulder pad. 519.
shoulder strap. 573.
shovel. 545.
shroud. 538.
shuttlecock. 526.
side line. 516, 522, 528.
side moulding. 581.
side wall. 527, 532.
side wall line. 527.
sideline. 519.
sideline. 523, 529.
sidestroke. 533.
silks. 554.
silly mid-off. 514.
single burner camp stove. 585.
single scull. 541.
single zero. 580.
singles pole. 524.
singles service court. 526.
singles sideline. 524, 526.
sinker. 567.
six-figure form. 555.
sixain. 580.
sixte. 563.
skate guard. 548.
skates, types of. 548.
skating. 548.
skeg. 537.
ski. 545.
ski boot. 546.
ski boot. 546.
ski goggles. 545.
ski instructor. 547.
ski jump. 547.
ski jumper. 547.
ski lift. 547.
ski pole. 545.
ski resort. 547.
ski stop. 545, 546.
ski suit. 545.
skier. 545.
skiing. 545, 546, 547.
skin diving. 536.
skirt. 516, 522, 525, 553.
skis, types of. 540.
slalom course. 547.
slalomist. 547.
sleeping bags. 584.
sleeve. 561, 562, 582.
small blade. 585.
snaffle bit. 553.
snaffle rein. 553.
snap shackle. 539.
snooker. 568, 569.
snorkel. 536.
snow goggles. 575.
soccer. 511.
soccer ball. 511.
sock. 516, 525.
sole. 546, 548, 572.
sole plate. 548.
South. 579.
South wind. 579.
spade. 541, 578.
spade mashie. 572.
speargun. 536.
speed skate. 536.
spike. 573, 574, 575.
spiked shoe. 521.
spinnaker boom. 538.
spinnaker sheet lead. 538.
spinner. 567.
spinning rod. 566.

split end. 518.
split link. 567.
spool. 566.
spoon. 572, 585.
sports. 509.
spot white ball. 569.
spring. 560.
spring hip throw. 564.
springboard. 534, 559, 560.
springboard diver. 534.
spur. 551.
square. 579.
square leg. 514.
squash. 527.
squash ball. 527.
squash racquet. 527.
stabilizer. 544.
stable type door. 581.
stanchion. 548.
standard poker hands. 578.
start. 552.
start line. 556.
start wall. 532.
startboard tack. 539.
starter. 532.
starting block. 532.
starting dive. 532.
starting grip. 532.
starting position. 535.
starting position (swimming). 532.
starting positions (diving). 534.
starting price. 555.
state of course. 555.
stationary bowl. 580.
steel bar. 559.
steeplechase. 556.
steering line. 544.
stern. 537.
stick. 516.
stirrup. 554.
stirrup iron. 553.
stirrup leather. 553.
stirrup sock. 521.
stitches. 521.
stocking. 562.
stopboard. 557.
straight. 552, 578.
straight flush. 578.
straight position. 534.
strainer. 582.
strand. 587.
strap. 521, 549, 559.
striking circle. 516.
stringing. 525.
strings. 527.
stroke guide. 532.
strokes, types of. 533.
strut. 560.
studded boot. 516.
stump. 514, 515.
submersible watch. 536.
substitute. 523, 529, 531.
suit tiles. 579.
support. 560.
surface of the water. 534.
suspension line. 544.
sweeper. 511.
sweeping loin throw. 564.
swimmer. 532.
swimming. 532.
swimming competition. 532.
swimming pool. 531.
swivel. 558, 567.
T-bar lift. 547.
tab. 553.
table. 528, 569.
table. 566.
table tennis. 528.
table tennis player. 528.
table tennis shoe. 528.
tack. 537.
tail. 540, 542, 543, 545, 567.
tail parachute. 542.
take-off board. 556, 557.
take-off line. 556.

tape. 521, 529.
taped handle. 516.
target areas. 563.
team bench. 531.
team playing positions. 513.
team shirt. 516, 521.
teapot. 585.
tee. 573.
teeing ground. 571.
teeth. 574.
telltale. 527, 538.
tendon guard. 548.
tennis. 524, 525.
tennis ball. 525.
tennis players. 525.
tennis racquet. 525.
tennis shoe. 525.
tenpin bowling. 576.
tents. 582, 583.
tents, types of. 583.
thigh pad. 519.
third base. 520.
third baseman. 520.
three-burner camp stove. 585.
three of a kind. 578.
threequarter backs. 512.
throat. 525, 567.
throat lash. 553.
throat protector. 521.
thrower-in. 513.
throwing arc. 557.
throwing circle. 556, 557.
throwing in a circle. 564.
thumb. 521.
tie flap. 582.
tierce. 563.
tight end. 518.
tight-head prop. 513.
tiller. 538.
timekeeper. 523, 531, 562, 565.
tin opener. 585.
tip. 540, 543, 545, 558, 567, 568, 570.
tip guard. 548.
tip-ring. 566.
tip section. 566.
tipster's choices. 555.
tipter's choice. 555.
toboggan. 549.
toe. 572.
toe box. 548.
toe pick. 548.
toe piece. 540, 545, 546.
toe-piece release setting indicator. 546.
toe stop. 548.
toe strap. 540.
tongue. 546, 548.
tools. 586.
top. 525.
top bar. 560.
top pocket. 569.
top surface. 542.
topping. 567.
touch in goal line. 512.
touch line. 511, 512, 513.
tow bar. 540.
tow-bar cover. 581.
tow hook. 542.
tow release knob. 542.
towing hitch. 581.
towrope. 540.
track. 547, 557.
track and field athletics. 556, 557.
trailing edge. 542, 543.
trainer. 565.
trainer's name. 555.
trampoline. 560.
transversale pleine. 580.
traveller. 539.
tread. 553.
treble. 552.
trebles ring. 550.
tree. 553.
triple bars. 551, 552.

The terms in **bold type** indicate the title of an illustration.

triple jump. 557.
trousers. 516, 564.
truck. 548.
trunks. 561.
tubular ice screw. 574.
tuck position. 534.
turn and bank indicator. 542.
turnbuckle. 539, 565.
turning judge. 532.
turtleneck. 545.
twin skis. 540.
twist dive. 535.
twisted rope. 587.
two-hand clean and jerk. 561.
two-hand snatch. 561.
two pairs. 578.
umbrella sheath. 573.
umpire. 514, 518, 524, 526, 528, 529.
umpire-in-chief. 520.
umpire position. 522.
umpire's stand. 526.
undershirt. 521.
uphaul. 537.
upper. 546.
upper cuff. 546.
upper edge. 528.
upper shell. 546.
upright. 556, 557, 559, 560.
vacuum flask. 586.
variometer. 542.
vaulting horse. 559, 560.
veil. 567.
vent hole. 544.
vertical side band. 529.
vertical stabilizer. 542.
vest. 565.
volleyball. 529.
volleyball. 529.
waders. 568.
wagon tent. 583.
wall. 551, 552, 579, 582.
wall and rails. 551, 552.
wardrobe. 582.
water bottle. 586.
water carrier. 586.
water ditch. 556.
water hazard. 571.
water jump. 551, 552.
water polo. 531.
water skiing. 540.
weapon, parts of the. 563.
web. 521.
weight. 558, 561.
weight belt. 536.
weightlifter. 561.
weightlifting. 561.
West. 579.
West wind. 579.
wet suit. 536.
wheel. 548, 581.
whip. 554.
whipping. 572.
White. 577, 578.
white cap. 531.
white cue ball. 569.
white dragon. 579.
white flag. 531, 564.
white front width light. 581.
white square. 577.
white tape. 526, 528.
wicket. 515.
wicket keeper. 514, 515.
width. 534, 581.
willow. 515.
winch. 539.
wind. 539.
wind abeam. 539.
wind baffle. 585.
wind indicator. 538.
window. 537, 582.
wing. 542, 543, 567.
wing forward. 512.
wing tip. 542.
wing wire. 543.
wire. 546, 558.

wire sling. 574.
wire support. 585.
wishbone boom. 537.
wood. 572.
wooden bar. 559.
wrist pad. 519.
wrist sling. 574.
wristband. 525.
yard line. 519.
yarn. 587.
yellow ball. 569.
zip. 583.
zipped screen door. 582.

SYMBOLS

access for physically handicapped. 705.
addition. 708.
airport. 707.
ampersand. 708.
ankh. 707.
Aquarius, the Water Bearer. 698.
argent. 696.
Aries, the Ram. 698.
azure. 696.
base. 695.
biology. 708.
birth. 708.
buffet. 705.
buses and taxis. 707.
camping and caravan site. 707.
camping prohibited. 707.
Cancer, the Crab. 698.
canton. 695.
Capricorn, the Goat. 698.
car rental. 707.
cattle. 701.
caution. 704.
caution, pedestrian crossing. 704.
caution, slippery floor. 704.
Celtic. 707.
cent. 708.
centre base. 695.
centre chief. 695.
charges. 696.
chevron. 696.
chief. 695, 696.
colours. 696.
common symbols. 704, 705, 706, 707.
constellations. 698.
copyright. 708.
crescent. 696.
cross. 696.
crosses. 707.
currency exchange. 706.
cyclists. 701.
danger, electrical hazard. 704.
danger, flammable. 704.
danger, poison. 704.
danger warning signs. 700, 701.
dangerous bend. 700.
dangerous descent. 700.
death. 708.
dexter. 695.
dexter base. 695.
dexter chief. 695.
dexter flank. 695.
direction to be followed. 703.
division. 708.
do not enter. 704.
do not use for wheelchairs. 705.
do not use luggage trolleys. 706.
dollar. 708.
double bend. 700.
double pennant. 697.
duty-free shop. 706.
eagle. 696.
emblem. 695.
empty set. 708.
end of motorway. 703.
end of priority. 701.
ermine. 696.
escalator, down. 705.

escalator, up. 705.
falling rocks. 700.
fanion. 697.
female. 708.
fess point. 695.
finial. 695.
fire extinguisher. 704.
fire hose. 704.
first aid. 704.
flag. 695.
flag, parts of a. 695.
flag shapes. 697.
flammule. 697.
fleur-de-lis. 696.
fly. 695.
furs. 696.
Gemini, the Twins. 698.
give priority to vehicles from opposite direction. 702.
give way. 701.
gonfalon. 697.
goods lift. 705.
graphic elements for symbols. 699.
Greek. 707.
gules. 696.
hairdresser. 706.
halyard. 695.
height limit. 702.
helicopters. 707.
hoist. 695.
honour point. 695.
hospital. 704.
infinity. 708.
information. 704.
informative signs. 703.
international road signs. 700, 701, 702, 703.
intersection. 700.
is a member of. 708.
is approximately equal to. 708.
is contained in. 708.
is equal to. 708.
is equal to or greater than. 708.
is equal to or less than. 708.
is equivalent to. 708.
is greater than. 708.
is identical with. 708.
is less than. 708.
is not equal to. 708.
is not identical with. 708.
Latin. 707.
Leo, the Lion. 698.
level crossing with barrier or gate. 701.
Libra, the Balance. 698.
lion passant. 696.
loose chippings. 700.
Lorraine. 707.
luggage claim. 706.
luggage lockers. 706.
luggage registration. 706.
luggage trolleys. 706.
male. 708.
Maltese. 707.
mandatory signs. 703.
mathematics. 708.
maximum speed limit. 702.
metals. 696.
motorway. 703.
mullet. 696.
multiplication. 708.
national speed limit applies. 702.
negative charge. 708.
no cycling. 702.
no dogs. 704.
no entry. 702.
no goods vehicles. 702.
no left turn. 702.
no motor vehicles. 702.
no motorcycles. 702.
no overtakin. 702.
no pedestrians. 702.
no stopping. 703.
no U-turn. 702.
no vehicles. 702.

nombril point. 695.
one-way traffic. 703.
or. 696.
ordinaries. 696.
oriflamme. 697.
other danger. 701.
pale. 696.
papal. 707.
parking. 703.
parking and stopping signs. 703.
parking prohibited or restricted. 703.
partitions. 696.
partriachal. 707.
passenger lift. 705.
pedestrian crossing. 700.
pennant. 697.
per bend. 696.
per cent. 708.
per fess. 696.
per pale. 696.
picnic area. 707.
Pisces, the Fishes. 698.
plus or minus. 708.
pole. 695.
police. 704.
positive charge. 708.
post office. 706.
pound. 708.
prescription. 708.
priority. 701.
priority junction. 701.
prohibitory signs. 702.
purpure. 696.
quarterly. 696.
radioactive material. 704.
ramp. 700.
reaction direction. 708.
rectangular. 697.
registered trademark. 708.
regulatory signs. 702.
restaurant. 705.
reversible reaction. 708.
right bend. 700.
road works. 701.
roadway narrows. 700.
roundabout. 701, 703.
sable. 696.
Sagittarius, the Archer. 698.
Saint Andrew's. 707.
schoolchildren. 700.
Schwenkel. 697.
Scorpio, the Scorpion. 698.
service station. 707.
shield. 695.
shield. 695.
signs showing priority at junctions. 701.
sinister. 695.
sinister base. 695.
sinister chief. 695.
sinister flank. 695.
slippery road. 700.
smoking permitted. 705.
smoking prohibited. 705.
square. 697.
square root of. 708.
staff. 695.
stairs. 705.
steep hill. 700.
stop. 701.
streamer. 697.
subtraction. 708.
swallowtail. 697.
swallowtail and tongue. 697.
swallowtail pennant. 697.
symbols. 693.
Taurus, the Bull. 698.
taxis. 706.
telephone. 704.
tinctures. 696.
toilet for men. 705.
toilet for men and women. 705.
toilet for women. 705.
traffic lights. 701.
trains. 707.

The terms in **bold type** indicate the title of an illustration.

two-way traffic. 701.
uneven surface. 700.
union. 708.
vair. 696.
vert. 696.
Virgo, the Virgin. 698.
waiting room. 706.
way. 706.
way out. 706.
weight limit. 702.
width clearance. 702.
wild animals. 701.
windcone. 697.

TOOLS AND EQUIPMENT

access panel. 263.
acetylene cylinder. 271.
acetylene valve. 272.
acorn nut. 254.
adapter. 275.
adjustable channel. 249.
adjustable frame. 252.
adjustable spanner. 248.
adjusting knob. 247.
adjusting ring. 250.
adjusting screw. 249, 272.
adjustment wheel. 277.
aerated filter. 267.
air cap. 270.
air chamber. 262.
air pressure adjusting screw. 270.
air valve. 270.
angle scale. 253.
anode. 263.
anti-slip shoe. 268.
anti-syphon vent. 257.
arc tube. 274.
arc tube mount structure. 274.
arc welding. 271.
arc welding machine. 271.
auger bit. 250.
auxiliary handle. 251.
back. 252, 255.
ball assembly. 261.
ball-cock supply valve. 258.
ball pein. 247.
ball pein hammer. 247.
base. 250, 251.
base elbow. 265.
base plate. 253.
bath. 259.
bathroom. 259.
belt. 251.
bench saw. 252.
bib tap. 261.
bit. 250.
blade. 247, 248, 252, 253, 277.
blade guard. 252, 270.
blade height adjustment. 252.
blade-locking bolt. 253.
blade tilt lock. 253.
blade tilting mechanism. 252.
blockboard. 255.
blowlamp. 271.
board. 255.
body. 250.
bolt. 254.
bolt. 249.
bolt follower. 256.
bottle cart. 271.
brace. 250.
brace. 269.
bradawl. 248.
branch. 257.
branching, examples of. 262.
bristles. 270.
brush. 270.
building sewer. 257.
bulb. 274.
butt welding. 272.
button. 274.
cabinet. 259.
cable. 251.

cable sleeve. 251.
cam ring. 250.
cap. 265, 271, 274.
cap iron. 247.
carpentry. 255.
carpentry: fasteners. 254.
carpentry: tools. 247, 248, 249, 250, 251, 252, 253.
cartridge fuse. 275.
cartridge stem. 261.
central ply. 255.
chain pipe wrench. 266.
check valve. 267, 272.
cheek. 247.
chipboard. 255.
chisel. 248.
chuck. 248, 250, 251.
chuck key. 251.
circular saw. 253.
circular saw blade. 253.
clamp. 267.
claw. 247.
claw hammer. 247.
cleaning plug. 260.
cold-water riser. 257.
cold-water supply. 258, 262, 263.
collet. 250.
collet nut. 250.
column. 251.
combination pliers. 277.
combination spanner. 248.
compression coupling. 260.
compression fitting. 264.
conical washer. 258.
container. 270.
continuity tester. 276.
copper pipe. 264.
copper to plastic. 265.
copper to steel. 265.
countersink. 250.
countersunk. 254.
cover. 259, 261.
crank. 250.
crimper. 277.
cross head (Phillips). 254.
curved jaw. 249.
cutting nozzle. 272.
cutting oxygen handle. 272.
cutting torch. 272.
cylinder. 256.
cylinder hole. 256.
cylinder lock. 256.
cylinder pressure gauge. 272.
dead bolt. 256.
decorative sheet. 255.
depth stop. 251.
disc seat. 261.
disc seat ring. 261.
discharge line. 267.
disposable gas cylinder. 271.
distribution field. 267.
diverter valve. 259.
domestic sink. 262.
double-bowl kitchen sink. 257.
double-twist auger bit. 250.
drain. 262.
drain hose. 262.
drain trap. 260.
drain valve. 263.
drill. 250.
drive wheel. 250.
earth clamp. 271.
earth green and yellow wire. 275.
edge. 255.
elbow. 265.
electric arc. 271.
electric drill. 251.
electric supply. 263.
electric water-heater tank. 263.
electrician's tools. 276, 277.
electricity. 274, 275, 276, 277.
electrode. 271, 274.
electrode holder. 271.
electrode lead. 271.
end grain. 255.
escutcheon. 256, 260.

exhaust tube. 274.
expansion bolt. 254.
extension ladder. 268.
external tooth lock washer. 254.
eye. 247.
face. 247.
face ply. 255.
face-shield. 273.
face side. 255.
faceplate. 256.
faces. 247.
feed lever. 251.
ferrule. 270.
filament. 274.
filler rod. 272.
filler tube. 258.
fitting. 264.
fittings. 265.
fixed jaw. 248, 249.
flame spreader tip. 271.
flange. 264.
flange bolt. 258.
flange nut. 264.
flare joint. 264.
flare nut. 264.
flat washer. 254.
flex. 275.
flexible hose. 259.
flexible rubber hose. 262.
flint. 273.
float. 258, 267.
float clamp. 267.
fluid adjustment screw. 270.
fluorescent tube. 274.
flush bushing. 265.
flush handle. 259.
flute. 250.
fluted land. 250.
frame. 249, 269.
front knob. 247.
fruit-picking ladder. 269.
fuse. 275.
fuse carrier. 275.
fuse pullers. 276.
G-clamp. 249.
gas. 274.
gasket. 261, 264.
gauntlet. 273.
goggles. 273.
grain. 255.
gravel. 267.
grease trap. 267.
grooved sleeve. 261.
guard. 251.
gun body. 270.
hacksaw. 252.
hacksaw. 266.
hammer. 277.
hand drill. 250.
hand shield. 273.
handle. 247, 248, 249, 250, 252, 253, 261, 270, 272.
handsaw. 252.
hardboard. 255.
head. 250, 254.
head tube. 272.
heat deflecting disc. 274.
heel. 247, 252.
hexagon bushing. 265.
high-temperature cutoff. 263.
high-voltage tester. 276.
hoisting rope. 268.
hollow-wood construction. 255.
hook ladder. 268.
hose. 274.
hot-water heater. 257.
hot-water riser. 257.
hot-water supply. 262, 263.
hot-water supply line. 262.
housing. 251.
inert gas. 274.
inner ply. 255.
inside knob. 256.
inspection chamber. 267.
inspection cover. 267.
insulated blade. 276.

insulated handle. 276, 277.
insulation. 263.
internal tooth lock washer. 254.
jaw. 248, 250, 251, 277.
key. 256.
keyway. 256.
knob. 256.
knob handle. 253.
knurled bolt. 270.
kraft paper. 255.
ladders. 269.
ladders and stepladders. 268.
laminate board. 255.
laminboard. 255.
land. 250.
latch. 256.
latch bolt. 256.
latch follower. 256.
latch lever. 256.
lateral adjusting lever. 247.
lead-in wire. 274.
lead screw. 250.
lever. 249, 260, 261.
lever cover. 261.
lever tap. 261.
light bulb. 274.
lip. 256.
live brown wire. 275.
lock. 256.
locking device. 268.
locking nut. 258.
locking ring. 248.
locknut. 260.
loft ladder. 268.
long-nose pliers. 277.
lower blade guard. 253.
lower guard retracting lever. 253.
lower heating element. 263.
lower thermostat. 263.
main electrode. 274.
main handle. 250.
main inspection eye. 257.
mallet. 247.
measuring drawtape. 277.
mechanical connectors. 264.
mercury. 274.
mercury-vapour lamp. 274.
metal bench top. 271.
metal washer. 260.
mitre gauge. 252.
mitre gauge slot. 252.
mitten. 273.
mixing chamber. 272.
mole wrench. 249.
monkey wrench. 266.
mortise lock. 256.
motor. 250, 251, 253.
moulded plywood. 255.
movable jaw. 248, 249.
multi-pliers. 249.
multi-ply plywood. 255.
multimeter. 276.
multipurpose ladder. 268.
multipurpose tool. 277.
nail. 254.
name plate. 251.
neon lamp. 276.
neon screwdriver. 276.
neutral blue wire. 275.
nipple. 265.
nitrogen. 274.
non-return air vent. 267.
nozzle. 270, 272.
nut. 254.
nut and bolt. 249.
o-ring. 261.
offset. 265.
on-off switch. 267.
one way head. 254.
open end spanner. 248.
outdoor drain cock. 257.
outside knob. 256.
overflow. 259.
overflow bend. 257.
overflow pipe. 263.
overflow tube. 258.

The terms in **bold type** indicate the title of an illustration.

oxyacetylene welding. 271.
oxygen cylinder. 271.
oxygen valve. 272.
[P] trap. 257.
packing. 261.
packing nut. 261.
packing retainer ring. 261.
paint roller. 270.
painting upkeep. 268, 269, 270.
pawl. 250.
pedestal drill. 251.
pedestal sump pump. 267.
peeled veneer. 255.
pencil point tip. 271.
perforated pipe. 267.
Phillips tip. 248.
phosphor coating. 274.
pin. 256, 274.
pinion. 250.
pipe. 264.
pipe coupling. 265.
pipe threader. 266.
pipe wrench. 266.
pistol grip handle. 251, 252.
pivot. 277.
plane. 247.
platform. 269.
platform ladder. 269.
plug. 275.
plumbing. 257, 258, 259, 260, 261, 262, 263, 264, 265, 266, 267.
plumbing system. 257.
plumbing tools. 266.
plumbing wrench. 266.
plunger. 266.
plywood. 255.
portable shower head. 259.
pressure regulator. 272.
pressure regulator. 271.
pressure relief valve. 263.
protective clothing. 273.
protective sheet. 255.
pulley. 251, 268.
pulley safety guard. 251.
pump motor. 267.
pump suction head. 267.
push-button. 256.
quill. 250, 251.
quill lock. 251.
raised head. 254.
ratchet. 248, 250.
reducing coupling. 265.
refill tube. 258.
reflector. 274.
release lever. 249.
removable blade. 270.
retainer nut. 261.
ring nut. 264.
ring spanner. 248.
rip fence. 252, 253.
rip fence adjustment. 252.
rip fence guide. 252.
rip fence lock. 252.
rising main. 257.
rivet. 249.
roller cover. 270.
roller frame. 270.
rolling ladder. 269.
roof flashing. 257.
roof vent. 265.
rope ladder. 268.
rose. 256.
rotor. 256.
round head. 254.
router. 250.
rubber gasket. 260.
rubber washer. 260.
rung. 268.
safety rail. 269.
scraper. 270.
screw. 254.
screw. 256.
screw base. 274.
screwdriver. 248.
scum. 267.

seal. 258, 263.
seat. 259.
septic tank. 267.
septic tank first compartment. 267.
septic tank second compartment. 267.
shank. 248, 250, 254.
shelf. 269.
shoulder. 254.
shoulder bolt. 254.
shower and bath fixture. 257.
shower head. 259.
shutoff valve. 260, 262.
side handle. 250.
side rail. 268.
single-handle kitchen tap. 261.
single-handle kitchen tap. 260.
single spring washer. 254.
single twist. 250.
sink. 260.
sink. 259.
sink strainer. 260.
slip joint. 249.
slip joint pliers. 249.
slot. 254.
slotted bit. 248.
slotted wall bracket. 259.
sludge. 267.
soap dish. 259.
socket. 275.
soil drain. 257.
soil-or-waste stack. 257.
soil vent. 257.
solder. 273.
soldering. 271, 272, 273.
soldering gun. 271.
soldering iron. 271.
spanners. 248.
spindle. 256, 261.
spindle hole. 256.
spiral. 248.
spiral ratchet screwdriver. 248.
spirit level. 248.
spout. 261.
spout assembly. 260.
spray head. 260.
spray hose. 260.
spray paint gun. 270.
spreader adjustment valve. 270.
spring. 249, 256, 261.
spring wing. 254.
spur. 250.
square head plug. 265.
standpipe. 262.
starting electrode. 274.
starting resistor. 274.
steel to plastic. 265.
stem. 274.
step. 269.
step stool. 269.
stepladder. 269.
stepladders. 269.
stopcock. 257, 258, 262, 263.
straight jaw. 249.
straight ladder. 268.
strainer. 261.
strainer body. 260.
strainer coupling. 260.
strainer plug. 261.
strainer sleeve. 260.
strap wrench. 266.
strike plate. 256.
striker. 273.
sump. 267.
supply tube. 260.
support. 274.
switch. 250, 251.
swivel base. 249.
swivel head. 249.
swivel lock. 249.
table. 251, 252.
table extension. 252.
table-locking clamp. 251.
tailpiece. 260.
tank lid. 259.
tank valve. 258.

tap body. 261.
tee. 262, 265.
teeth. 252.
test-lamp. 276.
tester probe. 276.
thread. 254, 261.
threaded cap. 265.
threaded rod. 254.
three-pin plug. 275.
throat. 249.
thumbscrew. 248.
tip. 248, 253, 254, 271.
tip cleaners. 273.
tipping valve tap. 261.
tissue holder. 259.
toe. 247, 252.
toggle bolt. 254.
toilet. 258.
toilet. 259.
toilet bowl. 258, 259.
toilet cistern. 259.
tool tray. 269.
tooth. 253.
toothed jaw. 249.
torch. 266.
towel rail. 259.
tower scaffold. 269.
transition fittings. 265.
trap. 260, 265.
trap and drain auger. 266.
trap coupling. 260.
tray. 270.
trigger. 270.
trigger switch. 253.
trip lever. 258.
tube cutter. 266.
tube end. 264.
tube flaring tool. 266.
tubular lock. 256.
tumbler holder. 259.
turning handle. 250.
twist drill. 250.
U-bend. 265.
union. 264.
union. 264.
union nut. 264.
upper blade guard. 253.
upper heating element. 263.
upper thermostat. 263.
valve seat. 261.
valve seat shaft. 258.
valve stem. 261.
vent hole. 270.
vent line. 265.
vice. 249.
warning plate. 251.
washer. 261.
washing machine. 262.
waste. 257.
waste disposal sink. 260.
waste disposal unit. 260.
waste pipe. 258.
waste tee. 262.
water authority main. 257.
water meter. 257.
water service pipe. 257.
waterproofed electrical supply. 267.
WC pedestal. 257.
wedge iron. 247.
wedge lever. 247.
weld bead. 271, 272.
welding. 271, 272, 273.
welding curtain. 273.
welding torch. 272.
welding torch. 271.
welding torch nozzle. 272.
wing nut. 254.
wing nut. 252.
wire cutter. 249, 277.
wire cutters. 277.
wire stripper. 277.
work lead. 271.
working pressure gauge. 272.
Y-branch. 265.

TRANSPORT

abutment. 400, 401, 402.
accelerator pedal. 386.
accommodation ladder. 420.
acoustic baffle. 421.
acoustic echo. 428.
acrylic window. 423.
adjustable seat. 407.
advance and retard capsule. 391.
advertising sign. 414.
aerial. 383.
aft stabilizer fin. 419.
after hydroplane. 424.
aftermast. 416.
aftermast topgallant staysail. 417.
aileron. 434.
air conditioning. 407.
air diffuser. 415.
air filter. 391.
air inlet. 436.
air intake. 404, 422, 441.
air-line. 387.
air transport. 434.
air warning radar. 425.
aircraft gate. 438.
airport. 438, 439.
alternator. 391, 404.
alternator indicator. 385.
anchor. 433.
anchor cable. 433.
anchor-windlass room. 419.
anchorage block. 402.
anchors, types of. 433.
annular combustion chamber. 436.
antenna. 433.
anti-aircraft gun. 425.
anti-collision light. 434.
anti-submarine mortar. 425.
approach ramp. 402.
approach span. 401.
apron. 438.
arc. 429.
arch. 401.
arch bridge. 401.
arch bridges, types of. 401.
arches, types of. 401.
arm. 433.
arm rest. 386.
arrivals concourse. 440.
arrivals timetable. 412.
articulated vehicle. 389.
articulation. 384.
astragal. 431.
automatic control system. 422.
automatically-controlled door. 440.
autopilot control. 437.
auxiliary tank. 388.
axial-flow compressor. 436.
axle. 404.
backstay. 416.
baggage check-in counter. 440.
baggage claim area. 440.
baggage compartment. 441.
baggage conveyor. 439.
baggage racks. 421.
baggage trailer. 439.
baggage trolley. 440.
Bailey bridge. 403.
balance beam. 426.
ballast. 408.
ballistic missile nuclear submarine. 424.
barrow. 413.
base. 409.
basecourse. 399.
battery. 392.
battery box. 388.
battery case. 392.
battery cover. 392.
battery pod. 423.
battery pod release hand pump. 423.
battery pod release lever. 423.
bead. 393.
beam bridge. 400.

The terms in **bold type** indicate the title of an illustration.

beam bridges, types of. 400.
bearing. 401.
bedroom. 431.
bell buoy. 430.
bellowslike joint. 444.
belted radial tyre. 393.
bench. 414.
Bermuda rigged ketch. 418.
bicycle. 397, 398.
bicycle horn. 398.
bill. 433.
blade lift fan. 421.
boarding step. 441.
boat deck. 419.
bobstay. 416.
body. 387, 407, 430.
body, types of. 384.
bogie. 415.
bogie. 404, 407.
bogie car-carrying wagon. 406.
bogie flat wagon. 406.
bogie frame. 404.
bogie open wagon. 406.
bogie tank wagon. 406.
bogie van. 406.
bogie wagon. 405.
bogie well wagon. 406.
boiler room. 419, 425.
bollard. 426.
bonnet. 383, 389.
booking hall. 412.
booster parachute. 443.
boot. 383.
bottom bracket axle. 398.
bottom-end transverse member. 411.
bottom retainer. 405.
bottom side rail. 411.
bow door ramp. 421.
bow horizontal thruster. 423.
bow plane. 423.
bow rudder. 420.
bowl. 429.
bowsprit. 416.
bowstring girder bridge. 401.
brace. 417.
bracket. 428.
brail. 417.
brake cable. 397.
brake lever. 397.
brake line. 393.
brake lining. 393.
brake pad. 393.
brake pedal. 386.
brake shoe. 393.
brake van. 406.
brakes. 393.
bridge. 420, 424.
bridge fin. 424.
brig. 418.
brigantine. 418.
bucket seat. 386.
buckle. 386.
buffer. 404.
bufferstop. 410.
bulk carrier. 427.
bulkhead deck. 420.
bulkhead flat wagon. 406.
bullseye. 432.
bulwark. 416.
bumper. 383, 389.
bunk. 424.
buoys. 430.
by-pass taxiway. 438.
bypass. 400.
cabin. 420, 441.
cable. 428.
cable stay anchorage. 402.
cable-stayed bridge. 402.
cage. 430.
caisson. 427.
caliper. 393.
camshaft. 391.
can. 430.
can buoy. 430.
canal lock. 426.

canal lock. 427.
cantilever bridge. 400.
cantilever span. 400.
capstan. 425.
captain's quarters. 419.
captain's seat. 437.
car. 383, 384, 385, 386.
car anchor. 433.
car deck. 421.
carburettor. 390, 391, 395.
cardinal system of marking. 430.
cargo-bay access hatch. 443.
cargo-bay door. 443.
cargo boom. 420.
cargo hatch. 419.
cargo hold. 419.
cargo terminal. 438.
carousel. 440.
carriageway. 399.
carrier. 397.
cash readout. 387.
catadioptric ring. 432.
catering vehicle. 439.
cell connector. 392.
central console. 437.
central instrument panel. 437.
centre-aisle. 407.
centre bearing. 436.
centre console. 385.
centre electrode. 392.
centre span. 402.
centre stand. 395.
chain. 398.
chain guide. 398.
chain stay. 397.
chain wheel. 397, 398.
change machine. 412.
channel. 409.
chapel. 419.
chassis. 389.
check-in area. 440.
check-rail. 408.
cherry-picker truck. 439.
classification yard. 411.
clearance light. 388.
clew line. 417.
clock. 385.
closure rail. 408.
clutch lever. 396.
clutch pedal. 386.
column. 401.
combustion chamber. 390, 436.
command module. 442.
compass card. 429.
composite topmark. 430.
compressor. 390.
compressor turbine. 390.
cone. 430.
conical buoy. 430.
conning tower. 423.
container. 411.
container. 420.
container flat wagon. 406.
container hold. 420.
container-loading bridge. 427.
container ship. 420.
container ship. 427.
container terminal. 427.
continuous beam. 400.
control cable. 398.
control column. 437, 441.
control room. 424, 431.
control stand. 404.
control tower. 438.
convertible. 384.
cooling air. 444.
cooling fan. 390, 391, 392.
cooling liquid pump. 444.
corner cap. 405.
corner fitting. 411.
corner structure. 411.
corridor. 407.
corridor connection. 407.
counterweight. 403, 408, 409.
coupé. 384.
coupler head. 405.

coupler knuckle. 405.
coupler knuckle pin. 405.
crank. 398, 426.
crankcase. 395.
crew quarters. 419.
cross-ply tyre. 393.
crossbar. 397.
crossing. 410.
crossing gate mechanism. 409.
crossover. 410.
crown. 433.
cupola. 431.
currency exchange counter. 440.
customs control. 440.
customs house. 427.
cut-out button. 396.
cylinder. 395.
cylinder-head. 395.
dashboard. 385.
dating nail. 408.
davit. 416.
deck. 400, 401, 402.
deck arch bridge. 401.
dehumidifier. 444.
delay indicator. 413.
delta wing. 435.
deluxe suite. 419.
departure time indicator. 413.
departures concourse. 440.
departures room. 440.
departures timetable. 412.
depth gauge. 423.
destination indicator. 413.
dial-type display. 428.
diesel-electric locomotive. 404.
diesel engine. 390.
diesel engine. 404, 422.
diesel shop. 410.
dining car. 407.
dining room. 419, 420.
dining section. 407.
dioptric ring. 432.
dip switch. 386, 396.
directional sign. 414.
disc. 393.
disc brake. 393.
disc brake. 395.
distributor. 391.
diver lockout compartment. 423.
door. 386.
door. 383.
door for driver and courier. 394.
door handle. 383.
door hasp. 405.
door hasp fastener. 405.
door lock. 383.
door mirror. 383, 389.
door panel. 415.
door pillar. 383.
door stop. 405.
double fluked anchor. 433.
double-leaf bascule bridge. 403.
double seat. 415.
down tube. 397.
drip moulding. 383.
drive chain. 397.
drive mechanism. 432.
drive shaft. 397.
driver's cab. 404.
driving turbine. 390.
drum. 393.
drum brake. 393.
dry-cell water alarm. 423.
dry dock. 427.
dual seat. 395.
duty-free counter. 440.
dynamics propeller. 421.
dynamo. 397.
east. 430.
echo sounder. 428.
electrical connection. 388.
electrical power unit. 439.
electrically illuminated point signal. 409.
electricity cable. 399.
element. 392.

elevator. 434.
elevon. 443.
emblem. 383.
emergency brake lever. 415.
emergency oxygen supply. 444.
end door. 411.
end ladder. 405.
engine. 391.
engine air intake. 421.
engine block. 391.
engine instruments. 437.
engine mounting pylon. 435.
engine room. 424, 425.
engines. 390.
engines. 443.
entrance turnstile. 414.
escalator. 414.
escape tower. 424.
estate car. 384.
exhaust cone. 436.
exhaust duct. 436.
exhaust gas inlet pipe. 390.
exhaust gas outlet pipe. 390.
exhaust manifold. 390, 391, 392.
exhaust nozzle. 436.
exhaust pipe. 390, 436, 441.
exhaust stack. 389.
exhaust system. 392.
exhaust valve. 390.
exit turnstile. 414.
expansion chamber. 429.
expansion space. 408.
exterior sign. 414.
external tank. 443.
F-1 engine. 442.
fan. 415, 436.
fan belt. 391, 392.
fan blade. 436.
fan cable stays. 402.
ferryboat. 427.
fifth wheel. 389.
filler hole. 391.
filler neck. 389.
filler plug. 429.
fin. 421, 434, 441.
fin-mounted tail unit. 435.
finial. 409.
first officer's seat. 437.
first stage. 442.
fishplate. 408.
fishplate bolt. 408.
fixed arch. 401.
fixed bridges. 400, 401, 402.
fixed distance marking. 438.
fixed stairs. 414.
flap guide rail. 435.
flap servo actuator. 422.
flashing light. 409.
flexible skirt. 421.
flight deck. 437.
flight deck. 434, 441, 443.
flight engineer's panel. 437.
flight engineer's seat. 437.
flight information board. 440.
float. 429.
floating bridge. 403.
floating crane. 427.
floating dock. 427.
fluke. 433.
flying instruments. 437.
flying jib. 417.
flywheel. 390, 391.
fog light. 389.
fold-out table. 407.
foot. 408.
foot brake pedal. 396.
foot rope. 416.
footbridge. 410, 414.
footrest. 396.
footway. 399.
fore royal sail. 417.
fore topmast staysail. 417.
forecourt. 387.
foremast. 416.
foresail. 417.
fork. 397.

The terms in **bold type** indicate the title of an illustration.

fork pocket. 411.
formation level. 399.
foundation of tower. 402.
four-door saloon. 384.
four-foot. 415.
four-masted bark. 416, 417.
frame. 395, 429.
framework. 432.
freight hold. 434.
freight station. 410.
freight wagons, types of. 406.
frigate. 425.
frog. 408.
front. 388.
front bearing. 436.
front brake. 397.
front brake lever. 396.
front bumper. 383.
front derailleur. 397, 398.
front foil. 422.
front footrest. 395.
front mudguard. 395.
front pipe. 392.
front spar. 435.
fuel indicator. 385.
fuel injector pump. 390.
fuel pump belt. 390.
fuel spray manifold. 436.
fuel tank. 389, 395, 422, 431, 441.
fuel tanker. 439.
fuel transfer pipe. 442.
funnel. 420.
funnel aileron. 419.
fuselage. 434.
fuselage mounted tail unit. 435.
gaff sail. 418.
gaff topsail. 417.
gallery. 431.
galley. 434.
garage. 419, 420.
gas inlet. 444.
gas main. 399.
gas outlet. 444.
gas turbine. 421.
gate arm. 409.
gate arm lamp. 409.
gate arm support. 409.
gear selector. 397, 398.
gearbox. 422.
gearchange lever. 385.
gearchange pedal. 395, 396.
gimbal ring. 429.
glass dome. 429.
glass-fibre cloth. 444.
glove. 444.
glove compartment. 385.
grab handle. 389.
grapnel. 433.
gravity band. 433.
gravity shackle. 433.
grille. 383.
ground airport equipment. 439.
ground electrode. 392.
group retarders. 411.
guide bar and live rail. 415.
guiding tower. 403.
gun mounting. 425.
gunter rig whale boat. 418.
gutter. 399.
gyro repeater. 423.
half-through arch bridge. 401.
hall. 419.
halyard. 417.
hand brake gear housing. 405.
hand brake wheel. 405.
hand brake winding chain. 405.
handbrake lever. 385.
handlebars. 397.
handrail. 415.
harbour. 427.
harbour station. 427.
harp cable stays. 402.
hatchback. 384.
head. 408.
head board. 388.
head tube. 397.

headlamp bezel. 384.
headlight. 384.
headlight. 383, 389, 395, 413.
headlight housing shell. 384.
headrest. 386, 407.
heat shield. 443.
heater control. 385.
helicopter. 441.
helicopter. 425.
helicopter hangar and flight deck. 425.
helium sphere. 442.
helmet. 444.
hex nut. 392.
high focal plane buoy. 430.
high-speed exit taxiway. 438.
high tension lead. 391.
highway crossing bell. 409.
hold yard. 411.
holding area marking. 438.
hopper ore wagon. 406.
hopper wagon. 406.
horizon mirror. 429.
horizon mirror shades. 429.
horizontal end handhold. 405.
horn. 385, 404.
horn button. 396.
hotel reservation desk. 440.
housing. 428.
hovercraft. 421.
hub. 397.
hubcap. 383.
hump. 411.
hump area. 411.
hurricane deck. 420.
hydrofoil. 422.
hydrofoil boat. 422.
ignition switch. 396.
immigration control. 440.
incandescent lamp. 432.
index bar. 429.
index mirror. 429.
index shades. 429.
indicator. 388.
indicator board. 413.
indicator lamp. 395.
indicator light. 383.
indicator switch. 386.
inflated carrying tyre. 415.
inflated guiding tyre. 415.
information counter. 440.
information office. 412.
injector. 390.
injector pipe. 390.
inlet guide vanes. 436.
inlet valve. 390, 391.
inner jib. 417.
inner lining. 393.
inner lockout hatch. 423.
instrument panel. 385.
instrument panel. 385.
instrument unit. 442.
insulator. 392.
inter-island ferry. 420.
interior door handle. 386.
interior door lock button. 386.
J-2 engine. 442.
jack staff. 425.
jetfoil. 422.
jewel cap. 429.
jockey roller. 398.
journal box. 404.
junction box. 409.
kerb. 399.
kerb weir. 399.
kerosene. 442.
ketch. 418.
kickstart pedal. 396.
king pin. 404.
kingpin. 388.
kitchen. 407.
knurled button. 428.
landing light. 441.
lantern. 431.
lantern of lighthouse. 432.
lantern pane. 431.

LASH ship. 427.
lateen sail. 418.
lateral system of marking. 430.
launch escape system. 442.
leading edge. 434.
leading edge flap. 434.
left-luggage office. 412.
lens carriage. 432.
level crossing. 409.
level crossing sign. 409.
level crossing with automatic gates. 410.
lever. 387.
life buoy. 422.
life raft. 421, 425.
lifeboat. 416.
lift bridge. 403.
lift-fan air intake. 421.
lift span. 403.
lifting lever. 405.
light. 415, 430.
lighthouse. 431.
limousine. 384.
line map. 414.
liquid compass. 429.
liquid-cooled garment. 444.
liquid hydrogen (fuel). 442.
liquid oxygen (lox). 442.
liquid oxygen (lox) transfer pipe. 442.
litter bin. 414.
livestock van. 406.
living quarters. 431, 443.
lock. 398.
lock-chamber. 426.
lock keeper's building. 427.
lockers. 412.
long-distance coach. 394.
long-range aircraft. 434.
loudspeaker. 415.
lounge. 419.
lower berth. 407.
lower chord. 401.
lower deck. 394.
lower fore topgallant sail. 417.
lower fore topsail. 417.
lower level. 426.
lower mast. 416.
lower side-rail. 388.
lox tank baffles. 442.
lubber's line. 429.
lubber's-line disk. 429.
luggage rack. 384.
lunar boot. 444.
lunar module. 442.
magnet. 429.
main beam warning light. 396.
main engines. 443.
main generator. 404.
main line. 410.
main lower topgallant sail. 417.
main lower topsail. 417.
main passenger entrance door. 394.
main petrol tap. 396.
main royal sail. 417.
main running track. 411.
main sail. 417.
main sewer. 399.
main spar. 435.
main undercarriage. 434.
main undercarriage mounting beam. 435.
main upper topgallant sail. 417.
main upper topsail. 417.
mainmast. 416.
maintenance hangar. 438.
manhole. 399.
manoeuvring engine. 443.
manually-operated points. 408.
maritime signals. 430, 431, 432.
maritime transport. 416.
mast. 409, 410, 441.
master retarders. 411.
masthead. 416.
masthead light. 420.

masting and standing rigging. 416.
medical injection disc. 444.
mercury bath. 432.
mezzanine. 414.
micrometer screw. 429.
mirror. 395.
missile. 424.
missile director. 425.
missile launcher. 425.
missile tube. 424.
mixed gas sphere. 423.
mizzen course. 417.
mizzenmast. 416.
mobile passenger stairs. 439.
motor car. 415.
motor compartment. 423.
motorcycle. 395, 396.
movable bridges. 403.
mud flap. 383, 388, 389.
mudguard. 397.
multiple-span beam bridge. 400.
murette. 431.
mushroom anchor. 433.
navigating bridge. 420.
navigation aids. 428, 429.
navigation light. 434.
navigational radar. 425.
neck ring. 444.
negative plate. 392.
negative plate group. 392.
negative terminal. 392.
north. 430.
nose. 434.
nose cone. 436.
nose wheel. 434.
nozzle. 442.
number of tracks sign. 409.
nut. 408, 428.
observation deck. 440.
observation window. 443.
observer's seat. 437.
odometer. 385.
oil-dip stick. 391.
oil drain plug. 391.
oil filter. 391.
oil indicator. 385.
oil pressure. 396.
oil tank cap. 396.
on-off switch. 428.
open flat semi-trailer. 388.
opening vent. 394.
orbiter. 443.
outbound. 411.
outer jib. 417.
outer lockout hatch. 423.
overbridge. 400.
overhead electric wire. 413.
overhead switch panel. 437.
overrider. 383.
oxygen supply pressure gauge. 444.
paddle valve. 426.
pallet and container transporter. 439.
palm. 433.
panoramic window. 407.
pantograph. 413.
parapet. 400.
parcels office. 412.
parking area. 438.
passenger cabin. 421, 434.
passenger car. 415.
passenger car interior. 415.
passenger coaches, types of. 407.
passenger liner. 419.
passenger platform. 413.
passenger seating. 422.
passenger station. 410.
passenger terminal. 440.
passenger terminal. 438.
passenger transfer vehicle. 439, 440.
passenger walkway. 438.
passport control. 440.

The terms in **bold type** indicate the title of an illustration.

pavement. 399.
payload. 442.
pedal. 397, 398.
pedestal. 387.
peep hole. 409.
periscope. 424.
petrol engine. 391.
petrol flap. 383.
petrol pump. 387.
petrol pump. 387, 391.
petrol pump hose. 387.
petrol tank cap. 396.
pier. 400, 401.
pier foundation. 400.
piggyback flat wagon. 406.
pillion footrest. 395.
pilots control consolette. 423.
pilots control station. 423.
piston. 390, 391, 393.
pitch link. 441.
pivot. 429.
pivot spindle. 384.
placard board. 405.
plate grid. 392.
platform. 388, 403.
platform edge. 413, 414.
platform number. 413.
platform shelter. 410.
platform trolley. 413.
playroom. 419.
point lever. 408.
point lock. 409.
point motor. 409.
point signal. 408.
point wire. 409.
points. 410.
pole. 416.
pole beacon. 430.
pontoon. 403.
poop. 416.
portable life support system. 444.
portable life support system
    control unit. 444.
portal bridge. 401.
porter. 413.
positive plate. 392.
positive plate group. 392.
positive terminal. 392.
potable water truck. 439.
power generators. 431.
power train. 398.
pressure gauge. 444.
pressure relief valve. 444.
pressure suit. 444.
pressure tight hatch. 423.
price per litre/gallon. 387.
primary power distribution panel.
    423.
prismatic section. 432.
prop stand. 395.
propeller. 419, 422, 424.
propeller gearbox. 421.
propeller shaft. 419, 420, 422.
pull rod. 408.
pulley. 391.
pulse of sound. 428.
pump attendant. 387.
pump nozzle. 387.
pushback tractor. 439.
pylon. 421.
quarter window. 383.
quayside crane. 427.
quayside railway. 427.
racing car. 384.
rack. 432.
radar. 421.
radar mast. 424.
radial passenger loading area. 438.
radial ply. 393.
radial tyre. 393.
radiator. 392.
radiator. 392, 404.
radiator hose. 392.
radiator pressure cap. 392.
radio antenna. 444.
radio mast. 424.

rail. 408.
rail anchor. 408.
rail joint. 408.
rail transport. 404.
railway map. 412.
railway station. 410.
railway track. 408, 409.
ramp. 410.
reactor. 424.
reactor compartment. 424.
rear brake. 397.
rear derailleur. 397.
rear foil. 422.
rear light. 383, 388, 395, 397.
rear load area. 384.
rear-mounted engine. 394.
rear of estate car. 384.
rear seat. 386.
rear suspension unit. 395.
rear window. 383.
rear window frame. 383.
rearview mirror. 385.
receiver-indicator. 428.
receiving yard. 411.
recovery vehicle. 387.
red marker light. 388.
reef band. 417.
reef point. 417.
reflector. 388.
refrigeration unit. 388.
refrigerator van. 406.
release bar. 389.
release handle. 386.
relief track. 410.
remote-control arm. 443.
remote-controlled points. 409.
reserve petrol tap. 396.
resonator. 392.
retaining ring. 384.
return spring. 393.
reversing light. 383.
revolution counter. 385.
rigs, types of. 418.
rim. 393, 395, 397.
rim flange. 393.
ring. 433.
road, cross section of a. 399.
road base. 399.
road transport. 383.
rock sample pocket. 444.
rocker cover. 391.
rocket. 442.
roll-on roll-off ramp. 427.
roller. 432.
roof. 383, 388, 411.
root rib. 435.
rotor blade. 436, 441.
rotor head. 441.
rotor hub. 441.
routing cardboard. 405.
royal mast. 416.
rub rail. 388.
rubber wall. 393.
rubbing strip. 393.
rudder. 419, 421, 424, 434, 443.
rudder pedal. 437.
running rail. 415.
running track. 411.
runway. 415, 438.
runway centre line markings. 438.
runway designation marking. 438.
runway end lights. 438.
runway side markings. 438.
runway threshold markings. 438.
runway touchdown zone marking.
    438.
saddle. 397.
safety bar. 388.
safety line. 414.
sail plan. 417.
sails, types of. 418.
saloon open coach. 407.
scissor-lift truck. 439.
screen wiper. 394.
scrubber. 423.
scuttle panel. 383.

sea anchor. 433.
sealed-beam mounting ring. 384.
seat belt. 386.
seat post. 397.
seat stay. 397.
seat tube. 397.
seats. 386.
second stage. 442.
security check. 440.
sediment chamber. 392.
semaphore. 410.
semi-trailer. 388.
semi-trailer. 389.
separator. 392.
service module. 442.
service room. 431.
service station. 387.
sextant. 429.
shank. 433.
sheet. 417.
ship's anchor. 433.
ship's motor boat. 425.
ship's side. 416.
shroud. 416.
shunting engine. 411.
side door. 411.
side handrail. 415.
side ladder. 405.
side ladder tread. 405.
side panel. 383.
side platform. 414.
side span. 402.
side wall. 411, 426.
side window. 389.
sidelight. 413.
sidewall. 388.
signal background plate. 409.
signal box. 410.
signal gantry. 410.
signalbox and yard office. 411.
signals. 409.
silencer. 392, 395.
sill step. 405.
simple-span beam bridge. 400.
simple topmarks. 430.
single-leaf bascule bridge. 403.
single seat. 415.
siren. 422.
skid. 441.
skid ramp. 389.
skirt finger. 421.
slat. 426.
sleeper. 408.
sleeping car. 407.
slide chair. 409.
sliding window. 407.
sluice hole. 426.
smoke filter. 419.
snort exhaust. 424.
snort induction. 424.
snow tyre. 393.
soleplate. 408.
solid-rocket booster. 443.
sonar display and control. 423.
sonar housing. 423.
sonic height sensor. 422.
south. 430.
space shuttle. 443.
space shuttle at take-off. 443.
space shuttle in orbit. 443.
space travel. 442.
spacelab. 443.
spacesuit. 444.
spanker. 417.
spanker boom. 416.
spanker gaff. 416.
spark plug. 392.
spark plug body. 392.
spark plug gap. 392.
spark plug gasket. 392.
spark plug terminal. 392.
speaking window membrane. 412.
speedometer. 385, 396.
sphere. 430.
spike. 408.
spleeping compartment. 407.

spline. 392.
spoiler. 434.
spoke. 397.
spotlight. 422.
spring. 404.
spring washer. 408.
sprocket cluster. 398.
squab. 386.
square sail. 418.
St George's cross. 430.
stabilizer. 420.
stabilizing fin. 442.
stabilizing plane. 423.
starter. 391.
starting signal. 413.
station concourse. 412.
station name. 414.
station platform. 413.
station platform. 410.
station sign. 413.
stator vane. 436.
stay. 416.
staysail-stay. 416.
steam generator. 424.
steam turbine. 420.
steel safety wheel. 415.
steering. 386.
steering column. 386.
steering damper. 396.
steering lock. 396.
steering wheel. 385, 386.
stem. 397, 416.
step. 389.
stern horizontal thruster. 423.
stern loading door. 420.
stern vertical thruster. 423.
stiffening girder. 402.
stock. 433.
stocked anchor. 433.
stockless anchor. 433.
straight wing. 435.
street, cross section of a. 399.
stretcher bar. 409.
stringer. 435.
strut. 422.
stud. 393, 428.
sub-base. 399.
subgrade. 399.
submerged foils. 422.
submersible. 423.
suburban commuter railway. 410.
subway to platforms. 412.
sump. 391.
sun roof. 383.
sun visor. 385.
sundeck. 419.
surface-piercing foils. 422.
surface water drain. 399.
suspended span. 400.
suspender. 402.
suspension bridge. 402.
suspension cable. 402.
swept-back wing. 435.
swimming pool. 419.
swing bridge. 403.
switch rail. 408.
T-tail unit. 435.
tachometer. 396.
tail. 434.
tail assembly. 434.
tail boom. 441.
tail pipe. 392.
tail pipe extension. 392.
tail plane. 434, 441.
tail rotor. 441.
tail shape. 435.
tailgate. 384.
tangent clamp. 429.
tanks. 443.
tapered wing. 435.
tarpaulin covered open wagon.
    406.
taxiway. 438.
telephone cable. 399.
telescope. 429.
telescopic corridor. 438.

The terms in **bold type** indicate the title of an illustration.

telescopic front fork. 395.
telescoping uncoupling rod. 405.
temperature indicator. 385.
tension roller. 398.
tension spring. 384.
theatre. 419.
third stage. 442.
three-hinged arch. 401.
throat. 433.
throttles. 437.
ticket collector's booth. 414.
ticket counter. 412, 440.
ticket office. 412.
timetables. 412.
toe clip. 397.
toilet. 407.
toilet truck. 439.
top. 416.
top-end transverse member. 411.
topgallant mast. 416.
topmark. 430.
topmast. 416.
topping lift. 416.
torpedo. 424.
torpedo storage compartment. 424.
tourist-class cabin. 419.
tow tractor. 439.
tower. 402.
tower crane. 427.
towing truck. 387.
track. 413, 414, 415.
traction motor. 404.
traction motor ventilator. 404.
tractor unit. 389.
tractor unit. 389.
trailer leg. 388.
trailer leg foot. 388.
trailer leg winding gear. 388.
trailing edge. 434.
trailing edge flap. 434.
train delays notice board. 412.
train set. 410.
transceiver. 444.
transducer. 428.
transit shed. 427.
transport. 381.
transporter bridge. 403.
tread bracing layer. 393.
tread design. 393.
trim system control valve. 423.
triple tail unit. 435.
trolley. 403.
trough. 409.
truck trailer. 389.
trussed arch. 401.
tuning control. 428.
turbine. 424, 436.
turbine blade. 436.
turbine-compressor shaft. 436.
turbine guide vane. 436.
turbo-charged engine. 390.
turbo-jet engine. 436.
turbocharger. 404.
turbofan engine. 436.
turbofan jet engine. 434.
turnbuckle. 409.
turntable. 403.
twin turret. 425.
twist grip throttle. 396.
two-door saloon. 384.
two-hinged arch. 401.
two-masted staysail schooner. 418.
type of fuel. 387.
tyre. 389, 397.
tyre pump. 397.
tyre rack. 387.
tyre valve. 397.
tyres. 393.
underground map. 414, 415.
underground railway. 415.
underground station. 414.
underground train. 415.
underwater communications set. 423.
universal step. 439.
upper berth. 407.

upper chord. 401.
upper deck. 394, 420.
upper fore topgallant sail. 417.
upper fore topsail. 417.
upper level. 426.
upper side-rail. 388.
upstream gate. 426.
upstream level. 426.
urine transfer fitting. 444.
valve spring. 390, 391.
vanity mirror. 385.
variable depth sonar. 425.
variable geometry wing. 435.
vent. 385.
vent cap. 392.
vent door. 388.
ventilating fan. 404.
vestibule. 407.
vestibule door. 407.
VHF aerial. 435.
viaduct. 400.
visor. 409, 444.
volume readout. 387.
wagon. 411.
waiting room. 412.
warning light. 396.
washroom and toilet. 394.
water bottle. 397.
water bottle clip. 397.
water main. 399.
water pump. 392.
water tank. 404, 407.
waterline. 425.
wearing course. 399.
weather radar. 434.
web. 408.
west. 430.
wheel. 393.
wheel. 383, 389.
wheel chock. 439.
wheel cylinder. 393.
wheelhouse. 421, 422.
whistle buoy. 430.
winch. 420, 425.
wind deflector. 389.
windlass. 422.
window. 383, 415, 434.
window winder handle. 386.
windscreen. 383, 389.
windscreen wiper. 384.
windscreen wiper blade. 384.
windshield. 434, 437.
wine cellar. 419.
wing. 383, 389, 434, 443.
wing rib. 435.
wing shape. 435.
wing structure. 435.
wing tip. 435.
wiper arm. 384.
wiper blade rubber. 384.
wiper switch. 386.
workshop. 387.
yard. 411.
yard. 416.

VEGETABLE KINGDOM

abruptly pinnate. 62.
achene. 66, 70.
almond. 67, 70.
Amanita virosa. 65.
anther. 64.
apple. 68.
apple. 68.
apricot. 67.
artichoke. 73.
asparagus. 77.
aubergine. 73.
autumn squash. 73.
avocado. 72.
axillary bud. 61, 62.
banana. 72.
bark. 63.
bean sprouts. 77.
beetroot. 76.

berries, major types of. 66.
berry, section of a. 66.
black currant. 66.
black salsify. 76.
blade. 62.
blueberry. 66.
bole. 63.
bract. 70.
branch. 63, 77.
branches. 63.
Brazil nut. 70.
broad beans. 77.
broad-leaved endive. 74.
broccoli. 73.
brush. 71.
Brussels sprouts. 74.
bud. 75.
bulb. 77.
bulb, section of a. 75.
bulb vegetables. 75.
bulbil. 75.
bundle. 77.
cabbage lettuce. 74.
calyx. 64, 66, 68, 71.
cambium. 63.
cantaloupe. 73.
cap. 65.
capitulum. 64.
capsule. 71.
capsule, section of a. 71.
cardoon. 77.
carrot. 76.
cashew. 70.
cauliflower. 73.
celeriac. 76.
celery. 77.
cep. 65.
chanterelle. 65.
chard. 74.
cherimoya. 72.
cherry. 67.
chestnut. 70.
chick peas. 77.
chicory. 74.
chilli pepper. 73.
Chinese cabbage. 74.
chive. 75.
ciliate. 62.
citrus fruit, section of a. 69.
citrus fruits, major types of. 69.
cob. 77.
coconut. 70.
collar. 61.
compound fleshy fruits. 66.
compound leaves. 62.
cordate. 62.
core. 68.
corn salad. 74.
corolla. 64.
corymb. 64.
cos lettuce. 74.
cotyledon. 61, 67, 71.
courgette. 73.
cranberry. 66.
crenate. 62.
crown. 63.
cucumber. 73.
cultivated mushroom. 65.
cupule. 70.
curled endive. 74.
curled kale. 74.
currant. 66.
dandelion. 74.
date. 67.
deadly mushroom. 65.
delicious lactarius. 65.
dentate. 62.
doubly dentate. 62.
druplet. 66.
dry fruits. 70, 71.
edible gyromitra. 65.
edible mushrooms. 65.
embryo. 67.
endocarp. 67, 68.
entire. 62.
epicalyx. 66.

exocarp. 66, 67, 68.
fennel. 77.
filament. 64.
flesh. 66, 67, 68.
fleshy fruits: berry fruits. 66.
fleshy fruits: citrus fruits. 69.
flower. 61.
flower, structure of a. 64.
flower bud. 61.
fly agaric. 65.
foliage. 63.
follicle. 71.
follicle, section of a. 71.
fruit vegetables. 73.
funiculus. 66, 71.
garden sorrel. 74.
garlic. 75.
germ. 71.
gill. 65.
gooseberry. 66.
grain of wheat, section of a. 71.
grape. 66.
grape. 66.
grapefruit. 69.
green bean. 73.
green cabbage. 74.
green peas. 77.
green russula. 65.
green walnut. 70.
guava. 72.
hazelnut. 70.
hazelnut, section of a. 70.
head. 77.
heartwood. 63.
horseradish. 76.
hot pepper. 73.
huckleberry. 66.
hull. 71.
husk. 70, 77.
hypha. 65.
Indian fig. 72.
inflorescences, types of. 64.
inflorescent vegetables. 73.
internode. 61.
Japan plum. 68.
Japanese persimmon. 72.
Jerusalem artichoke. 76.
juice sac. 69.
kernel. 70, 77.
kiwi. 72.
kohlrabi. 76.
kumquat. 69.
lanceolate. 62.
lateral root. 61.
leaf. 62.
leaf. 61, 77.
leaf axil. 61, 62.
leaf margin. 62.
leaf vegetables. 74.
leaves, types of. 62.
leek. 75.
legume, section of a. 71.
lemon. 69.
lentils. 77.
limb. 63.
linear. 62.
litchi. 72.
lobed. 62.
loculus. 68.
mandarin. 69.
mangetout. 77.
mango. 67.
margin. 62.
marrow. 73.
mesocarp. 66, 67, 68, 69.
midrib. 62, 71.
morel. 65.
mushroom, structure of a. 65.
mushrooms. 65.
muskmelon. 73.
mustard. 71.
mycelium. 65.
nectarine. 67.
node. 61.
nut. 70.
nuts, major types of. 70.

The terms in **bold type** indicate the title of an illustration.

okra. 73.
olive. 67.
orange. 69.
orange. 69.
orbicular. 62.
ovary. 64.
ovate. 62.
ovule. 62.
oyster mushroom. 65.
palmate. 62.
papaya. 72.
parsnip. 76.
partition. 70.
pea. 71.
pea. 71.
peach. 67.
peach. 67.
peanut. 70.
pear. 68.
pecan nut. 70.
pedicel. 64, 66, 68.
peltate. 62.
pericarp. 69, 70.
petals. 64.
petiole. 62.
phloem. 63.
pickling onion. 75.
pine kernel. 70.
pineapple. 72.
pinnate. 62.
pinnatifid. 62.
pip. 68, 69.
pistachio nut. 70.
pistil. 64.
pith. 63.
plant, structure of a. 61, 62.
plum. 67.
poisonous mushroom. 65.
pome fleshy fruits. 68.
pome fruit, section of a. 68.
pome fruits, principal types of. 68.
pomegranate. 72.
poppy. 71.
pore. 71.
potato. 76.
primary root. 61.
pulp. 69.
pumpkin. 73.
quince. 68.
raceme. 64.
radicle. 63.
radish. 76.
raspberry. 66.
receptacle. 64, 66.
reniform. 62.
rhubarb. 77.
rib. 77.
rind. 69.
ring. 63, 65.
root. 61.
root. 61, 75.
root cap. 61.
root-hair zone. 63.
root hairs. 61.
root vegetables. 76.
sagittate. 62.
salsify. 76.
sapwood. 63.
scale. 65.
scale leaf. 75.
secondary root. 61.
seed. 66, 67, 68, 69, 70, 71.
seed coat. 67, 71.
seed vegetables. 77.
segment. 69.
sepal. 66.
sepals. 64.
septum. 71.
shallot. 75.
shallow root. 63.
sheath. 62.
shell. 70.
shoot. 61, 63.
silique, section of a. 71.
silk. 77.

simple leaves. 62.
skin. 66, 67, 68.
soybeans. 77.
spadix. 64.
Spanish onion. 75.
spathulate. 62.
spear. 77.
spike. 64.
spinach. 74.
spores. 65.
spring onion. 75.
stalk. 66, 68, 77.
stalk vegetables. 77.
stamen. 64, 68.
star anise. 71.
starch. 71.
stem. 61.
stem. 61, 65, 75.
stigma. 64, 70.
stipule. 62.
stone. 66, 67.
stone fleshy fruits. 67.
stone fruit, section of a. 67.
stone fruits, major types of. 67.
strawberry, section of a. 66.
string. 77.
stump. 63.
style. 64, 66, 67, 68, 71.
suture. 71.
swede. 76.
sweet corn. 77.
sweet pepper. 73.
sweet potato. 76.
Swiss chard. 77.
taproot. 63.
terminal bud. 61.
tip. 62, 77.
tomato. 73.
top. 63.
tree. 63.
tree, structure of a. 63.
trifoliolate. 62.
tropical fruits. 72.
tropical fruits, major types of. 72.
truffle. 65.
trunk. 63.
trunk, cross section of a. 63.
tuber vegetables. 76.
turnip. 76.
twig. 61, 63.
umbel. 64.
valve. 71.
vegetable kingdom. 59.
vegetables. 73, 74, 75, 76, 77.
vein. 62.
vine leaf. 74.
volva. 65.
wall. 69.
walnut. 70.
walnut, section of a. 70.
water cress. 74.
watermelon. 73.
white cabbage. 74.
wild blackberry, section of a. 66.
wood ray. 63.
zest. 69.

WEAPONS

African warrior. 675.
aileron. 691.
air brake. 691.
air brake hydraulic jack. 691.
air cleaner. 690.
air-to-air missile. 691, 692.
air-to-surface missile. 692.
ammunition stowage. 690.
anti-tank missile. 692.
armet. 676.
armet. 676.
armour. 676.
arquebus. 682.
arrester hook. 691.
arrow. 677.

arrow rest. 677.
automatic rifle. 685.
auxiliary sighting telescope. 690.
back. 677.
ball. 682.
barrel. 681.
barrel. 680, 683, 684, 685, 686, 687, 688, 689.
barrel catch. 689.
barrel jacket. 683.
barrel nut. 685.
base. 688.
base plug. 682.
base ring. 680.
baseplate. 683.
bayonets. 679.
bayonets, major types of. 679.
bazooka. 686.
beaver. 676.
belly. 677.
bipod. 683, 687.
blade. 679.
bolt. 687.
bolt carrier. 685.
bolt catch. 685.
bolt guide. 677.
bore. 681.
bow. 677.
bow. 677.
bow irons. 677.
bows. 677.
bowstring. 677.
breastplate. 676.
breech. 680, 688.
breechblock. 684.
breechblock operating lever assembly. 684.
breeching rope. 680.
brow reinforce. 676.
buffer. 687.
bullet. 688.
butt. 677, 683, 685, 687, 689.
butt plate. 688.
cam lever. 689.
canister shot. 681.
canopy. 691.
cardboard case. 688.
carriage. 680.
carrying handle. 685, 687.
cartridge. 688, 689.
cartridge (rifle). 688.
cartridge (shotgun). 688.
cascable button. 680.
case. 688.
catch. 679.
catch spring. 679.
chain mail. 676.
chain shot. 681.
chamber. 689.
charge. 688.
charging handle. 685.
charging handle catch. 685.
chase. 680.
chase astragal. 680.
cheek. 690.
circuit test light. 686.
co-axial machine gun. 690.
cock. 682.
cocking handle. 687.
cocking lever. 686.
comb. 676.
combat aircraft. 691.
combustion chamber. 692.
command station. 692.
command system. 692.
command transmission. 692.
commander's seat. 690.
commando knife. 678.
core. 688.
cotton pagne. 675.
couter. 676.
cover. 687.
cradle. 684.
cross-guard. 679.
crossbow. 677.
crossbow. 677.

cuirass. 675.
cuisse. 676.
cup. 688.
cupola. 690.
cylinder. 689.
cylinder cam. 689.
daggers. 678.
dagger. 675, 678.
detonator. 682.
distance tube. 686.
dolphin. 680.
double barrel. 688.
double-edged swords. 678.
drawbar. 684.
drawbar lock. 684.
drive wheel. 690.
driver's seat. 690.
ejection port. 683, 685, 687.
ejection seat. 691.
elevating handle. 683.
elevating handwheel. 684.
elongating bar shot. 681.
equilibrator. 684.
exhaust nozzle. 691.
exhaust pipe. 690.
exploder. 686.
explosive. 682.
extractor. 689.
extractor spring. 689.
feather fletching. 677.
feed cover. 687.
feed tray. 687.
filling hole. 682.
fin. 692.
fin tip. 691.
fire control lever. 685.
firing, accessories for. 681.
firing chamber. 688.
firing lanyard. 684.
firing pin. 688.
firing pine. 689.
firing rod. 686.
firing shaft. 684.
first reinforce. 680.
first reinforce ring. 680.
flap. 691.
flap hydraulic jack. 691.
flash deflector. 686.
flash hider. 685, 687.
flint. 682.
flint arrowhead. 675.
flint knife. 675.
flintlock. 682.
float. 684.
forearm. 687, 688.
forward bolt assist mechanism. 685.
front grip. 686.
front sight. 686, 688, 689.
front sight housing. 685, 687.
front sight protector. 683.
fuel tank. 692.
fume extractor. 690.
gas cylinder. 687.
gas piston. 687.
gauntlet. 676.
gladius. 675.
gorget. 676.
grapeshot. 681.
greave. 676.
grip. 679.
guidance system. 692.
guide rods. 684.
gun. 690.
gunner's sight. 690.
hammer. 688, 689.
hand grenade. 682.
handguard. 685.
handle. 677.
hatch. 690.
headlight. 690.
heavy machine gun. 687.
helmet. 675.
hilted bayonet. 679.
hilted bayonet, parts of a. 679.
horizontal stabilizer. 691.

The terms in **bold type** indicate the title of an illustration.

THEMATIC INDEXES

hunting weapons. **688.**
in-flight refuelling probe. 691.
integral bayonet. 679.
jacket. 688.
javelin. 675.
jet engine. 691.
ladle. 681.
lance rest. 676.
lanyard ring. 689.
large bastard sword. 678.
leather garment. 675.
leather sandal. 675.
left-hand grip. 686.
lever. 682.
lifting handle. 684.
light machine gun. 687.
linstock. 681.
loader's seat. 690.
loading. 682.
locking ring. 684.
long-range radar system. 692.
lower limb. 677.
machete. 678.
machine gun. 690.
magazine. 683, 685, 688, 689.
magazine base. 689.
magazine catch. 685, 689.
magazine housing latch. 683.
magazine release. 685.
magazine spring. 689.
main shield bracket. 684.
main spring. 689.
main undercarriage wheel. 691.
missile. 692.
missile, structure of a. 692.
missile launch rail. 691.
missile tracking radar. 692.
missiles. 692.
missiles, major types of modern. 692.
modern bow. 677.
modern howitzer. 684.
mortar. 683.
muzzle. 680, 683, 688.
muzzle astragal. 680.
muzzle loading. 680, 681.
muzzle moulding. 680.
muzzle ring. 679.
nock. 677.
nocking point. 677.
nose. 676.
nozzle. 692.
nut. 677.
ogee. 680.
one-handed sword. 678.
operating rod. 687.
oxidizer tank. 692.
pan. 682.
pan cover. 682.
panoramic periscope. 690.
patch. 682.
pauldron. 676.
pellets. 688.
pistol. 689.
pistol grip. 683, 685, 687, 688.
Pitot tube. 691.
pivot. 683.
plug bayonet. 679.
point. 677.
poleyn. 676.
polished-stone hand axe. 675.
pommel. 679.
poniard. 678.
powder. 681.
powder flask. 682.
primer. 682, 688.
projectiles. 681.
propellant. 688.
quillon. 679.
quoin. 680.
radar warning receiver. 691.
radome. 691.
rammer. 681.
ramrod. 682.
rangefinder. 690.
rapier. 678.

rear end cap. 686.
rear sight. 683, 686, 687, 688, 689.
rear sight adjustment drum. 685.
rearview mirror. 690.
receiver. 683, 685, 687.
recoil sleigh. 684.
recoil spring. 689.
recoilless rifle. 686.
recuperator cylinder. 684.
recuperator cylinder front head. 684.
rerebrace. 676.
retractable boarding ladder. 691.
revolver. 689.
rifle (rifled bore). 688.
right elevating arc. 684.
right-hand grip. 686.
ring. 682.
Roman legionary. 675.
rondel. 676.
sabaton. 676.
sabre. 678.
safety. 683, 685.
safety pin. 682.
sandal. 675.
sear. 687.
second reinforce. 680.
second reinforce ring. 680.
serrated cast-iron casing. 682.
shaft. 677.
shell. 686, 690.
shield. 675.
ship's cannon. 680, 681.
shot. 681.
shotgun (smooth-bore). 688.
shoulder pad. 686.
shoulder stock. 686.
sight. 677, 683.
single-edged swords. 678.
skirt. 676.
skull. 676.
slide. 689.
sliding breech. 684.
sling. 680, 685, 686, 687.
sling swivel. 685.
slip ring. 685.
smoke bomb discharger. 690.
socket bayonet. 679.
solleret. 676.
spade. 684.
sponge. 681.
spring. 682, 686.
stabilizer. 677.
steel. 682.
steel spring. 682.
steering lever. 690.
stiletto. 678.
stirrup. 677.
stock. 688.
Stone Age arms. 675.
strap. 676.
striker. 682.
stroboscopic light. 691.
submachine gun. 683.
surface-to-air missile. 692.
surface-to-subsurface missile. 692.
surface-to-surface missile. 692.
swell of the muzzle. 680.
sword-breaker. 678.
swords. 678.
takedown pin. 685.
tank. 690.
tanker. 691.
target. 692.
target tracking radar. 692.
tasset. 676.
telescopic sight mounting. 686.
throwing spear. 675.
tiller. 677.
time fuse. 682.
towing eye. 684.
track. 690.
track link. 690.
trail. 684.

traversing and elevating mechanism. 687.
traversing handle. 683.
trigger. 677, 682, 683, 685, 686, 687, 688, 689.
trigger guard. 683, 688, 689.
tripod. 687.
trunnion. 680.
tube. 683, 686.
turbopump. 692.
turret. 690.
two-handed sword. 678.
UHF-IFF aerial. 691.
underlever. 688.
upper limb. 677.
vambrace. 676.
vane. 692.
vent. 680, 681.
vent field astragal. 680.
ventail. 676.
venturi. 686.
venturi fastening lever. 686.
visor. 676.
wad. 681, 688.
warhead. 692.
weapons. 673.
wheel. 680, 690.
winch. 690.
windscreen. 691.
wing. 676.
wing box. 691.
worm. 681.

The terms in **bold type** indicate the title of an illustration.

SPECIALIZED INDEXES

ATHLETICS

approach. 556, 557.
arena. 556, 557.
asymmetrical bars. 560.
balance beam. 560.
bar. 561.
base. 559.
beam. 560.
bed. 560.
belt. 561.
body. 558.
boot. 561.
cable. 561.
collar. 561.
cord grip. 558.
crossbar. 556, 557.
croup. 559.
disc. 561.
discus. 558.
discus throw. 556.
field events. 558.
finish line. 557.
finishing post. 557.
flight. 560.
frame. 559, 560.
gauze bandage. 561.
glove. 560.
guy cable. 559.
gymnast. 560.
gymnastics. 559, 560.
hammer. 558.
hammer throw. 556.
handle. 558.
head. 558.
high jump. 557.
horizontal bar. 559.
hurdle. 556.
javelin throw. 557.
javelins. 558.
knee pad. 561.
landing. 560.
landing area. 556, 557.
landing mat. 560.
lane. 557.
leg. 560.
long jump. 556.
low bar. 560.
metal head. 558.
neck. 559.
parallel bars. 559.
planting box. 556.
plasticine board. 556.
platform. 561.
pole. 556.
pole vault. 556.
pommel. 559.
pommel horse. 559.
rim. 558.
ring. 559.
rings. 559.
run. 560.
running track. 556.
saddle. 559.
safety cage. 556.
safety pad. 560.

second flight. 560.
sector flag. 556.
shaft. 558.
short-sleeved shirt. 561.
shot put. 557.
shots. 558.
sleeve. 561.
spring. 560.
springboard. 559, 560.
start line. 556.
steel bar. 559.
steeplechase. 556.
stopboard. 557.
strap. 559.
support. 560.
swivel. 558.
take-off board. 556, 557.
take-off line. 556.
throwing arc. 557.
throwing circle. 556, 557.
tip. 558.
top bar. 560.
track. 557.
**track and field athletics. 556,
557.**
trampoline. 560.
triple jump. 557.
trunks. 561.
two-hand clean and jerk. 561.
two-hand snatch. 561.
upright. 556, 557, 559, 560.
vaulting horse. 559, 560.
water ditch. 556.
weight. 558, 561.
weightlifter. 561.
weightlifting. 561.
wire. 558.
wooden bar. 559.

BASEBALL

backstop. 520.
bag. 520.
ball. 521.
baseball. 520, 521.
bat. 521.
bat. 521.
batter. 520.
batter's box. 520.
batter's helmet. 521.
batting glove. 521.
catcher. 521.
catcher. 520.
catcher's box. 520.
catcher's glove. 521.
centre field. 520.
centre fielder. 520.
chest protector. 521.
coach's box. 520.
cover. 521.
field (baseball). 520.
finger. 521.
first base. 520.
first baseman. 520.
foul line. 520.

glove. 521.
handle. 521.
heel. 521.
hitting area. 521.
home plate. 520.
infield. 520.
knee pad. 521.
knob. 521.
lace. 521.
left field. 520.
left fielder. 520.
mask. 521.
mound. 520.
on-deck circle. 520.
outfield. 520.
palm. 521.
pants. 521.
pitcher. 520.
pitcher's plate. 520.
player. 521.
players' bench. 520.
right field. 520.
right fielder. 520.
second base. 520.
second baseman. 520.
shin guard. 521.
shortstop. 520.
spiked shoe. 521.
stirrup sock. 521.
stitches. 521.
strap. 521.
tape. 521.
team shirt. 521.
third base. 520.
third baseman. 520.
throat protector. 521.
thumb. 521.
umpire-in-chief. 520.
undershirt. 521.
web. 521.

BICYCLE

bicycle. 397, 398.
bicycle horn. 398.
bottom bracket axle. 398.
brake cable. 397.
brake lever. 397.
carrier. 397.
chain. 398.
chain guide. 398.
chain stay. 397.
chain wheel. 397, 398.
control cable. 398.
crank. 398.
crossbar. 397.
down tube. 397.
drive chain. 397.
dynamo. 397.
fork. 397.
front brake. 397.
front derailleur. 397, 398.
gear selector. 397, 398.
handlebars. 397.
head tube. 397.

hub. 397.
jockey roller. 398.
lock. 398.
mudgard. 397.
pedal. 397, 398.
power train. 398.
rear brake. 397.
rear derailleur. 397.
rear light. 397.
rim. 397.
saddle. 397.
seat post. 397.
seat stay. 397.
seat tube. 397.
spoke. 397.
sprocket cluster. 398.
stem. 397.
tension roller. 398.
toe clip. 397.
tyre. 397.
tyre pump. 397.
tyre valve. 397.
water bottle. 397.
water bottle clip. 397.

CAMPING

4-berth caravan. 581.
air mattress. 584.
air pumps. 584.
aluminium panel. 581.
awning. 582.
awning channel. 581.
Baker tent. 583.
bed-mattress. 584.
belt loop. 585.
blade. 585.
bow saw. 586.
butane accessories. 585.
butane cylinder. 585.
**camping equipment. 584, 585,
586.**
canopy. 582.
canopy pole. 582.
canvas divider. 582.
caravan. 581.
chassis. 581.
control valve. 585.
cooking. 586.
cooking set. 585.
cool box. 586.
corkscrew. 585.
corner stay. 581.
cup. 585.
dome tent. 583.
double glazed window. 581.
family tent. 583.
family tents. 582.
file. 585.
flysheet. 583.
foam mattress. 584.
foam pad. 584.
folding camp bed. 584.
folding grill. 586.
folding shovel. 586.

The terms in **bold type** indicate the title of an illustration.

fork. 585.
frying pan. 585.
gauge. 585.
grab handle. 581.
grommet. 583.
guy line adapter. 583.
guy rope. 582.
handbrake lever. 581.
handle. 585.
hatchet. 586.
heater. 585.
height. 581.
hurricane lamp. 586.
inner tent. 583.
jockey wheel. 581.
jockey wheel handle. 581.
lantern. 585.
leather sheath. 585.
length. 581.
lighting. 586.
lighting cable. 581.
living room. 582.
maker's name. 581.
mud wall. 582.
mudguard. 581.
mummy. 584.
peg. 582, 583.
pegging-out point. 583.
penknife. 585.
plate. 585.
pole. 582.
pole loop. 582.
pressure regulator. 585.
pyramid tent. 583.
rain sill. 581.
rectangular. 584.
refrigerator vent. 581.
ridge pole. 582.
ridge tent. 583.
roof. 582.
roof vent and light. 581.
room. 582.
rubbing strake. 581.
saucepan. 585.
saw. 585.
scissors. 585.
screen window. 582.
screwdriver. 585.
self-erecting tent. 583.
semi-mummy. 584.
sewn-in groundsheet. 582.
sheath knife. 586.
side moulding. 581.
single burner camp stove. 585.
sleeping bags. 584.
sleeve. 582.
small blade. 585.
spoon. 585.
stable type door. 581.
strainer. 582.
teapot. 585.
tents. 582, 583.
tents, types of. 583.
three-burner camp stove. 585.
tie flap. 581.
tin opener. 585.
tools. 586.
tow-bar cover. 581.
towing hitch. 581.
vacuum flask. 586.
wagon tent. 583.
wall. 582.
wardrobe. 582.
water bottle. 586.
water carrier. 586.
wheel. 581.
white front width light. 581.
width. 581.
wind baffle. 585.
window. 582.
wire support. 585.
zip. 583.
zipped screen door. 582.

CAR

accelerator pedal. 386.
aerial. 383.
alternator indicator. 385.
arm rest. 386.
articulation. 384.
body, types of. 384.
bonnet. 383.
boot. 383.
brake pedal. 386.
bucket seat. 386.
buckle. 386.
bumper. 383.
car. 383, 384, 385, 386.
centre console. 385.
clock. 385.
clutch pedal. 386.
convertible. 384.
coupé. 384.
dashboard. 385.
dip switch. 386.
door. 386.
door. 383.
door handle. 383.
door lock. 383.
door mirror. 383.
door pillar. 383.
drip moulding. 383.
emblem. 383.
estate car. 384.
four-door saloon. 384.
front bumper. 383.
fuel indicator. 385.
gearchange lever. 385.
glove compartment. 385.
grille. 383.
handbrake lever. 385.
hatchback. 384.
headlamp bezel. 384.
headlight. 384.
headlight. 383.
headlight housing shell. 384.
headrest. 386.
heater control. 385.
horn. 385.
hubcap. 383.
indicator light. 383.
indicator switch. 386.
instrument panel. 385.
instrument panel. 385.
interior door handle. 386.
interior door lock button. 386.
limousine. 384.
luggage rack. 384.
mud flap. 383.
odometer. 385.
oil indicator. 385.
overrider. 383.
petrol flap. 383.
pivot spindle. 384.
quarter window. 383.
racing car. 384.
rear light. 383.
rear load area. 384.
rear of estate car. 384.
rear seat. 386.
rear window. 383.
rear window frame. 383.
rearview mirror. 385.
release handle. 386.
retaining ring. 384.
reversing light. 383.
revolution counter. 385.
road transport. 383.
roof. 383.
scuttle panel. 384.
sealed-beam mounting ring. 384.
seat belt. 386.
seats. 386.
side panel. 383.
speedometer. 385.
squab. 386.
steering. 386.
steering column. 386.
steering wheel. 385, 386.

sun roof. 383.
sun visor. 385.
tailgate. 384.
temperature indicator. 385.
tension spring. 384.
two-door saloon. 384.
vanity mirror. 385.
vent. 385.
wheel. 383.
window. 383.
window winder handle. 386.
windscreen. 383.
windscreen wiper. 384.
windscreen wiper blade. 384.
wing. 383.
wiper arm. 384.
wiper blade rubber. 384.
wiper switch. 386.

CARPENTRY

acorn nut. 254.
adjustable channel. 249.
adjustable frame. 252.
adjustable spanner. 248.
adjusting knob. 247.
adjusting ring. 250.
adjusting screw. 249.
angle scale. 253.
auger bit. 250.
auxiliary handle. 251.
back. 252, 255.
ball pein. 247.
ball pein hammer. 247.
base. 250, 251.
base plate. 253.
belt. 251.
bench saw. 252.
bit. 250.
blade. 247, 248, 252, 253.
blade guard. 252.
blade height adjustment. 252.
blade-locking bolt. 253.
blade tilt lock. 253.
blade tilting mechanism. 252.
blockboard. 255.
board. 255.
body. 250.
bolt. 254.
bolt. 249.
brace. 250.
bradawl. 248.
cable. 251.
cable sleeve. 251.
cam ring. 250.
cap iron. 247.
carpentry. 255.
carpentry: fasteners. 254.
carpentry: tools. 247, 248, 249, 250, 251, 252, 253.
central ply. 255.
cheek. 247.
chipboard. 255.
chisel. 248.
chuck. 248, 250, 251.
chuck key. 251.
circular saw. 253.
circular saw blade. 253.
claw. 247.
claw hammer. 247.
collet. 250.
collet nut. 250.
column. 251.
combination spanner. 248.
countersink. 250.
countersunk. 254.
crank. 250.
cross head (Phillips). 254.
curved jaw. 249.
decorative sheet. 255.
depth stop. 251.
double-twist auger bit. 250.
drill. 250.
drive wheel. 250.
edge. 255.

electric drill. 251.
end grain. 255.
expansion bolt. 254.
external tooth lock washer. 254.
eye. 247.
face. 247.
face ply. 255.
face side. 255.
faces. 247.
feed lever. 251.
fixed jaw. 248, 249.
flat washer. 254.
flute. 250.
fluted land. 250.
frame. 249.
front knob. 247.
G-clamp. 249.
grain. 255.
guard. 251.
hacksaw. 252.
hand drill. 250.
handle. 247, 248, 249, 250, 252, 253.
handsaw. 252.
hardboard. 255.
head. 250, 254.
heel. 247, 252.
hollow-wood construction. 255.
housing. 251.
inner ply. 255.
internal tooth lock washer. 254.
jaw. 248, 250, 251.
knob handle. 253.
kraft paper. 255.
laminate board. 255.
laminboard. 255.
land. 250.
lateral adjusting lever. 247.
lead screw. 251.
lever. 249.
locking ring. 248.
lower blade guard. 253.
lower guard retracting lever. 253.
main handle. 251.
mallet. 247.
mitre gauge. 252.
mitre gauge slot. 252.
mole wrench. 249.
motor. 250, 251, 253.
moulded plywood. 255.
movable jaw. 248, 249.
multi-pliers. 249.
multi-ply plywood. 255.
nail. 254.
name plate. 251.
nut. 254.
nut and bolt. 254.
one way head. 254.
open end spanner. 248.
pawl. 250.
pedestal drill. 251.
peeled veneer. 255.
Phillips tip. 248.
pinion. 250.
pistol grip handle. 251, 252.
plane. 247.
plywood. 255.
protective sheet. 255.
pulley. 251.
pulley safety guard. 251.
quill. 250, 251.
quill lock. 251.
raised head. 254.
ratchet. 248, 250.
release lever. 249.
ring spanner. 248.
rip fence. 252, 253.
rip fence adjustment. 252.
rip fence guide. 252.
rip fence lock. 252.
rivet. 254.
round head. 254.
router. 250.
screw. 254.
screwdriver. 248.
shank. 248, 250, 254.

The terms in **bold type** indicate the title of an illustration.

shoulder. 254.
shoulder bolt. 254.
side handle. 250.
single spring washer. 254.
single twist. 250.
slip joint. 249.
slip joint pliers. 249.
slot. 254.
slotted bit. 248.
spanners. 248.
spiral. 248.
spiral ratchet screwdriver. 248.
spirit level. 248.
spring. 249.
spring wing. 254.
spur. 250.
straight jaw. 249.
switch. 250, 251.
swivel base. 249.
swivel head. 249.
swivel lock. 249.
table. 251, 252.
table extension. 252.
table-locking clamp. 251.
teeth. 252.
thread. 254.
threaded rod. 254.
throat. 249.
thumbscrew. 248.
tip. 248, 253, 254.
toe. 247, 252.
toggle bolt. 254.
tooth. 253.
toothed jaw. 249.
trigger switch. 253.
turning handle. 250.
twist drill. 250.
upper blade guard. 253.
vice. 249.
warning plate. 251.
wedge iron. 247.
wedge lever. 247.
wing nut. 254.
wing nut. 252.
wire cutter. 249.

DOMESTIC APPLIANCES

air vent. 232.
automatic flex reel. 234.
backguard. 228, 231.
base. 232, 233.
beater. 225.
beater ejector. 225.
beaters. 225.
blade. 226.
blender. 225.
blending attachment. 225.
body. 233.
bottle opener. 233.
bowl. 226.
bowl with serving spout. 226.
bread guide. 227.
bumper. 234.
butter compartment. 229.
button notch. 233.
cabinet. 231.
canister vacuum cleaner. 234.
carpet nozzle. 234.
case. 232, 233, 234.
caster. 234.
citrus juicer. 226.
clamping handle. 226.
clamping nut. 226.
cleaning tools. 234.
cleaning tools. 234.
clock timer. 227, 228.
compressor. 229.
condenser coil. 229.
container. 226.
control knob. 228.
control panel. 227, 228, 231, 232.
cooking surface. 227.
cover. 226.
crevice tool. 234.

crisper. 229.
cutlery basket. 232.
cutting blade. 225.
cutting wheel. 233.
dairy compartment. 229.
dasher. 226.
defrost heater. 229.
defrost timer. 229.
detachable control. 227.
detergent dispenser. 232.
discs. 226.
dishwasher. 232.
domestic appliances. 225, 226, 227, 228, 229, 230, 231, 232, 233, 234.
door. 227, 230, 231.
door gasket. 230.
door shelf. 229.
door stop. 229.
door switch. 231.
dough hook. 225.
drain filter. 230.
drain hose. 232.
drain pan. 229.
drain pump. 230.
drip bowl. 228.
drive belt. 231.
drive wheel. 233.
drum. 226, 230, 231.
drum motor. 230.
dusting brush. 234.
egg tray. 229.
electric cooker. 228.
electric element. 228.
electric grill. 227.
electric tin-opener. 233.
end panel. 227.
evaporator coil. 229.
exhaust duct. 231.
exhaust hose. 231.
extension pipe. 234.
fabric guide. 233.
fan. 229, 231.
feed tube. 226.
fill opening. 233.
flex. 233.
flexible hose. 234.
floor brush. 234.
fluff trap. 231.
food processor. 226.
four blade beater. 225.
freezer bucket. 226.
freezer compartment. 229.
freezer door. 229.
fridge-freezer. 229.
front tip. 233.
gasket. 228, 232.
glass. 230.
glass cover. 229.
grater disc. 226.
grease well. 227.
griddle. 227.
grill element. 228.
groove. 227.
guard rail. 229.
hand blender. 225.
hand mixer. 225.
handle. 225, 226, 227, 228, 229, 233, 234.
heating duct. 231.
heating element. 230, 231, 232.
heel rest. 225, 233.
hinge. 227, 228, 232.
hob. 228.
ice-cream can. 226.
ice-cream freezer. 226.
ice cube tray. 229.
idler pulley. 231.
impeller. 232.
indicator. 232.
inlet hose. 232.
juice extractor. 226.
kettle. 233.
kickplate. 229.
latch. 227, 228, 232.
lever. 227.

lid. 226, 227.
magnetic gasket. 229.
magnetic lid holder. 233.
measuring cap. 225.
meat keeper. 229.
microwave oven. 227.
mixer. 225.
mixing bowl. 225.
motor. 231, 234.
motor unit. 225, 226.
on-off indicator. 228.
on-off switch. 234.
oven. 228.
oven lamp. 227, 228.
overflow protection switch. 232.
pierce lever. 233.
pipe. 234.
plate. 227.
pressure switch. 230.
probe receptacle. 227.
programmer. 228, 231, 232.
pulse button. 225.
pump. 232.
push-button control. 232.
pusher. 226.
rack. 228, 232.
reamer. 226.
refrigerator compartment. 229.
retractable flex. 234.
rinse-aid dispenser. 232.
roast sensor probe. 228.
roller. 232.
rotisserie. 228.
runner. 232.
safety thermostat. 231.
sensor probe. 227.
shag-carpet-rake. 234.
shelf. 229.
shelf channel. 229.
shock absorber. 230.
sight-glass tube. 233.
slide selector. 227, 233.
slot. 227.
soleplate. 233.
speed control. 225.
speed selector. 226.
spider (cross-piece). 230.
spindle. 226.
spiral beater. 225.
spout. 233.
spray. 233.
spray arm. 232.
spray button. 233.
stabilizer foot. 232.
stand. 225.
start switch. 231.
steam button. 233.
steam iron. 233.
storage door. 229.
strainer. 226.
stirrer cover. 227.
suction regulator. 234.
support wheel. 231.
surface element. 228.
switch. 228, 229.
temperature control. 227.
temperature dial. 233.
temperature selector. 231.
temperature sensing bulb. 228.
terminal. 227.
thermostat. 230.
thermostat control. 229.
thumb rest. 233.
tilt-back head. 225.
timer. 230.
toaster. 227.
trim ring. 228.
tub. 230, 232.
tubular element. 228.
tumble dryer. 231.
turntable. 225.
upholstery nozzle. 234.
vane. 231.
vapour discharge outlet. 230.
vertical flex support. 233.
wash tower. 232.

washing machine. 230.
water inlet valve. 230.
window. 227, 228.
wire beater. 225.
worktop surface. 232.

ELECTRICITY

access gallery. 641, 646.
access shaft. 646.
administrative building. 646.
afterbay. 637, 638, 641.
arch dam. 639.
arch dam, cross section of an. 639.
bank. 646.
base width. 644.
basin. 646.
basin side. 646.
berm. 638.
blade. 642, 643.
bottom ring. 643.
brace. 645.
bucket. 643.
bucket ring. 643.
bulb unit. 646.
busbar. 641.
bushing. 637, 645.
buttress. 639.
buttress dam. 639.
buttress dam, cross section of a. 639.
cable bundles. 644.
cantilever. 639.
circuit breaker. 641.
collector. 642.
concrete dam, cross section of a. 638.
connection point. 645.
control room. 637, 646.
core. 638.
crest of spillway. 637.
cross arm. 644.
crossarm. 645.
customer's service entrance. 645.
cut off trench. 638.
dam. 637, 646.
dams, major types of. 639.
diagonal. 644.
discharge liner. 643.
distribution board. 645.
distributor service loop. 645.
diversion canal. 637.
downstream face. 638.
downstream shoulder. 638.
downstream toe. 638.
draft tube. 641, 643.
drainage blanket. 638.
drainage layer. 638.
earth. 639.
electricity. 637, 638, 639, 640, 641, 642, 643, 644, 645, 646.
electricity, steps in production of. 640.
electricity meter. 645.
embankment dam. 639.
embankment dam, cross section of an. 638, 639.
equipment access shaft. 646.
fill. 638.
filter. 638.
fitted coupling bolt. 643.
foundation. 639.
foundation of dam. 638.
Francis turbine. 643.
fuse. 645.
fuse cut-out. 645.
fuse holder. 645.
gantry crane. 637, 641.
gate. 641, 646.
gate operating ring. 643.
generator. 642.
generator. 641, 642.
gravity dam. 639.

781

gravity dam, cross section of a. 639.
ground level. 644.
ground wire. 645.
ground-wire clamp. 645.
guide bearing. 642.
hand rail. 637.
headbay. 637.
horizontal member. 644.
hot line connector. 645.
hub. 643.
hub cover. 643.
hydraulic turbine, cross section of a. 643.
hydroelectric complex. 637.
hydroelectric power station, cross section of a. 641.
inactive dyke. 646.
insulator. 645.
Kaplan turbine. 643.
lightning arrester. 641, 645.
lock. 646.
log chute. 637.
low-tension distribution line. 645.
machine hall. 637, 641.
main leg. 644.
main switch. 645.
medium tension distribution line. 645.
neutral conductor. 645.
operating dam. 646.
operating floor. 646.
over read ground wire. 644.
overhead connection. 645.
panel. 644.
Pelton turbine. 643.
penstock. 637, 641, 646.
peripheral joint. 639.
phase conductor. 645.
pitching. 638.
power line. 637.
power plant, cross section of. 646.
power station. 646.
powerhouse. 637, 641.
pulvino. 639.
reservoir. 637, 638, 641.
rocks. 639.
rotor. 641, 642.
runner. 642, 643.
runner blade. 643, 646.
salient pole. 642.
screen. 641.
scroll case. 641.
sea. 646.
sea side. 646.
service box. 645.
shaft. 641, 642, 643.
soil. 639.
spacer. 644.
spillway. 637.
spillway chute. 637.
spillway gate. 637.
spiral case. 642, 643.
stator. 641, 642.
stay ring. 642, 643.
stay vane. 642, 643.
structure. 637.
strut. 646.
substation. 646.
supply point. 645.
suspension insulator string. 644.
suspension tower. 644.
tailrace. 641, 643.
terminal. 645.
tidal power plant. 646.
top of dam. 637, 638, 641.
tower foot. 644.
training wall. 637.
transformer. 641, 645.
transformer station. 641.
travelling crane. 641.
turbine. 641.
turbine runner. 646.
turbines, major types of. 643.
upstream blanket. 638.

upstream face. 638.
upstream shoulder. 638.
upstream toe. 638.
water intake. 641.
wave wall. 638.
wicket gate. 643.

ELECTRICITY (DO-IT-YOURSELF)

adapter. 275.
adjustment wheel. 277.
arc tube. 274.
arc tube mount structure. 274.
blade. 277.
bulb. 274.
button. 274.
cap. 274.
cartridge fuse. 275.
combination pliers. 277.
continuity tester. 276.
crimper. 277.
earth green and yellow wire. 275.
electrician's tools. 276, 277.
electricity. 274, 275, 276, 277.
electrode. 274.
exhaust tube. 274.
filament. 274.
flex. 275.
fluorescent tube. 274.
fuse. 275.
fuse carrier. 275.
fuse pullers. 276.
gas. 274.
hammer. 277.
heat deflecting disc. 274.
high-voltage tester. 276.
inert gas. 274.
insulated blade. 276.
insulated handle. 276, 277.
jaw. 277.
lead-in wire. 274.
light bulb. 274.
live brown wire. 275.
long-nose pliers. 277.
main electrode. 274.
measuring drawtape. 277.
mercury. 274.
mercury-vapour lamp. 274.
multimeter. 276.
multipurpose tool. 277.
neon lamp. 276.
neon screwdriver. 276.
neutral blue wire. 275.
nitrogen. 274.
phosphor coating. 274.
pin. 274.
pivot. 277.
plug. 275.
reflector. 274.
screw base. 274.
socket. 275.
starting electrode. 274.
starting resistor. 274.
stem. 274.
support. 274.
test-lamp. 276.
tester probe. 276.
three-pin plug. 275.
wire cutter. 277.
wire cutters. 277.
wire stripper. 277.

FISHING

antenna. 567.
anti-reverse lock. 566.
artificial fly. 567.
bail arm. 566.
barb. 567.
bend. 567.
blade. 567.
body. 567.
butt. 567.

butt cap. 566.
butt eye. 566.
butt grip. 566.
butt section. 566.
cheek. 567.
crank. 566.
drag. 566.
eye. 566, 567.
female ferrule. 566.
fishhook. 567.
fishing. 566, 567.
float. 567.
fly line. 566.
fly reel. 566.
fly rod. 566.
foot. 566.
foregrip. 566.
gap. 567.
gear housing. 566.
hackle. 567.
hand grip. 566.
handle. 566.
head. 567.
hook. 567.
joint. 567.
keeper ring. 566.
leader. 567.
leg. 566.
line. 566, 567.
line guide. 566.
lures. 567.
male ferrule. 566.
open-face spinning reel. 566.
point. 567.
reel seat. 566.
ribbing. 567.
screw locking nut. 566.
shank. 567.
shoulder. 567.
sinker. 567.
spinner. 567.
spinning rod. 566.
split link. 567.
spool. 566.
swivel. 567.
tail. 567.
throat. 567.
tip. 567.
tip-ring. 566.
tip section. 566.
topping. 567.
veil. 567.
wing. 567.

FRUITS

achene. 66, 70.
almond. 67, 70.
apple. 68.
apple. 68.
apricot. 67.
avocado. 72.
banana. 72.
berries, major types of. 66.
berry, section of a. 66.
black currant. 66.
blueberry. 66.
bract. 70.
Brazil nut. 70.
brush. 71.
calyx. 66, 68, 71.
capsule. 71.
capsule, section of a. 71.
cashew. 70.
cherimoya. 72.
cherry. 67.
chestnut. 70.
citrus fruit, section of a. 69.
citrus fruits, major types of. 69.
coconut. 70.
compound fleshy fruits. 66.
core. 68.
cotyledon. 67, 71.
cranberry. 66.
cupule. 70.

currant. 66.
date. 67.
druplet. 66.
dry fruits. 70, 71.
embryo. 67.
endocarp. 67, 68.
epicalyx. 66.
exocarp. 66, 67, 68.
flesh. 66, 67, 68.
fleshy fruits: berry fruits. 66.
fleshy fruits: citrus fruits. 69.
follicle. 71.
follicle, section of a. 71.
funiculus. 66, 71.
germ. 71.
gooseberry. 66.
grain of wheat, section of a. 71.
grape. 66.
grape. 66.
grapefruit. 69.
green walnut. 70.
guava. 72.
hazelnut. 70.
hazelnut, section of a. 70.
huckleberry. 66.
hull. 71.
husk. 70.
Indian fig. 72.
Japan plum. 68.
Japanese persimmon. 72.
juice sac. 69.
kernel. 70.
kiwi. 72.
kumquat. 69.
legume, section of a. 71.
lemon. 69.
litchi. 72.
loculus. 68.
mandarin. 69.
mango. 67.
mesocarp. 66, 67, 68, 69.
midrib. 71.
mustard. 71.
nectarine. 67.
nut. 70.
nuts, major types of. 70.
olive. 67.
orange. 69.
orange. 69.
papaya. 72.
partition. 70.
pea. 71.
pea. 71.
peach. 67.
peach. 67.
peanut. 70.
pear. 68.
pecan nut. 70.
pedicel. 66, 68.
pericarp. 69, 70.
pine kernel. 70.
pineapple. 72.
pip. 68, 69.
pistachio nut. 70.
plum. 67.
pome fleshy fruits. 68.
pome fruit, section of a. 68.
pome fruits, principal types of. 68.
pomegranate. 72.
poppy. 71.
pore. 71.
pulp. 69.
quince. 68.
raspberry. 66.
receptacle. 66.
rind. 69.
seed. 66, 67, 68, 69, 70, 71.
seed coat. 67, 71.
segment. 69.
sepal. 66.
septum. 71.
shell. 70.
silique, section of a. 71.
skin. 66, 67, 68.
stalk. 66, 68.

The terms in **bold type** indicate the title of an illustration.

stamen. 68.
star anise. 71.
starch. 71.
stigma. 70.
stone. 66, 67.
stone fleshy fruits. 67.
stone fruit, section of a. 67.
stone fruits, major types of. 67.
strawberry, section of a. 66.
style. 66, 67, 68, 71.
suture. 71.
tropical fruits. 72.
tropical fruits, major types of. 72.
valve. 71.
wall. 69.
walnut. 70.
walnut, section of a. 70.
wild blackberry, section of a. 66.
zest. 69.

GOLF

apron. 571.
bag well. 573.
ball. 573.
ball cross-section. 573.
brassie. 572.
bunker. 571.
caddie. 571.
canopy. 573.
cart path. 571.
casual water. 571.
club divider. 573.
clubhouse. 571.
core. 573.
course (golf). 571.
cover. 573.
cup. 573.
dimple. 573.
divot. 571.
driver. 572.
driving iron. 572.
electric golf cart. 573.
engine. 573.
face. 572.
fairway. 571.
ferrule. 572.
flagstick. 571.
golf. 571, 572, 573.
golf bag. 573.
golf clubs. 572.
golf clubs, types of. 572.
golf shoe. 573.
golf trolley. 573.
golfer. 571.
grip. 572.
groove. 572.
handle. 573.
head. 572.
head cover. 573.
heel. 572.
hole. 571.
hole. 571.
iron. 572.
mashie. 572.
mashie iron. 572.
mashie niblick. 572.
midiron. 572.
midmashie. 572.
neck. 572.
niblick. 572.
no. 1 iron. 572.
no. 1 wood. 572.
no. 2 iron. 572.
no. 2 wood. 572.
no. 3 iron. 572.
no. 3 wood. 572.
no. 4 iron. 572.
no. 4 wood. 572.
no. 5 iron. 572.
no. 6 iron. 572.
no. 7 iron. 572.
no. 8 iron. 572.
no. 9 iron. 572.

out of bounds. 571.
pitching niblick. 572.
pitching wedge. 572.
pocket. 573.
practice fairway. 571.
putter. 572.
putter. 572.
putting green. 571.
rough. 571.
rubber thread. 573.
sand wedge. 572.
shaft. 572.
shoulder strap. 573.
sole. 572.
spade mashie. 572.
spike. 573.
spoon. 572.
tee. 573.
teeing ground. 571.
toe. 572.
umbrella sheath. 573.
water hazard. 571.
whipping. 572.
wood. 572.

JET AND HELICOPTER

aileron. 434.
air inlet. 436.
air intake. 441.
air transport. 434.
aircraft gate. 438.
airport. 438, 439.
annular combustion chamber. 436.
antenna. 434.
anti-collision light. 434.
apron. 438.
arrivals concourse. 440.
automatically-controlled door. 440.
autopilot control. 437.
axial-flow compressor. 436.
baggage check-in counter. 440.
baggage claim area. 440.
baggage compartment. 441.
baggage conveyor. 439.
baggage trailer. 439.
baggage trolley. 440.
boarding step. 441.
by-pass taxiway. 438.
cabin. 441.
captain's seat. 437.
cargo terminal. 438.
carousel. 440.
catering vehicle. 439.
central console. 437.
central instrument panel. 437.
centre bearing. 436.
check-in area. 440.
cherry-picker truck. 439.
combustion chamber. 436.
control column. 437, 441.
control tower. 438.
currency exchange counter. 440.
customs control. 440.
delta wing. 435.
departures concourse. 440.
departures room. 440.
drive shaft. 441.
duty-free counter. 440.
electrical power unit. 439.
elevator. 434.
engine instruments. 437.
engine mounting pylon. 435.
exhaust cone. 436.
exhaust duct. 436.
exhaust nozzle. 436.
exhaust pipe. 436, 441.
fan. 436.
fan blade. 436.
fin. 434, 441.
fin-mounted tail unit. 435.
first officer's seat. 437.
fixed distance marking. 438.
flap guide rail. 435.
flight deck. 437.

flight deck. 434, 441.
flight engineer's panel. 437.
flight engineer's seat. 437.
flight information board. 440.
flying instruments. 437.
freight hold. 434.
front bearing. 436.
front spar. 435.
fuel spray manifold. 436.
fuel tank. 441.
fuel tanker. 439.
fuselage. 434.
fuselage mounted tail unit. 435.
galley. 434.
ground airport equipment. 439.
helicopter. 441.
high-speed exit taxiway. 438.
holding area marking. 438.
hotel reservation desk. 440.
immigration control. 440.
information counter. 440.
inlet guide vanes. 436.
landing light. 441.
leading edge. 434.
leading edge flap. 434.
long-range aircraft. 434.
main spar. 435.
main undercarriage. 434.
main undercarriage mounting beam. 435.
maintenance hangar. 438.
mast. 441.
mobile passenger stairs. 439.
navigation light. 434.
nose. 434.
nose cone. 436.
nose wheel. 434.
observation deck. 440.
observer's seat. 437.
overhead switch panel. 437.
pallet and container transporter. 439.
parking area. 438.
passenger cabin. 434.
passenger terminal. 440.
passenger terminal. 438.
passenger transfer vehicle. 439, 440.
passenger walkway. 438.
passport control. 440.
pitch link. 441.
potable water truck. 439.
pushback tractor. 439.
radial passenger loading area. 438.
root rib. 435.
rotor blade. 436, 441.
rotor head. 441.
rotor hub. 441.
rudder. 434.
rudder pedal. 437.
runway. 438.
runway centre line markings. 438.
runway designation marking. 438.
runway end lights. 438.
runway side markings. 438.
runway threshold markings. 438.
runway touchdown zone marking. 438.
scissor-lift truck. 439.
security check. 440.
skid. 441.
spoiler. 434.
stator vane. 436.
straight wing. 435.
stringer. 435.
swept-back wing. 435.
T-tail unit. 435.
tail. 434.
tail assembly. 434.
tail boom. 441.
tail plane. 434, 441.
tail rotor. 441.
tail shape. 435.
tapered wing. 435.
taxiway. 438.
telescopic corridor. 438.

throttles. 437.
ticket counter. 440.
toilet truck. 439.
tow tractor. 439.
trailing edge. 434.
trailing edge flap. 434.
triple tail unit. 435.
turbine. 436.
turbine blade. 436.
turbine-compressor shaft. 436.
turbine guide vane. 436.
turbo-jet engine. 436.
turbofan engine. 436.
turbofan jet engine. 434.
universal step. 439.
variable geometry wing. 435.
VHF aerial. 435.
weather radar. 434.
wheel chock. 439.
window. 434.
windshield. 434, 437.
wing. 434.
wing rib. 435.
wing shape. 435.
wing structure. 435.
wing tip. 435.

KITCHEN UTENSILS

back. 217.
baking sheet. 220.
baking utensils. 220.
baster. 221.
biscuit cutters. 220.
biscuit press. 220.
blade. 217.
bolster. 217.
boning knife. 217.
bottle opener. 219.
bread knife. 217.
butter curler. 217.
cake tin. 220.
carving fork. 217.
carving knife. 217.
citrus juicer. 218.
cleaver. 217.
colander. 218.
cook's knife. 217.
corer. 221.
cutting edge. 217.
draining spoon. 219.
egg beater. 220.
egg slicer. 221.
egg timer. 219.
filleting knife. 217.
fish slice. 219.
flan tin. 220.
funnel. 218.
garlic press. 218.
grapefruit knife. 217.
grater. 218.
guard. 217.
half handle. 217.
ham knife. 217.
heel. 217.
ice cream scoop. 221.
icing syringe. 220.
individual bun tin. 220.
kitchen knife. 217.
kitchen knives, types of. 217.
kitchen scales. 219.
kitchen timer. 219.
kitchen utensils. 217, 218, 219, 220, 221.
knife sharpener. 221.
ladle. 219.
lever corkscrew. 219.
measuring cups. 219.
measuring spoons. 219.
meat thermometer. 219.
mincer. 218.
mixing bowls. 220.
mortar. 218.
nutcracker. 218.
oyster knife. 217.

The terms in **bold type** indicate the title of an illustration.

paring knife. 217.
pasta maker. 218.
pastry brush. 220.
pastry cutting wheel. 220.
peeler. 217.
pestle. 218.
pie tin. 220.
point. 217.
potato masher. 219.
poultry shears. 221.
quiche tin. 220.
rivet. 217.
rolling pin. 220.
salad shaker. 218.
salad spinner. 218.
savoy bag and nozzles. 220.
set of utensils. 219.
shaker. 221.
sharpening steel. 217.
sieve. 218.
sifter. 220.
skimmer. 219.
snail dish. 221.
snail tongs. 221.
spaghetti tongs. 221.
spatula. 219.
stoner. 221.
tang. 217.
tea infuser. 221.
tin opener. 219.
tongs. 221.
vegetable brush. 221.
waiter's friend. 219.
whisk. 220.
zester. 217.

MEN'S CLOTHING

adjustable waist tab. 283.
adjustment slide. 284.
ankle length. 287.
armhole. 287.
astrakhan. 288.
back. 283.
back pocket. 284.
balaclava. 288.
belt. 284.
belt. 281.
belt buckle. 281.
belt carrier. 284.
belt loop. 281.
bikini briefs. 287.
binding. 288.
boater. 288.
bow. 288.
bow tie. 285.
bowler hat. 288.
boxer shorts. 287.
brace clip. 284.
braces. 284.
breast dart. 282.
breast pocket. 282, 285.
breast welt pocket. 283.
briefs. 287.
brim. 288.
broad welt side pocket. 281.
buckle. 284.
button. 288.
button loop. 284.
buttondown collar. 285.
buttoned placket. 285.
buttonhole. 281, 285, 286.
cardigan. 288.
carrier. 281, 284.
centre back vent. 283.
clip. 284.
cloth cap. 288.
collar. 281, 283, 285.
collar point. 285.
collar stay. 285.
combination. 287.
cravat. 285.
crease. 284.
crew neck sweater. 286.
crotch. 287.

crown. 288.
cuff. 285.
deerstalker. 288.
double-breasted buttoning. 281.
double-breasted jacket. 283.
drawstring. 282.
duffle coat. 282.
elastic webbing. 284.
elasticized leg opening. 287.
epaulet. 281.
eyelet. 281.
facing. 283.
felt hat. 288.
flap pocket. 282, 283.
flap side pocket. 283.
fly. 284, 287.
frog. 282.
front. 283, 285.
front apron. 285.
gun flap. 281.
half hoe. 287.
hanger loop. 286.
hatband. 288.
headgear. 288.
headgear, types of. 288.
heel. 287.
hood. 282.
instep. 287.
interfacing. 285.
inverness cape. 282.
knit shirt. 286.
lapel. 283.
leather end. 284.
leg. 287.
lining. 283.
long johns. 287.
loop. 285.
men's clothing. 281, 282, 283, 284, 285, 286, 287, 288.
neck end. 285.
neckhole. 287.
necktie. 285.
notch. 283.
notched lapel. 281.
outside ticket pocket. 283.
overcoat. 282.
panel. 284.
parka. 282.
peaked cap. 288.
peaked lapel. 282, 283.
pocket handkerchief. 283.
pointed tab end. 285.
prong. 284.
pullovers. 286.
raglan sleeve. 281.
raincoat. 281.
rear apron. 285.
ribbing. 286.
set-in-sleeve. 281, 285, 286.
sheepskin jacket. 282.
shirt. 285.
shirttail. 285.
short. 287.
side back vent. 283.
side pocket. 281.
single-breasted coat. 283.
skull cap. 288.
sleeve. 283.
sleeve strap. 281.
sleeve strap loop. 281.
slip-stitched seam. 285.
slipover. 286.
slit pocket. 284.
sock. 287.
sole. 287.
sou'wester. 288.
spread collar. 285.
straight-up ribbed top. 287.
tam-o'-shanter. 288.
three-quarter coat. 282.
tip. 284.
toe. 287.
toggle fastening. 282.
top collar. 283.
top hat. 288.
top stitching. 284.

trench coat. 281.
trilby. 288.
trousers. 284.
turn-up. 284.
turtleneck. 286.
two-way collar. 281.
underwear. 287.
V-neck. 283, 286.
V-neck cardigan. 286.
vest. 287.
waistband. 284, 287.
waistband extension. 284.
waistcoat. 283.
watch pocket. 283.
welt pocket. 286.
yoke. 285.

MICRO-COMPUTER

acoustic coupler. 457.
acoustic coupler. 454, 455.
alphanumeric keyboard. 456.
backspace key. 456.
cassette. 455.
cassette recorder. 455.
central processing unit. 454, 455.
configuration keys. 456.
connection cable. 457.
control key. 456.
control knob. 457.
control panel. 457.
cursor. 457.
cursor movement keys. 456.
data acquisition. 454.
data display. 454.
data processing. 454.
data processing devices. 454.
data recording on RAM* memory.
454.
data storage. 454.
disk. 455.
disk drive. 455.
dot matrix printer. 457.
enter key. 456.
escape key. 456.
extended character keys. 456.
feed pin. 457.
function keys. 456.
handset. 457.
home key. 456.
indicator light. 457.
input devices. 454.
joystick. 457.
joystick. 455.
keyboard. 456.
keyboard. 455.
lever. 456.
light pen. 455.
loudspeaker. 457.
microcomputer. 454, 455, 456,
457.
microphone. 457.
microprocessor. 455.
mouse. 455.
numeric keypad. 456.
output devices. 454.
paper guide roller. 457.
peripheral equipment. 457.
platen knob. 457.
plotter. 455.
print head. 457.
printer. 455.
push button. 457.
RAM: Random Access Memory.
454.
reset key. 456.
return key. 456.
ROM* memory. 454.
ROM: Read Only Memory. 454.
shift keys. 456.
shift lock key. 456.
soft keys. 456.
space bar. 456.
specific data processing program.
454.

switch. 457.
tab-key. 456.
template. 457.
visual display unit. 455.
word processing keys. 456.

MOTORCYCLE

carburettor. 395.
centre stand. 395.
clutch lever. 396.
crankcase. 395.
cut-out button. 396.
cylinder. 395.
cylinder-head. 395.
dip switch. 395.
disc brake. 395.
dual seat. 395.
foot brake pedal. 396.
footrest. 395.
frame. 395.
front brake lever. 396.
front footrest. 395.
front mudgard. 395.
fuel tank. 395.
gearchange pedal. 395, 396.
headlight. 395.
horn button. 396.
ignition switch. 396.
indicator lamp. 395.
kickstart pedal. 396.
main beam warning light. 396.
main petrol tap. 396.
mirror. 395.
motorcycle. 395, 396.
oil pressure. 396.
oil tank cap. 396.
petrol tank cap. 396.
pillion footrest. 395.
prop stand. 395.
rear light. 395.
rear suspension unit. 395.
reserve petrol tap. 396.
rim. 395.
silencer. 395.
speedometer. 396.
steering damper. 396.
steering lock. 396.
tachometer. 396.
telescopic front fork. 395.
twist grip throttle. 396.
warning light. 396.

NUCLEAR ENERGY

**advance gas-cooled reactor.
650.**
**advanced gas-cooled reactor.
648.**
air preheater. 647.
boiler house. 647.
boiler tube. 647.
burner. 647.
carbon dioxide gas coolant. 650.
carbon droxide coolant. 648.
chimney. 647.
closed circuit television/cathode
monitor. 652.
coal bunker. 647.
coal fired power station. 647.
coal upper. 647.
computer:control/alarm. 652.
concrete pressure vessel. 650.
concrete shield. 650, 651.
condenser. 647, 648, 649.
containment. 652.
containment building. 648.
control rod. 648, 650, 651.
control room. 652.
control room. 648.
control valve. 649.
conveyor belt. 647.
cool sodium. 651.
cooling pond. 648.
cooling water. 649.

The terms in **bold type** indicate the title of an illustration.

cylinder wall. 649.
double flow turbine. 649.
economizer. 647.
electrical distribution system. 652.
electrostatic precipitator. 647.
emergency core cooling. 652.
fast reactor. 651.
feed heater. 647.
forced draught fan. 647.
fuel element. 650, 651.
fuel handling control console. 652.
furnace. 647.
gas circulator. 648.
gas exit port. 648.
generator. 647, 648, 649, 652.
governor. 649.
graphite moderator. 650.
high activity spent fuel store. 648.
high pressure cylinder. 648.
high pressure steam. 648, 649.
hot air duct. 647.
hot sodium. 651.
induced draught fan. 647.
inner pressure cylinder. 648.
intermediate heat exchanger. 651.
intermediate pressure cylinder.
    649.
line printer. 652.
liquid sodium coolant. 651.
low pressure cylinder. 649.
Magnox reactor. 650.
main flue. 647.
main turbine shaft. 649.
miscellaneous auxiliary systems.
    652.
moderator. 648.
moderator/miscellaneous systems.
    652.
moving blade. 649.
new fuel store. 648.
**nuclear energy. 650, 651, 652,
    653.**
nuclear fuel cycle. 653.
nuclear power station. 648.
operator desk. 652.
outlet valve. 647.
power station. 649.
pressuriser. 651.
pressurized water reactor. 651.
primary air fan. 647.
primary heat transport system.
    652.
primary vessel. 651.
pulverizing mill. 647.
reactor jacket. 651.
reactor regulating system. 652.
refuelling machine. 648.
reheated steam. 648.
reheater. 647.
rotor. 649.
shutdown system. 652.
spent fuel chute. 648.
spent fuel storage and
    containment. 648.
stationery blade. 649.
stator. 649.
steam drum. 647.
steam from reheat. 649.
steam generator. 648, 650, 651.
steam generator system. 652.
steam to reheat. 649.
steam turbine. 648.
steel lined concrete pressure
    vessel. 648.
steel pressure vessel. 650, 651.
superheater. 647.
switchyard. 652.
travelling crane. 648.
turbine. 647, 652.
turbo-generator. 649.
turbo-generator. 650, 651.
uranium fuel element. 648.
water coolant and moderator. 651.
water to feed heaters and steam
    generator. 649.
weigher. 647.

OIL

above ground pipeline. 630.
**above ground pipeline support.
    630.**
administration office. 634.
anticline. 626.
aquifer. 636.
articulated trailer. 632.
asphalt. 635.
asphalt process. 634.
asphalt still. 635.
automatic tank gauge. 633.
autorefrigerating devices. 630.
baffle. 632.
ballast tank. 631.
barge. 631.
base rock. 626, 636.
beam pump. 627.
bit. 626.
bitumen. 636.
bitumen pumping. 636.
bitumen treatment. 636.
blowout preventer. 626.
booster intermediate station. 630.
bottom plate. 633.
breather valve. 633.
bridge. 631.
bucket wheel excavator. 636.
buffer tank. 630.
bulb. 631.
bund wall. 633.
bunker oil. 635.
burden. 636.
buried pipeline. 630.
butane carrier. 631.
canal boat. 631.
cap rock. 626, 636.
casing first string. 627.
casing second string. 627.
catalytic reformer. 634.
catalytic reforming plant. 635.
central pumping. 630.
centre Keelson. 631.
centre tank. 631.
chemical treatment. 635.
Christmas tree. 627.
Christmas tree. 630.
concrete drain. 633.
control room. 629.
conveyor. 636.
cooling tower. 634.
crane. 629.
crossover cargo deck line. 631.
crown block. 626.
crude oil. 635.
crude oil pipeline. 630.
derrick. 626, 629.
desasphalting. 634.
dewaxing. 634.
diesel oil. 635.
diluent. 636.
diluent recovery. 636.
discharge pipe. 632.
discharge pump. 632.
dispatch area. 634.
dragline. 636.
drain cock. 633.
drain valve. 633.
drawworks. 626.
drill collar. 626.
drill pipe. 626.
drill ship. 628.
drilling barge. 628.
drilling rig. 626.
elastic coupling. 631.
emptying outlet. 633.
engine. 626.
engine room. 631.
filling inlet. 633.
finished product storage. 634.
fire station. 634.
fixed platform. 628.
fixed-roof tank. 633.
flare. 629, 634.
floating platform. 628.

floating roof. 633.
floating-roof tank. 633.
flow bean. 627.
fluid coking plant. 634.
foam monitor. 631.
fore and aft gangway. 631.
fractionating tower. 635.
free-standing tanks. 631.
gas. 626.
gas lift. 627.
gas lift valve. 627.
gas oil. 635.
gas turbine. 634.
gas under pressure. 627.
greases. 635.
ground. 633.
hatch. 631.
heating oil. 635.
heavy petroleum. 635.
helideck. 629.
hook. 626.
hot water extraction. 636.
hydrofiner. 634.
jack-up platform. 628.
jacket. 629.
jet fuel. 635.
kelly. 626.
kerosene. 635.
laboratory. 634.
lagging. 633.
lifeboat. 629.
liquefied gas petroleum treatment.
    634.
liquefied petroleum gas storage.
    634.
liquid-level gauge. 633.
living quarters. 629.
logging unit. 629.
long residue. 635.
lubricants plant. 635.
lubricating oils. 635.
main inlet. 633.
manhole. 632, 633.
manometer. 633.
marine diesel. 635.
master gate valve. 627.
membrane tanks. 631.
methane carrier. 631.
mine. 636.
mud pit. 626.
mud pump. 626.
muskeg. 636.
offshore drilling. 628.
offshore well. 630.
**oil. 626, 627, 628, 629, 630, 631,
    635, 636.**
oil. 626.
oil and gas foam. 627.
oil/gas separator. 629.
oil refinery. 634.
oil sand. 636.
oil sands mining plant. 636.
oil storage. 633.
oil transport. 632.
oil trap. 626.
paraffins. 635.
petrochemical industry. 635.
petrochemicals. 635.
petrol. 635.
petroleum. 635.
pier. 628.
pile. 629.
pipeline. 630, 636.
plunger. 627.
polymerization and alkylation units.
    634.
potable water tank. 629.
power plant. 634.
pressure gauge. 627.
production platform. 629.
pumping station. 630.
pumping unit. 627.
pyrolysis. 636.
quarters. 631.
rail tank. 632.
reclaimed water. 636.

refinery. 634.
refinery. 630.
refinery products. 635.
rerunning. 634.
reserve mud tank. 629.
rigs. 628.
road tankers. 632.
rotary table. 626.
salt water. 626.
sand-rock. 636.
scale. 633.
sealing ring. 633.
secondary inlet. 633.
self-contained platform. 628.
semi-membrane tanks. 631.
semi-submersible. 628.
settling pond. 634, 636.
settling tank. 631.
shell. 633.
skid pad. 630.
solvent extraction unit. 635.
spiral staircase. 633.
splash plate. 633.
spray nozzle. 633.
stairs. 633.
steam cracker. 634.
**steam drive oil sands recovery
    process. 636.**
steam injection. 636.
stop. 630.
storage tank. 629, 635.
stove oil. 635.
straight run petroleum treatment.
    634.
strainer. 627.
submarine pipeline. 630.
submersible barge. 628.
sucker rod. 627.
support. 630.
swivel. 626.
tailing. 636.
tank. 632.
tank farm. 630, 634.
tank gauge float. 633.
tank wall. 632.
tankage. 635.
tanker. 631.
tender. 628.
terminal. 630.
thermal insulation. 630.
thermometer. 633.
thick-walled pipe. 626.
top central manhole. 632.
top plate. 633.
towboat. 631.
tractor. 632.
transverse baffle. 632.
transverse bulkhead. 631.
travelling block. 626.
tubing. 627.
tubing head. 627.
tubular heater. 635.
tubular member. 629.
utilities plant. 636.
vacuum distillation. 635.
vibrating mudscreen. 626.
watertight bulkhead. 631.
web frame. 631.
wing tank. 631.
workshop/store. 634.

PAINTING UPKEEP

air cap. 270.
air pressure adjusting screw. 270.
air valve. 270.
anti-slip shoe. 268.
blade guard. 270.
brace. 269.
bristles. 270.
brush. 270.
container. 270.
extension ladder. 268.
ferrule. 270.
fluid adjustment screw. 270.

The terms in **bold type** indicate the title of an illustration.

frame. 269.
fruit-picking ladder. 269.
gun body. 270.
handle. 270.
hoisting rope. 268.
hook ladder. 268.
knurled bolt. 270.
ladders. 269.
ladders and stepladders. 268.
locking device. 268.
loft ladder. 268.
multipurpose ladder. 268.
nozzle. 270.
paint roller. 270.
painting upkeep. 268, 269, 270.
platform. 269.
platform ladder. 269.
pulley. 268.
removable blade. 270.
roller cover. 270.
roller frame. 270.
rolling ladder. 269.
rope ladder. 268.
rung. 268.
safety rail. 269.
scraper. 270.
shelf. 269.
side rail. 268.
spray paint gun. 270.
spreader adjustment valve. 270.
step. 269.
step stool. 269.
stepladder. 269.
stepladders. 269.
straight ladder. 268.
tool tray. 269.
tower scaffold. 269.
tray. 270.
trigger. 270.
vent hole. 270.

PHOTOGRAPHY

air shutter release. 359.
aperture scale. 357.
ASA/DIN dial. 353.
ASA/DIN exposure index. 357.
background. 359.
barn doors. 358.
base of lamp. 357.
baseboard. 361.
battery. 357.
battery. 356.
bayonet mount. 353, 355.
bellows. 361.
between-the-lens shutter. 356.
boom arm. 359.
cable release. 359.
calculator. 357.
calculator dial. 357.
camera body. 353.
camera platform. 359.
camera screw. 359.
cartridge. 356.
cassette. 356.
cine scale. 357.
close-up lens. 355.
collet. 359.
colour analyser. 360.
colour filter. 355.
colour filter set. 358.
column. 359, 361.
column crank. 359.
column lock. 359.
condenser. 361, 362.
conical snoot. 358.
contact printer. 360.
cooling fan. 362.
darkroom. 360.
depth-of-field scale. 355.
developer bath. 360.
developing film. 356.
developing tank. 360.
diaphragm. 353.
diffuser. 358.

diffuser filter set. 358.
disc. 356.
disc camera. 354.
distance scale. 355.
dry mounting press. 360.
easel. 361.
easel. 360.
electric motor. 356.
electronic flash. 357.
enlarger. 361.
enlarger. 360.
enlarger timer. 360.
enlarging lens. 361.
exposure control. 356.
exposure meter. 357.
exposure-time scale. 357.
exposure-value. 357.
exposure value scale. 357.
extractor fan. 360.
eyecups. 355.
eyepiece. 356, 357.
eyepiece magnifier. 355.
fastening screw. 360.
film advance lever. 353.
film drying cabinet. 360.
film leader. 356.
film-pack. 356.
film take-up spool. 353.
film transport sprocket. 353.
films. 356.
filter drawer. 361.
fish-eye lens. 355.
fixing bath. 360.
flash. 358.
flash bracket. 357.
flash lamp. 357.
flash meter. 358.
flash outlet. 357.
flash sensor. 357.
flash synchronization terminal. 353.
flash umbrella. 358.
flash unit. 357.
flashbar socket. 356.
flashcube. 357.
focal plane shutter. 353.
focus magnifier. 361.
focusing knob. 361, 362.
focusing magnifier. 360.
focusing ring. 355.
folding camera. 354.
frame counter. 353.
gear train. 356.
glass bulb. 357.
grip. 357.
guillotine trimmer. 360.
hanger. 362.
head rotation lock. 361.
height control. 361.
height scale. 361.
honeycomb diffuser. 358.
hot shoe. 357.
incident-light measuring diffuser. 357.
indicator needle. 357.
infrared transmitter. 358.
interchangeable lens. 353.
interchangeable lenses. 355.
lamp. 361.
lamphouse. 361.
lead-in wire. 357.
lens. 356, 357, 362.
lens aperture ring. 355.
lens cap. 355.
lens hood. 355.
lens mount. 353.
levelling foot. 362.
light-reading scale. 357.
lightbox. 360.
lighttight box. 353.
lock ring. 362.
lower pan-head mounting screw. 359.
magnesium wire. 357.
mains lead. 362.
medium format SLR (6 x 6). 354.
mirror. 353.

motor. 362.
movable condenser. 361.
neckstrap lug. 353.
negative carrier. 361.
objective lens. 357.
pan handle. 359.
panoramic and tilting head. 359.
paper safe. 360.
parabolic reflector. 358.
pearl screen. 362.
pentaprism. 353.
perforation. 356.
photoelectric cell. 356.
photographic accessories. 359.
photography. 353, 354, 355, 356, 357, 358, 359, 360, 361, 362.
pocket instamatic camera. 354.
polarizing filter. 355.
Polaroid Land camera. 356.
press camera. 354.
print drying rack. 360.
print washer. 360.
printed circuit. 356.
processing rollers. 356.
projection lamp. 362.
projection screen. 362.
pull bail. 362.
push-button. 362.
rangefinder. 354.
red safelight filter. 361.
reel. 360.
reflecting screen. 358.
reflector. 359.
release button. 353.
remote control. 362.
resin-coated paper dryer. 360.
rewind crank. 353.
right angle finder. 355.
saddle. 362.
safelight. 360.
screen case. 362.
self timer. 353.
semi-fish-eye lens. 355.
shoe. 362.
shutter button. 356.
shutter release. 353.
shutter speed dial. 353.
side-tilt lock. 359.
single-lens reflex camera. 353.
sink. 360.
slide. 362.
slide changer. 362.
slide mount. 362.
slide projector. 362.
slide tray. 362.
softlight reflector. 358.
spot projector attachment. 358.
spotmeter. 357.
stand. 358, 359.
standard lens. 355.
stereo camera. 354.
still cameras. 354.
stop bath. 360.
studio accessories. 359.
studio lighting. 358.
subminiature camera. 354.
switch. 357.
sync cable. 358.
synchro cord. 357.
taking mirror. 356.
tele-converter. 355.
telephoto lens. 355.
telescoping leg. 359.
timer. 360.
transfer scale. 357.
transformer. 358.
tripod. 359.
tripod. 362.
tube. 362.
twin-lens reflex camera. 354.
view camera. 354.
viewfinder. 353.
voltage stabilizer. 361.
wide angle adapter. 357.
wide-angle lens. 355.
zoom lens. 355.

PLUMBING

access panel. 263.
aerated filter. 267.
air chamber. 262.
anode. 263.
anti-syphon vent. 257.
ball assembly. 261.
ball-cock supply valve. 258.
base elbow. 265.
bath. 259.
bathroom. 259.
bib tap. 261.
branch. 257.
branching, examples of. 262.
building sewer. 257.
cabinet. 259.
cap. 265.
cartridge stem. 261.
chain pipe wrench. 266.
check valve. 267.
clamp. 267.
cleaning plug. 260.
cold-water riser. 257.
cold-water supply. 258, 262, 263.
compression coupling. 260.
compression fitting. 264.
conical washer. 258.
copper pipe. 264.
copper to plastic. 265.
copper to steel. 265.
cover. 259, 261.
disc seat. 261.
disc seat ring. 261.
discharge line. 267.
distribution field. 267.
diverter valve. 259.
domestic sink. 262.
double-bowl kitchen sink. 257.
drain. 262.
drain hose. 262.
drain trap. 260.
drain valve. 263.
elbow. 265.
electric supply. 263.
electric water-heater tank. 263.
escutcheon. 260.
filler tube. 258.
fitting. 264.
fittings. 265.
flange. 258.
flange bolt. 258.
flange nut. 264.
flare joint. 264.
flare nut. 264.
flexible hose. 265.
flexible rubber hose. 262.
float. 258, 267.
float clamp. 267.
flush bushing. 265.
flush handle. 259.
gasket. 261, 264.
gravel. 267.
grease trap. 267.
grooved sleeve. 261.
hacksaw. 266.
handle. 261.
hexagon bushing. 265.
high-temperature cutoff. 263.
hot-water heater. 257.
hot-water riser. 257.
hot-water supply. 262, 263.
hot-water supply line. 262.
inspection chamber. 267.
inspection cover. 267.
insulation. 263.
lever. 260, 261.
lever cover. 261.
lever tap. 261.
locking nut. 258.
locknut. 260.
lower heating element. 263.
lower thermostat. 263.
main inspection eye. 257.
mechanical connectors. 264.
metal washer. 260.

The terms in **bold type** indicate the title of an illustration.

monkey wrench. 266.
nipple. 265.
non-return air vent. 267.
o-ring. 261.
offset. 265.
on-off switch. 267.
outdoor drain cock. 257.
overflow. 259.
overflow bend. 257.
overflow pipe. 263.
overflow tube. 258.
[P] trap. 257.
packing. 261.
packing nut. 261.
packing retainer ring. 261.
pedestal type sump pump. 267.
perforated pipe. 267.
pipe. 264.
pipe coupling. 265.
pipe threader. 266.
pipe wrench. 266.
plumbing. 257, 258, 259, 260, 261, 262, 263, 264, 265, 266, 267.
plumbing system. 257.
plumbing tools. 266.
plumbing wrench. 266.
plunger. 266.
portable shower head. 259.
pressure relief valve. 263.
pump motor. 267.
pump suction head. 267.
reducing coupling. 265.
refill tube. 258.
retainer nut. 261.
ring nut. 264.
rising main. 257.
roof flashing. 257.
roof vent. 265.
rubber gasket. 260.
rubber washer. 260.
scum. 267.
seal. 258, 263.
seat. 259.
septic tank. 267.
septic tank first compartment. 267.
septic tank second compartment. 267.
shower and bath fixture. 257.
shower head. 259.
shutoff valve. 260, 262.
single-handle kitchen tap. 261.
single-handle kitchen tap. 260.
sink. 260.
sink. 259.
sink strainer. 260.
slotted wall bracket. 259.
sludge. 267.
soap dish. 259.
soil drain. 257.
soil-or-waste stack. 257.
soil vent. 257.
spindle. 261.
spout. 261.
spout assembly. 260.
spray head. 260.
spray hose. 260.
spring. 261.
square head plug. 265.
standpipe. 262.
steel to plastic. 265.
stopcock. 257, 258, 262, 263.
strainer. 261.
strainer body. 260.
strainer coupling. 260.
strainer plug. 261.
strainer sleeve. 260.
strap wrench. 266.
sump. 267.
supply tube. 260.
tailpiece. 260.
tank lid. 259.
tank valve. 258.
tap body. 261.
tee. 262, 265.
thread. 261.

threaded cap. 265.
tipping valve tap. 261.
tissue holder. 259.
toilet. 258.
toilet. 259.
toilet bowl. 258, 259.
toilet cistern. 259.
torch. 266.
towel rail. 259.
transition fittings. 265.
trap. 260, 265.
trap and drain auger. 266.
trap coupling. 260.
trip lever. 258.
tube cutter. 266.
tube end. 264.
tube flaring tool. 266.
tumbler holder. 259.
U-bend. 265.
union. 264.
union. 264.
union nut. 264.
upper heating element. 263.
upper thermostat. 263.
valve seat. 261.
valve seat shaft. 258.
valve stem. 261.
vent line. 265.
washer. 261.
washing machine. 262.
waste. 257.
waste disposal sink. 260.
waste disposal unit. 260.
waste pipe. 258.
waste tee. 262.
water authority main. 257.
water meter. 257.
water service pipe. 257.
waterproofed electrical supply. 267.
WC pedestal. 257.
Y-branch. 265.

RAIL TRANSPORT

adjustable seat. 407.
advertising sign. 414.
air conditioning. 407.
air diffuser. 415.
air intake. 404.
alternator. 404.
arrivals timetable. 412.
axle. 404.
ballast. 408.
barrow. 413.
base. 409.
bench. 414.
body. 407.
bogie. 415.
bogie. 404, 407.
bogie car-carrying wagon. 406.
bogie flat wagon. 406.
bogie frame. 404.
bogie open wagon. 406.
bogie tank wagon. 406.
bogie van. 406.
bogie wagon. 405.
bogie well wagon. 406.
booking hall. 412.
bottom-end transverse member. 411.
bottom retainer. 405.
bottom side rail. 411.
brake van. 406.
buffer. 404.
bufferstop. 410.
bulkhead flat wagon. 406.
centre-aisle. 407.
change machine. 412.
channel. 409.
check-rail. 408.
classification yard. 411.
closure rail. 408.
container. 411.
container flat wagon. 406.

control stand. 404.
corner cap. 405.
corner fitting. 411.
corner structure. 411.
corridor. 407.
corridor connection. 407.
counterweight. 408, 409.
coupler head. 405.
coupler knuckle. 405.
coupler knuckle pin. 405.
crossing. 413.
crossing gate mechanism. 409.
crossover. 410.
dating nail. 408.
delay indicator. 413.
departure time indicator. 413.
departures timetable. 412.
destination indicator. 413.
diesel-electric locomotive. 404.
diesel engine. 404.
diesel shop. 410.
dining car. 407.
dining section. 407.
directional sign. 414.
door hasp. 405.
door hasp fastener. 405.
door panel. 415.
door stop. 405.
double seat. 415.
driver's cab. 404.
electrically illuminated point signal. 409.
emergency brake lever. 415.
end door. 411.
end ladder. 405.
entrance turnstile. 414.
escalator. 414.
exit turnstile. 414.
expansion space. 408.
exterior sign. 414.
fan. 415.
finial. 409.
fishplate. 408.
fishplate bolt. 408.
fixed stairs. 414.
flashing light. 409.
fold-out table. 407.
foot. 408.
footbridge. 410, 414.
fork pocket. 411.
four-foot. 415.
freight station. 410.
freight wagons, types of. 406.
frog. 408.
gate arm. 409.
gate arm lamp. 409.
gate arm support. 409.
group retarders. 411.
guide bar and live rail. 415.
hand brake gear housing. 405.
hand brake wheel. 405.
hand brake winding chain. 405.
handrail. 415.
head. 408.
headlight. 413.
headrest. 407.
highway crossing bell. 409.
hold yard. 411.
hopper ore wagon. 406.
hopper wagon. 406.
horizontal end handhold. 405.
horn. 404.
hump. 411.
hump area. 411.
indicator board. 413.
inflated carrying tyre. 415.
inflated guiding tyre. 415.
information office. 412.
journal box. 404.
junction box. 409.
king pin. 404.
kitchen. 407.
left-luggage office. 412.
level crossing. 409.
level crossing sign. 409.

level crossing with automatic gates. 410.
lifting lever. 405.
light. 415.
line map. 412.
litter bin. 414.
livestock van. 406.
lockers. 412.
loudspeaker. 415.
lower berth. 407.
main generator. 404.
main line. 410.
main running track. 411.
manually-operated points. 408.
mast. 409, 410.
master retarders. 411.
mezzanine. 414.
motor car. 415.
number of tracks sign. 409.
nut. 408.
outbound. 411.
overhead electric wire. 413.
panoramic window. 407.
pantograph. 413.
parcels office. 412.
passenger car. 415.
passenger car interior. 415.
passenger coaches, types of. 407.
passenger platform. 413.
passenger station. 410.
peep hole. 409.
piggyback flat wagon. 406.
placard board. 405.
platform edge. 413, 414.
platform number. 413.
platform shelter. 410.
platform trolley. 413.
point lever. 408.
point lock. 409.
point motor. 409.
point signal. 408.
point wire. 409.
points. 411.
porter. 413.
pull rod. 408.
radiator. 404.
rail. 408.
rail anchor. 408.
rail joint. 408.
rail transport. 404.
railway map. 412.
railway station. 410.
railway track. 408, 409.
ramp. 410.
receiving yard. 411.
refrigerator van. 406.
relief track. 410.
remote-controlled points. 409.
roof. 411.
routing cardboard. 405.
running rail. 415.
running track. 411.
runway. 415.
safety line. 414.
saloon open coach. 407.
semaphore. 410.
shunting engine. 411.
side door. 411.
side handrail. 415.
side ladder. 405.
side ladder tread. 405.
side platform. 414.
side wall. 411.
sidelight. 413.
signal background plate. 409.
signal box. 410.
signal gantry. 410.
signalbox and yard office. 411.
signals. 409.
sill step. 405.
single seat. 415.
sleeper. 408.
sleeping car. 407.
slide chair. 408.
sliding window. 407.

The terms in **bold type** indicate the title of an illustration.

soleplate. 408.
speaking window membrane. 412.
spike. 408.
spleeping compartment. 407.
spring. 404.
spring washer. 408.
starting signal. 413.
station concourse. 412.
station name. 414.
station platform. 413.
station platform. 410.
station sign. 413.
steel safety wheel. 415.
stretcher bar. 409.
suburban commuter railway. 410.
subway to platforms. 412.
switch rail. 408.
tarpaulin covered open wagon.
    406.
telescoping uncoupling rod. 405.
ticket collector's booth. 414.
ticket counter. 412.
ticket office. 412.
timetables. 412.
toilet. 407.
top-end transverse member. 411.
track. 413, 414, 415.
traction motor. 404.
traction motor ventilator. 404.
train delays notice board. 412.
train set. 410.
trough. 409.
turbocharger. 404.
turnbuckle. 409.
underground map. 414, 415.
underground railway. 415.
underground station. 414.
underground train. 415.
upper berth. 407.
ventilating fan. 404.
vestibule. 407.
vestibule door. 407.
visor. 409.
wagon. 411.
waiting room. 412.
water tank. 404, 407.
web. 408.
window. 415.
yard. 411.

SEWING

alteration line. 489.
arm. 485.
ball. 488.
bias. 488.
blade. 486, 487.
bobbin. 486.
bobbin case. 486.
bobbin winder. 485.
buckle. 488.
column. 485.
crosswise grain. 488.
cutting line. 489.
dart. 489.
dressmaker's model. 487.
edge. 487.
eye. 486, 487.
fabric structure. 488.
fasteners. 488.
feed dog. 486.
flat-bed. 485.
fold line. 489.
foot control. 485.
garment fabric. 488.
groove. 486.
hand wheel. 485.
handle. 487.
head. 485.
hemline. 488.
hinged presser foot. 485, 486.
hook. 486, 488.
hook and eyes. 488.
interfacing. 488.
interlining. 488.

latch lever. 486.
lenghtwise grain. 489.
lengthwise grain. 488.
lining. 488.
magnet. 487.
marking dot. 489.
motor. 485.
needle. 486.
needle. 485, 486, 487.
needle bar. 486.
needle clamp. 486.
needle clamp screw. 486.
needle plate. 485.
needle threader. 487.
needle threader. 486.
notch. 489.
pattern. 489.
pin. 487.
pin cushion. 487.
pinking shears. 487.
pivot. 487.
point. 486.
press-stud. 488.
presser bar. 486.
presser foot. 486.
presser foot lifter. 485.
ring. 488.
round eye. 488.
safety pins. 487.
scissors. 487.
seam allowance. 489.
seam line. 489.
selvage. 488.
sew-through buttons. 488.
sewing. 485, 486, 487, 488, 489.
sewing machine. 485, 486.
sewing spool. 485.
shank. 486, 487.
shank button. 488.
shuttle. 486.
skirt marker. 487.
slide. 488.
slide plate. 485.
socket. 488.
spool pin. 485.
stitch length regulator. 485.
stitch selector. 485.
stop. 488.
stop motion knob. 485.
straight eye. 488.
tab. 488.
tape. 488.
tape measure. 487.
teeth. 488.
tension dial. 486.
tension dial. 485, 486.
tension disc. 486.
tension spring. 486.
thimble. 487.
thread guide. 485, 486.
thread take-up lever. 485.
thread trimmer. 486.
tongue. 488.
tracing wheel. 487.
underlining. 488.
underlying fabrics. 488.
wheel. 487.
zip fastener. 488.
zip line. 489.

SKIING

anti-friction pad. 546.
automatic cable pulley. 547.
base plate. 546.
basket. 545.
beltbag. 545.
bottom. 545.
buckle. 546.
cabin. 547.
cable car. 547.
chalet. 547.
crash helmet. 545.
crossbar. 547.
disc. 547.

double chair lift. 547.
edge. 545.
flag. 547.
footrest. 547.
gaiter. 545.
gate. 547.
groove. 545.
handle. 547.
haulage cable. 547.
heel flange. 546.
heel piece. 545, 546.
heel release setting indicator. 546.
height adjustment screw. 546.
hinge. 546.
hook. 547.
inner boot. 546.
lower shell. 546.
manual release. 546.
mitten. 545.
pole. 547.
pylon. 547.
release setting screw. 546.
safety bar. 547.
safety binding. 546.
safety binding. 545.
safety strap. 546.
scarf. 545.
seat. 547.
shovel. 545.
ski. 545.
ski boot. 546.
ski boot. 545.
ski goggles. 545.
ski instructor. 547.
ski jump. 547.
ski jumper. 547.
ski lift. 547.
ski pole. 545.
ski resort. 547.
ski stop. 545, 546.
ski suit. 545.
skier. 545.
skiing. 545, 546, 547.
slalom course. 547.
slalomist. 547.
sole. 546.
T-bar lift. 547.
tail. 545.
tip. 545.
toe piece. 545, 546.
toe-piece release setting indicator.
    546.
tongue. 546.
track. 547.
turtleneck. 545.
upper. 546.
upper cuff. 546.
upper shell. 546.
wire. 546.

SOUND REPRODUCING SYSTEM

amplifier-tuner. 364.
analogue frequency meter. 364.
anti-skating device. 365.
arm elevator. 365.
arm rest. 365.
automatic frequency control. 364.
balance control. 364.
band. 365.
band selectors. 364.
base. 365.
base plate. 365.
bass tone control. 364.
cabinet. 363.
cassette deck. 363.
cassette holder. 366.
centre hole. 365.
cone. 363.
connecting cable. 363.
corrugation. 363.
counter reset button. 366.
counterweight. 365.
diaphragm. 363.

digital frequency display. 364.
Dolby noise reduction switch. 366.
drive belt. 365.
dust cover. 365.
ear cushion. 363.
earth lead. 365.
eject button. 366.
equalizer. 363.
fast-forward button. 366.
FM mode selector. 364.
FM stereo indicator. 364.
function lever. 365.
grille. 363.
groove. 365.
headband. 363.
headphone. 363.
headphone. 363.
headphone jack. 364, 366.
hinge. 365.
input selectors. 364.
jack. 363.
label. 365.
LED peak level meter. 366.
level controls. 363.
locked groove. 365.
loudness switch. 364.
loudspeaker. 363.
memory button. 364.
microphone. 363.
microphone jack. 366.
midrange. 363.
monitor indicator. 364.
motor pulley. 365.
output lead. 365.
pause button. 366.
platter. 365.
play button. 366.
power cord. 363, 365.
power switch. 364, 366.
preamplifier. 363.
preset tuning button. 364.
record. 365.
record button. 366.
record muting button. 366.
recording level button. 366.
rewind button. 366.
rubber mat. 365.
sound reproducing system. 363,
    364, 365, 366.
speaker. 363.
speaker selector. 364.
speed selector lever. 365.
spindle. 365.
spiral. 365.
spiral-in groove. 365.
stop button. 366.
stylus cartridge. 365.
supertweeter. 363.
system elements. 363.
tail-out groove. 365.
tape counter. 366.
tape deck. 366.
tape monitor switch. 364.
tape selector. 366.
tape-type indicator. 366.
tone arm. 365.
treble tone control. 364.
tuner. 363.
tuning buttons. 364.
turntable. 365.
turntable. 363.
tweeter. 363.
volume control. 363, 364.
woofer. 363.

TELEPHONE

acoustic resistance. 372.
automatic answer indicator. 373.
calls indicator. 373.
carbon granules. 372.
clapper. 372.
coil. 372.
coin slot. 373.
coinbox telephone. 373.

The terms in **bold type** indicate the title of an illustration.

cord. 372.
cordless telephone. 373.
cradle. 372.
cup. 372.
dial. 372.
diaphragm. 372.
diaphram. 372.
earpiece. 372.
electrode. 372.
erase button. 373.
facility telephone system. 373.
fast forward button. 373.
finger stop. 372.
gong. 372.
hands-free telephone. 373.
handset. 372, 373.
handset cord. 372.
housing. 372.
incoming message cassette. 373.
microphone. 373.
monitor button. 373.
mouthpiece. 372.
on/play button. 373.
outgoing announcement cassette.
    373.
permanent magnet. 372.
permanent wiring. 372.
plunger. 372.
pole piece. 372.
protected cable. 373.
push-button telephone. 373.
push buttons. 373.
receiver. 372.
receiver. 372.
record announcement button. 373.
reject chute. 373.
rewind button. 373.
ringer coil. 372.
stop button. 373.
switchhook. 372.
**telephone answering machine.
    373.**
telephone cord. 373.
telephone set. 372.
telephones, types of. 373.
transmitter. 372.
transmitter. 372.
varistor. 372.
volume control. 373.

TELEVISION

amplifier. 374.
base. 377.
blue beam. 377.
boom operator. 375.
brightness control. 377.
cabinet. 377.
camera. 376.
camera crane. 375.
camera pedestal. 375.
cameraman. 375.
catwalk. 375.
clock. 376.
contrast control. 377.
control panel. 374, 375, 376.
cue screen. 376.
cyclorama. 375.
deputy sound supervisor. 374.
director/producer. 376.
earphone jack. 377.
electron beam. 377.
electron gun. 377.
external conductive coating. 377.
faceplate. 377.
fine tuning knob. 377.
floodlight. 375.
floor crew. 375.
floor manager. 375.
funnel. 377.
green beam. 377.
hoist. 375.
lighting and vision assistant. 374.
lighting and vision control room.
    374.

lighting control panel. 374.
lighting director. 374.
loudspeaker. 375.
microphone boom. 375.
monitor. 376.
monitor pusher. 375.
monitor speaker. 376.
monitor stack. 376.
neck. 377.
off-on knob. 377.
phosphor dot. 377.
picture tube. 377.
presenter. 375.
preview monitor. 376.
production assistant. 376.
production control room. 376.
production control room. 374.
propman. 375.
protective window. 377.
red beam. 377.
screen. 377.
shadow mask. 377.
sound control room. 374.
sound desk. 374.
sound supervisor. 374.
speaker. 377.
special effects. 376.
spotlight. 375.
strip light. 375.
studio. 374.
studio and control rooms. 374.
studio floor. 375.
technical co-ordinator. 376.
teleprompter. 375.
telescopic aerial. 377.
television. 374, 375, 376, 377.
television set. 377.
test pattern. 376.
transmission monitor. 376.
UHF channel selector. 377.
utility speaker. 376.
VHF channel selector. 377.
video operator. 374.
video tape recorder. 374.
vision mixer. 376.

VEGETABLES

artichoke. 73.
asparagus. 77.
aubergine. 73.
autumn squash. 73.
bean sprouts. 77.
beetroot. 76.
black salsify. 76.
branch. 77.
broad beans. 77.
broad-leaved endive. 74.
broccoli. 73.
Brussels sprouts. 74.
bud. 75.
bulb. 77.
bulb, section of a. 75.
bulb vegetables. 75.
bulbil. 75.
bundle. 77.
cabbage lettuce. 74.
cantaloupe. 73.
cardoon. 77.
carrot. 76.
cauliflower. 73.
celeriac. 76.
celery. 77.
chard. 74.
chick peas. 77.
chicory. 74.
chilli pepper. 73.
Chinese cabbage. 74.
chive. 75.
cob. 77.
corn salad. 74.
cos lettuce. 74.
courgette. 73.
cucumber. 73.
curled endive. 74.

curled kale. 74.
dandelion. 74.
fennel. 77.
fruit vegetables. 73.
garden sorrel. 74.
garlic. 75.
green bean. 73.
green cabbage. 74.
green peas. 77.
head. 77.
horseradish. 76.
hot pepper. 73.
husk. 77.
inflorescent vegetables. 73.
Jerusalem artichoke. 76.
kernel. 77.
kohlrabi. 76.
leaf. 77.
leaf vegetables. 74.
leek. 75.
lentils. 77.
mangetout. 77.
marrow. 73.
muskmelon. 73.
okra. 73.
parsnip. 76.
pickling onion. 75.
potato. 76.
pumpkin. 73.
radish. 76.
rhubarb. 77.
rib. 77.
root. 75.
root vegetables. 76.
salsify. 76.
scale leaf. 75.
seed vegetables. 77.
shallot. 75.
silk. 77.
soybeans. 77.
Spanish onion. 75.
spear. 77.
spinach. 74.
spring onion. 75.
stalk. 77.
stalk vegetables. 77.
stem. 75.
string. 77.
swede. 76.
sweet corn. 77.
sweet pepper. 73.
sweet potato. 76.
Swiss chard. 77.
tip. 77.
tomato. 73.
tuber vegetables. 76.
turnip. 76.
vegetables. 73, 74, 75, 76, 77.
vine leaf. 74.
water cress. 74.
watermelon. 73.
white cabbage. 74.

WATER SPORTS

air hose. 536.
arm position. 535.
armstand. 534.
armstand dive. 535.
assistant timer. 531.
back binding. 540.
backstroke. 533.
backstroke start. 533.
backstroke swimmer. 533.
backstroke turn indicator. 532.
backward. 534.
backward dive. 535.
ball. 531.
bathing trunks. 531.
batten. 537, 538.
batten pocket. 537, 538.
beam reach. 539.
bear away (to). 537.
binding. 540.
blade. 536.

block. 539.
blue cap. 531.
blue flag. 531.
board. 537.
boat, types of. 541.
boom. 538.
boom vang. 538.
boot. 536.
bottom. 540.
bottom of the pool. 531, 534.
bow. 537, 538.
breaststroke. 533.
breaststroke kick. 533.
breaststroke swimmer. 533.
breaststroke turn. 533.
breathing in. 533.
breathing out. 533.
broad reach. 539.
buoyancy compensator. 536.
butterfly kick. 533.
butterfly stroke. 533.
butterfly swimmer. 533.
butterfly turn. 533.
centreboard. 538.
chief timekeeper. 532.
clam-cleat. 537, 539.
cleat. 538, 539.
clew. 537.
close hauled. 539.
close reach. 539.
cockpit. 538.
compass. 536.
competitive course. 532.
competitor. 532.
compressed-air cylinder. 536.
coxed four. 541.
coxed pair. 541.
coxless four. 541.
coxless pair. 541.
crawl swimmer. 533.
crossbar. 531.
crosstree. 538.
daggerboard. 537.
daggerboard well. 537.
depth gauge. 536.
dinghy. 538.
diver. 535.
dives, groups of. 535.
diving. 534.
diving installations. 534.
double handles. 540.
double scull. 541.
down wind. 539.
downhaul. 537.
eight. 541.
end of the lap. 533.
end wall. 532.
entries. 534.
entry. 535.
fairlead. 539.
false start rope. 532.
feet-first entry. 534.
figure ski. 540.
figure skiing handle. 540.
fin. 536, 540.
fixtures. 539.
flight. 535.
flights. 534.
flip turn. 533.
foot. 537.
foot pocket. 536.
forestay. 538.
forward. 534.
forward dive. 535.
front binding. 540.
front crawl stroke. 533.
fulcrum. 534.
full and by. 539.
glove. 536.
goal. 531.
goal. 531.
goal judge. 531.
goal line. 531.
goalkeeper. 531.
half-distance line. 531.
handle. 540.

The terms in **bold type** indicate the title of an illustration.

handles, types of. 540.
hank. 538, 539.
harness. 536.
head-first entry. 534.
head of sail. 537.
headwind. 539.
heel piece. 540.
height. 534.
height of the dive. 535.
hood. 536.
inhaul. 537.
inward dive. 535.
jib. 538.
jib halyard. 538.
jibsheet. 538.
jump ski. 540.
kick. 533.
knife. 536.
lane. 532.
lane number. 532.
lane rope. 532.
lane timekeeper. 532.
leech. 537.
leg position. 535.
length. 534.
light. 536.
luff. 537.
luff (to). 537.
macon. 541.
main halyard. 538.
mainsail. 538.
mainsheet. 538.
mask. 536.
mast. 537, 538.
mast foot. 537.
mast sleeve. 537.
masthead. 537.
mono-ski. 540.
mouthpiece. 536.
needle. 536.
oar, types of. 541.
on the wind. 539.
outhaul. 537.
pike position. 534.
placing judge. 532.
platform. 534.
platform diver. 534.
player. 531.
playing area (water polo). 531.
points of sailing. 539.
port tack. 539.
post. 531.
purge valve. 536.
rail. 536.
recorder. 532.
red cap. 531.
red flag. 531.
referee. 531, 532.
reverse dive. 535.
rowing. 541.
rowing (one oar). 541.
rowing (two oars). 541.
rudder. 538.
sail. 537.
sail panel. 538.
sailboard. 537.
scuba diver. 536.
sculling. 541.
secretary. 531.
shackle. 539.
sheet lead. 539.
shroud. 538.
side wall. 532.
sidestroke. 533.
single scull. 541.
skeg. 537.
skin diving. 536.
skis, types of. 540.
snap shackle. 539.
snorkel. 536.
spade. 541.
speargun. 536.
spinnaker boom. 538.
spinnaker sheet lead. 538.
springboard. 534.
springboard diver. 534.

start wall. 532.
startboard tack. 539.
starter. 532.
starting block. 532.
starting dive. 532.
starting grip. 532.
starting position. 535.
starting position (swimming). 532.
starting positions (diving). 534.
stern. 537.
straight position. 534.
stroke judge. 532.
strokes, types of. 533.
submersible watch. 536.
substitute. 531.
surface of the water. 534.
swimmer. 532.
swimming. 532.
swimming competition. 532.
swimming pool. 531.
tack. 537.
tail. 540.
team bench. 531.
telltale. 538.
tiller. 538.
timekeeper. 531.
tip. 540.
toe piece. 540.
toe strap. 540.
tow bar. 540.
towrope. 540.
traveller. 539.
tuck position. 534.
turnbuckle. 539.
turning judge. 532.
twin skis. 540.
twist dive. 535.
uphaul. 537.
water polo. 531.
water skiing. 540.
weight belt. 536.
wet suit. 536.
white cap. 531.
white flag. 531.
width. 534.
winch. 539.
wind. 539.
wind abeam. 539.
wind indicator. 538.
window. 537.
wishbone boom. 537.

WEAVING

back beam. 494.
ball. 496.
ball winder. 496.
basic weaves. 497.
beater. 494.
beater handtree. 494.
beater sley. 494.
bobbin. 495, 496.
bobbin winder. 496.
breast beam. 494.
clamp. 496.
cloth roller. 494.
comb. 495.
crossbar. 494.
crossbeam. 494.
crosspiece. 494.
driving wheel. 496.
eye. 495.
frame. 494.
gear. 496.
handle. 494.
harness. 494.
harnesses. 494.
hatching. 497.
heddle. 494, 495.
heddle rod. 495.
heddles. 495.
horizontal floor loom. 494.
interlock. 497.
knot. 497.

lam. 494.
leash rod. 494, 495.
nails. 495.
peg. 496.
plain weave. 497.
post. 494.
ratchet. 494.
ratchet wheel. 494.
reed. 494.
reed hook. 496.
release treadle. 494.
rod. 495.
satin weave. 497.
screw eye. 494.
shaft. 496.
shed stick. 495.
ski shuttle. 495.
slit. 497.
spool rack. 496.
stick shuttle. 495.
support. 495.
swift. 496.
take-up handle. 494.
tapestry bobbin. 495.
temple. 496.
thread guide. 496.
threading hook. 496.
top roller. 494.
treadle. 494.
treadle cord. 494.
twill weave. 497.
upright. 494, 495.
upright floor loom. 495.
vertical frame. 495.
warp. 494, 495.
warp roller. 494.
warp thread. 497.
warping mill. 496.
weaving. 494, 495, 496, 497.
weaving principle, diagram of. 497.
weft. 494.
weft thread. 497.
worm. 496.

WOMEN'S CLOTHING

accordion pleat. 294.
ankle sock. 301.
arm slit. 291.
armhole. 296.
baby doll. 301.
back. 294.
back belt. 290.
balaclava. 304.
barrel cuff. 296.
batwing sleeve. 296.
bell bottoms. 300.
beret. 304.
Bermuda shorts. 300.
bertha collar. 298.
bib. 300.
bikini. 303.
bishop sleeve. 296.
blazer. 297.
blouses. 295.
blouson. 291.
boa. 299.
boater. 304.
body shaper. 302.
body shirt. 295.
bolero. 297.
bottom of collar. 295.
bow collar. 298.
box jacket. 297.
box pleat. 294.
bra. 303.
brassiere cup. 303.
break line. 298.
breast pocket. 295.
breeches. 300.
briefs. 303.
brim. 304.
broad welt. 290.
broad welt side pocket. 294.

button-through smock. 295.
buttoned placket. 291, 295.
calf-lenght jeans. 300.
camisole. 302.
cap. 304.
cap sleeve. 296.
cape. 291.
car coat. 290.
cardigan. 297.
cartwheel hat. 304.
classic. 295.
cloche. 304.
coat dress. 292.
coats. 290, 291.
collar. 298.
collar point. 298.
collars, types of. 298.
corselette. 302.
corset. 303.
cowl collar. 298.
crew sweater. 297.
crotch piece. 295.
crown. 304.
culotte. 293.
cutaway armhole. 296.
dog ear collar. 298.
double breasted buttoning. 291.
double cuff. 296.
draped neck. 299.
draped neckline. 299.
dresses. 292.
dressing gown. 301.
drop waist dress. 292.
dungarees. 300.
epaulet sleeve. 296.
fall. 298.
fishnet tights. 301.
flap pocket. 294.
fly front closing. 290.
fold line. 294.
footstrap. 300.
foundation slip. 302.
frog. 298.
front top pocket. 300.
fur hood. 304.
garter. 302.
gather. 295.
gather skirt. 293.
girdle. 303.
gored skirt. 293.
gusset pocket. 294, 297.
half-slip. 303.
hand warmer pocket. 291.
hand warmer pouch. 294.
hat veil. 304.
head band. 304.
headgear. 304.
hold-up stocking. 301.
hose. 301.
inset pocket. 294.
inverted pleat. 294.
jabot. 298.
jeans. 300.
jumpsuit. 300.
kick pleat. 294.
kilt. 293.
kimono. 301.
kimono sleeve. 296.
knife pleat. 294.
lapel. 298.
leading edge. 298.
leg-of-mutton sleeve. 296.
long cardigan. 297.
loosely tied bow. 299.
mandarin collar. 298.
maternity dress. 292.
midriff band. 303.
mob-cap. 304.
mock pocket. 291.
modesty. 298.
narrow cuff. 296.
necklines. 299.
necks. 299.
necks. 299.
negligee. 301.
nightdress. 301.

The terms in **bold type** indicate the title of an illustration.

nightwear. 301.
notched lapel. 291, 298.
overshirt. 295.
pagoda sleeve. 296.
panel. 303.
pantee corselette. 302.
panty girdle. 303.
patch pocket. 290, 294.
patch pocket with turn-down flap. 290.
pea jacket. 291.
pedal pusher. 300.
pelerine. 290.
pelerine. 290.
Peter Pan collar. 298.
pillbox hat. 304.
pinafore. 292.
placket. 298.
pleat skirts. 294.
plunging neckline. 299.
pockets. 294.
pointed tab end. 296.
pompom. 304.
poncho. 291.
pop sock. 301.
princess dress. 292.
princess seaming. 302.
puff sleeve. 296.
pullover. 297.
pullovers. 297.
pyjamas. 301.
raglan. 290.
raglan sleeve. 290, 296.
ribbing. 291.
ridge. 294.
right side. 294.
roll. 298.
roll line. 298.
round neck. 299.
ruff. 298.
safari jacket. 297.
sailor collar. 298.
sailor tunic. 295.
sarong. 293.
scarf turban. 304.
seam pocket. 290, 294.
seaming. 290.
set-in sleeve. 296.
shawl collar. 298.
sheath dress. 292.
sheath skirt. 293.
shirt collar. 295, 298.
shirt sleeve. 295.
shirt-tail. 295.
shirtwaist dress. 292.
shirtwaist sleeve. 296.
short sock. 301.
shorts. 300.
shorts. 300.
shoulder-strap. 303.
showerproof hat. 304.
ski pants. 300.
skirts. 293.
slash neck. 299.
sleeves. 296.
slip. 302.
slipover. 297.
smock. 292, 295.
sock. 301.
soft cup bra. 303.
sou'wester. 304.
square neck. 299.
stand. 298.
stand-up collar. 298.
steel. 303.
stitched pleat. 294.
stocking. 301.
stocking cap. 304.
straight skirt. 293.
strapless brassiere. 303.
string. 304.
sundress. 292.
suspender. 303.
suspender belt. 303.
sweetheart neckline. 299.
T-shirt. 295.

T-shirt collar. 298.
T-shirt dress. 292.
tailored collar. 291, 298.
tailored sleeve. 296.
tam- o'-shanter. 304.
three-quarter sleeve. 296.
tiered skirt. 293.
tights. 301.
top coat. 290.
top stitched pleat. 294.
toque. 304.
trilby. 304.
trousers. 300.
tunic. 292, 295.
turban. 304.
turn-up. 300.
turtleneck. 297, 298.
twin-set. 297.
underwear. 302, 303.
underwired bra. 303.
underwiring. 303.
unmounted sleeve. 296.
V-shaped neck. 299.
waistband. 291.
waistcoat. 297.
waistcoats. 297.
welt pocket. 294, 297.
windcheater. 291.
women's clothing. 290, 291, 292, 293, 294, 295, 296, 297, 298, 299, 300, 301, 302, 303, 304.
wrap-over dress. 292.
wrap-over skirt. 293.
wrap-over top. 295.
yoke. 295.
yoke skirt. 293.

The terms in **bold type** indicate the title of an illustration.

SELECTIVE BIBLIOGRAPHY

Dictionaries:

Collins Dictionary of the English Language, London and Glasgow, Collins, 1986, 2nd edition, 1771 p.

The Concise Dictionary of Current English, Oxford, Clarendon Press, 1982, 7th edition, 1996 p.

Gage Canadian Dictionary, Toronto, Gage Publishing Limited, 1983, 1313 p.

Larousse Illustrated International, Paris, Larousse, McGraw-Hill, 1972.

Longman Dictionary of the English Language, Harlow, Longman, 1984, 1876 p.

The New Britannica/Webster Dictionary and Reference Guide, Encyclopedia Britannica, 1981.

The Oxford Illustrated Dictionary, Oxford, Clarendon Press, 1975, 2nd edition, 1018 p.

The Random House Dictionary of the English Language, the unabridged Edition, 1983, 2059 p.

Webster's New Collegiate Dictionary, Springfield, G. @ C. Merriam Company, 1980, 1532 p.

Webster's New Twentieth Century Dictionary of the Language, unabridged, Cleveland, Collins World, 1975.

Webster's new world dictionary of the American language, New York, The World Pub., 1953.

Encyclopedias:

Academic American Encyclopedia, Princeton, Arete Publishing Company, Inc., 1980, 21 vol.

Chamber's Encyclopedia, New rev. edition, London, International Learning Systems, 1969.

Collier's Encyclopedia, New York, Macmillan Educational Company, 1984, 24 vol.

Compton's Encyclopedia, F.E. Compton Company, Division of Encyclopedia Britannica Inc., The University of Chicago, 1982, 26 vol.

Encyclopedia Americana, Danbury, International ed., Conn.: Grolier, 1981, 30 vol.

Encyclopedia Britannica, E. Britannica, Inc., USA, 1970.

How it works — The illustrated science and invention encyclopedia, New York, H.S. Stuttman, Co., Inc. publishers, 1974.

McGraw-Hill Encyclopedia of Science @ Technology, New York, McGraw-Hill Book Company, 1982, 5th edition.

The Macmillan Encyclopedia, London and Basingstoke, Macmillan, 1986.

Merit Students Encyclopedia, New York, Macmillan Educational Company, 1984, 20 vol.

New Encyclopedia Britannica, Chicago, Toronto, Encyclopedia Britannica, 1985.

The Joy of Knowledge Encyclopedia, London, Mitchell Beazley Encyclopedias, 1976, 7 vol.

The Random House encyclopedia, New York, Random House, 1977, 2 vol.

The World Book Encyclopedia, Chicago, Field enterprises educational Corporation, 1973.

CONTENTS

Table of Contents 7
Introduction 15
Usage Guide 23

THEMES

ASTRONOMY 25
GEOGRAPHY 37
VEGETABLE KINGDOM 59
ANIMAL KINGDOM 79
HUMAN BEING 103
FOOD 133
FARMING 149
ARCHITECTURE 157
HOUSE 175
HOUSE FURNITURE 197
GARDENING 235
TOOLS AND EQUIPMENT 245
CLOTHING 279
PERSONAL ADORNMENT 313
PERSONAL ARTICLES 325
COMMUNICATIONS 343
TRANSPORT 381
OFFICE SUPPLIES AND EQUIPMENT 445
MUSIC 459
CREATIVE LEISURE ACTIVITIES 483
SPORTS AND LEISURE 509
MEASURING DEVICES 589
OPTICAL INSTRUMENTS 603
HEALTH 613
ENERGY 619
HEAVY MACHINERY 659
WEAPONS 673
SYMBOLS 693

General Index 711
Thematic Indexes 743
Specialized Indexes 779
Selective Bibliography 793